Lecture Notes in Computer Science   8250

Commenced Publication in 1973
Founding and Former Series Editors:
Gerhard Goos, Juris Hartmanis, and Jan van Leeuwen

T0213897

Goutam Paul   Serge Vaudenay (Eds.)

Progress in Cryptology – INDOCRYPT 2013

14th International Conference on Cryptology in India
Mumbai, India, December 7-10, 2013
Proceedings

 Springer

Volume Editors

Goutam Paul
Indian Statistical Institute
R. C. Bose Centre for Cryptology and Security
203 B. T. Road
Kolkata 700 108, India
E-mail: goutam.paul@isical.ac.in

Serge Vaudenay
EPFL - I&C - LASEC, INF 241 (INF Building)
Station 14
1015 Lausanne, Switzerland
E-mail: serge.vaudenay@epfl.ch

ISSN 0302-9743   e-ISSN 1611-3349
ISBN 978-3-319-03514-7   e-ISBN 978-3-319-03515-4
DOI 10.1007/978-3-319-03515-4
Springer Cham Heidelberg New York Dordrecht London

Library of Congress Control Number: 2013951885

CR Subject Classification (1998): E.3, K.6.5, D.4.6, C.2.0, J.1, G.2

LNCS Sublibrary: SL 4 – Security and Cryptology

Typesetting: Camera-ready by author, data conversion by Scientific Publishing Services, Chennai, India

Printed on acid-free paper

Springer is part of Springer Science+Business Media (www.springer.com)

Preface

Indocrypt 2013, the 14th International Conference on Cryptology in India, took place during December 7–10, 2013. It was hosted by the Homi Bhabha National Institute (HBNI), Mumbai. Indocrypt series of conferences began in 2000 under the leadership of Prof. Bimal Roy of Indian Statistical Institute and since 2003 it is organized under the aegis of Cryptology Research Society of India (CRSI), in association with an Indian institute or organization. This series is now well established as an international forum for presenting high-quality cryptography research. This year 76 papers were submitted for consideration. The authors of the submitted papers were from institutions across 12 countries and 4 continents.

Typically the submission deadline of Indocrypt is in July. But previous years' experience taught us that in this case the review time becomes very short. To ensure quality review, we brought forward the submission deadline by one month and set it for June 14. We received many requests for deadline extension, but we thought it would be unfair towards authors who submitted on time. Nevertheless, we opened a new call for *short* papers with July 15 as the deadline. We received 39 regular papers and 37 short papers.

After the Program Committee (PC) members selected their preferred papers, we assigned the articles for review. Most papers were refereed by three committee members, and papers co-authored by a PC member were refereed by five committee members. It was indeed a difficult challenge for the 40 PC members and 41 sub-reviewers to give every paper a fair assessment in such a short time.

Authors of regular papers were notified on August 26 and the authors of short papers were notified on September 2. We accepted a total of 21 papers, of which 15 are in the regular category and 6 are in the short papers category. The authors had to revise their papers according to the suggestions of the referees and submit the camera-ready versions by September 9.

The proceedings also contain the invited papers by Tatsuaki Okamoto, Kaisa Nyberg and Kenny Paterson. The organization of the conference involved many individuals. We express our heart-felt gratitude to the general chairs, namely, B.K. Dutta, Homi Bhabha National Institute, Mumbai, India, and Y.S. Mayya, Bhabha Atomic Research Centre, Mumbai, India. We are also extremely grateful to the Advisory Board members, in particular, to Prof. Bimal Roy, Director of Indian Statistical Institute, Kolkata. Special thanks to Subhadeep Banik for his help in preparing this proceedings version.

Finally, we would like to acknowledge Springer for their active cooperation and timely production of the proceedings.

December 2013

Goutam Paul
Serge Vaudenay

Organization

General Co-chairs

B.K. Dutta · Homi Bhabha National Institute, India
Y.S. Mayya · Bhabha Atomic Research Centre, India

Program Co-chairs

Goutam Paul · Indian Statistical Institute, Kolkata, India
Serge Vaudenay · EPFL, Lausanne, Switzerland

Program Committee

Martin R. Albrecht · Danmarks Tekniske Universitet, Denmark
Gildas Avoine · Université catholique de Louvain, Belgium
Rana Barua · Indian Statistical Institute, India
Daniel Bernstein · University of Illinois at Chicago, USA and Technische Universiteit Eindhoven, The Netherlands
A.K. Bhattacharjee · Bhabha Atomic Research Centre, India
Rishiraj Bhattacharyya · Ecole Normale Supérieure de Lyon, France
Ioana Boureanu · Ecole Polytechnique Fédérale de Lausanne, Switzerland
Claude Carlet · University of Paris 8, France
Sebastian Faust · Aarhus University, Denmark
Marc Fischlin · Darmstadt University of Technology, Germany
Pierre-Alain Fouque · University of Rennes 1, France
Steven Galbraith · University of Auckland, New Zealand
Sugata Gangopadhyay · Indian Institute of Technology Roorkee, India
Praveen Gauravaram · Tata Consultancy Services, India
Nathan Keller · Bar Ilan University, Israel
Dmitry Khovratovich · University of Luxembourg, Luxembourg
Kazukuni Kobara · National Institute of Advanced Industrial Science and Technology, Japan
Tanja Lange · Technische Universiteit Eindhoven, The Netherlands
Javier Lopez · University of Malaga, Spain
Kanta Matsuura · University of Tokyo, Japan
Miodrag Mihaljevic · Mathematical Institute SANU, Serbia

Ilya Mironov	Microsoft Research, USA
Katerina Mitrokotsa	University of Applied Sciences of Western Switzerland, Switzerland
P.V. Ananda Mohan	Electronics Corporation of India Limited, India
Debdeep Mukhopadhyay	Indian Institute of Technology Kharagpur, India
David Naccache	Ecole Normale Supérieure de Paris, France
Elisabeth Oswald	University of Bristol, UK
S.K. Parulkar	Bhabha Atomic Research Centre, India
Goutam Paul	Indian Statistical Institute, Kolkata, India (Co-chair)
Thomas Peyrin	Nanyang Technological University, Singapore
C. Pandu Rangan	Indian Institute of Technology Madras, India
Bimal Roy	Indian Statistical Institute, India
Santanu Sarkar	National Institute of Standards and Technology, USA
P.K. Saxena	Scientific Analysis Group, India
Jacob Schuldt	University of London, UK
Abhi Shelat	University of Virginia, USA
John A. Smolin	IBM T.J. Watson Research Center, USA
Francois-Xavier Standaert	Université Catholique de Louvain, Belgium
Serge Vaudenay	Ecole Polytechnique Fédérale de Lausanne, Switzerland (Co-chair)
Stefan Wolf	Universitá della Svizzera italiana, Switzerland

External Referees

Reza Azarderakhsh	Suvadeep Hajra	Rajesh Pillai
Nasour Bagheri	Kentaro Imafuku	Bertram Poettering
Abhishek Bajpai	Pascal Junod	Chester Rebeiro
Subhadeep Banik	Kohei Kishimoto	Arnab Roy
Bhagawan Bathe	Souvik Kolay	Sushmita Ruj
Aemin Baumeler	Martin Mehl Lauridsen	Subhabrata Samajder
Sonia Bogos	Wang Lei	Sumanta Sarkar
Ashish Choudhury	Takahiro Matsuda	Sourav Sen Gupta
Dhananjoy Dey	S.P. Mishra	SeongHan Shin
Cunsheng Ding	Kirill Morozov	Wu Shuang
Itai Dinur	Tetsushi Ohki	Izumi Takeuti
Alexandre Duc	Arpita Patra	Meltem Sönmez Turan
Sylvain Guilley	Christiane Peters	Frederik Vercauteren
Indivar Gupta	Marcel Pfaffhauser	

Invited Talks

Functional Encryption on the Decisional Linear Assumption*

Tatsuaki Okamoto

NTT
Tokyo, 180-8585 Japan
okamoto.tatsuaki@lab.ntt.co.jp

Abstract. Recently an advanced class of encryption systems, *functional encryption* (FE), formalized by Boneh, Sahai and Waters [TCC'11] and O'Neill [IACR ePrint'10], have been extensively studied, where a ciphertext of plaintext x is decrypted to $f(x)$ by a secret key associated with a function f, and there is a layered structure for keys such that a higher level key is a pair of master public and secret keys (for an authority) and a lower level key is a secret key with f (for a user) and is generated by a master secret key.

In my talk, we show two FE schemes for all (polynomial-size) circuits on the decisional linear (DLIN) assumption. Our FE schemes are adaptively secure and attribute-hiding in the indistinguishability-based security definition (not in the simulation-based security definition). In the first FE scheme, the number of secret keys is (polynomially) bounded, while that of ciphertexts is unbounded, and the security is proven solely under the DLIN assumption. The second FE scheme requires no bound on the number of secret keys and ciphertexts, but assumes the existence of the indistinguishability obfuscation, which was introduced by Barak et al. [Crypto'01] and recently instantiated by Garg et al. [FOCS'13] from the multi-linear maps, in addition to the DLIN assumption.

These FE schemes are constructed on the randomized encoding technique by Applebaum et al. [Computational Complexity'06] and (strongly) attribute-hiding inner-product encryption (IPE), which is instantiated by the Okamoto-Takashima IPE scheme [Eurocrypt'12] under the DLIN assumption.

---

* This is a joint work with Koutarou Suzuki.

Linear Cryptanalysis and Its Extensions

Kaisa Nyberg

Aalto University School of Science, Finland
`kaisa.nyberg@aalto.fi`

Abstract. During its 20 years of existence in public cryptographic literature, the method of *Linear cryptanalysis* has gained its position as one of the most significant generic methods of statistical cryptanalysis [8]. The main goal of this invited talk is to discuss some recent extensions of linear cryptanalysis for block ciphers. As these extensions typically exploit several linear approximations simultaneously, the statistical analysis involves distinguishing various types of probability distributions of the cipher data. We will present the details of the statistical model of the *Zero-correlation cryptanalysis* [2] and in particular its multidimensional version [3]. We will also present a proper statistical model for the *Statistical saturation attack* [5], which was recently shown in [7] to be mathematically equivalent with the *Multidimensional linear cryptanalysis* [6]. We will explain how this equivalence naturally extends itself to the statistical models of these attacks.

Recently we showed that linear approximations can be useful also outside the traditional domain of linear cryptanalysis [1]. Using the link between differential and linear cryptanalysis established in [4] we estimated expected differential probabilities using known strong linear approximations. As a final topic of this invited talk, we want to demonstrate that this link has potential applications also in the opposite direction. As an example, we will recall the classical statistical cryptanalysis method of *Index of coincidence*, where probabilities of differences, in particular zero-differences, are used to evaluate the nonuniformity of the ciphertext distribution.

References

1. Blondeau, C., Nyberg, K.: New links between differential and linear cryptanalysis. In: Nguyen, P.Q., Johansson, T. (eds.) Advances in Cryptology – EUROCRYPT 2013. Lecture Notes in Computer Science, vol. 7881, pp. 388–404. Springer (2013)
2. Bogdanov, A., Rijmen, V.: Linear hulls with correlation zero and linear cryptanalysis of block ciphers. Designs, Codes and Cryptography (2012)
3. Bogdanov, A., Leander, G., Nyberg, K., Wang, M.: Integral and multidimensional linear distinguishers with correlation zero. In: Wang, X., Sako, K. (eds.) Advances in Cryptology – ASIACRYPT 2012. Lecture Notes in Computer Science, vol. 7658, pp. 244–261. Springer (2012)
4. Chabaud, F., Vaudenay, S.: Links between differential and linear cryptanalysis. In: Santis, A.D. (ed.) Advances in Cryptology - EUROCRYPT '94, Workshop on the Theory and Application of Cryptographic Techniques, Perugia, Italy, May 9-

12, 1994, Proceedings. Lecture Notes in Computer Science, vol. 950, pp. 356–365. Springer (1995)

5. Collard, B., Standaert, F.X.: A statistical saturation attack against the block cipher PRESENT. In: Fischlin, M. (ed.) Topics in Cryptology - CT-RSA 2009, The Cryptographers' Track at the RSA Conference 2009, San Francisco, CA, USA, April 20-24, 2009. Proceedings. LNCS, vol. 5473, pp. 195–210. Springer (2009)

6. Hermelin, M., Cho, J.Y., Nyberg, K.: Multidimensional Extension of Matsui's Algorithm 2. In: Fast Software Encryption 2009. Lecture Notes in Computer Science, vol. 5665, pp. 209–227. Springer (2009)

7. Leander, G.: On linear hulls, statistical saturation attacks, PRESENT and a cryptanalysis of PUFFIN. In: Paterson, K.G. (ed.) Advances in Cryptology - EUROCRYPT 2011 - 30th Annual International Conference on the Theory and Applications of Cryptographic Techniques, Tallinn, Estonia, May 15-19, 2011. Proceedings. Lecture Notes in Computer Science, vol. 6632, pp. 303–322. Springer (2011)

8. Matsui, M.: Linear Cryptanalysis Method for DES Cipher. In: Helleseth, T. (ed.) Advances in Cryptology – EUROCRYPT '93, Workshop on the Theory and Application of Cryptographic Techniques Lofthus, Norway, May 2327, 1993 Proceedings. LNCS, vol. 765, pp. 386–397. Springer (1994)

Cryptographic Aspects of TLS

Kenneth G. Paterson*

Information Security Group,
Royal Holloway, University of London, U.K.

Abstract. TLS is one of the most important cryptographic protocols, being used daily by millions of people and their devices. In the last couple of years, TLS has become the focus of intense research attention, with a slew of papers reporting attacks on and security proofs for different parts of the protocol. In this talk, I will give a high-level overview of this recent work, focussed on explaining how the complexity and idiosyncratic design of TLS has raised barriers to its analysis. I'll also prognosticate on future developments in the TLS arena.

* Supported by EPSRC Leadership Fellowship EP/H005455/1.

Table of Contents

Key Exchange and Secret Sharing

Side Channel Attacks II

Efficient Implementation and Hardware

Coding Theory in Cryptography

Symmetric Key Cryptanalysis II

Key-Private Proxy Re-encryption under LWE

Yoshinori Aono[1], Xavier Boyen[2], Le Trieu Phong[1,*], and Lihua Wang[1,**]

[1] NICT, Japan
phong@nict.go.jp
[2] Queensland University of Technology, Australia

Abstract. Proxy re-encryption (PRE) is a highly useful cryptographic primitive whereby Alice and Bob can endow a proxy with the capacity to change ciphertext recipients from Alice to Bob, without the proxy itself being able to decrypt, thereby providing delegation of decryption authority. Key-private PRE (KP-PRE) specifies an additional level of confidentiality, requiring pseudo-random proxy keys that leak no information on the identity of the delegators and delegatees.

In this paper, we propose a CPA-secure PK-PRE scheme in the standard model (which we then transform into a CCA-secure scheme in the random oracle model). Both schemes enjoy highly desirable properties such as uni-directionality and multi-hop delegation.

Unlike (the few) prior constructions of PRE and KP-PRE that typically rely on bilinear maps under *ad hoc* assumptions, security of our construction is based on the hardness of the standard Learning-With-Errors (LWE) problem, itself reducible from worst-case lattice hard problems that are conjectured immune to quantum cryptanalysis, or "post-quantum".

Of independent interest, we further examine the practical hardness of the LWE assumption, using Kannan's exhaustive search algorithm coupling with pruning techniques. This leads to state-of-the-art parameters not only for our scheme, but also for a number of other primitives based on LWE published the literature.

Keywords: proxy re-encryption, key privacy, learning with errors, chosen ciphertext security, LWE practical hardness.

1 Introduction

Proxy re-encryption (PRE), introduced in [7], is a type of public key encryption, in which anyone can send encrypted messages to others using their public keys. The unique feature in PRE is the intermediation of delegation via "proxy re-encryption keys": Alice and Bob must set up a proxy key $rk_{A \to B}$ transforming Alice's ciphertexts to those Bob can decrypt. The proxy key $rk_{A \to B}$ is usually

---

* Corresponding author.
** This author is partially supported by JSPS KAKENHI Grant Number 23500031.

G. Paul and S. Vaudenay (Eds.): INDOCRYPT 2013, LNCS 8250, pp. 1–18, 2013.

put in a semi-trusted server: although the server cannot decrypt, its participation allows Alice to revoke delegation to Bob by revoking the key $rk_{A \to B}$ held at the server.

KP-PKE. Often, anonymity is a concern, and it is required that neither the delegator (Alice) nor the delegatee (Bob) be identifiable from the proxy re-encryption key $rk_{A \to B}$ that they set up. We speak of "key-private" proxy re-encryption (KP-PRE)—which, to be clear is a public-key primitive.

KP-PRE (a.k.a., anonymous PRE) is useful in various applications such as distributed file systems, digital rights management, credential system, and mailing lists as summarized in [2]. For example, in mailing list application, to securely send a message to all members $\{1, \ldots, N\}$ in the list, it suffices to send only *one* (instead of N if not using PRE) encrypted message under the public key represented that list. A proxy server will do the re-encrytion to all members in the list. The key privacy property of PRE ensures members[1] $\{1, \ldots, N\}$ in the mailing list remain anonymous.

We note that it is not a paradox for a re-encryption proxy to be granted the power to re-encrypt a ciphertext from Alice to Bob anonymously, without knowing the identity of either party. Not only can the proxy be prompted to perform re-encryption on the basis of an anonymous key (designated, e.g., as an index in a table), but the key index itself can be hidden using standard oblivious-transfer techniques if "unlinkability" across multiple re-encryptions is a requirement.

Related Works. Achieving key-private PRE has been acknowledged as a difficult task. In fact, many PRE schemes including [3,7,10,18,21] are not key-private, as shown in [2]. To our knowledge, there exist only two secure schemes with key privacy up to now: (1) the CPA-secure scheme in [2]; and (2) the CCA-secure in the random oracle model in [32]. Another PRE scheme had been claimed CCA-secure and key-private, in [33], but unfortunately its CCA security was recently broken as shown in [19].

There have also been a lot of works trying to achieve CCA security for PRE, even without the key privacy requirement: we mention [21] achieving the weaker notion of Replayable CCA from LWE per the corrected proof in [28], as well as [19,30,31,35] and [13] achieving full CCA respectively in bilinear groups and in groups where decisional Diffie-Hellman assumption holds. All of those schemes are single-hop schemes, in which a ciphertext can be re-encrypted once; and none of them is key-private.

Additionally, some works have looked at identity-based PRE: see for instance [29] for a key-private scheme using pairings and random oracles, and [34] for a construction focused on collusion safeness, to list just some recent ones.

With the exception of [21] (which is neither key-private nor truly CCA), all the foregoing PRE and KP-PRE constructions ultimately rely on the hardness of the

---

[1] When the system using PRE involves N users, they are conventionally represented as integers in $\{1, \ldots, N\}$.

Discrete Logarithm, and typically much stronger assumptions when pairings are involved. Those will never provide long-term safety guarantees (against quantum cryptanalysis in particular).

LWE. "Learning With Errors" or LWE [26] is rapidly emerging as a hardness assumption of choice when long-term security is an issue, both classical and quantum. As shown in [9,26], the LWE assumption theoretically has strong connection to lattice hardness assumptions, which are conjectured very safe in many respects. In practice, however, there are certain efficient "attacks" on LWE, such as those illustrated in [22–25]. Although none of those attacks comes anywhere close to breaking the LWE assumption in a theoretical sense, they force us to be careful in our choice of LWE parameters when concrete real-world security is a concern. Amongst the known "attacks", those of [22, 23] against the computational variant of LWE (namely, Search-LWE) are the most potent.

1.1   Our Contributions

The foregoing leaves us with the double interrogation, of whether it is possible to contruct KP-PRE from the theoretically very appealing LWE assumption, and whether one can then parametrize such construction in order to avoid the practical attacks. Specifically, in this study, we ask:

1. Can key-private PRE be efficiently constructed under the LWE assumption?
2. How hard is LWE, *practically*? This will affect the parameters of our schemes, as well as others.

Constructive Contributions: KP-PRE from LWE

- We design a key-private PRE against chosen plaintext attacks (CPA). This is achieved by transforming the public key encryption scheme of [22] in ways that are reminiscent of certain techniques developed in the context of fully homomorphic encryption schemes such as [8], notwithstanding certain impossibility results shown in [2]. At a very high level, we exploit two (new) facts about (our variant of) the encryption scheme of [22]: recipient anonymity, and additive homomorphism. We use those facts to show that our PRE scheme is CPA-secure under the LWE assumption, in the standard model. See Section 3.
- We then show that our scheme is eligible for conversion into a CCA-secure encryption scheme, using the well-known Fujisaki-Okamoto method [14,15], without losing the key-private PRE functionality. Consequently, this scheme is CCA-secure under the LWE assumption, in the random oracle model [6]. See Section 4.

Both CPA-secure and CCA-secure schemes are multi-hop (namely a ciphertext can be re-encrypted several times, albeit not indefinitely), and are uni-directional (namely one proxy key can only transform ciphertexts in one direction, not both).

Analytic Contributions: LWE Parameter Selection

- We evaluate the practical hardness of the LWE assumption. As with Lindner-Peikert [22] and Liu-Nguyen [23], our strategy is to solve a bounded distance decoding problem derived from a search LWE instance, and then employs Kannan's lattice exhaustive search algorithm [20]. However, using a new pruning strategy called *band pruning*, our attack on LWE can handle any Gaussian noise deviation (e.g., 4 or 5 used in our schemes), in contrast to [22, 23] (larger than 8 mandatorily. See footnote[2].). The computation, including lattice enumeration, cost of the attack is slightly better than [22], and is comparable with [23]. See Section 5.

2   Preliminaries and Definitions

We use $\overset{c}{\approx}$ for computational indistinguishability. For a matrix A, A^T is its transpose.

LWE Assumption. Succinctly, the assumption LWE(m, n, α, q) asserts that

$$(A, Ax + e) \overset{c}{\approx} (A, r)$$

in which

- $A \in \mathbb{Z}_q^{m \times n}$ and $r \in \mathbb{Z}_q^{m \times 1}$ are randomly chosen.
- $x \in \psi_{\alpha q}^{n \times 1}, e \in \psi_{\alpha q}^{m \times 1}$, and $Ax + e$ is computed over $\mathbb{Z}_q$. Moreover $\psi_{\alpha q}$ is the Gaussian distribution over the integers $\mathbb{Z}$, with mean 0 and deviation αq for real number $0 < \alpha < 1$. (Originally, x is chosen randomly from $\mathbb{Z}_q^{n \times 1}$ in [26]. However, as showed in [1, 24], one can take $x \in \psi_{\alpha q}^{n \times 1}$ as we do here.)

By a standard hybrid argument over columns of $X \in \psi_{\alpha q}^{n \times l}$, we have under the LWE assumption

$$(A, AX + E) \overset{c}{\approx} (A, R)$$

for random $R \in \mathbb{Z}_q^{m \times l}$ and Gaussian noise $E \in \psi_{\alpha q}^{m \times l}$. This fact is used in our security proofs.

Syntax of PRE. The scheme consists of following algorithms (ParamsGen, KeyGen, ReKeyGen, Enc, ReEnc, Dec). ParamsGen(λ) returns public parameters pp according to security parameter λ. KeyGen(pp) returns public-secret key pairs (pk, sk). Algorithm ReKeyGen(pp, sk_i, pk_j) returns $rk_{i \to j}$. Enc(pp, pk, m) returns a ciphertext CT. ReEnc$(pp, rk_{i \to j}, CT_i)$ transforms ciphertext CT_i of party i into a ciphertext that party j can decrypt. Dec(pp, sk, CT) recovers a message m.

Definition 1 (CPA security of PRE, [2]). *Consider below interactions between an adversary $\mathcal{A}$ and a challenger $\mathcal{C}$.*
Phase 1:

---

[2] Quoting from [22, Section 6]: "... to allow for a Gaussian parameter $s \geq 8$, so that the discrete Gaussian $D_{\mathbb{Z}^m, s}$ approximates the continuous Gaussian D_s extremely well." The same reason is for [23]. Our attack and its analysis in Section 5 do not rely on that approximation, and hence work for arbitrary noise deviation.

- $\mathcal{C}$ generates public parameters $pp \leftarrow \mathsf{ParamsGen}(\lambda)$ and gives them to $\mathcal{A}$.
- Uncorrupted key generation: $\mathcal{C}$ generates $(pk, sk) \leftarrow \mathsf{KeyGen}(pp)$ and gives $\mathcal{A}$ public key pk upon request. $\mathcal{A}$ can request many pk, and let Γ_H be the set of honest user indexes.
- Corrupted key generation: In this process, $\mathcal{C}$ generates key pair $(pk, sk) \leftarrow \mathsf{KeyGen}(pp)$ and $\mathcal{A}$ is given (pk, sk). $\mathcal{A}$ can request many times, and let Γ_C be the set of corrupted user indexes.

Phase 2:

- Re-encryption key generation: $\mathcal{A}$ submits pair of indexes (i, j) to get $rk_{i \to j} \leftarrow \mathsf{ReKeyGen}(pp, sk_i, pk_j)$. All requests where $i = j$ or where $i \in \Gamma_H, j \in \Gamma_C$ are ignored. (Remark here that it is sufficient to consider query (i, j) with $i, j \in \Gamma_H$, since if $i \in \Gamma_C$, then $\mathcal{A}$ can generate $rk_{i \to j}$ itself for all j.)
- Re-encryption: $\mathcal{A}$ submits query (i, j, C_i). The challenger in turn generates $rk_{i \to j} \leftarrow \mathsf{ReKeyGen}(pp, sk_i, pk_j)$ (if it is not yet created), and then returns $C_j \leftarrow \mathsf{ReEnc}(pp, rk_{i \to j}, C_i)$. All requests where $i = j$ or where $i \in \Gamma_H, j \in \Gamma_C$ are ignored. (Similarly to above, it is sufficient to consider queries (i, j) with $i, j \in \Gamma_H$.)
- Challenge: $\mathcal{A}$ submits (i^*, m_0, m_1). The challenger then chooses random bit $b \in \{0, 1\}$, and then returns $C_{i^*} = \mathsf{Enc}(pp, pk_{i^*}, m_b)$. This is done only once, and it is required that $i^* \in \Gamma_H$.

$\mathcal{A}$ finally outputs $b' \in \{0, 1\}$ as a guess of b. Define $\mathcal{A}$'s advantage as $|\Pr[b' = b] - 1/2|$. The PRE scheme is CPA-secure if this advantage is negligible for all poly-time adversary $\mathcal{A}$.

Definition 2 (Key privacy). *Consider following interactions of an adversary $\mathcal{A}$. Phase 1 is the same as in Definition 1.*
Phase 2:

- Re-encryption key generation: On input (i, j) for $i \neq j$ by the adversary, where $i \in \Gamma_H$, $j \in \Gamma_H \cup \Gamma_C$, return the key $rk_{i \to j}$. (There is no need to consider $i \in \Gamma_C$ since $\mathcal{A}$ holds sk_i in that case.)
- Re-encryption queries (i, j, C_i): The challenger returns to $\mathcal{A}$ the re-encrypted ciphertext $C_j = \mathsf{ReEnc}(pp, rk_{i \to j}, C_i)$. (If the re-encryption key $rk_{i \to j}$ was not generated yet, the challenger creates it.)
- Challenge: On input (i^*, j^*), the challenger takes a bit b randomly, returns $rk^* = rk_{i^* \to j^*} = \mathsf{ReKeyGen}(pp, sk_{i^*}, pk_{j^*})$ if $b = 1$ or returns a random key rk^* in the key space if $b = 0$. The constraints are: (1) $rk_{i^* \to j^*}$ was not queried before, (2) there is no chain of re-encryption keys from j^* to any $k \in \Gamma_C$, (3) $i^* \neq j^*$ and $j^* \in \Gamma_H$. Note there is no limitation on i^*, namely $i^* \in \Gamma_H \cup \Gamma_C$.

Eventually, $\mathcal{A}$ outputs a bit b', and its advantage is defined as $|\Pr[b' = b] - 1/2|$. The PRE scheme is key-private if this advantage is negligible for all poly-time adversary $\mathcal{A}$.

The above definition differs from its counterpart in [2] in some ways. The condition (3) with $j^* \in \Gamma_H$ while i^* is free in $\Gamma_H \cup \Gamma_C$ means that, regardless delegators, *honest* delegatees are enough to provide key privacy. This is stronger than [2] which requires both $i^*, j^* \in \Gamma_H$.

Our definition also removes the "collusion-safe" condition implicitly incorporated in that of [2] by requiring condition (2). This is for good because we think that collusion-safeness and key privacy are separate issues in applications.

Definition 3 (CCA security of PRE). *This is the same as Definition 1, with following additional decryption queries by adversary $\mathcal{A}$ in Phase 2: $\mathcal{A}$ repeatedly submits (i, C_i) to the challenger, who returns the decryption $\mathsf{Dec}(sk_i, C_i)$. The additional constraints here are: (1) $i \in \Gamma_H$ (since if $i \in \Gamma_C$ then $\mathcal{A}$ already held sk_i to do decryption itself), and (2) (i, C_i) is not a derivative of (i^*, C_{i^*}). Derivatives are defined as follows.*

- (i^*, C_{i^*}) *is a derivative of itself.*
- (i, C_i) *is computed from (i^*, C_{i^*}) via a chain of re-encryption by the re-encryption oracle.*
- *A chain of re-encryption keys from i^* to i is already hold by $\mathcal{A}$, and C_i is computed from C_{i^*} by using those keys.*

Our definition is slightly different from those in single-hop schemes [17, 19, 21] (in which two games are needed). The derivative notion is taken from [19], adapted for the multi-hop setting by considering chain conditions.

Definition 4 (Key privacy, CCA setting). *Phase 1, Phase 2 are the same as in Definition 2, except that in Phase 2, $\mathcal{A}$ can access to additional oracles $\mathsf{Dec}(sk_j, \cdot)$, where $j \in \Gamma_H$, handling queries of form (j, C_j). The queries cannot simultaneously satisfy: (1) $j = j^*$, and (2) C_j is computed involving rk^*.*

3   Our Key-Private, CPA-Secure PRE

Let us first recall some notions, originally used in fully homomorphic encryption. For matrices A, B, the notation $[A|B]$ stands for their column concatenation.

Functions Bits($\cdot$) and Power2($\cdot$). The functions $\mathsf{Power2}(\cdot)$ and $\mathsf{Bits}(\cdot)$ are described as follows. Let $v \in \mathbb{Z}_q^n$ and $\kappa = \lceil \lg q \rceil$ where $\lg(\cdot)$ is logarithm of base 2. Then there are bit vectors $v_i \in \{0,1\}^n$ such that $v = \sum_{i=0}^{\kappa-1} 2^i v_i$. Then

$$\mathsf{Bits}(v) = [v_0| \cdots |v_{\kappa-1}] \in \{0,1\}^{1 \times n\kappa}.$$

Let $X = [X_1| \cdots |X_l] \in \mathbb{Z}_q^{n \times l}$ where X_i are column vectors. Then

$$\mathsf{Power2}(X) = \begin{bmatrix} X_1 & \cdots & X_l \\ 2X_1 & \cdots & 2X_l \\ \vdots & & \vdots \\ 2^{\kappa-1}X_1 & \cdots & 2^{\kappa-1}X_l \end{bmatrix} \in \mathbb{Z}_q^{n\kappa \times l}.$$

It is easy to check that

$$\mathsf{Bits}(v)\mathsf{Power2}(X) = vX \in \mathbb{Z}_q^{1 \times l}.$$

This equality will be useful in checking the correctness of our schemes. Following PRE scheme is based on the public key encryption scheme given in [22]. In particular, the first three algorithms are basically the same as those in [22], while the last two are ours. Concrete parameters are given in Table 1.

Parameters Generation: Choose positive integers q, n, and take matrix $A \in \mathbb{Z}_q^{n \times n}$ randomly.

Key Generation: Let $s = \alpha q$ for $0 < \alpha < 1$. Take Gaussian noise matrices $R, S \in \psi_s^{n \times l}$. The public key is $pk = P$ for $P = R - AS \in \mathbb{Z}_q^{n \times l}$, and the secret key is $sk = S$. Here, l is the message length in bits, while n is the key dimension.

Encryption: To encrypt $m \in \{0,1\}^l$, take Gaussian noise vectors $e_1, e_2 \in \psi_s^{1 \times n}$, and $e_3 \in \psi_s^{1 \times l}$, and return ciphertext $c = (c_1, c_2) \in \mathbb{Z}_q^{1 \times (n+l)}$ where

$$c_1 = e_1 A + e_2 \in \mathbb{Z}_q^{1 \times n}, c_2 = e_1 P + e_3 + m \cdot \left\lfloor \frac{q}{2} \right\rfloor \in \mathbb{Z}_q^{1 \times l}.$$

Decryption: To decrypt $c = (c_1, c_2) \in \mathbb{Z}_q^{1 \times (n+l)}$ by secret key S, compute $\overline{m} = c_1 S + c_2 \in \mathbb{Z}_q^l$. Let $\overline{m} = (\overline{m}_1, \ldots, \overline{m}_l)$. If $\overline{m}_i \in [-\lfloor \frac{q}{4} \rfloor, \lfloor \frac{q}{4} \rfloor) \subset \mathbb{Z}_q$, let $m_i = 0$; otherwise $m_i = 1$.

Proxy Key Generation: Alice with keys (A, P_A, S_A) and Bob with keys (B, P_B, S_B) want to set up proxy key $rk_{A \to B}$. The proxy key $rk_{A \to B} = (P_B, Q)$ where

$$Q = \begin{bmatrix} X & -XS_B + E + \mathsf{Power2}(S_A) \\ \mathbf{0}_{l \times n} & \mathbf{I}_{l \times l} \end{bmatrix}$$

in which matrices $X \in \mathbb{Z}_q^{n\kappa \times n}$ ($\kappa = \lceil \lg q \rceil$) is chosen randomly. Noise matrix E is chosen from $\psi_s^{n\kappa \times l}$. Therefore, one way to generate Q is as follows

1. Bob creates X, E, and securely sends $X, -XS_B + E$ to Alice. This can be done without interaction by encrypting the tuple under a public key for which Alice holds the corresponding secret key. The resulting ciphertext is added to Bob's public key.
2. Alice with S_A uses above information from Bob to set up the proxy key.

Re-encryption: Let $rk_{A \to B} = (P_B, Q)$. To transform Alice's ciphertext $(c_1, c_2) \in \mathbb{Z}_q^{1 \times (n+l)}$ into Bob's ciphertext, return

$$f_1[A|P_B] + [f_2|f_3] + [\mathsf{Bits}(c_1)|c_2] \cdot Q \in \mathbb{Z}_q^{1 \times (n+l)}$$

in which $f_1, f_2 \in \psi_s^{1 \times n}$, and $f_3 \in \psi_s^{1 \times l}$ are chosen by the proxy.

Intuition on Key Privacy. The re-encryption key $rk_{A \to B}$ contains following information on Bob's secret $sk_B = S_B$: $(A, P_B = R_B - AS_B)$ and $(X, -XS_B + E)$. These together can be written in LWE form

$$\begin{bmatrix} A \\ X \end{bmatrix}, -\begin{bmatrix} A \\ X \end{bmatrix} S_B + \begin{bmatrix} R_B \\ E \end{bmatrix}$$

Table 1. The concrete parameters of our CPA-secure PRE

	n	q	s	$pk = P$ (bits)	$Q \in rk$ (bits)	Ciphertext (bits)	Rate $|CT|/|m|$	Bit security (cf. Table 3)
toy	160	2053	4.00	2.4×10^5	3.9×10^6	3456	27	45
low	192	4093	5.44	2.9×10^5	5.6×10^6	3840	30	62
medium	256	4093	5.13	3.9×10^5	9.8×10^6	4608	36	101
high	320	4093	4.88	4.9×10^5	15×10^6	5376	42	143

The CCA-secure scheme parameters are almost the same, except ciphertexts are a little lengthened by a symmetric encryption part. Intuitively, compared to [22], we have to decrease the noise deviation s to tolerate the noise increased in ciphertext transformation by proxy. In the table, message length $|m| = l = 128$.

and thus $rk_{A \to B}$ is pseudo-random if S_B is kept secret, namely if Bob is not corrupted. This also implies that public key P_B is pseudo-random and unrelated to Bob, which is the recipient-anonymous property of [22].

However, the above is still insufficient! If re-encryption is deterministic, for example using $[\mathsf{Bits}(c_1)|c_2] \cdot Q$ for $rk_{A \to B} = Q$ (and P_B is unused), there is an attack on key privacy as follows: (1) adversary $\mathcal{A}$ creates ciphertext (c_1, c_2) using Alice's public key; (2) $\mathcal{A}$ asks for challenge rk^* between Alice and Bob (which is either $rk_{A \to B} = Q$ or random); (3) $\mathcal{A}$ asks for re-encryption (c_1', c_2') of (c_1, c_2) from Alice to Bob, namely $(c_1', c_2') = [\mathsf{Bits}(c_1)|c_2] \cdot Q$; (4) $\mathcal{A}$ checks whether $(c_1', c_2') = [\mathsf{Bits}(c_1)|c_2] \cdot rk^*$. If the comparison holds true, $\mathcal{A}$ decides that rk^* is the re-encryption key between Alice and Bob. The idea of this attack is originated in [2, Lemma 2.7], and works well under the condition that re-encryption is deterministic.

To deal with the attack, we add the term $f_1[A|P_B] + [f_2|f_3]$ into the re-encryption. This is exactly an encryption of zero vector under the public key of Bob, so that decryption by Bob will not be affected by this term. Thus re-encryption is randomized, and we succeed in proving that the PRE scheme is key-private.

Multi-hop Property. A ciphertext $(c_1, c_2) \in \mathbb{Z}_q^{1 \times (n+l)}$, after re-encryption, is changed to a ciphertext in $\mathbb{Z}_q^{1 \times (n+l)}$. Namely, re-encryption does not change the format of ciphertexts. Original ciphertexts and transformed ciphertexts are decrypted by the same decryption algorithm (with different secret keys, of course). Thus our scheme is multi-hop, namely a ciphertext can be re-encrypted many times as long as the incurred noise is kept small enough.

Uni-directional Property. This property ensures that Alice and proxy together cannot decrypted Bob's ciphertexts. This is intuitively true because Alice and proxy can only get $(X, -XS_B + E)$ where X and E are chosen by Bob. The tuple is pseudo-random under the LWE assumption, so the information is useless.

Correctness. First, we check that normal ciphertext $c_1 = e_1 A + e_2$, $c_2 = e_1 P + e_3 + m \cdot \lfloor \frac{q}{2} \rfloor$ can be decrypted by secret S via the formula $c_1 S + c_2$.

Indeed,

$$c_1 S + c_2 = e_1 R + e_2 S + e_3 + m \cdot \left\lfloor \frac{q}{2} \right\rfloor$$

will yield m if the noise $e_1 R + e_2 S + e_3$ is small enough. Second, we check a transformed ciphertext can be decrypted by Bob. Namely, decryption of ciphertext $f_1[A|P_B] + [f_2|f_3] + [\mathsf{Bits}(c_1)|c_2] \cdot Q$ by Bob's secret S_B is the same as Alice's decryption on (c_1, c_2) with S_A. Indeed,

$$(f_1[A|P_B] + [f_2|f_3] + [\mathsf{Bits}(c_1)|c_2] \cdot Q) \begin{bmatrix} S_B \\ \mathbf{I}_{l \times l} \end{bmatrix}$$

$$= f_1(AS_B + P_B) + f_2 S_B + f_3 + [\mathsf{Bits}(c_1)|c_2] \begin{bmatrix} E + \mathsf{Power2}(S_A) \\ \mathbf{I}_{l \times l} \end{bmatrix}$$

$$= f_1 R_B + f_2 S_B + f_3 + \mathsf{Bits}(c_1)\,(E + \mathsf{Power2}(S_A)) + c_2$$

$$= \underbrace{f_1 R_B + f_2 S_B + f_3 + \mathsf{Bits}(c_1)E}_{\text{noise}} + c_1 S_A + c_2$$

will yield Alice's decryption on (c_1, c_2) since the incurred noise is sufficiently small. Technical details are deferred to Appendix A.

Theorem 1 (CPA security). *Under the LWE($n + q_{rk}n\lceil \lg q \rceil$, n, α, q) assumption, the above PRE scheme is CPA-secure. Here, q_{rk} is the number of re-encryption key queries the adversary can make.*

Proof. Consider an adversary $\mathcal{A}$ against the PRE. Let Game$_0$ be the interactions between $\mathcal{A}$ and a challenger as in Definition 1. In this initial game, $pp = (q, n, A)$, Γ_H is the set of honest users, Γ_C is the set of corrupted users. A key pair (P_i, S_i) satisfying $P_i = R_i - AS_i$ for Gaussian noise matrix R_i, S_i. The re-encryption key from party i to party j is $rk_{i \to j} = (P_j, Q_{ij})$ in which

$$Q_{ij} = \begin{bmatrix} X_{ij} & -X_{ij}S_j + E_{ij} + \mathsf{Power2}(S_i) \\ \mathbf{0}_{l \times n} & \mathbf{I}_{l \times l} \end{bmatrix}$$

in which X_{ij}, E_{ij} are generated by party j. The challenge ciphertext related to party i^* is (c_1^*, c_2^*) where

$$c_1^* = e_1^* A + e_2^* \text{ and } c_2^* = e_1^* P^* + e_3^* + m_b \cdot \left\lfloor \frac{q}{2} \right\rfloor$$

in which $b \in \{0, 1\}$ is the challenge bit, (e_1^*, e_2^*, e_3^*) are Gaussian noise, and P^* is the challenge public key.

For notational convenience, let $\Gamma_H = \{1, \ldots, N\}$. Following Game$_{1 \leq k \leq N}$ corresponds to honest party $k \in \Gamma_H$. Game$_k$ is identical to Game$_{k-1}$, except the following change:

– P_k ($= R_k - AS_k$ in Game$_{k-1}$) is changed into a random matrix P_k'.

- Re-encryption key query (i, k): return $rk_{i \to k} = (P'_k, Q_{ik})$ in which

$$Q_{ik} = \begin{bmatrix} X_{ik} & R_{ik} \\ \mathbf{0}_{l \times n} & \mathbf{I}_{l \times l} \end{bmatrix}$$

where R_{ik} is freshly random.
- Re-encryption query (i, k, C_i): return a random vector in $\mathbb{Z}_q^{1 \times (n+l)}$ to $\mathcal{A}$.

Game$_{\text{final}}$ is identical to Game$_N$ except that challenge ciphertext is

$$c_1^* = r_1^* \text{ and } c_2^* = r_2^* + m_b \cdot \lfloor \frac{q}{2} \rfloor$$

in which r_1^*, r_2^* are freshly random vectors over $\mathbb{Z}_q$ of proper lengths. By this change, the challenge bit b is information-theoretically hidden from $\mathcal{A}$, so $\Pr[b' = b] = 1/2$, and hence $\mathcal{A}$'s advantage in Game$_1$ is 0.

We now need to prove that the games are indistinguishable from the view of $\mathcal{A}$, under the LWE assumption. The change from Game$_{k-1}$ to Game$_k$ involves turning

$$P_k = R_k - AS_k, R_{ik} = E_{ik} - X_{ik}S_k$$

into random matrices. This is ensured by LWE with secret S_k of the form

$$\begin{bmatrix} A \\ \vdots \\ X_{ik} \\ \vdots \end{bmatrix}_i, -\begin{bmatrix} A \\ \vdots \\ X_{ik} \\ \vdots \end{bmatrix}_i S_k + \begin{bmatrix} R_k \\ \vdots \\ X_{ik} \\ \vdots \end{bmatrix}_i$$

where index i corresponds to all re-encryption key queries (i, k). Here we rely on the LWE$(n + q_{rk}n\lceil \lg q \rceil, n, \alpha, q)$ assumption. The change also relies on the fact that $f_1[A|P'_k] + [f_2|f_3]$ is pseudo-random under LWE$(n + l, n, \alpha, q)$ when dealing with re-encryption queries.

The change from Game$_N$ to Game$_{\text{final}}$ involves turning $e_1^*A + e_2^*$ and $c_2^* = e_1^*P^* + e_3^*$ into random vectors. This is ensured by LWE with secret $(e_1^*)^T$ (the transpose of e_1^*) of the form

$$[A|P^*]^T, (e_1^*[A|P^*] + [e_2^*|e_3^*])^T$$

where P^* is random by one of previous games. The assumption parameter is LWE$(n + l, n, \alpha, q)$. We consider $n + q_{rk}n\lceil \lg q \rceil > n + l$, ending with the LWE parameter stated in the theorem.   □

Theorem 2 (Key privacy). *Under the LWE$(n + q_{rk}n\lceil \lg q \rceil, n, \alpha, q)$ assumption, the above PRE scheme is key-private. Here, q_{rk} is the number of re-encryption key queries the adversary can make.*

Proof. Let Game$_0$ be the attack game as in Definition 2. In the game, the challenge re-encryption key is $rk_{i^* \to j^*} = (P_{j^*}, Q_{i^* j^*})$ where

$$Q_{i^* j^*} = \begin{bmatrix} X_{i^* j^*} & -X_{i^* j^*} S_{j^*} + E_{i^* j^*} + \mathsf{Power2}(S_{i^*}) \\ \mathbf{0}_{l \times n} & \mathbf{I}_{l \times l} \end{bmatrix}$$

for $j^* \in \Gamma_H$. For notational convenience, let $\Gamma_H = \{1, \dots, N\}$. Game$_{1 \le k \le N}$ corresponds to honest party $k \in \Gamma_H$. Game$_k$ is identical to Game$_{k-1}$, except that re-encryption key $rk_{i \to k}$ for any $i \in \Gamma_H \cup \Gamma_C$ is set to

$$rk_{i \to k} = \left(P_k, \begin{bmatrix} X_{ik} & R_{ik} \\ \mathbf{0}_{l \times n} & \mathbf{I}_{l \times l} \end{bmatrix} \right)$$

where P_k, R_{ik} are freshly random matrices over $\mathbb{Z}_q$ of proper sizes. Since $j^* \in \Gamma_H$ by the constraint in definition, $rk_{i^* \to j^*}$ is changed in Game$_{j^*}$ into

$$rk_{i^* \to j^*} = \left(P_{j^*}, \begin{bmatrix} X_{i^* j^*} & R_{i^* j^*} \\ \mathbf{0}_{l \times n} & \mathbf{I}_{l \times l} \end{bmatrix} \right)$$

for random matrices $P_{j^*}, R_{i^* j^*}$. Also, in Game$_k$, re-encryption queries (i, k, C_i) is answered by random vectors of length $\mathbb{Z}_q^{1 \times (n+l)}$ for all index i. Thus in Game$_N$, the challenge that $\mathcal{A}$ gets is random in both cases $b = 0$ and $b = 1$, and hence $\mathcal{A}$'s advantage is 0.

The games Game$_k$ and Game$_{k-1}$ are indistinguishable under LWE with secret S_k of the form

$$\begin{bmatrix} A \\ \vdots \\ X_{ik} \\ \vdots \end{bmatrix}_i, \quad - \begin{bmatrix} A \\ \vdots \\ X_{ik} \\ \vdots \end{bmatrix}_i S_k + \begin{bmatrix} R_k \\ \vdots \\ E_{ik} \\ \vdots \end{bmatrix}_i$$

where i depends on the re-encryption key queries, and LWE of form $f_1[A|P_k] + [f_2|f_3]$ for random matrix P_k and secret Gaussian noise vectors f_1, f_2, f_3. Thus all games above are indistinguishable to $\mathcal{A}$ under the LWE$(n + q_{rk} n \lceil \lg q \rceil, n, \alpha, q)$ and LWE$(n + l, n, \alpha, q)$ assumptions. Considering $n + q_{rk} n \lceil \lg q \rceil > n + l$, we end up with the LWE parameters as stated. □

4   Our Key-Private, CCA-Secure PRE

We apply Fujisaki-Okamoto method to the CPA-secure PRE to obtain following CCA-secure one. Succinctly, the encryption is as follows

$$\mathsf{Enc}_{cca}^{pre}(m; \sigma) = \mathsf{Enc}_{cpa}^{pre}(\sigma; H(\sigma, c_s)) || \mathsf{SE}_{G(\sigma)}(m)$$

in which

- σ is random; H and G are hash functions modeled as random oracles.
- $c_s = \mathsf{SE}_{G(\sigma)}(m)$ is the symmetric encryption of m under the key $G(\sigma)$.

Below is the detailed description of our CCA-secure scheme. Let (SE, SD) be a symmetric encryption scheme, which is one-time secure. (One example of (SE, SD) is the one-time-pad.) Let G, H are random oracles. Algorithms for parameters generation, key generation, proxy key generation are identical to the CPA-secure scheme in Section 3. The differences are in following algorithms.

Encryption: Choose random $\sigma \in \{0,1\}^l$. Symmetrically encrypt message $m \in \{0,1\}^*$: $c_s = \mathsf{SE}_{G(\sigma)}(m)$. Let $h = H(\sigma, c_s)$.
Encrypt σ: use randomness h, take Gaussian noise vectors $e_1, e_2 \in \psi_s^{1 \times n}$, and $e_3 \in \psi_s^{1 \times l}$, and return ciphertext $c = (c_1, c_2) \in \mathbb{Z}_q^{1 \times (n+l)}$ where

$$c_1 = e_1 A + e_2 \in \mathbb{Z}_q^{1 \times n}, c_2 = e_1 P + e_3 + \sigma \cdot \left\lfloor \frac{q}{2} \right\rfloor \in \mathbb{Z}_q^{1 \times l}.$$

Return (c_1, c_2, c_s).

Re-encryption: Do the re-encryption on (c_1, c_2) as in the CPA-secure scheme. Return the result together with unchanged c_s.

Decryption: To decrypt $c = (c_1, c_2, c_s)$ by secret key S, compute $\bar\sigma = c_1 S + c_2 \in \mathbb{Z}_q^l$. Let $\bar\sigma = (\bar\sigma_1, \ldots, \bar\sigma_l)$. If $\bar\sigma_i \in [-\lfloor \frac{q}{4} \rfloor, \lfloor \frac{q}{4} \rfloor) \subset \mathbb{Z}_q$, let $\sigma'_i = 0$; otherwise $\sigma'_i = 1$.
Let $\sigma' = \sigma'_1 \cdots \sigma'_l$ and $h' = H(\sigma', c_s)$. Using h', obtain c'_1, c'_2 as the encryption of σ' as in the encryption process. If $(c'_1, c'_2) \neq (c_1, c_2)$, return $\perp$; otherwise return $\mathsf{SD}_{G(\sigma')}(c_s)$ as the message.

Security Intuition. For CCA security, we need to ensure that the decryption oracles are useless to the adversary. In particular, the challenge ciphertext (c_1^*, c_2^*, c_s^*) cannot be converted to another ciphertext passing decryption without $\perp$. Some checks are as follows.

First, any modification on c_s^* will yield different hash value h', and hence $(c'_1, c'_2) \neq (c_1^*, c_2^*)$ in decryption, so $\perp$ is returned.

Second, consider the malformed ciphertext $(c_1^*, c_2^* + e, c_s^*)$, in which e is small noise. In decryption of $(c_1^*, c_2^* + e, c_s^*)$, we have $\bar\sigma = c_1^* S + c_2^* + e$, and suppose e is small enough compared to q, resulting $\sigma' \in \{0,1\}^l$ becomes the same as in the decryption of the challenge (c_1^*, c_2^*, c_s^*). Then h' is also the same since there is no change in c_s^*, and hence internal term (c'_1, c'_2) becomes exactly (c_1^*, c_2^*), since these terms encrypt the same message and randomness. But then $(c'_1, c'_2) \neq (c_1^*, c_2^* + e)$, so $\perp$ is returned.

Third, now consider the malformed ciphertext $(c_1^* + e, c_2^*, c_s^*)$, in which e is small noise. In this case $\bar\sigma = (c_1^* + e)S + c_2^* = c_1^* S + c_2^* + eS$. We can assume that eS is small since both e and S are so. The same argument as in the second case shows that the internal term in decryption (c'_1, c'_2) is exactly identical to (c_1^*, c_2^*). Then finally $\perp$ is returned since $(c'_1, c'_2) \neq (c_1^* + e, c_2^*)$.

Certainly, using the re-encryption algorithm, the adversary can re-encrypt (c_1^*, c_2^*, c_s^*) to other uncorrupted parties. Directly submitting the re-encrypted ciphertext is forbidden by the rules of derivatives, so the adversary changes it in some way, and then asks for decryption. But then the decryption oracle will act as above due to the modification of the ciphertext, preventing any information leakage on the challenge bit.

Theorem 3 (CCA security). *The above PRE scheme is CCA-secure under the LWE assumption, if G, H are random oracles.*

Theorem 4 (Key privacy). *The above PRE scheme is key-private in CCA setting under the LWE assumption.*

5 Practical Hardness of Search LWE Problem

Technical Reminders. Consider the search version of $LWE(m, n, \alpha, q)$. Recall $\psi_{s=\alpha q}$ is the discrete Gaussian distribution over $\mathbb{Z}$, whose density function at y is proportional to $\exp(-\pi y^2/s^2)$. Let $A \in \mathbb{Z}^{m \times n}$, $x \in \psi_{\alpha q}^{n \times 1}$, $e \in \psi_{\alpha q}^{m \times 1}$, $b = Ax + e \in \mathbb{Z}^{m \times 1}$. The search version of LWE is defined as the problem of finding x (or equivalently finding e) from given A and $b = Ax + e$. Denote $R_{\mathcal{O}}^{m \times m}$ the set of normalized orthogonal matrix of degree m.

Previous Attacks on LWE [22, 23]. The basic strategy is to solve a bounded distance decoding (BDD) problem. That is, consider the lattice $\Lambda_q(A) := \{z \in \mathbb{Z}^m : \exists x \text{ such that } z = Ax \ (\mod q)\}$ in which the desired vector is derived from the closest vector to $b = Ax + e$. Lindner and Peikert [22] use Babai's nearest plane algorithm, while Liu and Nguyen [23] employ [20]'s exhaustive search algorithm with linear pruning. As mentioned in the introduction, these attacks was analyzed with Gaussian deviation $s = \alpha q \geq 8$.

Our Attack on LWE. We use a modified version of the exhaustive search algorithm [20] with a new pruning strategy detailed below. Our attack works for any Gaussian noise deviation.

Throughout this section, we assume that the lattice $\Lambda_q(A)$ is given by a q-ary lattice, i.e., a lower triangle matrix with first $m - n$ and last n diagonal elements are q and 1, respectively. For this basis, we use $(b_1, \ldots, b_m)$ and $(\tilde{b}_1, \ldots, \tilde{b}_m)$ to denote a reduced basis and its Gram-Schmidt basis. Following Schnorr's geometric series assumption (GSA) [27] and experiments in [22], we assume that the graph of $\ln \|\tilde{b}_i\|$ consists of horizontal line $\|\tilde{b}_i\| = q$, slope of $0.5 \ln r$, and line $\|\tilde{b}_i\| = 1$. Here, r is a constant in GSA that assumes $\|\tilde{b}_i\|^2 / \|b_1\|^2 = r^{i-1}$ for a reduced basis. It connects to the Hermite factor by the relation $r = \delta^{-4m/(m-1)}$; here, δ is an algorithm-depended factor so that $\|b_1\| = \delta^n \det(L)^{1/n}$.

Following [22], we assume that such lattice basis can be computed in $t_{BKZ}(\delta) = 2^{1.8/\lg(\delta)-130}$ single-core seconds, while they expected it as $2^{1.8/\lg(\delta)-110}$. This is because the latest lattice reduction algorithm can solve 124 dimensional SVP instance [11] which achieves $\delta = 1.00862$ in 4 single core days[3]; it derives $\lg(t_{BKZ}(\delta)) - 1.8/\lg(\delta) \approx -127$. Thus, we rewrite the constant in [22] to -130. Since the record is the time to find a short vector, not to find a reduced basis, actual time for lattice reduction can be slightly larger than this. Therefore, the estimation is expected to be a lower bound of lattice reduction.

---

[3] Chen and Nguyen also announced a record for dimension 126, but the CPU time for solving one instance was not reported.

Table 2. Our re-estimation for [22, Figure 4]

n	q	$s=\alpha q$	Lattice dim	Hermite factor	lg(our time)	vs. lg([LP11]'s time) [secs]
128	2053	6.77	320	1.0086	**17**	32
192	4093	8.87	462	1.0067	**59**	78
256	4093	8.35	619	1.0054	**102**	132
320	4093	8.00	773	1.0045	**147**	189

Table 3. Estimation on our PRE schemes' parameters

	n	q	$s=\alpha q$	Lattice dim	Hermite factor	Bit security	lg(time) [secs]
toy	160	2053	4.00	362	1.0083	45	21
low	192	4093	5.44	451	1.0074	62	39
medium	256	4093	5.13	578	1.0060	101	78
high	320	4093	4.88	718	1.0050	143	120

New Strategy: Band Pruning. Our attack employs an exhaustive search algorithm [20] with pruning technique adopted for LWE. Since an error vector is sampled from a discrete Gaussian, we can upper and lower bound its projected length with high probability. Consider a search tree whose nodes at depth k are labeled by $b - \sum_{i=m-k+1}^{m} a_i \cdot b_i$, and a node is pruned if the length of projected vector $\pi_{m-k+1}(b - \sum_{i=m-k+1}^{m} a_i \cdot b_i)$ is outer of the range given below.

Write the error vector $e := b - z = (e_1, \ldots, e_m) = \sum_{i=1}^{m} \alpha_i \tilde{b}_i$ for some $z \in \Lambda_q(A)$. By $\langle e, \tilde{b}_i \rangle = \alpha_i \|\tilde{b}_i\|^2$, the projective length of each node is

$$\left\| \pi_{m-k+1}\left(b - \sum_{i=m-k+1}^{m} a_i \cdot b_i \right) \right\|^2 = \sum_{i=m-k+1}^{m} \alpha_i^2 \|b_i^*\|^2 = \sum_{i=m-k+1}^{m} \langle e, b_i^*/\|b_i^*\| \rangle^2.$$

Under the heuristic assumption [16, Heuristic 3] by Gama, Nguyen and Regev that claims the distribution of matrix $(\tilde{b}_1/\|\tilde{b}_1\|, \ldots, \tilde{b}_m/\|\tilde{b}_m\|)$ of a random reduced basis looks like a uniform distribution over $R_{\mathcal{O}}^{m \times m}$, we can predict the range of projected length of an error vector.

Theorem 5 (Band pruning). *Under [16, Heuristic 3], we can efficiently compute numbers L_k and R_k so that*

$$\Pr_{\substack{e \leftarrow D_{\mathbb{Z},\sigma}^m \\ (v_1,\ldots,v_m) \leftarrow R_{\mathcal{O}}^{m \times m}}} \left[L_k^2 < \sum_{i=1}^{k} \langle e, v_i \rangle^2 < R_k^2 \right] > 1 - 2/m^2.$$

The proof is given in the full version. Let the event E_k be $L_k^2 < \sum_{i=1}^{k} \langle e, v_i \rangle^2 < R_k^2$ holds, then the probability that the error vector is found is bounded by

$$\Pr[E_1 \cap \cdots \cap E_m] > 1 + \sum_{i=1}^{m} (\Pr[E_i] - 1) > 1 - 2/m. \tag{1}$$

Also, following [16], by the Gaussian heuristic assumption, the number of processed nodes during lattice enumeration is approximated by

$$N = \sum_{k=1}^{m} \frac{\mathrm{Vol}C(L_1, \ldots, L_k; R_1, \ldots, R_k)}{\prod_{i=m-k+1}^{m} ||\tilde{b}_i||}$$

where $C(L_1, \ldots, L_k; R_1, \ldots, R_k)$ is a k-dimensional Baumkuchen intersection defined by

$$\left\{ (x_1, \ldots, x_k) \in \mathbb{R}^k : L_i^2 < \sum_{\ell=1}^{i} x_\ell^2 < R_i^2 \text{ for } \forall i \in [k] \right\}.$$

Also, using their approximation technique, we compute the cost for lattice enumeration for various parameters. For each parameter tuple $(n, q, s = \alpha q)$, we search the optimal pair of (m, δ) so that the computational time in seconds

$$2^{1.8/\lg(\delta)-130} + (\sharp ENUM/(2.5 \cdot 10^7))$$

is minimized. Here, the first term is our lower bound estimation of lattice reduction algorithm, and the other term is the cost for enumeration from our benchmark testing of lattice enumeration that marks about 25 million nodes per single-thread second by Intel E5645 CPU. This CPU also marks about 9 million keys per single-thread second by RC5-72 benchmark testing published in distributed.net. Thus, our bit security estimation is given by following formula

$$\textbf{bit security} = \lg((\text{time in second}) \cdot (9 \cdot 10^6)).$$

By our new attack, we update the security estimation of parameters in Lindner and Peikert [22] in Table 2 and suggest parameter sets in Table 3 for our PRE schemes. The gap between our attack and [22] is mainly due to the improvement of lattice reduction algorithm, i.e., $t_{BKZ}(\delta)$, and new estimation of time to process one node. Improvement of the lattice enumeration part is slightly weaker because for [22]'s parameter (n, q, s, δ)=(128, 2053, 6.77, 1.0089) and (192, 4093, 8.87, 1.0067), the number of enumeration is about $2^{46.3}$ ($m = 325$) and $2^{83.2}$ ($m = 462$), while the original attacks estimated 2^{47} and 2^{87}, respectively.

References

1. Applebaum, B., Cash, D., Peikert, C., Sahai, A.: Fast cryptographic primitives and circular-secure encryption based on hard learning problems. In: CRYPTO 2009. LNCS, vol. 5677, pp. 595–618. Springer, Heidelberg (2009)
2. Ateniese, G., Benson, K., Hohenberger, S.: Key-private proxy re-encryption. In: Fischlin, M. (ed.) CT-RSA 2009. LNCS, vol. 5473, pp. 279–294. Springer, Heidelberg (2009), Full version at http://eprint.iacr.org/2008/463
3. Ateniese, G., Fu, K., Green, M., Hohenberger, S.: Improved proxy re-encryption schemes with applications to secure distributed storage. ACM Trans. Inf. Syst. Secur. 9(1), 1–30 (2006)

4. Banaszczyk, W.: New bounds in some transference theorems in the geometry of numbers. Mathematische Annalen 296(1), 625–635 (1993)
5. Banaszczyk, W.: Inequalities for convex bodies and polar reciprocal lattices in $\mathbb{R}^n$. Discrete & Computational Geometry 13(1), 217–231 (1995)
6. Bellare, M., Rogaway, P.: Random oracles are practical: A paradigm for designing efficient protocols. In: Denning, D.E., Pyle, R., Ganesan, R., Sandhu, R.S., Ashby, V. (eds.) ACM Conference on Computer and Communications Security, pp. 62–73. ACM Press, New York (1993)
7. Blaze, M., Bleumer, G., Strauss, M.J.: Divertible protocols and atomic proxy cryptography. In: Nyberg, K. (ed.) EUROCRYPT 1998. LNCS, vol. 1403, pp. 127–144. Springer, Heidelberg (1998)
8. Brakerski, Z.: Fully homomorphic encryption without modulus switching from classical gapSVP. In: Safavi-Naini, R., Canetti, R. (eds.) CRYPTO 2012. LNCS, vol. 7417, pp. 868–886. Springer, Heidelberg (2012)
9. Brakerski, Z., Langlois, A., Peikert, C., Regev, O., Stehlé, D.: Classical hardness of learning with errors. In: Boneh, D., Roughgarden, T., Feigenbaum, J. (eds.) STOC, pp. 575–584. ACM (2013)
10. Canetti, R., Hohenberger, S.: Chosen-ciphertext secure proxy re-encryption. In: Ning, P., di Vimercati, S.D.C., Syverson, P.F. (eds.) ACM Conference on Computer and Communications Security, pp. 185–194. ACM (2007)
11. T. D. S. Challenge, http://www.latticechallenge.org/svp-challenge/
12. Dawson, E. (ed.): CT-RSA 2013. LNCS, vol. 7779. Springer, Heidelberg (2013)
13. Deng, R.H., Weng, J., Liu, S., Chen, K.: Chosen-ciphertext secure proxy re-encryption without pairings. In: Franklin, M.K., Hui, L.C.K., Wong, D.S. (eds.) CANS 2008. LNCS, vol. 5339, pp. 1–17. Springer, Heidelberg (2008)
14. Fujisaki, E., Okamoto, T.: Secure integration of asymmetric and symmetric encryption schemes. In: Wiener, M. (ed.) CRYPTO 1999. LNCS, vol. 1666, pp. 537–554. Springer, Heidelberg (1999)
15. Fujisaki, E., Okamoto, T.: Secure integration of asymmetric and symmetric encryption schemes. J. Cryptology 26(1), 80–101 (2013)
16. Gama, N., Nguyen, P.Q., Regev, O.: Lattice enumeration using extreme pruning. In: Gilbert, H. (ed.) EUROCRYPT 2010. LNCS, vol. 6110, pp. 257–278. Springer, Heidelberg (2010)
17. Hanaoka, G., Kawai, Y., Kunihiro, N., Matsuda, T., Weng, J., Zhang, R., Zhao, Y.: Generic construction of chosen ciphertext secure proxy re-encryption. In: Dunkelman, O. (ed.) CT-RSA 2012. LNCS, vol. 7178, pp. 349–364. Springer, Heidelberg (2012)
18. Hohenberger, S., Rothblum, G.N., Shelat, A., Vaikuntanathan, V.: Securely obfuscating re-encryption. In: Vadhan, S.P. (ed.) TCC 2007. LNCS, vol. 4392, pp. 233–252. Springer, Heidelberg (2007)
19. Isshiki, T., Nguyen, M.H., Tanaka, K.: Proxy re-encryption in a stronger security model extended from CT-RSA2012. In: Dawson [12], pp. 277–292
20. Kannan, R.: Improved algorithms for integer programming and related lattice problems. In: Johnson, D.S., Fagin, R., Fredman, M.L., Harel, D., Karp, R.M., Lynch, N.A., Papadimitriou, C.H., Rivest, R.L., Ruzzo, W.L., Seiferas, J.I. (eds.) STOC, pp. 193–206. ACM (1983)
21. Libert, B., Vergnaud, D.: Unidirectional chosen-ciphertext secure proxy re-encryption. IEEE Transactions on Information Theory 57(3), 1786–1802 (2011)
22. Lindner, R., Peikert, C.: Better key sizes (and attacks) for LWE-based encryption. In: Kiayias, A. (ed.) CT-RSA 2011. LNCS, vol. 6558, pp. 319–339. Springer, Heidelberg (2011)

23. Liu, M., Nguyen, P.Q.: Solving BDD by enumeration: An update. In: Dawson [12], pp. 293–309

24. Micciancio, D., Regev, O.: Lattice-based cryptography. In: Bernstein, D.J., Buchmann, J., Dahmen, E. (eds.) Post-Quantum Cryptography, pp. 147–191. Springer, Heidelberg (2009)

25. Rckert, M., Schneider, M.: Estimating the security of lattice-based cryptosystems. Cryptology ePrint Archive, Report 2010/137 (2010), http://eprint.iacr.org/

26. Regev, O.: On lattices, learning with errors, random linear codes, and cryptography. In: Gabow, H.N., Fagin, R. (eds.) STOC, pp. 84–93. ACM (2005)

27. Schnorr, C.-P.: Lattice reduction by random sampling and birthday methods. In: Alt, H., Habib, M. (eds.) STACS 2003. LNCS, vol. 2607, Springer, Heidelberg (2003)

28. Seo, J.W., Yum, D.H., Lee, P.J.: Comments on "unidirectional chosen-ciphertext secure proxy re-encryption". IEEE Transactions on Information Theory 59(5), 32–56 (2013)

29. Shao, J.: Anonymous ID-based proxy re-encryption. In: Susilo, W., Mu, Y., Seberry, J. (eds.) ACISP 2012. LNCS, vol. 7372, pp. 364–375. Springer, Heidelberg (2012)

30. Shao, J., Cao, Z., Liu, P.: SCCR: a generic approach to simultaneously achieve cca security and collusion-resistance in proxy re-encryption. Security and Communication Networks 4(2), 122–135 (2011)

31. Shao, J., Liu, P., Cao, Z., Wei, G.: Multi-use unidirectional proxy re-encryption. In: ICC, pp. 1–5. IEEE (2011)

32. Shao, J., Liu, P., Wei, G., Ling, Y.: Anonymous proxy re-encryption. Security and Communication Networks 5(5), 439–449 (2012)

33. Shao, J., Liu, P., Zhou, Y.: Achieving key privacy without losing cca security in proxy re-encryption. Journal of Systems and Software 85(3), 655–665 (2012)

34. Wang, L., Wang, L., Mambo, M., Okamoto, E.: New identity-based proxy re-encryption schemes to prevent collusion attacks. In: Joye, M., Miyaji, A., Otsuka, A. (eds.) Pairing 2010. LNCS, vol. 6487, pp. 327–346. Springer, Heidelberg (2010)

35. Weng, J., Chen, M.-R., Yang, Y., Deng, R.H., Chen, K., Bao, F.: CCA-secure unidirectional proxy re-encryption in the adaptive corruption model without random oracles. SCIENCE CHINA Information Sciences 53(3), 593–606 (2010)

A   Correctness of Our PRE Scheme

We will use following lemmas, whose proofs can be derived from [4, 5]. Below $|\cdot|$ stands for either the Euclidean norm of a vector or the absolute value; $\langle \cdot, \cdot \rangle$ for inner product. Writing $|\psi_s^n|$ is a short hand for taking a vector from the distribution and computing its norm.

Lemma 1. Let $c \geq 1$ and $C = c \cdot \exp(\frac{1-c^2}{2})$. Then for any real $s > 0$ and any integer $n \geq 1$, we have $\Pr\left[|\psi_s^n| \geq \frac{c \cdot s \sqrt{n}}{\sqrt{2\pi}}\right] \leq C^n$.

Lemma 2. For any real $s > 0$ and $T > 0$, and any $x \in \mathbb{R}^n$, we have

$$\Pr\left[|\langle x, \psi_s^n \rangle| \geq Ts|x|\right] < 2\exp(-\pi T^2).$$

Theorem 6 (Correctness). *Let q, n, s be as in the scheme, and ρ $(= 0.01$ concretely) be the error of decryption per message symbol. For correctness of our PRE, we need $s^2 \leq \frac{\sqrt{2}\pi \cdot q}{16c\sqrt{n}\ln(2/\rho)}$ in which $c \in \{1.22, 1.20, 1.17, 1.16\}$ corresponds to $n \in \{160, 192, 256, 320\}$. These c are chosen so that $C^{4n} = (c \cdot \exp(\frac{1-c^2}{2}))^{4n} \leq 2^{-40}$.*

Proof. It suffices to check correctness of the transformed ciphertexts, since the noise is bigger than that in original ones. Continuing the main text, let us now check the decryption of transformed ciphertexts of (c_1, c_2), which is

$$f_1 R_B + f_2 S_B + f_3 + \mathsf{Bits}(c_1)E + c_1 S_A + c_2$$
$$= \underbrace{f_1 R_B + f_2 S_B + f_3 + \mathsf{Bits}(c_1)E + e_1 R + e_2 S + e_3}_{\text{noise}} + m \cdot \lfloor \tfrac{q}{2} \rfloor.$$

Suppose $\mathsf{Bits}(c_1)$ contains all 1's, each component in $\mathbb{Z}_q$ of the noise (in $\mathbb{Z}_q^{1 \times l}$) can be written as the inner product of two vectors $e = (f_1, f_2, f_3, E_1, \ldots, E_{n\kappa}, e_1, e_2, e_3)$ and $x = (r_B, s_B, 010_{1 \times l}, 1_{1 \times n\kappa}, r, s, 010_{1 \times l})$, where $010_{1 \times l}$ stands for a vector of length l with all 0's except one 1; $1_{1 \times n\kappa}$ for a vector of length $n\kappa$ with all 1's. We have $e \in \psi_s^{1 \times (n\kappa + 4n + 2l)}$ and $|x| \leq |(r_B, s_B, r, s)| + \sqrt{n\kappa + 2}$ where $(r_B, s_B, r, s) \in \psi_s^{1 \times 4n}$. Applying Lemma 1, we have with high probability (e.g., $\geq 1 - 2^{-40}$ when $c = 1.22, n = 160$)

$$|x| \leq \frac{c \cdot s\sqrt{4n}}{\sqrt{2\pi}} + \sqrt{n\kappa + 2}.$$

We now use Lemma 2 with x and $e \in \psi_s^{1 \times (n\kappa + 4n + 2l)}$. Let ρ (e.g., $= 0.01$) be the error per message symbol in decryption, we set $2\exp(-\pi T^2) = \rho$, so $T = \sqrt{\ln(2/\rho)}/\sqrt{\pi}$. For correctness, we need $Ts|x| \leq q/4$, which holds true provided that

$$\frac{\sqrt{\ln(2/\rho)}}{\sqrt{\pi}} \cdot s \cdot \left(\frac{c \cdot s\sqrt{4n}}{\sqrt{2\pi}} + \sqrt{n\kappa + 2} \right) \leq \frac{q}{4}.$$

With our choices of concrete parameters, $c \cdot s\sqrt{4n} \geq \sqrt{2\pi}\sqrt{n\kappa + 2}$, so the above holds true if

$$\frac{\sqrt{\ln(2/\rho)}}{\sqrt{\pi}} \cdot s \cdot \frac{2c \cdot s\sqrt{4n}}{\sqrt{2\pi}} \leq \frac{q}{4} \iff s^2 \leq \frac{\sqrt{2}\pi \cdot q}{16c\sqrt{n}\ln(2/\rho)}$$

as claimed. $\square$

Breaking the $\mathcal{O}(n|C|)$ Barrier for Unconditionally Secure Asynchronous Multiparty Computation (Extended Abstract)

Ashish Choudhury*

University of Bristol, UK
`ashish.choudhary@bristol.ac.uk`

Abstract. In PODC 2012, Dani et al. presented an unconditionally secure multiparty computation (MPC) protocol, which allows a set of n parties to securely evaluate any arithmetic circuit C of size $|C|$ on their private inputs, even in the presence of a computationally unbounded malicious adversary who can corrupt upto $t < (\frac{1}{3} - \epsilon)n$ parties, for any given non-zero ϵ with $0 < \epsilon < \frac{1}{3}$. The *total circuit-dependent* communication complexity of their protocol is $\mathcal{O}(\mathsf{PolyLog}(n) \cdot |C|)$, which is a significant improvement over the standard MPC protocols, which has *circuit-dependent* complexity of the form $\mathcal{O}(\mathsf{Poly}(n) \cdot |C|)$. The key innovation in their protocol is that instead of following the standard method of having every party communicate with every other party for evaluating each gate of C, it is sufficient to involve only a small subset of parties of size $\Theta(\mathsf{PolyLog}(n))$ to communicate with each other for evaluating each gate of the circuit. The protocol was presented in a synchronous setting and it was left as an open problem to design an asynchronous MPC (AMPC) protocol, with a similar characteristic. In this work, we solve this open problem by presenting the first unconditionally secure AMPC protocol where the circuit dependent complexity is $\mathcal{O}(\mathsf{PolyLog}(n) \cdot |C|)$.

1 Introduction

A milestone in the area of secure distributed computing is the following fundamental result by Ben-Or et al. [6] and independently by Chaum et al. [10]: let $\mathcal{P} = \{P_1, \ldots, P_n\}$ be a set of mutually distrusting parties, connected by pair-wise secure and authentic channels. Party P_i has a private input $\mathbf{x}_i \in \mathbb{F}$, where $\mathbb{F}$ is a finite field. Then there exists a protocol for the n parties, which allows them to "securely" compute any publicly known n-ary function $f : \mathbb{F}^n \to \mathbb{F}$ of their private inputs if less than $1/3$ fraction of the parties are corrupted. More specifically, let Adv be a computationally unbounded static malicious adversary, who can select any t parties to corrupt before the execution of a protocol and force them to behave in any arbitrary manner during the protocol execution. Then [6,10] showed that as long as $t < n/3$, there exists an MPC protocol satisfying the following requirements: **(1)** The honest parties (namely the parties not under the control of Adv) obtains $y_{\mathsf{out}} = f(\mathbf{x}_1, \ldots, \mathbf{x}_n)$. This property is often called the *correctness* property; **(2)** The inputs of the honest parties remain as private as possible; namely Adv does not learn anything about the inputs of the honest parties, beyond what

* This work has been supported in part by EPSRC via grant EP/I03126X.

G. Paul and S. Vaudenay (Eds.): INDOCRYPT 2013, LNCS 8250, pp. 19–37, 2013.

is revealed by the inputs of the corrupted parties, the description of the function f and the function output y_{out}. This property is often called the *privacy* property. The result of [6,10] is a very powerful result in distributed cryptography, since f can model any joint cryptographic task, which can be solved by the parties using an MPC protocol, even without deploying any public key machinery (which are computationally expensive and whose security is based on the assumption that adversary is computationally bounded).

The work of [6,10] laid the foundation of what is called *unconditionally secure* MPC, also known as *information theoretically secure* MPC. Due to its central importance in distributed cryptography, several papers have been written in the last three decades and various protocols have been proposed, addressing this problem (see for example [2,13,4] and their references). The common principle underlying all these protocols is the following: each party P_i (verifiably) secret-share its input $\mathbf{x}_i$ among *all* the parties, using a *linear secret-sharing scheme* (LSSS), say Shamir [22], with threshold t. Informally, such a scheme ensures that $\mathbf{x}_i$ remains private for an honest P_i, even if any set of t parties combine their shares of $\mathbf{x}_i$. On the other hand, given the shares of $\mathbf{x}_i$, then $\mathbf{x}_i$ can be efficiently reconstructed, even if upto $t < n/3$ shares are incorrect[1]. Once each party secret-share its input, the protocol performs what is called the *shared-circuit-evaluation*. More specifically, for simplicity and without loss of generality, assume that f is expressed as a (publicly known) arithmetic circuit C over $\mathbb{F}$, consisting of 2-input addition and multiplication gates; then the protocol tries to maintain the following invariant for each gate g of the circuit: let a and b be the inputs of g, such that both a and b are secret-shared (with threshold t) among the parties; then $g(a, b)$ is also secret-shared (with threshold t) among the parties. To maintain this invariant, *every* party in $\mathcal{P}$ interacts with *every other* party in $\mathcal{P}$; we refer to this as *all-to-all communication* paradigm. Finally, once y_{out} is available in secret-shared fashion, the parties exchange their shares of y_{out} and reconstruct y_{out}. Intuitively, the security follows as all intermediate values during the computation remain secret-shared with threshold t. The *communication complexity* of these protocols, namely the total number of elements of $\mathbb{F}$ communicated by the honest parties, is of the form $\mathcal{O}(\mathsf{Poly}(n)|C| + \mathsf{Poly}(n))$, where $|C|$ is the size of C. The research community focused on to improve the *circuit-dependent* communication complexity (which depends on $|C|$). This is because for most of the functions, $|C|$ is significantly larger than n; so in scenarios involving huge computations and large number of parties, a protocol with less circuit-dependent complexity is desirable. The initial protocols of [6,10] were highly inefficient, with circuit-dependent complexity of the form $\Omega(n^6|C|)$. Following a long series of work, the most efficient protocol was presented in [4], with communication complexity of $\mathcal{O}(n|C| + \mathsf{Poly}(n))$.

MPC with Poly-Log Circuit-Dependent Complexity: Even though an MPC protocol with linear circuit-dependent complexity (namely $\mathcal{O}(n|C|)$) looks promising, efforts were made to further improve it. Towards this, Damgård et al. [12] presented an MPC protocol with circuit-dependent complexity $\mathcal{O}(\mathsf{PolyLog}(|C|) \cdot \mathsf{PolyLog}(n) \cdot |C|)$. The protocol still follows the all-to-all communication paradigm; however instead of one gate, "several" gates are evaluated in parallel by a single "instance" of all-to-all

---

[1] Informally this is done by applying the standard Reed-Solomon (RS) error-correction and using the fact that a set of n Shamir shares is the same as an RS codeword of length n [19].

communication. Intuitively this is done by using packed secret-sharing [16], where several values are packed and then shared in a single instance of secret-sharing. Though the protocol of [12] has a better circuit-dependent complexity, it is highly complex mainly due to the use of packed secret-sharing. Moreover, instead of tolerating $t < n/3$ corruptions, it tolerates $t < (\frac{1}{3} - \epsilon)n$ corruptions, for any given constant ϵ, with $0 < \epsilon < \frac{1}{3}$.

In a different line of work, Dani et al. [14] tried to bypass the all-to-all communication paradigm for obtaining efficient MPC protocol with better circuit-dependent complexity. The key innovation was that for doing the shared circuit-evaluation, instead of involving *all* the n parties (as was the case in all the existing MPC protocols), it is sufficient to involve only a "small" subset of parties and do the shared circuit-evaluation only among this small subset of parties. More specifically, for each gate in the circuit, a designated subset of $\Theta(\log n)$ parties is involved, who do the all-to-all communication only among them for the shared evaluation of that gate. This is quite practical as it is highly unrealistic to ensure that every party communicates with every other party, particularly for real world applications where n is typically large. Based on this idea, they proposed an MPC protocol tolerating $t < (\frac{1}{3} - \epsilon)n$ corruptions for any given ϵ, where $0 < \epsilon < \frac{1}{3}$, with communication complexity $\mathcal{O}(\mathsf{PolyLog}(n)|C| + n\sqrt{n} \cdot \mathsf{PolyLog}(n))$, which is highly efficient as (asymptotically) it has better circuit-dependent complexity. The protocol is very simple and does not use packed secret-sharing; the only disadvantage is that it involves a negligible error probability in the correctness and privacy.

Our Results: All the above results are in the synchronous model, where there exists a global clock and the delay of every message in the network is upper bounded by a known constant. Though (theoretically) impressive, it does not model a real-life communication network, like the Internet, with no timing assumptions and where the messages can be arbitrarily (but finitely) delayed. Even though practically motivated, AMPC protocols received much less attention, due to the following general phenomena which is impossible to deal with in any asynchronous protocol and which makes the protocol highly involved: it is not possible to distinguish between a slow but honest sender (whose messages are delayed arbitrarily) and a corrupted sender (who does not send the messages at all). As a result, at every "stage" of an asynchronous protocol, a party cannot afford to listen from all the parties (to avoid endless waiting) and so communication from t (potentially honest) parties has to be ignored. This automatically implies that even the inputs of upto t parties have to be ignored for the computation of f; for an excellent introduction to the asynchronous protocols, see [9]. The best known unconditionally secure AMPC protocols [20,21,11] have communication complexity $\mathcal{O}(\mathsf{Poly}(n)|C| + \mathsf{Poly}(n))$ and are based on all-to-all communication paradigm. There does not exist any AMPC protocol whose circuit-dependent communication complexity is $\mathsf{PolyLog}(n)$; infact this was left as an open question in [14]. Motivated by the importance of asynchronous model, we solve this question and show the following:

Theorem 1 (Main Result). *Let $\mathcal{P} = \{P_1, \ldots, P_n\}$ be a set of n parties, connected by pair-wise secure and authentic channels. Moreover let Adv be a computationally unbounded static adversary, who can maliciously corrupt upto t parties, where $t < (\frac{1}{3} - \epsilon)n$ for any given ϵ, with $0 < \epsilon < \frac{1}{3}$. Furthermore, let $f : \mathbb{F}^n \to \mathbb{F}$ be an n-ary publicly known function, expressed as an arithmetic circuit C over $\mathbb{F}$. Then there exists* *a protocol for the n parties, which with high probability, is a secure AMPC protocol, with communication complexity $\mathcal{O}(\mathsf{PolyLog}(n)|C| + \mathsf{Poly}(n))$.*

Note: As in [14,17], in the rest of the paper the phrase with high probability means that an event happens with probability at least $1 - 1/n^c$ for every constant c and sufciently large n, where the probabilities are over the random coins of the honest parties.

2   Protocol Overview

We follow [14] and borrow few ideas from [20,1]. Without going into the full details of our protocol, we rather focus on the major idea behind the MPC protocol of [14] and the subtle problem in directly adapting the same to the asynchronous setting; this will be followed by a high level idea of our proposed solution to deal with this problem. Before that, we first state the following interesting result[2] by King et al. [17], based on [15]. This result lies at the heart of the MPC protocol of [14] as well as ours:

Theorem 2   (Universe Reduction Theorem [17]). *Let $\mathcal{P} = \{P_1, \ldots, P_n\}$ be a set of parties, connected by pair-wise secure and authentic (asynchronous) channels and let Adv be a computationally unbounded static adversary, corrupting upto t parties, where $t < (\frac{1}{3} - \epsilon)n$ and $0 < \epsilon < \frac{1}{3}$. Then there exists an efficient (asynchronous) protocol, say $\mathsf{Quorum}(\mathcal{P})$, with total communication complexity $\mathcal{O}(n\sqrt{n} \cdot \mathsf{PolyLog}(n))$. With high probability, the protocol outputs n publicly known (non-disjoint) sets $\mathcal{Q}_1, \ldots, \mathcal{Q}_n$ of parties called quorums, satisfying the following properties:*

(1). Each $|\mathcal{Q}_i| = \Theta(\log n)$; (2). A party $P_i \in \mathcal{P}$ appears in $\Theta(\log n)$ quorums and (3). For each $\mathcal{Q}_i$, the fraction of corrupted parties in $\mathcal{Q}_i$ is strictly less than $1/3$.

The above result states that it is possible to divide a large "universe" with a certain "property" into several smaller universe with the same property. Specifically, starting with the initial set $\mathcal{P}$ (the large universe) with more than $2/3$ fraction of honest parties, we can obtain n (non-disjoint) quorums of $\Theta(\log n)$ parties (smaller universe), such that in each quorum, more than $2/3$ fraction of the parties are honest. Intuitively the MPC protocol of [14] (and also our AMPC protocol) with poly-log circuit-dependent complexity uses the above result to implement the following idea for each gate of the circuit: instead of deploying the *entire* set $\mathcal{P}$ to do the shared evaluation of the gate, only *three* designated quorums, each of size $\Theta(\log n)$ are involved; the details follow.

Shared Gate Evaluation in the MPC Protocol of [14] Involving $\Theta(\log n)$ Parties: The MPC protocol of [14] maintains the following invariant for each gate g of the circuit C: let x_{left} and x_{right} be the two inputs of g. Then there will be a publicly known designated quorum, say $\mathcal{Q}_{\mathsf{out}}$ and a uniformly random mask, say m_{out}, such that:

- The masked gate output $g(x_{\mathsf{left}}, x_{\mathsf{right}}) + m_{\mathsf{out}}$ will be publicly known to $\mathcal{Q}_{\mathsf{out}}$, while the mask m_{out} will be Shamir-shared among $\mathcal{Q}_{\mathsf{out}}$ with threshold t_{out}. Here t_{out} is the maximum possible value satisfying $t_{\mathsf{out}} < \frac{|\mathcal{Q}_{\mathsf{out}}|}{3}$.

---

[2] Actually they showed the result in the more powerful adversarial model, namely the *full information model*, where the adversary can even see the communication of all the honest parties; obviously the result will hold in the point-to-point secure-channel setting.

It is easy to see that if $\mathcal{Q}_{out}$ contains at most t_{out} corrupted parties (which is indeed ensured by the quorum formation protocol Quorum with high probability), then m_{out} remains private and so is $g(x_{left}, x_{right})$. To maintain the above invariant, *two* more publicly known designated quorums, say $\mathcal{Q}_{left}$ and $\mathcal{Q}_{right}$ are involved (for simplicity, we assume $\mathcal{Q}_{left}$, $\mathcal{Q}_{right}$ and $\mathcal{Q}_{out}$ to be disjoint), with the following inputs:

- The masked input $x_{left} + m_{left}$ will be publicly known to the parties in $\mathcal{Q}_{left}$ and m_{left} will be a uniformly random mask, Shamir-shared among $\mathcal{Q}_{left}$ with threshold t_{left}; here t_{left} is the maximum value satisfying $t_{left} < \frac{|\mathcal{Q}_{left}|}{3}$.
- The masked input $x_{right} + m_{right}$ will be publicly known to $\mathcal{Q}_{right}$ and m_{right} will be a uniformly random mask, Shamir-shared among $\mathcal{Q}_{right}$ with threshold t_{right}; here t_{right} is the maximum value satisfying $t_{right} < \frac{|\mathcal{Q}_{right}|}{3}$.

Note that if $\mathcal{Q}_{left}$ and $\mathcal{Q}_{right}$ contain at most t_{left} and t_{right} corrupted parties respectively (which is indeed the case with high probability due to Quorum), then x_{left} and x_{right} remain private, as the respective masks remain private. To (securely) maintain the above mentioned invariant for g, the parties in $\mathcal{Q}_{left}$, $\mathcal{Q}_{right}$ and $\mathcal{Q}_{out}$ execute a protocol, say LightWeightGateEval, with the above public inputs and private inputs. The exact details of LightWeightGateEval were not provided in [14], but they refer to any standard $1/3$ fault-tolerant MPC protocol, say [6] for the same. Specifically, more than $2/3$ fraction of the parties in $\mathcal{Q}_{left} \cup \mathcal{Q}_{right} \cup \mathcal{Q}_{out}$ will be honest (with high probability) and so from [6], we know that there exists an MPC protocol for $\mathcal{Q}_{left} \cup \mathcal{Q}_{right} \cup \mathcal{Q}_{out}$, meeting the requirements of LightWeightGateEval. The interesting feature about LightWeightGateEval is that even though it involves all-to-all communication among $\mathcal{Q}_{left} \cup \mathcal{Q}_{right} \cup \mathcal{Q}_{out}$, instead of n parties, the all-to-all communication involves *only* $\Theta(\log n)$ parties and so it has communication complexity $\mathcal{O}(\mathsf{PolyLog}(n))$, rather than $\mathcal{O}(\mathsf{Poly}(n))$.

We now pause for a moment and discuss how *any potential* LightWeightGateEval protocol will work; this will help us to understand the subtle issue that bars us from directly extending LightWeightGateEval to the asynchronous setting. Perhaps the major bottleneck for LightWeightGateEval is that the *private* inputs, namely the masks m_{left}, m_{right} and m_{out} are individually shared among *different* quorums. Instead, if somehow we have these masks also (securely) "re-shared" among *all* the parties in $\mathcal{Q}_{combined} = \mathcal{Q}_{left} \cup \mathcal{Q}_{right} \cup \mathcal{Q}_{out}$, with threshold $t_{combined} = t_{left} + t_{right} + t_{out}$, then we are done. That is, the parties in $\mathcal{Q}_{combined}$ can then jointly do the following: **(1)**. Unmask m_{left} from $x_{left} + m_{left}$ and m_{right} from $x_{right} + m_{right}$ respectively in a shared fashion; as a result x_{left} and x_{right} will be now shared among $\mathcal{Q}_{combined}$ with threshold $t_{combined}$; **(2)**. Apply any existing $1/3$ fault-tolerant MPC protocol, say [6,4] on the shared x_{left} and x_{right} and obtain $g(x_{left}, x_{right})$ in a shared fashion with threshold $t_{combined}$. To this, add the mask m_{out} in a shared fashion and obtain $g(x_{left}, x_{right}) + m_{out}$ in a shared fashion with threshold $t_{combined}$; **(3)**. Finally, publicly reconstruct $g(x_{left}, x_{right}) + m_{out}$, which is possible as long as the maximum number of corrupted parties in $\mathcal{Q}_{combined}$ is $t_{combined}$ (which will be the case with high probability).

From the above discussion, it follows that all that LightWeightGateEval needs to do is to have m_{left}, m_{right} and m_{out} *reshared* among $\mathcal{Q}_{combined}$ with threshold $t_{combined}$ and without leaking any information about these masks. This can be done as follows: consider for example m_{left}; then each party in $\mathcal{Q}_{left}$ is asked to reshare its share of

m_{left} among $\mathcal{Q}_{\text{combined}}$ with threshold t_{combined}. Let $\mathbf{s} = (\mathbf{s}_1, \ldots, \mathbf{s}_{|\mathcal{Q}_{\text{left}}|})$ be the vector of *original* shares of m_{left} available with the respective parties in $\mathcal{Q}_{\text{left}}$ and let $\mathbf{s}' = (\mathbf{s}'_1, \ldots, \mathbf{s}'_{|\mathcal{Q}_{\text{left}}|})$ be the vector of *actual* shares, reshared by the parties in $\mathcal{Q}_{\text{left}}$. It is easy to see that $\mathbf{s}$ and $\mathbf{s}'$ will have distance at most t_{left}, assuming that $\mathcal{Q}_{\text{left}}$ has at most t_{left} corrupted parties. Since $t_{\text{left}} < \frac{|\mathcal{Q}_{\text{left}}|}{3}$, it follows that by applying the (RS) error-correction on $\mathbf{s}'$, we can error-correct t_{left} errors and recover $\mathbf{s}$ (and hence m_{left}). Interestingly, this is possible even if we have the shares of $\mathbf{s}'$, instead of the actual $\mathbf{s}'$ (which is the case for us). Thus we can perform the error-correction in a shared fashion and that too without revealing any information about the correct components of $\mathbf{s}'$ (namely the shares of m_{left} corresponding to the honest parties in $\mathcal{Q}_{\text{left}}$). Informally this is because the only information which is made public during the shared error-correction is the *syndrome* of the vector $\mathbf{s}'$; however it will be already known to the adversary, as the syndrome of $\mathbf{s}'$ is the same as the syndrome of the "error-vector" (which will be known to the adversary); see [1] for more details.

Problem in Extending LightWeightGateEval **to the Asynchronous Setting and Our Solution:** The major challenge for designing (a generic) LightWeightGateEval for the asynchronous setting is that it is not possible to ensure that *all* the *honest* parties in $\mathcal{Q}_{\text{left}}, \mathcal{Q}_{\text{right}}$ and $\mathcal{Q}_{\text{out}}$ participate with their private inputs. For example, consider $\mathcal{Q}_{\text{left}}$: assuming $\mathcal{Q}_{\text{left}}$ to have at most t_{left} corrupted parties, due to the asynchronicity, we can ensure that *only* $|\mathcal{Q}_{\text{left}}| - t_{\text{left}}$ parties from $\mathcal{Q}_{\text{left}}$ participate in LightWeightGateEval with their private inputs, namely the shares of m_{left}. However the t_{left} ignored parties may be honest, which implies that instead of having more than $2/3$ fraction of honest parties, we may only have more than $1/2$ fraction of honest parties participating in LightWeightGateEval with the correct shares of m_{left}. This seems to be insufficient for any existing generic $1/3$ fault-tolerant AMPC protocol, say $[7,20]$[3], to have m_{left} reshared among $\mathcal{Q}_{\text{combined}}$ with threshold t_{combined}. Indeed this will be the case for the LightWeightGateEval outlined in the previous section, as we will not have the sufficient "redundancy" (namely two-third), to perform the (shared) error-correction on the reshared shares of m_{left} and have it robustly reshared among $\mathcal{Q}_{\text{combined}}$ with threshold t_{combined}. Moreover, we may end up revealing some information about the correct shares of m_{left} during the shared error-correction. This is because due to the insufficient redundancy, the error-correction may report a correct share of m_{left} as incorrect, thus reporting an "incorrect" error-vector which was unknown to the adversary; as a result, the resultant syndrome may leak information about such correct shares of m_{left}.

To deal with the above problems, we apply the shared error-correction in an "online" fashion and that too without revealing anything about m_{left}. Specifically, we exploit the fact that if the (shared) error-correction algorithm fails to correct all the errors among the $|\mathcal{Q}_{\text{left}}| - t_{\text{left}}$ reshared shares, then we can always detect the same by applying error-detection[4] (in a shared fashion) on the output obtained at the end of error-correction. This is because we will still have enough redundancy left among the correctly reshared shares to perform the error-detection. If the error-detection indicates errors, then certainly we know that some of the missing t_{left} shares belonged to the honest parties and

---

[3] These are the only known $1/3$ fault-tolerant unconditionally secure AMPC protocols.

[4] The goal of the error-detection is to only detect (rather correct) the presence of any error.

so we wait for the completion of resharing of additional shares of m_{left} (by the "ignored" parties in $\mathcal{Q}_{\mathsf{left}}$) and repeat the process of error-correction followed by error-detection.

In a more detail, the online shared error-correction involves an iteration of length at most $(t_{\mathsf{left}} + 1)$. During the iteration r, where $0 \leq r \leq t_{\mathsf{left}}$, we wait for the completion of $2t_{\mathsf{left}} + 1 + r$ shares of m_{left} to be re-shared. Now *assuming* at most r of these reshared shares to be incorrect, we try to error-correct upto r errors (in a shared fashion), followed by the verification (aka shared error-detection) that the resultant (shared) vector constitutes a set of $2t_{\mathsf{left}} + 1 + r$ Shamir shares with threshold t_{left}. This process is repeated till in some iteration, the error-detection outputs no error, after which m_{left} will be robustly reshared among $\mathcal{Q}_{\mathsf{combined}}$. The idea is that if $\hat{r}$ denotes the number of parties in $\mathcal{Q}_{\mathsf{left}}$ who reshares an incorrect share of m_{left}, where $\hat{r} \leq t_{\mathsf{left}}$, then during the $\hat{r}$th iteration, we will have the resharing of $2t_{\mathsf{left}} + 1 + \hat{r}$ shares of m_{left} being completed, with $2t_{\mathsf{left}} + 1$ of them being the correct ones; so the error correction will correct $\hat{r}$ errors and the error-detection will confirm that no more errors are present.

To maintain the privacy of m_{out} during all the iterations, the above process is actually carried out on a masked vector $\mathbf{s'}_r + \mathbf{m}_r$ during the rth iteration. Here $\mathbf{s'}_r$ denotes the (shared) vector of $2t_{\mathsf{left}}+1+r$ shares of m_{left}, which have been reshared by the end of the rth iteration (and on which we would ideally like to apply the shared error-correction), while $\mathbf{m}_r$ denotes a uniformly random shared mask of length $2t_{\mathsf{left}} + 1 + r$, such that the components of $\mathbf{m}_r$ constitute a set of $2t_{\mathsf{left}} + 1 + r$ Shamir shares with threshold t_{left}. The idea is that if $\mathbf{s}_r$ constitutes the original vector of $2t_{\mathsf{left}} + 1 + r$ shares of m_{left} corresponding to $\mathbf{s'}_r$, then $\mathbf{s}_r + \mathbf{m}_r$ constitutes a set of $2t_{\mathsf{left}} + 1 + r$ Shamir shares with threshold t_{left}. So if the distance between $\mathbf{s'}_r$ and $\mathbf{s}_r$ is indeed r, then so will be between $\mathbf{s'}_r + \mathbf{m}_r$ and $\mathbf{s}_r + \mathbf{m}_r$. Thus if error-correction followed by error-detection is successful during the iteration r, then $\mathbf{s}_r + \mathbf{m}_r$ will be restored (in a shared fashion) and the parties can then unmask $\mathbf{m}_r$ in a shared fashion, resulting in $\mathbf{s}_r$ (and hence m_{left}) being reshared among $\mathcal{Q}_{\mathsf{combined}}$. On the other hand if the error-correction followed by error-detection is unsuccessful during the iteration r, then no information about the correct components of $\mathbf{s}_r$ (namely the correct shares of m_{left}) is revealed, as the error-correction and detection is done on a masked vector, where the mask is random, private and is independently generated for each iteration. Since $t_{\mathsf{left}} = \Theta(\log n)$, we may need to repeat the shared error-correction followed by error-detection $\mathcal{O}(\log n)$ times and so the communication complexity of the resultant protocol will be still $\mathcal{O}(\mathsf{PolyLog}(n))$.

3   Preliminaries and Definitions

We assume a set of n parties $\mathcal{P} = \{P_1, \ldots, P_n\}$, connected by pair-wise private and authentic channels. We assume a computationally unbounded static adversary Adv, who can corrupt any set of t parties at the beginning of a protocol, where $t < (\frac{1}{3} - \epsilon)n$ and $0 < \epsilon < \frac{1}{3}$ is a given constant. The adversary can force the parties under its control to behave in any arbitrary manner during the execution of a protocol. The channels are asynchronous and can have arbitrary (but finite) delay; i.e. the messages will reach to their destinations eventually. Moreover, the order in which the messages reach their destinations may be different from the order in which they were sent. To model the worst case scenario, Adv is given the power to schedule the delivery of every message in the network. Note that, while Adv can schedule the messages of the honest parties at its will, it has no access to the "contents" of these messages.

As in [9], we consider a protocol execution in the asynchronous model as a sequence of *atomic steps*, where a single party is *active* in each such step. A party gets activated by receiving a message after which it performs an internal computation and then possibly sends messages on its outgoing channels. The order of the atomic steps are controlled by a "scheduler", which is controlled by Adv. At the beginning of the computation, each party will be in a special *start* state. We say a party has *terminated/completed* the protocol if it reaches a *halt* state, after which it does not perform any further computation. A protocol execution is said to be *complete* if each (honest) party terminates the protocol. Notice that the executions that complete do so after a finite number of steps.

We assume that all computation and communication in our protocols is done over a finite field $\mathbb{F}$, where $|\mathbb{F}| > 3n$; there exists $3n$ publicly known non-zero distinct elements $\alpha_1, \ldots, \alpha_{3n} \in \mathbb{F}$, where α_i, α_{i+n} and α_{i+2n} will be associated as the *evaluation points* with party $P_i \in \mathcal{P}$. In our protocols, we will use two types of Shamir-shared values. One where the value is shared only among a *single* set of parties where each share holder receives one share. Second where the value is shared among *three* (possibly non-disjoint) sets of parties and where a party may receive more than one share, depending upon the number of sets in which is it present. More formally:

Definition 1 (d-sharing). *Let $s \in \mathbb{F}$ be a value and d be the degree of sharing.*

- d-**Sharing Involving a Single Quorum**: *Let $\mathcal{Q} \subseteq \mathcal{P}$ be a quorum of parties; then s is said to be d-shared among $\mathcal{Q}$ if there exists a polynomial, say $\mathbf{f}(\cdot)$, of degree at most d with $\mathbf{f}(0) = s$ and every (honest) $P_i \in \mathcal{Q}$ holds a share $\mathbf{s}_i = \mathbf{f}(\alpha_i)$ of s. The vector of shares of s corresponding to the (honest) parties in $\mathcal{Q}$ is called d-sharing of s, denoted as $[s]^d_{\mathcal{Q}}$.*
- d-**Sharing Involving Three Quorums**: *Let $\mathcal{A}, \mathcal{B}$ and $\mathcal{C}$ be three quorums of parties and let for each party $P_i \in \mathcal{A} \cup \mathcal{B} \cup \mathcal{C}$, k_i denotes the number of quorums (among $\mathcal{A}, \mathcal{B}$ and $\mathcal{C}$) in which P_i is present and so $k_i \in \{1, 2, 3\}$. Then s is said to be d-shared among $\mathcal{A} \cup \mathcal{B} \cup \mathcal{C}$ if there exists a polynomial, say $\mathbf{f}(\cdot)$, of degree at most d with $\mathbf{f}(0) = s$ and every (honest) party $P_i \in \mathcal{A} \cup \mathcal{B} \cup \mathcal{C}$ holds k_i shares[5] $\mathbf{s}_{i,1}, \ldots, \mathbf{s}_{i,k_i}$, with $\mathbf{s}_{i,k} = \mathbf{f}(\alpha_{i+(k-1)n})$ for $k \in \{1, \ldots, k_i\}$. The vector of (multi)shares of s corresponding to the (honest) parties in $\mathcal{A} \cup \mathcal{B} \cup \mathcal{C}$ is called d-sharing of s, denoted as $[[[s]]]^d_{\mathcal{A} \cup \mathcal{B} \cup \mathcal{C}}$.* □

Intuitively $[[[\cdot]]]$-sharing is the same as $[\cdot]$-sharing, where if P_i occurs in k_i quorums among $\mathcal{A}, \mathcal{B}$ and $\mathcal{C}$ then it plays the "role" of k_i share-holders. A well known property of d-sharings is the following *linearity* property: given $[x^{(1)}]^d_{\mathcal{Q}}, \ldots, [x^{(\ell)}]^d_{\mathcal{Q}}$ and publicly known constants $c_1, \ldots, c_\ell$, then we have $[c_1 \cdot x^{(1)} + \ldots + c_\ell \cdot x^{(\ell)}]^d_{\mathcal{Q}} = c_1 \cdot [x^{(1)}]^d_{\mathcal{Q}} + \ldots + c_\ell \cdot [x^{(\ell)}]^d_{\mathcal{Q}}$. We capture the above by saying that *the parties in $\mathcal{Q}$ (locally) compute $[c_1 \cdot x^{(1)} + \ldots + c_\ell \cdot x^{(\ell)}]^d_{\mathcal{Q}}$ from $[x^{(1)}]^d_{\mathcal{Q}}, \ldots, [x^{(\ell)}]^d_{\mathcal{Q}}$*; for this the parties apply the above linear function on their respective shares of $x^{(1)}, \ldots, x^{(\ell)}$. It is easy to see that the linearity property holds even with respect to $[[[\cdot]]]$-shared values. A well know property based on the linearity of d-sharings is the following: given at least $d+1$ distinct shares of

---

[5] A party may receive upto three shares, hence we require three evaluation points for each party.

a d-shared value s, then s can be expressed as a linear combination of these $d+1$ shares. This is because the $d+1$ shares constitute $d+1$ distinct points on the underlying sharing polynomial of degree at most d; and the free coefficient of this polynomial (i.e. s) can be expressed as a publicly known linear combination of the $d+1$ points.

3.1 Reed-Solomon (RS) Codes

Let $\mathcal{C}(N, k, d)$ be the family of RS codes of *length* N, *dimension* k and *distance* d. Associated with $\mathcal{C}(N, k, d)$ will be a publicly known $k \times N$ *generator matrix* G and a corresponding publicly known $(N - k) \times N$ *parity-check matrix* H defined as:

$$
G \stackrel{def}{=} \begin{pmatrix} 1 & \cdots & 1 \\ \alpha_1 & \cdots & \alpha_N \\ \vdots & & \vdots \\ \alpha_1^{k-1} & \cdots & \alpha_N^{k-1} \end{pmatrix} \quad \text{and} \quad H \stackrel{def}{=} \begin{pmatrix} 1 & \cdots & 1 \\ \alpha_1 & \cdots & \alpha_N \\ \vdots & & \vdots \\ \alpha_1^{N-k-1} & \cdots & \alpha_N^{N-k-1} \end{pmatrix} \cdot \begin{pmatrix} v_1 & & 0 \\ & \ddots & \\ 0 & & v_N \end{pmatrix},
$$

where $v_1, \ldots, v_N$ are publicly known non-zero values such that $G \cdot H^T = 0^{N-k}$. The encoding of a vector $a = (a_0, \ldots, a_{k-1}) \in \mathbb{F}^k$ is given by $a \cdot G$. If we consider the polynomial $\mathbf{f}(x) = a_0 + a_1 \cdot x + \ldots + a_{k-1} \cdot x^{k-1}$, then the RS codeword corresponding to a is the vector $(\mathbf{f}(\alpha_1), \ldots, \mathbf{f}(\alpha_N))$. It thus follows that the vector $(\mathbf{f}(\alpha_1), \ldots, \mathbf{f}(\alpha_N))$ constitutes $(k - 1)$-sharing of a_0. The *syndrome* of a word $y \in \mathbb{F}^N$ is given by $\mathfrak{s}(y) = y \cdot H^T \in \mathbb{F}^{N-k}$. The following facts about $\mathcal{C}(N, k, d)$ are well known:

Lemma 1 ([18]). *For $\mathcal{C}(N, k, d)$ the following holds:* **(1).** $d \geq N - k + 1$. *So if y_1 and y_2 are two codewords such that at least k components of y_1, y_2 are (position-wise) the same then $y_1 = y_2$.* **(2).** *If $y = a \cdot G$ (i.e. y is the RS codeword of a) then $\mathfrak{s}(y) = 0^{N-k}$.* **(3).** *The maximum number of errors that can be corrected by $\mathcal{C}(N, k, d)$ is $\lceil \frac{d}{2} \rceil$.*

RS Error-correction: We assume a (standard) efficient RS error-correcting procedure RSDec(N, k, Δ) for $\mathcal{C}(N, k, d)$ RS codes based on the syndrome decoding, where $d \geq (N - k + 1)$. The algorithm takes as input a vector $y' = (y'_1, \ldots, y'_N) \in \mathbb{F}^N$ with a *Hamming distance*[6] Δ from an *unknown* codeword $y = (y_1, \ldots, y_N) \in \mathcal{C}(N, k, d)$, such that $\Delta \leq \lceil \frac{d}{2} \rceil$. The goal of the algorithm is to "correct" the Δ errors in y' and recover the original codeword y. On a high level, RSDec works as follows: we first compute the syndrome $\mathfrak{s}(y')$ which further allows to compute the *error vector* $e = (e_1, \ldots, e_N)$, such that for every i, $y'_i - e_i = y_i$ holds; we stress that e can be computed from $\mathfrak{s}(y')$ alone. Moreover, e will have at most Δ *non-zero* components (corresponding to the error locations), as we are assuming that at most Δ components of y' are corrupted (different from y). Once e is computed, we can easily recover the original codeword y. As long as it is ensured that $\Delta \leq \lceil \frac{d}{2} \rceil$, it is guaranteed that the output is indeed y. A crucial observation about RSDec which we use later is that it is a *linear function* of the input vector y' as syndrome computation is a matrix multiplication operation; so we can deploy RSDec in a shared fashion on the shares of y'.

---

[6] Hamming distance between two vectors is the number of positions in which they differ.

4   The Various Existing Asynchronous Primitives

Asynchronous Verifiable Secret Sharing: The following result states that it is possible to verifiably share a secret, if the fraction of corrupted parties is less than $1/3$:

Theorem 3 ([7,20]). *Let $\mathcal{Q} \subseteq \mathcal{P}$ be a quorum of N parties containing at most t' corrupted parties where $t' < \frac{N}{3}$ and let $D \in \mathcal{P}$ be a dealer with a secret $s \in \mathbb{F}$. Then there exists a protocol, say $\mathsf{AVSS}(D, \mathcal{Q}, s)$ for D and the parties in $\mathcal{Q}$ satisfying:*

(1). TERMINATION: *With high probability, the following holds:* (A) *If D is honest and the parties in $\mathcal{Q}$ participate in AVSS then every honest party in $\mathcal{Q}$ eventually terminates;* (B) *If D is corrupted and some honest party in $\mathcal{Q}$ terminates, then every other honest party in $\mathcal{Q}$ eventually terminates.* (2). CORRECTNESS: *If some honest party in $\mathcal{Q}$ terminates, then with high probability, there exists a value, say $\bar{s}$, such that $\bar{s}$ will be t'-shared among $\mathcal{Q}$ (i.e. $[\bar{s}]_{\mathcal{Q}}^{t'}$). Moreover, if D is honest then $\bar{s} = s$.* (3). PRIVACY: *If D is honest, then the view of the corrupted parties in $\mathcal{Q}$ is independent of s.* (4). COMMUNICATION COMPLEXITY: *The protocol has communication complexity $\mathcal{O}(poly(N))$.*

The following corollary of Theorem 3 follows easily:

Corollary 1. *Let $\mathcal{A}, \mathcal{B}$ and $\mathcal{C}$ be three (possibly non-disjoint) quorums of parties, containing t_a, t_b and t_c corrupted parties respectively, where $t_a < \frac{|\mathcal{A}|}{3}, t_b < \frac{|\mathcal{B}|}{3}$ and $t_c < \frac{|\mathcal{C}|}{3}$. Let $t_{\mathsf{combined}} = t_a + t_b + t_c$ and $\mathcal{Q}_{\mathsf{combined}} = \mathcal{A} \cup \mathcal{B} \cup \mathcal{C}$. Moreover let $D \in \mathcal{P}$ be a dealer with a secret s. Furthermore let D invokes $\mathsf{AVSS}(D, \mathcal{Q}_{\mathsf{combined}}, s)$ and each $P_i \in \mathcal{Q}_{\mathsf{combined}}$ plays the role of k_i different parties in the protocol, where $k_i \in \{1, 2, 3\}$ is the number of quorums among $\mathcal{A}, \mathcal{B}$ and $\mathcal{C}$ where P_i is present; thus $t_{\mathsf{combined}} < \frac{|N|}{3}$, where $N = |\mathcal{A}| + |\mathcal{B}| + |\mathcal{C}|$. If $\mathsf{AVSS}(D, \mathcal{Q}_{\mathsf{combined}}, s)$ terminates then with high probability, there exists an $\bar{s}$, which is (t_{combined})-shared among $\mathcal{Q}_{\mathsf{combined}}$ (i.e. $[[[\bar{s}]]]_{\mathcal{Q}_{\mathsf{combined}}}^{t_{\mathsf{combined}}}$). Moreover, if D is honest then $\bar{s} = s$ and s remains private.* $\square$

In the rest of the paper we say that party P_i *t-share* s among $\mathcal{Q}$ (resp. $\mathcal{Q}_{\mathsf{combined}}$) to mean that P_i as a D invoke an instance $\mathsf{AVSS}(P_i, \mathcal{Q}, s)$ (resp. $\mathsf{AVSS}(P_i, \mathcal{Q}_{\mathsf{combined}}, s)$) and the parties in $\mathcal{Q}$ (resp. $\mathcal{Q}_{\mathsf{combined}}$) participate in the instance.

Asynchronous Reconstruction Protocol: Let $s \in \mathbb{F}$ be a value which is t'-shared among a quorum of parties $\mathcal{Q} \subseteq \mathcal{P}$, where $t' < \frac{|\mathcal{Q}|}{3}$ is the maximum number of corrupted parties in $\mathcal{Q}$ (i.e. $[s]_{\mathcal{Q}}^{t'}$). Then the well known asynchronous protocol $\mathsf{OEC}(\mathcal{Q}, [s]_{\mathcal{Q}}^{t'})$ (online error correction) [5,20], with communication complexity $\mathcal{O}(|\mathcal{Q}|^2)$, allows the parties in $\mathcal{Q}$ to robustly reconstruct s. In the rest of the paper we say that the *parties in $\mathcal{Q}$ robustly reconstruct $[s]_{\mathcal{Q}}^{t'}$* to mean that they execute $\mathsf{OEC}(\mathcal{Q}, [s]_{\mathcal{Q}}^{t'})$.

Let $\mathcal{A}, \mathcal{B}$ and $\mathcal{C}$ be three quorums, containing at most $t_a < \frac{|\mathcal{A}|}{3}, t_b < \frac{|\mathcal{B}|}{3}$ and $t_c < \frac{|\mathcal{C}|}{3}$ corrupted parties respectively. Moreover, let $t_{\mathsf{combined}} = t_a + t_b + t_c$, $\mathcal{Q}_{\mathsf{combined}} = \mathcal{A} \cup \mathcal{B} \cup \mathcal{C}$ and let s be t_{combined}-shared among $\mathcal{Q}_{\mathsf{combined}}$. Then by executing $\mathsf{OEC}(\mathcal{Q}_{\mathsf{combined}}, [[[s]]]_{\mathcal{Q}_{\mathsf{combined}}}^{t_{\mathsf{combined}}})$, the parties in $\mathcal{Q}_{\mathsf{combined}}$ can reconstruct s. This is because each $P_i \in \mathcal{Q}_{\mathsf{combined}}$ plays the role of k_i share-holders where $k_i \in \{1, 2, 3\}$ denotes the number of quorums among $\mathcal{A}, \mathcal{B}$ and $\mathcal{C}$ in which it is present. Thus $t_{\mathsf{combined}} < \frac{N}{3}$ holds where $N = |\mathcal{A}| + |\mathcal{B}| + |\mathcal{C}|$. In the rest of the paper we say that the *parties in $\mathcal{Q}_{\mathsf{combined}}$ robustly reconstruct $[[[s]]]_{\mathcal{Q}_{\mathsf{combined}}}^{t_{\mathsf{combined}}}$* to mean that they execute $\mathsf{OEC}(\mathcal{Q}_{\mathsf{combined}}, [s]_{\mathcal{Q}_{\mathsf{combined}}}^{t_{\mathsf{combined}}})$.

Asynchronous Broadcast and Agreement on a Common Subset: Bracha [8] presented an asynchronous protocol called A-Cast, which allows a sender Sen $\in \mathcal{P}$ to send some message m identically to all the n parties. If Sen is *honest* then all the honest parties eventually terminate with output m. If Sen is *corrupted* and some *honest* party terminates with output m', then every other honest party eventually does the same. The protocol has communication complexity $\mathcal{O}(n^2|m|)$ for a message m of size $|m|$. The details of A-Cast are available in [9].

Protocol ACS (agreement on a common subset) [5,7] allows the (honest) parties in a quorum $\mathcal{Q}$ of size N containing upto $t' < \frac{N}{3}$ corrupted parties, to agree on a common subset Com of $(N - t')$ parties, satisfying certain "property". The property will have the following characteristics: every honest party in $\mathcal{Q}$ will eventually satisfy the property; a corrupted party P_i in $\mathcal{Q}$ may not necessarily satisfy the property, but if some honest party in $\mathcal{Q}$ has found P_i to satisfy the property then it will hold that every other party in $\mathcal{Q}$ will also eventually find the same. The idea behind ACS is to execute $|\mathcal{Q}|$ instances of a $1/3$ fault-tolerant asynchronous Byzantine agreement (ABA) protocol [9], one on the behalf of each party in $\mathcal{Q}$ to decide if it satisfies the property and should be included in Com. The protocol has communication complexity $\mathcal{O}(\text{Poly}(N))$.

$1/3$ Fault-Tolerant AMPC Protocol: The following result states that it is possible to securely evaluate an arithmetic gate in a shared fashion as long as the fraction of corrupted parties is less than $1/3$:

Theorem 4 ([7,20]). *Let $\mathcal{Q} \subseteq \mathcal{P}$ be a quorum of N parties containing at most $t' < \frac{N}{3}$ corrupted parties and let a, b be t'-shared among $\mathcal{Q}$ (i.e. $[a]_{\mathcal{Q}}^{t'}, [b]_{\mathcal{Q}}^{t'}$). Moreover, let g be a publicly known 2-input gate over $\mathbb{F}$. Then there exists an efficient asynchronous protocol* AMPC$(g, \mathcal{Q}, [a]_{\mathcal{Q}}^{t'}, [b]_{\mathcal{Q}}^{t'})$ *for the parties in $\mathcal{Q}$ with the following properties:*

(1) TERMINATION*: With high probability, all the honest parties eventually terminate the protocol.* (2) CORRECTNESS*: With high probability, the protocol outputs $[g(a, b)]_{\mathcal{Q}}^{t'}$.* (3) PRIVACY*: The view of the adversary is independent of a and b and* (4) COMMUNICATION COMPLEXITY*: The protocol has communication complexity $\mathcal{O}(\text{Poly}(N))$.*

The following corollary to Theorem 4 follows easily:

Corollary 2. *Let $\mathcal{A}, \mathcal{B}$ and $\mathcal{C}$ be three quorums, containing at most t_a, t_b and t_c corrupted parties respectively, where $t_a < \frac{|\mathcal{A}|}{3}, t_b < \frac{|\mathcal{B}|}{3}$ and $t_c < \frac{|\mathcal{C}|}{3}$. Let $t_{\text{combined}} = t_a + t_b + t_c$ and $\mathcal{Q}_{\text{combined}} = \mathcal{A} \cup \mathcal{B} \cup \mathcal{C}$. Moreover let a, b be t_{combined}-shared among $\mathcal{Q}_{\text{combined}}$ and let the parties in $\mathcal{Q}_{\text{combined}}$ execute* AMPC$(g, \mathcal{Q}_{\text{combined}}, [[[a]]]_{\mathcal{Q}_{\text{combined}}}^{t_{\text{combined}}}, [[[b]]]_{\mathcal{Q}_{\text{combined}}}^{t_{\text{combined}}})$ *with each $P_i \in \mathcal{Q}_{\text{combined}}$ playing the role of k_i different parties, where $k_i \in \{1, 2, 3\}$ is the number of quorums in which P_i occurs. Then with high probability, the protocol terminates with output $[[[g(a, b)]]]_{\mathcal{Q}_{\text{combined}}}^{t_{\text{combined}}}$. The view of the adversary will be independent of a, b and the protocol has communication complexity $\mathcal{O}(\text{Poly}(|\mathcal{Q}_{\text{combined}}|))$.*

Generating Uniformly Random $[\cdot]$ and $[[[\cdot]]]$-Shared Vectors: Protocol Rand$(\mathcal{Q}, \ell)$ is a standard protocol, which allows a quorum of parties $\mathcal{Q}$ to generate a uniformly random t'-shared vector $[\mathbf{r}]_{\mathcal{Q}}^{t'} = ([r_1]_{\mathcal{Q}}^{t'}, \ldots, [r_\ell]_{\mathcal{Q}}^{t'})$ of length ℓ, where $t' < \frac{|\mathcal{Q}|}{3}$ is the maximum number of corrupted parties in $\mathcal{Q}$; thus the view of the adversary will be independent of $\mathbf{r}$. In the protocol each party in $\mathcal{Q}$ t'-share a uniformly random vector of length ℓ. Using ACS the parties in $\mathcal{Q}$ agree on a common subset Com of $|\mathcal{Q}| - t'$ parties who have correctly shared their vectors. Finally $[\mathbf{r}]_{\mathcal{Q}}^{t'}$ is set to be the sum of the vectors shared by the parties in Com. The protocol eventually terminates as there exists at least $|\mathcal{Q}| - t'$ honest parties in $\mathcal{Q}$ who correctly share their vectors. As there exists at least one honest party in Com (since $|\mathcal{Q}| - t' > 2t'$) whose shared vector is indeed random and private (follows from the property of AVSS), it follows that the shared $\mathbf{r}$ is indeed random and private. The protocol has communication complexity $\mathcal{O}(\text{Poly}(|\mathcal{Q}|, \ell))$.

Let $\mathcal{A}, \mathcal{B}$ and $\mathcal{C}$ be three quorums, containing at most t_a, t_b and t_c corrupted parties respectively, where $t_a < \frac{|\mathcal{A}|}{3}, t_b < \frac{|\mathcal{B}|}{3}$ and $t_c < \frac{|\mathcal{C}|}{3}$. Let $t_{\text{combined}} = t_a + t_b + t_c$ and $\mathcal{Q}_{\text{combined}} = \mathcal{A} \cup \mathcal{B} \cup \mathcal{C}$. It follows that using the above idea, the parties in $\mathcal{Q}_{\text{combined}}$ can execute $\text{Rand}(\mathcal{Q}_{\text{combined}}, \ell)$ to generate a uniformly random t_{combined}-shared vector $[[[\mathbf{r}]]]_{\mathcal{Q}_{\text{combined}}}^{t_{\text{combined}}} = ([[[\mathbf{r}_1]]]_{\mathcal{Q}_{\text{combined}}}^{t_{\text{combined}}}, \ldots, [[[\mathbf{r}_\ell]]]_{\mathcal{Q}_{\text{combined}}}^{t_{\text{combined}}})$ of length ℓ. For this, every party $P_i \in \mathcal{Q}_{\text{combined}}$ plays the role of k_i different parties and accordingly t_{combined}-share k_i uniformly random vectors among $\mathcal{Q}_{\text{combined}}$; here $k_i \in \{1, 2, 3\}$ denotes the number of quorums in which P_i is present. As a result, the relation $t_{\text{combined}} < \frac{N}{3}$ will hold where $N = |\mathcal{A}| + |\mathcal{B}| + |\mathcal{C}|$ and so the arguments used above hold here also.

5   Transforming a $[\cdot]$-Shared Value to a $[[[\cdot]]]$-Shared Value

We now present an asynchronous protocol Transform. The protocol takes as input a t_a-shared value s (i.e. $[s]_{\mathcal{A}}^{t_a}$), shared among the parties in a quorum $\mathcal{A}$, containing at most $t_a < \frac{|\mathcal{A}|}{3}$ corrupted parties. The protocol also takes as input two additional (possibly non-disjoint) quorums $\mathcal{B}$ and $\mathcal{C}$, containing at most t_b and t_c corrupted parties respectively, where $t_b < \frac{|\mathcal{B}|}{3}$ and $t_c < \frac{|\mathcal{C}|}{3}$. The protocol outputs $[[[s]]]_{\mathcal{Q}_{\text{combined}}}^{t_{\text{combined}}}$, with the view of the adversary being independent of s (thus s remains private); here $\mathcal{Q}_{\text{combined}} = \mathcal{A} \cup \mathcal{B} \cup \mathcal{C}$ and $t_{\text{combined}} = t_a + t_b + t_c$. The protocol has communication complexity $\mathcal{O}(\text{Poly}(|\mathcal{Q}_{\text{combined}}|))$. Looking ahead, protocol Transform will be the major component in our AMPC protocol for implementing the protocol LightWeightGateEval discussed in the introduction. For designing Transform we further need another subprotocol Cor&Det (standing for correct-and-detect) which we discuss next.

5.1   Protocol Cor&Det: Shared Error-Correction Followed by Error-Detection

The protocol takes as input quorums $\mathcal{A}, \mathcal{B}, \mathcal{C}$ and values t_a, t_b and t_c. Additionally, it takes input a parameter r, where $r \leq t_a$ and a t_{combined}-shared vector $[[[\mathbf{s}']]]_{\mathcal{Q}_{\text{combined}}}^{t_{\text{combined}}} = ([[[\mathbf{s}'_1]]]_{\mathcal{Q}_{\text{combined}}}^{t_{\text{combined}}}, \ldots, [[[\mathbf{s}'_{2t_a+1+r}]]]_{\mathcal{Q}_{\text{combined}}}^{t_{\text{combined}}})$. The vector $\mathbf{s}' = (\mathbf{s}'_1, \ldots, \mathbf{s}'_{2t_a+1+r})$ has a Hamming distance of *at most* t_a from an unknown vector $\mathbf{s} = (\mathbf{s}_1, \ldots, \mathbf{s}_{2t_a+1+r})$, which constitutes $2t_a + 1 + r$ distinct points on (an unknown) polynomial $\mathbf{f}(\cdot)$ of degree at most t_a; i.e. $\mathbf{f}(\alpha_i) = \mathbf{s}_i$ holds for $i = 1, \ldots, 2t_a + 1 + r$. The *exact value* of the Hamming distance between $\mathbf{s}$ and $\mathbf{s}'$ is not known (except that it is at most t_a). Moreover, Adv knows the components of $\mathbf{s}$ and $\mathbf{s}'$ in which they differ and thus Adv may know t_a points on[7] $\mathbf{f}(\cdot)$. The goal of Cor&Det is to error-correct upto r errors in $\mathbf{s}'$

---

[7] Looking ahead, for Transform, $\mathbf{s}$ will be a "truncated" t_a-sharing of s and $\mathbf{s}'$ will be the reshared shares of s, of which at most t_a may be incorrect.

and then identify if there are still more errors left. In a more detail, if *indeed* the Hamming distance between s and s′ is at most r, then the protocol outputs t_{combined}-shared s; i.e. $[[[s_1]]]_{\mathcal{Q}_{\text{combined}}}^{t_{\text{combined}}}, \ldots, [[[s_{2t_a+1+r}]]]_{\mathcal{Q}_{\text{combined}}}^{t_{\text{combined}}}$. Otherwise it outputs $\perp$. In any case, s remains private; the protocol has communication complexity $\mathcal{O}(\text{Poly}(|\mathcal{Q}_{\text{combined}}|))$.

The protocol (see Fig. 1) is based on the idea of shared error-correction, also used in [1]; however we need to make some modifications in our context (more on this in the sequel). Specifically we observe that s is an (N, k, d) RS codeword where $N = 2t_a+1+r, k = t_a+1$ and hence $d \geq t_a+r+1$ and so by applying RS error-correction, we can correct upto $\lceil \frac{t_a+r}{2} \rceil$ errors in s′. If indeed the Hamming distance between s and s′ is *at most* r, then we can error-correct the r errors in s′, as $r \leq \frac{t_a+r}{2}$; otherwise the recovered word may not be s. To detect this, we further apply the error-detection property of the RS codes. More specifically, let s* be the word obtained after correcting r errors in s′. We can verify whether s* is an (N, k, d) RS codeword by computing the syndrome of s* and checking it for 0. The idea is that if the syndrome of s* is 0 then s* = s. This is because s and s* will have *at least* $(2t_a+1+r) - t_a - r = t_a+1$ same components: in the worst case, at most t_a components of s′ could be corrupted and at most r correct components of s′ could have been incorrectly identified as corrupted by the error-correction algorithm. However from Lemma 1, if s and s* are different codewords then they can have *at most* t_a same components, which is a contradiction.

The above idea can be executed even with $[[[s′]]]_{\mathcal{Q}_{\text{combined}}}^{t_{\text{combined}}}$. This is because RSDec involves performing *linear* operations on s′ and so due to the linearity property of d-sharing, the same operations can be performed even on shared s′ and so we can compute the *shared syndrome* $\mathfrak{s}(s′)$. However, we also require the actual syndrome $\mathfrak{s}(s′)$ to be reconstructed, so as to compute the error-vector. But reconstructing $\mathfrak{s}(s′)$ seems to reveal information about the (unknown) components of s′, which we want to avoid. Specifically, if indeed at most r components of s′ are corrupted, then reconstructing the syndrome does not reveal any information about the unknown components of s. This is because in this case the adversary will known the *exact* error-vector that RSDec will output and so it can compute the syndrome itself (this follows from the fact that in this case the syndrome of the vector s′ will be the same as the syndrome of the reported error-vector); a detailed proof for the same appears in [1]. However, if *more* than $\frac{t_a+r}{2}$ errors have occurred, then Adv may not know the exact error-vector that RSDec will output because in this case, even some of the correct components of s′ may be incorrectly reported as corrupted (in the error-vector) by the algorithm, which may leak information about such correct components of s′.

To deal with the above privacy issue, we carry out the shared error-correction on s′+m instead of s′, where $m = (m_1, \ldots, m_{2t_a+1+r})$ constitutes a completely random and unknown *mask* subject to the condition that m constitutes $2t_a+1+r$ distinct points on a random unknown polynomial, say M($\cdot$) of degree at most t_a; i.e. m is an (N, k, d) RS codeword. To generate such a (shared) m, we use the protocol Rand to generate the coefficients of M($\cdot$) in a shared fashion and then generate the points on M($\cdot$) in a shared fashion. The idea is that s + m also constitutes an RS codeword. So if indeed at most r components of s′ are corrupted, then so will be in s′ + m and so we can correctly error-correct upto r errors in s′ + m obtaining s + m and then unmask m; else we

$$\text{Cor\&Det}(\mathcal{A}, \mathcal{B}, \mathcal{C}, r, t_a, t_b, t_c, [[[\mathbf{s}']]]_{\mathcal{Q}_{\text{combined}}}^{t_{\text{combined}}})$$

i. GENERATING t_{combined}-SHARED RANDOM MASK: The parties in $\mathcal{Q}_{\text{combined}}$ execute $\text{Rand}(\mathcal{Q}_{\text{combined}}, t_a + 1)$ and generate a uniformly random t_{combined}-shared vector $[[[\mathbf{M}]]]_{\mathcal{Q}_{\text{combined}}}^{t_{\text{combined}}} = ([[[\mathsf{m}_0]]]_{\mathcal{Q}_{\text{combined}}}^{t_{\text{combined}}}, \ldots, [[[\mathsf{m}_{t_a}]]]_{\mathcal{Q}_{\text{combined}}}^{t_{\text{combined}}})$ of length $t_a + 1$. Let $\mathsf{M}(x) = \mathsf{m}_0 + \mathsf{m}_1 \cdot x + \ldots + \mathsf{m}_{t_a} \cdot x^{t_a}$ be the *masking polynomial* of degree at most t_a. Using the linearity property, the parties in $\mathcal{Q}_{\text{combined}}$ compute the t_{combined}-shared vector $[[[\mathbf{m}]]]_{\mathcal{Q}_{\text{combined}}}^{t_{\text{combined}}} = [[[\mathsf{m}_1]]]_{\mathcal{Q}_{\text{combined}}}^{t_{\text{combined}}}, \ldots, [[[\mathsf{m}_{2t_a+1+r}]]]_{\mathcal{Q}_{\text{combined}}}^{t_{\text{combined}}}$, where $\mathsf{m}_i = \mathsf{M}(\alpha_i)$ for $i = 1, \ldots, 2t_a + 1 + r$. Thus $[[[\mathsf{m}_i]]]_{\mathcal{Q}_{\text{combined}}}^{t_{\text{combined}}} = [[[\mathsf{m}_0]]]_{\mathcal{Q}_{\text{combined}}}^{t_{\text{combined}}} + \alpha_i \cdot [[[\mathsf{m}_1]]]_{\mathcal{Q}_{\text{combined}}}^{t_{\text{combined}}} + \ldots + \alpha_i^{t_a} \cdot [[[\mathsf{m}_{t_a}]]]_{\mathcal{Q}_{\text{combined}}}^{t_{\text{combined}}}$.

ii. MASKING THE INPUT VECTOR: The parties in $\mathcal{Q}_{\text{combined}}$ (locally) compute $[[[\mathbf{s}' + \mathbf{m}]]]_{\mathcal{Q}_{\text{combined}}}^{t_{\text{combined}}} = [[[\mathbf{s}']]]_{\mathcal{Q}_{\text{combined}}}^{t_{\text{combined}}} + [[[\mathbf{m}]]]_{\mathcal{Q}_{\text{combined}}}^{t_{\text{combined}}}$.

iii. SHARED ERROR-CORRECTION, DETECTION AND TERMINATION: Let H be the publicly known $(t_a + r) \times (2t_a + 1 + r)$ parity-check matrix corresponding to the family of RS codes $\mathcal{C}(2t_a + 1 + r, t_a + 1, t_a + r + 1)$. The parties in $\mathcal{Q}_{\text{combined}}$ apply $\text{RSDec}(2t_a + 1 + r, t_a + 1, r)$ on $[[[\mathbf{s}' + \mathbf{m}]]]_{\mathcal{Q}_{\text{combined}}}^{t_{\text{combined}}}$ using H to error-correct r errors in a shared fashion followed by shared error-detection as follows:

   – The parties compute the t_{combined}-shared syndrome $([[[\mathsf{s}_1]]]_{\mathcal{Q}_{\text{combined}}}^{t_{\text{combined}}}, \ldots, [[[\mathsf{s}_{t_a+r}]]]_{\mathcal{Q}_{\text{combined}}}^{t_{\text{combined}}}) = [[[\mathbf{s}' + \mathbf{m}]]]_{\mathcal{Q}_{\text{combined}}}^{t_{\text{combined}}} \cdot H^T$. The parties then robustly reconstruct $[[[\mathsf{s}_i]]]_{\mathcal{Q}_{\text{combined}}}^{t_{\text{combined}}}$ for $i = 1, \ldots, t_a + r$ and obtain the syndrome $\mathbf{s} = (\mathsf{s}_1, \ldots, \mathsf{s}_{t_a+r})$.
   – From $\mathbf{s}$, the parties (locally) obtain the error vector $\mathbf{e} = (e_1, \ldots, e_{2t_a+1+r})$. If $\mathbf{e}$ has more than r *non-zero* components then the parties output $\perp$ and terminate.[a]
   – The parties compute a *default*[b] t_{combined}-sharing $[[[\mathbf{e}]]]_{\mathcal{Q}_{\text{combined}}}^{t_{\text{combined}}} = ([[[e_1]]]_{\mathcal{Q}_{\text{combined}}}^{t_{\text{combined}}}, \ldots, [[[e_{2t_a+1+r}]]]_{\mathcal{Q}_{\text{combined}}}^{t_{\text{combined}}})$ and set $[[[\mathbf{s}^\star]]]_{\mathcal{Q}_{\text{combined}}}^{t_{\text{combined}}} = [[[\mathbf{s}' + \mathbf{m}]]]_{\mathcal{Q}_{\text{combined}}}^{t_{\text{combined}}} - [[[\mathbf{e}]]]_{\mathcal{Q}_{\text{combined}}}^{t_{\text{combined}}}$.
   – The parties compute the shared syndrome $([[[\mathsf{s}_1^\star]]]_{\mathcal{Q}_{\text{combined}}}^{t_{\text{combined}}}, \ldots, [[[\mathsf{s}_{t_a+r}^\star]]]_{\mathcal{Q}_{\text{combined}}}^{t_{\text{combined}}}) = [[[\mathbf{s}^\star]]]_{\mathcal{Q}_{\text{combined}}}^{t_{\text{combined}}} \cdot H^T$ and then robustly reconstruct $[[[\mathsf{s}_i^\star]]]_{\mathcal{Q}_{\text{combined}}}^{t_{\text{combined}}}$ for $i = 1, \ldots, t_a + r$ to obtain the new syndrome $\mathbf{s}^\star = (\mathsf{s}_1^\star, \ldots, \mathsf{s}_{t_a+r}^\star)$. If $\mathbf{s}^\star \neq 0^{t_a+r}$ then the parties output $\perp$, else $[[[\mathbf{s}]]]_{\mathcal{Q}_{\text{combined}}}^{t_{\text{combined}}} = [[[\mathbf{s}^\star]]]_{\mathcal{Q}_{\text{combined}}}^{t_{\text{combined}}} - [[[\mathbf{m}]]]_{\mathcal{Q}_{\text{combined}}}^{t_{\text{combined}}}$ and then terminate.

[a] This clearly implies that more than r components in $[[[\mathbf{s}' + \mathbf{m}]]]_{\mathcal{Q}_{\text{combined}}}^{t_{\text{combined}}}$ are corrupted and so the parties stop further calculations.

[b] A default sharing of a value v is nothing but the *constant polynomial* v.

Fig. 1. Protocol for the shared error-correction followed by error-detection

detect that more than r errors are present in $\mathbf{s}' + \mathbf{m}$. But in any case, the privacy of the unknown components of $\mathbf{s}$ is preserved, as we compute syndrome of the masked $\mathbf{s}'$.

5.2 Designing Transform Using Cor&Det

The high level idea of Transform (see Fig. 2) is as follows: for simplicity and without loss of generality, let $\mathcal{A} = \{P_1, \ldots, P_{|\mathcal{A}|}\}$; moreover let $|\mathcal{A}| = 3t_a + 1$, which is the minimum possible value of $|\mathcal{A}|$. In the protocol, each party P_i in $\mathcal{A}$ reshare its share s_i of $\mathbf{s}$ among $\mathcal{Q}_{\text{combined}}$ with threshold t_{combined}. An honest P_i will indeed reshare s_i, however a corrupted P_i may not do the same. Moreover, due to the asynchronicity, we cannot wait for *all* the $|\mathcal{A}|$ shares of s to be reshared. So the parties in $\mathcal{Q}_{\text{combined}}$ perform what we call "online" shared error-correction, which is an iterative process of length at most $t_a + 1$. The iterations are indexed by a parameter r, whose value ranges from 0 to t_a. Namely during the iteration r, the parties in $\mathcal{Q}_{\text{combined}}$ agree on a common subset $\mathcal{SP}_r \subseteq \mathcal{A}$ of $2t_a + 1 + r$ "share-providers", such that the shares of each party in $\mathcal{SP}_r$ will be eventually reshared among $\mathcal{Q}_{\text{combined}}$. Let $\mathbf{s}_r$ denote the vector of *original* shares of the parties in $\mathcal{SP}_r$ and let $\mathbf{s'}_r$ denote the vector of *actual* values which are reshared by the individual parties in $\mathcal{SP}_r$; clearly the distance between $\mathbf{s}_r$ and $\mathbf{s'}_r$ is at most t_a, as $\mathcal{SP}_r$ may contain t_a corrupted parties, who could reshare an *incorrect* share. The parties optimistically *assume* that the distance between $\mathbf{s}_r$ and $\mathbf{s'}_r$ is at most r and try to error-correct the same; protocol Cor&Det is used for the same purpose. If $\perp$ is obtained as the output of Cor&Det then this clearly indicates that more than r parties in $\mathcal{SP}_r$ are corrupted, who shared an incorrect share; so the parties go to the next iteration and wait for more shares to be reshared (i.e. new parties are added to the set $\mathcal{SP}_r$) and repeat the process. The idea is that if $\hat{r}$ is the number of corrupted parties in $\mathcal{A}$ who reshare incorrect shares of s, where $\hat{r} \leq t_a$, then during the $\hat{r}$th iteration, $\mathcal{SP}_{\hat{r}}$ will be of size $2t_a + 1 + \hat{r}$ containing $\hat{r}$ corrupted parties, implying that the distance between $\mathbf{s}_{\hat{r}}$ and $\mathbf{s'}_{\hat{r}}$ will be $\hat{r}$ and so by the properties of Cor&Det, the vector $\mathbf{s}_{\hat{r}}$ will be "re-stored" and t_{combined}-shared at the end of iteration $\hat{r}$. Once this is done, t_{combined}-sharing of s can be computed using the linearity property. Specifically, the components of $\mathbf{s}_{\hat{r}}$ constitute distinct points on a polynomial of degree at most t_a and so the constant term of the polynomial (namely s) can be expressed as a linear combination of these points. It is easy to see that prior to the iteration $\hat{r}$, the instances of Cor&Det will output $\perp$ and s remains private, thanks to the property of Cor&Det and the fact that each honest $P_i \in \mathcal{A}$ independently reshare its share of s, where the degree of sharing is t_{combined}.

6   The High Level Description of Our AMPC Protocol

Our AMPC protocol is a sequence of the following stages:

(1) Quorum Assignment: The parties in $\mathcal{P}$ execute the protocol Quorum$(\mathcal{P})$ and obtain n public quorums $\mathcal{Q}_1, \ldots, \mathcal{Q}_n$ with the properties as stated in Theorem 2; to recall, each quorum will be of size $\Theta(\log n)$ and with high probability, the fraction of corrupted parties in each quorum is strictly less than $1/3$. For simplicity, we assume $|\mathcal{Q}_i| = 3t_i + 1$ for each $\mathcal{Q}_i$; so with high probability, the maximum number of corrupted parties in $\mathcal{Q}_i$ will be t_i. The next task is to assign a *unique* quorum for each gate of the circuit C, who will be involved in the shared evaluation of that gate, along with *two* other quorums (who will have the corresponding masked gate inputs); care is taken while doing this assignment to ensure "load-balancing". More specifically, corresponding to the circuit C, we construct a network G, with $|C| + n$ nodes: for every gate in C, there will be a node in G, called *internal node* and the remaining n nodes in G correspond to the n inputs of C and are called *input nodes*. For every (internal) wire from one gate to another gate in C, there will be an edge connecting the corresponding internal nodes in G. For every wire from an input to a gate in C, there will be an edge from the corresponding input node to the corresponding internal node in G. We next assume a canonical

---

Protocol Transform$(\mathcal{A}, \mathcal{B}, \mathcal{C}, t_a, t_b, t_c, [s]_{\mathcal{A}}^{t_a})$

Let $\mathcal{Q}_{\text{combined}} = \mathcal{A} \cup \mathcal{B} \cup \mathcal{C}$ and $t_{\text{combined}} = t_a + t_b + t_c$. For simplicity and without loss of generality, let $|\mathcal{A}| = 3t_a + 1$ and $\mathcal{A} = \{P_1, \ldots, P_{3t_a+1}\}$.

  i. RESHARING THE SHARES OF s: Every party $P_i \in \mathcal{A}$ acts as a D and t_{combined}-share its share $\mathbf{s}_i$ of s among $\mathcal{Q}_{\text{combined}}$.
 ii. ONLINE SHARED ERROR-CORRECTION AND TERMINATION—For $r = 0, \ldots, t_a$, the parties in $\mathcal{Q}_{\text{combined}}$ do the following:
   – Execute an instance of ACS and agree on a common set $\mathcal{SP}_r \subseteq \mathcal{A}$ of size $2t_a + 1 + r$, such that the share of each $P_i \in \mathcal{SP}_r$ is eventually reshared among $\mathcal{Q}_{\text{combined}}$. For simplicity, let $\mathcal{SP}_r = \{P_1, \ldots, P_{2t_a+1+r}\}$.
   – Let $[[[\mathbf{s}'_r]]]_{\mathcal{Q}_{\text{combined}}}^{t_{\text{combined}}} = ([[[\mathbf{s}'_1]]]_{\mathcal{Q}_{\text{combined}}}^{t_{\text{combined}}}, \ldots, [[[\mathbf{s}'_{2t_a+1+r}]]]_{\mathcal{Q}_{\text{combined}}}^{t_{\text{combined}}})$ be the vector of values reshared by the parties in in $\mathcal{SP}_r$. The parties in $\mathcal{Q}_{\text{combined}}$ execute $\text{Cor\&Det}(\mathcal{A}, \mathcal{B}, \mathcal{C}, r, t_a, t_b, t_c, [[[\mathbf{s}'_r]]]_{\mathcal{Q}_{\text{combined}}}^{t_{\text{combined}}})$. If $\perp$ is obtained at the end of Cor&Det then continue with the next iteration. Else let $[[[\mathbf{s}_1]]]_{\mathcal{Q}_{\text{combined}}}^{t_{\text{combined}}}, \ldots, [[[\mathbf{s}_{2t_a+1+r}]]]_{\mathcal{Q}_{\text{combined}}}^{t_{\text{combined}}}$ be the non-$\perp$ output obtained at the end of Cor&Det. Then using the linearity property, the parties compute $[[[s]]]_{\mathcal{Q}_{\text{combined}}}^{t_{\text{combined}}}$ from $[[[\mathbf{s}_1]]]_{\mathcal{Q}_{\text{combined}}}^{t_{\text{combined}}}, \ldots, [[[\mathbf{s}_{2t_a+1+r}]]]_{\mathcal{Q}_{\text{combined}}}^{t_{\text{combined}}}$ and terminate.

Fig. 2. Protocol for securely computing $[[[s]]]_{\mathcal{Q}_{\text{combined}}}^{t_{\text{combined}}}$ from $[s]_{\mathcal{A}}^{t_a}$

numbering of all the nodes in G and the n quorums and assign quorum $\mathcal{Q}_i$ to node j in G if $i = j \mod n$; thus a quorum is assigned to at most $\frac{|C|+n}{n}$ nodes in G.

(2) Random Shared Mask Generation for Each Node of G: For each node of the network G, the parties in the corresponding assigned quorum collectively generate a uniformly random and shared mask (the purpose of the mask will be clear in the sequel). More specifically, if a quorum say $\mathcal{Q}_k$ is assigned to a node in G, then corresponding to this node, the parties in $\mathcal{Q}_k$ collectively generate a uniformly random mask, say m, which is t_k-shared (recall that we assumed that $|\mathcal{Q}_k| = 3t_k + 1$) among $\mathcal{Q}_k$ (i.e. $[m]_{\mathcal{Q}_k}^{t_k}$); if $\mathcal{Q}_k$ is assigned to more than one node in G, then an independent shared mask is generated for each such node. For generating $[m]_{\mathcal{Q}_k}^{t_k}$, the parties in $\mathcal{Q}_k$ execute Rand$(\mathcal{Q}_k, 1)$, which will have communication complexity $\mathcal{O}(\text{Poly}(|\mathcal{Q}_k|)) = \mathcal{O}(\text{PolyLog}(n))$. If indeed t_k is the maximum number of corrupted parties in $\mathcal{Q}_k$ (which will be the case with high probability) then the view of the adversary will be independent of m. The total communication complexity of this stage will be $\mathcal{O}((|C| + n)\text{PolyLog}(n))$.

(3) Input Commitment: Here each party $P_i \in \mathcal{P}$ commits its private input $\mathbf{x}_i$ (for the computation of f) to the quorum which is assigned to the input node in G, corresponding to the input $\mathbf{x}_i$; for simplicity and without loss of generality, let $\mathcal{Q}_i$ be the designated quorum, then P_i t_i-share $\mathbf{x}_i$ among $\mathcal{Q}_i$ (i.e. $[\mathbf{x}_i]_{\mathcal{Q}_i}^{t_i}$). Recall that in a completely asynchronous setting, it is impossible to ensure input provision from all the n parties, as it will turn endless; as a result, the parties in $\mathcal{P}$ need to agree on a common subset Com of $(n - t)$ "input-providers", who have indeed correctly shared their private inputs to the respective assigned quorums. Towards this, corresponding to each party $P_i \in \mathcal{P}$, every party P_j in the assigned quorum $\mathcal{Q}_i$ broadcasts a confirmation after correctly receiving its share of $\mathbf{x}_i$ corresponding to $[\mathbf{x}_i]_{\mathcal{Q}_i}^{t_i}$. The idea is that if *majority* of the parties in $\mathcal{Q}_i$ broadcasts the confirmation, then with high probability, indeed P_i has correctly committed its input to $\mathcal{Q}_i$ and this will be known publicly; this is because with high probability, the quorum formation protocol Quorum($\mathcal{P}$) would ensure that $\mathcal{Q}_i$ has at most $t_i < \frac{\mathcal{Q}_i}{3}$ corrupted parties. Based on the broadcasted confirmations, the parties in $\mathcal{P}$ then agree on the set Com by executing an instance of ACS. For the remaining t parties not in Com, the parties in the quorum assigned to the corresponding input nodes in G consider a default sharing of 0 as the private input of those t parties. The interpretation is that the $(n - t)$ parties in Com have committed their inputs to the corresponding quorums, while the input for the remaining t parties is 0; and our goal is to securely compute the function f on the n-ary input vector $\mathbf{x} = (\mathbf{x}_1, \ldots, \mathbf{x}_n)$, where $\mathbf{x}_i$ is the value committed by P_i if $P_i \in$ Com, otherwise[8] $\mathbf{x}_i = 0$. It is easy to see that if $P_i \in$ Com and if indeed t_i is the maximum number of corrupted parties in $\mathcal{Q}_i$ (which will be the case with high probability), then $\mathbf{x}_i$ remains private (due to AVSS).

Finally once the inputs are committed, the parties in each $\mathcal{Q}_i$ (associated with the input nodes) do the following: they mask the shared input $[\mathbf{x}_i]_{\mathcal{Q}_i}^{t_i}$ with the corresponding shared mask $[m_i]_{\mathcal{Q}_i}^{t_i}$ (corresponding to the input node) generated in the previous stage; i.e. they compute $[\mathbf{x}_i + m_i]_{\mathcal{Q}_i}^{t_i}$. This is followed by (robust) reconstruction of the masked input $\mathbf{x}_i + m_i$ (the need to perform this step is to maintain the invariant for shared gate evaluation discussed in the sequel). Notice that $\mathbf{x}_i$ of the honest P_is in Com remains private because with high probability, the mask m_i will be random and private.

(4) Shared Gate Evaluation Involving Three Quorums: Using Transform as a sub-protocol, we design a protocol LightWeightGateEval, to maintain the following invariant for each gate g of the circuit C: let g takes inputs x_{left} and x_{right}, which we call the *left* and *right* inputs respectively. The input x_{left} (resp. x_{right}) may either be the output of some "previous" gate in C or it may be the private input (for f) of one of the parties in $\mathcal{P}$. In either case, there will be a node (either an internal node or an input node) in the network G and a corresponding assigned quorum $\mathcal{Q}_{\text{left}}$ (resp. $\mathcal{Q}_{\text{right}}$) called *left quorum* (resp. *right quorum*), where $|\mathcal{Q}_{\text{left}}| = 3t_{\text{left}} + 1$ (resp. $|\mathcal{Q}_{\text{right}}| = 3t_{\text{right}} + 1$). Correspondingly there will be a uniformly random mask m_{left} (resp. m_{right}) called *left mask* (resp. *right mask*), generated during the shared mask generation stage, such that m_{left} (resp. m_{right}) will be t_{left}-shared (resp. t_{right}-shared) among $\mathcal{Q}_{\text{left}}$ (resp. $\mathcal{Q}_{\text{right}}$); i.e. $[m_{\text{left}}]_{\mathcal{Q}_{\text{left}}}^{t_{\text{left}}}$ (resp. $[m_{\text{right}}]_{\mathcal{Q}_{\text{right}}}^{t_{\text{right}}}$). Furthermore, the masked left input $z_{\text{left}} = x_{\text{left}} + m_{\text{left}}$ and the masked right input $z_{\text{right}} = x_{\text{right}} + m_{\text{right}}$ will be publicly known to the parties in $\mathcal{Q}_{\text{left}}$ and $\mathcal{Q}_{\text{right}}$ respectively. Apart from $\mathcal{Q}_{\text{left}}$ and $\mathcal{Q}_{\text{right}}$, there will be an additional quorum $\mathcal{Q}_{\text{out}}$ called *output quorum* of size $|\mathcal{Q}_{\text{out}}| = 3t_{\text{out}} + 1$, assigned to the internal node corresponding to g in the network G; accordingly there will be a corresponding mask m_{out} called *output mask* from the shared mask generation stage, which will be t_{out}-shared among $\mathcal{Q}_{\text{out}}$ (i.e. $[m_{\text{out}}]_{\mathcal{Q}_{\text{out}}}^{t_{\text{out}}}$). Then LightWeightGateEval computes the masked output $z_{\text{out}} = g(x_{\text{left}}, x_{\text{right}}) + m_{\text{out}}$ and makes it publicly known to the

---

[8] Informally, this is the way we define an ideal-world AMPC functionality to prove security in the real-world/ideal-world paradigm; see for example [5,7].

parties in $\mathcal{Q}_{\text{combined}} = \mathcal{Q}_{\text{left}} \cup \mathcal{Q}_{\text{right}} \cup \mathcal{Q}_{\text{out}}$. If $\mathcal{Q}_{\text{left}}, \mathcal{Q}_{\text{right}}$ and $\mathcal{Q}_{\text{out}}$ contains $t_{\text{left}}, t_{\text{right}}$ and t_{out} parties respectively (which indeed will be the case with high probability), then $x_{\text{left}}, x_{\text{right}}, m_{\text{left}}, m_{\text{right}}$ and m_{out} remains private.

The high level idea behind LightWeightGateEval (discussed in the introduction) is the following: let $t_{\text{combined}} = t_{\text{left}} + t_{\text{right}} + t_{\text{out}}$. Then using Transform, the parties in $\mathcal{Q}_{\text{combined}}$ ensure that the private inputs, namely $x_{\text{left}}, x_{\text{right}}$ and the output mask m_{out} is t_{combined}-shared among them; i.e. they securely generate $[[[x_{\text{left}}]]]_{\mathcal{Q}_{\text{combined}}}^{t_{\text{combined}}}$ from z_{left} and $[m_{\text{left}}]_{\mathcal{Q}_{\text{left}}}^{t_{\text{left}}}$, $[[[x_{\text{right}}]]]_{\mathcal{Q}_{\text{combined}}}^{t_{\text{combined}}}$ from z_{right} and $[m_{\text{right}}]_{\mathcal{Q}_{\text{left}}}^{t_{\text{left}}}$ and $[[[m_{\text{out}}]]]_{\mathcal{Q}_{\text{combined}}}^{t_{\text{combined}}}$ from $[m_{\text{out}}]_{\mathcal{Q}_{\text{out}}}^{t_{\text{out}}}$ respectively. Then using AMPC, they compute $[[[g(x_{\text{left}}, x_{\text{right}})]]]_{\mathcal{Q}_{\text{combined}}}^{t_{\text{combined}}}$ followed by computing $[[[g(x_{\text{left}}, x_{\text{right}}) + m_{\text{out}}]]]_{\mathcal{Q}_{\text{combined}}}^{t_{\text{combined}}}$. Finally they reconstruct $g(x_{\text{left}}, x_{\text{right}}) + m_{\text{out}}$ using OEC. It is easy to see that if indeed the fraction of corrupted parties in each of $\mathcal{Q}_{\text{left}}, \mathcal{Q}_{\text{right}}$ and $\mathcal{Q}_{\text{out}}$ is less than $1/3$ (which will be the case with high probability), then the protocol LightWeightGateEval meets the promised security goals. Moreover, the communication complexity of LightWeightGateEval will be $\mathcal{O}(\text{PolyLog}(n))$; Transform involves $\Theta(\log n)$ parties while the instance of AMPC and OEC also involves $\Theta(\log n)$ parties. Thus the total complexity of this stage is $\mathcal{O}(|C|) \cdot \text{PolyLog}(n)$.

(5) Output Propagation: Let $\mathcal{Q}_{\text{final}}$ be the quorum of size $3t_{\text{final}} + 1$ which is assigned to the internal node in G corresponding to the output gate in the circuit C. Then due to the invariant maintained during the shared gate evaluation, the parties in $\mathcal{Q}_{\text{final}}$ will eventually have the publicly known masked function output $y_{\text{out}} + m_{\text{final}}$, where m_{final} will be a t_{final}-shared mask corresponding to this internal node, available to the parties in $\mathcal{Q}_{\text{final}}$ from the shared mask generation stage. The parties in $\mathcal{Q}_{\text{final}}$ then (robustly) reconstruct m_{final} and then unmask m_{final}, obtaining the function output y_{out}. The final task will be to "propagate" y_{out} to all the parties in $\mathcal{P}$. One obvious way of doing this is to ask each party in $\mathcal{Q}_{\text{final}}$ to broadcast the same and this will have communication complexity $\mathcal{O}(n^2 \cdot \text{PolyLog}(n))$; if $\mathcal{Q}_{\text{final}}$ has at most t_{final} corrupted parties (which will be the case with high probability), then every honest party will eventually receive y_{out} from the broadcast of majority of the parties in $\mathcal{Q}_{\text{final}}$. A more efficient output propagation method with communication complexity $\mathcal{O}(n \cdot \text{PolyLog}(n))$ was proposed in [14], which works even in the asynchronous setting.

Acknowledgement. The author would like to thank Arpita Patra for several helpful discussion.

References

1. Asharov, G., Lindell, Y.: A full proof of the BGW Protocol for perfectly-secure multiparty computation. Cryptology ePrint Archive, Report 2011/136 (2011)
2. Beerliová-Trubíniová, Z., Hirt, M.: Efficient multi-party computation with dispute control. In: Halevi, S., Rabin, T. (eds.) TCC 2006. LNCS, vol. 3876, pp. 305–328. Springer, Heidelberg (2006)
3. Beerliová-Trubíniová, Z., Hirt, M.: Simple and efficient perfectly-secure asynchronous MPC. In: Kurosawa, K. (ed.) ASIACRYPT 2007. LNCS, vol. 4833, pp. 376–392. Springer, Heidelberg (2007)

4. Beerliová-Trubíniová, Z., Hirt, M.: Perfectly-secure MPC with linear communication complexity. In: Canetti, R. (ed.) TCC 2008. LNCS, vol. 4948, pp. 213–230. Springer, Heidelberg (2008)
5. Ben-Or, M., Canetti, R., Goldreich, O.: Asynchronous secure computation. In: STOC, pp. 52–61. ACM (1993)
6. Ben-Or, M., Goldwasser, S., Wigderson, A.: Completeness theorems for non-cryptographic fault-tolerant distributed computation. In: STOC, pp. 1–10. ACM (1988)
7. Ben-Or, M., Kelmer, B., Rabin, T.: Asynchronous secure computations with optimal resilience. In: PODC, pp. 183–192. ACM (1994)
8. Bracha, G.: An asynchronous [(n-1)/3]-resilient consensus protocol. In: PODC, pp. 154–162. ACM (1984)
9. Canetti, R.: Studies in secure multiparty computation and applications. PhD thesis, Weizmann Institute, Israel (1995)
10. Chaum, D., Crépeau, C., Damgård, I.: Multiparty unconditionally secure protocols. In: STOC, pp. 11–19. ACM (1988)
11. Choudhury, A., Hirt, M., Patra, A.: Asynchronous multiparty computation with linear communication complexity. In: Afek, Y. (ed.) DISC 2013. LNCS, vol. 8205, pp. 388–402. Springer, Heidelberg (2013)
12. Damgård, I., Ishai, Y., Krøigaard, M.: Perfectly secure multiparty computation and the computational overhead of cryptography. In: Gilbert, H. (ed.) EUROCRYPT 2010. LNCS, vol. 6110, pp. 445–465. Springer, Heidelberg (2010)
13. Damgård, I.B., Nielsen, J.B.: Scalable and unconditionally secure multiparty computation. In: Menezes, A. (ed.) CRYPTO 2007. LNCS, vol. 4622, pp. 572–590. Springer, Heidelberg (2007)
14. Dani, V., King, V., Movahedi, M., Saia, J.: Brief announcement: Breaking the $\mathcal{O}(nm)$ Bit barrier, secure multiparty computation with a static adversary. In: PODC, pp. 227–228. ACM (2012), Full version available at http://arxiv.org/abs/1203.0289
15. Feige, U.: Noncryptographic selection protocols. In: FOCS, pp. 142–153. IEEE Computer Society (1999)
16. Franklin, M.K., Yung, M.: Communication complexity of secure computation. In: STOC, pp. 699–710. ACM (1992)
17. King, V., Lonargan, S., Saia, J., Trehan, A.: Load balanced scalable Byzantine agreement through quorum building, with full information. In: Aguilera, M.K., Yu, H., Vaidya, N.H., Srinivasan, V., Choudhury, R.R. (eds.) ICDCN 2011. LNCS, vol. 6522, pp. 203–214. Springer, Heidelberg (2011)
18. MacWilliams, F.J., Sloane, N.J.A.: The theory of error correcting codes. North-Holland Publishing Company (1978)
19. McEliece, R.J., Sarwate, D.V.: On sharing secrets and Reed-Solomon codes. Commun. ACM 24(9), 583–584 (1981)
20. Patra, A., Choudhary, A., Rangan, C.P.: Efficient statistical asynchronous verifiable secret sharing with optimal resilience. In: Kurosawa, K. (ed.) ICITS 2009. LNCS, vol. 5973, pp. 74–92. Springer, Heidelberg (2010)
21. Patra, A., Choudhury, A., Rangan, C.P.: Communication efficient perfectly secure VSS and MPC in asynchronous networks with optimal resilience. In: Bernstein, D.J., Lange, T. (eds.) AFRICACRYPT 2010. LNCS, vol. 6055, pp. 184–202. Springer, Heidelberg (2010); Full version available as Cryptology ePrint Archive, Report 2010/007, 2010
22. Shamir, A.: How to share a secret. Commun. ACM 22(11), 612–613 (1979)

Alternating Product Ciphers: A Case
for Provable Security Comparisons
(Extended Abstract)

John O. Pliam*

Institute for Data Intensive Engineering and Science (IDIES), Johns Hopkins
University, 3400 N. Charles St., Baltimore, MD 21218, USA
john.pliam@jhu.edu

Abstract. We formally study iterated block ciphers that alternate between two sequences of independent and identically distributed (i.i.d.) rounds. It is demonstrated that, in some cases the effect of alternating increases security, while in other cases the effect may strictly *decrease* security relative to the corresponding product of one of its component sequences. As this would appear to contradict conventional wisdom based on the ideal cipher approximation, we introduce new machinery for provable security comparisons. The comparisons made here simultaneously establish a coherent ordering of security metrics ranging from key-recovery cost to computational indistinguishability.

Keywords: block ciphers, product ciphers, multiple encryption, majorization.

1 Introduction

1.1 Overview

For many decades, various issues related to product ciphers have been raised and addressed. A large part of Shannon's seminal work [16] is devoted to both theoretical and practical aspects of products, and his invocation of the pastry dough mixing analogy [16, p. 712] captures a very intuitive idea that by alternating between two weakly mixing operations, we should eventually achieve strong mixing. Even today, many modern block cipher designs retain an element of this structure (see, e.g. [8]).

To model such mixing, we formalize the notion of an *alternating product cipher* as an interleaving product of independent ciphers as depicted in Fig. 3. We then ask: *How well does the mixing work, and how might it fail?* Various outcomes seem possible. We present a threefold alternating product with good security expansion. However, a related construction demonstrates somewhat surprisingly, an alternating product which is strictly less secure than the two-term product

---

* The author's position is supported in part by the U.S. National Science Foundation (NFS) Data-Scope grant CISE/ACI 1040114.

G. Paul and S. Vaudenay (Eds.): INDOCRYPT 2013, LNCS 8250, pp. 38–49, 2013.

of one of the component sequences by itself. On its face, this would appear to contradict an emerging conventional wisdom about multiple encryption based on the ideal cipher approximation, "that double encryption improves the security only marginally [...] triple encryption is significantly more secure than single and double encryption" [6]. The situation demands that we explore the problem of provable security *comparisons*. We find that certain security orderings transcend the (somewhat artificial) boundary between classical and modern cryptography.

We conclude that alternating product ciphers are, at a fundamental level, different from two-term products. Ascertaining their security is more nuanced and they provide evidence of further limits on the applicability of the ideal cipher approximation (see also [1]).

1.2 Motivation

We are initially motivated by how we might generalize the question, "is a cipher a group?", in the case of alternating products. Roughly, an encryption function $E : K \times M \to M$ is said to have the *group property* [16, p.673], if for each key pair (k_1, k_2), there is another key $k \in K$ such that $E(k_2, E(k_1, p)) = E(k, p)$ for each plaintext $p \in M$. Equivalently, the product of the cipher with itself produces *no new* permutations.

The group property obviously affords the cryptanalyst considerable advantage, if only because it reduces the cost of brute-force search against the product. Understandably, the question was raised as a possible weakness to multiple encryption schemes of DES [7]. These concerns were dismissed with increasing strength as researchers showed that DES was not likely to be a group [7], that it is not a group [3] and that it generates a large group [18].

Questions about whether a cipher is a group or whether multiple encryption improves security are really questions about ordering. That is to say, rather than quantifying specific models of attack against fixed encryption systems, we seek to establish the *correct ordering* between constructs of interest. In the case of alternating products, we find the comparison between XYZ and XZ to be the most intriguing since our intuition suggests that inserting statistically independent Y in between X and Z should improve security. Thus in comparing the two products of Fig. 1, we find that the order itself depends on the internal structure of the constituents.

Fig. 1. Motivating comparison between alternating product XYZ and XZ

1.3 Toward Coherent Security Ordering

Motivated by the above, we start by quantifying how the permutation count of an alternating product can grow or shrink. Numerically comparing these counts offers one possible ordering, since integers are *totally ordered* (every pair is comparable). But we argue that by relaxing this notion and considering *partial/pre orders* on ciphers, we pave the way to stronger and more broadly applicable security comparisons. There is a lucrative trade-off here: if we give up comparing *every* pair of ciphers, we are left with a *more meaningful* ordering of the remainder.

One powerful order (known to not be total) is *majorization*, and a great many interesting real-valued security metrics are known to respect majorization. These are called *Schur-convex* (concave if they reverse it). This covers the case of zero data complexity in the far left of Fig. 2; if a majorization relationship between two ciphers can be established, then the ciphers are also ordered by the real values of *any* Schur-convex(concave) function.

Better still, the comparisons of Fig. 1 in this paper possess additional structure, facilitating a coherent ordering of security metrics in arbitrary data complexity q. Specifically, we show in Sect. 3, that nonadaptive chosen-plaintext attack (ncpa) advantage [11,17] as well as conditional guesswork [13] are such metrics. This is depicted in the two rightmost diagrams in Fig. 2.

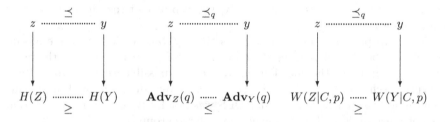

Fig. 2. We establish a coherent ordering of the ciphers in Fig. 1 by showing the consistency of a broad range of security metrics, crossing the divide between information-theoretic and modern cryptography.

2 Preliminaries

2.1 Prerequisites

We've tried to make this paper readable by nonspecialists conversant in contemporary cryptography. But in order to follow the proofs, we assume additional familiarity with the basics of permutation groups, probability theory and representation theory, referring the reader to [15], [5]. We also exploit aspects of the theory of majorization, treated very well in [9]. Since that is critical here, we provide a brief summary in §3.1.

2.2 Shannon's Model

We formalize Shannon's model [16] by representing an encryption system as a permutation-valued random variable. Precisely, given message space $\mathcal{M}$, let G be some subgroup of the full symmetric group $\mathfrak{S}_\mathcal{M}$ of all permutations on $\mathcal{M}$. An encryption system on $\mathcal{M}$, or G-cipher for short, is a G-valued random variable X. As a notational convention, for a G-cipher X (always uppercase), we shall denote the probability distribution from which it is drawn by lowercase function $x : G \to \mathbb{R}$ and write $X \sim x$.

Shannon observed that the set of encryption systems is endowed with the structure of an *unital associative algebra*[1] whose *sum* and *product* correspond to parallel and series composition, respectively. The composition in series of independent G-ciphers X, Y gives the notion of a product cipher $Z = XY$, which survives to this day. It is a standard observation that the probability distribution of the product $z(g) = \Pr[XY = g]$, is given by the *convolution* $z = x * y$:

$$z(g) = \sum_{h \in G} x(gh^{-1})y(h). \tag{1}$$

3   Models for Security Comparison

After a brief review of the theory of majorization, we explore ways in which claims of security ordering may be rigorously established as in Fig. 2.

3.1   Majorization and Schur-Convexity

Given vectors $x, y \in \mathbb{R}^n_+$ we say x is *majorized* by y and write $x \preceq y$, if their l_1 norms agree and for each $1 \leq k \leq n$,

$$\sum_{i=1}^{k} x_{[i]} \leq \sum_{i=1}^{k} y_{[i]},$$

with the values rearranged by $x_{[1]} \geq x_{[2]} \geq \cdots \geq x_{[n]}$ and similarly for y. The vector $x_\downarrow$ is the decreasing rearrangement of x (so $x_{[i]} = (x_\downarrow)_i$). Majorization is a *preorder* relation, so not all vectors are comparable in this way. We have, from the *Hardy-Littlewood-Pólya theorem*, that $x \preceq y$ is equivalent to the existence of a *doubly-stochastic* matrix D such that $x = Dy$. Furthermore, by the *Birkhoff-von Neumann theorem*, such a matrix is a convex sum of permutations, so $x \preceq y$ means:

$$x = \sum_{\pi \in \mathfrak{S}_n} p_\pi \pi \cdot y. \tag{2}$$

For our purposes, the vectors will usually be probability distributions, each with l_1 norm of 1. It is readily verified that the uniform distribution $u = (1/n, \ldots, 1/n)$ has $u \preceq x$ for all probability vectors x. If $x \preceq y$ and $y \preceq x$, then x is a permutation of y. If $x \preceq y$ but x is *not* a permutation of y, we'll write $x \prec y$.

---

[1] These days, it would be identified as the *group algebra* $\mathbb{R}G$.

Certain useful real-valued functions respect or reverse majorization. So if $\phi :$ $\mathbb{R}_+^n \to \mathbb{R}$ has $\phi(x) \leq \phi(y)$ $(\phi(x) \geq \phi(y))$ whenever $x \preceq y$, we call ϕ *Schur-convex (concave)*. If a Schur-convex (concave) function additionally satisfies $\phi(x) < \phi(y)$ $(\phi(x) > \phi(y))$ when $x \prec y$, we call ϕ *strictly Schur-convex (concave)*.

Examples and applications abound throughout science and engineering (see e.g. [4] for an interesting information-theoretic treatment). In particular, *Shannon entropy*, *Rényi entropy* and *guesswork* [10] are strictly Schur-concave. Furthermore *marginal guesswork* [12] and Bonneau's α-*guesswork* [2] are Schur-concave. For further details, see [9, pp. 562–564] and [14, Appx.]. As remarked, majorization treats the case of zero data complexity, which is sometimes useful by itself.

3.2   Nontrivial Data Complexity

For an adversary with access to q plaintext-ciphertext pairs or equivalently q queries to a chosen-plaintext oracle, we can often identify a vector mapping $\sigma : V \to \hat{V}$ and a Schur-convex function ϕ_q on $\hat{V}$ measuring in some way the cipher's resistance to attack. If $z \preceq y$ in V has additional structure so that $\hat{z} \preceq \hat{y}$ in $\hat{V}$, we write $z \preceq_{\phi_q \circ \sigma} y$ or just $z \preceq_q y$ when clear from context. This situation affords meaningful security comparisons for arbitrary data complexity. A proof of the following is sketched in the appendix and proved in the full version [14].

Theorem 1. *Given data complexity limit q and G-ciphers $X \sim x$, $Y \sim y$ and $Z \sim z$ with $Z = XY$, we have (for appropriate choices of σ)*

1. *$z \preceq_q y$ for conditional guesswork: $W(E|C, p)$, $p \in \mathcal{M}^{(q)}$ is Schur-concave as a function of $\hat{e}$,*
2. *$z \preceq_q y$ for distinguishing advantage: $\mathbf{Adv}_E^{\mathrm{ncpa}}(q)$ is Schur-convex as a function of $\hat{e}$,*

Here $E \sim e$ is a generic argument.

The relationship $z \preceq_q y$ can arise in many ways, but for our purposes, we'll use the fact that $Z = XY$.

4   Alternating Product Ciphers

4.1   The Formal Definition

We may now give a formal definition of an alternating product followed by an example.

Definition 1. *An **alternating product** is the product of independent G-ciphers alternating between two sequences of i.i.d. G-ciphers.*

Example 1. *Let $\{X_i\}_{i=1}^{r+1}$ be i.i.d. G-ciphers and let $\{Y_i\}_{i=1}^{r}$ be distinct i.i.d. G-ciphers. Then $E = X_{r+1} Y_r X_r \cdots Y_1 X_1$ is an alternating product of X_i and Y_i. Notice that Def. 1 permits either an even or an odd number of components in the product. We can imagine E as alternating between the "factors" of two products $X = X_{r+1} \cdots X_1$ and $Y = Y_r \cdots Y_1$ as depicted in Fig. 3 below.*

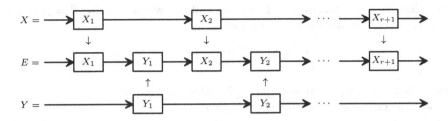

Fig. 3. An alternating product cipher seen as an interleaving of the terms of two iterated ciphers

4.2 Threefold Mixing Convolutions and Double Cosets

While most of this paper is devoted to alternating products, we treat a slightly more general case in this section to explicate a key observation, namely how mixing in typical iterated block ciphers is related to expansion along double cosets when randomness enters via a subgroup operation (like the XOR-ing of round subkeys).

Consider a threefold product $T = XYZ$ with Z confined to subgroup $K \leq G$, X confined to subgroup $H \leq G$, and Y deterministically taking single value $\pi \in G$. To understand how the convolution $t = x * y * z$ decomposes, it's instructive to employ an action of $g \in G$ on functions $\phi : G \to \mathbb{R}$ taking $\phi \mapsto \phi \circ g^{-1}$, in other words $(g \cdot \phi)(f) = \phi(g^{-1}f)$. With this in mind, we have the following useful lemma.

Lemma 1. *If the support of ϕ is confined to a left coset kH, then the support of $g \cdot \phi$ is confined to gkH.*

Proof: Assume $\mathrm{supp}(\phi) \subseteq kH$, and observe that $f \in \mathrm{supp}(g \cdot \phi) \implies (g \cdot \phi)(f) \neq 0 \implies \phi(g^{-1}f) \neq 0 \implies g^{-1}f \in \mathrm{supp}(\phi) \implies g^{-1}f \in kH \implies f \in gkH$. Thus $\mathrm{supp}(g \cdot \phi) \subseteq gkH$. □

It should be intuitively clear that T is spread out over the double coset $H\pi K$, but the following stronger result details some of the mechanics of the mixing, facilitating deeper security comparisons.

Theorem 2. *The cipher T has $\mathrm{supp}(t) \subseteq H\pi K$ and its distribution is a convex direct sum*

$$t = \bigoplus_{i=1}^{m} \alpha_i z_i,$$

of $m = [H : H \cap^{\pi} K]$ distinct probability vectors. Furthermore, each z_i is majorized by z.

Proof: The three terms in $T = XYZ$ are given by probability distributions $x(g), y(g)$ and $z(g)$ with $\mathrm{supp}(x) \subseteq H$, $\mathrm{supp}(y) = \{\pi\}$ and $\mathrm{supp}(z) \subseteq K$. First note that by the associativity of product ciphers, we may write $T = X(YZ)$, and the inner convolution $z' = y * z$ yields,

$$z'(g) = \sum_{h \in G} y(h)z(h^{-1}g) = z(\pi^{-1}g) = \pi \cdot z(g),$$

which by Lem. 1, precisely describes a function confined to πK.

Now the outer convolution $t = x * z'$ yields

$$t(g) = \sum_{h \in G} x(h)z'(h^{-1}g) = \sum_{h \in H} x(h)z'(h^{-1}g) = \sum_{h \in H} x(h)h \cdot z'(g).$$

Recognizing that z' is confined to πK, it is natural according to Lem. 1 to collect terms for which $h \cdot z'$ is confined to the same left coset of K. Indeed, recall that the left action of H on left cosets G/K (the supports of the various $h \cdot z'$) is equivalent to the double coset action $H \backslash G / K$. We may decompose the orbit $H\pi K = \bigcup_{i=1}^{m} \lambda_i K$, where the orbit size $m = [H : H \cap {}^{\pi}K]$ is given by the orbit-stabilizer theorem with

$$S \triangleq \mathrm{Stab}_{H \backslash (G/K)}(\pi K) = H \cap {}^{\pi}K.$$

Furthermore, we recognize $\{h \in H \mid h(\pi K) = \lambda_i K\} = h_i S$, for some left transversal $\{h_i\}$ of S in H. This gives us a recipe for collecting terms,

$$t = \sum_{h \in H} x(h)h \cdot z' = \sum_{i=1}^{m} \sum_{h \in h_i S} x(h)h \cdot z' = \sum_{i=1}^{m} x(h_i S) \underbrace{\left(\frac{1}{x(h_i S)} \sum_{h \in h_i S} x(h)h \cdot z' \right)}_{\triangleq z_i}$$

$$= \sum_{i=1}^{m} x(h_i S) z_i,$$

where, by construction, each z_i is confined to left coset $\lambda_i K$, so the sum is a direct sum. By the Hardy-Littlewood-Pólya and Birkhoff-von Neumann theorems,

$$z_i = \frac{1}{x(h_i S)} \sum_{h \in h_i S} x(h)h \cdot z'$$

is a convex sum of permuted copies of z', assuring majorization $z_i \preceq z' \preceq z$. Finally, taking $\alpha_i = x(h_i S)$ yields $\sum_i \alpha_i = 1$ and the theorem is proved.   □

Uniform distributions simplify the matter.

Corollary 1. *When both X and Z are uniformly distributed, T is uniformly distributed on $H\pi K$.*

Proof: The uniformity of Z implies $z \preceq z_i \preceq z$, so each z_i is uniform on $\lambda_i K$. The uniformity of X implies

$$t = \sum_{i=1}^{m} x(h_i S) z_i = \frac{|S|}{|H|} \sum_{i=1}^{m} z_i = \frac{|H \cap {}^{\pi}K|}{|H|} \sum_{i=1}^{m} z_i = \frac{1}{m} \sum_{i=1}^{m} z_i,$$

which precisely describes a function uniform on $H\pi K$.   □

The following is immediate.

Corollary 2. *If in addition to the conditions of the previous corollary,* $|H\pi K| > |K|$ *then* $t \prec z$.

REMARK. For noncommutative G, the additional condition in Coro. 2 is actually the typical case, even when $H = K$. For the remainder of this paper we assume $H \neq {}^{\pi}H$ so that $[H : H \cap {}^{\pi}H] > 1$ and thus $|H\pi H| > |H|$. This is always true in a simple group since $H = {}^{\pi}H$ means H is normal.   □

5   Applications

5.1   An Expanding Alternating Product

If, in Coro. 2, we further impose $H = K$, we obtain an alternating product cipher in the sense of Def. 1.

Proposition 1. *The alternating product cipher* $T = XYZ$ *is more secure than* $D = XZ$ *when* X *and* Z *are uniform* H-*ciphers and* Y *is deterministic on* $\{\pi\}$, *in the sense that:*

a). *The mixing of permutations in* T *produces dramatically more than* D.

b). $t \prec d$, *so by any strictly Schur-convave security metric,* T *is more secure than* D.

c). $t \preceq_q d$, *so by the security metrics of Thm. 1,* T *is no less secure than* D.

Proof: For (a) and (b), we need only apply Coro. 1 and Coro. 2. For (c), observe that since $D = XZ = Z$, $T = XYZ = (XY)D$, we have the necessary product relation for Thm. 1.   □

5.2   A Collapsing Alternating Product

Now let H be a subgroup of G and let $\pi \in G$ fall strictly outside H (so $H \neq \pi H$). Consider three independent G-ciphers X, Y, Z, where both X and Z are uniformly distributed on the left coset πH and Y takes the value π^{-1} deterministically. We seek to compare the products $T = XYZ$ vs $D = XZ$. Note that since X and Z are i.i.d., and Y is independent of these, T is also an alternating product. We have the following.

Proposition 2. *The product cipher* D *is more secure than the alternating product* T *in that:*

a). *The mixing of permutations in* D *produces dramatically more than* T.

b). $d \prec t$, *so by any strictly Schur-convex security metric,* D *is more secure than* T.

c). $d \preceq_q t$, *so by the security metrics of Thm. 1,* D *is no less secure than* T.

Proof: Without loss of generality, we may drop the trailing π, which poses no cryptanalytic barrier. We compare instead the products $T' = X'YZ$ and $D' = X'Z$, with X' uniform on H. Writing $T' = X'(YZ)$ the inner convolution $v = y*z$ trivially reduces to uniform on H. In this way, $T' = X'V$ is the double encryption of Prop. 1. On the other hand, D' is uniform on $H\pi H$ since it is of the form of the triple product of Prop. 1. The desired result follows at once from this reversal of roles of the double and triple product from Prop. 1. $\square$

5.3   A Collapsing General Alternating Product

Consider again the general alternating product cipher of Fig. 3 and Ex. 1, only now with each X_i uniform on πH and each Y_i deterministically taking π^{-1}. We seek to compare $E = X_{r+1}Y_rX_r \cdots Y_1X_1$ with $X = X_{r+1} \cdots X_1$. Again because products are associative, we may write $E = X_{r+1}((Y_rX_r) \cdots (Y_1X_1))$, and each of the inner convolutions $e_i = y_i * x_i$ trivially collapses to uniform on H. Further the sequence of convolutions $v = e_r * \cdots * e_1$ remains uniform on H and the final $x_{r+1} * v$ is uniform on πH. On the other hand $x_2 * x_1$ has support on translate of double coset $H\pi H$ and continued left convolution can only make this count go up. Clearly then, we have.

Proposition 3. *X is more secure than E.*

5.4   A Resource-Bounded Example of Extreme Expansion

It may seem from our treatment in the above examples that the ciphers here are purely information theoretic, applying only to infeasible and hypothetical ciphers. In this section, we present a positive example of a computationally efficient alternating product cipher $T = XYZ$ which has nearly optimal expansion of permutations along a huge double coset, yet where the $D = XY$ is trivially distinguishable from any idealized cipher.

To facilitate such a comparison, we exploit special properties of a polynomial-time cipher which achieves *every* permutation (given enough key construction data or equivalently a private random function oracle).

This construction from [13] called a *universal security amplifier* was originally put forth to decided whether any efficient block cipher possessed a property of the one-time pad, namely that when composed with a non-perfect cipher was strictly more secure.

For security parameter n, let $\mathcal{M}' = \{0, \ldots, 2^n\}$ and let X and Z independent universal security amplifiers on $\mathcal{M} = \{0, \ldots, 2^n - 1\}$, so they leave fixed the final plaintext 2^n. Let Y deterministically pick out any permutation $\pi \notin \mathfrak{S}_{\mathcal{M}}$. For example π could simply add $1 \mod 2^n + 1$, which is clearly computationally feasible. Now we'd like to compare $T = XYZ$ with $D = XZ$. Since X and Z clearly have the group property, $\mathrm{supp}(d) = \mathfrak{S}_{\mathcal{M}}$, and so encrypting once the plaintext 2^n will yield ciphertext 2^n with 100% probability. The following is thus immediate.

Proposition 4. *The product D is distinguishable from any idealized cipher.*

We may further exploit Thm. 2 and in this case, the expansion is huge.

Proposition 5. *The alternating product cipher T has* supp(t) *on about* $(2^n+1)!$ *permutations.*

Proof: Because the action $\mathfrak{S}_{\mathcal{M}'}$ on $\mathcal{M}'$ is multiply transitive we have by a standard result from group theory (see [15, Thm. 9.6]) that $\mathfrak{S}_{\mathcal{M}'} = \mathfrak{S}_{\mathcal{M}} \cup \mathfrak{S}_{\mathcal{M}} \pi \mathfrak{S}_{\mathcal{M}}$, in other words the double coset relevant to Thm. 2, $\mathfrak{S}_{\mathcal{M}} \pi \mathfrak{S}_{\mathcal{M}}$ is nearly the whole of $\mathfrak{S}_{\mathcal{M}'}$. This double coset has size $(2^n + 1)! - 2^n! \approx (2^n + 1)!$.

It remains then to show t has full support on the double coset. But z has *full* support on $\mathfrak{S}_{\mathcal{M}}$ [13], and by Thm. 2 each $z_i \preceq z$ so it cannot have fewer permutations on each of the left cosets $\lambda_i \mathfrak{S}_{\mathcal{M}}$. This forces supp$(t) = \mathfrak{S}_{\mathcal{M}} \pi \mathfrak{S}_{\mathcal{M}}$, and we are done. $\qquad\square$

References

1. Black, J.A.: The ideal-cipher model, revisited: An uninstantiable blockcipher-based hash function. In: Robshaw, M. (ed.) FSE 2006. LNCS, vol. 4047, pp. 328–340. Springer, Heidelberg (2006)
2. Bonneau, J.: Guessing human-chosen secrets. PhD thesis, University of Cambridge (May 2012)
3. Campbell, K.W., Wiener, M.: DES is not a group. In: Brickell, E.F. (ed.) CRYPTO 1992. LNCS, vol. 740, pp. 512–520. Springer, Heidelberg (1993)
4. Cicalese, F., Vaccaro, U.: Supermodularity and subadditivity properties of the entropy on the majorization lattice. IEEE Transactions on Information Theory 48(4), 933–938 (2002)
5. Diaconis, P.: Group Representations in Probability and Statistics. Institute of Mathematical Statistics, Hayward, CA (1988)
6. Gaži, P., Maurer, U.: Cascade encryption revisited. In: Matsui, M. (ed.) ASIACRYPT 2009. LNCS, vol. 5912, pp. 37–51. Springer, Heidelberg (2009)
7. Kaliski, B., Rivest, R., Sherman, A.: Is the Data Encryption Standard a group (results of cycling experiments on DES). Journal of Cryptology 1(1), 1–36 (1988)
8. Knudsen, L.R., Robshaw, M.J.B.: The block cipher companion. Springer-Verlag, New York (2011)
9. Marshall, A.W., Olkin, I., Arnold, B.C.: Inequalities: Theory of Majorization and Its Applications, 2nd edn. Springer, New York (2011)
10. Massey, J.L.: Guessing and entropy. In: Proc. 1994 IEEE Int'l Symp. on Information Theory, p. 204 (1994)
11. Morris, B., Rogaway, P., Stegers, T.: How to encipher messages on a small domain: Deterministic encryption and the Thorp shuffle. In: Halevi, S. (ed.) CRYPTO 2009. LNCS, vol. 5677, pp. 286–302. Springer, Heidelberg (2009)
12. Pliam, J.O.: On the Incomparability of Entropy and Marginal Guesswork in Brute-Force Attacks. In: Roy, B., Okamoto, E. (eds.) INDOCRYPT 2000. LNCS, vol. 1977, pp. 67–79. Springer, Heidelberg (2000)
13. Pliam, J.O.: A Polynomial-Time Universal Security Amplifier in the Class of Block Ciphers. Communications in Information and Systems 1(2), 181–204 (2001)
14. Pliam, J.O.: Alternating Product Ciphers: A Case for Provable Security Comparisons. arXiv preprint arXiv:1307.4107, Full version of this paper (2013)

15. Rotman, J.J.: An Introduction to the Theory of Groups, 4th edn. Springer (1995)
16. Shannon, C.E.: Communication theory of secrecy systems. Bell System Tech. Jour. 28, 656–715 (1949)
17. Vaudenay, S.: Decorrelation: a theory for block cipher security. Journal of Cryptology 16(4), 249–286 (2003)
18. Wernsdorf, R.: The one-round functions of the DES generate the alternating group. In: Rueppel, R.A. (ed.) EUROCRYPT 1992. LNCS, vol. 658, pp. 99–112. Springer, Heidelberg (1993)

Appendices

A.1   Variation Distance to Uniformity

The following lemma will prove quite useful.

Lemma 2. *The variation distance to uniformity is Schur-convex.*

Proof: Suppose $x \preceq y$ with $x, y \in \mathbb{R}^n_+$. As a consequence of the definition,

$$\|u - x\| = \sum_{i=1}^{k_x} x_{[i]} - \frac{k_x}{n}, \quad \text{and} \quad \|u - y\| = \sum_{i=1}^{k_y} y_{[i]} - \frac{k_y}{n},$$

where $k_x = \max\{i \mid x_{[i]} \geq 1/n\}$ and $k_y = \max\{i \mid y_{[i]} \geq 1/n\}$. If $k_x < k_y$, then

$$\sum_{i=1}^{k_y} y_{[i]} - \frac{k_y}{n} = \sum_{i=1}^{k_x} y_{[i]} + \sum_{i=k_x+1}^{k_y} y_{[i]} - \left(\frac{k_x}{n} + \frac{k_y - k_x}{n}\right)$$

$$= \sum_{i=1}^{k_x} y_{[i]} - \frac{k_x}{n} + \sum_{i=k_x+1}^{k_y} \left(y_{[i]} - \frac{1}{n}\right) \geq \sum_{i=1}^{k_x} x_{[i]} - \frac{k_x}{n}.$$

I.e., $\|u - y\| \geq \|u - x\|$. In case $k_x \geq k_y$ the result follows *mutatis mutandis*. $\square$

A.2   Sketch of Proof of Thm. 1

Proof Sketch of Thm. 1: For arbitrary q-tuple $p \in \mathcal{M}^{(q)}$, let $H = \mathrm{Stab}_G(p)$, and let $\{g_i\}$ be a left transversal for H in G. Then the two cases correspond to two different *induced representations* from H to G. Specifically, $\mathbb{R}\!\uparrow^G_H$ describes distributions over q-tuples for comparing values of $\mathbf{Adv}^{\mathrm{ncpa}}_X(q)$, while $\mathbb{R}H\!\uparrow^G_H$ describes the distributions over all permutations for comparing values of $W(X|C, p)$.

In either case, a general result adapted from [13, Lem. 3.3] is that if $z \preceq y$ in $V\!\uparrow^G_H \cong \bigoplus_i g_i \otimes V$ and the permutations for this majorization in (2) act on it by permuting direct summands $g_i \otimes V$ then

$$z_\downarrow^{(i)} = \sum_{i=1}^{[G:H]} \omega_{ij} D_{ij} y_\downarrow^{(i)}, \tag{3}$$

where $z^{(i)}$ and $y^{(i)}$ are projections of z and y into the direct summands of z and y, and where each D_{ij} is doubly stochastic as is the matrix $\Omega = [\omega_{ij}]$.

(*Case 1:*) Define σ taking $x \mapsto \hat{x} = \sum_i x_\downarrow^{(i)}$. The product relation assures (3), which by a result of Day [9, Prop. 5.A.6] implies $\hat{z} \preceq \hat{y}$. Since guesswork is Schur-concave and $W(X|C,p) = W(\sum_i x_\downarrow^{(i)})$ we have $z \preceq_q y$.

(*Case 2:*) Define σ taking $x \mapsto \hat{x} = [x(g_1 H), \dots, x(g_{[G:H]} H)]^{\mathrm{t}}$. Likely beginning with [17] and more recently [11] NCPA advantage $\mathbf{Adv}_X^{\mathrm{ncpa}}(q)$ is identified with variation distance to uniformity $\|\hat{x} - \hat{u}\|$, which by Lem. 2 is Schur-convex. Now the action of G on G/H also gives rise to a left module action of $\mathbb{R}G$ on $\mathbb{R}\!\uparrow_H^G$ consistent with (3), now with 1-dimensional summands. The 1×1 doubly stochastic matrices vanish and we obtain $\hat{z} = \Omega\hat{y}$ or $\hat{z} \preceq \hat{y}$. Again $z \preceq_q y$ by the Schur-convexity of $\mathbf{Adv}_X^{\mathrm{ncpa}}(q)$. $\qquad\square$

An Integral Distinguisher on Grøstl-512 v3[*]

Marine Minier[1] and Gaël Thomas[2]

[1] Université de Lyon, INRIA
INSA-Lyon, CITI, F-69621, Villeurbanne, France
marine.minier@insa-lyon.fr
[2] XLIM (UMR CNRS 7252), Université de Limoges
123 avenue Albert Thomas, 87060 Limoges Cedex - France
gael.thomas@unilim.fr

Abstract. This paper presents an improved integral distinguisher using 2^{913} computations against an 11-round version of the compression function of the SHA-3 candidate Grøstl-512 with the round 3 parameters. The original result presented in [18] was enhanced through the use of different integral properties.

Keywords: Hash functions, cryptanalysis, integral distinguishers, SHA-3 competition.

1 Introduction

The entire cryptographic community has been waiting until last October for the outcome of the SHA-3 competition[1]. Among the finalists, Grøstl [13] is a surviving proposal designed by P. Gauravaram et al. It is based on AES transformations and outputs 256 or 512 bits of hash according to the Grøstl-256/512 version.

During the second round, Grøstl has attracted a significant amount of cryptanalysis. For example, T. Peyrin presented rebound distinguishers against full version of the compression function Grøstl-256 [20]. This is one of the main reasons that forced the Grøstl designers to modify the parameters of Grøstl for the SHA-3 round 3. In the remainder of this paper, we refer to this last version as Grøstl v3 whereas the previous version is called Grøstl v2. Results against the compression function of Grøstl-256 v3 include a semi-free-start collision against 6 rounds that uses 2^{180} computations [22], a pseudo preimage against 8 rounds that uses $2^{507.32}$ computations [21], a rebound distinguisher against 10 rounds that uses 2^{392} computations [14], and an integral distinguisher against 11 rounds that requires 2^{953} computations [18]. In this paper, we improve this last distinguisher leading to an integral distinguisher on 11 rounds of the compression function of Grøstl-512 v3 with a complexity of 2^{913} computations.

---

[*] This work was partially supported by the French National Agency of Research: ANR-11-INS-011.

[1] see for example: http://ehash.iaik.tugraz.at/wiki/The_SHA-3_Zoo

G. Paul and S. Vaudenay (Eds.): INDOCRYPT 2013, LNCS 8250, pp. 50–59, 2013.

This paper is organized as follows: Section 2 introduces related work, notations of the paper and the description of Grøstl-512; Section 3 describes the integral distinguisher against Grøstl-512 v3 reduced to 11 rounds and finally Section 4 concludes this paper.

2 Related Work and Notations

2.1 Integral Attacks

Integral cryptanalysis was first introduced against the Square block cipher in the original paper [6] in the unknown key setting to retrieve information on some key bytes. Then, it was applied to AES in the original submission paper [7,8]. The original integral property on AES was extended by one round by Ferguson et al. in [10].

After those first attacks, many ciphers especially the ones that use a SPN structure have been studied with regard to this kind of distinguishers. Among all the integral cryptanalyses proposed in the literature, we could cite the attacks against SAFER [2], CRYPTON [9] and more recently on PRESENT [5]. The different Rijndael versions (Rijndael-192 and Rijndael-256) have also been attacked using integral properties [15,11]. Other contributions also analyze the general framework of Integral cryptanalysis and especially focus on the conditions that a block cipher must fulfill to be attacked using this method [17,3]. In [17], L. Knudsen and D. Wagner analyze integral cryptanalysis as a dual to differential attacks particularly applicable to block ciphers with bijective components. A first-order integral cryptanalysis considers a particular collection of m words in the plaintexts and ciphertexts that differ on a particular component. The aim of this attack is thus to predict the values in the sums (i.e. the integral) of the chosen words after a certain number of rounds of encryption. The same authors also generalize this approach to higher-order integrals: the original set to consider becomes a set of m^d vectors which differ in d components and where the sum of this set is predictable after a certain number of rounds. The sum of this set is called a d-th order integral.

More recently, in [16] Integral cryptanalysis has been proposed in the new model called known key settings where the key is known to the attacker. In the same settings, compression functions of hash functions could also be analyzed and some distinguishers have been proposed against SHA-3 candidates also using integral properties. Consider for instance integral distinguishers on the compression functions of Hamsi-256 [1,19] and Keccak [4].

2.2 Notations

In the remainder of this paper, we use the consistent notations introduced in [17] and extend them for expressing word-oriented integral attacks. For a d-th order integral, we have:

- The symbol 'C' (for "Constant") in the i-th entry, means that the values of all the i-th words in the collection of texts are equal.

- The symbol 'P' (for "Permutation") means that all words in the collection of texts are different.
- The symbol '?' means that the sum of words cannot be predicted.
- The symbol 'P^d' corresponds to the components that participate in a d-th order integral, i.e. if a word can take m different values then $\mathcal{P}^d$ means that in the integral, the particular word takes all values exactly m^{d-1} times.
- The symbol '0' means that the sum of all values is zero.

2.3   Description of the Grøstl-512 Hash Function

Grøstl [12] is a SHA-3 candidate designed by Guaravaram *et al.*, notably Grøstl-256 outputs hash values of lengths 224 and 256 bits whereas Grøstl-512 outputs hash values of lengths 384 or 512 bits. We focus on Grøstl-512. It is an iterated hash function with a compression function built from two distinct permutations P and Q. A t-block message (after padding) $(M_1, \cdots, M_t)$ is hashed by computing successive chaining values H_i using the compression function $f(H_{i-1}, M_i)$ and then applying the output transformation $g(H_t)$ as follows:

$$H_0 = IV$$
$$H_i = f(H_{i-1}, M_i) = H_{i-1} \oplus P(H_{i-1} \oplus M_i) \oplus Q(M_i) \text{ for } 1 \le i \le t$$
$$h = g(H_t) = trunc(H_t \oplus P(H_t))$$

where $trunc(\cdot)$ denotes the function that truncate its input by returning only the last 384 (or 512) bits.

The two permutations P and Q are constructed using the wide trail strategy, their design is very similar to AES with a fixed key input. Both permutations of the compression function of Grøstl-512 act on a 1024-bit state represented as a 8×16 matrix of bytes and have 14 rounds. The round transformations of Grøstl-512 are the following ones:

- AddRoundConstant (AC) adds a round-dependent constant to the state of P and Q.
- SubBytes (SB) is the non-linear layer that applies the AES Sbox to each byte of the state.
- ShiftBytes (ShB) rotates the bytes of row j in the following way: 0 for $j = 1$, 1 for $j = 2, \cdots 6$ for $j = 7$ and 11 for $j = 8$ for the P permutation and the shifted values are 1, 3, 5, 11, 0, 2, 4, 6 for the Q permutation.
- MixBytes (MB) is the linear diffusion layer where each column of the state is multiplied by a constant matrix B.

Note that the differences between Grøstl-512 v2 and the new version of Grøstl-512, Grøstl-512 v3 are localized in the two transformations AddRoundConstant and ShiftBytes.

3   Description of the 11-Round Distinguisher of the Grøstl-512 v3 Compression Function

3.1   The Divide-and-Conquer Method to Find Integral Properties

In [18], the authors propose a divide-and-conquer method to efficiently find integral properties on several rounds of an AES-like cipher or hash function. Their method works as follows: first, find some integral properties that sum to 0 before the last MixColumns (or MixBytes) operation. Then, combine several integral properties that sum together to 0 on a complete column and apply the MixColumns (or MixBytes) operation to fulfill the integral property. One thus obtain finally an integral property on a complete number of rounds.

3.2   Integral Properties for P and Q in the Forward Direction

We apply this method to the case of Grøstl-512 v3 and we find, for P and Q, the integral properties for 3.5 rounds shown in Fig. 1. In fact, we find the following integral properties with two active bytes for P:

- when the two active bytes are in position $(0,0)$ and $(1,1)$, then after 3.5 rounds, the bytes on three shifted columns have their sum equal to 0. This property also holds for two active bytes at positions $(3,0)$ and $(4,1)$; $(5,0)$ and $(6,1)$; $(0,1)$ and $(5,6)$; $(7,1)$ and $(0,6)$; $(7,0)$ and $(1,6)$. All those properties lead to three zero-sum shifted columns.

  and the following integral properties with two active bytes for Q:

- when the two active bytes are in position $(0,0)$ and $(5,1)$, then after 3.5 rounds, the bytes on three shifted columns have their sum equal to 0. This property also holds for two active bytes at positions $(1,0)$ and $(6,1)$; $(2,0)$ and $(7,1)$; $(4,0)$ and $(0,1)$; $(3,0)$ and $(0,6)$; $(3,1)$ and $(4,6)$; $(4,1)$ and $(2,6)$. All those properties lead to three zero-sum shifted columns.

Thus, we can combine those two bytes 3.5-round integral properties to mount integral properties on 4 rounds with respectively 12 active bytes for P and 14 active bytes for Q using the divide-and-conquer method of [18]. The deduced integral properties for P and Q are shown in Fig. 2. We are hence able to distinguish P and Q from random permutations using respectively 2^{96} and 2^{112} chosen texts that sum to 0 at byte level on three particular columns (i.e. on 192 bits) after four applications of the round function of P (respectively Q). This distinguisher has a complexity equal to 2^{96} cipher operations for P and 2^{112} cipher operations for Q.

Following the work of [15], we extended by two rounds at the beginning those 4-round integral properties using first a 24-th order integral property and second a 104-th order integral property as shown on Fig 3. We were able to distinguish P and Q from random permutations using 2^{832} chosen texts that sum to 0 at byte level on three particular columns (i.e. on 192 bits) after six applications of the round function of P (respectively Q). This distinguisher has a complexity equal to 2^{832} cipher operations.

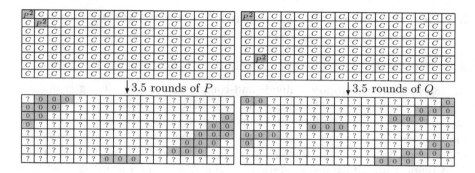

Fig. 1. The 3.5-round P integral property with 2 active bytes on the left and the 3.5-round Q integral property with 2 active bytes on the right

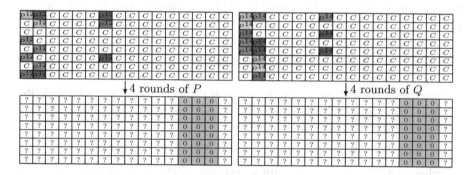

Fig. 2. The 4-round P integral property with 12 active bytes on the left and the 4-round Q integral property with 14 active bytes on the right

3.3   Integral Properties for P and Q in the Backward Direction

Let us now analyze which integral properties exist for the backward direction. We use the backward integral property already described in [19], a 2nd order integral property on 3 backward rounds presented in Fig. 4.

This property leads to a distinguisher on 3 backward rounds where the sums taken at byte level over all the inputs on the three shifted columns marked in blue in Fig. 4 are equal to 0. It requires 2^{16} chosen texts to work and has a complexity equal to 2^{16} cipher operations. This property could be extended by first one round and second two backward rounds at the beginning using a 80th order integral property as shown on Fig. 5. This leads to an integral distinguisher that uses 2^{640} chosen texts with a complexity equal to 2^{640} cipher operations to test if the sums taken at byte level over $3 \times 8 \times 8 = 192$ bits are equal to 0 or not.

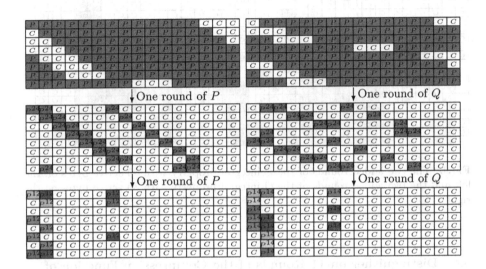

Fig. 3. The two added rounds of the integral property with 104 active bytes, for P on the left and Q on the right

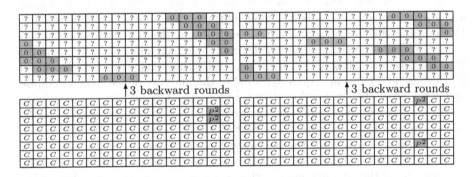

Fig. 4. The 2nd order Integral property on 3 backward rounds of P (left) and Q (right)

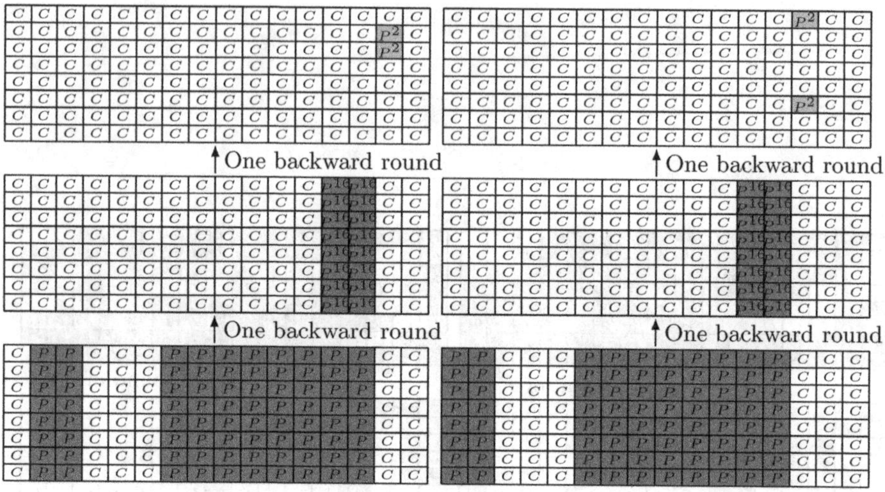

Fig. 5. The two added rounds of the P integral property with 80 active bytes on the left and the two added rounds of the Q integral property with 80 active bytes on the right

3.4 Distinguisher on 11 Rounds of the Compression Function of Grøstl-512 v3

We combined those two properties (in the backward and in the forward directions) starting from both the middle of P and the middle of Q to build a structural property on the compression function of Grøstl-512 when 11 rounds are considered (see Fig. 6). For the permutation P, start from the middle with 2^{912} middletexts with 114 active bytes (the other are taken equal to a constant) then, go backward on five rounds to obtain inputs that sum to 0 on 3 shifted columns and go forward on 6 rounds to obtain outputs that sum to 0 on 3 columns. Do the same for the permutation Q. Using Q, get the 2^{912} corresponding M_t messages. Using those messages and the inputs of P, compute the corresponding 2^{912} H_{t-1} values. Those 2^{912} values also verify that their sums taken over all 2^{912} values on 6 bytes are equal to 0 (due to the linearity of the XOR operation and considering the intersection of all 0-sum bytes). Considering the knowledge of H_{t-1}, of the outputs of P and of the outputs of Q, the corresponding H_t values are such that the sums taken over all the 2^{912} values on the intersection of the 6 common bytes (for the backward direction) and of the 3 columns (for the forward direction) are equal to 0. In other words, the sum taken over all the 2^{912} outputs of the compression function is null at 4 byte positions whereas the corresponding inputs H_{t-1} and M_t have 0-sum on 6 bytes (see Fig. 7).

Thus, we have exhibited a structural property of the Grøstl-512 compression function when P and Q are limited to 11 rounds. The computational cost of this property is about 2^{913} cipher operations with modest memory requirements to

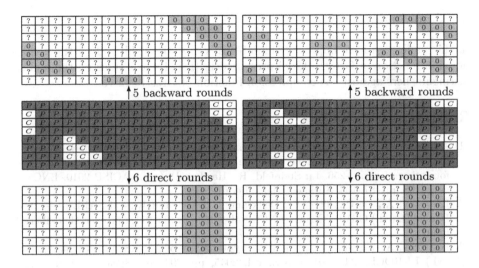

Fig. 6. Complete property on 11 rounds of P (on the left) and of Q (on the right) starting from the middle with a 114th order integral property

Fig. 7. Position of the 6 zero-sum bytes for H_{t-1} and M_t (left), and the 4 zero-sum bytes for H_t (right)

find some 0-sums at particular positions (4 bytes at the output of the compression function and 6 bytes at the input). This new structural property improves the one described in [18] that reaches 11 rounds also with a complexity equal to 2^{953} cipher operations.

Table 1. Summary of distinguishers against the compression function of Grøstl-512 v3

Nb rounds	Type of Attack	Time	Memory	Source
6	Semi-free-start Collision	2^{180}	2^{64}	[22]
8	Pseudo Preimage	$2^{507.32}$	2^{507}	[21]
10	Rebound Distinguisher	2^{392}	2^{64}	[14]
11	Integral Distinguisher	2^{953}	small	[18]
11	Integral Distinguisher	2^{913}	small	this paper

4   Conclusion

In this paper, we have improved the integral properties exhibited on the compression function of Grøstl-512 v3 presented in [18]. Table 1 sums up the main distinghuishers against the compression function of Grøstl-512 v3.

References

1. Aumasson, J.-P., Käsper, E., Knudsen, L.R., Matusiewicz, K., Ødegård, R., Peyrin, T., Schläffer, M.: Distinguishers for the compression function and output transformation of hamsi-256. In: Steinfeld, R., Hawkes, P. (eds.) ACISP 2010. LNCS, vol. 6168, pp. 87–103. Springer, Heidelberg (2010)
2. Biryukov, A., De Cannière, C., Dellkrantz, G.: Cryptanalysis of SAFER++. In: Boneh, D. (ed.) CRYPTO 2003. LNCS, vol. 2729, pp. 195–211. Springer, Heidelberg (2003)
3. Biryukov, A., Shamir, A.: Structural cryptanalysis of SASAS. In: Pfitzmann, B. (ed.) EUROCRYPT 2001. LNCS, vol. 2045, pp. 394–405. Springer, Heidelberg (2001)
4. Boura, C., Canteaut, A., De Cannière, C.: Higher-Order Differential Properties of KECCAK and Luffa. In: Joux, A. (ed.) FSE 2011. LNCS, vol. 6733, pp. 252–269. Springer, Heidelberg (2011)
5. Collard, B., Standaert, F.-X.: A statistical saturation attack against the block cipher PRESENT. In: Fischlin, M. (ed.) CT-RSA 2009. LNCS, vol. 5473, pp. 195–210. Springer, Heidelberg (2009)
6. Daemen, J., Knudsen, L.R., Rijmen, V.: The block cipher Square. In: Biham, E. (ed.) FSE 1997. LNCS, vol. 1267, pp. 149–165. Springer, Heidelberg (1997)
7. Daemen, J., Rijmen, V.: AES proposal: Rijndael. In: The First Advanced Encryption Standard Candidate Conference. N.I.S.T (1998)
8. Daemen, J., Rijmen, V.: The Design of Rijndael. Springer (2002)
9. Vitek, J., Bijnens, G., Rijmen, V., Preneel, B.: Attack on Six Rounds of Crypton. In: Knudsen, L.R. (ed.) FSE 1999. LNCS, vol. 1636, pp. 46–59. Springer, Heidelberg (1999)
10. Ferguson, N., Kelsey, J., Lucks, S., Schneier, B., Stay, M., Wagner, D., Whiting, D.L.: Improved cryptanalysis of rijndael. In: Schneier, B. (ed.) FSE 2000. LNCS, vol. 1978, pp. 213–230. Springer, Heidelberg (2001)
11. Galice, S., Minier, M.: Improving integral attacks against Rijndael-256 up to 9 rounds. In: Vaudenay, S. (ed.) AFRICACRYPT 2008. LNCS, vol. 5023, pp. 1–15. Springer, Heidelberg (2008)
12. Gauravaram, P., Knudsen, L.R., Matusiewicz, K., Mendel, F., Rechberger, C., Schläffer, M., Thomsen, S.S.: Grøstl – a SHA-3 candidate. Submission to NIST, Round 1/2 (2008)
13. Gauravaram, P., Knudsen, L.R., Matusiewicz, K., Mendel, F., Rechberger, C., Schläffer, M., Thomsen, S.S.: Grøstl addendum. Submission to NIST, Round 2 (2009)
14. Jean, J., Naya-Plasencia, M., Peyrin, T.: Improved rebound attack on the finalist Grøstl. In: Canteaut, A. (ed.) FSE 2012. LNCS, vol. 7549, pp. 110–126. Springer, Heidelberg (2012)
15. Nakahara Jr., J., de Freitas, D.S., Phan, R.C.-W.: New multiset attacks on Rijndael with large blocks. In: Dawson, E., Vaudenay, S. (eds.) Mycrypt 2005. LNCS, vol. 3715, pp. 277–295. Springer, Heidelberg (2005)

16. Knudsen, L.R., Rijmen, V.: Known-key distinguishers for some block ciphers. In: Kurosawa, K. (ed.) ASIACRYPT 2007. LNCS, vol. 4833, pp. 315–324. Springer, Heidelberg (2007)
17. Knudsen, L.R., Wagner, D.: Integral cryptanalysis. In: Daemen, J., Rijmen, V. (eds.) FSE 2002. LNCS, vol. 2365, pp. 112–127. Springer, Heidelberg (2002)
18. Li, Y., Wu, W., Dong, L.: Integral distinguishers of JH and Grøstl-512. Journal of Electronics (China) 29, 94–102 (2012)
19. Minier, M., Phan, R.C.-W., Pousse, B.: Integral distinguishers of some SHA-3 candidates. In: Heng, S.-H., Wright, R.N., Goi, B.-M. (eds.) CANS 2010. LNCS, vol. 6467, pp. 106–123. Springer, Heidelberg (2010)
20. Peyrin, T.: Improved differential attacks for ECHO and Grøstl. In: Rabin, T. (ed.) CRYPTO 2010. LNCS, vol. 6223, pp. 370–392. Springer, Heidelberg (2010)
21. Wu, S., Feng, D., Wu, W., Guo, J., Dong, L., Zou, J.: (Pseudo) Preimage attack on round-reduced Grøstl hash function and others. In: Canteaut, A. (ed.) FSE 2012. LNCS, vol. 7549, pp. 127–145. Springer, Heidelberg (2012)
22. Schläffer, M.: Updated differential analysis of Grøstl, Grøstl website (January 2011)

Warrant-Hiding Delegation-by-Certificate Proxy Signature Schemes

Christian Hanser and Daniel Slamanig

Institute for Applied Information Processing and Communications (IAIK),
Graz University of Technology (TUG), Inffeldgasse 16a, 8010 Graz, Austria
{christian.hanser,daniel.slamanig@tugraz.at}

Abstract. Proxy signatures allow an entity (the delegator) to delegate his signing capabilities to other entities (called proxies), who can then produce signatures on behalf of the delegator. Typically, a delegator may not want to give a proxy the power to sign *any* message on his behalf, but only messages from a well defined *message space*. Therefore, the so called *delegation by warrant* approach has been introduced. Here, a *warrant* is included into the delegator's signature (the so called certificate) to describe the message space from which a proxy is allowed to choose messages to produce valid signatures for. Interestingly, in all previously known constructions of proxy signatures following this approach, the warrant is made explicit and, thus, is an input to the verification algorithm of a proxy signature. This means, that a verifier learns the entire message space for which the proxy has been given the signing power. However, it may be desirable to hide the remaining messages in the allowed message space from a verifier. This scenario has never been investigated in context of proxy signatures, but seems to be interesting for practical applications. In this paper, we resolve this issue by introducing so called *warrant-hiding proxy signatures*. We provide a formal security definition of such schemes by augmenting the well established security model for proxy signatures by Boldyreva et al. Furthermore, we discuss strategies how to realize this warrant-hiding property and we also provide two concrete instantiations of such a scheme. They enjoy different advantages, but are both entirely practical. Moreover, we prove them secure with respect to the augmented security model.

1 Introduction

Proxy signatures, first introduced in [13], allow an entity (the delegator) to delegate his signing capabilities to other entities (called proxies), who can then produce signatures on behalf of the delegator. This concept has seen a considerable amount of interest since its introduction and numerous (secure) constructions have been proposed, see, e.g., [5]. Surprisingly, only quite recently a suitable security model for proxy signatures has been introduced [4], and adopted to multi-level and identity-based proxy signature schemes later on [16]. Apart from standard proxy signatures, various other "flavors" of proxy signatures have been introduced, including threshold [21], one-time [20], blind [18], ring [2], designated-verifier [19] as well as anonymous proxy signatures [9].

G. Paul and S. Vaudenay (Eds.): INDOCRYPT 2013, LNCS 8250, pp. 60–77, 2013.

In the initial paper [13], it was already observed that the delegator may not want to give a proxy the power to sign *any* message on behalf of the delegator, but only to sign messages from a well defined *message space*. To realize this feature, [13] introduced the so called *delegation by warrant* approach. Here, a signed *warrant* is included into the delegator's signature (the certificate) to describe the delegation. Thereby, any type of security policy may be included into this warrant to enforce the restrictions under which the delegation is valid. This approach seems to be particularly attractive and received the most attention, since the delegator can clearly define a *message space* for which the signing rights are delegated to the proxy. In state of the art schemes [16,5], a *warrant ω* is either the concatenation of all permitted messages or an abstract description of the message space for which signing is being delegated, together with a certificate, which is a signature on ω (and typically other values including the proxy's identity and public key), under the delegator's private signing key. An abstract description of a message space, thereby, could, for instance, be a context-free grammar, a regular expression, or as in [4], the description of a polynomial-time Turing machine computing the characteristic function of all potential messages, i.e., given a message to decide, whether the message is covered by ω or not.

Problem Statement: This plain inclusion of the warrant into the certificate, however, means that a verifier obtains a precise description of the message space a proxy is allowed to sign. However, this "feature" may not be desirable in some situations. Consider for instance a proxy, who is delegated the rights to sign a contract on behalf of the delegator and the proxy was given the power to sign different versions of the contract, e.g., including different contract conditions such as prices. Given such a signature from the proxy for one of these versions, the warrant would leak all conditions, e.g., more expensive prices, the delegator would have been willing to pay. Consequently, it would be desirable from the point of view of the delegator to *hide* the remaining options from the allowed message space, i.e., the warrant, from a verifier. Otherwise, this could compromise the delegator, as a verifier can learn for instance that the delegator would have been willing to pay a much higher price than he actually did.

In order to overcome this problem, which exists in all known proxy signature schemes supporting the delegation by warrant feature, we introduce the notion of a *warrant-hiding proxy signature scheme*. Basically, in such a signature scheme a proxy learns the warrant, but a proxy signature does not reveal the warrant, as it is not required as an explicit input to the proxy verification algorithm. Consequently, the warrant cannot be determined by a verifier when given a proxy signature. However, a proxy should only be able to produce valid signatures for messages that are *consistent* with the warrant, i.e., messages in the message space defined by the delegator. Thus, there must be an implicit mechanism to check membership in the warrant for a *given* message with corresponding proxy signature, but there should be no means to check membership for other messages.

Contribution: In this paper, we formally define *warrant-hiding proxy signature schemes* by augmenting the state of the art security model of [5] and introducing an additional property for proxy signatures called *privacy*. The latter property captures the fact that given a proxy signature, it is not possible to determine the warrant under which the proxy signer has produced the proxy signature. More precisely, this means that guessing the remaining messages in the warrant is intractable. Basically, this can be achieved by committing to the permitted message space and the proxy needs to provide a non-interactive proof that the message he has signed is contained in the warrant without revealing any other information about the remaining messages in the warrant. Consequently, we can base such a construction generally on zero-knowledge sets [14]. Since general constructions thereof heavily suffer from problems with efficiency, we propose two concrete practical constructions of such a proxy signature scheme based on the delegation-by-certificate approach. Our instantiations can be constructed from any secure digital signature scheme, a randomized version of the Merkle trees yielding hiding vector commitments (without updates) and the secure unconditionally hiding polynomial commitment scheme from [12] respectively. Note that in contrast to a naive approach, i.e., computing an independent certificate (signature of the delegator) for every allowed message, our approach uses a *single* certificate for all messages. After presenting our constructions, we compare them in terms of computational effort as well as bandwidth. Note that the proofs of the security of our constructions in the proposed security model are given in the full version [11]. Finally, we mention open problems for future work.

Outline: Section 2 discusses the cryptographic preliminaries. In Section 3, we present the formal framework for proxy signatures, the security model and our extensions to cover warrant-hiding proxy signature schemes. Section 4 discusses general design strategies and presents our two constructions of warrant-hiding proxy signatures as well as a comparison of their efficiency. Finally, Section 5 concludes the paper and lists open issues for future work.

2   Preliminaries

2.1   Basic Notions

Here, we briefly recall the definitions of bilinear maps, the t-SDH assumption, standard digital signature schemes as well as pseudorandom generators.

Definition 1 (Bilinear Map). Let G, G_T be two cyclic groups of the same prime order p, where G is additive and G_T is multiplicative. We call the map $e : G \times G \to G_T$ a *symmetric bilinear map* or *symmetric pairing* if it is efficiently computable and the following conditions hold:

Bilinearity: For all $P_1, P_2 \in G$ we have for all $P \in G$:
$$e(P_1 + P_2, P) = e(P_1, P) \cdot e(P_2, P) \quad \text{and} \quad e(P, P_1 + P_2) = e(P, P_1) \cdot e(P, P_2).$$
Non-degeneracy: If P generates G, then $g = e(P, P)$ generates G_T, i.e. $g \neq 1$.

In practice, G and G_T will typically be a suitable elliptic curve group of prime order and a torsion subgroup of some suitable finite field, respectively.

Definition 2 (t-Strong Diffie Hellman Assumption (t-SDH)). Let p be a prime of bitlength κ, G be a p-order group, $\alpha \in_R \mathbb{Z}_p^*$ and let $(P, \alpha P, \dots, \alpha^t P) \in G^{t+1}$ for some $t > 0$. Then, for every PPT adversary $\mathcal{A}$ there is a negligible function ϵ such that

$$\Pr\left(\mathcal{A}(P, \alpha P, \alpha^2 P, \dots, \alpha^t P) = \left(c, \frac{1}{\alpha + c} P \right) \right) \leq \epsilon(\kappa)$$

for any $c \in \mathbb{Z}_p \setminus \{-\alpha\}$.

Definition 3 (Digital Signature Scheme). A *digital signature scheme* DSS is a triple $(\mathsf{K}, \mathsf{S}, \mathsf{V})$ of PPT algorithms:

$\mathsf{K}(\kappa)$: Is a key generation algorithm that takes input a security parameter $\kappa \in \mathbb{N}$ and outputs a private (signing) key sk and a public (verification) key pk.

$\mathsf{S}(m, \mathsf{sk})$: Is a (probabilistic) algorithm, which takes as input a message $M \in \{0,1\}^*$ and a private key sk, and outputs a signature σ.

$\mathsf{V}(\sigma, m, \mathsf{pk})$: Is a deterministic algorithm, which takes as input a signature σ, a message $M \in \{0,1\}^*$ and a public key pk, and outputs a single bit $b \in \{\texttt{true}, \texttt{false}\}$ indicating whether σ is a valid signature for M under pk.

Furthermore, we require the digital signature scheme to be correct, i.e., for all $(\mathsf{sk}, \mathsf{pk}) \in \mathsf{K}(\kappa)$ and all $M \in \{0,1\}^*$ we have $\mathsf{V}(\mathsf{S}(M, \mathsf{sk}), M, \mathsf{pk}) = \texttt{true}$. A digital signature scheme is *secure*, if it is existentially unforgeable under adaptively chosen-message attacks (UF-CMA) [10]. Note that in practice, the sign and verify algorithms will typically use a hash function to map input messages to constant size strings, which is also known as the *hash-then-sign* paradigm.

Definition 4 (Pseudorandom Generator (PRG)). A *pseudorandom generator* $f : \{0,1\}^\kappa \to \{0,1\}^\ell$, with $\ell > \kappa$ being positive integers, is a function that can be computed in polynomial time. The input s_0 to the function is called *seed*. A PRG is called *secure* if its output is computationally indistinguishable from random when given a random seed s_0.

2.2 Commitments

A *commitment scheme* CS as a tuple $(\mathsf{CSetup}, \mathsf{CCommit}, \mathsf{COpen})$ of PPT algorithms:

$\mathsf{CSetup}(\kappa)$: Takes a security parameter κ and produces and outputs public parameters cpk which we assume to be implicitly input to the other two algorithms.

$\mathsf{CCommit}(\mathsf{M})$: Takes a value $M \in \mathcal{M}$ and outputs a tuple $(\mathcal{C}, O)$ representing the commitment $\mathcal{C}$ to M and the open information O.

$\mathsf{COpen}(\mathcal{C}, \mathsf{O})$: Gets $(\mathcal{C}, O)$ and outputs either $M \in \mathcal{M}$ or $\bot$ to indicate success or failure, respectively.

A commitment scheme is required to be *hiding* and *binding*. The former means that the value $M \in \mathcal{M}$ is hidden in $\mathcal{C}$ unless the open information O is available, whereas the latter means that is not possible to find an open information O' such that the given commitment $\mathcal{C}$ opens to $M' \neq M$. Besides hiding and binding, a commitment scheme needs to be *correct*, which means that for every honestly computed commitment $\mathcal{C}$, we have $\mathsf{COpen}(\mathsf{CCommit}(M)) = M$ for all $M \in \mathcal{M}$.

We call a commitment scheme *r-binding*, if it satisfies correctness, hiding and *relaxed-binding* [1]. Relaxed-binding is a weaker notion than binding and uses a modified security game. In this game the adversary A choses a value M. Then, is is given a commitment $(\mathcal{C}, O)$ to M (the randomness r for $\mathsf{CCommit}$ is randomly chosen but not controlled by A). If r-binding holds, A is not able to efficiently find O' computed with randomness r' such that $\mathsf{COpen}(\mathcal{C}, O') = M' \neq M$. We write $\mathsf{CCommit}(M, r)$ if we address an r-binding commitment scheme.

In order to support larger messages as input to the $\mathsf{CCommit}$ algorithm, it is common to use the so called *hash-then-commit* approach. It is not hard to see that this approach yields a secure commitment scheme assuming the existence of secure hash functions (collision resistance) and the security of the underlying commitment scheme. Subsequently, whenever we use commitment schemes, we assume that the hash-then-commit paradigm is being implicitly applied.

2.3 Polynomial Commitments

The constant-size unconditionally hiding $\mathsf{PolyCommit}_{\mathsf{Ped}}$ polynomial commitment scheme from [12] is based on Pedersen commitments [15] and uses an algebraic property of polynomials $f(X) \in \mathbb{Z}_p[X]$. Namely, that $(X - \gamma)$ perfectly divides the polynomial $f(X) - f(\gamma)$ for $\gamma \in \mathbb{Z}_p$. We briefly recall the construction:

$\mathsf{PSetup}(\kappa, t)$: Pick two groups G, G_T of the same prime order p (with p being a prime of bitlength κ) having a symmetric pairing $e : G \times G \to G_T$ such that the t-SDH assumption holds. Choose two generators $P, Q \in G$ and $\alpha \in_R \mathbb{Z}_p^*$ and output $\mathsf{ppk} = (G, G_T, p, e, P, \alpha P, \ldots, \alpha^t P, Q, \alpha Q, \ldots, \alpha^t Q)$ as well as $\mathsf{psk} = \alpha$.

$\mathsf{PCommit}(\mathsf{ppk}, f(X))$: Given $f(X) \in \mathbb{Z}_p[X]$ with $\deg(f) \leq t$, pick a random polynomial $r(X) \in \mathbb{Z}_p[X]$ with $\deg(f) \leq \deg(r) \leq t$ and compute the commitment $\mathcal{C} = f(\alpha)P + r(\alpha)Q \in G$ and output $\mathcal{C}$.

$\mathsf{POpen}(\mathsf{ppk}, \mathcal{C}, f(X), r(X))$: Output $(f(X), r(X))$.

$\mathsf{PVerify}(\mathsf{ppk}, \mathcal{C}, f(X), r(X))$: Verify whether

$$\mathcal{C} = \sum_{i=0}^{\deg(f)} f^{(i)}(\alpha^i P) + \sum_{i=0}^{\deg(r)} r^{(i)}(\alpha^i Q)$$

holds and output `true` on success and `false` otherwise.

$\mathsf{PCreateWit}(\mathsf{ppk}, f(X), r(X), \gamma)$: Compute $\phi(X) = \frac{f(X) - f(\gamma)}{X - \gamma}$, $\hat{\phi}(X) = \frac{r(X) - r(\gamma)}{X - \gamma}$ and $W_\gamma = \phi(\alpha)P + \hat{\phi}(\alpha)Q$ and output $(\gamma, f(\gamma), r(\gamma), W_\gamma)$.

PVerifyWit(ppk, $\mathcal{C}, \gamma, f(\gamma), r(\gamma), W_\gamma$): Verify that $f(\gamma)$ is the evaluation of un-known f at point γ. This is done by checking whether

$$e(\mathcal{C}, P) = e(W_\gamma, \alpha P - \gamma P) \cdot e(f(\gamma)P + r(\gamma)Q, P)$$

holds. Output true on success and false otherwise.

A polynomial commitment scheme is *secure* if it is correct, polynomial binding, evaluation binding and hiding. This scheme can be proven secure under the t-SDH assumption in G. Note that α must remain unknown to the committer (and thus the setup must be run by a TTP), since, otherwise, it would be a trapdoor commitment scheme.

In one of our constructions, we require an r-binding variant of PolyCommit$_\mathsf{Ped}$, since the random polynomial required for the hiding is not chosen implicitly in PCommit, but provided externally by computing it from a compact seed using a PRG.

Lemma 1. *The aforementioned modification of* PolyCommit$_\mathsf{Ped}$ *satisfies the r-binding property.*

Proof. In order to show that the r-binding property holds for this variant of PolyCommit$_\mathsf{Ped}$, we can follow the same strategy used to prove the binding of PolyCommit$_\mathsf{Ped}$ in [12]. Note, that now the adversary is allowed to choose $f(X)$, but $r(X)$ is randomly chosen by the challenger. Then, $\mathcal{C}, f(X), r(X)$ is given to the adversary and the adversary needs to deliver $f'(X), r'(X)$ with $f'(X) \neq f(X)$ such that PVerify(ppk, $\mathcal{C}, f'(X), r'(X)$) returns true. It is not hard to see, that the r-binding of this variant of PolyCommit$_\mathsf{Ped}$ can be proven using the the same reduction to the DL problem in G as in [12].   □

2.4   Randomized Merkle Trees

Let T be a complete binary tree of height h with n leaves and let N be the set of nodes of T. Furthermore, let $H : \{0,1\}^* \to \{0,1\}^\ell$ be a secure hash function, $\lambda : N \to \{0,1\}^\ell$ be a labeling function, κ be a security parameter and (CSetup, CCommit, COpen) be an unconditionally hiding commitment scheme CS producing commitments of length ℓ. Then, T is called *randomized Merkle tree* if the labeling function λ is recursively defined as follows:

$$\lambda(v) = \begin{cases} H(\lambda(v_L) || \lambda(v_R)) & \text{if } v \text{ has two children } v_L, v_R, \\ H(\lambda(v_L)) & \text{if } v \text{ has one child } v_L, \text{ and} \\ \mathcal{C}_i & \text{if } v \text{ is the } i\text{'th leaf,} \end{cases}$$

where $(\mathcal{C}_i, O_i) = $ CCommit(M_i) and $\mathcal{M} = (M_i)_{i=1}^n$ is the sequence of strings assigned to the leaves.

Let us additionally define the *authentication path* or *witness* of a leaf i with label $\mathcal{C}_i$ as $W_{M_i} = (w_j)_{j=1}^h$, where the value w_j at height j is defined to be the label of the sibling of the node of height j at the unique path from $\mathcal{C}_i$ to the root.

2.5 Hiding Vector Commitments from Randomized Merkle Trees

Vector commitments allow to commit to an ordered sequence of values represented as a compact commitment and to selectively open values at given positions. For a detailed description of vector commitments, we refer the reader to [6]. Below, we present a novel construction of vector commitments from randomized Merkles trees which are additionally hiding, but do not support updates and proofs of updates. Yet, it seems to be quite straight forward to modify the construction in order to support these two operations by replacing the leaf commitments with trapdoor commitments (chameleon hashes). Our construction uses an r-binding commitment scheme for the leaves, since we do not want the randomizers $\mathcal{R}$ required for the hiding to be generated implicitly, but from a compact seed. Clearly, one could also create a hiding vector commitment scheme in the ordinary sense using a binding and unconditionally hiding commitment scheme for the leaves.

Subsequently, let $\mathsf{VectorCommit}_{\mathsf{Merkle}} = (\mathsf{VKeyGen}, \mathsf{VCommit}, \mathsf{VOpen}, \mathsf{VVerify})$ be a tuple of PPT algorithms associated with a randomized Merkle tree T, such that:

$\mathsf{VKeyGen}(\kappa)$: Given the security parameter κ, run $\mathsf{CSetup}(\kappa)$ to obtain cpk of a suitable unconditionally hiding r-binding commitment scheme and output cpk.

$\mathsf{VCommit}(\mathcal{M}, \mathcal{R})$: Given a sequence of n messages $\mathcal{M}$ and a sequence of n randomizers $\mathcal{R}$, output the root hash $\mathcal{C}$ of T.

$\mathsf{VOpen}(i, \mathcal{M}, \mathcal{R})$: Takes a leaf index i, a sequence of n messages $\mathcal{M}$ and a sequence of n randomizers $\mathcal{R}$ and outputs the authentication path W_{M_i}.

$\mathsf{VVerify}(\mathcal{C}, i, M_i, r_i, W_{M_i})$: Takes a root hash $\mathcal{C}$ of a randomized Merkle tree T, the leaf index i, a message M_i, the randomizer r_i and an authentication path W_{M_i} and returns $\mathtt{true}$ if $\mathcal{C}$ equals the root hash reconstructed from M_i and the authentication path W_{M_i} and $\mathtt{false}$ otherwise.

We note that the auxiliary information in [6] essentially corresponds to $(\mathcal{M}, \mathcal{R})$ in our case. The security requirements are *correctness* and *position r-binding* as in [6] and additionally *hiding*.

Theorem 1. *Assuming the existence of secure hash functions and of secure, unconditionally hiding r-binding commitment schemes, the above construction of a hiding, r-binding vector commitment scheme is secure.*

Proof. The proof of the scheme's correctness can easily be verified. Since the above construction is essentially what Steinfeld et. al implicitly use in [17], the hiding as well as the r-binding properties follow directly from the proofs in [17]. The position binding of the above construction is immediate due to the structure of the Merkle tree (and the security of the used hash function) and the r-binding of the leaf commitments.   □

3 Proxy Signatures

In this section, we recall the formal model for proxy signatures and the security model of [4]. Then, we present an additional definition, capturing the warrant-hiding property and, finally, we define what constitutes a secure *warrant-hiding proxy signature scheme*.

Definition 5 (Proxy Signature Scheme [4]). A *proxy signature scheme* is a tuple PSS = (DSS, (D, P), PS, PV, ID) of PPT algorithms and the algorithms (D, P), PS, PV, ID are given access to a potentially empty common reference string P.[1] Furthermore, DSS is a secure digital signature scheme and the other algorithms are defined as follows:

- (D, P) is a pair of interactive probabilistic algorithms forming the (two-party) proxy-designation protocol. Each algorithm gets the two public keys pk_i, pk_j for the delegator i and the proxy j, respectively, as input. D also takes as input the private key sk_i of the delegator, the identity j of the proxy, and a message space descriptor (warrant) ω for which user i wants to delegate its signing rights to user j. P also takes as input the private key sk_j of the proxy. As a result of the interaction, the expected local output of P is skp, a proxy signing key that user j uses to produce proxy signatures on behalf of user i, for messages in ω. D has no local output. We write $skp = (D(pk_i, sk_i, j, pk_j, \omega), P(pk_j, sk_j, pk_i))$ for the result of this interaction.
- PS is the (probabilistic) proxy signing algorithm. As input it takes a proxy signing key skp and a message $M \in \{0,1\}^*$ and outputs a proxy signature σ_p.
- PV is the deterministic proxy verification algorithm. It takes a public key pk, a message $M \in \{0,1\}^*$ and a proxy signature σ_p as input, and outputs true or false. In the former case, we say that σ_p is a valid proxy signature for $M \in \omega$ relative to pk.
- ID is the proxy identification algorithm. It takes input a valid proxy signature σ_p, and outputs an identity $j \in \mathbb{N}$ or $\perp$ in case of an error.

As it is required by proxy signature schemes when used in practice, we assume the existence of a public key infrastructure. This means that the public keys of delegators and proxies are available in an authentic fashion, i.e., bound to their identities, to all participants.

Definition 6 (Security of a Proxy Signature Scheme [4]). Let PSS = (DSS, (D, P), PS, PV, ID) be a proxy signature scheme, A be an adversary and $\kappa \in \mathbb{N}$. We associate to PSS, A and κ the following game. First, if required, a TTP generates the common reference string P and makes it publicly available (we then implicitly assume that the challenger as well as A have access to P). Then, a public and private key pair (pk_1, sk_1) for user 1 is generated via $K(\kappa)$ and a counter n for the number of users is initialized to 1. The game initializes an empty array skp_1 to store the self-delegated proxy signing keys and corresponding message spaces, and empty sets DU and CS. The set DU stores the identities of the users designated by user 1 (together with the message spaces for which they are designated). The set CS keeps track of the set of messages for which

---

[1] If P is empty this definition exactly matches the definition given in [4,5].

the adversary can produce proxy signatures by user 1 on behalf of user 1 using compromised self-delegated proxy signing keys. Adversary A is given input pk_1 and it can make the following requests or queries in any order and any number of times:

- (i registers pk_i) A can request to register a public key pk_i for user $i = n + 1$ by outputting pk_i. The key is stored, counter n is incremented, and an empty array skp_i is created. This array will store the proxy signing keys of user 1 on behalf of user i together with the message spaces ω to which they correspond.
- (1 designates i) A can request to interact with user 1 running algorithm $D(\mathsf{pk}_1, \mathsf{sk}_1, i, \mathsf{pk}_i, \omega)$, for some $i \in \{2, \ldots, n\}$ and some message space ω (chosen by A). During the interaction, A plays the role of user i running $P(\mathsf{pk}_i, \mathsf{sk}_i, \mathsf{pk}_1)$. After a successful run, DU is set to $DU \cup \{(i, \omega)\}$.
- (i designates 1) A can request to interact with user 1 running $P(\mathsf{pk}_1, \mathsf{sk}_1, \mathsf{pk}_i)$, for some $i \in \{2, \ldots, n\}$. In the interaction, A plays the role of user i running $D(\mathsf{pk}_i, \mathsf{sk}_i, 1, \mathsf{pk}_1, \omega)$ for some message space ω selected by A. If skp is the resulting proxy signing key, then the pair (skp, ω) is stored in the last unoccupied position of skp_i. A does not have access to the elements in skp_i.
- (1 designates 1) A can request that user 1 runs the designation protocol with itself for some message space ω. A is given the transcript of the interaction. If skp is the resulting proxy signing key, the pair (skp, ω) is stored in the next available position of skp_1.
- (exposure of the l-th proxy signing key produced during self-delegation) A can request to see $\mathsf{skp}_1[l]$ for some $l \in \mathbb{N}$. If $\mathsf{skp}_1[l]$ contains a proxy signing key and message space pair (skp, ω), then skp is returned to A and CS is set to $CS \cup \omega$. Otherwise, $\perp$ is returned to A.
- (standard signature by 1) A can query oracle $O_S(\mathsf{sk}_1, \cdot)$ with a message M and obtain a standard signature for M by user 1, $\sigma = S(M, \mathsf{sk}_1)$.
- (proxy signature by 1 on behalf of i using the l-th proxy signing key) A can make a query (i, l, M), where $i \in [n], l \in \mathbb{N}$ and $M \in \{0, 1\}^*$, to oracle $O_{PS}((\mathsf{skp}_u)_{u \in [n]}, \cdot, \cdot, \cdot)$. If $\mathsf{skp}_i[l]$ contains a proxy signing key and message space pair (skp, ω), we say the query is valid and the oracle returns $PS(\mathsf{skp}, M)$. Otherwise, we say the query is invalid and the oracle returns $\perp$.

Eventually, A outputs a forgery (M, σ) or $(M, \sigma_p, \mathsf{pk})$. The output of the game is as follows:

Forgery of a Standard Signature: If the forgery is of the form (M, σ), where $V(\sigma, M, \mathsf{pk}_1) = \texttt{true}$, and M was not queried to oracle $O_S(\mathsf{sk}_1, \cdot)$, then return 1.

Forgery of a Proxy Signature by User 1 on Behalf of User $i \neq 1$: If the forgery is of the form $(M, \sigma_p, \mathsf{pk}_i)$, where $PV(\mathsf{pk}_i, M, \sigma_p) = 1$, $ID(\sigma_p) = 1$, for some $i \in \{2, \ldots, n\}$, and no valid query (i, l, M), for $l \in \mathbb{N}$, was made to the oracle $O_{PS}((\mathsf{skp}_u)_{u \in [n]}, \cdot, \cdot, \cdot)$, then return 1.

Forgery of a Proxy Signature by User 1 on Behalf of User 1: If the forgery is of the form $(M, \sigma_p, \mathsf{pk}_1)$, where $PV(\mathsf{pk}_1, M, \sigma_p) = 1$, $ID(\sigma_p) = 1$, no valid query $(1, l, M)$, for $l \in \mathbb{N}$, was made to $\mathsf{O}_{\mathsf{PS}}((\mathsf{skp}_u)_{u \in [n]}, \cdot, \cdot, \cdot)$, and $M \notin CS$ then return 1.

Forgery of a Proxy Signature by User $i \neq 1$ on Behalf of User 1; User i Was not Designated by User 1 to Sign M: If the forgery is of the form $(M, \sigma_p, \mathsf{pk}_1)$, where $\mathsf{PV}(\mathsf{pk}_1, M, \sigma_p) = 1$ and for each message space ω for which $(\mathsf{ID}(\sigma_p), \omega) \in DU$ it holds that $M \notin \omega$ then return 1.

Otherwise, return 0.

A wins the game, if it returns 1. We say that PSS is a secure proxy signature scheme, if the probability of winning the above game is negligible in the security parameter κ for all polynomial-time adversaries A.

For our privacy definition we have chosen an extractability style game instead of an indistinguishability style game, since it is not possible to find a meaningful notion of indistinguishability due to the fact that the adversary must not know the entire warrant. This requires the warrant to be chosen by the challenger.

Definition 7 (Privacy of a Proxy Signature Scheme). Let the setup be identical to the one in Definition 6. In query phase 1, A is allowed to issue the same types of queries as in the unforgeability game. At some point, A signals the challenger that it is ready to proceed to phase 2 by submitting the tuple (i, c) with $c > 1$. Now, the challenger chooses a warrant ω^*, consisting of c random messages from some message space $\mathbb{M}$ of minimum size $c + 1$, computes the proxy signing key $\mathsf{skp}^* = (\mathsf{D}(\mathsf{pk}_1, \mathsf{sk}_1, i, \mathsf{pk}_i, \omega^*), \mathsf{P}(\mathsf{pk}_i, \mathsf{sk}_i, \mathsf{pk}_1))$ and stores the proxy signing key to a new array skp'_i. Then, in query phase 2, A is allowed to issue queries as in phase 1. Additionally, A is allowed to query proxy signatures for the proxy key in skp'_i for all but one message M^* in the warrant ω^* (whereas on receiving query $l \in \{0, \dots, c - 2\}$ the challenger chooses an unused index l and takes message M_l from ω^*). At some point, A outputs a warrant ω' and wins if $\omega' = \omega^*$.

We say that PSS is *warrant-hiding*, if for all polynomial-time adversaries the probability of winning the above game is negligibly close to $1/|\mathbb{M}'|$, where $\mathbb{M}'$ represents the message space $\mathbb{M}$ minus all queried messages.

Definition 8 (Secure Warrant-Hiding Proxy Signature Scheme). If a secure PSS is warrant-hiding with respect to Definition 7, then we call PSS a *secure warrant-hiding* PSS (WHPSS).

4 Warrant-Hiding Proxy Signature Schemes

In this section we give the problem statement, discuss a generic design strategy and present concrete representation of the warrants which are used in our instantiations and present the two schemes.

Problem Statement: When trying to make the warrant implicit and hidden, one must, on the one hand, enforce that proxy signatures are only valid for messages within the warrant, which requires some suitable representation of the warrant, and, on the other hand, that verifiers cannot test messages against this representation by brute force to determine the remaining messages in the warrant. Furthermore, it is desirable that the representation of the warrant is compact, proxy signatures are compact and the verification of proxy signatures does not require interaction with the delegator, i.e., the verification of warrant-hiding proxy signatures should be non-interactive. Particular issues of interest, from the point of view of a designator, are:

- The verification of a proxy signature should hide the remaining messages in the warrant and
- the verification of a proxy signature should should not reveal (too much) information on the exact size of the warrant.

The first issue is satisfied by both of our constructions and concerning the second issue our constructions reveal an upper bound on the size of the warrant. In Section 4.6, we, however, discuss how the second issue can be achieved, although, reducing the efficiency of such a scheme.

A cryptographic building block that immediately comes to mind when being confronted with this problem statement is a commitment scheme. In particular, one seeks a commitment scheme that is capable of committing to a set of values resulting in a compact commitment and allows to selectively prove membership of a value in the commitment, while at the same time hiding the remaining values in the commitment. Primitives that satisfy both aforementioned properties are zero-knowledge sets [14] and vector commitments [6]. Latter, however, needs to be modified in a way such that it supports hiding. Another primitive, which seems suited at first glance, but actually turns out to be unsuitable, is the concept of a cryptographic accumulator. We briefly discuss these primitives in our context below.

(Nearly) Zero-Knowledge Sets: Zero-knowledge sets (ZKS) were introduced by Micali et. al [14]. They allow a prover to commit to an arbitrary finite set S in such a way that for any string x he can provide an efficient proof of whether $x \in S$ or $x \notin S$, without revealing any knowledge beyond this (non) membership. In particular, the verifier of the proof neither learns the remaining elements of the set S and nor the size of S. Follow up work [8,7] has instantiated ZKS from a variety of other assumptions and improved the efficiency. In [12], it is shown that when relaxing ZKS to nearly ZKS, which no longer require hiding an upper bound on the cardinality of S, the size of the proof that an element is (or is not) in a committed set is reduced by a factor of sixteen or more, when compared to the best known ZKS construction. One of our instantiations uses the polynomial commitment scheme introduced in [12]. Furthermore, note that we no not require non-membership proofs in our application and, thus, do not rely on costly general ZKS constructions. Doing so, we obtain a size of the public parameters of $\mathcal{O}(|\omega|)$ and a size of the proxy signature of $\mathcal{O}(1)$.

Hiding Vector Commitments: Vector commitments [6] allow to commit to an ordered sequence of values represented as a compact commitment and to selectively open values at given positions. However, the constructions of [6] do not provide hiding as it is, but can be extended to support hiding by applying the vector commitments to a sequence of hiding commitments instead of messages. They additionally support updates, which is not required in our application. Most importantly, the constructions of [6] require public parameters of size $\mathcal{O}(|\omega|^2)$. Our proposed construction uses an efficient hiding vector commitment from randomized Merkle trees as they are used implicitly in the construction of content extraction signatures in [17]. Our construction does not provide updates as it is. Nevertheless, it seems that it can easily be turned into a vector commitment scheme supporting updates. This could be achieved by exchanging the commitments of the leaves with trapdoor commitments (chameleon hash values). In contrast to the vector commitments of [6], the public parameters are $\mathcal{O}(1)$, but the size of the proxy signatures is $\mathcal{O}(\log |\omega|)$. As it is also the case with our first construction, an upper bound of the size of the warrant is revealed (vector commitments of [6] reveal the exact size).

Cryptographic Accumulators: A cryptographic accumulator [3] allows to represent a finite set of values S by a single value (the accumulator), whose size is independent of the size of S. For every accumulated value, one can compute a witness. Having such a witness, anybody can verify that the corresponding value has indeed been accumulated. However, it is infeasible to find a witness for a value that was not accumulated. The basic problem with accumulators is that they do not guarantee the hiding of the accumulated set S, which is crucial for our application.

4.1   Warrant Representation

In our constructions, the warrant ω is a sequence of messages $\omega = (M_i)_{i=1}^c$, which is being mapped into a compact representation, i.e., of constant size, which is then integrated into the certificate of the proxy. We stress that we do not require an explicit ordering and could also use a set representation instead, but we use the sequence notation for a consistent description of both schemes (in the second scheme, the messages are ordered, but the ordering is arbitrary and does not have any meaning for our construction). Note that in contrast to an abstract description of the message space, which allows the representation of a potentially unbounded message space, our construction supports only fixed message spaces in the sense that each message in this space must be known a priori. In particular, the number of messages is polynomially bounded and each message needs to be generated by a polynomial time algorithm. However, in most practical applications of proxy signatures such a message space is sufficient. Furthermore, this allows us to construct proxy signatures, which provide the warrant-hiding property. Considering potentially unbounded message spaces while hiding the warrant seems to be far from trivial and is an interesting aspect for future work.

Polynomial Commitments: Our first construction is based on the constant-size unconditionally hiding polynomial commitment scheme of Kate et al. [12]. Loosely speaking, this construction works in the following way. A delegator maps all c messages in the warrant to a polynomial of degree c, whereas the roots of this polynomial are defined to be hash values of messages in the warrant. Then, the delegator commits to this polynomial and signs the polynomial commitment resulting in a certificate for the proxy. A proxy signer is then allowed to produce proxy signatures by generating witnesses for the roots of the polynomial (representing valid messages in the warrant) and signs the witness along with the public key of the delegator. Then, any verifier can check both signatures and verify whether the message and the witness correspond to the committed polynomial and represent a root of the polynomial. Consequently, the verifier can check the correctness of a proxy signature without learning the remaining messages in the warrant. Latter is due to the unconditional hiding property of the polynomial commitment scheme.

Now, we need to discuss in detail how a set of valid messages (the warrant) is represented. Instead of using $\omega = (M_i)_{i=1}^c$ itself, we firstly construct a set $\omega_H = \{H(M_i) : i = 1, \dots, c\}$, where $H : \{0,1\}^* \to \mathbb{Z}_p$ is a secure hash function. From this set ω_H, we secondly derive the so-called *warrant polynomial* $m(X)$ using the map

$$\phi : 2^{\mathbb{Z}_p} \to \mathbb{Z}_p[X] \quad \text{with} \quad \omega_H \mapsto \prod_{H \in \omega_H} (X - H).$$

Note that the degree of $m(X)$ is polynomially bounded, i.e., represents the size of the warrant.

The intuition for this particular representation is that if the hash values of messages in ω are roots of the warrant polynomial $m(X)$, this polynomial uniquely captures the messages given by the warrant. More precisely, a message is in the warrant if and only if its hash value is a root of $m(X)$, i.e., there is a 1-to-1 correspondence between the set of valid witnesses and the warrant (up to collisions in the hash function H). Otherwise, if the valid messages did not correspond to the roots of $m(X)$ and were arbitrary evaluations, a dishonest proxy signer would be able to generate witnesses for arbitrary messages and, in further consequence, efficiently produce valid proxy signatures for messages outside the warrant.

Hiding Vector Commitments from Randomized Merkle Trees: Our second construction is based on hiding vector commitments from randomized Merkle trees. Loosely speaking, this construction works in the following way. A delegator generates an r-binding commitment for each of the c messages in the warrant and then computes the root of the randomized Merkle tree T with c leaves. This means that T aggregates commitments to all c messages in ω into a single root hash value. Then, the delegator signs the root hash of T resulting in a certificate for the proxy. A proxy signer is then allowed to produce proxy signatures by generating witnesses W_{M_i}, which is the respective authentication path for the leaf C_i, and signs the witness along with the public key of the delegator. Then, any verifier can check both signatures and verify whether the message and the witness correspond to the root hash of T. Consequently, the verifier can check the correctness of a proxy signature without learning the remaining messages in the warrant. Latter is due to the unconditional hiding property of the commitment scheme used at the leaf nodes.

4.2 The First Scheme (WHPSS$_{\mathsf{PolyCommit}}$)

Before Scheme 1 can be used, a TTP runs a setup in the following way to produce the common reference string, which is then accessible to all parties, i.e., delegators, proxy signers and verifiers, in an authentic fashion:

Setup: Given a security parameter κ and an upper bound $t \in \mathbb{N}$ for the size of the warrant, execute $\mathsf{PSetup}(\kappa, t)$ and obtain $(\mathsf{ppk}, \mathsf{psk})$. Choose a secure PRG $f : \mathbb{Z}_p \to \mathbb{Z}_p^{t+1}$ and output a suitable encoding of the tuple (f, ppk) as the common reference string P.

(D, P): D and P are given local inputs $\mathsf{pk}_i, \mathsf{sk}_i, j, \mathsf{pk}_j, \omega$ and $\mathsf{pk}_j, \mathsf{sk}_j, \mathsf{pk}_i$, where $\omega = (M_i)_{i=1}^c$ with $c \leq t$.
D picks a seed $s \in_R \mathbb{Z}_p$, computes $\omega_H = \{H(M_i) : i = 1, \ldots, c\}$ and $m(X) = \phi(\omega_H)$. Then, compute $r(X) \in \mathbb{Z}_p[X]$ with $\deg(r) = \deg(m) = c$ with coefficients obtained evaluating $f(s)$ as well as
$$\mathcal{C} = \mathsf{PCommit}(\mathsf{ppk}, m(X), r(X)) \quad \text{and} \quad \mathsf{cert} = \mathsf{S}(\mathcal{C}\|j\|\mathsf{pk}_j, \mathsf{sk}_i).$$

It sets the proxy signing key of user j as $\mathsf{skp}' = (\mathsf{pk}_i, s, \mathcal{C}, j, \mathsf{pk}_j, \omega, \mathsf{cert})$ and sends it to P. Now, P computes ω_H and $m(X) = \phi(\omega_H)$ as well as $r(X)$ from seed s. It checks whether
$$\mathsf{V}(\mathsf{cert}, \mathsf{PCommit}(\mathsf{ppk}, m(X), r(X))\|j\|\mathsf{pk}_j, \mathsf{pk}_i) = \mathtt{true}$$

If not, return $\perp$ and terminate. Otherwise, set $\mathsf{skp} = (\mathsf{sk}_j, \mathsf{skp}')$, output skp and terminate. If P returns $\perp$, D aborts. Otherwise, also D terminates correctly.

PS: Given skp, M so that there is an index l with $1 \leq l \leq c$ and $M_l = M$, this algorithm computes ω_H and $m(X) = \phi(\omega_H)$ as well as $r(X)$ from seed s. Then, it computes $h_M = H(M)$, $r_M = r(h_M)$ as well as
$$W_M = \mathsf{PCreateWit}(\mathsf{ppk}, m(X), r(X), h_M) \quad \text{and} \quad \sigma = \mathsf{S}(W_M\|r_M\|\mathsf{pk}_i, \mathsf{sk}_j),$$

and returns $\sigma_p = (j, \mathcal{C}, W_M, r_M, \mathsf{pk}_j, \mathsf{cert}, \sigma)$.

PV: Given $\mathsf{pk}_i, M, \sigma_p = (j, \mathcal{C}, W_M, r_M, \mathsf{pk}_j, \mathsf{cert}, \sigma)$, this algorithm verifies whether
$$\mathsf{V}(\mathsf{cert}, \mathcal{C}\|j\|\mathsf{pk}_j, \mathsf{pk}_i) \quad \wedge \quad \mathsf{V}(\sigma, W_M\|r_M\|\mathsf{pk}_i, \mathsf{pk}_j) \quad \wedge$$
$$\mathsf{PVerifyWit}(\mathsf{ppk}, \mathcal{C}, H(M), 0, r_M, W_M)$$

yields $\mathtt{true}$. On success return $\mathtt{true}$ and $\mathtt{false}$ otherwise.

ID: Given $\sigma_p = (j, \mathcal{C}, W_M, r_M, \mathsf{pk}_j, \mathsf{cert}, \sigma)$ output j.

Scheme 1: Warrant-hiding Proxy Signature Scheme from PolyCommit$_{\mathsf{Ped}}$ (WHPSS$_{\mathsf{PolyCommit}}$)

4.3 The Second Scheme (WHPSS$_{\mathsf{VectorCommit}}$)

In contrast to Scheme 1, here the requirement of a TTP for generating a common reference string depends on the commitment scheme used for labeling the leaves of the randomized Merkle tree.

(D, P):   D and P are given local inputs $\mathsf{pk}_i, \mathsf{sk}_i, j, \mathsf{pk}_j, \omega$ and $\mathsf{pk}_j, \mathsf{sk}_j, \mathsf{pk}_i$, where $\omega = (M_i)_{i=1}^c$. D picks a seed $s \in_R \{0,1\}^\kappa$, chooses a secure PRG $f : \{0,1\}^\kappa \to (\{0,1\}^\kappa)^c$ and computes $\mathcal{R} = f(s)$ and

$$\mathcal{C} = \mathsf{VCommit}(\omega, \mathcal{R}) \quad \text{and} \quad \mathsf{cert} = \mathsf{S}(\mathcal{C}\|j\|\mathsf{pk}_j, \mathsf{sk}_i).$$

It sets the proxy signing key of user j as $\mathsf{skp'} = (\mathsf{pk}_i, s, \mathcal{C}, j, \mathsf{pk}_j, \omega, \mathsf{cert})$ and sends it to P. Now, P computes $\mathcal{R}$ from s and checks whether

$$\mathsf{V}(\mathsf{cert}, \mathsf{VCommit}(\omega, \mathcal{R})\|j\|\mathsf{pk}_j, \mathsf{pk}_i) = \mathtt{true}$$

If not, return $\perp$ and terminate. Otherwise, set $\mathsf{skp} = (\mathsf{sk}_j, \mathsf{skp'})$, output skp and terminate. If P returns $\perp$, D aborts. Otherwise, also D terminates correctly.

PS: Given skp, M so that there is an index l with $1 \le l \le c$ and $M_l = M$, this algorithm computes $\mathcal{R}$ from seed s, sets $r_M = (r_l, l)$ and computes

$$W_M = \mathsf{VOpen}(l, \omega, \mathcal{R}) \quad \text{and} \quad \sigma = \mathsf{S}(W_M\|r_M\|\mathsf{pk}_i, \mathsf{sk}_j),$$

and returns $\sigma_p = (j, \mathcal{C}, W_M, r_M, \mathsf{pk}_j, \mathsf{cert}, \sigma)$.

PV: Given $\mathsf{pk}_i, M, \sigma_p = (j, \mathcal{C}, W_M, r_M, \mathsf{pk}_j, \mathsf{cert}, \sigma)$ with $r_M = (r_l, l)$, this algorithm verifies whether

$$\mathsf{V}(\mathsf{cert}, \mathcal{C}\|j\|\mathsf{pk}_j, \mathsf{pk}_i) \quad \wedge \quad \mathsf{V}(\sigma, W_M\|r_M\|\mathsf{pk}_i, \mathsf{pk}_j) \quad \wedge \quad \mathsf{VVerify}(\mathcal{C}, l, M, r_l, W_M)$$

yields $\mathtt{true}$. On success return $\mathtt{true}$ and $\mathtt{false}$ otherwise.

ID: Given $\sigma_p = (j, \mathcal{C}, W_M, r_M, \mathsf{pk}_j, \mathsf{cert}, \sigma)$ output j.

Scheme 2: Warrant-hiding Proxy Signature Scheme from Vector Commitments (WHPSS$_{\mathsf{VectorCommit}}$)

4.4   Security

Here, we discuss the security properties of our proposed WHPSS constructions. We are not dealing with the correctness of Scheme 1 and Scheme 2, since this is straight-forward to verify. Due to space constraints we omit the proofs here, and refer the reader for the full proofs of the subsequent theorems to the full version of the paper [11]. Subsequently, we informally discuss the security of both constructions.

In Scheme 1, the delegator, by running the delegation, commits to a message polynomial $m(X)$ based on an unconditionally hiding polynomial commitment $\mathcal{C}$ using a random polynomial $r(X)$. Hence, since the delegator does not sign the warrant itself, but a representation thereof (the commitment), we need to guarantee that the delegator is not able to change the warrant later on, i.e., finding polynomials $m'(X), r'(X)$ with $m(\alpha) = m'(\alpha)$ as well as $r(\alpha) = r'(\alpha)$, which would violate the binding of PolyCommit$_{\mathsf{Ped}}$. Now, we argue why the warrant-hiding property holds. Let $\mathcal{C}$ be a commitment to some warrant polynomial $m(X)$ of degree c. Note that PolyCommit$_{\mathsf{Ped}}$ unconditionally hides $m(X)$ in $\mathcal{C}$ as long as $r(X)$ is unknown ($r(X)$ is only known to the proxy). Along with a proxy signature, a root of $m(X)$ and an evaluation of the random polynomial $r(X)$ are being disclosed. It is not possible to interpolate $r(X)$ unless $c+1$ (with c being the size of the warrant) distinct evaluations of $r(X)$ are known, which will never happen and, thus, the hiding of PolyCommit$_{\mathsf{Ped}}$ and the security of the used PRG holds. The warrant polynomial $m(X)$ can only be reconstructed from all c roots, however, then, we no longer need the warrant to be hidden, since then all messages from the warrant are already known. Latter means that the unknown randomizers can not be determined.

Theorem 2. *Assuming the r-binding of* PolyCommit$_{\mathsf{Ped}}$, *the existence of secure hash functions and the security of the* DSS *scheme, Scheme 1 is a secure* PSS.

Theorem 3. *Assuming the unconditional hiding of* PolyCommit$_{\mathsf{Ped}}$ *and the existence of secure PRGs, Scheme 1 is a warrant-hiding* PSS.

In Scheme 2, the delegator, by running the delegation, commits to a sequence of messages and randomness based on VectorCommit$_{\mathsf{Merkle}}$ producing a root hash $\mathcal{C}$. As above, due to the binding of the commitment scheme we guarantee that the delegator cannot change the warrant afterwards. The warrant-hiding property holds, because even if an adversary gets to know all the leaf commitments, the respective messages are hidden due to the unconditionally hiding leaf commitment and the security of the used PRG. Latter means that the unknown randomizers can not be determined.

Theorem 4. *Assuming the r-binding of* VectorCommit$_{\mathsf{Merkle}}$, *the existence of secure hash functions and the security of the* DSS *scheme, Scheme 2 is a secure* PSS.

Theorem 5. *Assuming the unconditional hiding of* VectorCommit$_{\mathsf{Merkle}}$ *and the existence of secure PRGs, Scheme 2 is a warrant-hiding* PSS.

Taking the above results together, we obtain the following result:

Corollary 1. *Scheme 1 and Scheme 2 are both secure* WHPSS.

4.5 Efficiency Comparison

In Table 1, we analyze the complexity of both introduced schemes in terms of computational costs of all involved algorithms as well as the sizes of parameters, certificates (delegations) and proxy signatures. We now briefly highlight the major differences between both schemes. In terms of computational effort, WHPSS$_{\mathsf{PolyCommit}}$ has higher costs for signature generation, but requires constant time for signature verification. In contrast, WHPSS$_{\mathsf{VectorCommit}}$ is faster in signature generation, but has higher cost for verification (although in practice, the operations are cheap hash function evaluations). In terms of size, WHPSS$_{\mathsf{PolyCommit}}$

Table 1. Comparison of Costs of Scheme 1 and Scheme 2

Scheme	Computation					Size		
	$\mathcal{D}$	$\mathcal{P}$	$\mathcal{PS}$	$\mathcal{PV}$	$\mathcal{ID}$	P	cert	σ_p
WHPSS$_{\mathsf{PolyCommit}}$	$\mathcal{O}(|\omega|)$	$\mathcal{O}(|\omega|)$	$\mathcal{O}(|\omega|)$	$\mathcal{O}(1)$	$\mathcal{O}(1)$	$\mathcal{O}(|\omega|)$	$\mathcal{O}(1)$	$\mathcal{O}(1)$
WHPSS$_{\mathsf{VectorCommit}}$	$\mathcal{O}(|\omega|)$	$\mathcal{O}(|\omega|)$	$\mathcal{O}(\log|\omega|)$	$\mathcal{O}(\log|\omega|)$	$\mathcal{O}(1)$	$\mathcal{O}(1)$	$\mathcal{O}(1)$	$\mathcal{O}(\log|\omega|)$

has constant size proxy signatures, but the parameters P generated by a TTP are linear in the warrant size. In contrast, WHPSS$_{\text{VectorCommit}}$ has small constant size parameters P, but a proxy signature size logarithmic in the size of the warrant. We note that depending on the actual unconditionally hiding commitment scheme used in the construction of the randomized Merkle tree, also here a TTP may be required to be involved in the generation of P, e.g., when using Pedersen commitments.

4.6   On Hiding the Warrant Size

As already noted, both constructions reveal an upper bound on the warrant size. More precisely, in case of WHPSS$_{\text{PolyCommit}}$ this upper bound is t, which may be adjusted to be larger than any value that allows to draw meaningful conclusions for practical applications. Similarly to above, in case of WHPSS$_{\text{VectorCommit}}$ one can artificially enlarge the height of the hash tree and introduce dummy leaves to hide the warrant size. Clearly, both cases reduce practicality with increasing the upper bound. In theory, ZKS achieve hiding the cardinality of the set. However, the parameters therefore need to be chosen in a way that they are larger than any meaningful set size, which in practice does not improve on our modifications.

5   Conclusion

In this paper, we have introduced a new type of proxy signatures following the *delegation by warrant* approach. These so called *warrant-hiding proxy signatures* enable a delegator to restrict the message space for a proxy while hiding this message space (warrant) from verifiers.

An interesting question for future work is to construct such signature schemes for potentially unbounded message spaces which do not require exponential effort in producing a delegation. Nevertheless, this does not seem to be straight-forward when seeking efficient constructions suitable for practical applications. It may be interesting to study the security in context of multi-level proxy signatures [16].

Acknowledgements. Both authors have been supported by the European Commission through project FP7-FutureID, grant agreement number 318424.

References

1. An, J.H., Dodis, Y., Rabin, T.: On the security of joint signature and encryption. In: Knudsen, L.R. (ed.) EUROCRYPT 2002. LNCS, vol. 2332, pp. 83–107. Springer, Heidelberg (2002)
2. Awasthi, A.K., Lal, S.: ID-based Ring Signature and Proxy Ring Signature Schemes from Bilinear Pairings. I. J. Network Security 4(2), 187–192 (2007)
3. Benaloh, J.C., de Mare, M.: One-Way Accumulators: A Decentralized Alternative to Digital Signatures. In: Helleseth, T. (ed.) EUROCRYPT 1993. LNCS, vol. 765, pp. 274–285. Springer, Heidelberg (1994)

 4. Boldyreva, A., Palacio, A., Warinschi, B.: Secure proxy signature schemes for delegation of signing rights. IACR Cryptology ePrint Archive 2003, 96 (2003)
 5. Boldyreva, A., Palacio, A., Warinschi, B.: Secure Proxy Signature Schemes for Delegation of Signing Rights. J. Cryptology 25(1), 57–115 (2012)
 6. Catalano, D., Fiore, D.: Vector Commitments and Their Applications. In: Kurosawa, K., Hanaoka, G. (eds.) PKC 2013. LNCS, vol. 7778, pp. 55–72. Springer, Heidelberg (2013)
 7. Catalano, D., Fiore, D., Messina, M.: Zero-Knowledge Sets with Short Proofs. In: Smart, N.P. (ed.) EUROCRYPT 2008. LNCS, vol. 4965, pp. 433–450. Springer, Heidelberg (2008)
 8. Chase, M., Healy, A., Lysyanskaya, A., Malkin, T., Reyzin, L.: Mercurial Commitments with Applications to Zero-Knowledge Sets. In: Cramer, R. (ed.) EUROCRYPT 2005. LNCS, vol. 3494, pp. 422–439. Springer, Heidelberg (2005)
 9. Fuchsbauer, G., Pointcheval, D.: Anonymous Proxy Signatures. In: Ostrovsky, R., De Prisco, R., Visconti, I. (eds.) SCN 2008. LNCS, vol. 5229, pp. 201–217. Springer, Heidelberg (2008)
10. Goldwasser, S., Micali, S., Rivest, R.L.: A Digital Signature Scheme Secure Against Adaptive Chosen-Message Attacks. SIAM J. Comput. 17(2), 281–308 (1988)
11. Hanser, C., Slamanig, D.: Warrant-Hiding Delegation-by-Certificate Proxy Signature Schemes. Cryptology ePrint Archive, Report 2013/ (2013), http://eprint.iacr.org/2013/544
12. Kate, A., Zaverucha, G.M., Goldberg, I.: Constant-Size Commitments to Polynomials and Their Applications. In: Abe, M. (ed.) ASIACRYPT 2010. LNCS, vol. 6477, pp. 177–194. Springer, Heidelberg (2010)
13. Mambo, M., Usuda, K., Okamoto, E.: Proxy Signatures for Delegating Signing Operation. In: ACM Conference on Computer and Communications Security (CCS 1996), pp. 48–57. ACM (1996)
14. Micali, S., Rabin, M.O., Kilian, J.: Zero-Knowledge Sets. In: Symposium on Foundations of Computer Science (FOCS), pp. 80–91. IEEE (2003)
15. Pedersen, T.P.: Non-Interactive and Information-Theoretic Secure Verifiable Secret Sharing. In: Feigenbaum, J. (ed.) CRYPTO 1991. LNCS, vol. 576, pp. 129–140. Springer, Heidelberg (1992)
16. Schuldt, J.C.N., Matsuura, K., Paterson, K.G.: Proxy Signatures Secure Against Proxy Key Exposure. In: Cramer, R. (ed.) PKC 2008. LNCS, vol. 4939, pp. 141–161. Springer, Heidelberg (2008)
17. Steinfeld, R., Bull, L., Zheng, Y.: Content Extraction Signatures. In: Kim, K.-c. (ed.) ICISC 2001. LNCS, vol. 2288, pp. 285–304. Springer, Heidelberg (2002)
18. Tan, Z., Liu, Z., Tang, C.: Digital Proxy Blind Signature Schemes Based on DLP and ECDLP. Tech. rep., MM Research Preprints, MMRC, AMSS, Academia, Sinica, Beijing (2002)
19. Wang, G.: Designated-verifier proxy signatures for e-commerce. In: IEEE International Conference on Multimedia and Expo, ICME 2004, pp. 1731–1734 (2004)
20. Wang, H., Pieprzyk, J.: Efficient One-Time Proxy Signatures. In: Laih, C.-S. (ed.) ASIACRYPT 2003. LNCS, vol. 2894, pp. 507–522. Springer, Heidelberg (2003)
21. Zhang, K.: Threshold Proxy Signature Schemes. In: Okamoto, E., Davida, G., Mambo, M. (eds.) ISW 1997. LNCS, vol. 1396, pp. 282–290. Springer, Heidelberg (1998)

Improved Scan-Chain Based Attacks and Related Countermeasures

Subhadeep Banik[1] and Anusha Chowdhury[2]

[1] Applied Statistics Unit, Indian Statistical Institute,
203 B T Road, Kolkata 700 108, India
s.banik_r@isical.ac.in
[2] Dept. of Computer Science and Engineering,
Indian Institute of Technology Kanpur
anushac@iitk.ac.in

Abstract. Scan-chains are one of the most commonly-used DFT (Design for Testability) techniques. DFT refers to design techniques that add certain testability features to a micro-electronic hardware product design. However, the presence of scan-chains makes the device vulnerable to scan-based attacks from cryptographic point of view. Techniques to cryptanalyze stream ciphers like Trivium, with additional hardware for scan-chains, are already available in literature (Agrawal et. al. Indocrypt 2008). However, extending such ideas to more complicated stream ciphers like MICKEY 2.0, is not possible as the state update function used by MICKEY 2.0 is far more complex. In this paper, we will describe a general strategy to perform a scan-chain based attack on MICKEY 2.0. Furthermore, we will look at the XOR-CHAIN based countermeasure that was proposed by Agrawal et. al. in Indocrypt 2008, to protect Trivium from such scan-based attacks. We will show that such an XOR-CHAIN based countermeasure is vulnerable to a SET attack. As an alternative, we propose a novel countermeasure that can protect scan-chains against such attacks.

Keywords: MICKEY 2.0, Scan-Chain Attack, Stream Cipher.

1 Introduction

While manufacturing any hardware product, DFT techniques are design efforts that are specifically employed to ensure that a device is testable. Single scan-chains are one of the most popular and effective ways of providing testability to any hardware device. The objective of the scan-chain is to make testing easier by providing a way to set and observe every flip-flop in an IC. Unlike the functional tests that check chip functionality, scan tests cover stuck-at-faults, caused by manufacturing problems. Physical manufacturing defects, such as

- silicon defects, photo-lithography defects, mask contamination
- process variation or defective oxide etc.

G. Paul and S. Vaudenay (Eds.): INDOCRYPT 2013, LNCS 8250, pp. 78–97, 2013.

may lead to electrical defects such as shorts (bridging faults), opens, transistors stuck on open, changes in threshold voltage etc. which may lead to digital logic being stuck at either the 0 or 1 value at one or many of the flip-flops. It may also lead to slower transitions among the flip-flops causing delay faults which hamper the proper functioning of a cryptosystem.

Scan-chain testing can be done to check whether a chip is functioning normally or not. It provides the designer an easy way to ascertain whether the device has succumbed to the above mentioned defects or not. In this design methodology, all the flip-flops in the design are replaced with scan type flip-flops. The design is made controllable and observable by chaining all these flip-flops together and shifting test data in and out. Scan type flip-flop contains a multiplexer to select either a normal mode functioning or a scan mode functioning. By suitably alter-ing the control value to the multiplexer, the chip can be used for normal or scan test mode of operation. After selecting scan-test mode, the user is able to input test patterns of his choice into the device and thereafter scan out the contents of all the flip-flops connected to the scan-chain. It therefore gives the following opportunities to the user:

1. **Controllability**: The ability to set the flip-flops to certain states or logic values.
2. **Observability**: The ability to observe the state of these flip-flops.

The flip side of this design paradigm is that this makes certain cryptosystems implemented with such scan-chains in hardware, vulnerable to scan-based side channel attacks. Scan-based attack is a semi-intrusive side channel attack that does not require the attacker to actively tamper with the functioning of the cryptosystem as in optical/laser fault attacks. The attacker takes advantage of the scan-chain already implemented in the device and stops the normal mode of operation of the cryptosystem at some suitably chosen time instant and scans out the content of all the flip-flops in the system. The flip-flops usually store the internal state bits of the cryptosystem, and if the adversary can deduce the correspondence between the individual bits of the scanned out vector and the internal state bits, this may be enough to break the system. However, ascertain-ing such a correspondence is usually non-trivial and thus a fascinating area for cryptanalytic research. Scan-based attacks have already been reported against block ciphers like AES [19] and DES [20] and stream-ciphers like RC4 [16] and Trivium [2].

1.1   MICKEY 2.0

The stream cipher MICKEY 2.0 [3] was designed by Steve Babbage and Matthew Dodd as a submission to the eStream project. The cipher has been selected as a part of eStream's final hardware portfolio. MICKEY is a synchronous, bit-oriented stream cipher designed for low hardware complexity and high speed. After a TMD tradeoff attack [14] against the initial version of MICKEY (ver-sion 1), the designers responded by tweaking the design by increasing the state size from 160 to 200 bits and altering the values of some control bit tap locations. These changes were incorporated in MICKEY 2.0 and these are the only differences between MICKEY version 1 and MICKEY 2.0. While MICKEY 2.0 uses an 80-bit key and a variable length IV, a modified version of the cipher, MICKEY-128 2.0, that uses a 128-bit key [4], was also proposed by the designers.

The name MICKEY is derived from "Mutual Irregular Clocking Keystream generator" which describes the behavior of the cipher. The state consists of two 100-bit shift registers named R and S, each of which is irregularly clocked and controlled by the other. The cipher specification underlines that each key can be used with up to 2^{40} different IVs of the same length, and that 2^{40} keystream bits can be generated from each key-IV pair. Very little cryptanalysis of MICKEY 2.0 is available in literature. In [11], it was observed that unprotected implementations of MICKEY 2.0 may be vulnerable to power analysis attacks. In [18], non-smooth cryptanalysis of MICKEY 2.0 was performed. The attack, however, had time complexity more than exhaustive search. In [5], a differential fault attack has been reported against MICKEY 2.0. Apart from these, not many published results on MICKEY 2.0 are available.

1.2   Our Contribution

In [2], the stream cipher Trivium [8] was successfully cryptanalyzed using scan-based attack. We will show that due to the complex structure of the state-update functions used in MICKEY 2.0, extending the attack of [2] to MICKEY 2.0 is impossible. Our contributions are therefore threefold:

1. We will propose a strategy to perform the scan-based attack on MICKEY 2.0 that is independent of any specific physical implementation of the cipher.
2. In [2], the XOR-CHAIN based countermeasure was suggested to protect cryptosystems from such attacks. We will show that such a countermeasure is vulnerable to the SET attack.
3. As an alternative, we provide a countermeasure for scan-chains that will thwart a SET or RESET attack. We will prove that incorporating such a countermeasure will still allow the designer to control and test the scan-chain.

The organization of the paper is as follows. In Section 2 we will give some background on how scan-based attacks are mounted and carried out against cryptosystems. In Section 3, we will outline the details of the attack against MICKEY 2.0. In Section 4, we propose an attack against the XOR-CHAIN based countermeasure and show how MICKEY 2.0 can be attacked even in the presence of such a countermeasure. In Section 5 we will outline the proposed countermeasure and discuss its security features in detail. Section 6 concludes the paper.

2   Scan-Chain Attack: Background and Preliminaries

A scan-based test involves construction of one or more scan-chains in a chip by connecting the internal registers and flip-flops of a device and by making either ends of the chain available to the boundary scan interface, via the SCAN-IN and SCAN-OUT ports (See Fig 2). During testing, test vectors can be scanned in serially through the SCAN-IN pin. The contents of the chain can also be scanned out in a serial manner through the SCAN-OUT pin. During the testing phase, all flip-flops are disconnected from the combinatorial digital logic of the device and connected in single or multiple connected chains. As shown in Figure 2, this is done by placing a multiplexer infront of the D input of each flip-flop controlled by the SCAN-ENABLE signal. In normal mode of operation, the SCAN-ENABLE signal is set to 0, so the flip-flop accepts the D-input and the device behaves normally. In test mode, the SCAN-ENABLE signal is set to 1 and in this event the flip-flop accepts the SCAN-IN input. Scan-chains are automatically inserted into the design by a Computer aided synthesis tool. The chain is usually organized according to the physical positions of the flip-flops. One may note that any arbitrary pattern can be given as input into the scan-chain, and the state of every flip-flop can be read out. We will now discuss some salient features related

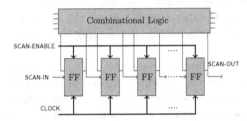 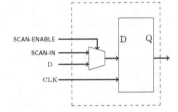

Fig. 1. Diagram of a Scan-chain   **Fig. 2.** Scan-enabled D FF

to scan-chains and state clearly the cryptographic model that is employed to mount a scan-based attack.

* **Ability to Assert the SCAN-ENABLE Signal :** We assume that the adversary is able to control the SCAN-ENABLE input to the device i.e. he has the ability to run the device under normal mode or test mode interchangeably. It is also reasonable to assume that the adversary can time the changing of the SCAN-ENABLE signal in synchronization with the system clock signal. In other words, he is able to stop the normal mode of operation of the device after any given number of clock rounds, drive the device into test mode and scan out the contents of the flip-flops of the scan-chain serially, via the SCAN-OUT port.
* **Knowledge of the Cryptosystem Used in the Device :** We   assume that the adversary knows the high-level algorithmic design details of the cryptosystem implemented in the device (in this case MICKEY 2.0). Although, the adversary is expected to know the general hardware structure of the cryptosystem, he does not know exactly how many flip-flops have been used in the design. For example, a typical implementation of MICKEY

2.0 ([6, 10, 12, 15, 17]) is expected to have around 211 flip-flops (100 each for the R and S registers, 7 for the counter register, and one each for INPUT_BIT_R, INPUT_BIT_S, CONTROL_BIT_R, CONTROL_BIT_S).[1] But different implementations of the cipher may use extra flip-flops as per the requirements of the designer. In this sense, the adversary must be able to come up with an attack strategy that is independent of any specific hardware implementation of the cipher.

* **Ability to Manipulate the Public Variables :** We assume that the adversary is able to operate the cryptosystem using any public variable of his choice. In this case, this implies that he can run the cipher using any IV of his choice, while the Key remains secret. The Secret Key is usually stored in the memory (RAM) which is not connected to the scan-chain.

* **Knowledge of Scan-Chain Structure :** Here, we assume that the adversary does not have any knowledge of the structure of the scan-chain that ties the flip-flops of the device together. The flip-flops in a scan-chain are not connected according to their positions in their respective registers. Rather, a Computer-aided tool optimizes the scan-chain according to the physical locations of the individual flip-flops. He also does not know the number of flip-flops in the scan-chain, but as shown in Section 3.1, finding this number is not difficult.

* **Putting It All Together :** The online attack procedure of the scan-based attack is very simple. The adversary lets the cryptosystem run in the normal mode for a fixed number of clock rounds. He then asserts the SCAN-ENABLE signal, which halts the normal operation mode, and scans out the content of the scan-chain serially via the SCAN-OUT port. He will get a scanned out vector $\mathbf{V}$, of the length of the scan-chain. This scanned out vector contains all the state bits of the cryptosystem at the clock round after which the normal mode of operation was halted. However, since the structure of the scan-chain is unknown to the adversary, he is unable to deduce the correspondence between the individual bits of $\mathbf{V}$ and individual state bits of the cryptosystem. For example, he knows with certainty that some element of $\mathbf{V}$ is equal to the 0th bit of the register R at the round when the normal mode was halted, but he does not know which element. In other words, he is unaware of the permutation π between the scanned out vector $\mathbf{V}$ and the internal state of the cipher.

So any scan-based attack usually proceeds in two phases :

(a) Pre-processing stage $\rightarrow$ In this stage, the adversary performs various tests on the device to gain information about the structure of the scan-chain and deduce the structure of the permutation π. This is the stage that requires rigorous cryptanalysis. Once the permutation π has been ascertained, the adversary proceeds to the online stage.

(b) Online stage $\rightarrow$ The adversary lets the device get initialized with some unknown Key and IV, and halts the device at some suitable clock round (in

---

[1] These are internal variables used in the description of MICKEY 2.0. For more please refer to [3].

the case of MICKEY 2.0, he stops the normal mode at the beginning of the PRGA). He then scans out the content of the flip-flops in the scan-chain through the SCAN-OUT port and therefore gets the vector $\mathbf{V}$. Since the permutation π is now known to him, he is able to reconstruct the internal state of the cipher from $\mathbf{V}$ and this completes the attack.

3   Attacking MICKEY 2.0

The keystream generator makes use of two registers R and S (100 bits each). The registers are updated in a non-linear manner using the control variables: INPUT_BIT_R, INPUT_BIT_S, CONTROL_BIT_R, CONTROL_BIT_S. As referred to earlier, any implementation of the cipher contains flip-flops for the R, S registers and the 4 control variables. Furthermore, there must be 7 flip-flops for the counter register to keep track of the number of rounds in the Preclock stage. For more details please refer to [3].

In [2], a scan-based attack on Trivium was presented. As we go along we will show that the attack idea of [2] can not be extended to MICKEY-like ciphers whose state update functions are much more complex. The keystream production stage in MICKEY 2.0 is preceded by the three stages:- IV Loading, Key Loading and Preclock. Initially the R, S registers are initialized to the all zero state. Then at each clock round, a variable length IV $[iv_0, iv_1, \ldots, iv_{v-1}]$ and the 80 bit Key $[k_0, k_1, \ldots, k_{79}]$ is used to update the state by successively executing the function CLOCK_KG$(R, S, 1, iv_i)$, (for $i \to 0$ to $v - 1$) and CLOCK_KG$(R, S, 1, k_i)$, (for $i \to 0$ to 79). The strategy of the adversary in our attack will be to operate the cipher in the IV loading stage using certain IV's of his choice and then halt the normal mode by asserting the SCAN-ENABLE signal and read out the contents of the scan-chain. He will repeat this exercise multiple number of times. By observing the scanned out vector in each case, he will attempt to deduce the structure of the scan-chain.

3.1   Finding the Length of the Scan-Chain

The attacker begins by resetting all the flip-flops of the scan-chain to zero and then asserts the SCAN-ENABLE signal. The first input to SCAN-IN port is set to 1. As is obvious from Figure 2, if there are n flip-flops in the chain, the scanned out vector will contain n zeros (which is the initial state of the scan-chain) followed by the single 1 which comes from the first input to the scan-chain. Thus the attacker can deduce the value of n easily.

3.2   Strategy to Find the Location of the Counter Bits

Initially, the task of the adversary is to ascertain the location of the bits of the counter register in the scanned out vector. In [2], the strategy to find the counter bits for Trivium was as follows (note that Trivium uses an 11-bit counter register). The attacker would initially RESET all the flip-flops in the scan-chain and run the cipher in the normal mode for $2^{10} - 1$ clock rounds. The structure of Trivium is such that if all the registers are initialized to the all-zero state, then it will continue to be in this state as long as the cipher runs. Hence, the only bits which will change are those in the flip-flops of the counter register which operates independently of the combinational logic of the cipher. After $2^{10} - 1$ rounds the 10 least significant bits of the counter become all 1s. If the adversary now asserts the SCAN-ENABLE signal and reads out the content of the scan-chain, he will observe exactly ten ones in the scanned-out vector. The bit locations of these 1s indicate the position of the ten LSBs of the counter register in the scan-chain. However, such an attack can not be extended to MICKEY 2.0. Initially, all the flip-flops in the R, S registers are set to 0. If the IV Loading stage runs even for a single clock round with the first IV bit equal to zero, the state of the S register evaluates to 085804128010408643BC42800. This vector itself has 24 ones and so it is clear that the strategy of [2] can not be extended to MICKEY 2.0. The strategy that we propose is as follows. To find the location of the LSB of the counter the attacker will use such IVs whose length is of the form $l_0 = 2\alpha + 1$ i.e. an odd number. Whatever be the value of the IV, after l_0 rounds, the LSB of the counter register will always evaluate to 1. After l_0 rounds of IV loading, the attacker asserts the SCAN-ENABLE signal and reads out the contents of the scan-chain. The attacker does this for n_0 many IVs of odd length and performs the bitwise AND of each of the n_0 scanned out vectors. If n_0 is sufficiently large, all but one of the elements of this product vector becomes 0. Clearly, the only non-zero element in the product vector corresponds to the location of the LSB of the counter register.

To find the location of the next LSB, the attacker chooses IVs of length $l_1 = 4\alpha + 2$ or $4\alpha + 3$. It is clear that irrespective of the values of the IV, after l_1 rounds of IV loading, the second LSB of the counter register always evaluates to 1. The attacker repeats the above process with n_1 IVs of this form and as above, computes the bitwise AND of all the scanned out vectors. If n_1 is sufficiently large, all but one of the elements of this product vector becomes 0 and the only non-zero element in the product vector corresponds to the location of the second LSB of the counter register. The process can similarly be extended to find the location of all the other bits of the counter register. The above arguments have been formalized in Algorithm 1.

Algorithm 1 returns the location β_k of the kth LSB of the counter register in the scan-chain. It also returns the IV set A_k which helps determine β_k. The values of $A_k \; \forall k \in [0, 6]$ for an implementation of MICKEY 2.0, that uses the 211 flip-flops given above, are included in Appendix A.

3.3   Strategy to Find the Location of the Other Internal State Bits

We will briefly recall the strategy of [2] to find the location of the state bits of Trivium. Note that Trivium has an internal register of 288 bits. The 80 bit Secret Key is directly loaded on to the first 80 bits of the register. The 80 bit IV is loaded on to the 94th to the 173rd bits of the register. The remaining 128 bits are loaded with a fixed initialization constant. In order to find the location of the 2nd

Input: The index of the counter LSB k
Output: The Set A_k of IVs which determine the location of the kth LSB of counter register
Output: The location index β_k of the kth LSB of counter register in the scan-chain

Let **P** be a vector of n elements (n is the length of the scan-chain)
$\mathbf{P} \leftarrow 1^n$;
$w \leftarrow 0$;
while $|\mathbf{P}| \neq 1$ **do**

    /* $|\mathbf{P}|$ denotes the number of 1s in **P** */

    Generate a random Initial Vector IV_w of length $l_k = 2^{k+1}\alpha + 2^k + r, \quad (0 \leq r < 2^k)$;

    Append IV_w to the Set A_k ;

    Reset cipher and perform IV Loading with IV_w ;

    Assert the SCAN-ENABLE signal and read the scanned out vector **V**.

    $\mathbf{P} = \mathbf{P}\&\mathbf{V}$ (& denotes bitwise AND);

    $w \leftarrow w + 1$;

end
for $i = 1$ TO n **do**

    if $\mathbf{P}[i] = 1$ **then**

        $\beta_k \leftarrow i$;

    end

end
Return A_k, β_k;

Algorithm 1. Algorithm to determine the location of counter bits

bit of the state register (say), the adversary initializes the cipher with the Key 8000 0000 0000 0000 and the all zero IV. The remaining bits of the register are initialized to all zero. As a result, before the initialization stage begins, only the first register bit holds the value 1 and the rest 0. The cipher is run in normal mode for one clock round, and then the SCAN-ENABLE signal is asserted and the contents of the chain are scanned out. The state update of Trivium is such that after the first initialization round, only the 2nd register bit has the value 1 and the rest 0. So the scanned out vector that the adversary obtains has two 1s: one in the location corresponding to the LSB of the counter register and the other in the position corresponding to the 2nd bit of the state register. Since the attacker already knows the location of the counter bits, he can easily deduce the location of the 2nd state register bit. This approach cannot be extended to MICKEY 2.0 for two reasons:

- As we have already seen, the state update function of MICKEY 2.0 is way too complex.
- Unlike Trivium, MICKEY 2.0 does not allow direct loading of Key and IV bits on to the state register. As mentioned earlier, initially the R, S registers are initialized to the all zero state. Then a variable length IV $[iv_0, iv_1, \ldots, iv_{v-1}]$ and the 80 bit Key $[k_0, k_1, \ldots, k_{79}]$ is used to update the state by successively executing CLOCK_KG$(R, S, 1, iv_i)$, (for $i \to 0$ to $v - 1$) and thereafter CLOCK_KG$(R, S, 1, k_i)$, (for $i \to 0$ to 79).

The strategy that we propose is as follows. To find the location of the ith bit of the register R (say), the attacker will use such Initial Vectors $IV_w = [iv_0, iv_1, \ldots, iv_{v-1}]$ which after the IV Loading stage i.e. executing the routine

CLOCK_KG($R, S, 1, iv_i$), (for $i \rightarrow 0$ to $v - 1$) successively, leaves the ith bit of the register R at value 1. Since the CLOCK_KG routine is known publicly, the attacker can easily select such IVs by random selection. By standard randomness assumptions, one out of every two randomly selected IVs will result in the ith bit of R being equal to 1 at the end of the IV Loading stage. The rest of the attack is same as before. After IV Loading, the attacker asserts the SCAN-ENABLE signal and reads out the scanned-out vector **V**. The attacker does this for m_i many IVs that result in the ith bit of R being 1 and performs the bitwise AND of each of the m_i scanned out vectors. If m_i is sufficiently large, all but one of the elements of this product vector becomes 0. Clearly, the only non-zero element in the product vector corresponds to the location of the ith bit of R.

Experimentally, the values of n_i, m_i for an implementation of MICKEY 2.0 with 211 flip-flops has been found to be around 8 to 20. To speed up the process, the attacker can omit those bit locations of the scanned out vector **V** whose correspondence to some flip-flop in the design have already been found out. For example, the attacker can omit the bits of **V** which correspond to the counter register. He may also omit any other bits of **V** whose correspondence with some internal state bit have already been determined. The arguments have been formalized in Algorithm 2.

Algorithm 2 returns the location β_χ of the state bit χ in the scan-chain. It also returns the IV set A_χ which helps determine β_χ. The values of A_χ for all bits of the registers R, S, for an implementation of MICKEY 2.0 that use the 211 flip-flops given above, are included in Appendix A.

4   Attacking the XOR-CHAIN Countermeasure Scheme

The Flipped-Scan countermeasure technique to protect scan-chains was proposed in [16]. This involved placing inverters at random points in the scan-chain. Security stemmed from the fact that an adversary could not guess the number and positions of the inverters. This technique was cryptanalyzed in [2] using a RESET attack. It was shown that if all flip-flops in the scan-chain are initially RESET, then the positions of the inverters can be completely determined by the $0 \rightarrow 1$ and $1 \rightarrow 0$ transitions in the scanned-out vector. As an alternative, the XOR-CHAIN based countermeasure was proposed in [2]. The technique involves placing XOR gates at random points of the chain as described in Figure 4. Security again stems from the fact that an adversary is unable to guess the number and positions of the XOR gates.

Notations. We assume that there are n flip-flops in the scan-chain. The state of the ith flip-flop ($1 \le i \le n$) at clock round t ($t \ge 0$) after the SCAN-ENABLE signal is asserted, is given by the symbol S_i^t. The τth ($\tau \ge 1$) round input to the scan-chain is given as x_τ. Similarly the τth round output of the scan-chain is denoted as y_τ. We also define the sequence a_i, ($1 \le i \le n$) over GF(2) as follows. If there is an XOR gate before the ith flip-flop then $a_i = 1$ else $a_i = 0$. The goal of the attacker is to determine the value of the vector $[a_1, a_2, \ldots, a_n]$.

Input: The internal state bit χ whose location in the scan-chain is to be determined
Input: The set of index locations scan-chain **T** whose correspondence has been determined
Output: The Set A_χ of IVs which determine the location of the state bit χ
Output: The location index β_χ of the state bit χ in the scan-chain

Let **P** be a vector of n elements (n is the length of the scan-chain)
$\mathbf{P} \leftarrow 1^n$;
$w \leftarrow 0$;

for $\forall\ i \in \mathbf{T}$ **do**
$\quad|\quad \mathbf{P}[i] = 0$;
end
while $|\mathbf{P}| \neq 1$ **do**
$\quad|\quad$ /* $|\mathbf{P}|$ denotes the number of 1s in **P** */
$\quad|\quad$ Generate a random Initial Vector $\mathrm{IV}_w = [iv_0, iv_1, \ldots, iv_{v-1}]$;
$\quad|\quad$ Set $R \leftarrow 0$, $S \leftarrow 0$;
$\quad|\quad$ Execute $\mathsf{CLOCK\_KG}(R, S, 1, iv_i)$, (for $i \to 0$ to $v - 1$);
$\quad|\quad$ **if** *The state bit* $\chi = 1$ **then**
$\quad|\quad\quad|\quad$ Append IV_w to the Set A_χ ;
$\quad|\quad\quad|\quad$ Reset cipher and perform IV Loading with IV_w ;
$\quad|\quad\quad|\quad$ Assert the $\mathsf{SCAN\text{-}ENABLE}$ signal and read the scanned out vector **V**.
$\quad|\quad\quad|\quad$ $\mathbf{P} = \mathbf{P}\&\mathbf{V}$ (& denotes bitwise AND);
$\quad|\quad$ **end**
$\quad|\quad$ $w \leftarrow w + 1$;
end
for $i = 1$ TO n **do**
$\quad|\quad$ **if** $\mathbf{P}[i] = 1$ **then**
$\quad|\quad\quad|\quad$ $\beta_\chi \leftarrow i$;
$\quad|\quad$ **end**
end
Append β_χ to the set **T**;
Return A_χ, β_χ;

Algorithm 2. Algorithm to determine location of the state bit χ

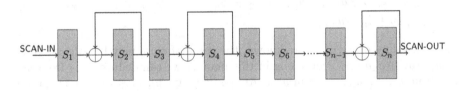

Fig. 3. Diagram of the XOR-CHAIN scheme proposed in [2]

4.1   The SET Attack on the **XOR-CHAIN** Structure

Most standard VLSI designs provide a GLOBAL SET/RESET (GSR) pin to initialize all flip-flops to some known state INIT during configuration [9]. The INIT value of flip-flop primitives like FDP, FDPE, FDS etc. in the Xilinx Virtex 6 library is 1 by default, i.e. these flip-flops are SET after configuration. Our strategy to attack the XOR-CHAIN would be to SET all the flip-flops in the chain and then assert the SCAN-ENABLE signal. We will prove in Theorem 1, that by observing the values of the scanned-out vector, the adversary will be able to determine the number and positions of the XOR gates in the chain.

Theorem 1. *If the scan-chain is initially* SET *i.e.* $S_i^0 = 1$, $\forall i \in [1, n]$, *and* $x_1 = 1$, *then the value of the vector* $[a_1, a_2, \ldots, a_n]$ *can be determined efficiently by observing the output bits* y_i, $\forall i \in [1, n]$ *of the scanned-out vector.*

Proof. Define the symbol $S_0^t = x_{t+1}$. Due to the architecture of the scan-chain, the following equation holds for any $t > 0$, $1 \le i \le n$:

$$S_i^t = S_{i-1}^{t-1} \oplus a_i \cdot S_i^{t-1} \tag{1}$$

We will give a general outline of the proof first and sort out the more technical details later. As can be seen from Figure 4, the first output bit y_1 is given by $y_1 = S_n^0 = 1$. The second output bit is given by

$$y_2 = S_n^1 = S_{n-1}^0 \oplus a_n \cdot S_n^0 = 1 \oplus a_n.$$

The value of a_n is therefore given by $1 \oplus y_2$. Now look at the equation governing y_3.

$$\begin{aligned} y_3 = S_n^2 &= S_{n-1}^1 \oplus a_n \cdot S_n^1 = S_{n-2}^0 \oplus a_{n-1} \cdot S_{n-1}^0 \oplus a_n \cdot (S_{n-1}^0 \oplus a_n \cdot S_n^0) \\ &= S_{n-2}^0 \oplus (a_{n-1} \oplus a_n) \cdot S_{n-1}^0 \oplus a_n \cdot S_n^0 \\ &= 1 \oplus a_{n-1}. \end{aligned}$$

The value of a_{n-1} is therefore given by $1 \oplus y_3$. Now look at the equation for y_4.

$$\begin{aligned} y_4 &= S_n^3 = S_{n-1}^2 \oplus a_n \cdot S_n^2 \\ &= S_{n-2}^1 \oplus a_{n-1} \cdot S_{n-1}^1 \oplus a_n \cdot \left(S_{n-2}^0 \oplus (a_{n-1} \oplus a_n) \cdot S_{n-1}^0 \oplus a_n \cdot S_n^0\right) \\ &= S_{n-3}^0 \oplus (a_{n-2} \oplus a_{n-1} \oplus a_n) \cdot S_{n-2}^0 \oplus (a_{n-1} \oplus a_n \oplus a_n a_{n-1}) \cdot S_{n-1}^0 \oplus a_n \cdot S_n^0 \\ &= 1 \oplus a_{n-2} \oplus a_n \oplus a_n a_{n-1}. \end{aligned}$$

Since the values of a_n, a_{n-1} are known, the value of a_{n-2} may be calculated as $1 \oplus y_4 \oplus a_n \oplus a_n a_{n-1}$. Proceeding in this manner we can deduce a_{n-3} from y_5, a_{n-4} from y_6, ..., a_{n-i+3} from y_{i-1}. At the ith stage, y_i, $(1 \le i \le n+1)$ can be written as

$$y_i = S_{n-i+1}^0 \oplus b_{i,n-i+2} \cdot S_{n-i+2}^0 \oplus b_{i,n-i+3} \cdot S_{n-i+3}^0 \oplus \cdots \oplus b_{i,n} \cdot S_n^0 \tag{2}$$

It can be shown that **(i)** $b_{i,n-i+2} = a_n \oplus a_{n-1} \oplus \cdots \oplus a_{n-i+2}$, **(ii)** $b_{i,n-i+3}, b_{i,n-i+4}$, ..., $b_{i,n}$ are functions of $a_n, a_{n-1}, \ldots a_{n-i+3}$ only. Since $a_n, a_{n-1}, \ldots a_{n-i+3}$ are already known, a_{n-i+2} equals

$$1 \oplus y_i \oplus a_n \oplus a_{n-1} \oplus \cdots \oplus a_{n-i+3} \oplus b_{i,n-i+3} \oplus \cdots \oplus b_{i,n}.$$

The values of $a_n, a_{n-1}, \ldots, a_1$ may be found out in this manner. Now all that remains to be shown are the proofs of **(i)**, **(ii)**. We will proceed by mathematical induction. Let $P(i)$ be the proposition defined as follows. For all $k \in [1, n]$, (and $k - i \ge 0$)

$$S_k^i = S_{k-i}^0 \oplus c_{k-i+1} \cdot S_{k-i+1}^0 \oplus \ldots \oplus c_k \cdot S_k^0$$

then **A.** $c_{k-i+1} = a_k \oplus a_{k-1} \oplus \cdots a_{k-i+1}$, **B.** $c_{k-i+2}, \ldots, c_k$ are functions of $a_{k-i+2}, a_{k-i+3}, \ldots, a_k$ only. For $i = 1$, $S_k^1 = S_{k-1}^0 \oplus a_k \cdot S_k^0$ and so $P(1)$ is true. Assume $P(i)$ is true for $i = 2, 3, \ldots, u$. For $i = u + 1$,

$$
\begin{aligned}
S_k^{u+1} &= S_{k-1}^u \oplus a_k \cdot S_k^u \\
&= S_{k-1-u}^0 \oplus (a_{k-1} \oplus a_{k-2} \oplus \cdots \oplus a_{k-u}) \cdot S_{k-u}^0 \oplus \eta_{k-u+1} \cdot S_{k-u+1}^0 \oplus \cdots \oplus \\
&\quad \eta_k \cdot S_k^0 \oplus a_k \cdot (S_{k-u}^0 \oplus \gamma_{k-u+1} \cdot S_{k-u+1}^0 \oplus \cdots \oplus \gamma_k \cdot S_k^0) \\
&= S_{k-u-1}^0 \oplus (a_k \oplus \cdots \oplus a_{k-u}) \cdot S_{k-u}^0 \oplus (\eta_{k-u+1} \oplus a_k \cdot \gamma_{k-u+1}) \cdot S_{k-u+1}^0 \\
&\quad \oplus \cdots \oplus (\eta_k \oplus a_k \cdot \gamma_k) \cdot S_k^0.
\end{aligned}
$$

This proves **A.** By induction hypothesis on $i = u$, $\eta_{k-u+1}, \ldots, \eta_k, \gamma_{k-u+1}, \ldots, \gamma_k$ are functions of $a_{k-u+1}, \ldots, a_k$ only and so this proves **B** as well. It can be seen that **(i)**, **(ii)** follow from **A, B.**

4.2 Attacking MICKEY 2.0 in Presence of XOR-CHAIN

One of the main difficulties of applying Algorithms 1 and 2, to any implementation of MICKEY 2.0 protected by an XOR-CHAIN structure is that the scanned-out vector will no longer represent the state of the scan-chain before the SCAN-ENABLE signal was asserted. Because of the random placement of the XOR gates in the chain, the scanned out vector $\mathbf{V} = [y_1, y_2, y_3, \ldots y_n]^T$ is a linear combination of the state of the scan-chain $\mathbf{S} = [S_1^0, S_2^0, S_3^0, \ldots, S_n^0]^T$. From Equation (2), the relation between $\mathbf{V}$ and $\mathbf{S}$ is given as :

$$
S_n^0 = y_1
$$
$$
S_{n-1}^0 \oplus b_{1,n} \cdot S_n^0 = y_2
$$
$$
S_{n-2}^0 \oplus b_{2,n-1} \cdot S_{n-1}^0 \oplus b_{2,n} \cdot S_n^0 = y_3
$$
$$
\vdots
$$
$$
S_1^0 \oplus b_{n,2} \cdot S_2^0 \oplus \cdots \oplus b_{n,n-2} \cdot S_{n-2}^0 \oplus b_{n,n-1} \cdot S_{n-1}^0 \oplus b_{n,n} \cdot S_n^0 = y_n
$$

In matrix form these equations may be written as $\mathcal{B} \cdot \mathbf{S} = \mathbf{V}$. Once the attacker has determined the values of $[a_1, a_2, \ldots, a_n]$ he can determine the values of $b_{i,j} \; \forall i, j$ and hence the matrix $\mathcal{B}$. Now we would like to point out that $\mathcal{B}$ is invertible over $GF(2)$. Clearly, $\mathcal{B}$ is a lower anti-triangular matrix with all the elements in the anti-diagonal equal to 1. Therefore, it follows that $Det(\mathcal{B}) = 1$, and hence the result. The attacker can now deduce the state of the scan-chain before the assertion of the SCAN-ENABLE signal, by computing $\mathbf{S} = \mathcal{B}^{-1} \cdot \mathbf{V}$. The adversary can now apply Algorithms 1 and 2 to the vector $\mathbf{S}$.

5 Securing the Scan-Chain: Double Feedback XOR-CHAIN

Our motivation was to find a structure that would resist the SET and RESET attacks. We found that a few simple tweaks to the XOR-CHAIN structure was sufficient to secure the chain from the aforementioned attacks. The structure we propose is this: We retain the idea of placing XOR gates at random points in the scan-chain. In the original proposal, if a_i was 1, the output of the ith flip-flop was fed back to the XOR gate placed before it. In the structure that we propose, if a_i is 1 ($\forall\ i \in [1, n-1]$), then the output of the ith and the $(i+1)^{th}$ flip-flop would be fed back to the XOR gate placed infront of the ith flip-flop (see Figure 5). For $i = n$, (i.e. for the last flip-flop in the chain) we keep $a_n = 0$. We call this the "Double Feedback XOR-CHAIN" structure. We will first prove that such a structure can be used to test the scan-chain efficiently. We will also prove that such a structure would resist the SET and RESET attacks.

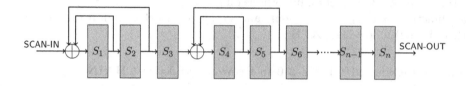

Fig. 4. Double Feedback XOR-CHAIN

5.1   Testability

Because of the structure of the Double Feedback XOR-CHAIN, the flip-flops are updated by the following recursive equation (See Figure 5).

$$
S_i^t = \begin{cases} S_{i-1}^{t-1} \oplus a_i \cdot (S_i^{t-1} \oplus S_{i+1}^{t-1}), & \text{if } 1 < i < n, \\ S_{i-1}^{t-1}, & \text{if } i = n, \\ x_t \oplus a_i \cdot (S_i^{t-1} \oplus S_{i+1}^{t-1}), & \text{if } i = 1. \end{cases} \tag{3}
$$

Let $X = [x_1, x_2, \ldots, x_n]$ be the inputs in the first n clock rounds, to the scan-chain after the assertion of SCAN-ENABLE signal. In the next n rounds, we read out the vector $Y = [y_{n+1}, y_{n+2}, \ldots, y_{2n}]$ from the SCAN-OUT pin. A necessary and sufficient condition to be able to use Double Feedback XOR-CHAIN structure for testing purposes is that the function mapping $X \to Y$ must be a bijection [2]. We will prove the bijection in two steps. Denote by $\mathcal{S}_t = [S_1^t, S_2^t, \ldots, S_n^t]^T$ the state of the scan-chain at the tth clock round. We will first prove that the map between $X \to \mathcal{S}_n$ is a bijection, and then we prove that the map between $\mathcal{S}_n \to Y$ is also a bijection. First we note that Equation (3) can be written in matrix form as follows:

$$
\begin{pmatrix} S_1^t \\ S_2^t \\ S_3^t \\ S_4^t \\ \vdots \\ S_n^t \end{pmatrix} = \begin{pmatrix} a_1 & a_1 & 0 & 0 & 0 & \cdots & 0 & 0 \\ 1 & a_2 & a_2 & 0 & 0 & \cdots & 0 & 0 \\ 0 & 1 & a_3 & a_3 & 0 & \cdots & 0 & 0 \\ 0 & 0 & 1 & a_4 & a_4 & \cdots & 0 & 0 \\ \vdots & \vdots & \vdots & \vdots & \vdots & \ddots & \vdots & \vdots \\ 0 & 0 & 0 & 0 & 0 & \cdots & 1 & 0 \end{pmatrix} \begin{pmatrix} S_1^{t-1} \\ S_2^{t-1} \\ S_3^{t-1} \\ S_4^{t-1} \\ \vdots \\ S_n^{t-1} \end{pmatrix} \oplus \begin{pmatrix} x_t \\ 0 \\ 0 \\ 0 \\ \vdots \\ 0 \end{pmatrix}.
$$

We can write this in compact form $S_t = A \cdot S_{t-1} \oplus X_t$. Here A is the tridiagonal matrix defined above and $X_t = [x_t, 0, 0, \ldots, 0]^T$. Before we prove the bijection we will look at a few useful results regarding the structure of A and its powers.

Lemma 1. *Consider the elements in the first column of A^p, $(1 \le p \le n-1)$. It can be shown that $A^p(p+1, 1) = 1$ and $A^p(i, 1) = 0$ for all $i \in [p+2, n]$. ($M(i,j)$ denotes the element in the ith row and j^{th} column of the matrix M)*

Lemma 2. *Consider the elements in the last row of A^p, $(1 \le p \le n-1)$. It can be shown that $A^p(n, n-p) = 1$ and $A^p(n, j) = 0$ for all $j \in [1, n-p-1]$.*

Lemma 3. *Let $\mathbf{e}_1 = [1, 0, 0, \ldots, 0]^T$. Then, the first columns of A^p, $(1 \le p \le n-1)$ and I_n i.e.*

$$I_n \cdot \mathbf{e}_1, \quad A \cdot \mathbf{e}_1, \quad A^2 \cdot \mathbf{e}_1, \quad \ldots, \quad A^{n-1} \cdot \mathbf{e}_1$$

are linearly independent over GF(2). (I_n is the $n \times n$ identity matrix.)

Lemma 4. *Let $\mathbf{e}_n = [0, 0, 0, \ldots, 1]$. Then, the last rows of A^p, $(1 \le p \le n-1)$ and I_n i.e.*

$$\mathbf{e}_n \cdot I_n, \quad \mathbf{e}_n \cdot A, \quad \mathbf{e}_n \cdot A^2, \quad \ldots, \quad \mathbf{e}_n \cdot A^{n-1}$$

are linearly independent over GF(2).

Lemma 1, 2, 3, 4 are quite standard results for tridiagonal matrices and hence we state them here without proof.

Theorem 2. *The function mapping the first n inputs to the scan-chain $X = [x_1, x_2, \ldots, x_n]$ to the state S_n of the scan-chain is a bijection.*

Proof. We have already shown that the successive state vectors S_t of the scan-chain are related by the equation $S_t = A \cdot S_{t-1} \oplus X_t$, $\forall t > 0$ where $X_t = [x_t, 0, 0, \ldots, 0]^T$. Combining these equations for $t = 1, 2, \ldots n$ we get

$$S_n = A^n \cdot S_0 \oplus A^{n-1} \cdot X_1 \oplus A^{n-2} \cdot X_2 \oplus \cdots \oplus A \cdot X_{n-1} \oplus X_n. \qquad (4)$$

The scan-chain is usually RESET before the SCAN-ENABLE signal is asserted, and so $S_0 = \mathbf{0}$ and therefore we have

$$S_n = A^{n-1} \cdot X_1 \oplus A^{n-2} \cdot X_2 \oplus \cdots \oplus A \cdot X_{n-1} \oplus X_n$$
$$= x_1 \cdot A^{n-1} \cdot \mathbf{e}_1 \oplus x_2 \cdot A^{n-2} \cdot \mathbf{e}_1 \oplus \cdots \oplus x_{n-1} \cdot A \cdot \mathbf{e}_1 \oplus x_n \cdot I_n \cdot \mathbf{e}_1.$$

Now, if possible let $X' = [x'_1, x'_2, \ldots, x'_n] \neq X$ be a vector that leads to the same value of S_n. So we have,

$$S_n = x'_1 \cdot A^{n-1} \cdot \mathbf{e}_1 \oplus x'_2 \cdot A^{n-2} \cdot \mathbf{e}_1 \oplus \cdots \oplus x'_{n-1} \cdot A \cdot \mathbf{e}_1 \oplus x'_n \cdot I_n \cdot \mathbf{e}_1.$$

Adding the equations we get

$$\mathbf{0} = (x_1 \oplus x'_1) \cdot A^{n-1} \cdot \mathbf{e}_1 \oplus (x_2 \oplus x'_2) \cdot A^{n-2} \cdot \mathbf{e}_1 \oplus \cdots \oplus (x_n \oplus x'_n) \cdot I_n \cdot \mathbf{e}_1.$$

By Lemma 3, $I_n \cdot \mathbf{e}_1$, $A \cdot \mathbf{e}_1$, $A^2 \cdot \mathbf{e}_1$, $\ldots$, $A^{n-1} \cdot \mathbf{e}_1$ are linearly independent, so we must have $x_i = x'_i$, $\forall i \in [1, n]$. Hence $X = X'$ and so the function mapping $X \to S$ is certainly an injection. Also both the domain and range of this map is the vector space $GF(2)^n$, which proves that the function is a bijection. $\qquad \square$

Theorem 3. *The function mapping the state $\mathcal{S}_n$ of the scan-chain to the output vector $Y = [y_{n+1}, y_{n+2}, y_{n+3}, \ldots, y_{2n}]$ is a bijection. Therefore the map between $X \rightarrow Y$ is also a bijection.*

Proof. We have $y_{n+1} = S_n^n = \mathbf{e}_n \cdot \mathcal{S}_n$. Similarly, $y_{n+2} = S_n^{n+1} = \mathbf{e}_n \cdot \mathcal{S}_{n+1} = \mathbf{e}_n \cdot (\mathcal{A} \cdot \mathcal{S}_n \oplus X_{n+1}) = \mathbf{e}_n \cdot \mathcal{A} \cdot \mathcal{S}_n$. Generalizing in this manner, we have for all $i \in [1, n]$,

$$y_{n+i} = S_n^{n+i-1} = \mathbf{e}_n \cdot \mathcal{S}_{n+i-1} = \mathbf{e}_n \cdot (\mathcal{A}^{i-1} \cdot \mathcal{S}_n \oplus \mathcal{A}^{i-2} \cdot X_{n+1} \oplus \cdots \oplus X_{n+i-1})$$

$$= \mathbf{e}_n \cdot (\mathcal{A}^{i-1} \cdot \mathcal{S}_n \oplus x_{n+1} \cdot \mathcal{A}^{i-2} \cdot \mathbf{e}_1 \oplus \cdots \oplus x_{n+i-1} \cdot I_n \cdot \mathbf{e}_1)$$

By Lemma 1, the last element of the column vectors $\mathcal{A}^{i-2} \cdot \mathbf{e}_1, \mathcal{A}^{i-3} \cdot \mathbf{e}_1, \ldots, I_n \cdot \mathbf{e}_1$ are all 0 and so their dot product with $\mathbf{e}_n$ will also be 0. And so we have $y_{n+i} = \mathbf{e}_n \cdot \mathcal{A}^{i-1} \cdot \mathcal{S}_n, \forall i \in [1, n]$. We can therefore write

$$Y^T = \begin{pmatrix} \mathbf{e}_n \cdot I_n \\ \mathbf{e}_n \cdot \mathcal{A} \\ \vdots \\ \mathbf{e}_n \cdot \mathcal{A}^{n-1} \end{pmatrix} \cdot \mathcal{S}_n = \mathcal{C} \cdot \mathcal{S}_n.$$

By Lemma 4, the rows of $\mathcal{C}$ are linearly independent and so $\mathcal{C}$ is invertible. This proves that the function mapping $\mathcal{S}_n \rightarrow Y$ is a bijection. Combining this result with Theorem 2, we can say that the function mapping $X \rightarrow Y$ is also a bijection. $\qquad\square$

5.2   Resistance against SET and RESET Attacks

In a Double Feedback XOR-CHAIN structure, it can be shown that if the scan-chain is initially RESET then the output in the first n rounds will be all 0. Similarly, if the chain is initially SET then the output in the first n rounds will be all 1. This is because, the initial contents of the scan-chain are simply shifted across each flip-flop regardless of whether there is a XOR gate placed infront of it. From Equation (3), we know that the value of $S_i^1 = S_{i-1}^0 \oplus a_i \cdot (S_i^0 \oplus S_{i+1}^0)$. If $a_i = 0$, i.e. if there is no XOR gate before the ith flip-flop, then the content of the $(i-1)^{th}$ flip-flop is simply shifted to the ith flip-flop in the next round. On the other hand, if $a_i = 1$, then we have $S_i^1 = S_{i-1}^0 \oplus S_i^0 \oplus S_{i+1}^0$. If the scan-chain is initially RESET i.e. $S_j^0 = 0$, $\forall j$, then the updated value of S_i^1 is also 0 and thus equal to S_{i-1}^0. If the scan-chain is initially SET i.e. $S_j^0 = 1$, $\forall j$, then the updated value of S_i^1 is also $1 \oplus 1 \oplus 1 = 1$ and thus also equal to S_{i-1}^0. In either event, the initial values of the flip-flops (whether all SET or RESET) are shifted across the chain and this is the output obtained in the first n rounds. Thus it is clear that in both attack scenarios no meaningful information about the vector $[a_1, a_2, \ldots, a_{n-1}]$ can be obtained from the first n scanned-out bits. Thus the attacker must look at the output bits $y_{n+1}, y_{n+2}, \ldots$ in hope of deducing $[a_1, a_2, \ldots, a_{n-1}]$. From equation (4), we have

$$\mathcal{S}_n = \mathcal{A}^n \cdot \mathcal{S}_0 \oplus \mathcal{A}^{n-1} \cdot X_1 \oplus \mathcal{A}^{n-2} \cdot X_2 \oplus \cdots \oplus \mathcal{A} \cdot X_{n-1} \oplus X_n.$$

Note that $\mathcal{S}_0$ is the all 1 or the all 0 column vector in the case of SET or RESET attack respectively. From Theorem 3, we have $Y^T = [y_{n+1}, y_{n+2}, \ldots, y_{2n}]^T = \mathcal{C} \cdot \mathcal{S}_n$. Note that, $\mathcal{A}^n, \mathcal{A}^{n-1}, \ldots, \mathcal{A}$ are dense $n \times n$ matrices over the polynomial ring $GF(2)[a_1, a_2, \ldots, a_{n-1}]$. The relation $Y^T = \mathcal{C} \cdot \mathcal{S}_n$ gives rise to n equations of degree $n-1$ each in $a_1, a_2, \ldots, a_{n-1}$. Solving such a system of equations does not seem to be easier than simply guessing the values $[a_1, a_2, \ldots, a_{n-1}]$ or breaking the cipher itself.

6   Conclusion

Although, scan-chains are a valuable tool to test an electrical device for faults, deployment of such scan-chains without having proper countermeasures in place can provide an attacker with a potent side channel to cryptanalyze the underlying cryptosystem. In this paper we outline a strategy to perform a scan-based side channel attack on MICKEY 2.0 that is independent of the actual implementation of the cipher. We then show that the XOR-CHAIN mechanism which was proposed in [2], is vulnerable to the SET attack. As a countermeasure we propose the Double Feedback XOR-CHAIN structure that resists the SET and RESET attacks. We have also presented detailed analysis, showing that such a structure may indeed be used for DFT purposes.

References

1. The ECRYPT Stream Cipher Project. eSTREAM Portfolio of Stream Ciphers (revised on September 8, 2008)
2. Agrawal, M., Karmakar, S., Saha, D., Mukhopadhyay, D.: Scan Based Side Channel Attacks on Stream Ciphers and Their Counter-Measures. In: Chowdhury, D.R., Rijmen, V., Das, A. (eds.) INDOCRYPT 2008. LNCS, vol. 5365, pp. 226–238. Springer, Heidelberg (2008)
3. Babbage, S., Dodd, M.: The stream cipher MICKEY 2.0. ECRYPT Stream Cipher Project Report, http://www.ecrypt.eu.org/stream/p3ciphers/mickey/mickey_p3.pdf
4. Babbage, S., Dodd, M.: The stream cipher MICKEY-128 2.0. ECRYPT Stream Cipher Project Report, http://www.ecrypt.eu.org/stream/p3ciphers/mickey/mickey128_p3.pdf
5. Banik, S., Maitra, S.: A Differential Fault Attack on MICKEY 2.0. IACR Cryptology ePrint Archive 2013: 29
6. Bulens, P., Kalach, K., Standaert, F.X., Quisquater, J.J.: FPGA Implementations of eSTREAM Phase-2 Focus Candidates with Hardware Profile, http://www.ecrypt.eu.org/stream/papersdir/2007/024.pdf
7. Cid, C., Robshaw, M. (eds.): S. Babbage, J. Borghoff and V. Velichkov (Contributors) The eSTREAM Portfolio in 2012, (January 16, 2012), Version 1.0, http://www.ecrypt.eu.org/documents/D.SYM.10-v1.pdf
8. De Cannière, C., Preneel, B.: Trivium Specifications, http://www.ecrypt.eu.org/stream/p3ciphers/trivium/trivium_p3.pdf
9. Floyd, T.L.: Digital Fundamentals, 10th edn. Prentice Hall (2009)
10. Gaj, K., Southern, G., Bachimanchi, R.: Comparison of hardware performance of selected Phase II eSTREAM candidates, http://www.ecrypt.eu.org/stream/papersdir/2007/026.pdf

11. Gierlichs, B., Batina, L., Clavier, C., Eisenbarth, T., Gouget, A., Handschuh, H., Kasper, T., Lemke-Rust, K., Mangard, S., Moradi, A., Oswald, E.: Susceptibility of eSTREAM Candidates towards Side Channel Analysis. In: Proceedings of SASC 2008 (2008), http://www.ecrypt.eu.org/stvl/sasc2008/

12. Good, T., Benaissa, M.: Hardware performance of eStream phase-III stream cipher candidates, http://www.ecrypt.eu.org/stream/docs/hardware.pdf

13. Helleseth, T., Jansen, C.J.A., Kazymyrov, O., Kholosha, A.: State space cryptanalysis of the MICKEY cipher. In: 2013 Information Theory and Applications Workshop, Catamaran Resort, San Diego, February 10-15 (2013)

14. Hong, J., Kim, W.-H.: TMD-Tradeoff and State Entropy Loss Considerations of stream cipher MICKEY. In: Maitra, S., Veni Madhavan, C.E., Venkatesan, R. (eds.) INDOCRYPT 2005. LNCS, vol. 3797, pp. 169–182. Springer, Heidelberg (2005)

15. Kitsos, P.: On the Hardware Implementation of the MICKEY-128 Stream Cipher, http://www.ecrypt.eu.org/stream/papersdir/2006/059.pdf

16. Sengar, G., Mukhopadhyay, D., Chowdhury, D.R.: Secured flipped scan-chain model for crypto-architecture. IEEE Transactions on CAD of Integrated Circuits and Systems 26(11), 2080–2084 (2007)

17. Rogawski, M.: Hardware evaluation of eSTREAM Candidates: Grain, Lex, Mickey128, Salsa20 and Trivium, http://www.ecrypt.eu.org/stream/papersdir/2006/015.pdf

18. Tischhauser, E.: Nonsmooth cryptanalysis, with an application to the stream cipher MICKEY. Journal of Mathematical Cryptology 4(4), 317–348 (2011)

19. Yang, B., Wu, K., Karri, R.: Secure scan-chain: a design-for-test architecture for crypto-chips. IEEE Transactions on CAD of Integrated Circuits and Systems 25(10), 2287–2293 (2006)

20. Yang, B., Wu, K., Karri, R.: Scan based side channel attack on dedicated hardware implementations of data encryption standard. In: ITC 2004, pp. 339–344 (2004)

Appendix A: Set of IVs to Ascertain the Location of the Internal State Bits

Table 1. Set A_k of IVs which can determine the location of the kth LSB of counter register (The IVs are of the form 0^i. The values of i are listed in the table.)

k^{th} LSB of counter	Set A_k of IVs to find k^{th} LSB
0th bit (LSB):	3, 5, 7, 9, 11, 13, 15, 17
1st bit:	3, 7, 11, 15, 19, 23, 27, 31
2nd bit:	4, 12, 20, 28, 36, 44, 52, 60
3rd bit:	8, 9, 10, 11, 12, 13, 14, 15
4th bit:	16, 17, 18, 19, 20, 21, 22, 23
5th bit:	32, 33, 34, 35, 36, 37, 38, 39
6th bit:	64, 65, 66, 67, 68, 69, 70, 71

Table 2. The Set A_χ of IVs which can determine the location of the bits of Registers R, S. (The IVs are of the form 0^i. The values of i are listed in the table.)

i	Set A_χ of IVs to find $R[i]$	Set A_χ of IVs to find $S[i]$
0	3, 10, 11, 12, 14, 16, 17, 19, 20, 21, 22, 25, 26, 29, 30, 31, 34, 35, 36, 37	13, 16, 19, 22, 23, 25, 27, 28, 29, 33, 34, 36, 37, 38, 40
1	3, 4, 10, 12, 13, 16, 18, 22, 23, 25, 27, 28, 29, 31, 32, 34, 36	13, 14, 16, 17, 19, 20, 21, 22, 23, 25, 26, 27, 30, 31, 33, 34, 36, 39
2	4, 5, 6, 7, 11, 12, 14, 15, 17, 19, 23, 24, 26, 28, 29, 32, 33, 34, 37, 38, 39	13, 14, 16, 17, 19, 21, 24, 25, 26, 27, 29, 31, 32, 35, 36, 37, 38
3	3, 5, 7, 8, 10, 11, 14, 15, 18, 21, 22, 24, 27, 28, 30, 31, 33, 34, 39, 40	14, 17, 19, 22, 23, 26, 28, 30, 32, 33, 36, 39
4	3, 4, 6, 7, 8, 9, 10, 12, 14, 15, 20, 21, 28, 31, 32, 35, 36, 37, 40	1, 4, 7, 10, 16, 18, 21, 22, 23, 24, 26, 27, 28, 30, 31, 33, 35, 36, 37, 39
5	3, 4, 5, 6, 8, 9, 11, 12, 13, 19, 20, 22, 25, 26, 33, 36	2, 4, 5, 8, 10, 11, 13, 15, 16, 17, 23, 24, 26, 28, 30, 31, 32, 33, 37, 39
6	3, 4, 5, 7, 9, 12, 13, 14, 16, 17, 19, 25, 27, 28, 29, 30, 31, 37	3, 5, 9, 11, 13, 14, 15, 17, 22, 24, 25, 27, 28, 29, 31, 32, 36, 38, 39, 40
7	4, 5, 8, 10, 11, 12, 14, 17, 18, 19, 20, 26, 28, 29, 31, 38, 39	4, 5, 6, 7, 10, 11, 12, 14, 16, 17, 18, 26, 28, 30, 32, 33, 34, 38, 39, 40
8	5, 9, 11, 13, 14, 18, 20, 21, 22, 23, 27, 28, 29, 32, 39, 40	5, 7, 8, 11, 12, 15, 17, 23, 24, 29, 30, 34, 35, 36, 38, 39
9	3, 6, 7, 12, 16, 17, 20, 22, 23, 24, 25, 26, 28, 30, 31, 33, 38, 39, 40	1, 5, 6, 10, 12, 13, 17, 18, 19, 23, 24, 29, 30, 31, 33, 35, 36, 39, 40
10	4, 7, 8, 13, 14, 15, 17, 18, 19, 21, 22, 24, 25, 27, 28, 29, 30, 32, 34, 35, 36, 37, 38, 40	2, 3, 6, 11, 13, 14, 18, 20, 21, 22, 24, 25, 27, 30, 32, 34, 36, 38, 40
11	5, 6, 7, 8, 9, 14, 16, 17, 18, 20, 22, 25, 28, 29, 31, 32, 33, 34, 36, 38	1, 3, 4, 8, 11, 12, 13, 14, 15, 16, 18, 25, 26, 27, 29, 31, 34, 35, 36, 38, 39, 40
12	3, 6, 8, 9, 13, 16, 18, 19, 20, 25, 30, 31, 32, 33, 34, 37, 39	1, 2, 4, 5, 8, 9, 13, 14, 15, 19, 21, 22, 23 25, 26, 28, 29, 30, 32, 33, 34, 35, 37, 38, 39
13	3, 4, 7, 9, 13, 14, 16, 23, 25, 29, 30, 33, 34, 40	2, 3, 6, 8, 9, 10, 13, 14, 15, 17, 22, 24, 25, 26, 28, 31, 33, 38, 39
14	4, 5, 6, 7, 8, 10, 11, 12, 13, 15, 17, 24, 26, 30, 34	3, 4, 7, 16, 18, 19, 21, 26, 28, 29, 31, 32, 33, 34, 36, 37, 38, 39, 40
15	5, 7, 8, 9, 11, 13, 16, 17, 18, 19, 25, 26, 27, 28, 31, 32, 35, 36, 37, 38, 39	4, 8, 9, 10, 13, 14, 16, 19, 20, 27, 30, 31, 32, 33, 35, 37, 38, 39
16	3, 6, 7, 8, 9, 12, 15, 16, 18, 19, 21, 22, 25, 27, 33, 36, 39, 40	5, 7, 10, 11, 14, 15, 17, 19, 20, 21, 24, 31, 32, 33, 34, 37, 38, 39, 40
17	4, 7, 8, 9, 10, 11, 12, 16, 19, 20, 22, 26, 28, 34, 35, 36, 40	6, 7, 8, 11, 15, 18, 20, 21, 23, 24, 27, 32, 34, 35, 36, 39
18	5, 6, 7, 8, 9, 10, 12, 17, 20, 21, 22, 27, 28, 29, 30, 31, 32, 35, 37, 38, 39	7, 8, 12, 13, 19, 20, 24, 25, 26, 27, 29, 30, 31, 32, 34, 37, 38
19	3, 6, 8, 9, 11, 12, 13, 15, 16, 17, 18, 20, 22, 23, 25, 26, 28, 30, 33, 36, 37, 38, 40	8, 9, 14, 19, 20, 21, 22, 23, 25, 26, 28, 29, 30, 31, 32, 34, 35, 36, 37, 39, 40

Table 2. (Contd.)

i	Set A_χ of IVs to find $R[i]$	Set A_χ of IVs to find $S[i]$
20	3, 4, 7, 9, 12, 13, 14, 17, 18, 19, 20, 24, 25, 27, 28, 31, 37, 38	9, 15, 19, 20, 22, 24, 25, 26, 27, 29, 31, 32, 35, 40
21	3, 4, 5, 6, 7, 8, 16, 17, 18, 19, 23, 26, 28, 34, 35, 36, 37, 38	1, 5, 9, 10, 12, 16, 20, 21, 23, 26, 29, 30, 33, 35, 36, 37, 38
22	3, 4, 5, 7, 8, 9, 10, 11, 12, 14, 16, 18, 19, 21, 22, 24, 25, 26, 27, 28, 32, 34, 36, 39	2, 3, 6, 7, 10, 13, 14, 15, 16, 17, 19, 21, 23, 24, 25, 26, 30, 33, 36, 39, 40
23	4, 5, 8, 9, 10, 12, 15, 17, 19, 20, 22, 25, 27, 29, 30, 31, 32, 33, 34, 37, 38, 39, 40	3, 4, 7, 8, 11, 16, 17, 18, 19, 20, 23, 24, 26, 28, 29, 31, 36, 38, 40
24	5, 9, 10, 13, 14, 15, 16, 17, 18, 19, 20, 21 22, 26, 28, 30, 32, 33, 35, 36, 37, 39, 40	4, 8, 12, 13, 14, 15, 16, 17, 18, 20, 23, 24, 29, 32, 38, 39
25	3, 6, 7, 11, 12, 17, 18, 19, 22, 23, 25, 26, 27, 28, 31, 33, 34, 35, 37, 38, 39, 40	5, 7, 9, 11, 16, 17, 18, 21, 23, 24, 27, 34, 36, 37, 38, 39, 40
26	4, 7, 8, 12, 18, 20, 23, 24, 26, 27, 29, 30, 31, 34, 36, 37, 39, 40	6, 7, 10, 11, 12, 13, 14, 16, 17, 18, 23, 24, 27, 29, 33, 35, 39, 40
27	5, 6, 7, 8, 9, 13, 14, 15, 19, 21, 22, 23, 24, 25, 26, 27, 30, 32, 35, 36, 38, 39, 40	1, 4, 9, 11, 12, 14, 15, 16, 17, 18, 20, 22, 23, 24, 26, 27, 29, 30, 36, 37, 38
28	3, 6, 8, 9, 13, 14, 15, 19, 21, 24, 26, 27, 29, 30, 32, 33, 36, 38, 40	2, 5, 10, 11, 13, 14, 15, 16, 17, 18, 21, 24, 28, 29, 30, 31, 33, 34, 39
29	4, 7, 9, 10, 11, 12, 13, 15, 16, 17, 20, 22, 23, 25, 26, 27, 30, 33, 37, 38	2, 3, 5, 6, 8, 12, 14, 15, 16, 17, 18, 19 21, 22, 24, 25, 27, 29, 30, 31, 32, 34, 35, 39, 40
30	5, 6, 7, 8, 10, 12, 14, 15, 16, 18, 19, 21, 22, 24, 26, 27, 31, 32, 34, 35, 36, 37, 39	1, 3, 4, 6, 7, 10, 16, 17, 18, 19, 20, 22, 23, 25, 26, 34, 35, 38
31	6, 8, 9, 11, 12, 15, 16, 19, 20, 22, 25, 26, 27, 32, 33, 34, 36, 38, 39, 40	2, 3, 4, 5, 7, 11, 12, 13, 17, 20, 24, 26, 27, 33, 35, 36, 38, 39
32	7, 9, 10, 11, 13, 14, 15, 16, 20, 21, 22, 26, 27, 33, 35, 36, 39, 40	1, 3, 4, 5, 6, 8, 13, 14, 16, 18, 19, 23, 27, 32, 33, 35, 37, 38, 39
33	8, 10, 12, 13, 15, 16, 21, 23, 27, 34, 35, 37, 38, 39, 40	2, 3, 4, 5, 7, 8, 9, 10, 13, 15, 17, 18, 19, 22, 23, 24, 25, 29, 30, 33, 38
34	9, 11, 12, 14, 15, 16, 22, 23, 24, 28, 35, 38, 40	3, 4, 6, 8, 10, 11, 14, 16, 18, 20, 23, 25, 26, 30, 31, 32, 33, 39
35	10, 11, 13, 14, 16, 23, 24, 25, 26, 29, 30, 31, 32, 36, 37, 38	4, 5, 8, 9, 15, 18, 19, 21, 23, 24, 27, 29, 31, 32, 33, 34, 36, 38
36	11, 14, 17, 24, 25, 27, 28, 30, 32, 33, 34, 35, 36, 38	5, 6, 7, 9, 10, 11, 16, 17, 18, 19, 22, 23, 25, 28, 29, 32, 33, 35, 36, 37, 38, 39, 40
37	3, 10, 11, 13, 16, 17, 18, 20, 21, 22, 26, 28, 31, 33, 34, 36, 38	6, 8, 10, 12, 13, 14, 16, 17, 19, 20, 21, 22 23, 24, 26, 27, 28, 29, 33, 34, 35, 37, 39, 40
38	3, 4, 10, 12, 15, 16, 18, 19, 20, 22, 23, 25, 26, 27, 28, 35, 36, 38	7, 8, 9, 11, 12, 14, 15, 16, 18, 19, 21, 22, 23, 24, 25, 27, 30, 31, 35, 36, 38
39	4, 5, 6, 7, 11, 12, 16, 19, 20, 21, 22, 24, 26, 27, 29, 30, 31, 32, 36, 39	8, 9, 12, 13, 14, 15, 17, 20, 22, 23, 24, 25, 27, 31, 32, 36, 38
40	5, 7, 8, 12, 17, 20, 21, 23, 25, 26, 27, 30, 32, 33, 34, 35, 36, 40	9, 13, 15, 18, 19, 21, 22, 24, 25, 27, 28, 29, 32, 33, 34, 38
41	3, 6, 7, 8, 9, 10, 11, 12, 13, 15, 16, 17, 18 20, 22, 24, 25, 27, 29, 30, 32, 33, 34, 36, 38, 39	10, 14, 16, 17, 18, 19, 22, 26, 27, 29, 30, 31, 34, 35, 36, 37, 39
42	3, 4, 7, 8, 9, 11, 15, 17, 18, 19, 20, 26, 28, 29, 31, 33, 34, 37, 39, 40	11, 15, 16, 17, 18, 19, 20, 23, 27, 30, 32, 33, 35, 37, 40
43	4, 5, 6, 7, 8, 9, 10, 11, 16, 17, 18, 20, 21, 22, 23, 27, 28, 29, 32, 34, 38, 39, 40	1, 5, 8, 11, 12, 14, 16, 17, 18, 19, 20, 21, 23, 24, 26, 31, 33, 34, 36
44	5, 7, 8, 9, 10, 12, 13, 14, 15, 17, 18, 21, 23, 24, 28, 29, 33, 34, 39, 40	2, 3, 6, 9, 12, 15, 17, 20, 21, 23, 24, 28, 29, 30, 32, 35, 38, 39, 40
45	3, 6, 7, 8, 9, 11, 12, 13, 14, 15, 18, 19, 20, 21, 23, 24, 30, 31, 35, 36, 37, 40	3, 4, 6, 7, 9, 10, 12, 18, 20, 21, 23, 24, 25, 27, 28, 30, 31, 39,
46	3, 4, 7, 8, 9, 12, 13, 14, 15, 22, 24, 29, 30, 34, 35, 37, 38, 39	4, 5, 6, 8, 10, 11, 12, 19, 20, 22, 23, 24, 25, 26, 27, 28, 31, 32, 33, 40,
47	4, 5, 6, 7, 8, 9, 10, 11, 12, 14, 16, 17, 23, 25, 26, 30, 35, 38, 40	5, 6, 7, 11, 12, 16, 18, 19, 20, 21, 22, 26, 28, 32, 34, 38,
48	5, 7, 8, 9, 10, 12, 15, 17, 18, 19, 24, 26, 27, 28, 31, 32, 36, 37, 38	6, 7, 8, 12, 16, 17, 19, 20, 21, 23, 27, 33, 35, 36, 39, 40,
49	6, 7, 8, 9, 10, 13, 14, 15, 16, 17, 18, 20, 25, 26, 27, 29, 30, 31, 33, 34, 35, 36, 38	1, 4, 10, 14, 26, 27, 28, 31, 33, 34, 37, 38,
50	3, 7, 8, 9, 11, 12, 17, 18, 19, 20, 23, 25, 27, 29, 31, 32, 35, 37, 39	2, 5, 11, 15, 27, 29, 32, 33, 34, 38,
51	4, 8, 9, 10, 11, 13, 14, 15, 18, 20, 21, 22 23, 24, 26, 28, 30, 31, 33, 34, 35, 38, 39, 40	3, 6, 12, 16, 17, 18, 19, 20, 21, 23, 25, 27, 30, 31, 32, 34, 37, 38,
52	3, 5, 6, 7, 9, 11, 13, 14, 15, 20, 22, 23, 24, 27, 28, 31, 32, 35, 38, 40	4, 7, 16, 17, 19, 20, 24, 26, 27, 29, 30, 31, 33, 34, 36, 38, 40,
53	4, 6, 8, 10, 11, 14, 16, 17, 21, 22, 24, 25, 26, 28, 29, 30, 31, 33, 34, 35, 39	5, 6, 8, 9, 17, 20, 25, 26, 28, 29, 31, 32, 34, 37, 38,
54	3, 5, 6, 9, 10, 12, 14, 15, 16, 18, 20, 21, 26, 27, 28, 30, 35, 38, 39, 40	6, 7, 9, 10, 18, 19, 23, 27, 31, 32, 35, 39,
55	4, 6, 10, 13, 14, 16, 19, 21, 27, 29, 30, 36, 37, 38, 40	7, 10, 19, 20, 24, 25, 26, 27, 28, 29, 30, 32, 36, 40
56	3, 5, 6, 10, 13, 14, 15, 16, 19, 21, 23, 25, 26, 28, 29, 31, 34, 35, 36, 39	1, 5, 8, 12, 13, 15, 16, 18, 19, 20, 21, 22, 23, 27, 30, 31, 33, 34, 36
57	4, 6, 11, 12, 13, 15, 16, 20, 22, 23, 24, 26, 27, 28, 29, 32, 35, 37, 38, 39, 40	2, 3, 6, 7, 9, 13, 16, 20, 21, 24, 27, 28, 29, 31, 33, 35, 36, 38,
58	3, 5, 6, 10, 11, 15, 17, 19, 20, 24, 27, 30, 31, 33, 36, 37, 38, 40	3, 7, 8, 9, 14, 17, 19, 20, 22, 27, 29, 32, 34, 36, 37, 38
59	4, 6, 11, 16, 17, 18, 19, 20, 21, 22, 23, 25, 26, 28, 31, 34, 35, 36, 38	3, 4, 6, 8, 9, 10, 12, 13, 16, 19, 20, 21, 22, 24, 25, 27, 29, 30, 32, 35, 36, 38, 39, 40

Table 2. (Contd.)

i	Set A_χ of IVs to find $R[i]$	Set A_χ of IVs to find $S[i]$
60	3, 5, 6, 10, 11, 13, 15, 16, 18, 19, 22, 23, 24, 25, 27, 28, 34, 36, 38	2, 5, 9, 10, 11, 14, 16, 17, 21, 22, 23, 30, 31, 33, 35, 36, 37, 39, 40
61	3, 4, 6, 10, 12, 15, 17, 21, 22, 23, 24, 26, 28, 32, 34, 37, 39	1, 3, 5, 6, 9, 10, 11, 12, 14, 15, 19, 21, 22, 24, 25, 27, 34, 36, 39, 40,
62	4, 5, 6, 11, 12, 16, 17, 18, 19, 22, 24, 25, 26, 27, 28, 29, 30, 31, 32, 33, 34, 38, 39, 40	1, 2, 5, 6, 7, 10, 11, 12, 15, 18, 21, 23, 25, 26, 28, 29, 33, 34, 35, 36, 37, 39
63	3, 5, 7, 10, 11, 14, 16, 18, 19, 21, 22, 23, 26, 27, 30, 33, 34, 38, 40	2, 6, 8, 9, 11, 13, 14, 16, 22, 23, 24, 26, 29, 30, 31, 33, 35, 40
64	3, 4, 6, 7, 8, 10, 12, 14, 15, 16, 21, 24, 25, 26, 27, 29, 30, 32, 35, 36, 37, 39	3, 4, 7, 9, 12, 14, 16, 22, 23, 25, 26, 28, 29, 31, 40,
65	3, 4, 5, 6, 8, 9, 10, 14, 15, 17, 19, 20, 21, 23, 26, 27, 29, 31, 33, 36, 40	1, 4, 5, 7, 8, 11, 18, 19, 21, 22, 27, 28, 30, 35, 36, 37, 38
66	3, 4, 5, 7, 9, 11, 12, 14, 15, 18, 22, 24, 25, 26, 27, 29, 37	2, 3, 5, 8, 12, 13, 19, 22, 28, 29, 30, 36, 38,
67	3, 4, 5, 8, 12, 13, 20, 21, 22, 23, 26, 27, 29, 32, 34, 35, 36, 37, 38, 39	3, 4, 9, 11, 13, 14, 20, 28, 31, 33, 34, 37
68	4, 5, 9, 13, 21, 23, 24, 27, 30, 31, 32, 33, 34, 36, 38, 40	4, 5, 10, 12, 13, 14, 15, 21, 22, 29, 32, 34, 35, 38, 39, 40
69	5, 10, 11, 12, 13, 22, 23, 24, 25, 26, 28, 31, 33, 35, 36, 39	2, 4, 5, 6, 8, 10, 11, 13, 14, 15, 17, 19, 22, 23, 25, 27, 28, 29, 30, 32, 33, 34, 35, 37
70	6, 7, 11, 13, 23, 24, 25, 27, 28, 29, 30, 31, 34, 35, 37, 38, 39, 40	1, 3, 5, 6, 7, 9, 11, 12, 14, 15, 16, 18, 21, 23, 24, 26, 28, 29, 30, 31, 33, 34, 35, 36, 38,
71	3, 7, 8, 10, 11, 13, 14, 16, 17, 19, 20, 21, 22, 24, 26, 28, 31, 32, 34, 35, 36, 37, 39,	1, 2, 4, 6, 7, 8, 10, 12, 13, 15, 16, 17, 21, 22, 24, 25, 27, 31, 32, 34, 35, 36, 37, 39,
72	3, 4, 8, 9, 10, 12, 16, 18, 22, 23, 27, 28, 31, 34, 37, 38	1, 2, 3, 5, 7, 8, 9, 11, 13, 14, 19, 22, 23, 25, 26, 30, 32, 33, 34, 35, 37, 38
73	4, 5, 6, 7, 9, 10, 13, 14, 15, 17, 19, 23, 24, 28, 29, 30, 31, 35, 36, 37, 39	3, 4, 6, 8, 9, 10, 14, 15, 19, 20, 22, 23, 24, 27, 31, 34, 35, 36, 38, 39,
74	5, 7, 8, 10, 14, 16, 17, 18, 19, 20, 24, 25, 26, 29, 31, 36, 38, 39, 40	1, 11, 14, 15, 18, 20, 21, 22, 23, 24, 25, 31, 32, 35, 39
75	6, 7, 8, 9, 11, 12, 13, 14, 17, 18, 20, 21, 22, 23, 25, 27, 28, 30, 31, 37, 38, 40,	1, 2, 5, 7, 10, 14, 15, 16, 19, 21, 22, 26, 27, 29, 31, 32, 34, 37, 38, 40,
76	7, 8, 9, 10, 11, 13, 15, 18, 21, 23, 24, 26, 28, 29, 30, 32, 38	1, 2, 3, 7, 8, 12, 17, 20, 24, 25, 31, 32, 36, 37, 39
77	8, 9, 10, 12, 13, 16, 17, 19, 22, 23, 24, 25, 26, 27, 28, 29, 31, 32, 33, 34, 35, 36, 37, 38	1, 2, 3, 4, 7, 8, 9, 12, 13, 16, 19, 22, 24, 25, 26, 28, 31, 32, 33, 36, 37, 38
78	9, 10, 13, 17, 18, 19, 20, 23, 24, 25, 27, 29, 32, 33, 35, 37, 39	2, 3, 5, 8, 10, 14, 16, 19, 22, 26, 28, 29, 32, 33, 34, 36, 37, 38, 40,
79	3, 11, 12, 15, 16, 17, 18, 19, 23, 24, 26, 28, 29, 32, 33, 34, 35, 40	3, 4, 6, 8, 9, 13, 15, 16, 17, 19, 20, 27, 28, 30, 32, 33, 35, 36, 37, 38, 39, 40
80	3, 4, 10, 11, 14, 17, 18, 19, 21, 22, 24, 27, 28, 30, 31, 33, 34, 36, 37	4, 7, 9, 10, 13, 17, 18, 19, 21, 22, 31, 33, 37, 38, 39
81	3, 4, 5, 6, 7, 10, 12, 14, 15, 16, 17, 18, 19, 21, 28, 31, 32, 35, 36	1, 4, 5, 12, 13, 14, 16, 18, 19, 20, 25, 27, 28, 29, 35, 36
82	3, 4, 5, 7, 8, 10, 14, 15, 17, 18, 19, 21, 23, 25, 26, 33, 36, 38, 39	2, 4, 5, 6, 8, 12, 13, 14, 15, 17, 19, 20, 21, 23, 27, 28, 29, 30, 32, 33, 36, 39
83	4, 5, 8, 9, 11, 12, 13, 14, 16, 17, 18, 20, 22, 23, 24, 26, 27, 28, 34, 35, 36, 39, 40	3, 6, 7, 11, 13, 14, 15, 18, 19, 20, 21, 23, 24, 25, 29, 30, 31, 33, 37, 38, 40,
84	5, 9, 10, 11, 13, 15, 17, 18, 21, 22, 24, 25, 26, 27, 29, 30, 31, 32, 35, 37, 38, 39, 40	3, 4, 6, 7, 8, 10, 12, 13, 14, 15, 21, 23, 24, 25, 26, 28, 29, 30, 31, 32, 35, 36, 38, 39, 40
85	6, 7, 10, 12, 13, 16, 17, 18, 22, 25, 27, 30, 32, 33, 34, 35, 38, 40	2, 5, 7, 8, 9, 13, 14, 15, 18, 19, 22, 23, 24, 28, 30, 31, 32, 34, 36, 38, 39
86	7, 8, 11, 12, 14, 15, 17, 18, 23, 26, 28, 31, 32, 33, 35, 39	1, 3, 7, 8, 9, 10, 12, 13, 14, 15, 17, 21, 22, 25, 28, 30, 31, 32, 35, 36, 39
87	3, 8, 9, 10, 11, 14, 15, 18, 19, 20, 21, 22, 24, 25, 26, 27, 28, 33, 34, 35, 38, 39, 40	2, 3, 4, 8, 10, 14, 18, 25, 27, 28, 31, 34, 35, 38, 39,
88	3, 4, 9, 11, 13, 22, 23, 26, 27, 32, 35, 38, 40	1, 3, 4, 5, 9, 12, 16, 20, 23, 27, 28, 29, 33, 35, 36, 39, 40,
89	3, 4, 5, 6, 7, 12, 15, 16, 17, 19, 20, 21, 22, 23, 24, 25, 26, 27, 29, 30, 31, 33, 36, 37, 39	2, 4, 5, 6, 7, 8, 9, 13, 17, 21, 24, 28, 30, 34, 35, 37, 38, 40
90	3, 4, 5, 7, 8, 10, 11, 12, 13, 15, 17, 18, 22, 23, 24, 26, 27, 29, 31, 32, 37, 38, 39, 40	3, 6, 7, 8, 9, 10, 14, 16, 22, 23, 25, 28, 29, 31, 34, 35, 36, 37, 39
91	3, 4, 5, 8, 9, 10, 12, 13, 14, 18, 19, 20, 21, 22, 23, 24, 27, 29, 33, 39, 40	4, 7, 8, 10, 15, 17, 18, 24, 26, 27, 29, 32, 33, 35, 40,
92	3, 4, 5, 9, 11, 12, 13, 14, 15, 16, 17, 22, 23, 24, 28, 29, 32, 38, 39, 40	5, 6, 8, 9, 10, 11, 16, 17, 18, 23, 24, 28, 29, 30, 31, 34, 35, 36, 38, 39
93	4, 5, 10, 11, 13, 15, 16, 18, 19, 23, 24, 25, 26, 29, 33, 34, 35, 36, 37, 38, 40	6, 7, 8, 10, 11, 17, 18, 24, 25, 26, 29, 31, 35, 37, 39
94	3, 5, 10, 12, 15, 17, 21, 22, 24, 26, 27, 28, 29, 32, 35, 37, 38	7, 8, 11, 12, 16, 18, 22, 25, 27, 29, 30, 31, 34, 35, 36, 38, 39, 40
95	3, 4, 6, 7, 10, 14, 18, 20, 21, 27, 30, 31, 33, 36, 37, 38	8, 12, 17, 18, 25, 27, 30, 31, 32, 33, 34, 35, 38, 39
96	3, 4, 5, 6, 8, 10, 13, 16, 17, 20, 22, 25, 26, 28, 29, 30, 37, 38	9, 10, 13, 18, 23, 24, 26, 28, 29, 30, 31, 32, 34, 36, 38, 40
97	3, 4, 5, 7, 9, 10, 13, 14, 16, 18, 20, 25, 27, 28, 30, 32, 34, 35, 36, 37, 38	10, 11, 13, 14, 16, 18, 19, 21, 25, 30, 31, 32, 33
98	4, 5, 8, 10, 14, 17, 19, 21, 22, 23, 26, 28, 29, 30, 33, 34, 36, 38	11, 12, 14, 15, 17, 20, 23, 25, 26, 28, 31, 32, 33, 34, 36, 38, 40
99	5, 9, 11, 12, 13, 14, 18, 19, 20, 22, 24, 27, 28, 29, 31, 32, 34, 37, 38	12, 15, 18, 21, 22, 24, 26, 27, 28, 32, 33, 35, 36, 37, 39, 40

Correlation Analysis against Protected SFM Implementations of RSA

Aurélie Bauer and Éliane Jaulmes

ANSSI
51, boulevard de La Tour-Maubourg
75700 PARIS-07 SP
{Aurelie.Bauer,Eliane.Jaulmes}@ssi.gouv.fr

Abstract. Since Kocher's first attacks in 1996, the field of side-channel analysis has widely developed, and new statistical tools have competed against new countermeasures to threaten cryptosystems. Among existing algorithms, RSA has always been a privileged target. It seems generally admitted that a combination of SPA protection such as regular exponentiation associated with blinding techniques such as randomization of the exponent and of the input message offers in practice sufficient protection against all known side-channel attacks. Indeed, known attacks either require building statistical information over several executions of the algorithm, which is countered by exponent randomization, or rely on partial SPA leakage, which implies an incorrect implementation of known countermeasures, or require specific internal knowledge of the implementation and hard-to-obtain experimental conditions, as for the recent horizontal correlation analysis of Clavier *et al.* [10]. In this paper, we show that it is possible to attack a state-of-the-art implementation of Straightforward Method (SFM) RSA. Our attack requires a small public exponent (no greater than $2^{16} + 1$) and a reasonable exponent blinding factor (no greater than 32 bits). It does not require additional internal knowledge of the implementation, neither does it have special experimental requirements. From a practical point of view, it thus compares with classical correlation analysis. We provide simulations of our attack demonstrating its efficiency, even in noisy scenarios. This shows that SFM implementations of RSA may be much more difficult to protect against side-channel attacks than CRT implementations.

Keywords: Side-Channel Attacks, Correlation Power Analysis, Collision Correlation Power Analysis, RSA scheme, Exponent Blinding, Message Blinding.

1 Introduction

Physical components included in embedded systems may leak information on data manipulated throughout cryptographic computations. *Side-channel analysis*, which was first introduced by Kocher *et al.* [17] in 1996, exploits such leakages and retrieves information on the secret parameters. This field covers nowadays a large range of statistical and cryptanalytic techniques such as timing attacks [17], simple power analysis (SPA) [17], differential power analysis (DPA) [18], correlation power analysis (CPA) [7], mutual information analysis (MIA) [3, 14] and many others.

G. Paul and S. Vaudenay (Eds.): INDOCRYPT 2013, LNCS 8250, pp. 98–115, 2013.

To counter these threats, research has been focusing on devising implementations that are resistant to side-channel analysis. While there exists generic countermeasures designed such that they can protect any given implementation (for instance clock jitter), most of them stay dedicated to specific algorithms or particular operations. One set of countermeasures still widely used up to now in the public key setting, is that introduced by Coron [11] in 1999.

Focusing on the well-known RSA scheme, it can be seen that the modular exponentiation phase, which consists in raising a given message to a secret exponent modulo a public integer, is a promising target for side-channel attackers. An unprotected RSA implementation can easily be threatened by a simple power analysis (SPA) where only one power curve is sufficient to recover the whole secret key. Thus, implementing RSA while avoiding classical side-channel attacks requires a set of well-chosen countermeasures. A first idea is to use a regular exponentiation, for example the "Square-and-Multiply Always" algorithm [11], the Montgomery ladder [16], the Joye ladder [15] or the atomic Square-and-Multiply exponentiation [8]. These techniques allow to proceed the same operations independently from the value of the key bits. Among all these solutions, the later one is often preferred due to its efficiency. Obviously these countermeasures offer protection against SPA, but are not sufficient to protect the scheme against more advanced attacks such as DPA or CPA [7, 18]. Those methods exploit leakage information from several executions of the algorithm and use statistical tools to extract the secret information. As a consequence, protecting the scheme against those kinds of attacks requires to execute the algorithm differently from one call to the next. Random values should thus be added to the computation, either in the secret exponent, which refers to the technique called "Exponent Blinding", or in the original message, namely using "Message Blinding".

In this work, we focus on SPA-resistant RSA implementations that use both exponent blinding and message blinding. As far as we are aware, this scenario represents the academic state of the art of secure RSA implementations. In fact, there are few side-channel attacks that threaten this scheme [9,10,12,13,19–23] and they apply only in particular settings. Indeed, the attack performed by Walter [22] on RSA with small public exponent, the one proposed by Fouque *et al.* [12] or the recent attack of Schindler and Itoh [19], all require partial SPA leakage exploitable on a single power curve. In Walter's Big-Mac attack [20] and Clavier *et al.* [9, 10] horizontal correlation analysis the authors exploit leakage information coming from each of the elementary operations involved in the Long Integer Multiplication. These attacks are very powerful but may be difficult to apply in practice. Indeed, they require to obtain additional internal information such as detailed knowledge of the implementation of the modular multiplication. Moreover, the adversary should also work with experimental tools of high quality as this attack requires a huge memory on the acquisition device and a precise timing to separately observe the leakage corresponding to each register operation.

In This Paper. We propose a side-channel attack against SPA-resistant SFM-RSA[1] scheme, implemented using both message blinding and exponent blinding. This attack can be seen as an alternative to Clavier *et al.* ROSETTA attack [9], where no specific information concerning the implementation of the modular multiplication is required. In fact, it exploits only general leakage information

---

[1] As mentioned before, SFM stands for Straightforward Method, *i.e.* a non-CRT implementation of RSA.

from each modular operation and does not assume high end metrology. Moreover, no additional SPA leakage is needed that could allow the attacker to distinguish multiplications from squaring operations on a unique power curve. Our attack is described on the Square-and-Multiply always algorithm and on the atomic Square-and-Multiply implementation of the exponentiation, but it also works for other choices of algorithms. It applies when the exponent masking technique suggested by Coron [11] is used and for any kind of message blinding. It works for small public exponents. The masking factor used for exponent randomization should either be less than 32-bit long or reduced in this range through fault injection.[2]

The paper is organised as follows. Section 2 recalls some basic notions related to the RSA scheme with exponent blinding and message blinding, and gives statistical definitions required for correlation power analysis. Section 3 presents existing side-channel attacks on RSA implementations using various counter-measures. In Section 4, we describe our attack against protected RSA implementations for a public exponent e equal to 3 and known inputs. In Section 5, we explain how to adapt this attack when the input is blinded by using the collision correlation technique [23]. Then Section 6 provides simulation results for various signal-to-noise ratios. Section 7 concludes the analysis.

2   Preliminaries

2.1   State-of-the-Art Implementation of RSA

Description. Let N be an n-bit RSA modulus, defined as the product of two large primes p and q. In the sequel, we focus on the *balanced* case meaning that the prime factors p and q are equal-sized. The public exponent e is chosen to be coprime to the Euler's totient function $\phi(N) = (p-1)(q-1)$. The corresponding private key d satisfies the well-known RSA equation $ed \equiv 1 \bmod \phi(N)$. In other words, there exists an integer $k \in \mathbb{Z}$ such that:

$$ed = 1 + k\phi(N) . \tag{1}$$

By definition, the private key satisfies $0 < d < \phi(N)$. Its binary representation is expressed as $d = (d[0] \ldots d[n-1])$, where the least significant bit is referred as $d[0]$ and the most significant one as $d[n-1]$. Note that the variable k verifies $0 < k < e$ since otherwise it would imply $d > \phi(N)$, which is not possible [6].

Implementation. In this paper, we focus on *StraightForward Method* (SFM) implementations of RSA. It means that the decryption of a ciphertext C using the private key d is computed as $C^d \bmod N$. In order to resist "side-channel attacks", several steps must be taken into account to protect the sensitive operations where secrets bits are manipulated. In the particular case of RSA, this concerns the modular exponentiation $C^d \bmod N$, where secrets bits are processed sequentially and combined to the known value C.[3]

---

[2] Even if a 32-bit long masking factor is not recommended, this scenario still corresponds to some implementation designs of RSA on embedded devices.

[3] The attack is presented on a RSA decryption but could also apply on a RSA signature.

The first threat to address is the *Simple Power Analysis* (SPA). In order to resist this attack, the algorithm should behave similarly when the bits of the secret exponent are equal to 0 or 1. Regular algorithms have been designed to address this issue: the well-known *Square-and-Multiply Always* technique, provided in Fig. 1, Algorithm 1 and the *Atomic Square-and-Multiply* method [8], provided in Fig. 1, Algorithm 2, which is one of the most efficient technique. In Section 5, we focus on these two implementations. Other implementations choices are studied in Appendix A.

Algorithm 1. "Square-and-Multiply-Always" (*from left to right*)

$R_0 \leftarrow 1$
for $i = n - 1$ to 0 do
$\quad R_0 \leftarrow R_0^2$
$\quad$ if $d[j] = 1$ then
$\quad \quad R_0 \leftarrow R_0 \cdot C$
$\quad$ else
$\quad \quad R_1 \leftarrow R_0 \cdot C$
return R_0

Algorithm 2. "Atomic Square-and-Multiply" (*from left to right*)

$R_0 \leftarrow 1; R_1 \leftarrow C$
$k \leftarrow 0, i \leftarrow n - 1$
while $i \geq 0$ do
$\quad R_0 \leftarrow R_0 \cdot R_k$
$\quad k \leftarrow k \oplus d[i]$
$\quad i \leftarrow i - \neg k$
return R_0

Fig. 1. Two well-known regular SFM-RSA implementations

Additionally to that SPA-protection, the RSA scheme is also assumed to be implemented using exponent masking. This countermeasure prevents an attacker to gain information on the secret exponent d by studying several power consumption curves corresponding to computations of $C^d \bmod N$, for different values of C. In that case, the adversary could apply a *Differential Power Analysis* (DPA) or use an improved version called *Correlation Power Analysis* (CPA) (further details on this attack are provided in Section 2.2). To prevent such scenarios, the key should be masked before its use inside the modular exponentiation. A suitable idea, originally described by Coron [11], is to blind the exponent d using a random value λ. Thus a new secret key $d^{(i)} = d + \lambda^{(i)} \phi(N)$ is generated, each time the modular exponentiation has to be performed on $C^{(i)}$, with $\lambda^{(i)}$ a random l-bit integer. That way, the decryption (similarly the signature) process is performed as $\left(C^{(i)}\right)^{d^{(i)}} \bmod N$. In our attack, we require l to be no greater than 32. In real implementations, this could be the case for low end devices where generating random bits have a non negligible cost or it could be the result of a fault injection during the generation of $\lambda^{(i)}$ or during the computation of $d^{(i)}$.

Finally, in order to make the scheme fully secure, we also assume that it has been implemented using message blinding. Several techniques have been proposed in the literature, but we will not detail them here, since our attack applies independently from the chosen method.

2.2 Correlation Power Analysis

The attack proposed in this paper against secure SFM-RSA schemes, implemented as described in the previous section, makes use of the *Correlation Power Analysis* technique, introduced in [7]. For the sake of completeness, we remind the basic principle of this method, which can be seen as an extension of the Differential Power Analysis of Kocher *et al.* [18].

As all side-channel attacks, correlation power analysis works by first registering leakage information from the power consumption or electromagnetic emanation of the device during the computation. Such leakage can come from several instants of a single execution, in the case of horizontal power analysis [9,10], or from a single instant of several executions, in the case of classical power analysis [7]. More generally, any combination of the two above is also possible, see for instance a unified description of CPA in both contexts in [4]. In the leakage traces, the attacker needs to identify the *points of interest*, namely the points in the traces where the leakage corresponds to the manipulation of the targeted sensitive information. For example, in vertical attacks, there is only one such point on each execution trace. In the case of horizontal analysis, several points of interest must be identified on the unique trace used to perform the attack. Let us denote as $(\ell_i)_{i \in I}$ the leakage values at the identified points of interest extracted from the power consumption curve(s).

Then, the adversary makes an hypothesis on a sub-part of the secret. Using his hypothesis and following the algorithm, the attacker is able to predict the operations $\mathcal{O}_i$ that took place during the execution(s) at each identified point of interest. He determines the contributions of these predicted operations to the global leakage. Therefore he chooses a leakage model $\mathcal{M}$ and computes the quantities $\mathsf{m}_i = \mathcal{M}(\mathcal{O}_i)$, all related to the hypothesis on the secret parameter. The choice of a given leakage model should of course be based on the knowledge of the attacked device architecture. A common choice for $\mathcal{M}$ is to take the Hamming Weight of register size values manipulated during the operation $\mathcal{O}_i$. For instance, in the case of a multiplication on a 32-bit architecture, one could choose the Hamming Weight of the 32 least significant bits of the result.

Finally, the adversary validates or invalidates his hypothesis by computing the so-called *correlation coefficient* between the modelization values and the leakages. If L denotes the random variable corresponding to the observed leakages $(\ell_i)_{i \in I}$ and M the one corresponding to the modelized predictions $(\mathsf{m}_i)_{i \in I}$, then this coefficient can be expressed as:

$$\rho = \rho(\mathsf{L}, \mathsf{M}) = \frac{cov(\mathsf{L}, \mathsf{M})}{\sigma_\mathsf{L} \sigma_\mathsf{M}},$$

where "*cov*" is the covariance function and "σ" the standard deviation. For the sample $(\mathsf{m}_1, \mathsf{m}_2 \ldots \mathsf{m}_{|I|})$ of predicted leakages and $(\ell_1, \ell_2, \ldots \ell_{|I|})$ of registered power consumption values, an approximation $\tilde{\rho}(\mathsf{L}, \mathsf{M})$ of $\rho(\mathsf{L}, \mathsf{M})$ is given by the Pearson coefficient:

$$\tilde{\rho}(\mathsf{L}, \mathsf{M}) = \frac{\sum_i (\ell_i - \ell)(\mathsf{m}_i - \mathsf{m})}{\sqrt{\sum_i (\ell_i - \ell)^2 \sum_i (\mathsf{m}_i - \mathsf{m})^2}},$$

where $\mathsf{m} = \frac{1}{|I|} \sum_i \mathsf{m}_i$ and $\ell = \frac{1}{|I|} \sum_i \ell_i$, with a sum taken over $i \in I$.

When the value of this correlation coefficient is high, it means that the random variables L and M are related, implying that the hypothesis on the sub-part of the secret was correct. In the other case, it means that the initial guess was wrong. In practice, the good hypothesis is often determined as that giving the highest correlation value among all possible hypotheses.

Remark: In practice, the identification of the points of interest is in fact done *a posteriori* by running the same attack on all points of the traces (or in a selected interval). The points of interest are then the points for which one of the key hypotheses produced a correlation peak.

3   Previous Attacks on RSA Implementations

In this section, we recall some existing side-channel attacks on RSA implementations. In particular, we study their applicability to the implementation we attack in this paper.

3.1   Statistical Analyses on Several Consumption Traces

Most existing side-channel attacks, such as Differential Power Analysis, Correlation Power Analysis or Mutual Information Analysis, require a high number – at least several – consumption traces to be efficient. Indeed, statistical analyses are performed on the collected curves, all related to the same sub-part of the secret, allowing to validate or invalidate hypotheses on the secret key. Such attacks target SPA-protected implementations, where the observation of a single power consumption trace does not provide enough information on the key.

Among such attacks, one can cite, for instance the work of Amiel *et al.* [2] describing a classical correlation power analysis on RSA or the work in [1] where the study of the Hamming weight distributions allows to distinguish multiplications from squaring operations. In [23], the collision correlation technique can be used to distinguish products with a common operand (key bit equal to 0) and products with independent operands (key bit equal to 1). Finally the well-known *doubling attack* of Fouque *et al.* [13] observes common intermediate values between the exponentiation of C and that of C^2.

In our context. Clearly these techniques are powerful on SPA-protected implementations. However they are successful only when sufficiently many traces, relied to the same sub-part of the secret, are available. As a consequence, the use of exponent blinding, which consists in changing the secret exponent at each new modular exponentiation performed by the device, make such attacks ineffective.

3.2   Attacks that Exploit an SPA Leak

Another approach is to assume that the SPA protection is not perfect and that some information can be extracted from a single execution of the secret computation. Indeed, in particular configurations, such as, for instance, when using sliding windows or implementing special types of multiplication algorithms such as MMM the "Montgomery Modular Multiplication", leakages might be obtained revealing partial information about the secret key. For a practical example, see Fouque *et al.*'s attack on RSA when e is small [12] and the improvement proposed by Walter in 2007 [22]. In 2011 [19], Schindler and Itoh generalized this technique by showing that any partial SPA information can be used to reconstruct the secret exponent, even when exponent blinding is used. They have no limitation on the size of the public key.

In our context. These techniques are efficient, since they are successful even against exponent blinding in the RSA exponentiation. However, they also rely on a strong hypothesis, which is the presence of SPA leaks. In this paper, we focus on implementations, that do not leak any exploitable SPA information. All the attacks mentioned in this section become ineffective in this context.

3.3   Horizontal Attacks

Up to now, the only attacks successful against protected implementations using exponent blinding, and which do not require any SPA leak, are horizontal correlation analyses. Indeed, these attacks use a unique power consumption curve. Their main idea can be explained as follows: when considering the leakage from the result of a modular multiplication or squaring, the attacker only gets a single information. However, modular operations in the case of RSA consist in multiplying 1024-bit or 2048-bit long numbers. In an embedded device, this is done by splitting the numbers into several smaller registers. The attacker could then consider the leakage coming from each register operation and thus gain much more information from a single modular operation. This idea was first studied by Walter in [20,21] in the so-called Big-Mac attack. It consists in cutting the power consumption trace – obtained from one or many execution of the algorithm on a single input – in many sub-traces, each of them containing information on a single internal operation such as, for instance, an elementary multiplication inside a LIM. This attack has then been extended in the work of Clavier *et al.* [9,10] giving the Horizontal correlation analysis. A unified version of these two approaches can be found in [4].

In our context. This kind of attack is very efficient and provides strong results even for message blinding and exponent blinding implementations. However, it relies on two assumptions. First, the attacker needs a precise knowledge of the internal modular operations implementation (*e.g.* performed using LIM or MMM, parallelized or not, *etc.*). Secondly, the power consumption curve must be sufficiently precise to obtain several points of interest from one modular multiplication[4]. Thus correct time synchronisation and patterns identification will

---

[4] By comparison, a classical CPA on RSA like [2] will use one point of interest for each modular multiplication. In [9] the authors exploit $(\ell^2 - \ell)/2$ points per multiplication, where $\ell = n/w$ for a modulus of size n on a w-bit architecture.

become a critical factor. As a matter of fact, in some experimental settings, horizontal analysis might not be applicable. In such configurations, our attack could be an interesting alternative, since it uses the same metrology as classical CPA on RSA schemes.

3.4   Attack Proposed in this Paper

Our attack applies against protected implementations of RSA using a regular exponentiation algorithm, with exponent masking of the form $d^{(i)} = d + \lambda^{(i)} \phi(N)$ and any kind of message blinding. We do not assume any partial SPA leakage nor require a precise knowledge of the internal implementation of modular operations. Our attack uses only one point of interest for each modular operation, as for vertical CPA attacks [2], and thus have less constraints on the metrology than horizontal attacks. For this reason, it represents an interesting alternative in noisy or black box scenarios.

4   The Attack on Protected RSA with Known Inputs

This section provides a description of our attack in a simplified setting, when the inputs[5] are known and for a public-key e equal to 3. The generalization for implementations using messages blinding will be discussed later, see Section 5. Other implementation choices are discussed in Appendix A. Additional considerations required for a practical implementation of the attack are provided in Appendix B.

4.1   Special Properties of the RSA Scheme

Let us first recall some well-known facts about the RSA cryptosystem, that will be useful in the following. For a more complete description of RSA properties, see [5].

Known Bits on $\phi(N)$. Since the factorization of the modulus N is a private information, the totient Euler's function is unknown to the attacker. However, half of its bits can easily be recovered. Indeed, knowing that $\phi(N) = (p-1)(q-1) = N - p - q + 1$ and assuming that p and q are balanced (*e.g.* $p, q \simeq \sqrt{N}$), the half[6] most significant bits of $\phi(N)$ is known and is equal to the half most ones of N.

Relation between d and $\phi(N)$. In the relation $ed = 1 + k\phi(N)$, see RSA Equation (1), the parameters d, k and $\phi(N)$ refer to unknown values. However when $e = 3$, the relation becomes:

$$3d = 1 + 2\phi(N). \tag{2}$$

The knowledge of the half most significant bits of $\phi(N)$ allows to deduce the half most significant ones of the secret key d. This result remains valid if more significant bits are known or guessed on $\phi(N)$. Conversely, guessing additional bits on d automaticaly implies recovering the corresponding ones on $\phi(N)$.

---

[5] Known inputs can either represent known messages for RSA signature or known ciphertexts for RSA decryption.

[6] Of course, there could be some carries issues, but this point will be discussed in Appendix B.

4.2 Description of the Attack

Let us now explain the details of our correlation analysis on protected RSA implementations. We recall that the secret exponent d is masked before each modular exponentiation as $d^{(i)} = d + \lambda^{(i)}\phi(N)$, see implementation details in Section 2.1, and that we first focus here on a simplified setting where each input data $C^{(i)}$ is known to the attacker.

General idea. Let $\mathcal{T}^{(1)}, \ldots, \mathcal{T}^{(L)}$ be L power consumption curves, registered by the adversary during the computation of $\left(C^{(1)}\right)^{d^{(1)}} \bmod N, \ldots, \left(C^{(L)}\right)^{d^{(L)}} \bmod N$. In these expressions, the notation $d^{(i)}$ refers to the i-th masked value of d. The random masking factor $\lambda^{(i)}$ belongs to $[0, 2^{32} - 1]$. The attack, which mainly consists in two steps, works as follows. First, the goal consists in guessing, for each i, the value of the masking factor $\lambda^{(i)}$ associated to the curve $\mathcal{T}^{(i)}$. To do so, several separate correlation analyses are made on each curve, using the first half of the exponentiation. In a second step, the adversary tries to guess the unknown bits of d by small increments using a classical correlation analysis, similar to the one described in [2]. For this step, the adversary uses the information gathered during the first part, namely the value of the masking factors $\lambda^{(i)}$. Thus a guess on d can easily be transformed into as many guesses on the masked values $d^{(i)}$.

Step 1: Learning Masking Factors with Correlation Attacks. First, we know that the half most significant bits of d can easily be recovered using Equation (2) of Section 4.1. From this information, the attacker wants to learn the value of the masking factors $\lambda^{(i)}$ that have been used to blind the exponent d as $d^{(i)} = d + \lambda^{(i)} \cdot \phi(N)$ for each exponentiation and thus for each curve $\mathcal{T}^{(i)}$. To do so, the attacker should perform the following operations:

1. Try all possible values for $\lambda^{(i)}$. Since each masking factor has been chosen as a 32-bit random value, this step requires 2^{32} operations.
2. For each possible $\lambda^{(i)}$, deduce the $n/2$ most significant bits of $d^{(i)}$. Indeed, observe that once $\lambda^{(i)}$ is known, we can use the knowledge on the most significant bits of d and $\phi(N)$ (see Section 4.1) to deduce the most significant bits of $d^{(i)}$ thanks to the relation $d^{(i)} = d + \lambda^{(i)}\phi(N)$. Note that we may know a few less bits than that, due to carries coming from the unknown parts of $\phi(N)$ and d that cannot be predicted.
3. From that point, since the adversary knows the input value $C^{(i)}$ together with the half most significant bits of $d^{(i)}$, it can predict the first half of the intermediate operations that have been performed during the modular exponentiation $(C^{(i)})^{d^{(i)}} \bmod N$. Depending on the exponentiation algorithm, the number η of intermediate operations the adversary is able to predict will vary from $n/2$ to n. In what follows, we denote as $\mathcal{O}_j^{(i)}$ such operations. Then, the attacker chooses a leakage model function $\mathcal{M}$ and computes some predicted values $\mathfrak{m}_j^{(i)} = \mathcal{M}(\mathcal{O}_j^{(i)})$ for $j \in \{1, \eta\}$. These values are then stored in a vector $\mathsf{M}^{(i)} = (\mathfrak{m}_j^{(i)})_{1 \leq j \leq \eta}$.
4. Perform a correlation analysis between the values $\mathsf{M}^{(i)} = (\mathfrak{m}_j^{(i)})_{1 \leq j \leq \eta}$, that have been predicted, and the leakages $\mathsf{L}^{(i)} = (\ell_j^{(i)})_{1 \leq j \leq \eta}$ coming from the

trace $\mathcal{T}^{(i)}$ at the identified points of interest. To do so, the adversary computes the Pearson correlation coefficient $\tilde{\rho}(\mathsf{L}^{(i)}, \mathsf{M}^{(i)})$, as described in Section 2.2. (See Figure 2 for an illustration.)

5. Eventually keep the mask $\lambda^{(i)}$ that gives the best correlation value.

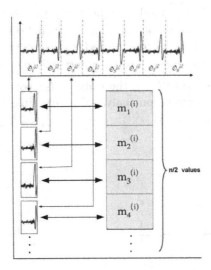

Fig. 2. Step 1: Correlation between predicted values $\mathsf{m}_\ell^{(i)}$ and points on the curve $\mathcal{T}^{(i)}$

At the end of the process, the attacker is able to link each curve $\mathcal{T}^{(i)}$ to its corresponding masked factor $\lambda^{(i)}$.

Step 2: Recovering d. Assume now that we have guessed sufficiently many λ's corresponding to given power consumption curves, say L for instance. In this case, the final step consists in recovering the whole secret key d, namely guessing its $n/2$ least significant bits. To do so, the adversary performs a correlation power analysis as described in [2]. The idea is to make an hypothesis on a few bits on d, say w at a time, from the most significant bits to the least significant ones, then to (in)validate it using a CPA on the obtained consumption curves. So until we have guessed the whole secret key d or until the remaining bits can simply be recovered by a final exhaustive search, we repeat the following operations[7]:

1. Try all possible values for w bits of d. In practice, w may be taken quite small, as an example 8 bits could be a good choice, the idea being to make this exhaustive search step as fast as possible. From that hypothesis, we get a truncated value named $\overline{d}$, corresponding to the known most significant bits of d, concatenated with our guess and padded with 0's on the least significant positions (except for the last bit which we know is 1 since d is odd).

---

[7] The following process starts from the most significant unknown bits of d after execution of step 1 of the attack.

2. For each obtained value $\overline{d}$, compute $\overline{\phi(N)}$ as $\frac{3\overline{d}-1}{2}$, see Equation (2).

3. For each curve $\mathcal{T}^{(i)}$, deduce an approximation of $d^{(i)}$ by computing $\overline{d^{(i)}} = \overline{d} + \lambda^{(i)}\overline{\phi(N)}$. From these guessed bits on $d^{(i)}$, the adversary is able to determine the corresponding intermediate operations $\mathcal{O}_j^{(i)}$ during the modular exponentiation $\left(C^{(i)}\right)^{d^{(i)}}$ mod N. One can notice that, depending on the size of $\lambda^{(i)}$, the place of the w bits in $\overline{d^{(i)}}$ will slightly vary From that point, the adversary uses a model function $\mathcal{M}$ and computes the predicted values $\mathrm{m}_j^{(i)} = \mathcal{M}(\mathcal{O}_j^{(i)})$ corresponding to the intermediate operations.

4. Extract from the curves $(\mathcal{T}^{(i)})_i$ the leakages $\ell_j^{(i)}$ corresponding to the same operations. Use the correlation analysis described in Section 2.2 and compute the correlation coefficient $\tilde{\rho}\left((\ell_j^{(i)})_{i,j}, (\mathrm{m}_j^{(i)})_{i,j}\right)$. (See Figure 3 to illustrate the process.)

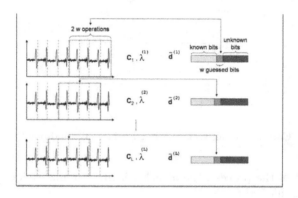

Fig. 3. Correlation Analysis between L curves $\mathcal{T}^{(i)}$ and the corresponding guessed bits on $\overline{d^{(i)}}$

5. Validate the w bits on d that give the best correlation coefficient.

5   The Attack on Protected RSA with Masked Inputs

In the previous attack, since we use a correlation analysis, we need to know the input in order to evaluate our predictions. When the input is unknown, the attack can be modified by performing a *Collision Correlation Analysis*, as described in [23]. Indeed, even if the input is unknown, we can still predict, from our guess on the exponent, the sequence of operations that should occur, according to the implemented exponentiation algorithm. In the following, we especially focus on two implementation cases.

5.1   The Atomic Square-and-Multiply Exponentiation Algorithm

This exponentiation technique has been proposed in [8] and is provided by Algorithm 2, see Figure 1. Here, from the guess on the exponent, we are able to deduce the sequence of operations. That is, we know when a squaring written as a multiplication is followed by a multiplication by $R_1 = C$ (case $d[j] = 1$) and when it is followed by another squaring (case $d[j] = 0$). In the first case, the result R_0 of the first squaring is then multiplied by $R_1 = C$, which value is independent from R_0. In the second case, this result is multiplied by R_0 itself. Thus, in this second case we expect a correlation between the result of the first squaring and the second operand of the next operation.

Following this exponentiation algorithm, a bit $d^{(i)}[j]$ of the exponent corresponds to 1 or 2 modular operations. Let us denote as $\mathcal{O}^{(i)}_{f(j)}$ the first squaring that always occurs. The next modular operation $\mathcal{O}^{(i)}_{f(j)+1}$ is then either a multiplication by C or the squaring associated to $d^{(i)}[j-1]$. When we know the most significant bits of $d^{(i)}$ down to j, we are able to determine the corresponding values of $f(j)$. In the following, we denote as $(\ell_{in})^{(i)}_{f(j)}$ the leakage associated to the loading of the second operand of $\mathcal{O}^{(i)}_{f(j)}$ and $(\ell_{out})^{(i)}_{f(j)}$ the one related to the output of $\mathcal{O}^{(i)}_{f(j)}$.

First Part of the Attack. From a guess on $\lambda^{(i)}$, we obtain the half most significant bits of $d^{(i)}$. Let L_1 and L_2 be two sets initially empty. For all known bits of $d^{(i)}$ such that $d^{(i)}[j] = 0$, we add $(\ell_{out})^{(i)}_{f(j)}$ to L_1 and $(\ell_{in})^{(i)}_{f(j)+1}$ to L_2. Thus the correlation coefficient $\tilde{\rho}(\mathsf{L}_1, \mathsf{L}_2)$ is maximal for the good hypothesis, which gives us the correct value for $\lambda^{(i)}$.

Second Part of the Attack. We proceed as above, except that one guess on the bits of the private exponent d corresponds to different values for the corresponding bits of the masked exponents $d^{(i)}$. We use the same sets L_1 and L_2 initially empty. For all i and all new known bits of $d^{(i)}$ such that $d^{(i)}[j] = 0$, we add $(\ell_{out})^{(i)}_{f(j)}$ to L_1 and $(\ell_{in})^{(i)}_{f(j)+1}$ to L_2. Again, the correlation coefficient $\tilde{\rho}(\mathsf{L}_1, \mathsf{L}_2)$ is maximal for the good hypothesis, which gives us the correct value for the targeted bits of d.

5.2   The Square-and-Multiply-Always Exponentiation Algorithm

This exponentiation is given by Algorithm 1, see Figure 1. Here, from a guess on the private exponent, we can predict when two consecutive multiplications will have a common operand. Indeed when $d[j] = 0$, the Square-and-Multiply-Always algorithm computes $R_1 \leftarrow R_0 \cdot C$ followed by $R_0 \leftarrow R_0 \cdot R_0$. The R_0 input value is the same for both operations. When $d[j] = 1$, the algorithm computes $R_0 \leftarrow R_0 \cdot C$ followed by $R_0 \leftarrow R_0 \cdot R_0$. The R_0 value is updated after the first multiplication and thus the two operations have no common operand.

Following this exponentiation algorithm, a bit $d^{(i)}[j]$ of the exponent always corresponds to 2 modular operations. We denote $\mathcal{O}^{(i)}_{f(j)}$ the first squaring. The next modular operation $\mathcal{O}^{(i)}_{f(j)+1}$ is the multiplication by C and $\mathcal{O}^{(i)}_{f(j)+2}$ corresponds to the squaring associated with $d^{(i)}[j-1]$. Let $\ell^{(i)}_{f(j)}$ be the leakage associated to the loading of the first operand of $\mathcal{O}^{(i)}_{f(j)}$.

First Part of the Attack. From a guess on $\lambda^{(i)}$, we obtain the half most significant bits of $d^{(i)}$. Let L_1 and L_2 be two sets initially empty. For all known bits of $d^{(i)}$ such that $d^{(i)}[j] = 0$, we add $\ell^{(i)}_{f(j)+1}$ to L_1 and $\ell^{(i)}_{f(j)+2}$ to L_2. The correlation coefficient $\tilde{\rho}(\mathsf{L}_1, \mathsf{L}_2)$ is maximal for the good hypothesis, which gives us the correct value for $\lambda^{(i)}$.

Second Part of the Attack. We proceed as above, except that one guess on the bits of the private exponent d corresponds to different values for the corresponding bits of the masked exponents $d^{(i)}$. We use the same sets L_1 and L_2 initially empty. For all i and all new known bits of $d^{(i)}$ such that $d^{(i)}[j] = 0$, we add $\ell^{(i)}_{f(j)+1}$ to L_1 and $\ell^{(i)}_{f(j)+2}$ to L_2. That way, the correlation coefficient $\tilde{\rho}(\mathsf{L}_1, \mathsf{L}_2)$ is maximal for the good hypothesis, which gives us the correct value for the targeted bits of d.

6   Simulation Results

In order to check the validity of our attack, we performed many simulations on RSA implementations, using a public key e equal to 3, a modulus of size 1024 and 2048 bits and exponent blinding with 8-bit and 16-bit random masked factors[8]. For each scenarios, we performed a hundred simulations, each of them following the same process: simulating and storing the leakage of the implementation at each loop iteration, then performing our attack using either correlation power analyses or collision correlation attacks depending whether the inputs are known or not. More precisely, in order to simulate the leakage of the operation $Z = X.Y \bmod N$, we produce the three consecutive leakages $(\mathrm{HW}_{32}(X), \mathrm{HW}_{32}(Y), \mathrm{HW}_{32}(Z))$, where $\mathrm{HW}_{32}(X)$ denotes the Hamming weight of the 32 least significant bits of X. Then, we add to this value a random noise of zero mean and standard deviation σ. Finally, each experiment has been performed for different number of traces. Obviously, when this number increases, the Pearson coefficient better estimates the value of the correlation. Thus, the attack works better. However, it also takes longer to compute since the random blinding factor must first be guessed for each trace.

Figure 4 presents the success rate observed over the hundred experiments for the two steps of the known input attack. The first number represents the success rate for guessing the correct value of $\lambda^{(i)}$. The second number represents the success rate for guessing the correct value of d. Note that success consists in recovering the whole secret exponent. Thus we observe that when the noise becomes too high the success rate drops quickly since we need to accumulate 128 correct guesses ($w = 8$) in step 2 to obtain the whole secret key, for a 1024-bit modulus.

---

[8] The exponent blinding factor was chosen quite small in order to be able to launch hundreds of attacks for comparison. However, simulations indicate that when this factor increases it mainly impacts the computation time.

On the same figure, we show two variations on the main experiments. In the first one, we used moduli of size 2048 bits instead of 1024 bits and kept $\lambda^{(i)}$ of size 8 bits with 500 traces. We observe in this case that the success rate for the whole attack drops quicker since a success requires more correct guesses. On the other hand, even in high noise the guesses on $\lambda^{(i)}$ stay quite good. Further experiments suggest that, at a given noise level, decreasing the success rate of the first step has a negligible impact on the success of the second step. In the second scenario, we used $\lambda^{(i)}$ of size 16 bits and kept moduli of size 1024 bits with 500 traces. We observe in this case that the success rate for the first step of the attack drops when the noise is high. However, it has no impact when the noise stays reasonable and the overall success rate is unchanged. This observation was confirmed on our simulations for moduli of size 256 to 2048 bits.

On Figure 5, we show the attack on unknown inputs with the Square-and-Multiply-Always algorithm and with the Atomic Square-and-Multiply algorithm. In these last two cases, the success rate of the attack is more impacted by noise. Indeed here noise impacts the two sets we try to correlate instead of one. This observation shows that our attack is similar to second order attacks classically applied on symmetric algorithm. We also observe in the "no noise" scenario that some wrong guesses have the same correlation than the correct one. These wrong branches could be detected by a more elaborating backtracking algorithm since the correlation coefficient then drops for the next guesses. This would also improve the results in the noisy case.

N	λ	Traces	Deviation σ											
			0		1		5		10		15		20	
1024	8	500	100	100	100	100	100	96	100	71	99.8	0	93.9	0
1024	8	1000	100	100	100	100	100	100	100	100	99.8	61	93.9	0
1024	8	2000	100	100	100	100	100	100	100	100	99.8	96	93.9	55
2048	8	500	100	100	100	100	100	95	100	29	100	0	99.9	0
1024	16	500	100	100	100	100	100	96	100	71	94	0	58	0

Fig. 4. Percentage of success in the known input attack

Traces	Square-and-Multiply Always								Atomic Square-and-Multiply							
	$\sigma = 0$		$\sigma = 1$		$\sigma = 3$		$\sigma = 5$		$\sigma = 0$		$\sigma = 1$		$\sigma = 3$		$\sigma = 5$	
1000	100	97	100	97	99.8	74	53.9	0	100	99	100	98	99.7	83	21.9	0
2000	100	99	100	98	99.8	76	51.4	4	100	97	100	96	98.8	84	30.6	0

Fig. 5. Percentage of success for regular algorithms, with input blinding ($N = 1024$ bits and $\lambda = 8$ bits)

7   Conclusion

We have described an attack against an SFM implementation of RSA protected against SPA by a regular exponentiation algorithm and against DPA by exponent and message blinding. Our attack does not require any assumption concerning the details of the modular multiplication. It works in two steps, combining the results of several correlation analyses. The attack only applies when the exponent blinding factor allows an exhaustive search. This could limit the applicability of our attack. However, in a scenario where the blinding factor may be reduced in a small interval through fault injection, our attack may find a renewed interest.

One can observe that RSA-CRT implementations do not suffer from this attack since the private exponents d_p and d_q corresponding to the prime factors p and q are completely unknown from the attacker. Indeed, even if e is small, we cannot deduce useful information about the first bits of d_p and d_q.

References

1. Amiel, F., Feix, B., Tunstall, M., Whelan, C., Marnane, W.P.: Distinguishing Multiplications from Squaring Operations. In: Avanzi, R.M., Keliher, L., Sica, F. (eds.) SAC 2008. LNCS, vol. 5381, pp. 346–360. Springer, Heidelberg (2009)
2. Amiel, F., Feix, B., Villegas, K.: Power Analysis for Secret Recovering and Reverse Engineering of Public Key Algorithms. In: Adams, C., Miri, A., Wiener, M. (eds.) SAC 2007. LNCS, vol. 4876, pp. 110–125. Springer, Heidelberg (2007)
3. Bastina, L., Gierlichs, B., Prouff, E., Rivain, M., Standaert, F.-X., Veyrat-Charvillon, N.: Mutual Information Analysis: A Comprehensive Study. Journal of Cryptology 24(2), 269–291 (2011)
4. Bauer, A., Jaulmes, E., Prouff, E., Wild, J.: Horizontal and vertical side-channel attacks against secure RSA implementations. In: Dawson, E. (ed.) RSA 2013. LNCS, vol. 7779, pp. 1–17. Springer, Heidelberg (2013)
5. Boneh, D.: Twenty years of attacks on the RSA cryptosystem. Notices of the American Mathematical Society, AMS (1999)
6. Boneh, D., Durfee, G., Frankel, Y.: An Attack on RSA Given a Small Fraction of the Private Key Bits. In: Ohta, K., Pei, D. (eds.) ASIACRYPT 1998. LNCS, vol. 1514, pp. 25–34. Springer, Heidelberg (1998)
7. Brier, E., Clavier, C., Olivier, F.: Correlation Power Analysis with a Leakage Model. In: Joye, M., Quisquater, J.-J. (eds.) CHES 2004. LNCS, vol. 3156, pp. 16–29. Springer, Heidelberg (2004)
8. Chevallier-Mames, B., Ciet, M., Joye, M.: Lowcost Solutions for Preventing Simple Side-Channel Cryptanalysis: Side-Channel Atomicity. IEEE Transactions on Computers 53(6), 760–768 (2004)
9. Clavier, C., Feix, B., Gagnerot, G., Giraud, C., Roussellet, M., Verneuil, V.: ROSETTA for Single Trace Analysis – Recovery of Secret Exponent by Triangular Trace Analysis. In: Galbraith, S., Nandi, M. (eds.) INDOCRYPT 2012. LNCS, vol. 7668, pp. 140–155. Springer, Heidelberg (2012)
10. Clavier, C., Feix, B., Gagnerot, G., Roussellet, M., Verneuil, V.: Horizontal Correlation Analysis on Exponentiation. In: Soriano, M., Qing, S., López, J. (eds.) ICICS 2010. LNCS, vol. 6476, pp. 46–61. Springer, Heidelberg (2010)
11. Coron, J.-S.: Resistance against Differential Power Analysis for Elliptic Curve Cryptosystems. In: Koç, Ç.K., Paar, C. (eds.) CHES 1999. LNCS, vol. 1717, pp. 292–302. Springer, Heidelberg (1999)
12. Fouque, P.-A., Kunz-Jacques, S., Martinet, G., Muller, F., Valette, F.: Power Attack on Small RSA Public Exponent. In: Goubin, L., Matsui, M. (eds.) CHES 2006. LNCS, vol. 4249, pp. 339–353. Springer, Heidelberg (2006)

13. Fouque, P.-A., Valette, F.: The Doubling Attack – Why Upwards is Better than Downwards. In: Walter, C.D., Koç, Ç.K., Paar, C. (eds.) CHES 2003. LNCS, vol. 2779, pp. 269–280. Springer, Heidelberg (2003)
14. Gierlichs, B., Batina, L., Tuyls, P., Preneel, B.: Mutual Information Analysis. In: Oswald, E., Rohatgi, P. (eds.) CHES 2008. LNCS, vol. 5154, pp. 426–442. Springer, Heidelberg (2008)
15. Joye, M.: Highly regular m-ary powering ladders. In: Jacobson Jr., M.J., Rijmen, V., Safavi-Naini, R. (eds.) SAC 2009. LNCS, vol. 5867, pp. 350–363. Springer, Heidelberg (2009)
16. Joye, M., Yen, S.-M.: The Montgomery Powering Ladder. In: Kaliski Jr., B.S., Koç, Ç.K., Paar, C. (eds.) CHES 2002. LNCS, vol. 2523, pp. 291–302. Springer, Heidelberg (2003)
17. Kocher, P.C.: Timing Attacks on Implementations of Diffie-Hellman, RSA, DSS, and Other Systems. In: Koblitz, N. (ed.) CRYPTO 1996. LNCS, vol. 1109, pp. 104–113. Springer, Heidelberg (1996)
18. Kocher, P.C., Jaffe, J., Jun, B.: Differential Power Analysis. In: Wiener, M. (ed.) CRYPTO 1999. LNCS, vol. 1666, pp. 388–397. Springer, Heidelberg (1999)
19. Schindler, W., Itoh, K.: Exponent Blinding Does Not Always Lift (Partial) SPA resistance to Higher-Level Security. In: Lopez, J., Tsudik, G. (eds.) ACNS 2011. LNCS, vol. 6715, pp. 73–90. Springer, Heidelberg (2011)
20. Walter, C.D.: Sliding Windows Succumbs to Big Mac Attack. In: Koç, Ç.K., Naccache, D., Paar, C. (eds.) CHES 2001. LNCS, vol. 2162, pp. 286–299. Springer, Heidelberg (2001)
21. Walter, C.D.: Longer Keys May Facilitate Side Channel Attacks. In: Matsui, M., Zuccherato, R.J. (eds.) SAC 2003. LNCS, vol. 3006, pp. 42–57. Springer, Heidelberg (2004)
22. Walter, C.D.: Longer Randomly Blinded RSA Keys May Be Weaker Than Shorter Ones. In: Kim, S., Yung, M., Lee, H.-W. (eds.) WISA 2007. LNCS, vol. 4867, pp. 303–316. Springer, Heidelberg (2008)
23. Witteman, M.F., van Woudenberg, J.G.J., Menarini, F.: Defeating RSA Multiply-Always and Message Blinding Countermeasures. In: Kiayias, A. (ed.) CT-RSA 2011. LNCS, vol. 6558, pp. 77–88. Springer, Heidelberg (2011)

A   Our Attack in Other Implementation Cases

A.1   Right-to-Left Implementation

The description can be adapted to the right-to-left case by going backward from the result of the computation. Indeed if we look at a right-to-left "Square-and-Multiply Always" implementation (see Algorithm 3), we see that knowing the last t bits of d, we can deduce the last t squares and multiplies.

Algorithm 3. "Square-and-Multiply-Always" *(from right to left)*

```
R_0 ← 1 ; R_1 ← C
for j = 0 to n − 1 do
    if d[j] = 1 then
        └ R_0 ← R_0 · R_1
    else
        └ t ← R_0 · R_1
    └ R_1 ← R_1²
return R_0
```

A.2   Montgomery

Our attack in the known input case can be adapted to the improved version of the "Square-and-Multiply Always" algorithm based on Montgomery [16] (see Algorithm 4).

Algorithm 4. "Montgomery ladder"

$R_0 \leftarrow 1$; $R_1 \leftarrow C$
for $j = n - 1$ **to** 0 **do**
    if $d[j] = 0$ **then**
        $R_1 \leftarrow R_1 \cdot R_0$
        $R_0 \leftarrow R_0 \cdot R_0$
    else
        $R_0 \leftarrow R_0 \cdot R_1$
        $R_1 \leftarrow R_1 \cdot R_1$

return R_0

In the masked input case, we can distinguish a transition from '0' to '1' or '1' to '0' from no transition. Indeed when a transition occurs, the output of the square is used as the first operand of the next multiplication. When there is no transition the output of the squaring is used as the second operand.

A.3   Larger Public Key

When e is greater than 3, the coefficient k is no longer known for certain (see Equation (1)). Thus it must be guessed together with the $\lambda^{(i)}$ in order to apply the first part of the attack. Since k verifies $0 < k < e$, this means that the exhaustive search factor is multiplied by the value of the public key. In most RSA implementations, the RSA public exponent does not exceed $2^{16} + 1$. This means that a 2^{16} factor should be added to the exhaustive search complexity.

B   Attack Implementation: Carries and Wrong Guesses

There is an issue when performing "Step 2" of the attack: how to deal with the carries and their potential wrong guesses implication. Indeed, in this part of the algorithm, we are trying to guess the bits of d by small increments, setting the lower unknown bits to 0. When the intermediate value $\overline{d}$ is used to compute $\overline{\phi(N)}$ and $\overline{d^{(i)}}$, we may be confronted to the fact that the bits we are guessing are wrong because of unknown carries coming up to this point in the real values. More precisely, we may be wrong on two points:

1. **When We Compute $\overline{d^{(i)}}$ from $\overline{d}$ and $\overline{\phi(N)}$.** In this case, an error means that the prediction given by the corresponding curve will be incorrect: this adds some noise in the correlation coefficient computation. If we are not wrong too often, this will not change the overall decision about $\overline{d}$.

2. **When We Compute $\overline{\phi(N)}$ from $\overline{d}$.** In this configuration, an error means that we will be wrong for all curves. Indeed, if $\overline{\phi(N)}$ is incorrect, then all $\overline{d^{(i)}}$ will also be incorrect. But let us have a look at the kind of error it implies. Assume that we predict some value a for the w bits of d we are

considering at this point. Thus, we can write $\overline{d}$ as $[d]_{(j+1)w} + a2^{jw} + 1$, where $[d]_{(j+1)w} = d - (d \bmod 2^{(j+1)w})$. In that case, we compute $\overline{\phi(N)}$ as:

$$\overline{\phi(N)} = \frac{3\overline{d}-1}{2} = \frac{3[d]_{(j+1)w} + a2^{jw} + a2^{jw+1} + 2}{2}$$

$$= \frac{3[d]_{(j+1)w}}{2} + a2^{jw} + a2^{jw-1} + 1.$$

Let b be the value of the corresponding bits of $\overline{\phi(N)}$, that is:

$$b = \left(\frac{3[d]_{(j+1)w}}{2^{jw+1}} + a + \lfloor a/2 \rfloor \right) \bmod 2^w$$

If we assume that b is incorrect, this means that a carry should have appeared in the computation of b and the correct value is $b + 1$. In this case, the predictions of $d^{(i)}$ for the guess a will all be wrong. On the other hand, the predictions for $a + 1$ will give:

$$\overline{\phi(N)} = \frac{3[d]_{(j+1)w}}{2} + (a+1)2^{jw} + a2^{jw-1} + 2^{jw-1} + 1.$$

As a consequence, if b' denotes the value of the corresponding bits of $\overline{\phi(N)}$, we obtain:

$$b' = \left(\frac{3[d]_{(j+1)w}}{2^{jw+1}} + a + 1 + \lfloor a/2 \rfloor \right) \bmod 2^w = b + 1.$$

This time, we reach the correct value for $\overline{\phi(N)}$. Since $\overline{d^{(i)}} = \overline{d} + \lambda^{(i)}\overline{\phi(N)}$, with high probability, we also have the correct value for the bits of $\overline{d^{(i)}}$ we are considering. The guess $a+1$ will have a better correlation coefficient than the guess a. At the next step, however, the correlation will drop suddenly. When this happens, we know that the previous guess $a + 1$ was incorrect and we just have to back up one step, subtract 1 to the guess, and go on. The simulations we have done confirm that this approach is correct.

Complete SCARE of AES-Like Block Ciphers by Chosen Plaintext Collision Power Analysis*,**

Christophe Clavier, Quentin Isorez, and Antoine Wurcker

XLIM-CNRS, Université de Limoges,
Limoges, France
christophe.clavier@unilim.fr
quentin.isorez@etu.unilim.fr
antoine.wurcker@xlim.fr

Abstract. Despite Kerckhoffs's principle, proprietary or otherwise secret cryptographic algorithms are still used in real life. For security and
efficiency reasons a common design practice simply modifies some parameters of widely used and well studied encryption standards. In this paper,
we investigate the feasibility of reverse engineering the secret specifications of an AES-like block cipher by SCARE techniques based on collision
power analysis. In the considered observational model, we demonstrate
that an adversary who does not know the secret key can recover the full
set of secret parameters of an AES-like software implementation even if
it is protected by common first-order Boolean masking and shuffling of
independent operations. We study possible countermeasures and recall
some simple guidelines to mitigate the side-channel information with the
aim to thwart our attacks.

Keywords: embedded devices, side-channel analysis, collisions, SCARE,
reverse engineering, AES.

1 Introduction

Side Channel Analysis (SCA) has been introduced by Kocher et al. [10,11] as an
efficient means to recover the secret key of cryptographic algorithms on embedded devices. Since then many new attack techniques have been discovered and
new efficient countermeasures against these attacks have been proposed. Most
of this research activity concerned the classical context of key recovery where
the target encryption function is publicly known as in the emblematic cases of
DES [12] and AES [13] standards.

* This work has been conducted under the framework of the MARSHAL+ (Mecha-
  nisms Against Reverse-engineering for Secure Hardware and Algorithms) research
  project, subsidized by FUI 12, and co-sponsored by the competitiveness clusters
  System@tic and SCS.
** Simulations presented in this paper have been partly performed on the CALI computing cluster of university of Limoges, funded by the Limousin region, XLIM, IPAM
  and GEIST institutes, as well as the university of Limoges.

G. Paul and S. Vaudenay (Eds.): INDOCRYPT 2013, LNCS 8250, pp. 116–135, 2013.

Nevertheless, despite Kerckhoffs's principle, the security is sometimes expected through obscurity, and proprietary or otherwise secret cryptographic algorithms are still used in civil applications such as GSM or Pay-TV systems and for diplomatic or military usages. For sake of simplicity a strategy for designing a secret encryption function may consist in only modifying some parameters of a well studied and widely used public function. Doing this, the design and development costs are reduced, and provided that the secret parameters are carefully chosen the designer can expect inheriting the strength of the public function structure like the Substitution Permutation Network in the exemplary case of AES.

It is thus of interest to study to which extent SCA techniques – essentially through power or electromagnetic measurements – can be used to recover the structure details and/or the parameter values of an encryption algorithm whose specifications are kept secret. Novak [14] has first described a SCARE[1] technique that reveals the content of one of the two substitution tables used in an authentication and key agreement secret GSM algorithm. His attack considers the observational model where the adversary is able to decide whether two instances of precisely located intermediate data collide or not – without identifying their values – based on the side-channel observation of their execution trace(s). In the same model, Clavier [5] later improved this attack by revealing both S-Boxes without prior knowledge of the encryption key. In [7] Daudigny et al. proposed a SCARE of the standard DES. They used DPA to infer so-called *scheduling information* which reveals when particular bits are manipulated, from which the supposedly unknown permutation functions are derived. Two other contributions extended the usage of SCARE to whole classes of ciphers sharing the same structure: Real et al. [17] first revealed the round function of any unknown hardware Feistel implementation while Rivain et al. [19] recently show how to exploit S-Boxes collisions to retrieve an equivalent representation of any secret Substitution-Permutation Network based encryption function. Although other publications [8,15] also deal with side-channel analysis to reveal information about secret algorithms, as far as we know all methods described so far either target a specific component – often the non linear substitution table – of the algorithm or only applies to unprotected implementations.

In this paper, we investigate the feasibility of reverse engineering the secret specifications of an AES-like block cipher. In the collision power analysis model, we demonstrate that an adversary who does not know the secret key can efficiently recover the full set of secret parameters of an AES-like software implementation even if it is protected by a common set of countermeasures. While our work has much in common with [19] (same attacker model, same attacker goal) they still have distinct contributions. On one hand Rivain et al. recover any SPN-based function while our method only applies to AES with secret parameters. On the other hand they assume an unprotected implementation while we describe a variant of our attack that deals with some classical side-channel countermeasures.

---

[1] SCARE stands for Side-Channel Analysis for Reverse Engineering.

The paper is organized as follow: Section 2 briefly describes the AES and defines what we call an AES-like function which is the target of our attacks. We also present the considered attacker model. In Section 3 we explain step by step how to recover the full set of parameters of the AES-like function in the case of an unprotected implementation, whereas Section 4 deals with the adaptation of our attack to an implementation which features a classical set of countermeasures including first-order Boolean masking of the encryption path together with shuffling of independent operations. We discuss possible countermeasures to our attacks in Section 5 and conclude the paper in Section 6.

2   AES-Like Block Cipher and the Attacker Model

We give hereafter a brief description of the 128-bit version of AES, and define what we mean in this paper by an AES-like block cipher. For more precise information about the AES we refer the reader to the NIST standard [13] which includes its full specifications.

2.1   Description of the AES

In the process of AES computation, a byte is considered as an element of the finite field $GF(2^8)$, and each 16-byte internal state may be represented as a square 4×4 matrix. The mapping between the vector and matrix representations is done by numbering the elements column by column.

Given a 128-bit plaintext $M = (m_0, \ldots, m_{15})$ and a 128-bit ciphering key $K = (k_0, \ldots, k_{15})$ the AES computes a 128-bit ciphertext $C = (c_0, \ldots, c_{15})$ by first XOR-ing M with K and then updating the result state S_0 through 10 rounds. For $r = 1, \ldots, 9$, each AES round number r computes its output state S_r by successively applying four transformations SubBytes, ShiftRows, MixColumns and AddRoundKey to its input S_{r-1}. The ciphertext is finally defined as the output of a 10th and last round which does not include the MixColumns operation. The encryption process is summarized as follow:

$$S_0 \leftarrow M \oplus K_0 \qquad (K_0 = K)$$
$$S_r \leftarrow \texttt{MixColumns}(\texttt{ShiftRows}(\texttt{SubBytes}(S_{r-1}))) \oplus K_r \qquad (r = 1, \ldots, 9)$$
$$C \leftarrow \texttt{ShiftRows}(\texttt{SubBytes}(S_9)) \oplus K_{10}$$

The SubBytes transformation is a permutation over $GF(2^8)$ defined by an S-Box table S. The ShiftRows consists in rotating each row number i ($i = 0, \ldots, 3$) by i bytes to the left. The MixColumns computes each column of its output as the product of a constant matrix by the corresponding input column. Finally the AddRoundKey computes the XOR (addition in $GF(2^8)$) between the current state and the round key K_r. The different round keys K_r involved in the encryption process are derived from K through the key scheduling function depicted on Figure 1. The RotWord operation simply rotates each byte of a column by one position upward, SubWord applies the S-Box to each byte of the column, and Rcon[r] is a round dependent constant word equal to $(\rho^{r-1}, 0, 0, 0)$ with $\rho = 2$.

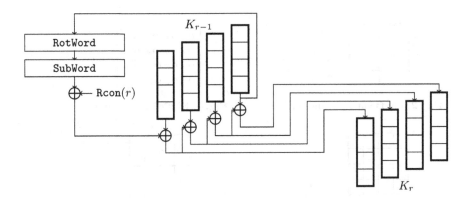

Fig. 1. The AES key schedule

2.2   Definition of an AES-Like Block Cipher

From the definition of the 128-bit AES it is possible to derive a large class of encryption functions which differ from the standard AES while preserving its essential structure of a Substitution Permutation Network as well as the number and width of its internal values.

We define an AES-like block cipher as any function which is derived from AES by modifications of the following parameters:

1. the S-Box table S can be replaced by any other one that preserves the property that the SubBytes function is a permutation over $GF(2^8)$ elements,
2. in the ShiftRows transformation each row number i is rotated by σ_i bytes to the left, where σ_i can be any value from 0 to 3 ($\sigma_i = i$ for the standard AES),
3. the constant matrix which defines the MixColumns operation can be replaced by any 16-tuple $(\alpha_0, \ldots, \alpha_{15})$ of $GF(2^8)$ elements[2] provided that the resulting matrix remains invertible,
4. the RotWord operation in the key schedule rotates the column by η bytes upward, where η can be any value from 0 to 3 ($\eta = 1$ for the standard AES),
5. the round dependent constant word Rcon$[r]$ involved in the key schedule for the computation of K_r is defined as $(\rho^{r-1}, 0, 0, 0)$ where ρ can take any byte value ($\rho = 2$ for the standard AES).

Figures 2 to 5 depict the possible degrees of freedom on the parameters of ShiftRows, MixColumns, RotWord and Rcon respectively.

For sake of simplicity, in the following sections, we shall simply denote by *AES* the secret AES-like function that the attacker aims at reverse-engineer, and we shall refer to the standard AES function as *standard AES*.

---

[2] Note that we do not require that the modified MixColumns matrix is circulant as is the standard one.

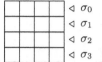

Fig. 2. ShiftRows parameters

Fig. 3. MixColumns matrix

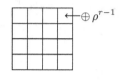

Fig. 4. RotWord parameter

Fig. 5. Rcon[r] parameter

2.3   The Attacker Model

We consider the chosen plaintext scenario which is relevant as we assume that the attacker owns a device (e.g. a smartcard) embedding a software implementation of a secret AES-like encryption function. He can query the device with chosen plaintexts and receives the corresponding ciphertexts. He is assumed to ignore the value of the key K and his goal is to reverse-engineer all the secret parameters of the encryption function by analysing the power traces of each encryption.

It is obvious that the cryptographic strength of an AES-like block cipher defined as above may range from very weak to reasonably strong functions. Even, probably a quite small fraction of them can be acceptable for a safe cryptographic usage. Nevertheless, as a conservative option, we choose to consider a blind attacker who does not disqualify a possible function regarding the relevance of its parameters, but rather accepts a priori any set of parameters $(S, \{\sigma_i\}_i, \{\alpha_i\}_i, \eta, \rho)$ modifiable according to our definition.

We make the observation assumption that the attacker can identify S-Box collisions by side-channel analysis. More precisely, given two power trace segments T and T' corresponding to two table lookups $y = S(x)$ and $y' = S(x')$ in the AES computation[3], the attacker can decide whether $(x, y) = (x', y')$ or not, based on a side-channel distinguisher. This side-channel collision model has already been used in many key recovery attacks [21,20,1,2,3,6] as well as for reverse-engineering purpose [14,5]. Notably Bogdanov [3] used exactly the same model as ours applied on AES S-Boxes.

It may be argued that detecting collisions between two S-Boxes based on traces from two different executions is more difficult than from a unique trace and may result in less reliable decisions due to possible differences in the experimental conditions (temperature,...). As we think that this is a debatable question, we

---

[3] The two S-Box lookups may be located at different rounds, and possibly on different traces with different inputs.

choose to present our attack in both settings: the *inter-traces* scenario where the attacker can detect collisions from different traces, and the *intra-trace* one where he can not.

2.4   Notations

We introduce the following further notations:

- $K_r = (k_{r,0}, \ldots, k_{r,15})$, the rth round key   (for $r = 0, \ldots, 10$)
- $\mu_{r,i,j} = k_{r,i} \oplus k_{r,j}$ (for $r = 1, \ldots, 10$ and $i, j = 0, \ldots, 15$)
- $X_r = (x_{r,0}, \ldots, x_{r,15})$, the SubBytes input of round r (for $r = 1, \ldots, 10$)
- $Y_r = (y_{r,0}, \ldots, y_{r,15})$, the SubBytes output of round r (for $r = 1, \ldots, 10$)

3   Attacking an Unprotected Implementation

In this section we describe how to recover the secret parameters of an AES implementation that does not feature any side-channel countermeasure. We proceed step by step, and the order of these steps has importance as each of them depends on the information retrieved in previous ones.

When this is relevant, we propose methods for both inter-traces and intra-trace settings.

3.1   Retrieving ShiftRows Parameters

In the inter-traces setting we can easily recover the σ_i parameters. We first acquire a trace for a random plaintext, then we compare this trace with the four ones corresponding to a single modification of plaintext byte m_i ($i = 0, \ldots, 3$). For each line i, observing which quadruplet of consecutive second round S-Boxes do not collide with the reference trace reveals the value of σ_i.

In the intra-trace scenario, things are a little more complex :

Lemma 1. *Assume a collision occurring between S-Box i in the first round, and S-Box j in the second round. There are two ways to destroy this collision by modification of a single plaintext byte: (i) either the active plaintext byte is at position i or, (ii) the active byte is any of the four bytes involved in the computation of $x_{2,j}$.*

Depending whether one of the four plaintext positions involved in the computation of $x_{2,j}$ is equal to i itself or not, there are respectively 4 or 5 active bytes that destroy the collision.

Definition 1. *We denote by 4-Collision and 5-Collision collisions that can be destroyed by 4 and 5 plaintext bytes respectively.*

Lemma 2. *The four bytes involved in the calculation of a same $x_{2,j}$ belong to different lines of the state matrix and are aligned on a same column after ShiftRows operation.*

To retrieve the `ShiftRows` parameters we first encrypt random plaintexts until a single collision occurs between a first round S-Box at position i and a second round S-Box at position j. Then for all $k \neq i$ we encrypt a modified plaintext where only m_k has changed, and identify whether 3 or 4 positions destroy the collision.

The first case (cf. red and $*$ in Figure 6) corresponds to a `4-Collision` and the three identified positions together with i are involved in the computation of $x_{2,j}$. The second case (cf. green and $\odot$ in Figure 6) corresponds to a `5-Collision` and the four identified positions are related to $x_{2,j}$. In both cases, these four positions are equal to $\{4((u + \sigma_i) \bmod 4) + i\}_{i=0,\dots,3}$ where $u = \lfloor j/4 \rfloor$ is the column of the collision. They are all different modulo 4 so that it is easy to infer the σ_i parameters from them.

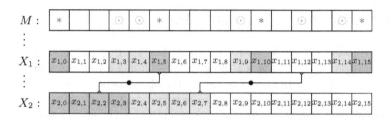

Fig. 6. Collision between $x_{1,5}$ and $x_{2,2}$ revealing a `4-Collision`(medium gray/red,$*$). And collision between $x_{1,12}$ and $x_{2,7}$ revealing a `5-Collision`(light gray/green,$\odot$).

3.2   Retrieving K_0 and K_{10} Up to a XOR with a Constant Byte

The first step consists in detecting collisions between first round S-Boxes at two indices i and i' (cf. light gray/green boxes on Figure 7) either on a same trace or on two different ones. Each such collision implies equality of two S-Boxes inputs and provides us with a linear relation between two key bytes:

$$x_{1,i} = x_{1,i'} \;\Leftrightarrow\; (m_i \oplus k_{0,i}) = (m_{i'} \oplus k_{0,i'})$$
$$\Leftrightarrow\; k_{0,i} \oplus k_{0,i'} = m_i \oplus m_{i'}$$

Gathering several relations with random plaintexts eventually allows to relate all key bytes together. We now know each differential $\mu_{0,i,i'} = k_{0,i} \oplus k_{0,i'}$ and the key K_0 is thus retrieved up to a XOR with a constant byte. For example, it suffices to know the value of $k_{0,0}$ to compute other key bytes as $k_{0,i} = k_{0,0} \oplus \mu_{0,0,i}$.

Since we already retrieved the `ShiftRows` parameters we know which last round S-Box index any ciphertext byte is linked to. Similarly to the recovery of K_0, encrypting random plaintexts and observing collisions in the last round S-Boxes (cf. medium gray/red boxes on Figure 7) makes it possible to gather linear relations $\mu_{10,i,i'} = k_{10,i} \oplus k_{10,i'} = c_i \oplus c_{i'}$ which eventually reveal K_{10} up to a XOR with a constant byte. Note that the same set of traces can be used to recover both K_0 and K_{10} up to a constant.

3.3   Retrieving the S-Box Table

A collision between first round S-Box at index i and last round S-Box at index j (cf. dark gray/blue boxes on Figure 7) implies that $x_{1,i} = x_{10,j}$ and $y_{1,i} = y_{10,j}$. Denoting $x = x_{1,i}$ and $y = y_{10,j}$, the collision reveals an S-Box relation $S(x) = y$ for two values $x = x' \oplus k_{0,0}$ and $y = y' \oplus k_{10,0}$ where $x' = m_i \oplus \mu_{0,0,i}$ and $y' = c_{j'} \oplus \mu_{10,0,j'}$ [4] are known from the attacker.

The S-Box table can thus be recovered by encrypting random plaintexts and observing such collisions (possibly on different traces) between first and last round S-Boxes. Once all 256 S-Box relations

$$S(x' \oplus k_{0,0}) = y' \oplus k_{10,0}$$

have been identified for all couples (x', y') the table S is recovered up to two XOR permutations on its inputs and outputs respectively.

When only collisions on the same trace are exploited, the relations are gathered like in the coupon collector problem. In that case we can save a large amount of traces by choosing the plaintexts so that all $x'_i = m_i \oplus \mu_{0,0,i}$ are different from each others and do not belong to already known relations.

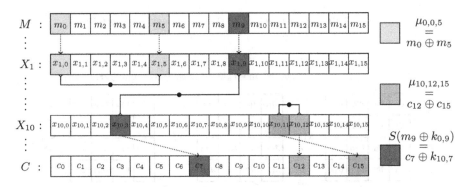

Fig. 7. Examples of collisions used in different attack steps in order to retrieve K_0 (light gray/green), K_{10} (medium gray/red) or the S-Box (dark gray/blue)

3.4   Retrieving K and All Key Schedule Parameters

The next step is simply a 2^{26} offline exhaustive search that aims at recovering the absolute value of the key K as well as the key schedule parameters which are the amount of rotation η of the RotWord operation and the constant byte ρ that defines the Rcon vector.

---

[4] Due to the ShiftRows the ciphertext byte related to the collision is located at index $j' = 4((u - \sigma_k) \bmod 4) + (j \bmod 4)$ where $u = \lfloor j/4 \rfloor$.

For each candidate about $k_{0,0}$ and $k_{10,0}$ we know K_0, K_{10} and the S-Box table. It is then sufficient to make guesses also about the 2^2 values of η and the 2^8 values of ρ in order to be able to compute the key schedule and derive all round keys. Each of these 2^{26} candidates suggests a K_{10} value which is checked against the 128-bit known K_{10}. As this check on K_{10} is a 128-bit constraint, the probability of finding a false positive is overwhelmingly low, which has been confirmed by our simulations.

Note that a natural extension of the definition of Rcon would be to define each constant word as $\text{Rcon}[r] = (\rho_0^{r-1}, \rho_1^{r-1}, \rho_2^{r-1}, \rho_3^{r-1})$. Then the exhaustive search takes 2^{50} computations which may is unaffordable. We propose in Appendix A an adaptation of our attack that can deal with such 32-bit entropy Rcon as well as with a full 320-bit entropy Rcon where all words are independent.

3.5 Retrieving the MixColumns Matrix

At this point we have retrieved all secret parameters of the AES except the coefficients $\{\alpha_i\}_{i=0,...,15}$ of the MixColumns matrix. We are so able to know the input of the first round MixColumns for each already acquired trace. As can be seen on Figure 8, each byte u_{4i+j} of the MixColumns output depends on 4 same-row parameters $\{\alpha_j, \alpha_{j+4}, \alpha_{j+8}, \alpha_{j+12}\}$:

$$u_{4i+j} = \alpha_j * v_{4i} \oplus \alpha_{j+4} * v_{4i+1} \oplus \alpha_{j+8} * v_{4i+2} \oplus \alpha_{j+12} * v_{4i+3}$$

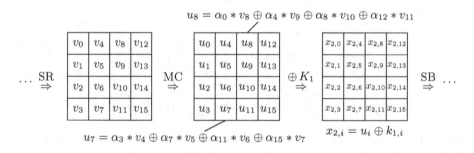

Fig. 8. Propagation of value v through MixColumns of first round

The goal is thus to obtain such equations by determining some input values $x_{2,\ell}$ of the second round S-Boxes, from which u_ℓ is inferred as $u_\ell = x_{2,\ell} \oplus k_{1,\ell}$ and the MixColumns input is derived from the plaintext. Gathering 4 independent equations involving the same set of parameters, and solving offline this system of equations, allows to recover a row of 4 parameters of MixColumns matrix. Finding 4 equations for each row allows to determine the whole matrix.

In both inter-traces and intra-trace settings no more traces are required for obtaining these equations as we can exploit traces already acquired for the previous steps. Amongst these traces we can find some $x_{2,\ell}$ values by noticing collisions occurring between $x_{2,\ell}$ and either some byte of known X_1 or some byte of known X_{10}. Our simulations demonstrate that the number of previously acquired traces always happens to be far from sufficient to get enough independent equations.

3.6   Experimental Results

In order to verify the soundness of our attack and estimate the number of traces necessary to fully recover the AES secret specifications we have performed PC-based simulations. For each of the successive steps we developed a program that simulates only that part of the attack so that we can evaluate the individual cost of each step. All these programs have been executed on a large number of simulation runs that comprise the following features:

1. a secret AES-like block cipher is generated by drawing at random the set of its parameters complying with properties stated as in Section 2.2,
2. a secret key K is generated at random,
3. all parameters (or key knowledge) that are supposed to have been retrieved in previous steps are considered as known,
4. an oracle simulates a perfect collision detection: it takes as input all the AES parameters, the key, a plaintext and two S-Box positions (possibly at different rounds and/or on different traces) and returns a Boolean value which indicates whether the input/output pairs of these two S-Boxes are equal or not,
5. the attack step is performed by following the method described in the relevant section, and the number of traces used in the oracle queries is counted.

Table 1 presents the number of traces – averaged on 10 000 runs – required by each step in both intra-trace and inter-traces settings. For sake of clarity we also mention the two last steps that do not necessitate any further trace.

Our attack on an unprotected implementation recovers the full set of secret AES parameters as well as the key within less than 400 traces on average by intra-trace analysis, and less than 100 traces when collisions between different traces can be exploited.

Table 1. Experimental results on an unprotected implementation

Step	# of traces		# of
	intra	inter	runs
Section 3.1 - Retrieving `ShiftRows`	11.4	5.	10 000
Section 3.2 - Reducing K_0 and K_{10} entropies to 8 bits	69.5	7.8	10 000
Section 3.3 - Retrieving the S-Box	287.7	81.2	10 000
Section 3.4 - Retrieving K and the key schedule	0.	0.	–
Section 3.5 - Retrieving `MixColumns`	0.	0.	10 000
Total	**368.6**	**94.0**	

4   Attacking an Implementation with Both First-Order Masking and Shuffling

In this section we consider a first-order side channel protected implementation of the AES. Precisely we assume an implementation that jointly features two countermeasures:

The first countermeasure makes use of an 8-bit Boolean masking all along the data and the key schedule paths. Due to the considered attacker model, we are only concerned by the effect of this countermeasure on the inputs and outputs of the SubBytes operation. The masking of all other operations have no consequence on our attack. SubBytes uses a randomized version $\widetilde{S}$ of the S-Box table by means of two independent 8-bit input and output Boolean masks r_{in} and r_{out} such that $\widetilde{S}(x \oplus r_{in}) = S(x) \oplus r_{out}$ for all x. Due to memory and time constraints, typical embedded implementations of this countermeasures refresh the S-Box randomization only at each execution. We thus assume that the same randomized table is used for each input index and at each round of a same execution[5]. The main negative effect of this countermeasure for the attacker is that he is no more able to detect and exploit S-Box collisions from two different traces. Though, note that it is still possible to interpret collisions on $\widetilde{S}$ on a same trace as revealing collisions on the non-randomized S-Box. Thus, with this single countermeasure only, the intra-trace version of the attack described in Section 3 perfectly applies.

We also assume a second countermeasure which shuffles the 16 computations of $\widetilde{y}_i = \widetilde{S}(\widetilde{x}_i)$ at each round[6]. As a consequence, the observation of a collision between two (or more) computations of $\widetilde{S}(\widetilde{x})$ (possibly at different rounds) gives no information about the index of the $\widetilde{x} = x \oplus r_{in}$ input bytes. The attacker is thus limited to observe the number of different S-Box inputs at each round, and how many occurrences of each of them there are. To capture this limited attacker capacity, we introduce the following definition :

Definition 2. *Let's define an n-structure (or more simply a structure) of type $n_1^{(t_1)} n_2^{(t_2)} \ldots n_s^{(t_s)}$ of elements of E the set of all n-tuples of elements of E (with $n = \Sigma_k t_k n_k$) such that $t = \Sigma_k t_k$ distinct elements appear in the tuple with $n_1, n_2, \ldots, n_s$ occurrences of each of them respectively.*

For example, any X_r made of all distinct S-Box input bytes belongs to a structure of type $1^{(16)}$ of elements of $GF(2^8)$. As another example, the 16-tuple:

$$X_1 = (13, 47, 173, 47, 86, 119, 13, 47, 119, 223, 205, 119, 37, 88, 200, 5)$$

is a $1^{(8)}2^{(1)}3^{(2)}$ structure as 13 appears twice, and 47 and 119 appear three times each.

---

[5] A mask conversion is applied to masked intermediate values before or at the end of each round to adapt from the r_{out} of one round to the r_{in} of the next one.

[6] Here also the shuffling of other AES operations such as ShiftRows, MixColumns, AddRoundKey, etc. have no influence on the attack proposed in the considered S-Box collision model.

4.1 Retrieving K_0 Up to a XOR with a Constant Byte

The first step consists in executing the AES with random plaintexts until finding one such that the first round SubBytes presents a unique n-fold colliding value (a $1^{(16-n)}n^{(1)}$ structure). Only about a couple of traces are needed on average to find such a reference trace. Then, for each $i = 0, \ldots, 15$, one modifies m_i and observes whether the collision disappears (or its multiplicity n is reduced). The set I of indices for which this happens verifies:

$$\forall\, i, i' \in I, \; k_{0,i} \oplus k_{0,i'} = m_i \oplus m_{i'}$$

where m_i and $m_{i'}$ are the byte values from the reference plaintext.

By comparing the reference trace with at most 16 modified ones, one should result with $|I| = n$. However, if $n = 2$, a non-detection may occur when the change of an input byte involved in the initial collision makes it collide with another not initially colliding one. In such rare case, it should be sufficient to change again the different message bytes to reveal all which of them are involved in the initial collision.

Once a set of n colliding indices is identified, n different key bytes are linearly related together. Repeating this process to exploit different reference plaintexts exhibiting $1^{(16-n)}n^{(1)}$ structures, eventually allows to relate all key bytes to each others. K_0 is then retrieved up to a XOR with a constant byte (e.g. $k_{0,0}$).

Notice that two tricks allow to reduce the number of traces required to relate all key bytes together. First, when the linear relation that some subset J of key bytes verify is known, one should choose the reference plaintext such that X_1 bytes belonging to J are all different. The second trick is an early abort of the process of determining the set I for a reference plaintext: as soon as a new relation is found that involves a key byte from J, one can skip considering other indices from J .

4.2 Retrieving K_{10} Up to a XOR with a Constant Byte

If the attacker can query a decipher oracle with chosen ciphertexts, it is possible to recover the value of K_{10} up to a XOR with a constant by a similar method than that used to recover K_0. One first encrypts random plaintexts until finding one such that the last round SubBytes presents a $1^{(16-n)}n^{(1)}$ structure. Let C be the ciphertext. For modified ciphertexts C', differing from C by only one byte c_i, one then encrypts $M' = \text{AES}_K^{-1}(C')$ and observes whether the collision in the last round S-Boxes disappeared. By the same principle as for K_0, it is thus possible to identify relations like $k_{10,i} \oplus k_{10,i'} = c_i \oplus c_{i'}$. Accumulating sufficiently many such relations eventually reveals K_{10} up to a XOR with a constant, with the same complexity than for K_0.

When the attacker does not have access to a decipher oracle, it is still possible to recover K_{10}. For random plaintexts, we exploit only traces which show no collision in the last round S-Boxes (a $1^{(16)}$ structure). In that case we know that for each index pair (i, i'), $\mu_{10,i,i'}$ is not equal to $c_i \oplus c_{i'}$. Starting from lists of all possible values for all $\mu_{10,i,i'}$, and accumulating such negative information, we end up with sufficiently many lists containing only one remaining value so that K_{10} is finally recovered up to a XOR with a constant byte (e.g. $k_{10,0}$).

Note that we can do better by exploiting (possibly a posteriori) traces with collisions as well. Whenever some $\mu_{10,i,i'}$ is known one can detect when a collision occurs between S-Boxes related to bytes c_i and $c_{i'}$. If it happens that this identified collision on X_{10} is the only one on this trace, then one can infer negative information as above for all index pairs (j, j') not involved in the collision.

4.3   Retrieving the S-Box Table

At this point, we know K_0 and K_{10}, each up to a XOR with a constant. We now show how to recover the S-Box table for each candidate about these two constants. We are seeking couples $(x' = x \oplus k_{0,0}, y' = y \oplus k_{10,0})$ verifying $S(x) = y$ as in Section 3.3. To that end we select wisely chosen plaintexts such that X_1 contains five different byte values $x^{(1)}$, $x^{(2)}$, $x^{(3)}$, $x^{(4)}$ and $x^{(6)}$. As depicted on Figure 9 each value is repeated a different number of times, so that when a collision occurs the colliding value can be identified based on the collision order.

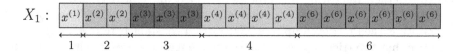

Fig. 9. Example of state X_1 having five values with different numbers of occurrences

If a collision occurs between one (or several) of the five input values $x^{(i)}$ and some X_{10} byte then at least 240 values y' are invalidated for pairing with $x' = x^{(i)} \oplus k_{0,0}$. For any other non-colliding $x^{(j)}$, one can invalidate up to 16 values y' for pairing with $x' = x^{(j)} \oplus k_{0,0}$. After each execution one should propagate the negative information as much as possible. For example if it is known that x' is necessarily paired with y' then one can invalidate all couples (x', y'') and (x'', y') with $x'' \neq x'$ and $y'' \neq y'$. This, in turn can reveal another assured pair, and so on.

The same set of $x^{(i)}$ can be used multiple times if needed by just changing their positions. Nevertheless, as a wise strategy for choosing the $x^{(i)}$ values, we suggest to select values $x' = x^{(i)} \oplus k_{0,0}$ with the least number of invalidated y' values. The rational behind this criterion is to maximize the expected gained information.

4.4   Retrieving K and All Key Schedule Parameters

The same offline 2^{26} exhaustive search (not impacted by the countermeasures) as in Section 3.4 can be conducted to retrieve K and the key schedule parameters.

We also provide in Appendix B an adaptation of our attack that can deal with the case of a 32-bit or a full entropy Rcon constants set.

4.5   Retrieving the `MixColumns` Matrix and the `ShiftRows` Parameters

Knowing K and the S-Box we are able to fully control vectors X_1 and Y_1. Let's encrypt the plaintext M_0 defined by $m_i = k_{0,i} \oplus S^{-1}(0)$ for all i, such that $Y_1 = (0, \ldots, 0)$. For that reference plaintext the output of the `MixColumns` is also all zeroes and we have $X_2 = K_1$. By analysing the trace of this execution (or simply because we know K_1) we obtain the number n_0 of second round S-Box inputs which collide with the value $S^{-1}(0)$ of X_1 in the first round (cf. Figure 10).

Without loss of generality, assume that we want to recover the first column $(\alpha_0, \alpha_1, \alpha_2, \alpha_3)$ of the `MixColumns` matrix. Let's modify only one message byte m_{4u} and denote by $v = y_{1,4u}$ the value of the active cell at S-Box output. The column number $(u - \sigma_0) \bmod 4$ takes value $(v, 0, 0, 0)$ at input, and $(\alpha_0 v, \alpha_1 v, \alpha_2 v, \alpha_3 v)$ at output of the `MixColumns`, whereas all other columns remain unchanged. Assuming that the active quadruplet of bytes of X_2 does not contain the value $S^{-1}(0)$ in the reference execution[7], by exhausting v we can identify four values[8] v_0, v_1, v_2 and v_3 which induce more than n_0 occurrences of $S^{-1}(0)$ in the second round S-Box inputs (cf. Figure 11). Since each of these values has provoked an extra $S^{-1}(0)$ in X_2, we know that for some unknown permutation π of $\{0, 1, 2, 3\}$ the following holds:

$$\forall i = 0, \ldots, 3 \qquad \alpha_i v_{\pi(i)} \oplus k_{1,4((u-\sigma_0) \bmod 4)+i} = S^{-1}(0)$$

For each possible σ_0 this system of equations suggests a set of 24 values (one per candidate about π) for the targeted column of coefficients $(\alpha_0, \alpha_1, \alpha_2, \alpha_3)$.

At this point, we can change the value of u and repeat this process with the active cell at the top of another column. For each possible σ_0 we obtain a new set of 24 candidates for the column of coefficients. By intersecting the two sets, with high probability, there remains only one column value for the correct σ_0 and none for the incorrect ones, which therefore reveals $(\alpha_0 v, \alpha_1 v, \alpha_2 v, \alpha_3 v)$ and σ_0.

We can do better by having two active bytes on the same row. This allows the attacker to gather the eight v values that produce extra collisions with only one stone. The number of permutation candidates to exhaust becomes 8! (instead of $2 \times 4!$) which is still affordable.

By repeating this attack with the active cell located on the other rows, we can successively recover the three other columns of coefficients together with the corresponding `ShiftRows` parameters.

In the rare cases where it remains an indecision about some column(s) of `MixColumns` coefficients (and possibly `ShiftRows` parameters), it can be solved

---

[7] The opposite case should be rare and is easily detectable by observing a reduction of the number of occurrences of $S^{-1}(0)$. In that case, simply modify u to change the column of the active cell.

[8] It may happen that less than four values are identified when one or two of them produce multiple extra $S^{-1}(0)$ values. In such case, these special v values should be counted as many times as their collision order.

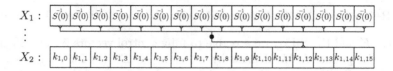

Fig. 10. Collision revealing that $n_0 = 1$

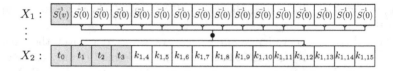

Fig. 11. Presence of an extra collision $(n = 2)$ gives exploitable information

by checking the few AES-like candidates against a known plaintext/ciphertext pair.

4.6   Experimental Results

We performed simulations of the different attack steps described in this section in a similar way as for the unprotected implementation case described in Section 3.

Table 2 presents the number of traces – averaged on 10 000 runs – required by each step of the attack. For sake of clarity we also mention the offline exhaustive search of Section 4.4 that does not necessitate any further trace.

Overall, less than 4 000 traces are required to fully recover to whole set of secret AES parameters in the more realistic scenario of a classical first-order protected implementation and no prior information about the key.

We emphasize that the entropy of secret information in the case of a SCARE attack is usually much important compared to a classical key recovery. In the considered AES-like case, the total entropy to be retrieved amounts to about 1 830 bits[9] of information in addition to the 128 key bits.

Table 2. Experimental results on a masked and shuffled implementation

Step	# of traces	# of runs
Section 4.1 - Reducing K_0 entropy to 8 bits	245.6	10 000
Section 4.2 - Reducing K_{10} entropy to 8 bits	1 407.7	10 000
Section 4.3 - Retrieving the S-Box	1 263.4	10 000
Section 4.4 - Retrieving K and the key schedule	0.	–
Section 4.5 - Retrieving MC and SR	910.0	10 000
Total	**3 826.7**	

---

[9] Taking account of all secret components: S-Box($\log_2(256!) \simeq 1684$ bits), ShiftRows (4 x 2 bits), MixColumns (16 x 8 bits), RotWord (2 bits), Rcon (8 bits).

5   Countermeasures

We showed in Section 4 that our attack applies to a first-order protected implementation even if this countermeasure comes together with shuffling of independent operations.

First, we notice that our attack should not be feasible on an hardware AES implementation or if the attacker is not able to choose the plaintexts.

While it is a quite memory consuming countermeasure, we have envisaged a high-order masking and shuffling protected implementation where 16 randomized S-Box tables are computed at the beginning of each execution, each table being masked with independent couples of input and output masks. This 128-bit mask countermeasure, which necessitates 4 kilo-bytes of RAM to store the different S-Boxes, prevents the attacker to exploit collisions occurring at two different S-Box indices. Nevertheless vertical collisions between S-Boxes at the same position in different rounds are still observable and provide the advantage that the attacker knows that the two colliding indices are equal. We have also found an attack against this strong countermeasure provided that the attacker has the prior knowledge of K_0 up to a XOR with a constant. We intend to describe this attack in an extended version of this paper. While we have not yet precisely estimated its complexity, we think that it may require many dozens of thousands traces which may be considered as dissuasive.

We have also studied the T-Box equivalent implementation which merges SubBytes and MixColumns steps in four 1 kilo-bytes 8-bit to 32-bit tables. This implementation may be considered as a countermeasure attempt since the four tables are different which reduces the potential of collisions occurrence. Unfortunately, such implementation option (even in 32-bit or 128-bit masked versions) is still vulnerable to small adaptations of the attacks described in this paper provided the prior knowledge of K_0 up to a constant.

Considering the powerful potential of information retrieval provided by the S-Box collision model, we think that a full higher-order masking scheme of the AES such as the ones recently proposed [18,9,4] is an efficient countermeasure against our attack.

As another safe option we advice the developers to also include generic hardware and/or software countermeasures such as random delays or current scramblers that can mitigate the side-channel signal and make the observation of collisions difficult or even impossible.

6   Conclusion

We proposed a new application of SCARE attack to reverse engineer secret specifications of a modified AES where every parameter can be changed provided that its SPN structure and sizes are preserved. Our chosen plaintext attacks, which use collisions detected when two S-Box operations have same inputs and outputs, apply on 8-bit processor implementations and do not necessitate the knowledge of the encryption key.

On unprotected implementations the full set of secret parameters and the key are recovered within an average of only 94 or 369 traces depending whether the attacker can detect collisions on different traces or not.

We also considered protected implementations which feature a common set of countermeasures including both first-order masking and shuffling of independent operations. Those countermeasures do not prevent from retrieving the secret parameters which is still possible and necessitates to analyse about 3 800 traces.

This study illustrates the powerful potential of information retrieval provided by the S-Box collision model and confirms the need to protect AES implementations against high-order side channel analysis.

References

1. Biryukov, A., Bogdanov, A., Khovratovich, D., Kasper, T.: Collision Attacks on AES-Based MAC: Alpha-MAC. In: Paillier, P., Verbauwhede, I. (eds.) CHES 2007. LNCS, vol. 4727, pp. 166–180. Springer, Heidelberg (2007)
2. Bogdanov, A.: Improved Side-Channel Collision Attacks on AES. In: Adams, C., Miri, A., Wiener, M. (eds.) SAC 2007. LNCS, vol. 4876, pp. 84–95. Springer, Heidelberg (2007)
3. Bogdanov, A.: Multiple-Differential Side-Channel Collision Attacks on AES. In: Oswald, E., Rohatgi, P. (eds.) CHES 2008. LNCS, vol. 5154, pp. 30–44. Springer, Heidelberg (2008)
4. Carlet, C., Goubin, L., Prouff, E., Quisquater, M., Rivain, M.: Higher-Order Masking Schemes for S-Boxes. In: Canteaut, A. (ed.) FSE 2012. LNCS, vol. 7549, pp. 366–384. Springer, Heidelberg (2012)
5. Clavier, C.: An Improved SCARE Cryptanalysis Against a Secret A3/A8 GSM Algorithm. In: McDaniel, P., Gupta, S.K. (eds.) ICISS 2007. LNCS, vol. 4812, pp. 143–155. Springer, Heidelberg (2007)
6. Clavier, C., Feix, B., Gagnerot, G., Roussellet, M., Verneuil, V.: Improved Collision-Correlation Power Analysis on First Order Protected AES. In: Preneel and Takagi (eds.) [16], pp. 49–62
7. Daudigny, R., Ledig, H., Muller, F., Valette, F.: SCARE of the DES. In: Ioannidis, J., Keromytis, A.D., Yung, M. (eds.) ACNS 2005. LNCS, vol. 3531, pp. 393–406. Springer, Heidelberg (2005)
8. Guilley, S., Sauvage, L., Micolod, J., Réal, D., Valette, F.: Defeating Any Secret Cryptography with SCARE Attacks. In: Abdalla, M., Barreto, P.S.L.M. (eds.) LATINCRYPT 2010. LNCS, vol. 6212, pp. 273–293. Springer, Heidelberg (2010)
9. Kim, H., Hong, S., Lim, J.: A Fast and Provably Secure Higher-Order Masking of AES S-Box. In: Preneel and Takagi (eds.) [16], pp. 95–107.
10. Kocher, P.C.: Timing Attacks on Implementations of Diffie-Hellman, RSA, DSS, and Other Systems. In: Koblitz, N. (ed.) CRYPTO 1996. LNCS, vol. 1109, pp. 104–113. Springer, Heidelberg (1996)
11. Kocher, P.C., Jaffe, J., Jun, B.: Differential Power Analysis. In: Wiener, M. (ed.) CRYPTO 1999. LNCS, vol. 1666, pp. 388–397. Springer, Heidelberg (1999)
12. National Bureau of Standards. Data Encryption Standard. Federal Information Processing Standard #46 (1977)
13. National Institute of Standards and Technology. Advanced Encryption Standard (AES). Federal Information Processing Standard #197 (2001)

14. Novak, R.: Side-Channel Attack on Substitution Blocks. In: Zhou, J., Yung, M., Han, Y. (eds.) ACNS 2003. LNCS, vol. 2846, pp. 307–318. Springer, Heidelberg (2003)
15. Novak, R.: Sign-Based Differential Power Analysis. In: Chae, K.-J., Yung, M. (eds.) WISA 2003. LNCS, vol. 2908, pp. 203–216. Springer, Heidelberg (2004)
16. Preneel, B., Takagi, T. (eds.): CHES 2011. LNCS, vol. 6917. Springer (2011)
17. Réal, D., Dubois, V., Guilloux, A.-M., Valette, F., Drissi, M.: SCARE of an Unknown Hardware Feistel Implementation. In: Grimaud, G., Standaert, F.-X. (eds.) CARDIS 2008. LNCS, vol. 5189, pp. 218–227. Springer, Heidelberg (2008)
18. Rivain, M., Prouff, E.: Provably Secure Higher-Order Masking of AES. In: Mangard, S., Standaert, F.-X. (eds.) CHES 2010. LNCS, vol. 6225, pp. 413–427. Springer, Heidelberg (2010)
19. Rivain, M., Roche, T.: SCARE of Secret Ciphers with SPN structures. In: Sako, K., Sarkar, P. (eds.) ASIACRYPT 2013 Part I. LNCS, vol. 8269, pp. 526–544. Springer, Heidelberg (2013)
20. Schramm, K., Leander, G., Felke, P., Paar, C.: A Collision-Attack on AES: Combining Side Channel- and Differential-Attack. In: Joye, M., Quisquater, J.-J. (eds.) CHES 2004. LNCS, vol. 3156, pp. 163–175. Springer, Heidelberg (2004)
21. Schramm, K., Wollinger, T., Paar, C.: A New Class of Collision Attacks and Its Application to DES. In: Johansson, T. (ed.) FSE 2003. LNCS, vol. 2887, pp. 206–222. Springer, Heidelberg (2003)

A Attack against Extended Rcon on Unprotected Implementation

In the main part of the paper we assumed an 8-bit entropy Rcon vector made of 10 words $\text{Rcon}[r] = (\rho^{r-1}, 0, 0, 0)$. Two natural extensions would be to define a 32-bit entropy or a full entropy Rcon vectors of constant words respectively equal to $(\rho_0^{r-1}, \rho_1^{r-1}, \rho_2^{r-1}, \rho_3^{r-1})$ and $(\rho_{r,0}, \rho_{r,1}, \rho_{r,2}, \rho_{r,3})$ for $r = 1, \ldots, 10$. In the first case the exhaustive search of Sections 3.4 and 4.4 necessitates 2^{50} computations which is a quite intensive task, while it is completely infeasible in the second case.

In this appendix we present an adaptation of this attack step that exploits new collisions to recover Rcon parameters in both extended cases.

A.1 Inter-traces Version

The first step uses 2^8 particular plaintexts in order to accumulate information about K_1. The attacker already knows every couples (x, y) verifying $S(x \oplus k_{0,0}) = y \oplus k_{10,0}$. So for each candidate for $k_{10,0}$ he knows the plaintext that produces an all zeroes Y_1 vector. For each candidate for $k_{0,0}$, by observing collisions between first round of already acquired traces and second round of those particular traces, the attacker can determine the values $x_{2,i}$. For the correct guess on $(k_{0,0}, k_{10,0})$ the identified X_2 vector is equal to K_1 while it is considered as random for incorrect guesses.

The second step uses the key schedule offline step to obtain other informations about K_1. For each candidate for $(k_{0,0}, k_{10,0})$, the attacker can determine the S-Box. For each further candidates for η and $\rho_{1,0}$ he can compute the set $\{k_{1,0}, k_{1,4}, k_{1,8}, k_{1,12}\}$. So for each $(k_{0,0}, k_{10,0})$ there are 2^{10} candidates for 4 bytes of K_1 which are checked against the K_1 value suggested by the first step. With high probability there will be only one match which reveals the correct $(k_{0,0}, k_{10,0}, \eta, \rho_{1,0})$. At this point, the attacker knows K_0, K_{10}, the S-Box, η, K_1 and $\rho_{1,0}$. Knowing K_0, η, and K_1, he can easily compute $\rho_{1,1}$, $\rho_{1,2}$ and $\rho_{1,3}$.

The MixColumns parameters can now be recovered as described in Section 3.5 since only first round parameters are required for this step. Then, iteratively, it is possible to compute successive values of K_r and $(\rho_{r,0}, \rho_{r,1}, \rho_{r,2}, \rho_{r,3})$ for each round $r = 2, \ldots, 9$. The attacker computes the values just before the AddRoundKey of round r. He is also able to recover X_{r+1} by collisions on already acquired traces. This gives K_r from which the ρ parameters for this round are derived. Rcon[10] is finally inferred from K_9 and K_{10}.

A.2 Intra-trace Version

In case where only intra-trace collisions are available, attacker can adapt the previous method.

To identify $x_{2,i}$ values for each $k_{10,0}$ candidate, he places zeroes in the first 8 bytes of Y_1 and chooses the last 8 plaintext bytes to place 8 different values in the right part of X_1 at each execution. Each collision observed between the right part of X_1 and the left part of X_2 reveals the value of some $x_{2,i}$ up to $k_{0,0}$. The same can be done be inverting the roles of the right and left parts. For each $k_{0,0}$, known $x_{2,i}$ values are checked against one of the four sets of 2^{10} K_1 computed offline. When sufficiently many $x_{2,i}$ have been identified all sets become empty which invalidates $k_{10,0}$ except for the correct candidate.

The collisions on last step in order to learn informations on bytes of round keys can be done intra-trace too. For each trace already acquired we know the exact values of S-Boxes of first, second and last rounds. So the attacker will learn the value of one $x_{i,j}$ at each collision with any one of known S-Boxes. Notice that the attacker progressively learns values for other rounds S-Boxes making progressively grow the number of instructive collisions.

B   Attack against Extended Rcon on Protected Version

In case of joint 8-bit masking and shuffling countermeasures, attacker applies the method described in Appendix A with some modifications.

For the first step, attacker will uses intra-trace method with 12 fixed bytes and 4 free bytes at first round in order to have 12 fixed bytes in second round and 4 bytes considered as random (impacted by the free bytes). He cannot determine exactly where a collision between X_1 and X_2 occurs but can determine if it occurs between the fixed parts, between the free parts or between a free and a fixed part.

If the collision occurs between the fixed parts it will not disappear when he changes the free part. He learns that the fixed value of first round collides with one of the fixed values of second round.

If the collision occurs between a first round byte and one from the random part of second round, it will disappear every time he changes only one byte of the free part. He does not learn anything and waits for other cases.

If the collision occurs between the fixed part of second round and the free part of first round, it will disappear only when he changes the colliding free byte. He learns which byte from the free part collides with a fixed byte.

The attacker can so accumulate the values of the 12 first bytes of X_2 without knowing their precise positions. Remind that $X_2 = K_1$ if $k_{10,0}$ is correct. He can then use this knowledge to intersect with offline candidates of K_1 lines.

For the last step collisions, the attacker gathers data about X_r when there are no collision between the rth round values and a known round. When a collision occurs he cannot determine the colliding bytes, but when a no-collision occurs he learns 16 byte values that are not used in those S-Boxes. By accumulation he is finally able to determine the value of K_r and then the values of Rcon[r].

Security Analysis of GFN: 8-Round Distinguisher for 4-Branch Type-2 GFN

Donghoon Chang, Abhishek Kumar, and Somitra Sanadhya

Indraprashtha Institute of Information Technology Delhi (IIIT-Delhi), India
{donghoon,abhishek1101,somitra}@iiitd.ac.in

Abstract. Generalized Feistel network (GFN) is a widely used design for encryption algorithm such as DES, IDEA and others. Generally, block ciphers are used not only for symmetric encryption but also as building blocks of cryptographic hash functions in modes such as Matyas-Meyer-Oseas (MMO) and Miyaguchi-Preneel. For these compression function modes, block ciphers are used with a key that is known to the attacker. Therefore a known-key distinguisher on the internal block cipher can be directly converted into a distinguisher on the compression function. In other words, the security of a compression mode relies on the security of the internal block cipher used.

The security of the cipher in known-key setting is only due to the round function. Block ciphers popularly use sub-key XOR-ing followed by one or more SP-functions as the building block of a round function. The general understanding is that increasing the number of active S-boxes will cause more confusion and guarantee more secure ciphers against differential and linear cryptanalysis. In Indocrypt 2012, Sasaki compared the security of single-SP function with double-SP function and successfully mounted a distinguisher up to 7-round for 4-branch type-2 GFN with double-SP functions and up to 11-rounds of 2-branch single-SP functions by using the rebound attack technique. Based on the total number of S-boxes used and the number of rounds attacked, he argued that double-SP is in fact weaker than single-SP. The basis of this result is the number of rounds that the author could attack. In this work, we successfully increase the number of rounds attacked from 7 to 8 for 4-branch type-2 double-SP. The presented distinguisher is the first known distinguisher for 8 round 4-branch type-2 GFN with double SP-function. In our attack, we use an improved matching technique which is simpler than the byte-by-byte matching. This simple matching technique results in better complexity than the previously known 7 round distinguisher for most of the practical cases, allowing us to attack one extra round.

Keywords: Block cipher, rebound attack, generalized Feistel network, SP-functions, known-key distinguisher, active S-box.

1 Introduction

Design of block ciphers has been a challenging and interesting topic for cryptographers for a long time. Fesitel network and its variants have been a popular

G. Paul and S. Vaudenay (Eds.): INDOCRYPT 2013, LNCS 8250, pp. 136–148, 2013.
© Springer International Publishing Switzerland 2013

choice for block cipher designers since the seminal work of Luby and Rackoff [5] on proving its security.

Moreover, these primitives are also used as building blocks of compression functions, authenticated encryption schemes, signcryption schemes and many others. Typical examples of block cipher based constructions are Davies-Meyer, Matyas-Meyer-Oseas and Miyaguchi-Preneel hashing modes. The security of these designs lies on two parameters: the round function and the secret key. Recently, many attacks were proposed in the context of known-key setting [4] where the value of the key is already known to the attacker. In this case only the randomness of the key and the round function provides the security.

The security of round function can be understood in terms of the paradigm of confusion and diffusion. There are various ways to achieve high confusion and high diffusion in the design. Many block ciphers use a subkey XOR-ing followed by a non-linear component called S-box transformation and a linear transformation called P-box. This design paradign is popularly known as the SP-layer (single SP). Since only the S-boxes are responsible for non-linearity in the round function, it is generally understood that larger active S-boxes will provide a more secure design against differential [1] and liner attacks [6].

Recently, cryptographers analyzed the security of Block-ciphers in terms of repetition of SP-functions. In 2011, Bogdanov and Shibutani [2] analyzed 4-branch GFN with double SP-function and single SP-function in terms of number of the active S-boxes and concluded that double SP-function is more secure than single SP-function against differential and linear cryptanalysis. Note that [2] analyzed the design assuming infinite number of SP rounds. In 2011, Sasaki and Yasuda [9] used rebound attack technique on 2-branch single SP-function and successfully mounted distinguisher up to 11 rounds against it. More recently in Indocrypt 2012, Sasaki [8] presented the first cryptanalysis for 4-branch type-2 GFN with double SP-functions and showed a distinguisher against 7 rounds. He compared the two designs and opined that double SP is weaker than single SP when the number of rounds is finite.

Our Contribution: In this paper, we extend the number of rounds attacked from 7 to 8 for 4-branch type-2 GFN with double SP-function. We use a simple matching technique described by Sasaki in [8] and improve it further, which allows us to extend the distinguisher for an extra round. Our result is the first cryptanalytic result for 8 rounds of the above mentioned GFN. Moreover, our 7 round distinguisher has lesser complexity that the previously known best 7 round attack on the same GFN. Our result strengthens the belief of [8] that double SP is indeed weaker than single SP.

The rest of the paper is organized as follows. In § 2, we provide the notation used in this work and describe related prior work. Our attack on 4-branch type-2 GFN with double SP-function is presented in § 3 In § 4, we provide the summary of the attack with results. Finally, we conclude the work in § 5 with some open problems.

2   Preliminaries

2.1   The Generalized Feistel Network (GFN)

An N-bit block size is represented by m lines and the size of each line is n bits i.e $n = N/m$. This block cipher is called GFN, if the m lines satisfy the following restrictions [2].

1. After each round, lines are rotated by one position to the either right or left. [1]
2. Each lines follows one of the three criteria:
   (a) It is the source of a keyed, domain preserving, nonlinear function acting on n bits.
   (b) It is the output of a keyed, domain preserving, nonlinear function acting on n bits. The line is updated by XORing the output of the function to it.
   (c) It is neither source nor destination.
3. The structure should attain full diffusion after a finite number of rounds.

A schematic diagram of 4-line type-2 GFN is shown in Figure 1. A 4-line GFN divides an input of N-bit equally in four parts such that $N = (n_1, n_2, n_3, n_4)$ and a round of type-2 GFN outputs $[n_4 \oplus f_2(n_3), n_1, n_2 \oplus f_1(n_1), n_3]$ for keyed nonlinear functions f_1 and f_2. For details on the type of GFNs, please refer to [12].

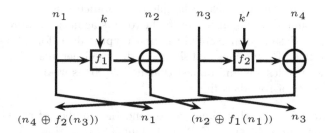

Fig. 1. GFN 4-line type-2

Based on the above criteria, we introduce the following notation to fix the parameters of the Generalized Feistel Network.

1. N:Length of the block in bits. Popular choices are 64 bits (e.g. in DES) and 128 bits (e.g. in AES).
2. n: Size of the input and output of the round function. In other words it is the size of one word. Therefore, for a 4-branch Feistel network $n = N/4$.
3. c: Input/output size of an S-box in bits. Popular choices are 8 bits or 4 bits. [2]

---

[1] In this paper lines are rotated one position right.
[2] For subsequent discussion c-bit will be termed as one byte.

4. r: Number of S-box used in one S-box layer, i.e., $r = n/c$.

As an example, the design of the CLEFIA block cipher [10] is very similar to 4-branch type-2 GFN with parameters $(N, n, c, r) = (128, 32, 8, 4)$.

2.2   Double SP Round Function

Round function of a 4-branch type-2 GFN with double SP-function has these six operations: XORing of subkey, S-box layer, permutation layer, again XORing of subkey, an S-box layer and finally a permutation layer at the end (since SP layer used twice, hence named as double SP) [2]. The design of double SP round function is described in Figure 2 and Figure 3 next. Next we briefly explain the operations used in the round function [11].

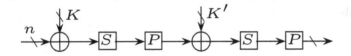

Fig. 2. Simplified Double-SP round function

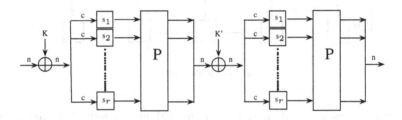

Fig. 3. Double-SP round function

Subkey XOR : This is the first layer of the round function. The input of the round function gets XOR'ed with the round key in this step. Note that the round key is generated by the key scheduling algorithm.

S-Box : S-box layer is used to create confusion. This layer may contain several S-boxes which could all be same (as in AES) or be different (as in DES). Each group of input bits is substituted by using one or more S-boxes. Usually, the S-boxes are represented in the form of tables.

If all the S-boxes of the S-box layer are different then the operation of the layer can be defined as $S[X] = S_1[X_1] \| S_2[X_2] \| S_3[X_3] \| \ldots \| S_r[X_r]$, where $X = X_1 \| X_2 \| X_3 \| \ldots \| X_r$.

On the other hand, if all the S-boxes are the same then the S-box layer operations can be defined as $S[X] = S[X_1] \| S[X_2] \| S[X_3] \| \ldots S[X_r]$.

Permutation Layer : Permutation layer is used to introduce diffusion in the cipher. It makes sure that local differences in the internal state before P-layer propagate to larger area of the state after this layer.

2.3 Rebound-Attack Technique

Rebound attack was first introduced by Mendel et al. [7] at FSE 2009 to attack hash functions Whirlpool and Grøstl. It has become a very useful technique to analyze the security of block cipher based compression functions. The aim of the technique is to get message pairs which will satisfy certain truncated differential trail. Truncated differential cryptanalysis, developed by Knudsen in 1994 [3], is a generalization of the differential cryptanalysis [1]. While the attacker is interested in differential on the full state in differential cryptanalysis, the truncated differential attack relaxes this condition and looks for partial state differentials.

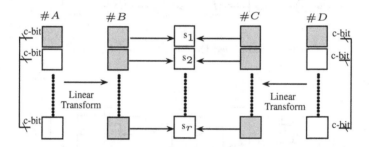

Fig. 4. Inbound phase

The entire truncated differential trail is divided into the following three phases:

1. Backward outbound phase,
2. Inbound phase,
3. Forward outbound phase.

Among these three phases, the inbound phase corresponds to a low probability part of the truncated differential trail. The basic attack strategy of Rebound attack is to find at least one starting point i.e. one paired values, which will follow the characteristics of inbound phase. After getting one starting point, the attacker checks whether or not the starting point satisfies the truncated differential path of the outbound phase. The criteria of success is to find at least one starting point which will follow the outbound phase.

We briefly describe the rebound attack idea now. The inbound phase consists of a linear layer, a non-linear layer and finally another linear layer. An example is shown in Figure 4 where truncated differential path for inbound phase is $1 \rightarrow F \rightarrow 1$. [3] To get a starting point, one chooses all possible differences of c bits

---
[3] F is any full active difference, i.e., a word where all bytes are active.

(size of an S-box) from both sides of the cipher. For both the directions, the attacker finds the truncated differential characteristic just before the component which causes non-linearity. The next step is to store all the input differences and the output differences for the non-linear component (set of S-boxes). Finally, we choose any one difference as input and try to find a matching output difference. We know that given any random input and output differences for an S-box, matching probability in the ideal case is 2^{c-1} where c is the input/output size of an S-box. For a randomly chosen input and output differences, there exist difference pairs following the given input/output differences with a probability roughly half (this probability is very close to the best possible probability, the actual probability depends upon DDT of S-box under consideration). Thus, if the non-linear component has r number of S-boxes then the matching probability for any randomly selected input/output difference pair is 2^{-r}. After matching all possible input and output differences, total number of matched difference will be 2^{2c-r}. So as long as $2c \geq r$, we will get at least one matched input and output difference and hence, 2^{2c} matching pairs.

We can describe the Rebound attack with reference to Figure 4 in the following steps.

1. Prepare differential distribution table (DDT) for all c-bit r S-boxes (in case the design uses the same S-boxe repeatedly, only one table is required).
2. For all possible $2^c - 1$ (in Figure 4 colored boxes represents active S-boxes) possible differences of state $\#A$, compute corresponding r-byte difference of state $\#B$, and store them in a table T.
3. Repeat Step 2, for state $\#D$, and after getting differences at state $\#C$, check whether this output difference of S-boxes will match with any input differences stored in table T by using DDT. After getting any such matched input/output pair, produce it as a matching result. The matching probability of one difference is 2^{-r}, so after matching all $2^c - 1$ differences, we have 2^{c-r} matched differences and hence 2^c matching pairs.
4. Repeat Step 2 and Step 3, form backward direction.

Since Step 4 will also result in the same number of matches as Step 3, we will have 2^{2c-r} matched differences and 2^{2c} matching pairs after completing all the Steps from 1 to 4.

2.4   Previous Rebound Attack on 4-Branch Double-SP Feistel

In 2011, Sasaki and Yasuda [9] successfully mounted distinguishers for 9-round and 11-rounds for single SP-function. In order to compare the security of GFN in the context of single SP-function with double SP-function, Sasaki again applied the same technique for 4-branch type-2 GFN with double SP-function for 6-rounds [8] and presented a distinguisher. He exploited the fact that an attacker may control the behavior of S-boxes for a few rounds. He interpreted the result that double SP-function is weaker than single SP-function.[4] The metric of his comparison is the number of rounds attacked. In the same work, he used byte-by-byte matching approach in place of simple rebound technique for matching and extended number of rounds attacked. He could find a distinguisher for one more round i.e up to 7-rounds, which is the best known attack in terms of the number of rounds distinguished.

The complexity of the 7-round distinguisher was shown to be 2^{3c-r} 7-round 4-branch computations in [8]. Note that the complexity in the case of random permutation will be $2^{(n-c)/2}$ queries to the permutation.

3   8-Round Distinguishing Attack on Type-2 4-Branch GFN with Double-SP Layer

In this section, we present our new known-key distinguishing attack on a block cipher $E_K(\cdot)$ which is 8-round type-2 4-branch double-SP GFN. The key K is known to the attacker.

Theorem 1 (Our Result). *Let $E_K(\cdot)$ be a block cipher with block size $N(= 4n)$, where K is a randomly chosen and public N-bit key. For any given c-bit constant a, we show that we can find a message pair (M, M') and the corresponding ciphertext pair (C, C') with complexity 2^{2c} such that*

– $M \oplus M' = (bin_n(0), X, ?, ?)$, *and*
– $C \oplus C' = (?, ?, P[1_a], ?)$,

where each ? represents any n-bit value out of the possible 2^n, $C = E_K(M)$, $C' = E_K(M')$, c is the bit size of an S-box, r is the number of such S-boxes, $n = c \times r$, 1_a is the n-bit constant, where only one predetermined (j-th) byte is active defined by $1_a := (bin_1(0), bin_2(0), bin_3(0), \ldots bin_j(a) \ldots, bin_r(0))$, $bin_j(x)$ is the c-bit representation of x which is j-th byte of word, $P[\cdot]$ is the underlying n-bit permutation of the block cipher E and X is any full-active difference determined in the middle of the attack. [5]

On the other hand, in case of a random permutation over N-bit, we show that it requires a complexity of $32 \times r \times 2^{n/2}$ to find such plaintext and ciphertext pairs, in terms of number of S-box operations. Therefore, our construction will work as a distinguisher for 4-branch type-2 GFN with double SP-functions.

Proof. **In case of Random permutation:** For a random permutation, given any two messages (M, M') such that $M \oplus M' = (bin_n(0), X, ?, ?)$ the probability

---

[4] Note that Bogdanov et al. had earlier proved that double SP is stronger than single SP, however there are two differences in their approach with that of Sasaki. Firstly they consider infinite number of rounds in the design and secondly they consider key-xor after each SP. In comparison, Sasaki [8] considers finite number of rounds and consider key xor after double SP. The second point should not make any difference since the results being considered are in the known-key setting.

[5] j is any predetermined byte i.e. $1 \leq j \leq r$.

that the corresponding ciphertext (C, C') satisfies $C \oplus C' = (?, ?, P[1_a], ?)$, is 2^{-n}, where n is the size of a word in bits. So, for getting one such message pair we need $2^{n/2}$ message-ciphertext pairs.

Since, each round is using 4 S-box layers and each layer contains r S-boxes, the total number of S-boxes used in our construction is $32 \times r$. Therefore, the complexity of calculating $2^{n/2}$ message-ciphertext pairs can be described as the time complicity of $32 \times r \times 2^{n/2}$ S-box operations.

For example, let's consider a case of $(N, n, c, r) = (128, 32, 8, 4)$. For a block cipher with a known key, we can find a message pair satisfying the condition discussed with about 2^{18} operations, on the other hand, for a random permutation, we can find it with about 2^{23} operations. This fact leads to a distinguishing attack against the block cipher.

In case of $E_K(\cdot)$:

The aim of the our attack is to prduce a pair of messages having differences of the form $(0, X, ?, ?)$, such that they produce an output difference of the form $(?, ?, P[1_a], ?)$ for all known keys.

The truncated differential characteristic followed by our 8-round attack is as follows.

$(0, X, ?, ?) \rightarrow (0, 0, X, ?) \rightarrow (0, 0, 0, X) \rightarrow (X, 0, 0, 0) \rightarrow (0, X, P[1_\alpha], 0) \rightarrow (P[1_a], 0, X, P[1_a]) \rightarrow (0, P[1_a], ?, X) \rightarrow (?, 0, P[1_a], ?) \rightarrow (?, ?, P[1_a], ?)$.

Our differential trail starts with an input message pair having no difference in the first word, some specific difference X in the second word (X is a full active difference determined in the middle of the attack) and any arbitrary difference in the next two words.

Given such an input difference, we will get a ciphertext pair which can have arbitrary differences in first, second and fourth words, but the difference in the third word will be a fixed value. That is, we show that we can get a specific difference out of the possible $2^c - 1$ differences. Our work shows that we can create such a differential trail with lower complexity in comparison to a random permutation. This can be used as a valid distinguisher against the cipher.

Out of the 8 rounds, first three rounds are backward outbound phase, next three rounds are inbound phase and last two rounds are forward outbound phase. Complexity of the attack is only in finding a pair of values satisfying truncated differential path of the inbound phase. This is due to the fact that after getting any suitable pair, both the forward and the backward outbound phases will satisfy with probability 1.

Three-Round Inbound Phase: The truncated differential trail for inbound phase will propagate as:

$(X, 0, 0, 0) \rightarrow (0, X, P[1_\alpha], 0) \rightarrow (P[1_a], 0, X, P[1_\alpha]) \rightarrow (0, P[1_a], ?, X)$

The complexity of inbound phase is cost of finding a pair of values which will follow truncated differential path as shown in given Figure 5.

Definition: We say that Δ and ∇ are *matched* if we can find at least one X such that $S[X] \oplus S[X \oplus \Delta] = \nabla$.

To get inbound phase with desired differential characteristic, the following steps are followed.

1. Make difference distribution table (DDT) for all S-boxes.
2. (a) See Figure 5. Fix the difference at position (5) as 1_a, where a is an already provided value at the beginning of the attack process as mentioned in our result (theorem 1). Using DDT, choose any matched β such that differences 1_β and 1_a at positions (4) and (5) are matched.
   (b) Since P is linear, the difference at position (3) will be $P^{-1}[1_\beta]$.
   (c) For every α such that $1 \leq \alpha \leq 2^c - 1$, we define the difference at position (1) as 1_α, and repeat the following procedure.
      i. Since the difference at position (1) is 1_α, the difference at the position (2) will be $P[1_\alpha]$.
      ii. If the differences at positions (2) and (3) are matched, for each matched difference we can generate 2^r possible matching massage pairs at position (2) from the DDT, where the difference of each matching pair (M, M') is $P[1_\alpha]$ and the difference of $(S[M], S[M'])$ is $P^{-1}[1_\beta]$.
      iii. For each matching pair (M, M') of 2^r pairs, repeat the following procedure.
         A. If the difference of $S[P[S[M]] \oplus K'_9]$ and $S[P[S[M']] \oplus K'_9]$ at position (5) is 1_a, then fix it and fix all the corresponding values in between position (10) and (12) from the knowledge of (M, M'). Find difference X at position (11) from the knowledge of (M, M'), and go to Step 2-(d).
         B. Else if there remain matched pairs we have not considered, go to Step 2-(c)-iii, otherwise go to Step 2-(c).
   (d) Fix the difference at position (10) as 1_α, where α is already fixed in Step 2-(c).
   (e) For every λ such that $1 \leq \lambda \leq 2^c - 1$, repeat the following procedure.
      i. Calculate the difference $P^{-1}[1_\lambda]$ at position (8). Note that we already know that the difference at position (7) should be X.
      ii. If the differences at positions (7) and (8) are matched, we generate 2^r possible matching pairs at position (7) from the DDT, where the difference of each matching pair (W, W') is X and the difference of $(S[W], S[W'])$ is $P^{-1}[1_\lambda]$.
      iii. For each matching pair (W, W') of 2^r pairs, repeat the following procedure.
         A. If the difference of $S[P[S[W]] \oplus K'_{11}]$ and $S[P[S[W']] \oplus K'_9]$ at position (10) is 1_α, then fix it and calculate the value at position (6) from the knowledge of (M, M') and (W, W'), fix the value at position (13) and stop the inbound phase and exit.
         B. Else if there remain matched pairs we have not considered, go to Step 2-(e)-iii, otherwise go to Step 2-(e).

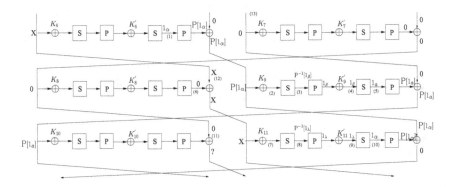

Fig. 5. 3-round inbound phase

Complexity Calculation for the Inbound Phase: Next, we provide the time and memory complexity for the procedure described above in a step by step fashion.

1. a). If the S-box layer has same S-boxes, Step 1 requires 2^{2c} time and 2^{2c} memory.
   b). If the S-box layer has all different S-boxes, Step 1 requires $r \times 2^{2c}$ time as well as memory.
2. Step 2-(a) requires constant complexity by DDT look up.
3. Step 2-(b) requires only one operation, so the complexity is constant.
4. Step 2-(c)-i again requires constant complexity.
5. Step 2-(c)-ii: Since we are using r S-boxes in the S-box layer, the matching probability is 2^{-r}. And after getting one matched difference we have 2^r matching pair, so the complexity of Step 2-(c)-ii is 2^r.
6. Step 2-(c)-iii requires 2^c complexity, since after completion of this step we found all 2^{c-r} matched differences and used all 2^c matching pairs.
7. Step 2-(d) requires constant complexity.
8. Step 2-(e)-i again requires constant complexity.
9. Step 2-(e)-ii: Since we are using r S-boxes in the S-box layer the matching probability is 2^{-r}. After getting one matched difference, we have 2^r matching pairs, so the complexity of Step 2-(e)-ii is 2^r.
10. Step 2-(e)-iii requires 2^c complexity. After completion of this step we found all 2^{c-r} matched differences and used all 2^c matching pairs.
11. Overall complicity of finding one starting point i.e. one message pair, which may follow entire differential characteristic of inbound phase is $r \times 2^{2c}$, both in terms of time and memory.

Three-Round Backward Outbound Phase :

The truncated differential path of backward outbound phase is as follows.
$(0, X, ?, ?) \rightarrow (0, 0, X, ?) \rightarrow (0, 0, 0, X)$.

After getting one starting point for inbound phase, the truncated differential path for backward outbound phase will propagate with probability 1.

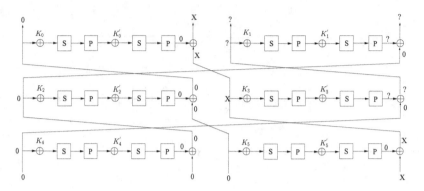

Fig. 6. 3-round backward outbound phase

Two-Round Forward Outbound Phase :
The truncated differential path of forward outbound phase is as follows.
$(0,\mathrm{P}[1_a], ?, X) \rightarrow (?, 0, \mathrm{P}[1_a], ?) \rightarrow (?, ?, \mathrm{P}[1_a], ?)$.

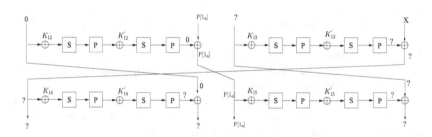

Fig. 7. 2-round forward outbound phase

Similar to the backward outbound phase, after getting any paired values which will satisfy inbound phase, i.e., one starting point, truncated differential path will follow the forward outbound phase with probability 1.

4   Summary of the Attack

As shown in Table 1, the complexity of the proposed distinguisher is much lower than for a random permutation.

We have presented the complexity of our attack in terms of the number of S-box look ups. In [8], Sasaki showed a 6-round distinguisher with the complexity of 2^c 6-round 4-branch double SP-function computation and a 7-round distinguisher with complexity 2^{3c-r} 7-round 4-branch double SP-functions computations. Similarly, complexity of our distinguisher is 2^c 8-round 4-branch type-2

Table 1. Complexity comparison between random permutation and our distinguisher. N is block length in bits, n is size of a word, c is size of S-box and r number of S-boxes used in an S-box layer.

N	n	c	r	complexity for random permutation	complexity of our attack same S-box	different S-box
64	16	4	4	2^{15}	2^8	2^{10}
128	32	8	4	2^{23}	2^{16}	2^{18}
256	64	8	8	2^{40}	2^{16}	2^{19}

double SP-function computations. For random permutation, the required complexity is $2^{n/2}$ 8-round 4-branch type-2 double SP-function computations. Hence the proposed distinguisher has lower complexity than any known distinguisher for GFN, provided that the input size of S-boxes is $\geq$ the number of S-boxes used.

5 Conclusions

We extended the number of rounds which can be distinguished from a random permutation by one more round in comparison to previous work by Sasaki, i.e., from 7 to 8 rounds, by using the rebound attack technique.

We have shown an attack on 32 SP-layers for double SP-functions, while in the case of single SP-function the maximum number of layers attacked is 22. The limitation of the proposed distinguisher is that it is useful only for those cases where the input size of S-boxes is greater than or equal to the number of S-boxes used. Increasing the numbers of rounds attacked is an interesting open problem.

References

1. Biham, E., Shamir, A.: Differential Cryptanalysis of DES-like Cryptosystems. In: Menezes, A., Vanstone, S.A. (eds.) CRYPTO 1990. LNCS, vol. 537, pp. 2–21. Springer, Heidelberg (1991)
2. Bogdanov, A., Shibutani, K.: Double SP-Functions: Enhanced Generalized Feistel Networks - Extended Abstract. In: Parampalli, U., Hawkes, P. (eds.) ACISP 2011. LNCS, vol. 6812, pp. 106–119. Springer, Heidelberg (2011)
3. Knudsen, L.R.: Truncated and Higher Order Differentials. In: Preneel, B. (ed.) FSE 1994. LNCS, vol. 1008, pp. 196–211. Springer, Heidelberg (1995)
4. Knudsen, L.R., Rijmen, V.: Known-Key Distinguishers for Some Block Ciphers. In: Kurosawa, K. (ed.) ASIACRYPT 2007. LNCS, vol. 4833, pp. 315–324. Springer, Heidelberg (2007)
5. Luby, M., Rackoff, C.: How to Construct Pseudo-Random Permutations from Pseudo-Random Functions (Abstract). In: Williams, H.C. (ed.) CRYPTO 1985. LNCS, vol. 218, pp. 447–447. Springer, Heidelberg (1986)

6. Matsui, M.: Linear Cryptoanalysis Method for DES Cipher. In: Helleseth, T. (ed.) EUROCRYPT 1993. LNCS, vol. 765, pp. 386–397. Springer, Heidelberg (1994)

7. Mendel, F., Rechberger, C., Schläffer, M., Thomsen, S.S.: The Rebound Attack: Cryptanalysis of Reduced Whirlpool and Grøstl. In: Dunkelman, O. (ed.) FSE 2009. LNCS, vol. 5665, pp. 260–276. Springer, Heidelberg (2009)

8. Sasaki, Y.: Double-SP Is Weaker Than Single-SP: Rebound Attacks on Feistel Ciphers with Several Rounds. In: Galbraith, S., Nandi, M. (eds.) INDOCRYPT 2012. LNCS, vol. 7668, pp. 265–282. Springer, Heidelberg (2012)

9. Sasaki, Y., Yasuda, K.: Known-Key Distinguishers on 11-Round Feistel and Collision Attacks on Its Hashing Modes. In: Joux, A. (ed.) FSE 2011. LNCS, vol. 6733, pp. 397–415. Springer, Heidelberg (2011)

10. Shirai, T., Shibutani, K., Akishita, T., Moriai, S., Iwata, T.: The 128-Bit Blockcipher CLEFIA (Extended Abstract). In: Biryukov, A. (ed.) FSE 2007. LNCS, vol. 4593, pp. 181–195. Springer, Heidelberg (2007)

11. Stinson, D.R.: Cryptography - theory and practice, 3rd edn. Discrete mathematics and its applications series. Chapman and Hall/CRC Press (2005)

12. Zheng, Y., Matsumoto, T., Imai, H.: On the Construction of Block Ciphers: Provably Secure and Not Relying on Any Unproved Hypotheses. In: Brassard, G. (ed.) CRYPTO 1989. LNCS, vol. 435, pp. 461–480. Springer, Heidelberg (1990)

Improbable Differential from Impossible Differential: On the Validity of the Model

Céline Blondeau

Aalto University, School of Science,
Department of Information and Computer Science
celine.blondeau@aalto.fi

Abstract. Differentials with low probability are used in improbable differential cryptanalysis to distinguish a cipher from a random permutation. Due to large diffusion, finding such differentials for actual ciphers remains a challenging task. At Indocrypt 2010, Tezcan proposed a method to derive improbable differential distinguishers from impossible differential ones. In this paper, we discuss the validity of the assumptions made in the computation of the improbable differential probabilities. In particular, we show based on experiments that such improbable differential cryptanalysis can fail. The validity of the improbable differential cryptanalyses on PRESENT and CLEFIA is discussed.

Keywords: improbable differential, impossible differential, truncated differential, PRESENT, CLEFIA.

1 Introduction

Since the introduction of differential cryptanalysis [2] in the beginning of the 90's, many generalizations of this attack have been proposed to cryptanalyse a large number of block ciphers. While most of them exploit differentials with high probability, in the impossible differential cryptanalysis context [1] attackers take advantage of zero-probability differentials. Recently a variation of this attack called improbable differential cryptanalysis have been introduced by Tezcan [21] at Indocrypt 2010 and by Mala, Dakhilalian and Shakiba [15]. In this context, differentials with low probabilities are used to distinguish the cipher from a random permutation.

While in theory this attack could be efficient on some ciphers, in practice, it may be hard to find differentials or truncated differentials with such small probabilities. In [15,21] a method based on the knowledge of impossible differentials is proposed. The computation of improbable differential probabilities is then obtained based on the assumption that all other differentials than the known impossible ones on the r_1 last rounds of the cipher are uniformly distributed.

In this paper, we recall and explain the assumptions made in [15,21] to derive improbable differentials from impossible ones. Based on experiments on SPN and Feistel ciphers, we show that the assumptions made in the computation of the improbable differential probabilities are not correct. In particular, the

G. Paul and S. Vaudenay (Eds.): INDOCRYPT 2013, LNCS 8250, pp. 149–160, 2013.

validity of the improbable differential attack by Tezcan on 11, 12 and 13 rounds of PRESENT [22,23] and 13, 14 and 15 rounds of respectively CLEFIA-128, CLEFIA-192 and CLEFIA-256 [21] is discussed.

This paper is organized as follows. In Section 2, we recall the principle of improbable differential cryptanalysis and the method described in [21] to derive improbable differentials from impossible ones. In Section 3, based on experiments on a 24-bit block cipher, we show that the assumptions made in the computation of the improbable differential probabilities are not valid and that the corresponding key-recovery attack can fail. In Section 4, a comparison between the assumptions in truncated differential cryptanalysis and in the method proposed by Tezcan is made to support the discussion regarding the validity of the latter one. Section 5 is dedicated to the two improbable differential cryptanalyses proposed in the literature on PRESENT and CLEFIA and constructed from that model.

2   Improbable Differential Cryptanalysis

2.1   Improbable Differential Distinguisher

In this paper, iterated block ciphers E with block size n parameterized by a key K are considered. Among the different cryptanalyses on block ciphers, the statistical ones make use of a non-uniform behavior of the cipher. A key-recovery attack is often derived from a distinguisher that compares the probability of a particular characteristic, such as the probability of a differential with the uniform one. By a slight abuse of notation, as in this paper we will focus on the distinguishing part of the statistical attack (adaptation to a key-recovery attack can be done easily), we will denote by E the part of the cipher we aim at distinguishing.

While contemporary ciphers are designed to be resistant to the classical differential cryptanalysis, by improving the different existing methods, attackers are often able to show a non-random behavior of a reduced number of rounds of the cipher. Among the different generalizations of differential cryptanalysis, we focus in this paper on the truncated differential cryptanalysis [12], the impossible differential cryptanalysis [1], and the improbable differential cryptanalysis [22]. As all of these attacks rely on truncated differentials[1], we first recall the definition of a truncated differential.

Definition 1. *A truncated differential on E is a pair (A, C) where $A \subset (\mathbb{F}_2^n)^*$ (where $(\mathbb{F}_2^n)^* = \mathbb{F}_2^n \backslash \{0\}$) is a set of input differences and $C \subset (\mathbb{F}_2^n)^*$ a set of output differences.*

---

[1] Notice that in impossible differential cryptanalysis if only one output difference is taken into consideration, the complexity of the attack will be close to the full codebook, as in the case of the simple zero-correlation presented in [8].

The expected probability of the truncated differential (A, C) *on the cipher* E *is defined by*

$$p = P[A \xrightarrow{E} C] = \frac{1}{|A|} \sum_{a \in A} P_{\mathbf{X}, \mathbf{K}}[E_K(X) \oplus E_K(X \oplus a) \in C]. \tag{1}$$

The probability of such truncated differential (A, C) for a random permutation is $p_U = \frac{|C|}{2^n - 1}$ and is usually called uniform probability.

Depending on the probability p different key-recovery attacks are implemented. As in the impossible differential setting $p = 0$, all the key candidates for which the truncated differential occurs are discarded. In the truncated and improbable differential key-recovery attacks a threshold T is introduced to reduce the set of potential candidates. The number S_k of occurrences of the truncated differential is then compared with the threshold T for each key candidate k. In classical truncated differential cryptanalysis, as $p > p_U$, the correct key should be among the ones such that $S_k \geq T$, whereas in improbable differential cryptanalysis, as $p < p_U$, the correct key should satisfy $S_k \leq T$. To avoid confusion, we call "*probable differential*" a truncated differential with probability $p > p_U$.

For most of the cases in the probable differential context or for the described improbable differential cryptanalyses in [21,22], the probability p of a truncated differential can be expressed relative to the uniform probability p_U. The sign of the bias $\varepsilon = p - p_U$ indicates if the truncated differential is probable or improbable.

The data complexity of such distinguishing attacks has been heavily studied. While tight estimates of their complexities can be obtained from the algorithms presented in [4] and [21], an asymptotic behavior can be derived from an expansion of the Kullback-Leibler divergence between two binomial distributions with respective probabilities p_U and $p_U \pm \varepsilon$. As presented in Table 3 of [4], the number N_S of samples[2] required to distinguish two distributions with probabilities p_U and $p = p_U \pm \varepsilon$ is proportional to $\frac{2p_U}{\varepsilon^2}$.

The data complexity of an impossible differential distinguisher is inverse proportional to p_U. A discussion regarding the advantages and the disadvantages of an improbable, or almost impossible, differential in comparison with an impossible differential in key-recovery attack on the same number of rounds of a cipher is provided in [15].

2.2   Construction of Improbable Differentials: Using Impossible Differential

In practice, due to the large number of trails composing a differential, having a good estimate of its probability can be challenging. Based on assumptions, such as the *Markov assumption* [14], the probability of a differential trail is often computed by multiplying the probabilities round by round. Nevertheless, it is

---

[2] The ratio between the number N_S of samples and the data complexity depends of the number of input differences.

well known that this kind of assumption is not always true and in particular a key dependency can occur [11,3]. Although, finding all trails relative to a differential is impossible for almost all ciphers, underestimate of a differential probability can be obtained by summing up the probability of trails in a subset. Therefore, using standard methods, finding improbable differentials for a particular cipher can be a challenging task.

In [21,15], the authors proposed a method based on the knowledge of impossible differentials. Without loss of generality[3], we assume that an impossible distinguisher (B, C) on the r_1 last rounds of E is combined with a truncated differential (A, B) on the r_0 first rounds of E. We denote by E_0 and E_1 the corresponding partial ciphers: $E = E_1 \circ E_0$ and by q the probability of the truncated differential (A, B) on E_0: $q = P[A \overset{E_0}{\looparrowright} B]$ (see Figure 1). From these two partial distinguishers, Tezcan proposed a method to compute the probability of the truncated differential (A, C) on E. While in [21], the following assumption is not explicitly written, this one seems necessary to compute the probability of the distinguisher as in Proposition 1.

Assumption 1. *For all $\bar{b} \notin B$, $\bar{b} \neq 0$, the probabilities $P[\bar{b} \overset{E_1}{\looparrowright} C]$ on the r_1 rounds of E_1 are equal.*

Notice that for any permutation, for any fix input difference we have: $\sum_{c \in \mathbb{F}_2^n} P[b \to c] = 1$ and $\sum_{b \in \mathbb{F}_2^n} \sum_{c \in \mathbb{F}_2^n} P[b \to c] = 2^n$.

As depicted in Figure 1, in the improbable differential context of Tezcan the set $(\mathbb{F}_2^n)^* \backslash B$ of intermediate differences which are not in B play an important role. In the following, we denote by $\bar{B}$ this set: $\bar{B} = (\mathbb{F}_2^n)^* \backslash B$.

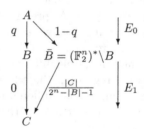

Fig. 1. Improbable differential from impossible differential

Based on the previous assumption, the probability of the improbable differential can be computed as followed:

Proposition 1. *Let $E = E_1 \circ E_0$ be a Markov cipher with probable truncated differential (A, B) on E_0 and impossible differential (B, C) on E_1 with $|B| < 2^n - |C| - 1$. Let $q = P[A \overset{E_0}{\looparrowright} B]$ be the probability of the differential (A, B).*

---

[3] A more general description can be found in [21].

Assuming independent rounds keys and under Assumption 1, the truncated differential (A, C) has probability $p = \dfrac{|C|}{2^n - |B| - 1}(1 - q) \approx \dfrac{|C|}{2^n}(1 - q)$ and is improbable.

Proof. Based on Assumption 1, as E_1 is a permutation of $\mathbb{F}_2^n$ we deduce from that for all $\bar{b} \notin B$, $\bar{b} \neq 0$, we have $P[\bar{b} \overset{E_1}{\mapsto} C] = \dfrac{|C|}{2^n - |B| - 1}$.

Then assuming that the cipher is a Markov cipher, we have

$$p = \frac{1}{|A|} \sum_{a \in A} \sum_{c \in C} P[a \overset{E}{\mapsto} c]$$

$$= \frac{1}{|A|} \sum_{a \in A} \sum_{\bar{b} \in \bar{B}} \sum_{c \in C} P[a \overset{E_0}{\mapsto} \bar{b}] P[\bar{b} \overset{E_1}{\mapsto} c]$$

$$= \frac{|C|}{2^n - |B| - 1} \frac{1}{|A|} \sum_{a \in A} \sum_{\bar{b} \in \bar{b}} P[a \overset{E_0}{\mapsto} \bar{b}]$$

$$= \frac{|C|}{2^n - |B| - 1}(1 - q)$$

$\square$

In the following sections, the validity[4] of Assumption 1 is discussed using a comparison between the expected probability p of the improbable differential with the experimental one p_E for different ciphers. In particular, we show that the different cases can occur: $p_E = p$, $p_E < p$, $p_E > p$ and even $p_E > p_U$. In the last two cases, the attack can fail due to an overestimate of the data complexity or a wrong threshold selection.

3   Experimental Improbable Distinguisher

As accurate experiments are possible on a 24-bit cipher, we design[5] a 24-bit generalized Feistel Network with 6 branches to test the validity of Assumption 1. The experiments aim at computing the probability of some 11-round improbable differential of the cipher with round function given by Figure 2. In order to limit the number of assumptions in the computation of the experimental probability, independent round keys have been selected. For the presented experimental results of this section, the 4-bit Sbox S of the cipher PRESENT [7] has been chosen[6]. Using an impossible differential on 10 rounds of this cipher, and a

---

[4] In some cases Assumption 1 on the last rounds can be replaced by an assumption on the first rounds. The validity can nevertheless be discussed in the same way.

[5] This example is proposed in an illustrative and easy to understand purpose. For different reasons, experiments on reduced versions of existing ciphers such as CLEFIA may not reflect the behavior of the real ciphers.

[6] Experiments with different Sboxes have also been performed and the provided results are similar.

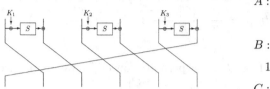

$$A : X \quad Y \quad 0 \quad 0 \quad 0 \quad 0$$
$$\text{1 round} \Downarrow \quad q = 2^{-3.91}$$
$$B : 0 \quad X \quad 0 \quad 0 \quad 0 \quad 0$$
$$\text{10 rounds} \Downarrow \quad Impossible$$
$$C : 0 \quad 0 \quad 0 \quad Z \quad 0 \quad 0$$

Fig. 2. Round function of a 24-bit cipher build for experimental purpose and the 11-round improbable distinguisher where X, Y, Z are non-zero nibble values

truncated differential on the first round (see Figure 2) we conducted experiments to determine the probability p_E of the truncated differential (A, C).

The results of the experiments are shown in Table 1 for different sets of input differences. In this table we can see that the experimental probabilities are different from the theoretical ones. In particular, we always have that $p_E > p$ and $\varepsilon_E^2 > \varepsilon^2$. A theoretical estimate of the data complexity would then have been overestimated. The first attack setting presented in Table 1 illustrates a failed attack since $p_E > p_U$.

Table 1. Experiments of 11 rounds of the experimental cipher for different sets of input differences defined regarding the quantity $\delta(a, b) = \#\{x \in (\mathbb{F}_2^4)^* | S(x) \oplus S(x \oplus a) = b\}$

$X, Y \in \{\texttt{0x1}..\texttt{0xF}\}$ such that	q	p	p_E	$2^{-19.88}(1-q)$
All	$2^{-3.90}$	$2^{-20.10}$	$2^{-19.94}$	$2^{-19.98}$
$\delta(X, Y) \geq 2$	$2^{-2.68}$	$2^{-20.24}$	$2^{-20.14}$	$2^{-20.12}$
$\delta(X, Y) \geq 4$	2^{-2}	$2^{-20.42}$	$2^{-20.28}$	$2^{-20.29}$

As Proposition 1 requires Assumption 1, these experiments show that this assumption may not be correct. More detailed experiments targeting the claim proposed in Assumption 1 confirm the non-equality of the probabilities $P[\bar{b} \xrightarrow{E_1} C]$. In particular, we observe a large deviation between expected probabilities $P[\bar{b} \xrightarrow{E_1} C]$ and the uniform probability p_U: while some are impossible, some are of order of magnitude $2^3 p_U$ or $2^{-3} p_U$.

As Assumption 1 has some similarities with the assumptions made in probable differential cryptanalysis, in the next section, we recall the assumptions made in the truncated differential cryptanalysis context and discuss the difference between the two cryptanalysis methods.

4   Validity of the Assumptions

Assumptions similar to Assumption 1 are made in probable differential cryptanalysis when computing truncated differential probabilities using a truncated differential trails. For this section, we denote by F_{K_i} ($1 \leq i \leq r$) the round functions of the cipher E_K and by $(A_0, A_1, \cdots, A_{r-1}, A_r)$ a truncated differential trail. To compute the truncated differential probability of the differential (A_0, A_r), the following assumption is commonly made.

Assumption 2. *For all $a_i \in A_i$ and for all $a_{i+1} \in A_{i+1}$, the probabilities $P[a_i \overset{F_{K_i}}{\to} a_{i+1}]$ are equal.*

Proposition 2. *Assuming a Markov cipher for differential cryptanalysis. If the rounds keys are independent under Assumption 2 the probability of the truncated differential trail $(A_0, A_1, \cdots, A_{r-1}, A_r)$ is equal to $\prod_{i=0}^{r-1} P[A_i \overset{F_{K_i}}{\to} A_{i+1}]$.*

In many of the published truncated differential cryptanalysis (see for instance [18,17]) a comparison between the experimental probability of a truncated differential and the formula provided in Proposition 2 on a reduced number of rounds of the cipher is made to check if Assumption 2 can be bypassed. Some of them, such as [17], show that the experimental probabilities can be larger than the theoretical ones, which in the context of truncated differential cryptanalysis provides an underestimate of the attack complexity but does not challenge its validity.

By comparing Assumption 2 with Assumption 1, we observe that the latter is stronger and the probabilities $P[\bar{b} \overset{E_1}{\to} C]$ are less likely to be equal. Indeed a simple comparison between the different existing attacks show that often in truncated differential cryptanalysis, the sets A_i correspond to a small number of Sboxes while in improbable differential setting, the intermediate state is of size $2^n - |B|$ meaning that more probabilities are required to be equal. Since the diffusion grows with the number of rounds, the number r_1 of involved rounds in the improbable differential context may also influence deviations of the probabilities and contradiction with Assumption 2 may be more likely.

In the literature, there is no complete match between the truncated differentials $(A, \bar{B})$ on E_0 and $(\bar{B}, C)$ on E_1. In particular it may occur that the set D such that $P[A \overset{E_0}{\to} D] = 1$ is a small subset of $\mathbb{F}_2^n$. In that case, if we know the truncated probability $P[D \overset{E_1}{\to} C]$ (which may be different from $\dfrac{|C|}{2^n - |B| - 1}$) we may, based on Assumption 2, be able to compute the probability of the truncated differential (A, C).

To illustrate this behavior, we provide some explanations on the cryptanalysis presented in Section 3. In particular we show that based on Assumption 2, we are able to explain the experimental probabilities provided in Table 1. As $r_0 = 1$, it is easy to see from Figure 2 that $D = \{0XW000 \mid X, W \in \mathbb{F}_2^4,\ X \neq 0\}$. An experimental computation of the probability show that $P[D \backslash B \overset{E_1}{\to} C] =$

$2^{-19.88}$ and is far from the uniform probability $p_U = 2^{-20}$. Using Proposition 2, and the knowledge of $P[A \xrightarrow{E_0} B]$ we are able to compute the probability of the truncated differential (A, C). The results of this computation are provided in the last column of Table 1. The quasi-nonexistent deviation between these new theoretical probabilities and the experimental ones illustrates that a tight estimate of the probability $P[D \xrightarrow{E_1} C]$ is necessary to the computation, and can not be derived directly from the impossible differential (B, C).

5   Improbable Differential in the Literature

5.1   The Improbable Attack on PRESENT

PRESENT is a 64-bit lightweight block cipher designed in 2008 [7] by Bogdanov *et al.* The description of this cipher can be found in [7]. The security of a version reduced to 26 out of the 31 rounds have been threaten by a multidimensional linear cryptanalysis [10].

In [22], Tezcan presents an improbable differential cryptanalysis on this block cipher. This attack on a version reduced to 11 rounds is derived from a 9-round improbable distinguisher. In Table 2, we describe this distinguisher based on combination of a 3-round differential with the 6-round impossible differential.

Table 2. A 3-round truncated differential combined with a 6-round impossible differential on PRESENT as in [22]. The four bits x can not be zero at the same time. $X_{i,S}$ denotes the state after the non-linear layer and $X_{i,P}$ after the permutation at round i.

A	0000 0000 0000 0000 0000 0000 0000 0000 0000 0000 0000 0000 0001 0000 0000 0001	
$X_{1,S}$	0000 0000 0000 0000 0000 0000 0000 0000 0000 0000 0000 0000 1001 0000 0000 1001	Differential
$X_{1,P}$	0000 0000 0000 1001 0000 0000 0000 0000 0000 0000 0000 0000 0000 0000 0000 1001	
$X_{2,S}$	0000 0000 0000 0100 0000 0000 0000 0000 0000 0000 0000 0000 0000 0000 0000 0100	
$X_{2,P}$	0000 0000 0000 0001 0000 0000 0000 0001 0000 0000 0000 0000 0000 0000 0000 0000	with $q = 2^{-12}$
$X_{3,S}$	0000 0000 0000 0011 0000 0000 0000 0011 0000 0000 0000 0000 0000 0000 0000 0000	
$X_{3,P}$	0000 0000 0000 0000 0000 0000 0000 0000 1001 0000 0000 0000 1001 0000 0000 0000	
B	0000 0000 0000 0000 0000 0000 0000 0000 0000 ???0 0000 0000 0000 ???0 0000 0000	
$X_{4,P}$	0000 0000 0?00 0000 0000 0000 0?00 0?00 0000 0000 0?00 0?00 0000 0000 0000 0000	
$X_{5,S}$	0000 0000 ???? ???? 0000 0000 ???? ???? 0000 0000 ???? ???? 0000 0000 0000 0000	
$X_{5,P}$	00?? 00?? 00?? 0000 00?? 00?? 00?? 0000 00?? 00?? 00?? 0000 00?? 00?? 00?? 0000	
$X_{6,S}$	???? ???? ???? 0000 ???? ???? ???? 0000 ???? ???? ???? 0000 ???? ???? ???? 0000	
$X_{6,P}$	???0 ???0 ???0 ???0 ???0 ???0 ???0 ???0 ???0 ???0 ???0 ???0 ???0 ???0 ???0 ???0	
$X_{6,P}$	???? ???? ???? ???? ???? ???? ???? ???? ???? ???? ???? ???? ???x ???x ???x ???x	Impossible
$X_{7,S}$	???? ???? ???? ???? ???? ???? ???? ???? ???? ???? ???? ???? 000x 000x 000x 000x	
$X_{7,P}$	???? ???? ???? 0000 ???? ???? ???? 0000 ???? ???? ???? 0000 ???? ???? ???? xxxx	
$X_{8,S}$	???? ???? ???? 0000 ???? ???? ???? 0000 ???? ???? ???? 0000 ???? ???? ???? ???1	
C	???0 ???0 ???0 ???? ???0 ???0 ???0 ???? ???0 ???0 ???0 ???? ???0 ???0 ???0 ???1	$p_U = 2^{-13}$
$X_{9,S}$	0101 0101 0101 ???? 0101 0101 0101 ???? 0101 0101 0101 ???? 0101 0101 0101 0001	
$X_{9,P}$	000? 000? 000? 0000 111? 111? 111? 1110 000? 000? 000? 0000 111? 111? 111? 1111	$p_U = 2^{-48}$

As depicted in Table 2, the truncated output difference describes a set of size 2^{12}. Therefore, an experimental verification of the expected probability of this distinguisher on 9 rounds of PRESENT is out of reach since $p_U \approx 2^{-48}$.

Nevertheless, by piling-up only one round of this distinguisher, we are able to compute the probability of the 8 first rounds of the improbable distinguisher of Table 2. As depicted in Table 2, this distinguisher is derived from a 3-round differential composed with a 5-round impossible differential. As the uniform probability to obtain the truncated output differences is $p_U = 2^{-13}$, according to Proposition 1 if Assumption 1 was true, the theoretical probability of the truncated differential on the 8-round distinguisher would be smaller than p_U. Our experiments with 300 keys and 2^{32} plaintexts show that this truncated differential have a probability which vary depending of the key between $2^{-12.96}$ and $2^{-12.98}$ and is not improbable.

We thus believe that if the improbable differential distinguisher does not work on these 8 rounds, the proposed attack on 11 rounds of PRESENT derived from the 9-round distinguisher of Table 2 is not correct. From the fact that 22 rounds of PRESENT can be distinguished from a random permutation [10], we can also deduce that Assumption 1 is not true for 6 rounds.

In [23], Tezcan proposed an attack on 12 and 13 rounds of PRESENT. In this extended version of [22], Tezcan explains how to use undisturbed bits to find impossible differentials on some ciphers. Using the theory a 5-round and a 6-round impossible distinguisher on PRESENT are proposed. While the 6-round distinguisher correspond to the one of Table 2, the probability of the (5+5)-rounds distinguisher is estimated $p = 2^{-16}(1 - 2^{-17.84})$. No experiments on the full improbable distinguisher can be performed. To derive the attack on 12 and 13 rounds, the 5-round impossible distinguisher is combined with a 5-round differential. As based on the previous discussions, Assumption 1 is not valid on 5 rounds of PRESENT, the different cases presented at the end of Section 2.2 can occur.

As impossible differentials are harder to find on a large number of rounds of an SPN cipher with diffusion similar to the one of PRESENT than a linear or differential distinguisher (even using undisturbed bits as in [23]), it may be impossible to build improbable differentials using this technique for this type of cipher. Additionally due to the large diffusion, it is hard to believe that Assumption 1 can be true for SPN ciphers.

5.2   The Improbable Attack on CLEFIA

In Appendix C of [21], an experimental attack on 5 rounds of CLEFIA [19] is proposed to illustrate the theory developed in the same paper. In this section, we discuss the choices taken to run these experiments. The sets A, B, C chosen for the experimental attack in [21] are such that a truncated differential on 1 round with probability $q = \frac{10}{256}$ is combined with an impossible differential on 4 rounds. By the choice taken for the set C, the uniform probability $p_U = 1 - 2^{-32}$ is very close to 1 and is the deterministic factor which made this experimental attack succeed. Indeed under Assumption 1, the probability of the improbable differential is $p = (1 - 2^{-32})(1 - q) \approx (1 - q)$ and the conducted experiments confirm this probability. Notice that even if the probability $P[D \mapsto C]$ would be slightly different from $(1-2^{32})$, it will only marginally influence the probability p which is close to $1 - \frac{10}{256}$ and no experiment will be able to detect this deviation.

In [21], an attack on 13 rounds of CLEFIA-128 using an improbable distinguisher on 1+9 rounds is proposed. As CLEFIA is a 128-bit word oriented block cipher, it is more difficult to conduct sensible experiment on a reduced number of rounds than it is for the SPN cipher PRESENT. Nevertheless, the number of impossible differentials on 9 rounds of this cipher presented in [24] tends to induce that the probability of the truncated differential $(\bar{B}, C)$ is not close to the uniform one p_U. Based on this believe and on the discussion provided in Section 4, we want to say that the probability of the truncated differential (A, C) on 10 rounds of CLEFIA may be badly estimated. If this is the case, the whole improbable differential attack on this cipher may be wrong. Nevertheless others attacks [20,16] on 13 rounds of CLEFIA using one of the 9-round impossible differential are done by taking into consideration the key-schedule of the cipher. To our knowledge[7], in the single key model, the best known attack which were proposed at SAC 2013[6] are zero-correlation attacks on 14 rounds of CLEFIA-192 and 15 rounds of CLEFIA-256.

Similar arguments as the ones provided for CLEFIA, may hold for many generalized Feistel constructions since many impossible and multidimensional zero-correlation distinguishers[8] are often derived from the same number of rounds of the cipher and the validity of Assumption 1 can be challenged in the same way. Therefore, we claim that it may be hard to use the method proposed in [21] to derive an improbable distinguisher using impossible differentials.

6   Conclusion

In this paper, we discussed the assumptions made when deriving improbable differential distinguishers from impossible differential distinguishers. In particular we show that assuming that almost all differentials of the cipher have similar probability is a strong assumption which leads to a wrong estimate of the truncated differential probability and which can turn out to not be improbable.

Other improbable differential attacks exist in the literature [9,13]. As the computation of the truncated differential probability does not depend on the same assumption we believe that these attacks remain valid. This article provides then new insights on improbable differential cryptanalysis.

Acknowledgments. I would like to thank Kaisa Nyberg and Hadi Soleimany for the advices provided when writing this article.

---

[7] Notice that the recent proposed attack [25] on the full CLEFIA is not a valid one due to the involved complexities.

[8] Using the link between zero-correlation and impossible differential provided in [5] we can convert a zero-correlation distinguisher to an impossible differential one.

References

1. Biham, E., Biryukov, A., Shamir, A.: Cryptanalysis of Skipjack Reduced to 31 Rounds Using Impossible Differentials. In: Stern, J. (ed.) EUROCRYPT 1999. LNCS, vol. 1592, pp. 12–23. Springer, Heidelberg (1999)
2. Biham, E., Shamir, A.: Differential Cryptanalysis of DES-like Cryptosystems. In: Menezes, A., Vanstone, S.A. (eds.) CRYPTO 1990. LNCS, vol. 537, pp. 2–21. Springer, Heidelberg (1991)
3. Blondeau, C., Gérard, B.: Links Between Theoretical and Effective Differential Probabilities: Experiments on PRESENT. In: Ecrypt Workshop on Tools for Cryptanalysis (2010)
4. Blondeau, C., Gérard, B., Tillich, J.-P.: Accurate estimates of the data complexity and success probability for various cryptanalyses. Des. Codes Cryptography 59(1-3), 3–34 (2011)
5. Blondeau, C., Nyberg, K.: New Links Between Differential and Linear Cryptanalysis. In: Johansson, T., Nguyen, P.Q. (eds.) EUROCRYPT 2013. LNCS, vol. 7881, pp. 388–404. Springer, Heidelberg (2013)
6. Bogdanov, A., Geng, H., Wang, M., Wen, L., Collard, B.: Zero-Correlation Linear Cryptanalysis with FFT and Improved Attacks on ISO Standards Camellia and CLEFIA. In: SAC (to appear, 2013)
7. Bogdanov, A.A., Knudsen, L.R., Leander, G., Paar, C., Poschmann, A., Robshaw, M., Seurin, Y., Vikkelsoe, C.: PRESENT: An Ultra-Lightweight Block Cipher. In: Paillier, P., Verbauwhede, I. (eds.) CHES 2007. LNCS, vol. 4727, pp. 450–466. Springer, Heidelberg (2007)
8. Bogdanov, A., Rijmen, V.: Zero-Correlation Linear Cryptanalysis of Block Ciphers. IACR Cryptology ePrint Archive, 2011:123 (2011)
9. Borst, J., Knudsen, L.R., Rijmen, V.: Two Attacks on Reduced IDEA. In: Fumy, W. (ed.) EUROCRYPT 1997. LNCS, vol. 1233, pp. 1–13. Springer, Heidelberg (1997)
10. Cho, J.Y.: Linear Cryptanalysis of Reduced-Round PRESENT. In: Pieprzyk, J. (ed.) CT-RSA 2010. LNCS, vol. 5985, pp. 302–317. Springer, Heidelberg (2010)
11. Daemen, J., Rijmen, V.: Probability distributions of correlation and differentials in block ciphers. J. Mathematical Cryptology 1(3), 221–242 (2007)
12. Knudsen, L.R.: Truncated and Higher Order Differentials. In: Preneel, B. (ed.) FSE 1994. LNCS, vol. 1008, pp. 196–211. Springer, Heidelberg (1995)
13. Knudsen, L.R., Rijmen, V.: On the Decorrelated Fast Cipher (DFC) and Its Theory. In: Knudsen, L.R. (ed.) FSE 1999. LNCS, vol. 1636, pp. 81–94. Springer, Heidelberg (1999)
14. Lai, X., Massey, J.L., Murphy, S.: Markov Ciphers and Differentail Cryptanalysis. In: Davies, D.W. (ed.) EUROCRYPT 1991. LNCS, vol. 547, pp. 17–38. Springer, Heidelberg (1991)
15. Mala, H., Dakhilalian, M., Shakiba, M.: Cryptanalysis of Block Ciphers Using Almost-Impossible Differentials. IACR Cryptology ePrint Archive, 2010:485 (2010)
16. Mala, H., Dakhilalian, M., Shakiba, M.: Impossible Differential Attacks on 13-Round CLEFIA-128. J. Comput. Sci. Technol. 26(4), 744–750 (2011)
17. Matsui, M., Tokita, T.: Cryptanalysis of a Reduced Version of the Block Cipher E2 (1999)
18. Reichardt, B., Wagner, D.: Markov Truncated Differential Cryptanalysis of Skipjack. In: Nyberg, K., Heys, H.M. (eds.) SAC 2002. LNCS, vol. 2595, pp. 110–128. Springer, Heidelberg (2003)

19. Shirai, T., Shibutani, K., Akishita, T., Moriai, S., Iwata, T.: The 128-Bit Block-cipher CLEFIA (Extended Abstract). In: Biryukov, A. (ed.) FSE 2007. LNCS, vol. 4593, pp. 181–195. Springer, Heidelberg (2007)

20. Tang, X., Sun, B., Li, R., Li, C.: Impossible differential cryptanalysis of 13-round CLEFIA-128. Journal of Systems and Software 84(7), 1191–1196 (2011)

21. Tezcan, C.: The Improbable Differential Attack: Cryptanalysis of Reduced Round CLEFIA. In: Gong, G., Gupta, K.C. (eds.) INDOCRYPT 2010. LNCS, vol. 6498, pp. 197–209. Springer, Heidelberg (2010)

22. Tezcan, C.: Improbable Differential Attack on PRESENT using Undisturbed Bits. In: International Conference on Applied and Computational Mathematics, Page Book of Abstracts, 2012, Ankara, Turkey, (October 3, 2012), http://cihangir.forgottenlance.com/papers/ICACM_Extended_Abstract.pdf

23. Tezcan, C.: Improbable differential attacks on PRESENT using undisturded bits. Journal of Computational and Applied Mathematics (in press, 2013)

24. Tsunoo, Y., Tsujihara, E., Shigeri, M., Saito, T., Suzaki, T., Kubo, H.: Impossible Differential Cryptanalysis of CLEFIA. In: Nyberg, K. (ed.) FSE 2008. LNCS, vol. 5086, pp. 398–411. Springer, Heidelberg (2008)

25. Yuan, Z., Li, X., Liu, H.: Impossible Differential-Linear Cryptanalysis of Full-Round CLEFIA-128. IACR Cryptology ePrint Archive, 2013:301 (2013)

Compact Authenticated Key Exchange from Bounded CCA-Secure KEM

Kazuki Yoneyama

NTT Secure Platform Laboratories
3-9-11 Midori-cho Musashino-shi Tokyo 180-8585, Japan
yoneyama.kazuki@lab.ntt.co.jp

Abstract. How to reduce communication complexity is a common important issue to design cryptographic protocols. This paper focuses on authenticated key exchange (AKE). Several AKE schemes have been studied, which satisfy strong security such as exposure-resilience in the standard model (StdM). However, there is a large gap on communication costs between schemes in the StdM and in the random oracle model. In this paper, we show a generic construction that is significantly compact (i.e., small communication cost) and secure in the StdM. We follow an existing generic construction from key encapsulated mechanism (KEM). Our main technique is to use a bounded chosen-ciphertext secure KEM instead of an ordinary chosen-ciphertext secure KEM. The communication cost can be reduced to half by this technique, and we achieve the most compact AKE scheme in the StdM. Moreover, our construction has instantiations under wider classes of hardness assumptions (e.g., subset-sum problems and multi-variate quadratic systems) than existing constructions. This work pioneers the first meaningful application of bounded chosen-ciphertext secure KEM.

Keywords: authenticated key exchange, key encapsulation mechanism, bounded CCA.

1 Introduction

1.1 Background

Authenticated Key Exchange (AKE) is a cryptographic primitive to share a common *session key* among multiple parties through unauthenticated networks such as the Internet. In the ordinary PKI-based setting, each party locally keeps his own *static secret key* (SSK) and publish a *static public key* (SPK) corresponding to the SSK. Validity of SPKs is guaranteed by a certificate authority. In a key exchange session, each party generates an *ephemeral secret key* (ESK) and sends an *ephemeral public key* (EPK) corresponding to the ESK. A session key is derived from these keys with a *key derivation procedure*. Parties can establish a secure channel with the session key.

Bellare and Rogaway [1,2] first proposed a provably secure AKE scheme in the random oracle model (ROM). Their security model (denoted as the BR model) captures natural security requirements of AKE such as impersonation resistance and known key secrecy. However, as studies on AKE make progress, various advanced attacks that cannot be prevented in the BR model have been proposed. For example, key-compromise

G. Paul and S. Vaudenay (Eds.): INDOCRYPT 2013, LNCS 8250, pp. 161–178, 2013.

impersonation (KCI) [3] can be a practical threat. Suppose a party A's SSK is disclosed. Though, clearly, an adversary that knows the SSK can now impersonate A, it may be desirable that this loss does not enable an adversary to impersonate other entities to A. Also, ESK-exposure attacks [4] are another concern. If an adversary can guess the ESK of one or both parties (e.g., thanks to a poor implementation of pseudo-random number generator), the secrecy of session keys should not be affected. Therefore, most of advanced attacks use *exposure of secret information*; thus, the security model must capture such exposure.

There have been several security models that can guarantee *exposure-resilience*. Canetti and Krawczyk [5] propose a model (denoted as the CK model) formulating exposure of SSKs and session state (i.e., some intermediate computation result). The CK model captures more security requirements than the BR model such as forward secrecy. However, the CK model only guarantees partial exposure-resilience because resistances to KCI and ESK-exposure attacks are not guaranteed. LaMacchia et al. [4] propose a very strong security model (denoted as the eCK model) formulating exposure of both SSKs and ESKs. The eCK model captures resistances to KCI and ESK-exposure attacks. However, it is clarified that the eCK model is not stronger than the CK model because of the difference on session state reveal property [6,7]. Fujioka et al, [8] revisit security attributes of HMQV [9] as a model (denoted as the CK^+ model) formulating exposure of SSKs, ESKs and session state. The CK^+ model captures all known advanced attacks, and is stronger than the CK model.

Concrete AKE schemes satisfying these models have been studied. HMQV [9] is one of the most efficient protocols and satisfies the CK^+ model. However, the security proof is given in the ROM under the knowledge-of-exponent assumption [10] that is a widely criticized assumption [11]. Various variants of HMQV (e.g., NAXOS [4] and CMQV [12]) have been studied and proved in the ROM. Okamoto [13,14] first proposes a specific construction (i.e., not generic construction) of eCK secure AKE in the StdM. However, the schemes rely on a strong building block, πPRF. It is not known how to construct πPRF concretely. Boyd et al. [15,16] propose a generic construction (BCGNP construction) of AKE from key encapsulation mechanism (KEM), which is secure in the CK model in the standard model (StdM). Because the CK model does not capture exposure of ESKs in the test session, unfortunately, it is unclear whether the BCGNP construction is secure when the ESK of the test session is exposed. Fujioka et al, [8] show that the BCGNP construction is insecure in the CK^+ model, and propose another generic construction (FSXY construction) of AKE from KEM, which is secure in the CK^+ model in the StdM.

1.2 Motivation

Most of exposure-resilient AKE schemes in the ROM is optimally *compact* (i.e., achieving the optimal communication cost); that is, each party only sends one group element like the Diffie-Hellman key exchange (DHKE). On the other hand, schemes in the StdM need larger communication costs than in the ROM. The existing most compact exposure-resilient AKE scheme in the StdM is the BCGNP construction (a variant that the DHKE is added) or the FSXY construction. These constructions use chosen ciphertext secure (IND-CCA secure) KEM as a building block. For example, in the BCGNP construction, each party exchanges a ciphertext of IND-CCA secure KEM and a EPK (one group element) of the DHKE. Thus, if the ciphertext length of underlying IND-CCA secure KEM is compact, the instantiated AKE scheme is also compact. However, Hanaoka et al. [17] show that it is impossible to construct IND-CCA secure KEM that the ciphertext length is shorter than two group elements with standard assumptions in the StdM. Hence, a limitation of these generic constructions is that the communication cost must be larger than three group elements.

1.3   Our Contribution

We overcome the barrier of communication costs by showing an exposure-resilient compact AKE scheme that the communication cost is lower than three group elements. Specifically, we introduce a new generic construction of CK^+ secure AKE in the StdM.

Our technique is to use *bounded* chosen-ciphertext secure (IND-q-CCA secure) KEM [18] instead of ordinary IND-CCA secure KEM. The difference between IND-q-CCA security and IND-CCA security is whether the number q of decryption queries by an adversary is bounded in advance. We carefully examine the security proofs of generic constructions from KEM, and find that the number of decryption queries depends on the number of sessions that each party owns. Because the number of sessions must be bounded in advance, a simulator can handle simulations only with an a-priori bounded number of decryption queries. We further discuss this issue in Section 3.3.

The distinguished advantage of IND-q-CCA secure KEM is compactness of the ciphertext. The decisional DH (DDH) based KEM [18], the computational DH (CDH) based KEM [19,20], the decisional bilinear DH (DBDH) based KEM [21] and the computational bilinear DH (CBDH) based KEM [20] can be constructed with one group element ciphertexts. Moreover, based on the fact that the factoring assumption implies the CDH assumption on a group of $\mathbb{Z}_N^*$ [22], the CDH-based KEM is secure under the factoring assumption if it is implemented on $\mathbb{Z}_N^*$. Thus, our result includes the most compact factoring-based AKE.

Another merit is that our generic construction can be instantiated by wider classes of hardness assumptions than existing constructions. Since the BCGNP construction and the FSXY construction are based on IND-CCA secure KEM, these cannot be instantiated under assumptions that IND-CCA secure KEM in the StdM is not known (e.g., subset-sum problems [23] and multi-variate quadratic systems [24]). Conversely, our generic construction covers these assumptions, because IND-q-CCA secure KEM is constructed from semantically secure (IND-CPA secure) KEM in the black-box manner [18], and IND-CPA secure KEM schemes in the StdM are known under these assumptions.

Furthermore, though the BCGNP construction and the FSXY construction adapt a strong randomness extractor as a part of the session key derivation procedure, we can replace it with a weaker building block, a *key derivation function* (KDF). The KDF is weaker and more efficient primitive than the strong randomness extractor; the output of the KDF is just guaranteed computationally indistinguishable from random value but the strong randomness extractor guarantees statistical indistinguishability. We can prove the security of our construction only with the computational property; thus, we can improve efficiency of the session key derivation procedure. This technique is proposed in [25,26]

This paper pioneers the first meaningful application of IND-q-CCA secure KEM because it was just a theoretical notion (i.e., to examine how strong security is achieved only from CPA-PKE) and any application is previously unknown.

2 CK$^+$ Security Model

In this section, we recall and quote the CK$^+$ model [9,8].

Notations. Throughout this paper we use the following notations. If Set is a set, then by $m \in_R$ Set we denote that m is sampled uniformly from Set. If $\mathcal{ALG}$ is an algorithm, then by $y \leftarrow \mathcal{ALG}(x; r)$ we denote that y is output by $\mathcal{ALG}$ on input x and randomness r (if $\mathcal{ALG}$ is deterministic, r is empty).

We denote a party by U_P, and party U_P and other parties are modeled as probabilistic polynomial-time (PPT) Turing machines w.r.t. security parameter κ. For party U_P, we denote static secret (public) key by SSK_P (SPK_P) and ephemeral secret (public) key by ESK_P (EPK_P). Party U_P generates its own keys, ESK_P and EPK_P, and the static public key EPK_P is linked with U_P's identity in some systems like PKI.[1]

Session. An invocation of a protocol is called a *session*. Session activation is done by an incoming message of the forms $(\Pi, \mathcal{I}, U_P, U_{\bar{P}})$ or $(\Pi, \mathcal{R}, U_{\bar{P}}, U_P, X_P)$, where we equate Π with a protocol identifier, $\mathcal{I}$ and $\mathcal{R}$ with role identifiers, and U_P and $U_{\bar{P}}$ with party identifiers. If U_P is activated with $(\Pi, \mathcal{I}, U_P, U_{\bar{P}})$, then U_P is called the session *initiator*. If $U_{\bar{P}}$ is activated with $(\Pi, \mathcal{R}, U_{\bar{P}}, U_P, X_P)$, then $U_{\bar{P}}$ is called the session *responder*. The initiator U_P outputs X_P, then may receive an incoming message of the forms $(\Pi, \mathcal{I}, U_P, U_{\bar{P}}, X_P, X_{\bar{P}})$ from the responder $U_{\bar{P}}$, U_P then computes the session key SK if U_P received the message. On the contrary, the responder $U_{\bar{P}}$ outputs $X_{\bar{P}}$, and computes the session key SK.

If U_P is the initiator of a session, the session is identified by sid $= (\Pi, \mathcal{I}, U_P, U_{\bar{P}}, X_P)$ or sid $= (\Pi, \mathcal{I}, U_P, U_{\bar{P}}, X_P, X_{\bar{P}})$. If $U_{\bar{P}}$ is the responder of a session, the session is identified by sid $= (\Pi, \mathcal{R}, U_{\bar{P}}, U_P, X_P, X_{\bar{P}})$. We say that U_P is the *owner* of session sid, if the third coordinate of session sid is U_P. We say that U_P is the *peer* of session sid, if the fourth coordinate of session sid is U_P. We say that a session is *completed* if its owner computes the session key. The *matching session* of $(\Pi, \mathcal{I}, U_P, U_{\bar{P}}, X_P, X_{\bar{P}})$ is session $(\Pi, \mathcal{R}, U_{\bar{P}}, U_P, X_P, X_{\bar{P}})$ and vice versa.

Adversary. The adversary $\mathcal{A}$, which is modeled as a probabilistic polynomial-time Turing machine, controls all communications between parties including session activation by performing the following adversary query.

---

[1] Static public keys must be known to both parties in advance. They can be obtained by exchanging them before starting the protocol or by receiving them from a certificate authority. This situation is common for all PKI-based AKE schemes.

- Send(message): The message has one of the following forms: $(\Pi, \mathcal{I}, U_P, U_{\bar{P}})$, $(\Pi, \mathcal{R}, U_{\bar{P}}, U_P, X_P)$, or $(\Pi, \mathcal{I}, U_P, U_{\bar{P}}, X_P, X_{\bar{P}})$. The adversary $\mathcal{A}$ obtains the response from the party.

To capture exposure of secret information, the adversary $\mathcal{A}$ is allowed to issue the following queries.

- KeyReveal(sid): The adversary $\mathcal{A}$ obtains the session key SK for the session sid if the session is completed.
- StateReveal(sid): The adversary $\mathcal{A}$ obtains the session state of the owner of session sid if the session is not completed (the session key is not established yet). The session state includes all ephemeral secret keys and intermediate computation results except for immediately erased information but does not include the static secret key.
- Corrupt(U_i): This query allows the adversary $\mathcal{A}$ to obtain all information of the party U_i. If a party is corrupted by a Corrupt(U_i, S_i) query issued by the adversary $\mathcal{A}$, then we call the party U_i *dishonest*. If not, we call the party *honest*.

Freshness. For the security definition, we need the notion of freshness.

Definition 1 (Freshness). *Let* $\mathsf{sid}^* = (\Pi, \mathcal{I}, U_P, U_{\bar{P}}, X_P, X_{\bar{P}})$ *or* $(\Pi, \mathcal{R}, U_P, U_{\bar{P}}, X_{\bar{P}}, X_P)$ *be a completed session between honest parties* U_P *and* $U_{\bar{P}}$. *If the matching session exists, then let* $\overline{\mathsf{sid}^*}$ *be the matching session of* sid^*. *We say session* sid^* *is fresh if none of the following conditions hold:*

1. *The adversary* $\mathcal{A}$ *issues* KeyReveal(sid^*), *or* KeyReveal($\overline{\mathsf{sid}^*}$) *if* $\overline{\mathsf{sid}^*}$ *exists,*
2. $\overline{\mathsf{sid}^*}$ *exists and the adversary* $\mathcal{A}$ *makes either of the following queries*
   - StateReveal(sid^*) *or* StateReveal($\overline{\mathsf{sid}^*}$),
3. $\overline{\mathsf{sid}^*}$ *does not exist and the adversary* $\mathcal{A}$ *makes the following query*
   - StateReveal(sid^*).

Security Experiment. For the security definition, we consider the following security experiment. Initially, the adversary $\mathcal{A}$ is given a set of honest parties and makes any sequence of the queries described above. During the experiment, the adversary $\mathcal{A}$ makes the following query.

- Test(sid^*): Here, sid^* must be a fresh session. Select random bit $b \in_U \{0, 1\}$, and return the session key held by sid^* if $b = 0$, and return a random key if $b = 1$.

The experiment continues until the adversary $\mathcal{A}$ makes a guess b'. The adversary $\mathcal{A}$ *wins* the game if the test session sid^* is still fresh and if the guess of the adversary $\mathcal{A}$ is correct, i.e., $b' = b$. The advantage of the adversary $\mathcal{A}$ in the AKE experiment with the PKI-based AKE protocol Π is defined as

$$\mathrm{Adv}_{\Pi}^{\mathrm{AKE}}(\mathcal{A}) = \Pr[\mathcal{A} \ wins] - \frac{1}{2}.$$

We define the security as follows.

Definition 2 (Security). *We say that a PKI-based AKE protocol Π is secure in the CK^+ model if the following conditions hold:*

1. *If two honest parties complete matching sessions, then, except with negligible probability, they both compute the same session key.*
2. *For any PPT bounded adversary $\mathcal{A}$, $\mathrm{Adv}_{\Pi}^{\mathrm{AKE}}(\mathcal{A})$ is negligible in security parameter κ for the test session sid^*,*
   (a) *if $\overline{\mathsf{sid}^*}$ does not exist, and the static secret key of the owner of sid^* is given to $\mathcal{A}$.*
   (b) *if $\overline{\mathsf{sid}^*}$ does not exist, and the ephemeral secret key of sid^* is given to $\mathcal{A}$.*
   (c) *if $\overline{\mathsf{sid}^*}$ exists, and the static secret key of the owner of sid^* and the ephemeral secret key of $\overline{\mathsf{sid}^*}$ are given to $\mathcal{A}$.*
   (d) *if sid^* exists, and the ephemeral secret key of sid^* and the ephemeral secret key of $\overline{\mathsf{sid}^*}$ are given to $\mathcal{A}$.*
   (e) *if $\overline{\mathsf{sid}^*}$ exists, and the static secret key of the owner of sid^* and the static secret key of the peer of sid^* are given to $\mathcal{A}$.*
   (f) *if $\overline{\mathsf{sid}^*}$ exists, and the ephemeral secret key of sid^* and the static secret key of the peer of sid^* are given to $\mathcal{A}$.*

3 Compact AKE from BCCA-KEM

In this section, we propose a generic construction of compact CK^+-secure AKE from BCCA-KEM.

3.1 Preliminaries

Security Notions of KEM Schemes. Here, we recall the definition of IND-q-CCA and IND-CPA security for KEM, and min-entropy of KEM keys as follows.

Definition 3 (Model for KEM Schemes). *A KEM scheme consists of the following 3-tuple* (KeyGen, EnCap, DeCap)*:*

- *$(ek, dk) \leftarrow$ KeyGen$(1^\kappa, r_g)$: a key generation algorithm which on inputs 1^κ and $r_g \in \mathcal{RS}_G$, where κ is the security parameter and $\mathcal{RS}_G$ is a randomness space, outputs a pair of keys (ek, dk).*
- *$(K, CT) \leftarrow$ EnCap$_{ek}(r_e)$: an encryption algorithm which takes as inputs encapsulation key ek and $r_e \in \mathcal{RS}_E$, outputs KEM session key $K \in \mathcal{KS}$ and ciphertext $CT \in \mathcal{CS}$, where $\mathcal{RS}_E$ is a randomness space, $\mathcal{KS}$ is a KEM session key space, and $\mathcal{CS}$ is a ciphertext space.*
- *$K \leftarrow$ DeCap$_{dk}(CT)$: a decryption algorithm which takes as inputs decapsulation key dk and ciphertext $CT \in \mathcal{CS}$, and outputs KEM session key $K \in \mathcal{KS}$.*

Definition 4 (IND-q-CCA and IND-CPA Security for KEM). *A KEM scheme is IND-q-CCA-secure if the following property holds for security parameter κ; For any PPT adversary $\mathcal{A} = (\mathcal{A}_1, \mathcal{A}_2)$, $\mathbf{Adv}^{\mathrm{ind-cca}} = |\Pr[r_g \leftarrow \mathcal{RS}_G; (ek, dk) \leftarrow$ KeyGen$(1^\kappa, r_g);$ state $\leftarrow \mathcal{A}_1^{\mathcal{DO}(dk, \cdot)}(ek); b \leftarrow \{0, 1\}; r_e \leftarrow \mathcal{RS}_E; (K_0^*, CT_0^*) \leftarrow$ EnCap$_{ek}(r_e); K_1^* \leftarrow \mathcal{K};$*

$b' \leftarrow \mathcal{A}_2^{\mathcal{DO}(dk,\cdot)}(ek, (K_b^*, CT_0^*), state); b' = b] - 1/2| \leq negl$, where $\mathcal{A}_1$ and $\mathcal{A}_2$ are restricted to pose at most q queries to decryption oracle $\mathcal{DO}$ in total, $\mathcal{K}$ is the space of session key and state is state information that $\mathcal{A}$ wants to preserve from $\mathcal{A}_1$ to $\mathcal{A}_2$. $\mathcal{A}$ cannot submit the ciphertext $CT = CT_0^*$ to $\mathcal{DO}$.

We say a KEM scheme is IND-CCA-secure for KEM if q is unbounded. We say a KEM scheme is IND-CPA-secure for KEM if $\mathcal{A}$ does not access $\mathcal{DO}$.

Definition 5 (Min-Entropy of KEM Key). *A KEM scheme is k-min-entropy KEM if for any ek, distribution $D_{\mathcal{KS}}$ of variable K defined by $(K, CT) \leftarrow \mathsf{EnCap}_{ek}(r_e)$, distribution D_{pub} of public information and random $r_e \in \mathcal{RS}_E$, $H_\infty(D_{\mathcal{KS}}|D_{pub}) \geq k$ holds, where H_∞ denotes min-entropy.*

Security Notion of Key Derivation Function. Let $KDF : Salt \times Dom \rightarrow Rng$ be a function with finite domain Dom, finite range Rng, and a space of non-secret random salt $Salt$.

Definition 6 (Key Derivation Function [27]). *We say function KDF is a key derivation function (KDF) if the following condition holds for a security parameter κ: For any PPT adversary $\mathcal{A}$ and any distribution D_{Rng} over Rng with $H_\infty(D_{Rng}) \geq \kappa$, $| \Pr[y \in_R Rng; 1 \leftarrow \mathcal{A}(y)] - \Pr[x \in_R Dom; s \in_R Salt; y \leftarrow KDF(s, x); 1 \leftarrow \mathcal{A}(y)]| \leq negl$.*

For example, concrete constructions of such a computationally secure KDF are given in [28,29] from a computational extractor and a PRF.

Security Notion of Pseudo-Random Function. Let κ be a security parameter and $\mathsf{F} = \{F_\kappa : Dom_\kappa \times \mathcal{FS}_\kappa \rightarrow Rng_\kappa\}_\kappa$ be a function family with a family of domains $\{Dom_\kappa\}_\kappa$, a family of key spaces $\{\mathcal{FS}_\kappa\}_\kappa$ and a family of ranges $\{Rng_\kappa\}_\kappa$.

Definition 7 (Pseudo-Random Function [16]). *We say that function family $\mathsf{F} = \{F_\kappa\}_\kappa$ is a PRF family if for any PPT distinguisher $\mathcal{D}$, $\mathbf{Adv}^{prf} = | \Pr[1 \leftarrow \mathcal{D}^{F_\kappa(\cdot)}] - \Pr[1 \leftarrow \mathcal{D}^{RF_\kappa(\cdot)}]| \leq negl$, where $RF_\kappa : Dom_\kappa \rightarrow Rng_\kappa$ is a truly random function.*

3.2 Protocol of FSXY Construction

First, we recall the protocol of the FSXY construction.

It is a generic construction from IND-CCA secure KEM (KeyGen, EnCap, DeCap) and IND-CPA secure KEM (wKeyGen, wEnCap, wDeCap), where the randomness space of encapsulation algorithms is $\mathcal{RS}_E$, the randomness space of key generation algorithms is $\mathcal{RS}_G$ and the KEM key space is $\mathcal{KS}$. Other building blocks are PRFs and a strong randomness extractor. For a security parameter κ, let $F : \{0, 1\}^* \times \mathcal{FS} \rightarrow \mathcal{RS}_E$, $F' : \{0, 1\}^* \times \mathcal{FS} \rightarrow \mathcal{RS}_E$, and $G : \{0, 1\}^* \times \mathcal{FS} \rightarrow \{0, 1\}^\kappa$ be PRFs, where $\mathcal{FS}$ is the key space of PRFs ($|\mathcal{FS}| = \kappa$). Let $Ext : \mathcal{SS} \times \mathcal{KS} \rightarrow \mathcal{FS}$ be a strong randomness extractor with randomly chosen seed $s \in \mathcal{SS}$, where $\mathcal{SS}$ is the seed space.

Party U_P randomly selects $\sigma_P \in_R \mathcal{FS}$ and $r \in_R \mathcal{RS}_G$, and runs $(ek_P, dk_P) \leftarrow \mathsf{KeyGen}(1^\kappa, r)$. Party U_P's SSK and SPK are $((dk_P, \sigma_P), ek_P)$. Fig. 1 shows the protocol.

$$\boxed{\begin{array}{l}
\textbf{Common public parameter}: F, F', G, Ext, s \\
\textbf{SSK and SPK for party } U_A : SSK_A := (dk_A, \sigma_A), SPK_A := ek_A \\
\textbf{SSK and SPK for party } U_B : SSK_B := (dk_B, \sigma_B), SPK_B := ek_B
\end{array}}$$

Party U_A (Initiator)   Party U_B (Responder)

$$r_A, r'_A \in_R \mathcal{FS}; r_{TA} \in_R \mathcal{RS}_G$$
$$(CT_A, K_A) \leftarrow$$
$$\mathsf{EnCap}_{ek_B}(F_{\sigma_A}(r_A) \oplus F'_{r'_A}(\sigma_A))$$

$$(ek_T, dk_T) \leftarrow \mathsf{wKeyGen}(1^\kappa, r_{TA}) \xrightarrow{\quad U_A, U_B, CT_A, ek_T \quad}$$

$$r_B, r'_B \in_R \mathcal{FS}; r_{TB} \in_R \mathcal{RS}_E$$
$$(CT_B, K_B) \leftarrow$$
$$\mathsf{EnCap}_{ek_A}(F_{\sigma_B}(r_B) \oplus F'_{r'_B}(\sigma_B))$$

$$\xleftarrow{\quad U_A, U_B, CT_B, CT_T \quad} (CT_T, K_T) \leftarrow \mathsf{wEnCap}_{ek_T}(r_{TB})$$

$$
\begin{array}{ll}
K_B \leftarrow \mathsf{DeCap}_{dk_A}(CT_B) & \\
K_T \leftarrow \mathsf{wDeCap}_{dk_T}(CT_T) & K_A \leftarrow \mathsf{DeCap}_{dk_B}(CT_A) \\
K'_1 \leftarrow Ext(s, K_A); K'_2 \leftarrow Ext(s, K_B) & K'_1 \leftarrow Ext(s, K_A); K'_2 \leftarrow Ext(s, K_B) \\
K'_3 \leftarrow Ext(s, K_T) & K'_3 \leftarrow Ext(s, K_T) \\
ST := (U_A, U_B, ek_A, ek_B, & ST := (U_A, U_B, ek_A, ek_B, \\
\quad CT_A, ek_T, CT_B, CT_T) & \quad CT_A, ek_T, CT_B, CT_T) \\
SK = G_{K'_1}(ST) \oplus G_{K'_2}(ST) \oplus G_{K'_3}(ST) & SK = G_{K'_1}(ST) \oplus G_{K'_2}(ST) \oplus G_{K'_3}(ST)
\end{array}
$$

Fig. 1. FSXY construction

The FSXY construction uses the twisted PRF trick [13]; that is, computing $F_\sigma(r) \oplus F'_{r'}(\sigma)$ from ESK (r, r') and SSK σ. The trick ensures that if either of the ESK or the SSK is revealed, $F_\sigma(r) \oplus F'_{r'}(\sigma)$ is still hidden. Thus, it is guaranteed that randomness of EnCap for honest parties is never revealed.

3.3 Construction

Next, we show our generic construction.

Design Principle. First, we examine the role of IND-CCA secure KEM in the security proof of the FSXY construction. The proof is divided by game transitions. A simulator must manage such transitions so that an adversary cannot distinguish two games. In some game, K_A or K_B in the test session is replaced with a random value. It is ensured that the adversary cannot distinguish this change from the IND-CCA security of (KeyGen, EnCap, DeCap). Then, the simulator (as the attacker in the IND-CCA game) must embed the challenge encapsulation key ek^* into the SPK and the challenge ciphertext CT^* into the EPK of the test session to manage the simulation. Because the simulator does not know the decapsulation key corresponding to ek^*, the simulator poses EPKs, that are sent to the party assigned ek^* in sessions except the test session, to the decryption oracle and can simulate session key derivation procedures. On the other hand, in the CK$^+$ model, the adversary can initiate multiple sessions for arbitrary two honest parties, and can designate a session as the test session from completed sessions. Because the simulator cannot know which session is designated, a possible way is to guess the session that the adversary poses Test query. Therefore, it is inevitable to limit the number of candidates in the proof; e.g., N parties exist in a system and each party is activated in at most ℓ sessions.[2] It means that the number of EPKs that are sent to the party assigned ek^* in sessions except the test session is at most $\ell - 1$. Hence, the maximum number of queries to the decryption oracle is also $\ell - 1$.

This fact implies that the IND-CCA security is not necessary to prove the security in the CK$^+$ model. Our main idea is to use IND-q-CCA secure KEM instead of IND-CCA secure KEM. Specifically, $q = \ell - 1$. It is known that IND-q-CCA secure KEM is constructed from IND-CPA secure KEM in a black-box manner [18]. Thus, we can instantiate the generic construction with various hard problems. Especially, we have compact instantiations based on DH problems and the factoring problem. We have DH-based IND-q-CCA secure KEM schemes [18,19,21,20] that a ciphertext contains only one group element. If we use the ElGamal KEM as IND-CPA secure KEM, the communication cost of DH-based AKE schemes is only two group elements. Moreover, the CDH-based KEM [19,20] is also used as the factoring-based thanks to the fact [22] that the factoring assumption implies the CDH assumption on $\mathbb{Z}_N^*$. Hence, we can also reduce the communication cost of factoring-based AKE schemes.

Also, the session key derivation procedure is more efficient than the FSXY construction because a KDF is used instead of a strong randomness extractor. On input a value having sufficient min-entropy, a strong randomness extractor outputs a value which is *statistically indistinguishable* from a uniformly chosen random value. Indeed, such statistical indistinguishability is not necessary to prove security of our construction. *Computational indistinguishability* is sufficient, and the KDF is suitable.

To adjust a small change of the security proof, we add a random κ bits element σ'_P to the SSK of each party.

Protocol. The protocol of our generic construction is shown in Fig. 2. We use IND-q-CCA secure KEM (bKeyGen, bEnCap, bDeCap).

Public Parameters. Let κ be the security parameter, $F : \{0, 1\}^* \times \mathcal{FS} \to \mathcal{RS}_E$, $F' : \{0, 1\}^* \times \mathcal{FS} \to \mathcal{RS}_E$, and $G : \{0, 1\}^* \times \mathcal{FS} \to \{0, 1\}^\kappa$ be pseudo-random functions, where $\mathcal{FS}$ is the key space of PRFs ($|\mathcal{FS}| = \kappa$), $\mathcal{RS}_E$ is the randomness space of encapsulation algorithms, and $\mathcal{RS}_G$ is the randomness space of key generation algorithms, and let $KDF : Salt \times \mathcal{KS} \to \mathcal{FS}$ be a KDF with a non-secret random salt $s \in Salt$, where $Salt$ is the salt space and $\mathcal{KS}$ is a space of KEM session keys. These are provided as some of the public parameters.

Secret and Public Keys. Party U_P randomly selects $\sigma_P \in_R \mathcal{FS}$, $\sigma'_P \in_R \{0, 1\}^\kappa$ and $r \in_R \mathcal{RS}_G$, and runs $(ek_P, dk_P) \leftarrow$ bKeyGen$(1^\kappa, r)$. Party U_P's SSK and SPK are $((dk_P, \sigma_P, \sigma'_P), ek_P)$.

---

[2] It is one of the most different aspects between security models for KEM and AKE. In KEM, the simulator can embed an instance of a hard problem into the challenge ciphertext without guessing because the challenge ciphertext is unique in the game. In AKE, as mentioned, candidates of the test session are multiple and the test session is chosen from all completed sessions.

Common public parameter : F, F', G, KDF, s
SSK and SPK for party U_A : $SSK_A := (dk_A, \sigma_A, \sigma'_A), SPK_A := ek_A$
SSK and SPK for party U_B : $SSK_B := (dk_B, \sigma_B, \sigma'_B), SPK_B := ek_B$

Party U_A (Initiator)   Party U_B (Responder)

$r_A \in_R \{0,1\}^\kappa; r'_A \in_R \mathcal{FS}; r_{TA} \in_R \mathcal{RS}_G$

$(CT_A, K_A) \leftarrow$
     $\mathsf{bEnCap}_{ek_B}(F_{\sigma_A}(r_A) \oplus F'_{r'_A}(\sigma'_A))$

$(ek_T, dk_T) \leftarrow \mathsf{wKeyGen}(1^\kappa, r_{TA})$ $\xrightarrow{\quad U_A, U_B, CT_A, ek_T \quad}$

                         $r_B \in_R \{0,1\}^\kappa; r'_B \in_R \mathcal{FS}; r_{TB} \in_R \mathcal{RS}_E$

                         $(CT_B, K_B) \leftarrow$

                               $\mathsf{bEnCap}_{ek_A}(F_{\sigma_B}(r_B) \oplus F'_{r'_B}(\sigma'_B))$

$\xleftarrow{\quad U_A, U_B, CT_B, CT_T \quad}$ $(CT_T, K_T) \leftarrow \mathsf{wEnCap}_{ek_T}(r_{TB})$

$K_B \leftarrow \mathsf{bDeCap}_{dk_A}(CT_B)$ $K_A \leftarrow \mathsf{bDeCap}_{dk_B}(CT_A)$

$K_T \leftarrow \mathsf{wDeCap}_{dk_T}(CT_T)$

$K'_1 \leftarrow KDF(s, K_A); K'_2 \leftarrow KDF(s, K_B)$ $K'_1 \leftarrow KDF(s, K_A); K'_2 \leftarrow KDF(s, K_B)$

$K'_3 \leftarrow KDF(s, K_T)$ $K'_3 \leftarrow KDF(s, K_T)$

$ST := (U_A, U_B, ek_A, ek_B,$ $ST := (U_A, U_B, ek_A, ek_B,$

      $CT_A, ek_T, CT_B, CT_T)$ $CT_A, ek_T, CT_B, CT_T)$

$SK = G_{K'_1}(ST) \oplus G_{K'_2}(ST) \oplus G_{K'_3}(ST)$ $SK = G_{K'_1}(ST) \oplus G_{K'_2}(ST) \oplus G_{K'_3}(ST)$

Fig. 2. Our construction

Session State. The session state of a session owned by U_A contains ephemeral secret keys (r_A, r_{TA}), encapsulated KEM key K_A and ad-hoc decryption key dk_T. Other information that is computed after receiving the message from the peer is immediately erased when the session key is established. Similarly, the session state of a session owned by U_B contains ephemeral secret keys (r_B, r_{TB}) and encapsulated KEM key K_B.

Security. We show the following theorem.

Theorem 1. *If* $(\mathsf{bKeyGen}, \mathsf{bEnCap}, \mathsf{bDeCap})$ *is IND-$(\ell - 1)$-CCA secure and κ-min-entropy KEM,* $(\mathsf{wKeyGen}, \mathsf{wEnCap}, \mathsf{wDeCap})$ *is IND-CPA secure and κ-min-entropy KEM, F, F', G are PRFs, and KDF is a KDF, then our construction is* CK^+*-secure.*

The proof of Theorem 1 is shown in Appendix A. Here, we give an overview of the security proof.

The proof outline is almost same as that of the FSXY construction except the difference between the strong randomness extractor and the KDF. We have to consider the following four exposure patterns in the CK^+ security model (matching cases):

2-(c) the static secret key of the initiator and the ephemeral secret key of the responder

2-(d) both ephemeral secret keys

2-(e) both static secret keys

2-(f) the ephemeral secret key of the initiator and the static secret key of the responder

In case 2-(c), K_A is protected by the security of CT_A because r'_A is not revealed; therefore, $F'_{r'_A}(\sigma'_A)$ is hidden and dk_B is not revealed. In case 2-(d), K_A and K_B are protected by the security of CT_A and CT_B because σ_A and σ_B are not revealed; therefore, $F_{\sigma_A}(r_A)$ and $F_{\sigma_B}(r_B)$ are hidden and dk_A and dk_B are not revealed. In case 2-(e), K_T is protected by the security of CT_T because dk_T and r_{TB} are not revealed. In case 2-(f), K_B is protected by the security of CT_B because r'_B is not revealed; therefore, $F'_{r'_B}(\sigma'_B)$ is hidden and dk_A is not revealed.

We transform the CK$^+$ security game since the session key in the test session is randomly distributed. First, the simulator guesses the test session. The guess matches with an adversary's choice with probability $1/N^2\ell$. Secondly, we change part of the twisted PRF in the test session into a random function because the key of part of the twisted PRF is hidden from the adversary; therefore, the randomness of the protected KEM can be randomly distributed. Thirdly, we change the protected KEM key into a random key for each pattern; therefore, the input of KDF is randomly distributed and has sufficient min-entropy. In this case, though the simulator is limited to pose only $\ell - 1$ queries to the decryption oracle, it is no problem because the maximum number of sessions for the target party is at most $\ell - 1$ except the test session. Fourthly, we change the output of KDF into randomly chosen values. Finally, we change one of the PRFs (corresponding to the protected KEM) into a random function. Therefore, the session key in the test session is randomly distributed; thus, there is no advantage to the adversary. We can show a similar proof in non-matching cases.

4   Instantiations

4.1   Diffie-Hellman-Based

We can instantiate our generic construction with IND-q-CCA secure KEM from various assumptions: DDH-based [18], CDH-based [19,20], DBDH-based [21] and CBDH-based [20]. The DDH-based instantiation is with the Cramer et al.'s KEM [18] as an IND-q-CCA secure KEM, and with the ElGamal KEM as an IND-CPA KEM. The communication cost (for two parties) is $4|p|$, where $|p|$ is the length of a group element. The computational cost (for two parties) is 11 regular exponentiations (all symmetric operations such as hash function/KDF/PRF and multiplications are ignored). Therefore, our instantiation is more efficient both in communication and computation than the DDH-based instantiation of the FSXY construction.

A disadvantage of using IND-q-CCA secure KEM is the encapsulation key size. The Cramer et al.'s KEM needs the encapsulation key and the decapsulation key consisting of $O(\kappa q^2) \cdot |p|$ group elements, respectively. Thus, our instantiation also needs the EPK and SPK consisting of the same order group elements. Therefore, our instantiation is suitable for environments that the bandwidth is constrained, but the storage size is sufficiently large. A typical example is to use smartphones outdoors.

We show a comparison between this instantiation and previous schemes in Table 1.

4.2   Factoring-Based

Moreover, we can instantiate our generic construction with IND-q-CCA secure KEM from the factoring assumption. We use the fact [22] that if a scheme is secure under the

Table 1. Comparison of exposure-resilient DH-based schemes and instantiations of our construction

	Instantiations	Model	Assumption	Computation (#parings +#[multi,regular]-exp)	Communication complexity		EPK size
[9]	–	ROM	gap DH & KEA1	$0 + [2, 2]$	$2|p|$	512	$O(1) \cdot |p|$
[13]	–	StdM	DDH & πPRF	$0 + [6, 6]$	$9|p|$	2304	$O(1) \cdot |p|$
[8]	Cramer-Shoup [30] ElGamal [31]	StdM	DDH	$0 + [4, 12]$	$8|p|$	2048	$O(1) \cdot |p|$
Ours	Cramer et al. [18] ElGamal [31]	StdM	DDH	$0 + [0, 11]$	$4|p|$	1024	$O(\kappa(\ell - 1)^2) \cdot |p|$
Ours	Yamada et al. [21] ElGamal [31]	StdM	DDH & DBDH	$(2\kappa(\ell - 1)^2 + 4)$ $+[0, 10]$	$4|p|$	1024	$O(\sqrt{\kappa}(\ell - 1)) \cdot |p|$

Table 2. Comparison of exposure-resilient factoring-based schemes and instantiations of our construction

	Instantiations	Model	Assumption	Computation (#[multi,regular]-exp)	Communication complexity		EPK size
[8]	Hofheinz-Kiltz [32] Blum-Goldwasser [33]	StdM	factoring	$[3, 13]$	$6|p|$	18k	$O(1) \cdot |p|$
Ours	Pereira et al. [19] Blum-Goldwasser [33]	StdM	factoring	$[0, 4\kappa^2 + 8]$	$4|p|$	12k	$O(\kappa^2(\ell - 1)^2) \cdot |p|$
Ours	anonymous [20] Blum-Goldwasser [33]	StdM	factoring	$[0, 4\kappa + 8]$	$4|p|$	12k	$O(\kappa(\ell - 1)^2) \cdot |p|$

For concreteness expected communication costs for 128-bit security implementations are also given. Note that computational costs are estimated without any pre-computation technique.

CDH assumption in $\mathbb{Z}_N^*$, it is also secure under the factoring assumption. Because the CDH-based IND-q-CCA secure KEM schemes [19,20] remain the security when implemented in $\mathbb{Z}_N^*$, we enjoy this fact to obtain factoring-based instantiations. For example, the CDH-based instantiation is with the Pereira et al.'s KEM [19] as an IND-q-CCA secure KEM, and with the Hofheinz-Kiltz KEM [32] as an IND-CPA KEM. The communication cost (for two parties) is $6|p|$, where $|p|$ is the length of a group element. The computational cost (for two parties) is 2 multi exponentiations and $4\kappa^2 + 7$ regular exponentiations (all symmetric operations such as hash function/KDF/PRF and multiplications are ignored). Therefore, our instantiation is more efficient in communication than the factoring-based instantiation of the FSXY construction.

We show a comparison between this instantiation and previous schemes in Table 2.

4.3   Others

Cramer et al. [18] showed that IND-q-CCA secure KEM is generically constructed only from IND-CPA secure KEM. There have many efficient IND-CPA KEM (or PKE) schemes based on code-based problems [34], lattice problems [35], subset-sum problems [23], and multi-variate quadratic systems [24]. Therefore, we have AKE instantiations from various types of assumptions other than the DH and the factoring assumption.

References

1. Bellare, M., Rogaway, P.: Entity Authentication and Key Distribution. In: Stinson, D.R. (ed.) CRYPTO 1993. LNCS, vol. 773, pp. 232–249. Springer, Heidelberg (1994)
2. Bellare, M., Rogaway, P.: Provably secure session key distribution: the three party case. In: STOC 1995, pp. 57–66 (1995)
3. Blake-Wilson, S., Johnson, D., Menezes, A.: Key Agreement Protocols and Their Security Analysis. In: IMA Int. Conf. 1997, pp. 30–45 (1997)
4. LaMacchia, B.A., Lauter, K., Mityagin, A.: Stronger Security of Authenticated Key Exchange. In: Susilo, W., Liu, J.K., Mu, Y. (eds.) ProvSec 2007. LNCS, vol. 4784, pp. 1–16. Springer, Heidelberg (2007)
5. Canetti, R., Krawczyk, H.: Analysis of Key-Exchange Protocols and Their Use for Building Secure Channels. In: Pfitzmann, B. (ed.) EUROCRYPT 2001. LNCS, vol. 2045, pp. 453–474. Springer, Heidelberg (2001)
6. Cremers, C.J.F.: Session-state Reveal Is Stronger Than Ephemeral Key Reveal: Attacking the NAXOS Authenticated Key Exchange Protocol. In: Abdalla, M., Pointcheval, D., Fouque, P.-A., Vergnaud, D. (eds.) ACNS 2009. LNCS, vol. 5536, pp. 20–33. Springer, Heidelberg (2009)
7. Cremers, C.J.F.: Examining Indistinguishability-Based Security Models for Key Exchange Protocols: The case of CK, CK-HMQV, and eCK. In: ASIACCS 2011, pp. 80–91 (2011)
8. Fujioka, A., Suzuki, K., Xagawa, K., Yoneyama, K.: Strongly Secure Authenticated Key Exchange from Factoring, Codes, and Lattices. In: Fischlin, M., Buchmann, J., Manulis, M. (eds.) PKC 2012. LNCS, vol. 7293, pp. 467–484. Springer, Heidelberg (2012)
9. Krawczyk, H.: HMQV: A High-Performance Secure Diffie-Hellman Protocol. In: Shoup, V. (ed.) CRYPTO 2005. LNCS, vol. 3621, pp. 546–566. Springer, Heidelberg (2005)
10. Damgård, I.B.: Towards Practical Public Key Systems Secure Against Chosen Ciphertext Attacks. In: Feigenbaum, J. (ed.) CRYPTO 1991. LNCS, vol. 576, pp. 445–456. Springer, Heidelberg (1992)
11. Naor, M.: On Cryptographic Assumptions and Challenges. In: Boneh, D. (ed.) CRYPTO 2003. LNCS, vol. 2729, pp. 96–109. Springer, Heidelberg (2003)
12. Ustaoglu, B.: Obtaining a secure and efficient key agreement protocol from (H)MQV and NAXOS. In: Des. Codes Cryptography, vol. 46(3), pp. 329–342 (2008)
13. Okamoto, T.: Authenticated Key Exchange and Key Encapsulation in the Standard Model. In: Kurosawa, K. (ed.) ASIACRYPT 2007. LNCS, vol. 4833, pp. 474–484. Springer, Heidelberg (2007)
14. Moriyama, D., Okamoto, T.: An eCK-Secure Authenticated Key Exchange Protocol without Random Oracles. In: Pieprzyk, J., Zhang, F. (eds.) ProvSec 2009. LNCS, vol. 5848, pp. 154–167. Springer, Heidelberg (2009)
15. Boyd, C., Cliff, Y., Gonzalez Nieto, J.M., Paterson, K.G.: Efficient One-Round Key Exchange in the Standard Model. In: Mu, Y., Susilo, W., Seberry, J. (eds.) ACISP 2008. LNCS, vol. 5107, pp. 69–83. Springer, Heidelberg (2008)
16. Boyd, C., Cliff, Y., González Nieto, J.M., Paterson, K.G.: One-round key exchange in the standard model. IJACT 1(3), 181–199 (2009)
17. Hanaoka, G., Matsuda, T., Schuldt, J.C.N.: On the Impossibility of Constructing Efficient Key Encapsulation and Programmable Hash Functions in Prime Order Groups. In: Safavi-Naini, R., Canetti, R. (eds.) CRYPTO 2012. LNCS, vol. 7417, pp. 812–831. Springer, Heidelberg (2012)
18. Cramer, R., Hanaoka, G., Hofheinz, D., Imai, H., Kiltz, E., Pass, R., Shelat, A., Vaikuntanathan, V.: Bounded CCA2-Secure Encryption. In: Kurosawa, K. (ed.) ASIACRYPT 2007. LNCS, vol. 4833, pp. 502–518. Springer, Heidelberg (2007)
19. Pereira, M., Dowsley, R., Hanaoka, G., Nascimento, A.C.A.: Public Key Encryption Schemes with Bounded CCA Security and Optimal Ciphertext Length Based on the CDH Assumption. In: Burmester, M., Tsudik, G., Magliveras, S., Ilić, I. (eds.) ISC 2010. LNCS, vol. 6531, pp. 299–306. Springer, Heidelberg (2011)

20. anonymous: Reducing Public Key Sizes in Bounded CCA-Secure KEMs with Optimal Ciphertext Length (manuscript)

21. Yamada, S., Hanaoka, G., Kunihiro, N.: Two-Dimensional Representation of Cover Free Families and Its Applications: Short Signatures and More. In: Dunkelman, O. (ed.) CT-RSA 2012. LNCS, vol. 7178, pp. 260–277. Springer, Heidelberg (2012)

22. Hofheinz, D., Kiltz, E.: The Group of Signed Quadratic Residues and Applications. In: Halevi, S. (ed.) CRYPTO 2009. LNCS, vol. 5677, pp. 637–653. Springer, Heidelberg (2009)

23. Lyubashevsky, V., Palacio, A., Segev, G.: Public-Key Cryptographic Primitives Provably as Secure as Subset Sum. In: Micciancio, D. (ed.) TCC 2010. LNCS, vol. 5978, pp. 382–400. Springer, Heidelberg (2010)

24. Huang, Y.-J., Liu, F.-H., Yang, B.-Y.: Public-Key Cryptography from New Multivariate Quadratic Assumptions. In: Fischlin, M., Buchmann, J., Manulis, M. (eds.) PKC 2012. LNCS, vol. 7293, pp. 190–205. Springer, Heidelberg (2012)

25. Yoneyama, K.: One-Round Authenticated Key Exchange with Strong Forward Secrecy in the Standard Model against Constrained Adversary. IEICE Transactions 96-A(6), 1124–1138 (2013)

26. Yoneyama, K.: Generic Construction of Two-Party Round-Optimal Attribute-Based Authenticated Key Exchange without Random Oracles. IEICE Transactions 96-A(6), 1112–1123 (2013)

27. Gennaro, R., Shoup, V.: A Note on An Encryption Scheme of Kurosawa and Desmedt. In: Cryptology ePrint Archive: 2004/194 (2004)

28. Krawczyk, H.: Cryptographic Extraction and Key Derivation: The HKDF Scheme. In: Rabin, T. (ed.) CRYPTO 2010. LNCS, vol. 6223, pp. 631–648. Springer, Heidelberg (2010)

29. Dachman-Soled, D., Gennaro, R., Krawczyk, H., Malkin, T.: Computational Extractors and Pseudorandomness. In: Cramer, R. (ed.) TCC 2012. LNCS, vol. 7194, pp. 383–403. Springer, Heidelberg (2012)

30. Cramer, R., Shoup, V.: A Practical Public Key Cryptosystem Provably Secure Against Adaptive Chosen Ciphertext Attack. In: Krawczyk, H. (ed.) CRYPTO 1998. LNCS, vol. 1462, pp. 13–25. Springer, Heidelberg (1998)

31. Elgamal, T.: A public key cryptosystem and a signature scheme based on discrete logarithms. IEEE Transactions on Information Theory 31(4), 469–472 (1985)

32. Hofheinz, D., Kiltz, E.: Practical Chosen Ciphertext Secure Encryption from Factoring. In: Joux, A. (ed.) EUROCRYPT 2009. LNCS, vol. 5479, pp. 313–332. Springer, Heidelberg (2009)

33. Blum, M., Goldwasser, S.: An Efficient Probabilistic Public-Key Encryption Scheme Which Hides All Partial Information. In: Blakely, G.R., Chaum, D. (eds.) CRYPTO 1984. LNCS, vol. 196, pp. 289–302. Springer, Heidelberg (1984)

34. Kobara, K., Imai, H.: Semantically Secure McEliece Public-Key Cryptosystems-Conversions for McEliece PKC. In: Kim, K. (ed.) PKC 2001. LNCS, vol. 1992, pp. 19–35. Springer, Heidelberg (2001)

35. Lyubashevsky, V., Peikert, C., Regev, O.: On Ideal Lattices and Learning with Errors over Rings. In: Gilbert, H. (ed.) EUROCRYPT 2010. LNCS, vol. 6110, pp. 1–23. Springer, Heidelberg (2010)

A   Proof of Theorem 1

In the experiment of CK^+ security, we suppose that sid^* is the session identity for the test session, and that there are at most N parties and at most ℓ sessions are activated for each party. Let κ be the security parameter, and let $\mathcal{A}$ be a PPT (in κ) bounded adversary. Suc denotes the event that $\mathcal{A}$ wins. We consider the following events that cover all cases of the behavior of $\mathcal{A}$.

- Let E_1 be the event that the test session sid* has no matching session $\overline{\text{sid}}^*$, the owner of sid* is the initiator and the static secret key of the initiator is given to $\mathcal{A}$.
- Let E_2 be the event that the test session sid* has no matching session $\overline{\text{sid}}^*$, the owner of sid* is the initiator and the ephemeral secret key of sid* is given to $\mathcal{A}$.
- Let E_3 be the event that the test session sid* has no matching session $\overline{\text{sid}}^*$, the owner of sid* is the responder and the static secret key of the responder is given to $\mathcal{A}$.
- Let E_4 be the event that the test session sid* has no matching session $\overline{\text{sid}}^*$, the owner of sid* is the responder and the ephemeral secret key of sid* is given to $\mathcal{A}$.
- Let E_5 be the event that the test session sid* has matching session $\overline{\text{sid}}^*$, and both static secret keys of the initiator and the responder are given to $\mathcal{A}$.
- Let E_6 be the event that the test session sid* has matching session $\overline{\text{sid}}^*$, and both ephemeral secret keys of sid* and $\overline{\text{sid}}^*$ are given to $\mathcal{A}$.
- Let E_7 be the event that the test session sid* has matching session $\overline{\text{sid}}^*$, and the static secret key of the owner of sid* and the ephemeral secret key of $\overline{\text{sid}}^*$ are given to $\mathcal{A}$.
- Let E_8 be the event that the test session sid* has matching session $\overline{\text{sid}}^*$, and the ephemeral secret key of sid* and the static secret key of the owner of $\overline{\text{sid}}^*$ are given to $\mathcal{A}$.

To finish the proof, we investigate events $E_i \land Suc$ $(i = 1, \ldots, 8)$ that cover all cases of event Suc. In this paper, we show the proof of event $E_1 \land Suc$. Other events are given in the full version.

A.1   Event $E_1 \land Suc$

We change the interface of oracle queries and the computation of the session key. These instances are gradually changed over seven hybrid experiments, depending on specific sub-cases. In the last hybrid experiment, the session key in the test session does not contain information of the bit b. Thus, the adversary clearly only output a random guess. We denote these hybrid experiments by $\mathbf{H}_0, \ldots, \mathbf{H}_6$ and the advantage of the adversary $\mathcal{A}$ when participating in experiment $\mathbf{H}_i$ by $\mathbf{Adv}(\mathcal{A}, \mathbf{H}_i)$.

Hybrid Experiment $\mathbf{H}_0$: This experiment denotes the real experiment for CK$^+$ security and in this experiment the environment for $\mathcal{A}$ is as defined in the protocol. Thus, $\mathbf{Adv}(\mathcal{A}, \mathbf{H}_0)$ is the same as the advantage of the real experiment.

Hybrid Experiment $\mathbf{H}_1$: In this experiment, if session identities in two sessions are identical, the experiment halts.

When two ciphertexts from different randomness are identical and two public keys from different randomness are identical, session identities in two sessions are also identical. In the IND-q-CCA secure KEM and IND-CPA secure KEM, such an event occurs with negligible probability. Thus, $|\mathbf{Adv}(\mathcal{A}, \mathbf{H}_1) - \mathbf{Adv}(\mathcal{A}, \mathbf{H}_0)| \leq negl$.

Hybrid Experiment $\mathbf{H}_2$: In this experiment, the experiment selects a party U_A and integer $i \in [1, \ell]$ randomly in advance. If $\mathcal{A}$ poses Test query to a session except i-th session of U_A, the experiment halts.

Since guess of the test session matches with $\mathcal{A}$'s choice with probability $1/N^2\ell$, $\mathbf{Adv}(\mathcal{A}, \mathbf{H}_2) \geq 1/N^2\ell \cdot \mathbf{Adv}(\mathcal{A}, \mathbf{H}_1)$.

Hybrid Experiment $\mathbf{H}_3$: In this experiment, the computation of (CT_A^*, K_A^*) in the test session is changed. Instead of computing $(CT_A^*, K_A^*) \leftarrow \mathsf{bEnCap}_{ek_B}(F_{\sigma_A}(r_A) \oplus F'_{r'_A}(\sigma'_A))$, it is changed as $(CT_A^*, K_A^*) \leftarrow \mathsf{bEnCap}_{ek_B}(F_{\sigma_A}(r_A) \oplus RF(\sigma'_A))$, where we suppose that U_B is the intended partner of U_A in the test session.

We construct a distinguisher $\mathcal{D}$ between PRF $F^* : \{0,1\}^* \times \mathcal{FS} \to \mathcal{RS}_E$ and a random function RF from $\mathcal{A}$ in $\mathbf{H}_2$ or $\mathbf{H}_3$. $\mathcal{D}$ performs the following steps.

Setup. $\mathcal{D}$ chooses pseudo-random functions $F : \{0,1\}^* \times \mathcal{FS} \to \mathcal{RS}_E$ and $G : \{0,1\}^* \times \mathcal{FS} \to \{0,1\}^k$, where $\mathcal{FS}$ is the key space of PRFs, and a KDF $KDF : Salt \times \mathcal{KS} \to \mathcal{FS}$ with a salt $s \in Salt$. Also, $\mathcal{D}$ embeds F^* into F'. These are provided as a part of the public parameters. Also, $\mathcal{D}$ sets all N parties' static secret and public keys. $\mathcal{D}$ selects $\sigma_P \in \mathcal{FS}$, $\sigma'_P \in \{0,1\}^{kappa}$ and $r \in \mathcal{RS}_G$ randomly, and runs key the generation algorithm $(ek_P, dk_P) \leftarrow \mathsf{bKeyGen}(1^k, r)$ and U_P's static secret and public keys are $((dk_P, \sigma_P, \sigma'_P), ek_P)$.

Next, $\mathcal{D}$ sets the ephemeral public key of i-th session of U_A (i.e., the test session) as follows: $\mathcal{D}$ selects ephemeral secret keys $r_A^* \in \mathcal{FS}$ and $r_{TA}^* \in \mathcal{RS}_G$ randomly. Then, $\mathcal{D}$ poses σ'_A to his oracle (i.e., F^* or a random function RF) and obtains $x \in \mathcal{RS}_E$. $\mathcal{D}$ computes $(CT_A^*, K_A^*) \leftarrow \mathsf{bEnCap}_{ek_B}(F_{\sigma_A}(r_A^*) \oplus x)$ and $(dk_T^*, ek_T^*) \leftarrow \mathsf{wKeyGen}(r_{TA}^*)$, and sets the ephemeral public key (CT_A^*, ek_T^*) of i-th session of U_A.

Simulation. $\mathcal{D}$ maintains the list $\mathcal{L}_{SK}$ that contains queries and answers of KeyReveal. $\mathcal{D}$ simulates oracle queries by $\mathcal{A}$ as follows.

1. $\mathsf{Send}(\Pi, \mathcal{I}, U_P, U_{\bar{P}})$: If $P = A$ and the session is i-th session of U_A, $\mathcal{D}$ returns the ephemeral public key (CT_A^*, ek_T^*) computed in the setup. Otherwise, $\mathcal{D}$ computes the ephemeral public key (CT_P, ek_T) obeying the protocol, returns it and records $(\Pi, U_P, U_{\bar{P}}, (CT_P, ek_T))$.
2. $\mathsf{Send}(\Pi, \mathcal{R}, U_{\bar{P}}, U_P, (CT_P, ek_T))$: $\mathcal{D}$ computes the EPK $(CT_{\bar{P}}, CT_T)$ and the session key SK obeying the protocol, returns the ephemeral public key, and records $(\Pi, U_P, U_{\bar{P}}, (CT_P, ek_T), (CT_{\bar{P}}, CT_T))$ as the completed session and SK in the list $\mathcal{L}_{SK}$.
3. $\mathsf{Send}(\Pi, \mathcal{I}, U_P, U_{\bar{P}}, (CT_P, ek_T), (CT_{\bar{P}}, CT_T))$: If $(\Pi, U_P, U_{\bar{P}}, (CT_P, ek_T), (CT_{\bar{P}}, CT_T))$ is not recorded, $\mathcal{D}$ records the session $(\Pi, U_P, U_{\bar{P}}, (CT_P, ek_T), (CT_{\bar{P}}, CT_T))$ is not completed. Otherwise, $\mathcal{D}$ computes the session key SK obeying the protocol, and records $(\Pi, U_P, U_{\bar{P}}, (CT_P, ek_T), (CT_{\bar{P}}, CT_T))$ as the completed session and SK in the list $\mathcal{L}_{SK}$.
4. $\mathsf{KeyReveal}(sid)$:
   (a) If the session sid is not completed, $\mathcal{D}$ returns an error message.
   (b) Otherwise, $\mathcal{D}$ returns the recorded value SK.
5. $\mathsf{StateReveal}(sid)$: $\mathcal{D}$ responds the ephemeral secret key and intermediate computation results of sid as the definition. Note that the StateReveal query is not posed to the test session from the freshness definition.
6. $\mathsf{Corrupt}(U_P)$: $\mathcal{D}$ responds the static secret key and all unerased session states of U_P as the definition.

7. **Test(sid):** $\mathcal{D}$ responds to the query as the definition.
8. If $\mathcal{A}$ outputs a guess $b' = 0$, $\mathcal{D}$ outputs that the oracle is the PRF F^*. Otherwise, $\mathcal{D}$ outputs that the oracle is a random function RF.

Analysis. For $\mathcal{A}$, the simulation by $\mathcal{D}$ is same as the experiment $\mathbf{H}_2$ if the oracle is the PRF F^*. Otherwise, the simulation by $\mathcal{D}$ is same as the experiment $\mathbf{H}_3$. Thus, if the advantage of $\mathcal{D}$ is negligible, then $|\mathbf{Adv}(\mathcal{A}, \mathbf{H}_3) - \mathbf{Adv}(\mathcal{A}, \mathbf{H}_2)| \leq negl$.

Hybrid Experiment $\mathbf{H}_4$: In this experiment, the computation of K_A^* in the test session is changed again. Instead of computing $(CT_A^*, K_A^*) \leftarrow \mathsf{bEnCap}_{ek_B}(F_{\sigma_A}(r_A) \oplus RF(\sigma_A'))$, it is changed as choosing $K_A^* \leftarrow \mathcal{KS}$ randomly, where we suppose that U_B is the intended partner of U_A in the test session.

We construct an IND-CCA adversary S from $\mathcal{A}$ in $\mathbf{H}_3$ or $\mathbf{H}_4$. S performs the following steps.

Init. S receives the public key ek^* as a challenge.

Setup. S chooses pseudo-random functions $F : \{0, 1\}^* \times \mathcal{FS} \rightarrow \mathcal{RS}_E$, $F' : \{0, 1\}^* \times \mathcal{FS} \rightarrow \mathcal{RS}_E$ and $G : \{0, 1\}^* \times \mathcal{FS} \rightarrow \{0, 1\}^k$, where $\mathcal{FS}$ is the key space of PRFs, and a KDF $KDF : Salt \times \mathcal{KS} \rightarrow \mathcal{FS}$ with a salt $s \in Salt$. These are provided as a part of the public parameters. Also, S sets all N parties' static secret and public keys except U_B. S selects $\sigma_P \in \mathcal{FS}$, $\sigma_P' \in \{0, 1\}^{k}appa$ and $r \in \mathcal{RS}_G$ randomly, and runs key the generation algorithm $(ek_P, dk_P) \leftarrow \mathsf{bKeyGen}(1^\kappa, r)$ and U_P's static secret and public keys are $((dk_P, \sigma_P, \sigma_P'), ek_P)$.

Next, S sets ek^* as the static public key of U_B. Also, S receives the challenge (K^*, CT^*) from the challenger.

Simulation. S maintains the list $\mathcal{L}_{SK}$ that contains queries and answers of **KeyReveal**. S simulates oracle queries by $\mathcal{A}$ as follows.

1. **Send($\Pi, \mathcal{I}, U_P, U_{\bar{P}}$):** If $P = A$ and the session is i-th session of U_A, S computes ek_T^* obeying the protocol and returns the ephemeral public key (CT^*, ek_T^*). Otherwise, S computes the ephemeral public key (CT_P, ek_T) obeying the protocol, returns it and records $(\Pi, U_P, U_{\bar{P}}, (CT_P, ek_T))$.
2. **Send($\Pi, \mathcal{R}, U_{\bar{P}}, U_P, (CT_P, ek_T)$):** If $\bar{P} = B$ and $CT_P \neq CT^*$, S poses CT_P to the decryption oracle, obtains K_P, computes the ephemeral public key $(CT_{\bar{P}}, CT_T)$ and the session key SK obeying the protocol, returns the ephemeral public key, and records $(\Pi, U_P, U_{\bar{P}}, (CT_P, ek_T), (CT_{\bar{P}}, CT_T))$ as the completed session and SK in the list $\mathcal{L}_{SK}$. Else if $\bar{P} = B$ and $CT_P = CT^*$, S sets $K_P = K^*$, computes the ephemeral public key $(CT_{\bar{P}}, CT_T)$ and the session key SK obeying the protocol, returns the ephemeral public key, and records $(\Pi, U_P, U_{\bar{P}}, (CT_P, ek_T), (CT_{\bar{P}}, CT_T))$ as the completed session and SK in the list $\mathcal{L}_{SK}$. Otherwise, S computes the ephemeral public key $(CT_{\bar{P}}, CT_T)$ and the session key SK obeying the protocol, returns the ephemeral public key, and records $(\Pi, U_P, U_{\bar{P}}, (CT_P, ek_T), (CT_{\bar{P}}, CT_T))$ as the completed session and SK in the list $\mathcal{L}_{SK}$.

3. Send(Π, $\mathcal{I}$, U_P, $U_{\bar{P}}$, (CT_P, ek_T), $(CT_{\bar{P}}, CT_T)$): If (Π, U_P, $U_{\bar{P}}$, (CT_P, ek_T), $(CT_{\bar{P}}, CT_T)$)) is not recorded, S records the session ($\Pi, U_P, U_{\bar{P}}, (CT_P, ek_T), (CT_{\bar{P}}, CT_T)$) is not completed. Else if $P = A$ and the session is i-th session of U_A, S computes the session key SK obeying the protocol except that $K_A^* = K^*$, and records ($\Pi, U_P, U_{\bar{P}}, (CT_P, ek_T), (CT_{\bar{P}}, CT_T)$) as the completed session and SK in the list $\mathcal{L}_{SK}$. Otherwise, S computes the session key SK obeying the protocol, and records ($\Pi, U_P, U_{\bar{P}}, (CT_P, ek_T), (CT_{\bar{P}}, CT_T)$) as the completed session and SK in the list $\mathcal{L}_{SK}$.
4. KeyReveal(sid):
   (a) If the session sid is not completed, S returns an error message.
   (b) Otherwise, S returns the recorded value SK.
5. StateReveal(sid): S responds the ephemeral secret key and intermediate computation results of sid as the definition. If the owner of sid is U_B, S poses ciphertexts received by U_B to the decryption oracle and can simulate all intermediate computation results. Note that the StateReveal query is not posed to the test session from the freshness definition.
6. Corrupt(U_P): S responds the static secret key and all unerased session states of U_P as the definition.
7. Test(sid): S responds to the query as the definition.
8. If $\mathcal{A}$ outputs a guess b', S outputs b'.

Analysis. S must pose ciphertexts to the decryption oracle when the receiver is U_B and sessions are not the test session. The maximum number of sessions activated with U_B is $\ell - 1$ except the test session. Thus, the number of queries to the decryption oracle is equal or smaller than $\ell - 1$.

The simulation by S is same as the experiment $\mathbf{H}_3$ if the challenge is (K_1^*, CT_0^*). Otherwise, the simulation by S is same as the experiment $\mathbf{H}_4$. Also, both $K_{A,1}^*$ in two experiments have κ-min-entropy because (bKeyGen, bEnCap, bDeCap) is κ-min-entropy KEM. Thus, if the advantage of S is negligible, then $|\mathbf{Adv}(\mathcal{A}, \mathbf{H}_4) - \mathbf{Adv}(\mathcal{A}, \mathbf{H}_3)| \le negl$.

Hybrid Experiment $\mathbf{H}_5$: In this experiment, the computation of $K_1'^*$ in the test session is changed. Instead of computing $K_1'^* \leftarrow KDF(s, K_A^*)$, it is changed as choosing $K_1'^* \in \mathcal{FS}$ randomly.

Since K_A^* is randomly chosen in $\mathbf{H}_4$, it has sufficient min-entropy. Thus, by the definition of the strong randomness extractor, $|\mathbf{Adv}(\mathcal{A}, \mathbf{H}_5) - \mathbf{Adv}(\mathcal{A}, \mathbf{H}_4)| \le negl$.

Hybrid Experiment $\mathbf{H}_6$: In this experiment, the computation of SK in the test session is changed. Instead of computing $SK = G_{K_1'}(\mathsf{ST}) \oplus G_{K_2'}(\mathsf{ST}) \oplus G_{K_3'}(\mathsf{ST})$, it is changed as $SK = x \oplus G_{K_2'}(\mathsf{ST}) \oplus G_{K_3'}(\mathsf{ST})$ where $x \in \{0, 1\}^\kappa$ is chosen randomly and we suppose that U_B is the intended partner of U_A in the test session.

The proof of $|\mathbf{Adv}(\mathcal{A}, \mathbf{H}_6) - \mathbf{Adv}(\mathcal{A}, \mathbf{H}_5)| \le negl$ is similar to that in experiment $\mathbf{H}_3$. Thus, we omit it.

In $\mathbf{H}_6$, the session key in the test session is perfectly randomized. Thus, $\mathcal{A}$ cannot obtain any advantage from Test query.

Therefore, $\mathbf{Adv}(\mathcal{A}, \mathbf{H}_6) = 0$ and $\Pr[E_1 \wedge Suc]$ is negligible.

On the Share Efficiency of Robust Secret Sharing and Secret Sharing with Cheating Detection*

Mahabir Prasad Jhanwar and Reihaneh Safavi-Naini

Department of Computer Science
University of Calgary, Canada

Abstract. In a basic (t, n)-threshold secret sharing scheme the adversary is passive and the security goal is to ensure that unauthorized subsets do not learn any information about the secret. In this paper we consider the case that the corrupted parties submit *incorrect* shares and there are extra security goals with respect to incorrect shares. We consider two such security requirements: in a (t, n)-threshold robust secret sharing (RSS) scheme we require that the shared secret can be recovered from the set of *all* n shares even if up to t of them are incorrect; and in a (t, n)-threshold secret sharing scheme with cheating detection (SSCD) property we require to prevent cheaters who try to make another player reconstruct an invalid secret.

We make the following contributions. Firstly, we construct a robust (t, n)-threshold secret sharing (RSS) scheme with the lowest known share size for $n = 2t + 1$. In our RSS scheme the share size is $\log_2 s + \log_2 \frac{1}{\delta} + n$ bits which is less than the share size of the best known scheme by $\log_2 \frac{1}{\delta} + n$ bits. Here $\log_2 s$ bits denotes secret size and δ denotes error probability in reconstructing the correct secret. We then consider the problem of reducing the size of public information in RSS. We will motivate this problem and propose a scheme that nearly halves the amount of public information. For this we first construct a new variant of Shamir secret sharing scheme and then modify it to provide robustness. The construction achieves the least total share storage/communication among all known threshold robust secret sharing schemes.

The final contribution of this paper is the constriction of an optimal threshold secret sharing with *cheating detection* property. We propose a scheme that achieves the lower bound on the share size of cheating detection schemes, and hence is optimal. The scheme is the first to achieve the bound without having special requirements.

1 Introduction

Secret sharing is one of the most important primitive in cryptography and in particular distributed systems. In a (t, n)-threshold secret sharing scheme [26,1], a dealer $\mathcal{D}$ distributes a secret s to n players, say $P_1, \ldots, P_n$ in such a way that

---

* Financial support for this research was provided in part by Alberta Innovates - Technology Futures, in the Province of Alberta in Canada.

G. Paul and S. Vaudenay (Eds.): INDOCRYPT 2013, LNCS 8250, pp. 179–196, 2013.

any $t+1$ or more players can recover the secret s, but any t or fewer players have no information on s. A piece of information given to P_i is called a share and is denoted by σ_i. The scheme is said to be *perfect* if no subset of t or less shares can leak any information about the secret s, where the leakage is in information theoretic sense and without assuming any limit on the computational resources of the adversary. An important efficiency parameter in secret sharing scheme is the size of shares. Let Σ_i be the set of possible shares for P_i. Let S be the set of possible secrets. Then it is well known that $|\Sigma_i| \geq |S|$ for any perfect (t,n)-threshold secret sharing scheme [15], i.e., $\log_2 \sigma_i \geq \log_2 s$. Schemes with $\log_2 \sigma_i = \log_2 s$ are called *ideal*.

In its basic form, secret sharing assumes that the corrupted participants are passive (or semi-honest) and follow the protocol during the reconstruction phase. In practice however one needs to consider stronger adversaries who deviate from the protocol, collude and submit wrong shares. There are a wide range of settings and security requirements that address active adversaries in secret sharing. In this paper we consider two particular formulation of security requirements for threshold secret sharing, known as robust secret sharing [4] and secret sharing with cheating detection [22]. In the following we briefly describe these two and then present our contributions. A closely related problem of *identifying cheaters* in secret sharing has also been studied [17,21,6,13] in the literature.

Robust Secret Sharing (RSS): In a *perfect (t,n)-threshold robust secret sharing* scheme, in addition to the requirement of perfect threshold secret sharing it is also required that the secret can be reconstructed with high probability from the set of all shares, even if up to t shares are incorrect. Requiring that the set of uncorrupted shares have sufficient information to recover the secret implies that $n - t \geq t + 1$ and so $n \geq 2t + 1$ ($t \leq \frac{n-1}{2}$). When $n = 2t + 1$, the number of honest users is only one more than the colluders. It is known that in this case colluders will always succeed with some probability and that the share size of the users is always larger than the secret size. The extra share size is called the *share redundancy* and is defined as $\max_i\{\log_2 \sigma_i\} - \log_2 s$. Construction of schemes with the lowest probability of failure and the least share redundancy has been an active research area in recent years. The construction in [7] has the lowest known share redundancy equal to $2\log_2 \frac{1}{\delta} + 2n$ bits where δ is the probability of error in reconstructing the correct secret.

We also consider a new property for secret sharing schemes and study it for RSS. Secret sharing schemes, including robust schemes, use some public data during reconstruction. This public data enables users to store smaller shares. For example in Shamir secret sharing the public data is the interpolation points which is assigned to players individually but does not need to be made secret. The information is used during the reconstruction. By making these points public, the share size of the users is effectively halved. To implement such a scheme however one needs to provide a broadcast channel or authenticated bulletin board that will be used to make the required public data available for reconstruction. Reducing this public data is not only important from practical view point, but also raises interesting theoretical questions and in particular possible tradeoff between the amount of public and private data in various schemes. To our knowledge this has not been considered before. We will discuss this in our contributions.

Secret Sharing with Cheating Detection (SSCD): The goal of secret sharing schemes with cheating detection property is to ensure detection of cheating by the malicious players who aim to cheat an honest player by opening incorrect shares and causing the honest player to reconstruct wrong secret. Specifically, suppose that t players, say $P_1, \ldots, P_t$, want to cheat a $(t+1)$th player, P_{t+1}, by opening modified shares $\sigma'_1, \ldots, \sigma'_t$. They succeed if the secret s' that is reconstructed from $\sigma'_1, \ldots, \sigma'_t$ and σ_{t+1} is different from the original secret s. In this case, we say that the *player P_{t+1} is cheated by the wrong shares $\sigma'_1, \ldots, \sigma'_t$*. Tompa and Woll [27] first considered this problem (see also [3,2,22]). Two different model exists for such a system. In the first one, known as CDV model, we suppose that the cheaters somehow know the value of the secret s. The other model OKS is characterized by the property that t cheaters (corrupted players) $P_1, \ldots, P_t$ does not have any idea about the secret s before they cheat P_{t+1}. Ogata, Kurosawa, and Stinson showed the following tight lower bound on share size in OKS model:

$$\log_2 \sigma_i \geq \log_2 s + \log_2 \frac{1}{\delta_c}, \tag{1}$$

where δ_c denotes the cheating probability. In OKS model, the only two known share-optimal schemes [23,22] impose *restrictions on the secret set*. Construction of SSCD schemes in this model that meet the lower bound is an interesting open problem.

1.1 Our Contribution

The contribution of this paper is three fold.

[i] A Threshold Robust Secret Sharing with the Lowest Redundancy. We propose a new (t, n)-threshold robust secret sharing scheme that has redundancy, $\log_2 \frac{1}{\delta} + n$ bits. Each user's share consists of two field elements and system's public parameters, in addition to the interpolation points, consists of two filed elements that are used to verify correctness of a reconstructed candidate secret. For share generation the scheme uses polynomials over finite fields, and for reconstruction Lagrange interpolation(s) to construct a candidate secret. The reconstruction algorithm loops over all subsets of size $t+1$ of n participants and so is computationally inefficient. A similar inefficiency exists in [7], which has had the shortest share size before this paper. It is worth noting that the best scheme [4] with computationally efficient reconstruction has share size which is substantially larger than our proposed scheme (see Sect. 3.3). Construction of RSS schemes with computationally efficient reconstruction and share size similar to ours is an interesting open question.

[ii] Reducing System's Public Information. In polynomial based schemes such as Shamir's scheme, each user is associated with two pieces of information:

one is an index/identity that can be made public, and a second that is the share of the secret. In some cases [27] to add extra security properties, the public part is also made private. On the other hand in some cases [14] to provide extra properties such as robustness, the public part of the user is enlarged, and/or the secret part of the share grows [4]. An interesting question is to what extent private *and* public information associated with a user can be reduced. In this paper we ask this question in the context of RSS and in particular our proposed RSS scheme. We show that the public information can be nearly halved. To achieve this we first construct a variant of Shamir secret sharing. We will then use this scheme to construct an RSS with the same share length (for the secure part of share) as the scheme in Sect. 3, but with the extra property that it has only $t+1$ field elements for its public values. This nearly halves the amount of public information and effectively results in the least total share storage/communication among all known threshold robust secret sharing schemes.

[iii] **Secret Sharing with Cheating Detection.** The robust secret sharing scheme in Sect. 3 builds on a secret sharing scheme with cheating detection property. We describe the underlying scheme in Sect. 5. In the previous section we noted the two common security models for secret sharing with cheating detection. We evaluate security of our scheme in OKS model and show that it has the smallest possible share size, satisfying with equality the lower bound in (1) for such schemes. There are two other known optimal schemes [22,23] in OKS model, both imposing restrictions on the secret set. In particular the scheme in [23] requires that the secret set be a finite field with characteristic different from 2, and the construction in [22] requires a number q such that q be a prime power and $q^2 + q + 1$ is a prime. The latter scheme also assumes that secret is *chosen with uniform distribution* hence using a weaker security notion. In our scheme secret can be from any finite field and the only requirement is that the field size to be $\geq n$ which is a general requirement for all schemes. We use the strong definition of security which requires security for any distribution on the secret set.

1.2   Related Work

It is known that, in the range $\frac{n}{3} \leq t < \frac{n}{2}$, robust secret sharing is possible, but only if one admits a small but positive failure probability (denoted as δ) in reconstructing the correct secret. The first solution to the problem of designing robust secret sharing schemes with absolute correctness in reconstruction (i.e., the error probability $\delta = 0$) was presented by McElice and Sarwate [20], where error correcting technique for Reed-Solomon codes are used to enhance the original Shamir secret sharing scheme with the robustness property. Their scheme assumes $n \geq 3t + 1$. Moreover, it follows immediately from the theory of Reed-Solomon error correcting codes that the condition $n \geq 3t + 1$ ($t \leq \frac{n-1}{3}$) is also necessary for Shamir's scheme to be robust with $\delta = 0$. In fact, the above is true for any (t, n)-threshold secret sharing scheme. It was shown in [16] that a secret sharing scheme realizing an access structure Γ has robustness property with $\delta = 0$ precisely when the access structure Γ satisfies a condition called $\mathcal{Q}^3$ [12]. A monotone access structure Γ for a set $\mathcal{P}$ of participants is said to satisfy $\mathcal{Q}^3$ condition if $A_1 \cup A_2 \cup A_3 \neq \mathcal{P}$ for any $A_1, A_2, A_3 \in \Gamma^c$, where Γ^c is $2^{\mathcal{P}} \backslash \Gamma$. The (t, n)-threshold access structure satisfies $\mathcal{Q}^3$ precisely when $n \geq 3t + 1$.

Constructions for threshold robust secret sharing schemes with unconditional security for $n = 2t + 1$ can be broadly divided into two classes. We briefly describe the best scheme in each class. The scheme due to Cramer et al. [7] follows the approach of [2]. It uses standard Shamir secret sharing and distributes the shares of three field elements that are algebraically related: the dealer shares independently the actual secret $s \in \mathbb{F}_q$, a randomly chosen field element $r \in \mathbb{F}_q$, and their product $\rho = s \cdot r$. The reconstructor does the following: for every subset of $t + 1$ players, he reconstructs s', r' and ρ' and checks if $s' \cdot r' = \rho'$, and halts and outputs s' if it is the case. One can show that for any subset of $t + 1$ players: if $s' \neq s$ then $s' \cdot r' \neq \rho'$ except with probability $1/|\mathbb{F}_q|$. Thus if $\lfloor \log_2 |\mathbb{F}_q| \rfloor = k$, taking into account union bound over all subsets of size t + 1, gives a robust secret sharing scheme with failure probability $\delta = \frac{1}{2^{k-n}}$ and shares of size $3k$ ($= k + 2 \log_2 \frac{1}{\delta} + 2n$) bits. Therefore the redundancy in share size is $2 \log_2 \frac{1}{\delta} + 2n$. The reconstruction procedure of this scheme has running time which is exponential in the number of players.

The second scheme is given by Cevellos, Fehr, Ostrovsky and Rabani [4], and is based on the scheme of Rabin and Ben-Or [25]. The Share distribution algorithm of this scheme is the same as the well-known scheme of Rabin and Ben-Or [25] which is the standard Shamir secret sharing scheme, but enhanced by means of an (unconditionally secure) message authentication code (MAC : $\mathcal{M} \times \mathcal{K} \rightarrow \mathcal{T}$, $\mathcal{M} = \mathbb{F}_q$, $\mathcal{K} = \mathbb{F}_q \times \mathbb{F}_q$, and $\mathcal{T} = \mathbb{F}_q$). In particular, for every pair of players P_i and P_j, P_i's Shamir share $s_i \in \mathcal{M}$ is authenticated with an authentication tag $\tau_{ij} \in \mathcal{T}$, where the corresponding authentication key $k_{ji} \in \mathcal{K}$ is given to player P_j. Therefore, beyond the actual Shamir share, every player gets $3n$ field elements as part of his share. The scheme by [4] uses a message authentication code with *short* tags and keys and with the resulting weak security. The short tags and keys result in the required saving (improvement over Rabin and Ben-Or scheme) in the share size. The weakened security of authentication (and so higher chance of forging) is compensated with a more sophisticated reconstruction procedure which runs in polynomial time and results in an exponentially small failure probability. Finally the redundancy in share size for the scheme is $3 \log_2 \frac{1}{\delta} + 3n \log_2(n\lambda)$ bits, where λ is an independent security parameter and δ is the scheme's error probability.

Cheating detection was first consisted by Tompa and Woll [27]. Their work was followed by a number of authors including [3,2,22]. In OKS model, the only two known share-optimal schemes [23,22] impose *restrictions on the secret set*. Construction of SSCD schemes in this model that meet the lower bound is an interesting open problem.

Applications. Threshold robust secret sharing schemes provide a powerful tool for building secure and reliable distributed data storage systems. Users' data (files) can be broken into pieces (shares) and stored on multiple servers such that privacy of data against servers is provided, and the system ensures recovery of the data when a subset of servers corrupt their stored shares, accidentally or intentionally. In recent years, systems and architectures based on this primitive have emerged [18,28,9] which shows importance of threshold robust secret sharing in practice. Threshold robust secret sharing has also direct application to Secure Message Transmission (SMT) [8,10,11]. In an unconditionally secure SMT, a sender is connected to a receiver through n wires such that up to t of which are controlled by an adversary. The goal of an SMT protocol is to ensure that the message sent by the sender is received correctly by the receiver, and no information about the message is leaked to the adversary. Good threshold robust secret sharing schemes lead to good secure message transmission schemes [8,19]. Robust secret sharing schemes may also be seen as an stepping stone towards the construction of verifiable secret sharing (VSS) schemes [5,24], in which, in addition to the corrupted players, the dealer is dishonest and may hand out inconsistent shares. Finally robust secret sharing is an important primitive for secure multi-party computation.

2 Preliminaries

2.1 Robust Secret Sharing

Secret sharing schemes, that satisfy the additional property, that the secret can be reconstructed from the set of *all* shares even if some players provide incorrect shares, are called *robust secret sharing schemes*. In order to clearly define the robustness property of a secret sharing, we describe a secret sharing scheme by means of two interactive protocols, Share and Rec, where Share involves a dealer $\mathcal{D}$ and n players $P_1, \ldots, P_n$, and the reconstruction protocol Rec involves the n players and the reconstructor $\mathcal{R}$, a trusted third party. The dealer is connected to every player by a secure, untappable channel. There is also a broadcast channel that can be used by everyone in the system. We now describe the protocols Share and Rec. Let $[n] = \{1, \ldots, n\}$.

- Share: The dealer $\mathcal{D}$ takes as input a secret $s \in S$, locally computes shares $\sigma_1, \ldots, \sigma_n$, and for every $i \in [n]$, sends the i-th share σ_i privately to player P_i.
- Rec: During reconstruction, each player P_i, communicates, possibly by means of several synchronous communication rounds[1], its share σ_i to $\mathcal{R}$. The reconstructor uses the received shares to produce an output s', which is supposed to be the secret s.

Security. We now define the security goals of a (t, n)-threshold robust secret sharing scheme. We begin by defining the adversary.

Adversarial Capability. We consider unbounded adversary. In the reconstruction phase Rec, the adversary $\mathcal{A}$ adaptively corrupts up to t players. The corruption can be done between communication rounds and continue as long as

---

[1] In each round, every player P_i sends *a part* of its full share σ_i. In case, when the Rec is *single round*, each player sends σ_i.

the total number of corrupted players does not exceed t. Once a player P_i is corrupted, the adversary learns P_i's share σ_i, and from then on, he controls the information that P_i send to $\mathcal{R}$. By a **rushing** adversary we mean, in every communication round, he can decide for every corrupted player on what this player should send to $\mathcal{R}$, depending on what he has seen so far and depending on what the honest players have sent to $\mathcal{R}$ in the current round. By contrast, a **non-rushing**[2] adversary is one who selects the corrupted shares before the start of each round.

Privacy. By the perfect privacy of a (t, n)-threshold RSS scheme we mean that at the end of the share distribution protocol Share, no t players has any information about the secret. Formally, for any subset $B \subset \{P_1, \ldots, P_n\}$ of size at most t and for every two elements $s_1, s_2 \in S$, we have

$$\text{Prob[Secret is } s_1 \mid \text{view}_B] = \text{Prob[Secret is } s_2 \mid \text{view}_B],$$

where view_B denotes the total available information for the members of B to see. The probabilities are taken over the random coins of Share.

Robustness. We now define the (t, δ)-robustness property of an n-player robust secret sharing scheme $\Pi = (\text{Share}, \text{Rec})$. To describe it clearly, we consider the following game called the "robustness game".

Robustness Game

1. **Share distribution phase:** The dealer $\mathcal{D}$ picks a secret $s \in S$, and uses Share to compute shares $\sigma_1, \ldots, \sigma_n$ for the n players; σ_i is given privately to $P_i, 1 \leq i \leq n$.
2. **Reconstruction Phase:** In this phase, the adversary $\mathcal{A}$ adaptively corrupts up to t players as described above.
3. **Final Phase:** At the end of reconstruction phase, $\mathcal{R}$ has all the n shares and at most t of them are incorrect. Based on the shares, $\mathcal{R}$ outputs the secret s'. The adversary is said to win if $s' \neq s$.

We now define the advantage of $\mathcal{A}$ in the above game as

$$\text{Adv}_{\Pi,(t,n)}^{\text{Robust}}(\mathcal{A}) = \text{Prob}[s' \neq s].$$

Definition 1. *A (t, n)-threshold robust secret sharing scheme $\Pi = (\text{Share}, \text{Rec})$ is said to be unconditionally secure with (t, δ)-robustness property against non-rushing adversary, if it has both perfect privacy and $Adv_{\Pi,(t,n)}^{\text{Robust}}(\mathcal{A}) \leq \delta$ in the above game.*

In this paper, we present RSS schemes with single round reconstruction. The schemes are secure against non-rushing adversary.

---

[2] Security against non-rushing adversary makes sense in a communication model enhanced with a simultaneous broadcast channel, i.e., one by means of which all players broadcast their information at the same time.

2.2 Lagrange Interpolation

Let t be a positive integer and $\mathbb{F}$ be a field. Given any $t+1$ pairs of field elements $(x_1, y_1), \ldots, (x_{t+1}, y_{t+1})$ with the x_i's distinct, there exists a unique polynomial $f(x) \in \mathbb{F}[x]$ of degree at most t such that $f(x_i) = y_i$ for $1 \leq i \leq t+1$. The polynomial can be obtained using the Lagrange interpolation formula as follows,

$$f(x) = y_1 \lambda_{x_1}^A(x) + \cdots + y_{t+1} \lambda_{x_{t+1}}^A(x), \tag{2}$$

where $A = \{x_1, \ldots, x_{t+1}\}$ and $\lambda_{x_i}^A(x)$'s are Lagrange basis polynomials, given by

$$\lambda_{x_i}^A(x) = \frac{\prod_{1 \leq j \leq t+1, j \neq i}(x - x_j)}{\prod_{1 \leq j \leq t+1, j \neq i}(x_i - x_j)} .$$

To simplify the notation, we write $\lambda_{x_i}(x)$ for $\lambda_{x_i}^A(x)$ when the description of the set A is clear from the context. We define Lagrange coefficients as $\lambda_{x_i} = \lambda_{x_i}(0)$. Therefore, from equation (2) we have $f(0) = \sum_{i=1}^{t+1} y_i \lambda_{x_i}$. One may also note that $\sum_{i=1}^{t+1} \lambda_{x_i} = 1$.

2.3 Shamir Secret Sharing

Let $f(x) = s + a_1 x + \cdots + a_t x^t$. The secret is $f(0) = s$. Player P_i will receive an ordered pair $(\alpha_i, f(\alpha_i))$. It is easy to show that this is a threshold scheme, since for any $t+1$ participants, there is only one polynomial of degree at most t passing through their $t+1$ points. Also it is a perfect threshold scheme since for any t points and any point $(0, s')$, there is a unique polynomial of degree at most t passing through their t points and $(0, s')$. The scheme becomes ideal if the values $\{\alpha_i\}_{i=1}^n$ are publicly revealed (the values does not yield any information about s) so that the share of player P_i is just the value $f(\alpha_i)$.

3 The New Scheme: RSSS-Basic

We noted that in the scheme in [7], the relation $\rho = s \cdot r$ is formed and ρ, r and s individually shared. Our first observation is that in [7] one only needs to distribute (Shamir secret sharing) shares of s and r and make ρ the public parameter. We note that, knowledge of ρ and t shares does not reveal any information about the secret and so this appears as a promising approach. This approach however does not guarantee the required robustness. Following this direction, we use the Rabin and Ben-Or's Information Checking [25] vectors[3] (relation) and construct an efficient RSS with unconditional security. We now describe our scheme.

---

[3] Information Checking Vector (α, β): Let $s \in \mathbb{F}_q$. Let $\alpha \neq 0$ and y be randomly chosen from $\mathbb{F}_q$ and $\beta = s + \alpha y$. Then the tuple (α, β) will reveal no information about s.

We have a group of n players $\{P_1, \ldots, P_n\}$. Let t and n are positive integers such that $n = 2t + 1$. We fix a finite field $\mathbb{F}_q$ with $q > n$, and n distinct points, $\alpha_1, \ldots, \alpha_n \in \mathbb{F}_q$, known to all players. We now present a (t, n)-threshold robust secret sharing scheme.

- Share: On input a secret $s \in \mathbb{F}_q$, the share generation algorithm Share outputs a list of shares as follows:
  - The dealer $\mathcal{D}$ chooses random $r, X (\neq 0) \in \mathbb{F}_q$ with uniform distribution and computes $Y = s + Xr$.
  - $\mathcal{D}$ chooses t random elements $f_1, \ldots, f_t$ from $\mathbb{F}_q$ independently with uniform distribution. These random elements together with s define a polynomial $f(x) = s + \sum_{i=1}^{t} f_i x^i$. $\mathcal{D}$ then computes $s_i = f(\alpha_i)$ for all $i \in [n]$.
  - $\mathcal{D}$ also picks t random elements $g_1, \ldots, g_t \in \mathbb{F}_q$ independently with uniform distribution. These random elements together with r define a polynomial $g(x) = r + \sum_{i=1}^{t} g_i x^i$. $\mathcal{D}$ then computes $r_i = g(\alpha_i)$ for all $i \in [n]$.
  - Every player P_i gets his/her share $\sigma_i = (s_i, r_i)$. The tuple (X, Y) is part of system's public parameters.
- Rec: The secret reconstruction algorithm Rec outputs the secret as follows:
  - Every player sends (s'_i, r'_i) to the reconstructor $\mathcal{R}$. Therefore, $\mathcal{R}$ receives n shares, at most t of which are possibly incorrect.
  - To reconstruct the secret, $\mathcal{R}$ does the following for *every subset* of $t + 1$ players $\{P_{i_1}, \ldots, P_{i_{t+1}}\}$:
    * Computes, $s' = \sum_{j=1}^{t+1} \lambda_{i_j} s'_{i_j}$ and $r' = \sum_{j=1}^{t+1} \lambda_{i_j} r'_{i_j}$ (Lagrange interpolation).
    * Checks, if $Y = s' + Xr'$.
    * If yes, $\mathcal{R}$ then outputs the secret as s'.

3.1 Privacy

The following theorem shows, that no t players has any information about the secret.

Theorem 1. *For any subset $B \subset \{P_1, \ldots, P_n\}$ of size t and its view_B*

$$Prob[Secret\ is\ s_1 \mid \mathsf{view}_B] = Prob[Secret\ is\ s_2 \mid \mathsf{view}_B],$$

for all $s_1, s_2 \in \mathbb{F}_q$, where view_B denotes the elements, that the members of B see: $\mathsf{view}_B = (X, Y, \{(s_i, r_i)_{P_i \in B}\})$.

Proof: Without loss of generality, let $B = \{P_1, \ldots, P_t\}$. Then $\mathsf{view}_B = (X, Y, \{(s_i, r_i)_{i=1}^{t}\})$. For every choice of $s \in \mathbb{F}_q$ for secret, we have: a unique value for $r = X^{-1} \cdot (Y - s)$, a unique polynomial f of degree at most t such that $f(0) = s; f(\alpha_i) = s_i$ for $1 \leq i \leq t$, and a unique polynomial g of degree at most t such that $g(0) = r; g(\alpha_i) = r_i$ for $1 \leq i \leq t$. As the set of actual unknowns were chosen independently with uniform distribution, hence, for every $s \in \mathbb{F}_q$, $\Pr[s$ is secret $\mid (s_i, r_i)_{P_i \in B}] = \frac{1}{q^{2t+1}}$. Since the probability is the same for every $s \in \mathbb{F}_q$, the privacy follows.

3.2 Robustness

Theorem 2. *Let $\mathbb{F}_q$ be any finite field with q elements. Let $k = \lfloor \log_2 q \rfloor$. Then for any positive integers n, t with $n = 2t + 1$, $q > n$, and secret space $\mathbb{F}_q$, RSSS-Basic forms an unconditional secure (t, n)-threshold robust secret sharing scheme with (t, δ) robustness against non-rushing adversary such that*

$$\delta \leq \frac{1}{2^{k-n}} \ .$$

Proof: Consider an arbitrary set A of $t+1$ shares revealed in the reconstruction phase. If A consists exclusively of shares of honest players, then the secret s' reconstructed by $\mathcal{R}$ would certainly be the correct secret s. Else, either a failure would be detected, or an incorrect secret $s' \neq s$ is accepted based on the shares in A. We now compute the probability for the case when $s' \neq s$ but $Y = s' + Xr'$. Let $s' = s + \epsilon_s$ and $r' = r + \epsilon_r$. The value s' is accepted for the secret if and only if the corrupted shares in A leads to a pair $(\epsilon_s, \epsilon_r) \in \mathbb{F}_q \times \mathbb{F}_q$ such that $\epsilon_s \neq 0$ and $Y = (s + \epsilon_s) + X(r + \epsilon_r)$. But $Y = (s + \epsilon_s) + X(r + \epsilon_r) = s + Xr + \epsilon_s + X\epsilon_r$ implies $\epsilon_s + X\epsilon_r = 0$. Thus we see that, for every $(\epsilon_s, \epsilon_r) \in \mathbb{F}_q \times \mathbb{F}_q$ with $\epsilon_s \neq 0$, there is a unique value of $\epsilon_r = -X^{-1}\epsilon_s$ ($X \neq 0$) such that $Y = (s + \epsilon_s) + X(r + \epsilon_r)$. Hence, for any set of $t+1$ shares containing at most t corrupted shares, a wrong secret is accepted with probability at most $\frac{1}{q}$. Therefore, taking into account, the union bound of probabilities over all subsets of size $t+1$, the probability that an incorrect secret is accepted in the reconstruction process is at most $\frac{2^n}{q} = \frac{1}{2^{k-n}}$.

3.3 Efficiency Comparison

Set the secret space $S = \mathbb{F}_q$. We now compare the share efficiency of our construction with the schemes of [7,4]. One may note that, for all the three schemes, the error probability δ is determined directly by the cardinality of the secret space. For our construction and [7], we have $\delta = \frac{2^n}{|\mathbb{F}_q|}$, i.e., $\log_2 \frac{1}{\delta} + n = \log_2 |\mathbb{F}_q|$. For [4], δ is dictated by $|\mathbb{F}_q|$ and an independent parameter λ^4; specifically $\delta = \frac{1}{2^{\frac{\log_2 |\mathbb{F}_q|}{\lambda} - n \log_2(n \cdot \lambda)}}$ (improved error probability over the other two schemes). We set $k = \lfloor \log_2 |\mathbb{F}_q| \rceil$ (in bits). The following table exhibit the individual share redundancy (in bits).

Table 1. Comparison Table

Scheme	Secret size	Redundancy	δ	Rec Complexity
[7]	k	$2(\log_2 \frac{1}{\delta} + n)$	$2^{-(k-n)}$	$\exp(n)$
[4]	k	$3 \log_2 \frac{1}{\delta} + 3n \log_2(n\lambda)$	$2^{-(n\frac{k}{\lambda} - n \log_2(n \cdot \lambda))}$	$\text{poly}(n)$
RSSS-Basic	k	$\log_2 \frac{1}{\delta} + n$	$2^{-(k-n)}$	$\exp(n)$

---

[4] In [4], each player gets n tags and n keys beside the actual share. The length of tags and keys are determined by $MAC : \mathbb{F}_q \times (\mathbb{F}_q/2^\lambda)^2 \to \mathbb{F}_q/2^\lambda$. The tag space $\mathcal{T} = \mathbb{F}_q/2^\lambda$ and key space $\mathcal{K} = (\mathbb{F}_q/2^\lambda)^2$. Therefore, the share size redundancy is $3n \frac{\log_2 |\mathbb{F}_q|}{\lambda} = 3 \log_2 \frac{1}{\delta} + 3n \log_2(n\lambda)$ bits.

4   Robust Secret Sharing with Savings on Public Data

In a secret sharing scheme shares carry information about the secret and need to be securely stored and so the share size is the main efficiency parameter of a secret sharing scheme. For reconstruction, secret sharing schemes may also use some public values associated with each player. For example in Shamir's secret sharing each user has an associated field element $\alpha_i \in \mathbb{F}_q$. The share of the player is $f(\alpha_i)$ which is securely stored by the user. The reconstruction needs the tuple $(\alpha_i, f(\alpha_i))$. The value α_i can be stored publicly and so is not considered in measuring share efficiency of schemes. This means without extra setup assumptions such as existence of a public bulletin board that allows access to the non-sensitive part of the secret when needed, for a $\log_2 |\mathbb{F}_q|$ bit secret in Shamir's scheme, $2 \log_2 |\mathbb{F}_q|$ bits need to be stored and presented at the reconstruction time. Taking into account the interpolation points, for the robust secret sharing scheme in Section 3, a user's storage is essentially $3 \log_2 |\mathbb{F}_q|$ bits and therefore the total communication[5] during reconstruction is $3n \log_2 |\mathbb{F}_q|$ bits. An interesting question is if the total share storage can be reduced.

In the following we present a threshold robust secret sharing for $n = 2t + 1$ with the property that we can save on t interpolation points. This is the least total share storage/communication among all known threshold robust secret sharing schemes. The scheme follows the approach of RSSS-Basic, in achieving robustness, but replaces the Shamir secret sharing with a new ideal polynomial based secret sharing that allows us to reduce the public values. We begin by first describing our variant of Shamir's scheme.

4.1   A Variant of Shamir Secret Sharing

We have a group of n players $\{P_1, \ldots, P_n\}$. Let t be a positive integer such that $1 \le t \le n$. We fix a prime $q > n$, and n distinct points, $\alpha_1, \ldots, \alpha_n \in \mathbb{F}_q$, known to all players. We now present a (t, n)-threshold secret sharing scheme.

- Share: On input a secret $s \in \mathbb{F}_q$, the share generation algorithm Share outputs a list of shares as follows:
    - The dealer $\mathcal{D}$ chooses t random elements $f_1, \ldots, f_t$ from $\mathbb{F}_q$ independently with uniform distribution. These random elements together with s define a polynomial $f(x) = s + \sum_{i=1}^{t} f_i x^i$. $\mathcal{D}$ then computes $s_i = f(\alpha_i)$ for all $i \in [n]$.
    - He then computes $\sigma_i = s + \alpha_i s_i$ for all $i \in [n]$.
    - For every $i \in [n]$, the dealer sends to player P_i the share σ_i.
- Rec: Any $t+1$ players $\{P_{i_1}, \ldots, P_{i_{t+1}}\}$ with their shares $\{\sigma_{i_1}, \ldots, \sigma_{i_{t+1}}\}$, compute the secret as follows: $s = \left(\lambda_{i_1} \prod_{j \ne 1} \alpha_{i_j} + \cdots + \lambda_{i_{t+1}} \prod_{j \ne t+1} \alpha_{i_j} + \prod_{j=1}^{t+1} \alpha_{i_j} \right)^{-1} \cdot \left(\lambda_{i_1} \prod_{j \ne 1} \alpha_{i_j} \sigma_{i_1} + \cdots + \lambda_{i_{t+1}} \prod_{j \ne t+1} \alpha_{i_j} \sigma_{i_{t+1}} \right).$

---

[5] We are not counting the information which is same for all the players, like the threshold parameter or the description of the underlying field.

4.2   Correctness

The correctness of the scheme requires that any $t+1$ correct shares would output the original secret.

$$\lambda_{i_1} \prod_{j \neq 1} \alpha_{i_j} \sigma_{i_1} + \cdots + \lambda_{i_{t+1}} \prod_{j \neq t+1} \alpha_{i_j} \sigma_{i_{t+1}}$$

$$= \lambda_{i_1} \prod_{j \neq 1} \alpha_{i_j} (s + \alpha_{i_1} s_{i_1}) + \cdots + \lambda_{i_{t+1}} \prod_{j \neq t+1} \alpha_{i_j} (s + \alpha_{i_{t+1}} s_{i_{t+1}})$$

$$= s(\lambda_{i_1} \prod_{j \neq 1} \alpha_{i_j} + \cdots + \lambda_{i_{t+1}} \prod_{j \neq t+1} \alpha_{i_j}) + \prod_{j=1}^{t+1} \alpha_{i_j} (\sum_{j=1}^{t+1} \lambda_{i_j} s_{i_j})$$

$$= s(\lambda_{i_1} \prod_{j \neq 1} \alpha_{i_j} + \cdots + \lambda_{i_{t+1}} \prod_{j \neq t+1} \alpha_{i_j}) + \prod_{j=1}^{t+1} \alpha_{i_j} s$$

$$= s(\lambda_{i_1} \prod_{j \neq 1} \alpha_{i_j} + \cdots + \lambda_{i_{t+1}} \prod_{j \neq t+1} \alpha_{i_j} + \prod_{j=1}^{t+1} \alpha_{i_j}).$$

Remark 1. In the scheme, a user's share is $\sigma_i = s + \alpha_i s_i$, where $\{\alpha_1, \ldots, \alpha_n\}$ denotes the interpolation points. We observe that, correctness will still holds if a user's share is computed as follows: $(\beta_i, \sigma_i = s + \beta_i s_i)$ for $1 \leq i \leq n$, where $\{\beta_1, \ldots, \beta_n\}$ are random field elements and the interpolation points $\{\alpha_1, \ldots, \alpha_n\}$ are kept public as usual. This fact would help us derive the correctness of our robust secret sharing scheme in the next section.

4.3   Privacy

The privacy of the scheme follows as a special case of the privacy of information checking procedure from [25]. We first prove the following lemma for completeness.

Lemma 1. *([25]) Let $s \in \mathbb{F}_q$ be the secret. Let random elements $\alpha \neq 0$ and y are chosen from $\mathbb{F}_q$ independently with uniform distribution. Compute $\beta = s + \alpha y$. Then the tuple (α, β) will reveal no information about s.*

Proof: Note that for every value of s in $\mathbb{F}_q$, there exists a unique value for y in $\mathbb{F}_q$, namely $y = \alpha^{-1}(\beta - s)$, such that $\beta = s + \alpha y$. Therefore, Prob[secret is $s \mid (\alpha, \beta)$] = Prob[$y = \alpha^{-1}(\beta - s)$ is chosen] = $\frac{1}{|\mathbb{F}_q|}$. Thus (α, β) gives no information about s.

Rabin and Ben-Or [25] observed that, the above lemma immediately generalizes to the following. For a secret $s \in \mathbb{F}_q$, any positive integer ℓ, and $\alpha_1, \ldots, \alpha_\ell \in \mathbb{F}_q \backslash \{0\}$ choose random elements $y_1, \ldots, y_\ell \in \mathbb{F}_q$ independently with uniform distribution. Compute $\beta_i = s + \alpha_i y_i$ for $1 \leq i \leq \ell$. Then the tuples $\{(\alpha_i, \beta_i)\}_{1 \leq i \leq \ell}$ will reveal no information about s. We know that for Shamir secret sharing scheme, any t shares are independent from the secret s. Thus for any t Shamir shares $(s_{i_1}, \ldots, s_{i_t})$, the values $\sigma_{i_j} = s + \alpha_{i_j} s_{i_j}, 1 \leq j \leq t$ will give no information about the secret s. This shows the perfect privacy of the above scheme.

4.4 The New Scheme: RSSS

Let $\mathbb{F}_q$ be a field. Let t and n are positive integers such that $n = 2t + 1$. We now present an n-player robust secret sharing scheme.

- Share: On input a secret $s \in \mathbb{F}_q$, the share generation algorithm Share outputs a list of shares as follows:
  - The dealer $\mathcal{D}$ chooses random $r, X (\neq 0) \in \mathbb{F}_q$ with uniform distribution and computes $Y = s + Xr$.
  - The dealer chooses two sets of random t points $s_1, \ldots, s_t$ and $r_1, \ldots, r_t$ from $\mathbb{F}_q$ independently with uniform distribution.
  - It then computes unique set of t points $\alpha_1, \ldots, \alpha_t$, where $\alpha_i = r_i s_i^{-1}$, $1 \leq i \leq t$.
  - The dealer $\mathcal{D}$ then interpolates the unique polynomial f of degree at most t such that $f(0) = s$ and $f(\alpha_i) = s_i$ for all $1 \leq i \leq t$. The dealer also interpolates the unique polynomial g of degree at most t such that $g(0) = r$ and $g(\alpha_i) = r_i$ for all $1 \leq i \leq t$.
  - $\mathcal{D}$ picks $t+1$ random points $\beta_{t+1}, \ldots, \beta_n \in \mathbb{F}_q$ with uniform distribution, and also sets $\beta_i = \alpha_i$ for $1 \leq i \leq t$.
  - It then computes $s_i = f(\beta_i)$ for $t+1 \leq i \leq n$, $r_i = g(\beta_i)$ for $t+1 \leq i \leq n$, and $\alpha_i = r_i s_i^{-1}$ for $t + 1 \leq i \leq n$.
  - The dealer finally computes $\sigma_i = s + r_i$ for all $i \in [n]$. Every participant P_i will receive an ordered pair (σ_i, α_i). The tuple (X, Y) along with $t+1$ points $\beta_{t+1}, \ldots, \beta_n$ are part of system's public parameters (Note that the players $\{P_1, \ldots, P_t\}$ have interpolation points $\beta_i = \alpha_i$, $1 \leq i \leq t$, respectively).
- Rec: The secret reconstruction algorithm Rec outputs the secret as follows:
  - Every player sends their share (σ_i', α_i') to the reconstructor $\mathcal{R}$.
  - To reconstruct the secret, $\mathcal{R}$ does the following for *every subset* of $t + 1$ players $\{P_{i_1}, \ldots, P_{i_{t+1}}\}$:
    * $\mathcal{R}$ computes, $s' = \left(\lambda_{i_1} \prod_{j \neq 1} \alpha_{i_j}' + \cdots + \lambda_{i_{t+1}} \prod_{j \neq t+1} \alpha_{i_j}' + \prod_{j=1}^{t+1} \alpha_{i_j}' \right)^{-1} \cdot$ $\left(\lambda_{i_1} \prod_{j \neq 1} \alpha_{i_j}' \sigma_{i_1}' + \cdots + \lambda_{i_{t+1}} \prod_{j \neq t+1} \alpha_{i_j}' \sigma_{i_{t+1}}' \right).$
    * It then computes $r_{i_j}' = \sigma_{i_j}' - s'$ for all $1 \leq j \leq t+1$.
    * It computes $r' = \sum_{j=1}^{t+1} \lambda_{i_j} r_{i_j}$ and checks if $Y = s' + Xr'$.
    * If yes, then $\mathcal{R}$ outputs the secret as s'.

4.5 Correctness and Efficiency

During the reconstruction, if the $t + 1$ shares $(\sigma_{i_j}', \alpha_{i_j}')$'s are all correct i.e., $(\sigma_{i_j}', \alpha_{i_j}') = (\sigma_{i_j}, \alpha_{i_j})$ for all $1 \leq j \leq t + 1$, then $s' = s$, the correct secret. This follows immediately from Remark 1 in Sect. 4.2. We now give a table to summarize the efficiency of the scheme.

Table 2. Comparison Table

Scheme	Redundancy	Rec Complexity	δ	Saving on Interpolation Pts
[7]	$2(\log_2 \frac{1}{\delta} + n)$	$\exp(n)$	$2^{-(k-n)}$	-
[4]	$3\log_2 \frac{1}{\delta} + 3n\log_2(n\lambda)$	$\text{poly}(n)$	$2^{-(n\frac{k}{\lambda} - n\log(n\cdot\lambda))}$	-
RSSS	$\log_2 \frac{1}{\delta} + n$	$\exp(n)$	$2^{-(k-n)}$	t

4.6 Privacy

The following theorem shows, that any t players get no information about the secret.

Theorem 3. *For any subset $B \subset \{P_1, \ldots, P_n\}$ of size t and its* view$_B$

$$Prob[\textit{Secret is } s_1 \mid \text{view}_B] = Prob[\textit{Secret is } s_2 \mid \text{view}_B],$$

for all $s_1, s_2 \in \mathbb{F}_q$, where view$_B$ *denotes the elements, that the members of B see:* view$_B = (X, Y, \{(\sigma_i, \alpha_i)_{P_i \in B}\})$.

Proof: Consider any set $B = \{P_{i_1}, \ldots, P_{i_t}\}$ of t players. Therefore, we have view$_B$ $= (X, Y, \{(\sigma_{i_j}, \alpha_{i_j})_{j=1}^t\})$. For every choice of $s \in \mathbb{F}_q$ for secret, we have: unique values for $r = X^{-1} \cdot (Y - s); r_{i_j} = \sigma_{i_j} - s,\ 1 \leq j \leq t; s_{i_j} = \alpha_{i_j}^{-1} \cdot (\sigma_{i_j} - s) = \alpha_{i_j}^{-1} \cdot r_{i_j},\ 1 \leq j \leq t$, a unique polynomial f of degree at most t satisfying $f(0) = s; f(\beta_{i_j}) = s_{i_j}$ for $1 \leq j \leq t$, and a unique polynomial g of degree at most t such that $g(0) = r; g(\beta_{i_j}) = r_{i_j}$ for $1 \leq j \leq t$. Therefore, the t players in B cannot rule out any element of $\mathbb{F}_q$ as a possibility for secret. This shows that view$_B$ does not contain any information about the original secret.

4.7 Robustness

One may note that, both the schemes, RSSS-Basic and RSSS are similar. The later scheme achieves some advantage due to the restructuring of the former. In the previous section, we proved, the restructuring did not affect the privacy of the scheme and therefore the robustness property of RSSS remain the same as for RSSS-Basic. For completeness, we now state the theorem. The proof is similar to RSSS-Basic.

Theorem 4. *Let $\mathbb{F}_q$ be any finite field with q elements. Let $k = \lfloor \log_2 q \rceil$. Then for any positive integers n, t with $n = 2t + 1$, $q > n$, and secret space $\mathbb{F}_q$, RSSS forms an unconditional secure (t, n)-threshold robust secret sharing scheme with (t, δ) robustness against non-rushing adversary such that*

$$\delta \leq \frac{1}{2^{k-n}}\ .$$

5   Secret Sharing with Cheating Detection

Tompa and Woll [27] introduced the problem of cheating detection in secret sharing. Suppose that, in a (t, n) threshold secret sharing scheme, t players, say $P_1, \ldots, P_t$, want to cheat a $(t + 1)$th player, P_{t+1}, by opening modified shares $\sigma'_1, \ldots, \sigma'_t$. They succeed if the secret s' that is reconstructed from $\sigma'_1, \ldots, \sigma'_t$ and σ_{t+1} is different from the original secret s (see Section 2.1 of [22] for a thorough definition). There are two different models, CDV and OKS, for secret sharing schemes capable of detecting such cheating. The CDV model is characterized by the property that t cheaters (corrupted players) $P_1, \ldots, P_t$ somehow know the secret s before they cheat P_{t+1}, whereas in OKS model, they does not have any idea about the secret. In [22], a lower bound on share size has been derived for secret sharing schemes with cheating detection property in OKS model; $\log_2 \sigma_i \geq \log_2 s + \log_2 \frac{1}{\delta_c}$, where δ_c is the cheating probability. Therefore, in the above model, the redundancy in share size is at least $\log_2 \frac{1}{\delta_c}$.

One may easily note that our robust secret sharing scheme RSSS-Basic in Section 3 is build upon a secret sharing scheme with cheating detection property. We see that the share size, for the underlying secret sharing scheme with the property of cheating detection, meets the lower bound of [22]. We observe that this is the first such scheme. To the best of our knowledge, there exists two schemes [22,23] in the literature that satisfy the above lower bound, but both the schemes admit some limitations whereas our scheme is free from any such limitation. In particular, the scheme of [23] requires that the secret should lie in a field whose characteristic is different from 2, and the construction of [22] requires a number q such that q be a prime power and $q^2 + q + 1$ is also prime. The latter scheme also assumes that secret is *chosen with uniform distribution* and so effectively has a weaker security notion. In our scheme secret can be from any filed and only requires the field size to be $\geq n$. This is a general restriction on all scheme. We use the strong definition of security which requires security for any distribution on the secret set. For completeness, we now describe our scheme.

5.1   The Scheme

We have a group of n players $\{P_1, \ldots, P_n\}$. Let t be a positive integer such that $1 \leq t \leq n$. We fix a prime $q > n$, and n distinct points, $\alpha_1, \ldots, \alpha_n \in \mathbb{F}_q$, known to all players. We now present a (t, n)-threshold secret sharing scheme with cheating detection property.

- Share: On input a secret $s \in \mathbb{F}_q$, the share generation algorithm Share outputs a list of shares as follows:
  - The dealer $\mathcal{D}$ chooses random $r, X(\neq 0) \in \mathbb{F}_q$ with uniform distribution and computes $Y = s + Xr$.
  - The dealer $\mathcal{D}$ chooses t random elements $f_1, \ldots, f_t$ from $\mathbb{F}_q$ independently with uniform distribution. These random elements together with s define a polynomial $f(x) = s + \sum_{i=1}^{t} f_i x^i$. $\mathcal{D}$ then computes $s_i = f(\alpha_i)$ for all $i \in [n]$.

- $\mathcal{D}$ also chooses t random elements $g_1, \ldots, g_t$ from $\mathbb{F}_q$ independently with uniform distribution. These random elements together with r define a polynomial $g(x) = r + \sum_{i=1}^{t} g_i x^i$. $\mathcal{D}$ then computes $r_i = g(\alpha_i)$ for all $i \in [n]$.
- Every participant P_i will receive its share $\sigma_i = (s_i, r_i)$.
- The tuple (X, Y) is part of system's public parameters.
- Rec: Any qualified set of players $(t + 1$ players$)$ $\{P_{i_1}, \ldots, P_{i_{t+1}}\}$ will reconstruct the secret as follows.
  - They obtain $s = \sum_{j=1}^{t+1} \lambda_{i_j} s_{i_j}$ and $r = \sum_{j=1}^{t+1} \lambda_{i_j} r_{i_j}$ from their shares.
  - If $Y = s + Xr$, they take s as the correct value of the secret.

5.2   Security and Share Size Efficiency

The privacy of the scheme follows from Theorem 1. The cheating probability of the above scheme follows from Theorem 2, in particular the cheating probability δ_c is $\frac{1}{q} = \frac{1}{2^k}$ and it holds for arbitrary distribution on the secret space. The individual share size of each player is $\log_2 \sigma_i = 2k = \log_2 s + \log_2 \frac{1}{\delta_c}$. Therefore this scheme meets the lower bound of [22] in the OKS model. One may also note that, a secret sharing scheme with cheating detection property can also extracted from RSSS with the added property of saving t interpolation points.

Acknowledgments. The authors would like to thank Pengwei Wang for useful discussions. The Authors would also like to thank the reviewers for their comments.

References

1. Blakley, G.: Safeguarding cryptographic keys. AFIPS National Computer Conference 48, 313–317 (1979)
2. Cabello, S., Padró, C., Sáez, G.: Secret sharing schemes with detection of cheaters for a general access structure. In: Ciobanu, G., Păun, G. (eds.) FCT 1999. LNCS, vol. 1684, pp. 185–194. Springer, Heidelberg (1999)
3. Carpentieri, M., De Santis, A., Vaccaro, U.: Size of shares and probability of cheating in threshold schemes. In: Helleseth, T. (ed.) EUROCRYPT 1993. LNCS, vol. 765, pp. 118–125. Springer, Heidelberg (1994)
4. Cevallos, A., Fehr, S., Ostrovsky, R., Rabani, Y.: Unconditionally-secure robust secret sharing with compact shares. In: Pointcheval, D., Johansson, T. (eds.) EUROCRYPT 2012. LNCS, vol. 7237, pp. 195–208. Springer, Heidelberg (2012)
5. Chor, B., Goldwasser, S., Micali, S., Awerbuch, B.: Verifiable secret sharing and achieving simultaneity in the presence of faults (extended abstract). In: FOCS 1985, pp. 383–395. IEEE Computer Society (1985)
6. Choudhury, A.: Brief announcement: optimal amortized secret sharing with cheater identification. In: Kowalski, D., Panconesi, A. (eds.) PODC, pp. 101–102. ACM (2012)
7. Cramer, R., Damgård, I.B., Fehr, S.: On the cost of reconstructing a secret, or VSS with optimal reconstruction phase. In: Kilian, J. (ed.) CRYPTO 2001. LNCS, vol. 2139, pp. 503–523. Springer, Heidelberg (2001)

8. Dolev, D., Dwork, C., Waarts, O., Yung, M.: Perfectly secure message transmission. In: FOCS 1990, pp. 36–45. IEEE Computer Society (1990)
9. Ganger, G.R., Khosla, P.K., Bakkaloglu, M., Bigrigg, M.W., Goodson, G.R., Oguz, S., Pandurangan, V., Soules, C.A.N., Strunk, J.D., Wylie, J.J.: Survivable storage systems. In: Proceedings of DARPA Information Survivability Conference amp; Exposition II, DISCEX 2001, vol. 2, pp. 184–195 (2001)
10. Garay, J., Givens, C., Ostrovsky, R.: Secure message transmission with small public discussion. In: Gilbert, H. (ed.) EUROCRYPT 2010. LNCS, vol. 6110, pp. 177–196. Springer, Heidelberg (2010)
11. Garay, J., Givens, C., Ostrovsky, R.: Secure message transmission by public discussion: A brief survey. In: Chee, Y.M., Guo, Z., Ling, S., Shao, F., Tang, Y., Wang, H., Xing, C. (eds.) IWCC 2011. LNCS, vol. 6639, pp. 126–141. Springer, Heidelberg (2011)
12. Hirt, M., Maurer, U.M.: Complete characterization of adversaries tolerable in secure multi-party computation (extended abstract). In: Burns, J.E., Attiya, H. (eds.) PODC, pp. 25–34. ACM (1997)
13. Ishai, Y., Ostrovsky, R., Seyalioglu, H.: Identifying cheaters without an honest majority. In: Cramer, R. (ed.) TCC 2012. LNCS, vol. 7194, pp. 21–38. Springer, Heidelberg (2012)
14. Jhanwar, M.P., Safavi-Naini, R.: Unconditionally-secure robust secret sharing with minimum share size. In: Sadeghi, A.-R. (ed.) FC 2013. LNCS, vol. 7859, pp. 96–110. Springer, Heidelberg (2013)
15. Karnin, E.D., Greene, J.W., Hellman, M.E.: On secret sharing systems. IEEE Transactions on Information Theory 29(1), 35–41 (1983)
16. Kurosawa, K.: General error decodable secret sharing scheme and its application. IACR Cryptology ePrint Archive, Report 2009/263 (2009), http://eprint.iacr.org/
17. Kurosawa, K., Obana, S., Ogata, W.: t-cheater identifiable (k, n) threshold secret sharing schemes. In: Coppersmith, D. (ed.) CRYPTO 1995. LNCS, vol. 963, pp. 410–423. Springer, Heidelberg (1995)
18. Lakshmanan, S., Ahamad, M., Venkateswaran, H.: Responsive security for stored data. IEEE Trans. Parallel Distrib. Syst. 14(9), 818–828 (2003)
19. Martin, K.M., Paterson, M.B., Stinson, D.R.: Error decodable secret sharing and one-round perfectly secure message transmission for general adversary structures. Cryptography and Communications 3(2), 65–86 (2011)
20. McEliece, R.J., Sarwate, D.V.: On sharing secrets and Reed-Solomon codes. Commun. ACM 24(9), 583–584 (1981)
21. Obana, S.: Almost optimum t-cheater identifiable secret sharing schemes. In: Paterson, K.G. (ed.) EUROCRYPT 2011. LNCS, vol. 6632, pp. 284–302. Springer, Heidelberg (2011)
22. Ogata, W., Kurosawa, K., Stinson, D.R.: Optimum secret sharing scheme secure against cheating. SIAM J. Discrete Math. 20(1), 79–95 (2006)
23. Padro, C., Sáez, G., Villar, J.L.: Detection of cheaters in vector space secret sharing schemes. Des. Codes Cryptography 16(1), 75–85 (1999)
24. Pedersen, T.P.: Non-interactive and information-theoretic secure verifiable secret sharing. In: Feigenbaum, J. (ed.) CRYPTO 1991. LNCS, vol. 576, pp. 129–140. Springer, Heidelberg (1992)
25. Rabin, T., Ben-Or, M.: Verifiable secret sharing and multiparty protocols with honest majority (extended abstract). In: Johnson, D.S. (ed.) STOC 1989, pp. 73–85. ACM (1989)

26. Shamir, A.: How to share a secret. Communications of the ACM 22(11), 612–613 (1979)
27. Tompa, M., Woll, H.: How to share a secret with cheaters. J. Cryptology 1(2), 133–138 (1988)
28. Waldman, M., Rubin, A.D., Cranor, L.F.: The architecture of robust publishing systems. ACM Trans. Internet Techn. 1(2), 199–230 (2001)

There's Something about m-ary
Fixed-Point Scalar Multiplication Protected against Physical Attacks

Benoit Feix[1] and Vincent Verneuil[2],[*]

[1] Underwriters Laboratories, Security Lab, Basingstoke, England
benoit.feix@ul.com
[2] NXP Semiconductors, Hamburg, Germany
vincent.verneuil@nxp.com

Abstract. In this paper, we study the fixed-point scalar multiplication operation on elliptic curves in the context of embedded devices prone to physical attacks. We propose efficient algorithms based on Yao and BGMW algorithms that are suited for embedded computing, with various storage-efficiency trade-offs. In particular, we study their security towards side-channel and fault analysis and propose a set of low-cost yet efficient countermeasures against these attacks.

Keywords: elliptic curve cryptography, scalar multiplication, embedded devices, side-channel analysis, fault analysis.

1 Introduction

Elliptic Curve Cryptography (ECC) is involved in many cryptographic protocols for signature (ECDSA), key exchange (ECDH), encryption (ECIES), etc. These protocols are used in many applications such as payment, pay-TV, transport and identity. It is thus of strong interest for the industry to improve the computation efficiency of the point scalar multiplication — the most time-consuming operation in ECC protocols.

Implementations must withstand *Side-Channel Analysis* (SCA) and *Fault Analysis* (FA). In general, the *Simple Side-Channel Analysis* (SSCA) operates the secret recovery through a single side-channel execution trace. Alternatively, *Advanced Side-Channel Analysis* (ASCA) uses multiple traces and associated data (messages, ciphertexts...) to recover the secret value through statistical processing [27]. On the other hand, FA consists in perturbing the chip activity and infer information from the possibly faulty results returned by the device [9].

The fixed base-point property of protocols relying on ElGamal or Diffie-Hellman schemes can be exploited to speed up the scalar multiplication computation. For instance, an ECDSA signature generation requires a single scalar multiplication involving a fixed base point. Yao and Pippenger showed first that

---

[*] This work was initiated when both authors were with Inside Secure.

G. Paul and S. Vaudenay (Eds.): INDOCRYPT 2013, LNCS 8250, pp. 197–214, 2013.
© Springer International Publishing Switzerland 2013

values depending on the generator only can be precomputed to save computations during a group exponentiation or scalar multiplication [5,34].

Subsequent works have improved these methods to fit implementers needs. First, Brickell, Gordon, McCurley, and Wilson have proposed a method based on Yao's algorithm, often referred to as BGMW algorithm [11]. In an other direction, Lim and Lee presented a fixed-base comb technique [28], later improved by Tsaur and Chou [32] and by Mohamed, Hashim, and Hutter [29] in the context of elliptic curve cryptography.

In this paper, we study how simple algorithms inspired by Yao's method can be protected against physical attacks, including SSCA, ASCA and FA. All of them are suited to the context of embedded devices, since nowadays microprocessors have storage capabilities from many hundreds of kilobytes to a few megabytes, which was not the case a decade ago. Moreover, our methods are designed to ensure reasonable RAM requirements, they are thus very practical on embedded devices. In particular, we show that the point additions performed in our algorithms can be computed in a random sequence, hence providing a novel and cheap countermeasure. In addition, internal point blinding can be applied for a negligible extra cost. Finally, we propose an adaptation of a FA countermeasure proposed by Boscher, Naciri and Prouff [10] and improved by Baek [3] and Joye and Karroumi [26].

Roadmap. The paper is organized as follows. Section 2 reminds the reader of the necessary background on elliptic curve scalar multiplication and embedded security. In Section 3 we present fast fixed-point scalar multiplication algorithms and compare their cost with classical methods. In Section 4 we devise side-channel and fault analysis countermeasures for our algorithms. We also discuss their cost and compare the performances obtained with our techniques with classical ones. Finally we conclude our paper in Section 5.

2 Scalar Multiplication Background

2.1 Elliptic Curves Background

We focus on general elliptic curves defined over fields of large characteristic as they are the most used in practice. However, most of our study applies also to curves of specific shape such as Montgomery and Edwards curves, or to elliptic curves defined over binary fields.

An elliptic curve over a field $\mathbb{F}_q$ of characteristic greater than 3 is defined by an affine equation of the form:

$$y^2 = x^3 + ax + b \tag{1}$$

where a, b are elements of $\mathbb{F}_q$ such that $4a^3 + 27b^2 \neq 0$.

The set of the affine points of $\mathcal{E}$ with coordinates in $\mathbb{F}_q$, together with the *point at infinity* $\mathcal{O}$ is denoted $\mathcal{E}(\mathbb{F}_q)$. It has an abelian group structure considering the well-known *chord and tangent* group law denoted $[+]$. The addition of two same points is generally computed using a specific *doubling* formula and is thus denoted $P[+] P = [2] P$ in the following.

Homogeneous ($\mathcal{H}$) and Jacobian ($\mathcal{J}$) projective coordinates are generally used to implement elliptic curve arithmetic to avoid the costly field inversion of affine ($\mathcal{A}$) point addition formulas. Jacobian coordinates offer a faster doubling than homogeneous coordinates, but the addition is more expensive.

Table 1 recalls the cost of additions, mixed affine-projective additions and doublings using homogeneous projective coordinates and Jacobian projective coordinates on prime fields of large characteristic [6]. Throughout the rest of this paper, M denotes the cost of a field multiplication, S the cost of a field squaring and A the cost of a field addition or subtraction.

Table 1. Cost of point operation in homogeneous and Jacobian coordinates over large-characteristic fields

Operation	Cost	Operation	Cost
$\mathcal{H} \leftarrow \mathcal{H}[+]\mathcal{H}$	$12M + 2S + 7A$	$\mathcal{J} \leftarrow \mathcal{J}[+]\mathcal{J}$	$11M + 5S + 13A$
$\mathcal{H} \leftarrow \mathcal{H}[+]\mathcal{A}$	$9M + 2S + 7A$	$\mathcal{J} \leftarrow \mathcal{J}[+]\mathcal{A}$	$7M + 4S + 14A$
$\mathcal{H} \leftarrow [2]\mathcal{H}$	$6M + 6S + 12A$	$\mathcal{J} \leftarrow [2]\mathcal{J}$	$2M + 8S + 17A$
$\mathcal{H} \leftarrow [2]\mathcal{H}$ $(a = -3)$	$7M + 3S + 11A$	$\mathcal{J} \leftarrow [2]\mathcal{J}$ $(a = -3)$	$3M + 5S + 18A$

2.2 Scalar Multiplication

The addition of a point P to itself d times is called the *scalar multiplication* of P by d and denoted $[d] P$. A well-known method to compute the scalar multiplication is the *double-and-add* algorithm. Considering $(d_{\ell-1}d_{\ell-2}\ldots d_0)_2$, the binary representation of d, the *right-to-left* version of this method relies on the following decomposition:

$$[d] P = \sum_{i=0}^{\ell-1} d_i \left[2^i\right] P \tag{2}$$

We focus in this study on the right-to-left version of this algorithm on which Yao's algorithm is based, whereas fixed-base comb algorithms are based on its left-to-right counterpart. This algorithm requires on average ℓ doublings and $\ell/2$ point additions.

Because a point addition $P[+]Q$ and a subtraction $P[-]Q$ have the same cost in $\mathcal{E}(\mathbb{F}_q)$, a common option to speed up the scalar multiplication consists in using a signed representation in order to decrease the number of additions to be computed.

A base b signed representation of k is $(k_{\ell_b-1}k_{\ell_b-2}\ldots k_0)$ such that:

$$k = \sum_{i=0}^{\ell_b-1} k_i b^i \quad \text{with} \quad |k_i| < b \tag{3}$$

Among them the binary *Non-Adjacent Form* (NAF) is defined as follows. The NAF representation of a positive non-zero integer k is $(k_{\ell-1}k_{\ell-2}\ldots k_0)_{\text{NAF}}$ with $k_i \in \{-1, 0, 1\}$, $0 \le i < \ell - 1$ and $k_{\ell-1} = 1$, such that for all pairs of consecutive digits, at least one of them is zero. As a consequence, the number of non-zero digits of ℓ-digit NAF representations is approximately $\ell/3$.

The right-to-left double-and-add scalar multiplication algorithm using the NAF representation is presented in Alg. 2.1. Compared to the binary algorithm, it requires only ℓ doublings and $\ell/3$ point additions on average, thus saving $\ell/6$ point additions.

Alg. 2.1. Right-to-left NAF double-and-add scalar multiplication

---

Input: $P \in \mathcal{E}(\mathbb{F}_q)$, ℓ-NAF-digit scalar $d = (d_{\ell-1}d_{\ell-2}\ldots d_0)_{\text{NAF}}$
Output: $Q = [d]\,P$
1: $Q \leftarrow \mathcal{O}$
2: $R \leftarrow P$
3: **for** $i = 0$ **to** $\ell - 1$ **do**
4:    **if** $d_i = 1$ **then**
5:        $Q \leftarrow Q\,[+]\,R$
6:    **if** $d_i = -1$ **then**
7:        $Q \leftarrow Q\,[-]\,R$
8:    $R \leftarrow [2]\,R$
9: **return** Q

Remark. For a sake of simplicity, the binary length of d and the length of its signed representation — which may differ by 1 — are both denoted ℓ through the rest of this paper.

2.3   Side-Channel Analysis and Countermeasures

Countering SSCA on scalar multiplication can be achieved using regular implementations [25]. Considering ASCA, most countermeasures stem from Coron's propositions [14]: scalar blinding, projective coordinates randomization and input point blinding. Among them, the multiplicative blinding of the projective coordinates requires the lowest computational overhead but does not protect against chosen input-point attacks [19,1]. It is then necessary to use extra countermeasures such as additive point randomization [14,1] or scalar blinding, which are much more expensive.

Another category of attacks inspired by the Big Mac attack from Walter [33] has been recently extended to several other attacks referred to as *horizontal* techniques [13,4]. They are more difficult to mount in practice than classical ASCA but necessitate only one side-channel trace, contrary to classical ASCA.

To thwart FA on scalar multiplication, Biehl, Meyer, and Müller proposed that implementations verify that the output point of a computation belongs to the curve [7]. Ciet and Joye advise to check the curves parameters also [12].

Nevertheless Blömer, Otto, and Seifert have proven that such countermeasures are circumvented by a so-called *sign change* attack which takes advantage of the signed NAF representation [8]. To provide a robust protection against fault attacks, *self-secure* algorithms [18,10,3,26] detect a fault injected during the execution of the scalar multiplication by checking an invariant property on the manipulated variables during or at the end of the computation.

Recently, Fan, Gierlichs, and Vercauteren presented a combined FA and SSCA [16]. A well-chosen input point and a single fault injection lead to the manipulation of the point at infinity during the scalar multiplication, which can be observed by SSCA. Input point blinding is thus necessary to thwart this attack.

2.4   Fixed-Point Scalar Multiplication Methods

Assuming that $(d_{v-1}d_{v-2} \ldots d_0)_h$ is the base-h representation of d, the BGMW [11] algorithm relies on the following decomposition:

$$[d] P = \sum_{i=1}^{h-1} i \sum_{d_j=i} [h^j] P \qquad (4)$$

If all $[h^j] P$, such that $0 \le j \le v - 1$, are precomputed, Alg. 2.2 computes $[d] P$ using in average $v(h-1)/h - 1$ point additions[1] in the inner loop (step 5) and $h - 2$ additions in the main loop (step 6).

Alg. 2.2. BGMW fixed-point scalar multiplication

Input: $P \in \mathcal{E}(\mathbb{F}_q)$, $d = (d_{v-1}d_{v-2} \ldots d_0)_h$, $\{P_j = [h^j] P, \text{ for } j \in [0, v-1]\}$
Output: $Q = [d] P$
1: $Q, R \leftarrow \mathcal{O}$
2: **for** $i = h - 1$ **to** 1 **by** -1 **do**
3:      **for** $j = 0$ **to** $v - 1$ **do**
4:          **if** $d_j = i$ **then**
5:              $Q \leftarrow Q [+] P_j$
6:      $R \leftarrow R [+] Q$
7: **return** R

Other fixed-point scalar multiplication techniques are generally derived from the Lim and Lee comb method [28] which uses more precomputations but provides a better efficiency. For instance, Tsaur and Chou [32] and Mohamed et al. [29] improve this method by using signed representations. Besides, Hedabou, Pinel and Bénéteau [21] show that comb algorithms can be rendered regular to counter SSCA by recoding the scalar and propose a point blinding method against ASCA. Unfortunately, this method does not allow to refresh the blinding

---

[1] The initial point addition with $\mathcal{O}$ is free.

point without recomputing the whole array of precomputed points, which is an issue in practice. Finally, we are not aware of any work addressing the protection of these algorithms against FA.

3 Revisiting the BGMW Algorithm

Following Brickell et al. observation [11], the sequence of intermediate results stored in R in Alg. 2.1 does not depend on the scalar:

$$R \leftarrow P \leftarrow [2]\, P \leftarrow \cdots \leftarrow [2^{\ell-1}]\, P$$

We propose in this section to rewrite the BGMW algorithm to make use of signed representations of the scalar and benefit of the lower number of non-zero digits thereof.

3.1 NAF Scalar Multiplication

Let T refer to an ℓ-point pre-computation table such that:

$$T_i = [2^i]\, P \quad \text{with} \quad 0 \leq i \leq \ell - 1$$

With d_i the binary or NAF digits of d, the scalar multiplication can then be written as:

$$[d]\, P = \sum_{i=0}^{\ell-1} [d_i]\, T_i$$

In this manner, the computation complexity drops to $\ell/3$ point additions, see below Alg. 3.1. On the other hand, $2(\ell - 1) \lceil \ell/8 \rceil$ bytes in memory are required if the additional $\ell - 1$ points are stored in affine coordinates.

Alg. 3.1. Add-only NAF scalar multiplication using precomputations

---

Input: $P \in \mathcal{E}(\mathbb{F}_q)$, ℓ-NAF-digit scalar $d = (d_{\ell-1} d_{\ell-2} \ldots d_0)_{\mathrm{NAF}}$, $T = \left([2^i]\, P\right)_{0 \leq i \leq \ell-1}$
Output: $Q = [d]\, P$
1: $Q \leftarrow \mathcal{O}$
2: **for** $i = 0$ to $\ell - 1$ **do**
3:     **if** $d_i = 1$ **then**
4:         $Q \leftarrow Q\,[+]\,T_i$
5:     **if** $d_i = -1$ **then**
6:         $Q \leftarrow Q\,[-]\,T_i$
7: **return** Q

The storage requirements of this method amounts to 16 kB for a 256-bit elliptic curve and 64 kB for a 512-bit curve. In the next section, we discuss using window methods to improve both efficiency and memory requirements.

3.2   Application to m-ary NAF Scalar Multiplication

Window algorithms are well-known to improve scalar multiplication efficiency by reducing the number of point additions in left-to-right algorithms [20]. Yet less widely known among implementers, window methods apply to right-to-left algorithms also [30,34]. Considering an m-ary scalar multiplication algorithm, with $m = 2^t$, this strategy generally requires $m - 1$ point registers instead of one register Q to perform a general m-ary scalar multiplication — thus it requires more RAM —, and an additional computation phase at the end of the main loop known as *aggregation*.

On the other hand, only one precomputed point out of t is required, therefore the size of T drops ℓ to $\ell' = \lceil \ell/t \rceil$. Consequently, the precomputed values are:

$$T_i = \left[2^{ti}\right] P \quad \text{with} \quad 0 \le i \le \ell' - 1$$

We consider in this section an ℓ-NAF-digit integer which digits are scanned using a fixed window of size t. As two consecutive NAF digits cannot be both non-zero, the set of possible integers coded by t NAF digits is:

$$\{0, \pm 1\} \text{ for } t = 1,$$
$$\{0, \pm 1, \pm 2\} \text{ for } t = 2,$$
$$\{0, \pm 1, \pm 2, \pm 3, \pm 4, \pm 5\} \text{ for } t = 3,$$
$$\{0, \pm 1, \pm 2, \ldots, \pm \nu(t)\} \text{ for any } t \ge 1,$$
$$\text{with } \nu(t) = \frac{2^{t+1} - \frac{3+(-1)^t}{2}}{3}.$$

The m-ary NAF scalar multiplication strategy requires that $\nu(t)$ registers R_j, $j \in \{1, 2, \ldots, \nu(t)\}$ are available to store the internal sums of points $\left[2^{ti}\right] P$ such that the ith scanned window holds the value j. We obtain the final result by computing the aggregation:

$$\sum_{i=1}^{\nu(t)} [i] \, R_i$$

Our fixed-point scalar multiplication using the m-ary NAF scalar scanning is presented in Alg. 3.2. The average number of point additions performed in the main loop is:

$$\left\lceil \frac{\ell}{t} \right\rceil \left(1 - \left(\frac{2}{3}\right)^t\right)$$

The aggregation is computed using the efficient technique from Joye and Karroumi [26]. It requires $2(\nu(t) - 1)$ additional additions.

It is worth noticing that the storage requirement and the number of additions performed in the main loop decrease when t increases. On the other hand, the cost of the aggregation rises rapidly with t. The optimal value for t thus depends on ℓ, as discussed in Section 3.4.

Alg. 3.2. Add-only m-ary NAF scalar multiplication using precomputations

---

Input: $P \in \mathcal{E}(\mathbb{F}_q)$, ℓ-NAF-digit scalar $d = (d_{\ell-1}d_{\ell-2} \ldots d_0)_{\mathrm{NAF}}$, $T = \left(\left[2^{ti}\right] P\right)_{0 \leq i \leq \ell'-1}$

Output: $Q = [d] P$

    Initialization

1: $R_1 \leftarrow \mathcal{O}$, $R_2 \leftarrow \mathcal{O}$, $\ldots$, $R_{\nu(t)} \leftarrow \mathcal{O}$

    Main loop

2: **for** $i = 0$ **to** $\ell' - 1$ **do**

3:      $u = \sum_{j=0}^{t-1} 2^j d_{ti+j}$ [Assume $d_i = 0$ if $i \geq \ell$]

4:      **if** $u > 0$ **then**

5:          $R_u \leftarrow R_u \, [+] \, T_i$

6:      **if** $u < 0$ **then**

7:          $R_{-u} \leftarrow R_{-u} \, [-] \, T_i$

    Aggregation

8: **for** $i = \nu(t) - 1$ **to** 1 **by** -1 **do**

9:      $R_i \leftarrow R_i \, [+] \, R_{i+1}$

10:     $R_{\nu(t)} \leftarrow R_{\nu(t)} \, [+] \, R_i$

11: **return** $R_{\nu(t)}$

On-the-fly Table Computation. Although we focus on the context where the base point is known in advance and the precomputations table can be calculated off-line — this is the context of ECDSA signature, where the input point is a generator defined in the public parameters —, we can also consider the case of an unknown base point that will be used for several scalar multiplications. This may be the case in applications such as ECDSA verification, ECDH key exchange, ECIES decryption, etc.

In such a case, one may run a first scalar multiplication using the classical right-to-left algorithm, and populates on-the-fly the table T. However, points T_i will likely be computed in projective coordinates which involves general additions during further scalar multiplications instead of mixed affine-projective additions.

An option is thus to convert these points to affine coordinates at the end of the first scalar multiplication using Montgomery's trick for multiple inversions [31]. It requires expensive computations to be put in balance with the gain obtained in further scalar multiplications.

3.3 Application to Width-w NAF Scalar Multiplication

We recall the *width-w* NAF representation [20]: given an integer $w \geq 2$, the width-w NAF representation of a non-zero positive integer k, denoted $(k)_{\mathrm{NAF}_w}$ is a base 2^{w-1} signed representation[2], cf. expression (3) and the aggregation consists in computing:

$$\sum_{i=0}^{2^{w-2}-1} [2i + 1] \, R_{2i+1}$$

---

[2] In particular, $(k)_{\mathrm{NAF}} = (k)_{\mathrm{NAF}_2}$ for any positive integer k.

Algorithm 3.3 presents our fixed-point scalar multiplication method using the width-w representation. The number of point additions performed in the main loop is $\ell/(w+1)$ in the average. The aggregation is computed using an efficient technique inspired by Joye and Karroumi [26] and requires $3(2^{w-2}-1)$ additions.

Alg. 3.3. Add-only width-w NAF scalar multiplication using precomputations

Input: $P \in \mathcal{E}(\mathbb{F}_q)$, $d = (d_{\ell-1}d_{\ell-2}\ldots d_0)_{\text{NAF}_w}$, $T = \left([2^i]\,P\right)_{0 \le i \le \ell-1}$

Output: $Q = [d]\,P$

   Initialization

1: $R_1 \leftarrow \mathcal{O}$, $R_3 \leftarrow \mathcal{O}$, $\ldots$, $R_{2^{w-1}-1} \leftarrow \mathcal{O}$

   Main loop

2: **for** $i = 0$ **to** $\ell - 1$ **do**

3:    **if** $d_i > 0$ **then**

4:       $R_{d_i} \leftarrow R_{d_i}\,[+]\,T_i$

5:    **if** $d_i < 0$ **then**

6:       $R_{-d_i} \leftarrow R_{-d_i}\,[-]\,T_i$

   Aggregation

7: **for** $i = 2^{w-1} - 3$ **to** 1 **by** -2 **do**

8:    $R_i \leftarrow R_i\,[+]\,R_{i+2}$

9:    **if** $i = 2^{w-1} - 3$ **and** $i \neq 1$ **then**   [First loop iteration, $w \neq 3$]

10:      $R_{2^{w-1}-1} \leftarrow [2]\,R_{2^{w-1}-1}\,[+]\,[2]\,R_i$

11:    **if** $i \neq 2^{w-1} - 3$ **and** $i \neq 1$ **then**   [Not first/last loop iteration]

12:      $R_{2^{w-1}-1} \leftarrow R_{2^{w-1}-1}\,[+]\,[2]\,R_i$

13:    **if** $i \neq 2^{w-1} - 3$ **and** $i = 1$ **then**   [Last loop iteration, $w \neq 3$]

14:      $R_{2^{w-1}-1} \leftarrow R_{2^{w-1}-1}\,[+]\,R_i$

15:    **if** $i = 2^{w-1} - 3$ **and** $i = 1$ **then**   [Single loop iteration ($w = 3$)]

16:      $R_{2^{w-1}-1} \leftarrow [2]\,R_{2^{w-1}-1}\,[+]\,R_i$

17: **return** $R_{2^{w-1}-1}$

This methods requires less registers than Alg. 3.2 as only odd digits appear in the width-w NAF representation. On the other hand, it requires the full ℓ-point precomputed table T.

Remark. The width parameter w allow to control the aggregation cost vs. main loop speed-up trade-off. Intermediate trade-offs can be obtained using sliding-window NAF techniques [20] for instance, or, more generally, *fractional* window techniques [30].

3.4   Efficiency and Storage Requirements Analysis

We study hereafter the efficiency and storage (RAM & non-volatile memory) requirements of the previous fixed-point scalar multiplication methods.

Coordinates Choice. Since our algorithms involve point additions only, the best representation for registers R_i is the homogeneous projective coordinates. All additions performed in the main loop use a mixed affine-projective formula, as precomputed points T_i are stored in affine coordinates. Only the aggregation stage requires general additions.

As a matter of reference, we provide the cost of a classical left-to-right NAF double-and-add algorithm, denoted *LR-NAF-DA*. It is computed assuming the use of Jacobian coordinates, mixed affine-projective additions and $a = -3$ to provide a fair comparison. We compare our algorithms with BGMW Alg. 2.2 with $h = 2^t$ for $t=2$, 3, 4, 5, assuming the use of homogeneous projective coordinates and mixed affine-projective additions when possible.

Efficiency Comparison. Costs are expressed in field multiplications M, assuming $S/M = 0.8$ and $A/M = 0$. The storage requirement corresponds to the size of table T for our algorithms and to the size of the array $\{P_j\}$ for the BGMW algorithm. The RAM estimation is based on the number of registers used in algorithms — i.e. it does not include the RAM required to compute point operations.

We provide in Fig. 1 a graphical comparison of the cost per scalar bit of our fixed base-point scalar multiplication algorithms depending on ℓ for common key lengths.

Table 2. Comparison of scalar multiplication algorithms cost (in M), storage requirement (in kB), and used RAM (in B) for 256 and 512-bit elliptic curves over large characteristic fields, assuming $a = -3$

Algorithm	$\ell = 256$			$\ell = 512$		
	Cost	Storage	RAM	Cost	Storage	RAM
LR-NAF-DA	2662	0	160	5324	0	320
BGMW Alg. 2.2 $h = 4$	1034	8	256	2052	32	512
BGMW Alg. 2.2 $h = 8$	862	5.3	256	1654	21.3	512
BGMW Alg. 2.2 $h = 16$	**816**	4	256	1452	16	512
BGMW Alg. 2.2 $h = 32$	923	3.2	256	**1449**	12.8	512
Alg. 3.1	901	16	160	1806	64	320
Alg. 3.2, $t = 2$	775	8	256	1529	32	512
Alg. 3.2, $t = 3$	**743**	5.3	544	1377	21.3	1088
Alg. 3.2, $t = 4$	781	4	1024	**1325**	16	2048
Alg. 3.3, $w = 3$	717	16	256	1395	64	512
Alg. 3.3, $w = 4$	**663**	16	448	1206	64	896
Alg. 3.3, $w = 5$	736	16	832	**1188**	64	1664

Non-volatile Memory Transfers. We consider in Table 2 arithmetic operations only. On embedded devices, the comparison must also takes into account the numerous transfers from non-volatile memory to RAM performed in algorithms, but such costs highly depends on devices (frequency, bus width, etc.) To

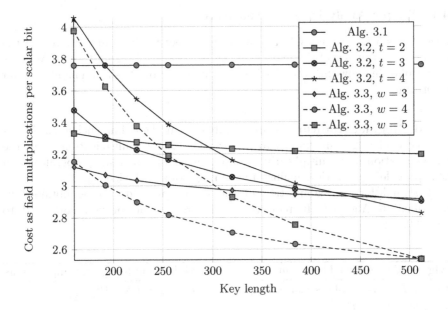

Fig. 1. Comparison of fixed-point scalar multiplication algorithms cost depending on the key length

estimate the practical expected overhead, we take as an example an 8-bit AVR chip provided with the Ad-X coprocessor, both running at 30 MHz. Considering Alg. 3.2 with $t = 2$ and $\ell = 256$, the transfer of 8kB of EEPROM to RAM takes about 5 % of the full computation time. This is far from negligible, but makes our method still very attractive. In addition, the overhead would be much smaller for higher window sizes, for 16 or 32-bit devices, or if transfers can be performed while the coprocessor is running.

Results Analysis. Considering Fig. 1, the best choice for an efficient and practical implementation is the m-ary NAF add-only scalar multiplication with $t = 3$ or 4, depending on the key length.

The better efficiency of our algorithms over the classical BGMW method, cf. Table 2, is due to the use of signed representations. On the opposite, the strategy of using separate registers and a final aggregation requires a few more computations and more RAM than the strategy applied in the BGMW algorithm. However, we will see in the next section that our choices allow very efficient countermeasures.

4   Side-Channel Analysis Countermeasures

We discuss in this section the means to protect our fixed-point algorithms against side-channel and fault attacks.

4.1   Simple Analysis Countermeasure

Algorithms 3.1, 3.2, and 3.3 are obviously subject to the simple analysis if the conditional branches of the main loop can be observed by an attacker. We show in the following how this source of leakage can be removed using an highly regular algorithm.

Highly Regular Addition Loop. Highly regular algorithms such as the Montgomery ladder [24] are known to perform the scalar multiplication — or the exponentiation in a multiplicative group — without any dummy operation and thus provide a protection against a wide range of attacks [25,26].

A straightforward adaptation of the m-ary method can be obtained as described in Alg. 4.1. It requires t registers instead of $\nu(t)$ compared to Alg. 3.2.

Alg. 4.1. Regular add-only m-ary scalar multiplication using precomputations

---

Input: $P \in \mathcal{E}(\mathbb{F}_q)$, ℓ-bit scalar $d = (d_{\ell-1}d_{\ell-2}\ldots d_0)_2$, $T = \left(\left[2^{ti}\right]P\right)_{0 \le i \le \ell'-1}$

Output: $Q = [d]P$

  Initialization
1: $R_0 \leftarrow \mathcal{O}$, $R_1 \leftarrow \mathcal{O}$, ... , $R_{m-1} \leftarrow \mathcal{O}$
  Main loop
2: **for** $i = 0$ **to** $\ell' - 1$ **do**
3:     $u = \sum_{j=0}^{t-1} d_{ti+j}2^j$ [Assume $d_i = 0$ if $i \ge \ell$]
4:     $R_u \leftarrow R_u \,[+]\, T_i$

  Aggregation
5: **for** $i = m - 2$ **to** 1 **by** -1 **do**
6:     $R_i \leftarrow R_i \,[+]\, R_{i+1}$
7:     $R_{m-1} \leftarrow R_{m-1} \,[+]\, R_i$
8: **return** R_{m-1}

This algorithm requires exactly ℓ' point additions in the main loop. It is worth noticing that the overhead introduced by this method over Alg. 3.2 tends to 0 as t grows. Note also that the NAF representation does not help reducing the number of performed additions here, as zero digits are now treated in the same way as other digits.

Efficiency Analysis. Table 3 gives the precise cost of Alg.4.1 assuming the use of homogeneous coordinates and mixed affine-projective additions in the main loop. Under our assumptions, the window width minimizing the number of field operations is $t = 3$ for $\ell \le 224$, and $t = 4$ for $\ell \ge 256$.

Table 3. Cost of Alg. 4.1 (in M), storage requirement (in kB), and used RAM (in B) for 256 and 512-bit elliptic curves over large characteristic fields

Algorithm	$\ell = 256$			$\ell = 512$		
	Cost	Storage	RAM	Cost	Storage	RAM
Alg. 4.1, $t = 1$	2740	16	256	5454	64	512
Alg. 4.1, $t = 2$	1438	8	448	2795	32	896
Alg. 4.1, $t = 3$	1102	5.3	832	2003	21.3	1664
Alg. 4.1, $t = 4$	**1086**	4	1600	**1764**	16	3200
Alg. 4.1, $t = 5$	1394	3.2	3136	1935	12.8	6272

4.2   Advanced Analysis Countermeasures

Let us now focus on the protection of our algorithms towards ASCA. Commonly used countermeasures consist in randomizing the projective coordinates of points, blinding the scalar with a random multiple of the subgroup order and input point blinding.

While the projective coordinates randomization is generally a low-cost countermeasure, it would imply a non-negligible overhead here. Indeed, each point T_i of the precomputed table should have its coordinates randomized, which in turn requires a general addition, instead of a mixed affine-projective one.

The scalar blinding countermeasure $d^* \leftarrow d + rn$, with r a random nonce and n the order of the generator point P, has two drawbacks: first it induces an overhead of $(|r| + \ell)/\ell$, second its efficiency is uncertain when n has a particular form as with NIST prime curves [17].

We present in the rest of this section two ASCA countermeasures ensuring high protection and little overhead for the fixed-point scalar multiplication algorithms.

Shuffling the Sequence of Point Additions. As the main loop of our algorithms performs additions only, and as points to be added are all stored in a table, the sequence of additions can be performed in any order. Not only it can be processed in left-to-right direction as well as right-to-left, but it is even possible to pick the points T_i to be added in a random order[3].

Considering our proposed highly regular algorithm, a random permutation σ of $\{0, 1, \dots, \ell' - 1\}$ can be generated and used in a similar way to shuffle the iterations of the main loop. This solution is detailed at the end of the section in Alg. 4.2.

The extra cost brought by this countermeasure lies principally in the generation of the random permutation. Generating efficiently a random permutation is an issue that merits a whole study by itself. As it is not the core subject of this paper, we suggest to use the method proposed by Coron [15,4] for generating a pseudo-random permutation.

---

[3] Permutations of the points added in Yao's algorithm already appear in a paper by Avanzi [2] for efficiency purpose.

Internal Point Blinding. Assuming a random point R lying on the curve, a naïve blinding of the form $[d] (P [+] R) [-] [d] R$ requires two scalar multiplications instead of one, which is an overkill for most applications. In specific cases such as fixed-scalar multiplication, efficient point blinding is possible as shown by Coron [14]. Itoh, Izu, and Takenaka have also proposed a modified left-to-right algorithm using internal point blinding [22,23].

Due to the specific structure of our algorithms the countermeasure is straightforward to apply. For instance, considering Alg. 3.1, initialize Q to some random point R from $\mathcal{E}(\mathbb{F}_q)$ at step 1 and subtract this point from Q before the return statement. Thus the point blinding requires only an extra point addition.

For m-ary algorithms using accumulators $R_1, R_2, \ldots, R_q$, $q > 1$, we propose the following strategy to keep a low overhead. Find a sequence of integers $(e_i)_{1 \leq i \leq q} \in \{-1, 1\}^q$ such that:

$$\sum_{i=1}^q i \cdot e_i \in \{0, 1\}$$

Then, modifying the initialization step of the algorithm to $R_i \leftarrow [e_i] R$, for $1 \leq i \leq q$, yields $R_q = [d] P$ or $R_q = [d] P [+] R$ at the end of the aggregation step. In the first case no extra operation is required to remove the mask, and a single subtraction by R has to be performed in the second case.

Our experimentations show that a sequence (e_i) with $i \cdot e_i$ summing to 1 can be easily found if $q = \nu(t)$ — i.e. using the m-ary NAF algorithm — or summing to 0 if $q = 2^t - 1$ — i.e. using the highly regular m-ary algorithm[4]. For instance:

$$(e_i) = (-1, 1) \text{ for } q = 2,$$
$$(e_i) = (-1, -1, 1) \text{ for } q = 3,$$
$$(e_i) = (1, -1, 1, 1, -1) \text{ for } q = 5.$$
$$(e_i) = (-1, 1, -1, -1, 1, -1, 1) \text{ for } q = 7.$$

Random Point Generation. Generating a random point on the curve may be an overkill in practice as it requires a square root computation in $\mathbb{F}_q$. The following strategy can thus be applied: a random point R is generated once for all offline before any computation and stored in non-volatile memory together with T. After each scalar multiplication, R is updated as follows:

for $i = 1$ **to** r **do**
    Pick at random $j \in \{0, 1, \ldots, \ell' - 1\}$
    Pick a random bit b
    $R \leftarrow R [+] [(-1)^b] T_j$

where r is a security parameter depending on the size of T and on the required security level.

Randomizing the projective coordinates of R before each scalar multiplication provides an additional level of blinding at a very low cost.

---

[4] In this case, R_0 can be initialized to R as it has no consequence on the result.

4.3   Fault Analysis Countermeasures

We finally consider the protection of our scalar multiplication algorithms against FA.

Following an observation by Joye and Karroumi [26], register R_1 holds the value $\left[\sum_{i=1}^{m-1}\right] R_i^*$ at the end of the aggregation, where R_i^* is the value stored in R_i prior to the aggregation. It follows that, after the aggregation, $R_0 + R_1 = \left[\sum_{i=0}^{\ell'-1}\right] T_i$. We can use this invariant to check the computation consistency.

Therefore, we propose to store an extra point S, together with the table T, equal to the sum of all the points in T. The fault detection stage then requires only a point addition $R_0 \, [+] \, R_1$ after the aggregation and a comparison with S.

If the point blinding countermeasure presented in the last section is used, an extra subtraction is required to unmask $R_0 \, [+] \, R_1$. Alternatively, one may initialize R_0 to $\left[-\sum_{i=1}^{m-1} e_i\right] R$, such that no extra addition at all is required in the fault verification stage.

We present in Alg. 4.2 an updated version of the highly regular m-ary algorithm with the main loop shuffling and point blinding countermeasures presented in the previous section, and the present fault detection method.

Alg. 4.2. Regular Add-only m-ary scalar multiplication using precomputations with ASCA and FA countermeasures

Input: $P \in \mathcal{E}(\mathbb{F}_q)$, ℓ-bit scalar $d = (d_{\ell-1} d_{\ell-2} \ldots d_0)_2$, $T = \left(\left[2^{ti}\right] P\right)_{0 \le i \le \ell'-1}$, $S =$
$\sum_{i=0}^{\ell'-1} T_i$, $(e_i)_{1 \le i \le t-1}$ s.t. $\sum_{i=1}^{m-1} i \cdot e_i = 0$ and $\sum_{i=1}^{m-1} e_i = -1$

Output: $Q = [d] \, P$

    Initialization
1: Generate a random permutation $\sigma = (\sigma_0 \ldots \sigma_{\ell'-1})$ of $[0, \ldots, \ell'-1]$
2: Generate a random point $R \in \mathcal{E}(\mathbb{F}_q) \setminus \mathcal{O}$
3: $R_0 \leftarrow R$, $R_1 \leftarrow [e_1] \, R$, ..., $R_{t-1} \leftarrow [e_{t-1}] \, R$

    Main loop
4: **for** $i = 0$ **to** $\ell' - 1$ **do**
5:     $u = \sum_{j=0}^{t-1} 2^j d_{t\sigma_i + j}$ [Assume $d_i = 0$ if $i \ge \ell$]
6:     $R_u \leftarrow R_u \, [+] \, T_{\sigma_i}$

    Aggregation
7: **for** $i = m - 2$ **to** 1 **by** -1 **do**
8:     $R_i \leftarrow R_i \, [+] \, R_{i+1}$
9:     $R_{m-1} \leftarrow R_{m-1} \, [+] \, R_i$

    Fault detection
10: $R_0 \leftarrow R_0 \, [+] \, R_1$
11: **if** $R_0 \ne S$ **then**
12:     **return** FAULT DETECTED
13: **return** R_{t-1}

4.4 Security Analysis

The regular structure of Alg. 4.2 provides a standard protection against classical SSCA, i.e. against attacks targeting conditional branches leakages. The additive blinding of internal point registers thwarts classical ASCA that requires the knowledge of manipulated data. It also counteracts chosen input-point attacks when the attacker controls the value of the internal registers. Shuffling the sequence of point additions adds an additional layer of protection against ASCA by increasing the number of required traces by a factor of ℓ'.

Let us now consider the attacks based on potential noticeable additions involving the point at infinity in the main loop of the scalar multiplication. Obviously no point in T should be the point at infinity and its integrity should further be checked. As specified in Alg. 4.2, the pseudo-random generation of R should also verify that $R \neq \mathcal{O}$. The possibility that the point at infinity appears in one computation of the main loop is thus very unlikely considering the size of the groups. Due to the masking and shuffling countermeasures, even in this case, an attacker would not be able to identify the addition or the register involved.

Finally, as no value nor any result is ever discarded during the computation, the fault countermeasure ensures that a perturbation introduced in any point addition or any point register would be detected and no result returned.

5   Conclusion

We propose in this paper fixed-point scalar multiplication algorithms derived from Yao and BGMW algorithms. These algorithms benefit from the use of signed representations for the scalar and have a small code size footprint. They can be used in embedded devices provided with a few dozen kilobytes of storage and a few kilobytes of RAM. We propose a novel countermeasure towards side-channel analysis with a very low cost and adapt some others to our algorithms. We present a combination of them and hence provide our regular m-ary algorithm with state-of-the-art protection against SSCA, ASCA and FA. The question of comparing the efficiency, storage requirement, and protection against physical attacks of our methods with fixed-base comb algorithms is left open for further research.

Acknowledgements. The authors would like to thank Christophe Clavier for his support and fruitful discussions. We also thank the anonymous referees for their valuable comments.

References

1. Akishita, T., Takagi, T.: Zero-value point attacks on elliptic curve cryptosystem. In: Boyd, C., Mao, W. (eds.) ISC 2003. LNCS, vol. 2851, pp. 218–233. Springer, Heidelberg (2003)

2. Avanzi, R.M.: Delaying and merging operations in scalar multiplication: Applications to curve-based cryptosystems. In: Biham, E., Youssef, A.M. (eds.) SAC 2006. LNCS, vol. 4356, pp. 203–219. Springer, Heidelberg (2007)

3. Baek, Y.-J.: Regular 2^w-ary right-to-left exponentiation algorithm with very efficient dpa and fa countermeasures. Int. J. Inf. Sec. 9(5), 363–370 (2010)

4. Bauer, A., Jaulmes, E., Prouff, E., Wild, J.: Horizontal and vertical side-channel attacks against secure RSA implementations. In: Dawson, E. (ed.) CT-RSA 2013. LNCS, vol. 7779, pp. 1–17. Springer, Heidelberg (2013)

5. Bernstein, D.J.: Pippenger's exponentiation algorithm, To be incorporated into author's High-speed cryptography book (January 2002), http://cr.yp.to/papers.html#pippenger

6. Bernstein, D.J., Lange, T.: Explicit-formulas database, http://www.hyperelliptic.org/EFD

7. Biehl, I., Meyer, B., Müller, V.: Advances in cryptology - crypto 2000. In: Bellare, M. (ed.) CRYPTO 2000. LNCS, vol. 1880, pp. 131–146. Springer, Heidelberg (2000)

8. Blömer, J., Otto, M., Seifert, J.-P.: Sign change fault attacks on elliptic curve cryptosystems. In: Breveglieri, L., Koren, I., Naccache, D., Seifert, J.-P. (eds.) FDTC 2006. LNCS, vol. 4236, pp. 36–52. Springer, Heidelberg (2006)

9. Boneh, D., DeMillo, R.A., Lipton, R.J.: On the Importance of Checking Cryptographic Protocols for Faults. In: Fumy, W. (ed.) EUROCRYPT 1997. LNCS, vol. 1233, pp. 37–51. Springer, Heidelberg (1997)

10. Boscher, A., Naciri, R., Prouff, E.: CRT RSA algorithm protected against fault attacks. In: Sauveron, D., Markantonakis, K., Bilas, A., Quisquater, J.-J. (eds.) WISTP 2007. LNCS, vol. 4462, pp. 229–243. Springer, Heidelberg (2007)

11. Brickell, E.F., Gordon, D.M., McCurley, K.S., Wilson, D.B.: Fast exponentiation with precomputation. In: Rueppel, R.A. (ed.) EUROCRYPT 1992. LNCS, vol. 658, pp. 200–207. Springer, Heidelberg (1993)

12. Ciet, M., Joye, M.: Elliptic curve cryptosystems in the presence of permanent and transient faults. Des. Codes Cryptography 36(1), 33–43 (2005)

13. Clavier, C., Feix, B., Gagnerot, G., Roussellet, M., Verneuil, V.: Horizontal correlation analysis on exponentiation. In: Soriano, M., Qing, S., López, J. (eds.) ICICS 2010. LNCS, vol. 6476, pp. 46–61. Springer, Heidelberg (2010)

14. Coron, J.-S.: Resistance against Differential Power Analysis for Elliptic Curve Cryptosystems. In: Koç, Ç.K., Paar, C. (eds.) CHES 1999. LNCS, vol. 1717, pp. 292–302. Springer, Heidelberg (1999)

15. Coron, J.-S.: A new DPA countermeasure based on permutation tables. In: Ostrovsky, R., De Prisco, R., Visconti, I. (eds.) SCN 2008. LNCS, vol. 5229, pp. 278–292. Springer, Heidelberg (2008)

16. Fan, J., Gierlichs, B., Vercauteren, F.: To infinity and beyond: Combined attack on ECC using points of low order. In: Preneel, B., Takagi, T. (eds.) CHES 2011. LNCS, vol. 6917, pp. 143–159. Springer, Heidelberg (2011)

17. FIPS PUB 186-3. Digital Signature Standard. National Institute of Standards and Technology (October 2009)

18. Giraud, C.: An rsa implementation resistant to fault attacks and to simple power analysis. IEEE Trans. Computers 55(9), 1116–1120 (2006)

19. Goubin, L.: A refined power-analysis attack on elliptic curve cryptosystems. In: Desmedt, Y.G. (ed.) PKC 2003. LNCS, vol. 2567, pp. 199–211. Springer, Heidelberg (2002)

20. Hankerson, D., Menezes, A.J., Vanstone, S.: Guide to Elliptic Curve Cryptography. Springer Professional Computing Series (January 2003)

21. Hedabou, M., Pinel, P., Bénéteau, L.: Countermeasures for preventing comb method against SCA attacks. In: Deng, R.H., Bao, F., Pang, H., Zhou, J. (eds.) ISPEC 2005. LNCS, vol. 3439, pp. 85–96. Springer, Heidelberg (2005)

22. Itoh, K., Izu, T., Takenaka, M.: Efficient countermeasures against power analysis. In: Quisquater, J.-J., Paradinas, P., Deswarte, Y., El Kalam, A.A. (eds.) CARDIS, pp. 99–114. Kluwer (2004)

23. Itoh, K., Izu, T., Takenaka, M.: Improving the Randomized Initial Point Countermeasure against DPA. In: Zhou, J., Yung, M., Bao, F. (eds.) ACNS 2006. LNCS, vol. 3989, pp. 459–469. Springer, Heidelberg (2006)

24. Joye, M., Yen, S.-M.: The Montgomery Powering Ladder. In: Kaliski Jr., B.S., Koç, Ç.K., Paar, C. (eds.) CHES 2002. LNCS, vol. 2523, pp. 291–302. Springer, Heidelberg (2003)

25. Joye, M.: Highly regular m-ary powering ladders. In: Jacobson Jr., M.J., Rijmen, V., Safavi-Naini, R. (eds.) SAC 2009. LNCS, vol. 5867, pp. 350–363. Springer, Heidelberg (2009)

26. Joye, M., Karroumi, M.: Memory-efficient fault countermeasures. In: Prouff, E. (ed.) CARDIS 2011. LNCS, vol. 7079, pp. 84–101. Springer, Heidelberg (2011)

27. Kocher, P.C., Jaffe, J., Jun, B.: Differential Power Analysis. In: Wiener, M. (ed.) CRYPTO 1999. LNCS, vol. 1666, pp. 388–397. Springer, Heidelberg (1999)

28. Lim, C.H., Lee, P.J.: More flexible exponentiation with precomputation. In: Desmedt, Y.G. (ed.) CRYPTO 1994. LNCS, vol. 839, pp. 95–107. Springer, Heidelberg (1994)

29. Mohamed, N.A.F., Hashim, M.H.A., Hutter, M.: Improved fixed-base comb method for fast scalar multiplication. In: Mitrokotsa, A., Vaudenay, S. (eds.) AFRICACRYPT 2012. LNCS, vol. 7374, pp. 342–359. Springer, Heidelberg (2012)

30. Möller, B.: Improved techniques for fast exponentiation. In: Lee, P.J., Lim, C.H. (eds.) ICISC 2002. LNCS, vol. 2587, pp. 298–312. Springer, Heidelberg (2003)

31. Montgomery, P.L.: Speeding the Pollard and elliptic curve methods of factorization. Mathematics of Computation 48, 243–264 (1987)

32. Tsaur, W.-J., Chou, C.-H.: Efficient algorithms for speeding up the computations of elliptic curve cryptosystems. Applied Mathematics and Computation 168(2), 1045–1064 (2005)

33. Walter, C.D.: Sliding Windows Succumbs to Big Mac Attack. In: Koç, Ç.K., Naccache, D., Paar, C. (eds.) CHES 2001. LNCS, vol. 2162, pp. 286–299. Springer, Heidelberg (2001)

34. Yao, A.C.: On the evaluation of powers. SIAM J. Comput. 5(1), 100–103 (1976)

On the Relationship between Correlation Power Analysis and the Stochastic Approach: An **ASIC** Designer Perspective

Fabrizio De Santis[1,2], Michael Kasper[3,4], Stefan Mangard[2],
Georg Sigl[1], Oliver Stein[4,5], and Marc Stöttinger[6]

[1] Technische Universität München, Germany
desantis@tum.de
[2] Infineon Technologies AG, Germany
stefan.mangard@infineon.com
[3] Fraunhofer Institute for Secure Information Technology, Germany
michael.kasper@sit.fraunhofer.de
[4] Center for Advanced Security Research Darmstadt, Germany
{michael.kasper,oliver.stein}@cased.de
[5] Technische Hochschule Regensburg, Germany
oliver.stein@hs-regensburg.de
[6] Nanyang Technological University, Singapore
mstottinger@ntu.edu.sg

Abstract. The design and the security verification of side-channel resistant cryptographic hardware often represent an iterative process. This process essentially consists of a *detection phase* ($\mathcal{DP}$), where the information leakage is identified and a *correction phase* ($\mathcal{CP}$), where design flaws are corrected. Correlation Power Analysis (**CPA**) and the Stochastic Approach (**SA**) are two candidate tools to perform the $\mathcal{DP}$ and to *support* designers in the $\mathcal{CP}$. However, until now, the relationship between these two tools has not been discussed yet and it is uncertain from a designer point of view, what informative feedback can be gained from these methods, especially when it comes to evaluate high-dimensional leakage models. In this work, we investigate the relationship between **CPA** and the **SA** from both a mathematical and empirical point of view. In particular, we demonstrate that the informative feedback provided by the **SA** is transferable to a linear combination of **CPA** attacks and discuss the implications of this entanglement, when it comes to pinpoint the high-dimensional leakage of simulated leakage data and simulated power traces of an **ASIC** implementation of PRESENT.

1 Introduction

The analysis of side-channel leakage is an integral part of the design of secure cryptographic hardware, which is performed at early stages of development already. Typically, the earlier a design flaw is discovered, the less re-engineering effort has to be spent in correcting the issue [1,19]. In practice, two different challenges have to be accomplished during the development of side-channel resistant

G. Paul and S. Vaudenay (Eds.): INDOCRYPT 2013, LNCS 8250, pp. 215–226, 2013.
© Springer International Publishing Switzerland 2013

cryptographic hardware: first, the *leakage* must be identified in a so-called *detection phase* ($\mathcal{DP}$). Secondly, the *design flaws*, which have caused the leakage, must be repaired in a so-called *correction phase* ($\mathcal{CP}$).

Recently, different works have been published addressing the $\mathcal{DP}$, cf. [7,17,23], whereas the $\mathcal{CP}$ was not addressed. However, previous contributions have shown how the Correlation Power Analysis (CPA) and the Stochastic Approach (SA) are indeed useful tools to constructively *support* designers in the correction of design flaws: in [15, 16] CPA was used to pinpoint a design flaw of a masked ASIC implementation of AES, while a constructive usage of the SA is reported in [9], where the SA was used to pinpoint a design flaw in the routing of an FPGA implementation of AES. Yet, it remains uncertain from a designer perspective, which different informative feedback can be gained from CPA and the SA to support designers in the $\mathcal{CP}$. Also, it remains unclear, to which extent these tools can be used to pinpoint the *leakage* of bit interactions using high-dimensional leakage models. In fact, aforementioned works only considered the switching activity of *independent* leakage contributions, whereas [3, 8, 20] have shown that dependent contributions may also produce exploitable information leakage *e.g.* due to the occurrence of glitches in the combinational logic path or due to technology factors like the scaling of the CMOS technology.

In this work, we address these open questions by investigating the relationship between CPA and the SA from both a mathematical and empirical point of view. In particular, we provide the following contributions:

– We proof that the SA can be expressed as a linear combination of CPA attacks and provide two Corollaries, which demonstrate that the informative feedback provided by CPA and the SA is indeed equivalent, in some specific, yet practically relevant cases.
– We extend previous works [9, 15, 16] by considering high-dimensional leakage models. In particular, we show that the SA can precisely identify and quantify each contribution to the leakages, once an adequate approximation subspace is selected and properly estimated. On the other hand, we show that CPA can only loosely point to individual leakage contributions, being inherently unable to capture bit interactions when high-dimensional leakage models are used.

The rest of the paper is structured as follows. In Sect. 2, we provide the necessary background information. In Sect 3, we discuss the *mathematical* relationship between CPA and the SA. In Sect. 4, we *empirically* evaluate and discuss the application of CPA and the SA to simulated high-dimensional leakage data as well as to simulated power traces of an ASIC implementation of PRESENT. Finally, we draw conclusions in Sect. 5.

2 Background

The Leakage Model. During the execution of a cryptographic implementation θ, *sensitive* intermediate values $v_{\theta,t}(x, k) \in \{0, 1\}^w$ are computed at certain time t. Sensitive intermediate values typically depends on a public input

$x \in \{0,1\}^p$ and a secret key $k \in \{0,1\}^s$ and their size w depends on the particular design specifications. The computation of sensitive intermediate values $v_{\theta,t}(x,k)$ for randomly chosen inputs $x \in \{0,1\}^p$ and a random, but fixed, key $k \in \{0,1\}^s$ can be interpreted as a random experiment, which defines the random variable $V_{\theta,t}(\cdot, k)$. Similarly, the measurable leakage $\ell_{\theta,t}$, which is observed during the computation of $v_{\theta,t}(\cdot, k)$, can be treated as the realization of yet another random variable $L_{\theta,t}(\cdot, k)$ taking values in $\mathbb{R}$. A central assumption in side-channel analysis is to consider the leakage as the sum of a deterministic contribution $\delta_{\theta,t}$ and *independent* noise R_t:

$$L_{\theta,t}(\cdot, k) = \delta_{\theta,t}(V_{\theta,t}(\cdot, k)) + R_t. \qquad (1)$$

Tools for Side-Channel Analysis. CPA and the SA are side-channel analysis tools which are typically employed by designers to analyse the leakages of cryptographic hardware implementations and identify possible design flaws [9,15,16]. Both techniques consider the leakage $\ell_{\theta,t}(\cdot, k)$ of N cryptographic operations under public inputs $x_0, \ldots, x_{N-1}$, being observed at M points in time $T = \{t_0, t_1, \ldots, t_{M-1}\}$. Let the matrix $\mathbf{L}_\theta = \left(\ell_{\theta,t_j}(x_i, k)\right)_{\substack{0 \leq i \leq N-1 \\ 0 \leq j \leq M-1}}$ denote the $N \times M$ *leakage matrix* and $\ell_{\theta,t}$ a column vector thereof. For any $u \geq 0$, let $\mathbf{A}_\theta$ be the $N \times (u+1)$ *model matrix* defined as follows:

$$\mathbf{A}_\theta := \begin{pmatrix} g_{\theta,0}(x_0, k^*) & \cdots & g_{\theta,u}(x_0, k^*) \\ \vdots & \ddots & \vdots \\ g_{\theta,0}(x_{N-1}, k^*) & \cdots & g_{\theta,u}(x_{N-1}, k^*) \end{pmatrix}. \qquad (2)$$

where $g_{\theta,j} \colon \{0,1\}^p \times \{0,1\}^q \to \mathbb{R}$ are the analytical *model functions*, which model the leakages of arbitrary selected *target* intermediate values. The target intermediate values are typically a function of the public inputs $x_0, \ldots, x_{N-1}$ and a *small* key hypothesis $k^* \in \{0,1\}^q$ ($q \ll s$) and do not necessarily correspond to $v_{\theta,t}(\cdot, k)$, being arbitrarily selected by designers during the security verifications (*e.g.* only a subset of bits can be targeted).

Correlation Power Analysis (CPA). The basic idea of CPA is to evaluate the linear strength between the observed leakages and the leakage models specified via the $\mathbf{A}_\theta$ matrix, cf. [4]. Hence, given the leakages $\ell_{\theta,t}$ and the corresponding model matrix $\mathbf{A}_\theta$, CPA computes the sample Pearson's correlation coefficient $\widetilde{\rho}$ between the measured leakages $\ell_{\theta,t}$ and each column $\mathbf{A}_{\theta,j}$ of the model matrix $\mathbf{A}_\theta$, as follows:

$$\widetilde{\rho}_{\theta,j,t}(\mathbf{A}_{\theta,j}, \ell_{\theta,t}) := \frac{\sum_{n=0}^{N-1}(g_{\theta,j}(x_n, k^*) - \widetilde{\mathbb{E}}(\mathbf{A}_{\theta,j}))(\ell_{\theta,t}(x_n, k) - \widetilde{\mathbb{E}}(\ell_{\theta,t}))}{\sqrt{\sum_{n=0}^{N-1}(g_{\theta,j}(x_n, k^*) - \widetilde{\mathbb{E}}(\mathbf{A}_{\theta,j}))^2 \sum_{n=0}^{N-1}(\ell_{\theta,t}(x_n, k) - \widetilde{\mathbb{E}}(\ell_{\theta,t}))^2}},$$

where $\widetilde{\mathbb{E}}(\cdot)$ denotes the sample mean operator.

The Stochastic Approach (SA). The core idea of the SA is to estimate the leakage function, which underlies the origin of the leakage, by approximating the deterministic part $\delta_{\theta,t}$ and the noise R_t of Eq. (1) in a chosen subspace. In here, we only recall the approximation of the deterministic part, and refer to [9,11,22] for a comprehensive study of the SA. The SA approximates the deterministic part in a $(u + 1)$-dimensional subspace $\mathcal{F}_{u+1,t}$ spanned by the analytical model functions $g_{\theta,j}(\cdot, \cdot)$ as follows:

$$\mathcal{F}_{u+1,t} := \left\{ \widetilde{\delta} : \{0,1\}^p \times \{0,1\}^q \to \mathbb{R}; \quad \widetilde{\delta} = \sum_{j=0}^{u} \widetilde{\beta}_{\theta,j,t} g_{\theta,j} \right\}. \tag{3}$$

The ordinary least square method, cf. [18], is used to derive the optimal approximation $\widetilde{\delta}_{\theta,t}(\cdot)$ in terms of square errors. The least square estimators $\widetilde{\beta}_\theta$ are uniquely determined by the solution which minimizes $\|\mathbf{L}_\theta - \mathbf{A}_\theta \beta_\theta\|_2^2$:

$$\widetilde{\beta}_\theta = (\mathbf{A}_\theta^T \mathbf{A}_\theta)^{-1} \mathbf{A}_\theta^T \mathbf{L}_\theta, \tag{4}$$

where $\mathbf{A}_\theta^T \mathbf{A}_\theta$ must be an invertible $(u + 1) \times (u + 1)$-matrix and, typically, $\mathbf{A}_{\theta,0} = \mathbf{1}_N$. In side-channel analysis, the regression coefficients β_θ are usually referred to as the *leakage characteristic* of the design θ under test or, simply, β_θ-characteristic [9].

Other Tools. For the sake of completeness, we briefly recall the Kocher's original DPA attack [10] and the Mutual Information Analysis (MIA) [2]. Kocher's original DPA attack assumes a single-bit model (*e.g.* $\mathbf{A}_\theta$ defined over $\{0,1\}$) and computes $\widetilde{\mathbb{E}}[\ell_{\theta,t}|\mathbf{A}_{\theta,j} = 1] - \widetilde{\mathbb{E}}[\ell_{\theta,t}|\mathbf{A}_{\theta,j} = 0]$. Similarly, MIA estimates the mutual information between leakages and models as $\widetilde{I}(\ell_{\theta,t}, \mathbf{A}_{\theta,j})$ to quantify the leakage amount in bits of information. Interestingly, these attacks are *asymptotically* equivalent to CPA attacks when single-bit models are employed [14].

Security Verification. The goal of a side-channel security analysis is to make conclusive statements about the side-channel security of a design θ under test. However, since both leakages and models are realizations of random experiments, security statements are only possible in a stochastic sense, that is, only relatively to selected $(\mathbf{A}_\theta, \mathsf{T}, \gamma)$-adversaries, where $\mathbf{A}_\theta$ denotes the selected leakage models, T denotes the selected side-channel analysis tool (*e.g.* CPA or the SA) and γ denotes the desired statistical confidence[1], unless equivalences are demonstrated, cf. [6,14]. Hence, the experience of designers play a fundamental role to select appropriate adversaries in order to anticipate the attackers working conditions and pre-emptively remove possible design flaws. Clearly, an improper selection of the adversaries could possibly leave exploitable flaws behind and, consequently, lead to an overestimated security confidence and produce higher security risks. In this respect, the task of designers is to properly define the model matrix $\mathbf{A}_\theta$ by accurately choosing the target intermediate values, the model selection functions and the side-channel analysis tools. A typical choice for designers is to select those intermediate values which can be computed from a small key hypothesis

---

[1] In this view, we can speak of $(\mathbf{A}_\theta, \mathsf{T}, \gamma)$-security. The number of traces N is implicitly accounted in by γ.

and then use Boolean model functions in the form $g_{\theta,j} : \mathbb{F}_2^p \times \mathbb{F}_2^q \to \mathbb{F}_2$ to map intermediate values to single-bits [15, 16], possibly considering any polynomial of the target bits, as follows:

$$g_{\theta,j}(x, k^*) = \prod_{p \in P_j} f_{\theta,p}(x, k^*), \quad j = 1, \ldots, \sum_{i=1}^{b} \binom{b}{i} - 1, \qquad (5)$$

where $f_{\theta,p}$ denotes the pth bit of the target intermediate values obtained by combining the public and secret material by an algorithm specific function $f_\theta(\cdot, \cdot)$, b is the size of target intermediate values, $\mathcal{P}$ denotes the power set operator and P_j is the jth element of the set $\mathcal{P}(b) \backslash \{\emptyset\}$. The choice of using single-bit models is well-known to be suboptimal for attackers in terms of efficiency [13]. However, using the single-bit models of Eq. (5) still represents the most effective way for designers to understand the leakage characteristic of digital circuits. In fact, single-bit models make the least assumptions on the leakages and enable designers to collect informative feedback relatively to every single signal in the design. Additionally, using quadratic or higher-degree polynomials of the target bits, denoted as *high-dimensional models* in [8], allow to capture also those effects which arise from the interactions of logical transitions *e.g.* like those occurring during the asynchronous activity of the combinational logic. It is worth noting that, contrary to attackers, hardware designers typically work under more favourable conditions during security verifications for at least three reasons: first, designers have *full* control over the design under test and possess the knowledge of the secret key processed by the device. Therefore, they can skip over testing multiple key hypothesis and *significant* computational effort can be saved. Second, designers are not only interested in exploiting the leakage in the most efficient way, rather they are mainly interested in identifying and correcting design flaws. Third, hardware designers can simulate the switching activity of their implementation, or even single parts of it, with a sampling frequency in the range of THz, which is typically not available to real attackers. For instance, designers can simulate the switching activity of individual hardware modules at gate or transistor level, with a resolution of a few picoseconds [1, 19].

3 On the Relation between CPA and the SA

In this section we discuss the *mathematical* relation between CPA and the SA by proving that the leakage characteristic of the SA can be expressed as a linear combination of CPA attacks. Therefore, we derive two Corollaries of specific, yet practical relevance.

Proposition 1. *Let $\mathbf{A}_\theta$ and $\widetilde{\beta}_{\theta,t}$ be defined as in Eq. (2) and (4). Let $\widetilde{\beta}_{\theta,t}^*$ be the vector $\widetilde{\beta}_{\theta,t} \backslash \{\widetilde{\beta}_{\theta,0,t}\}$ and $\mathbf{A}_{\theta,0} = \mathbf{1}_N$. Then, the $\widetilde{\beta}_{\theta,t}^*$-characteristic can be expressed as a linear combination of sample correlation coefficients:*

$$\widetilde{\beta}_{\theta,i,t} = \sum_{j=1}^{u} w_{i,j}\widetilde{\rho}_{\theta,j,t}(\mathbf{A}_{\theta,j}, \boldsymbol{\ell}_{\theta,t}), \ i \in [1, u], \ w_{i,j} \in \mathbf{W} \ as \ defined \ in \ Eq. \ (8)$$

Proof. Starting from Eq. (2) and (4), we derive:

$$
\begin{aligned}
(\mathbf{A}_\theta^T \mathbf{A}_\theta)\widetilde{\boldsymbol{\beta}}_{\theta,t} &= \mathbf{A}_\theta^T \boldsymbol{\ell}_{\theta,t} &\Longleftrightarrow \\
\left(\textstyle\sum_{n=0}^{N-1} g_{\theta,i}(x_n, k^*) g_{\theta,j}(x_n, k^*)\right)_{0 \le i,j \le u} \widetilde{\boldsymbol{\beta}}_{\theta,t} &= \left(\textstyle\sum_{n=0}^{N-1} g_{\theta,i}(x_n, k^*)\ell_{\theta,t}(x_n, k^*)\right)_{0 \le i \le u} &\Longleftrightarrow \\
\left(\textstyle\sum_{j=0}^{u} \widetilde{\mathbb{E}}\left[\mathbf{A}_{\theta,i} \cdot \mathbf{A}_{\theta,j}\right] \widetilde{\beta}_{\theta,j,t}\right)_{0 \le i \le u} &= \left(\widetilde{\mathbb{E}}\left[\mathbf{A}_{\theta,i} \cdot \boldsymbol{\ell}_{\theta,t}\right]\right)_{0 \le i \le u},
\end{aligned}
$$
$$(6)$$

where the $\cdot$ operator denotes the element-by-element multiplication between vectors. From Eq. (6): $\widetilde{\beta}_{\theta,0,t} = \widetilde{\mathbb{E}}\left[\boldsymbol{\ell}_{\theta,t}\right] - \sum_{j=1}^{u} \widetilde{\beta}_{\theta,j,t}\widetilde{\mathbb{E}}\left[\mathbf{A}_{\theta,j}\right]$ for $i = 0$, since $\mathbf{A}_{\theta,0} = \mathbf{1}_N$. By replacing $\widetilde{\beta}_{\theta,0,t}$ in Eq. (6) and grouping terms together, we obtain:

$$\left(\sum_{j=1}^{u} \widetilde{\sigma}(\mathbf{A}_{\theta,i}, \mathbf{A}_{\theta,j})\widetilde{\beta}_{\theta,j,t}\right)_{0 \le i \le u} = \left(\widetilde{\sigma}(\mathbf{A}_{\theta,i}, \boldsymbol{\ell}_{\theta,t})\right)_{0 \le i \le u}, \tag{7}$$

where $\widetilde{\sigma}(\cdot, \cdot)$ is the sample covariance estimator. By rewriting Eq. (7) in a matrix form we obtain $\widetilde{\boldsymbol{\Sigma}}_{\mathbf{A}_{\theta,i}, \mathbf{A}_{\theta,j}}\widetilde{\boldsymbol{\beta}}_{\theta,t}^{*} = \widetilde{\boldsymbol{\Sigma}}_{\mathbf{A}_{\theta,i}, \boldsymbol{\ell}_{\theta,t}}$, where the matrices $\widetilde{\boldsymbol{\Sigma}}_{\mathbf{A}_{\theta,i}, \mathbf{A}_{\theta,j}} = (\widetilde{\sigma}(\mathbf{A}_{\theta,i}, \mathbf{A}_{\theta,j}))_{1 \le i,j \le u}$ and $\widetilde{\boldsymbol{\Sigma}}_{\mathbf{A}_{\theta,i}, \boldsymbol{\ell}_{\theta,t}} = (\widetilde{\sigma}(\mathbf{A}_{\theta,i}, \boldsymbol{\ell}_{\theta,t}))_{1 \le i \le u}$ are sample covariance matrices. Therefore, solving for $\widetilde{\boldsymbol{\beta}}_{\theta,t}^{*}$:

$$\widetilde{\boldsymbol{\beta}}_{\theta,t}^{*} = \mathbf{W}\mathbf{R}_{\mathbf{A}_{\theta,i}, \boldsymbol{\ell}_{\theta,t}}, \tag{8}$$

where $\mathbf{R}_{\mathbf{A}_{\theta,i}, \boldsymbol{\ell}_{\theta,t}} = (\widetilde{\rho}_{\theta,i,t}(\mathbf{A}_{\theta,i}, \boldsymbol{\ell}_{\theta,t}))_{1 \le i \le u}$ is a sample correlation matrix and the weighting matrix is $\mathbf{W} = \text{diag}\left((\widetilde{\sigma}(\mathbf{A}_{\theta,i})\widetilde{\sigma}(\boldsymbol{\ell}_{\theta,t}))_{1 \le i \le u}\right)\widetilde{\boldsymbol{\Sigma}}_{\mathbf{A}_{\theta,i}, \mathbf{A}_{\theta,j}}^{-1}$. ∎

Proposition 1 establishes a mathematical relation between CPA and the SA, which entails the following theoretical, yet practical, consequences. First, the $\widetilde{\beta}_{\theta,t}^{*}$-characteristic can be computed from CPA attacks. For instance, designers can evaluate CPA attacks in first place and then estimate the $\widetilde{\beta}_{\theta,t}^{*}$-characteristic only afterwards, with a consequent saving of computational resources. It is worth noting that $\widetilde{\beta}_{\theta,t}$ and $\widetilde{\beta}_{\theta,t}^{*}$ are equivalent from a designer perspective, since $\widetilde{\beta}_{\theta,0,t}$ only accounts to an offset in the leakages, which is typically not relevant for the sake of side-channel analysis. Secondly, Eq. (8) clearly shows that the information feedback provided by the $\widetilde{\beta}_{\theta,t}$-characteristic results necessarily biased, in case the leakages contain dependent contributions which are not accounted by the selected subspace. In this respect, only an appropriate selection of the subspace can precisely identify the leakage contributions. In contrast, an improper selection would provide a biased leakage characteristic and therefore lead designers to misinterpret the leakage contributions and the design flaws there of.

Finally, it can be observed from Eq. (8) that, if all the correlations $\rho_{\theta,i,t}$ equal zero, then also the $\beta^*_{\theta,t}$-characteristic necessarily equal zero. This is of course most unlikely to happen for any particular leakage realization, but hypothesis testing can be used to verify if there exists enough evidence in the realizations to reject the idea that populations values equal zero [13, 18].

Corollary 1. *If all the columns of the model matrix $\mathbf{A}_\theta$ are pairwise uncorrelated, then the $\widetilde{\beta}^*_{\theta,t}$-characteristic can be expressed as scaled correlation coefficients:*

$$\widetilde{\beta}_{\theta,i,t} = \widetilde{\rho}_{\theta,i,t}(\mathbf{A}_{\theta,i}, \boldsymbol{\ell}_{\theta,t})\frac{\widetilde{\sigma}_{\boldsymbol{\ell}_{\theta,t}}}{\widetilde{\sigma}_{\mathbf{A}_{\theta,i}}}, \ \forall i \in [1, u]$$

Proof. If $\forall i \neq j$: $\ \widetilde{\sigma}(\mathbf{A}_{\theta,i}, \mathbf{A}_{\theta,j}) = 0$, then $\left(\widetilde{\boldsymbol{\Sigma}}_{\mathbf{A}_{\theta,i}, \mathbf{A}_{\theta,j}}\right)^{-1} = \mathrm{diag}\left(\widetilde{\boldsymbol{\Sigma}}_{\mathbf{A}_{\theta,i}, \mathbf{A}_{\theta,j}}\right)^{-1}$. Therefore, the Corollary follows immediately from Equation (8). ∎

Corollary 2. *If all the columns of the model matrix $\mathbf{A}_\theta$ are pairwise uncorrelated and all $\mathbf{A}_{\theta,i}$ are defined over two constants $\{a_{0,i}, a_{1,i}\}$, then the $\widetilde{\beta}^*_{\theta,t}$-characteristic can be expressed as a scaled difference of means:*

$$\widetilde{\beta}_{\theta,i,t} = \frac{1}{a_{1,i} - a_{0,i}}\left(\widetilde{\mathbb{E}}\left[\boldsymbol{\ell}_{\theta,t}|\mathbf{A}_{\theta,i} = a_{1,i}\right] - \widetilde{\mathbb{E}}\left[\boldsymbol{\ell}_{\theta,t}|\mathbf{A}_{\theta,i} = a_{0,i}\right]\right), \ \forall i \in [1, u]$$

Proof. If $\forall i \neq j$: $\ \widetilde{\sigma}(\mathbf{A}_{\theta,i}, \mathbf{A}_{\theta,j}) = 0$, then $\widetilde{\beta}_{\theta,i,t} = \widetilde{\sigma}(\mathbf{L}_{\theta,t}, \mathbf{A}_{\theta,i})/\widetilde{\sigma}^2(\mathbf{A}_{\theta,i})$ from Corollary 1. Since each $\mathbf{A}_{\theta,i}$ can be viewed as the realization of a binary random variable with probability p_i, then $\sigma^2(\mathbf{A}_{\theta,i}) = p_i(1 - p_i)(a_{1,i} - a_{0,i})^2$ and $\sigma(\mathbf{L}_{\theta,t}, \mathbf{A}_{\theta,i}) = p_i(1 - p_i)(a_{1,i} - a_{0,i})(\mathbb{E}[\mathbf{L}_{\theta,t}|\mathbf{A}_{\theta,i}=a_{1,i}] - \mathbb{E}[\mathbf{L}_{\theta,t}|\mathbf{A}_{\theta,i} = a_{0,i}])$. Therefore, the Corollary follows immediately. ∎

The Corollaries above are valid if and only if $\mathbf{A}_{\theta,i}, \mathbf{A}_{\theta,j}$ are uncorrelated, that is $\widetilde{\sigma}(\mathbf{A}_{\theta,i}, \mathbf{A}_{\theta,j}) = 0$. As previously discussed, it is very unlikely to happen that $\widetilde{\sigma}(\mathbf{A}_{\theta,i}, \mathbf{A}_{\theta,j}) = 0$. However, the model matrix $\mathbf{A}_\theta$ is under the control of designers and can be constructed in such a way that the condition $\widetilde{\sigma}(\mathbf{A}_{\theta,i}, \mathbf{A}_{\theta,j}) = 0$ holds true. This is indeed the practical case when *balanced* inputs go through bijective functions (or, composition thereof, *e.g.* $S \circ \oplus$) and only first degree polynomials of the target intermediates are considered [5]. In particular, Corollary 1 implies that, under the conditions stated, the informative feedback provided by the $\widetilde{\beta}^*_{\theta,t}$-characteristic corresponds to CPA attacks. They are indeed equivalent, in case both $\boldsymbol{\ell}_{\theta,t}$ and $\mathbf{A}_{\theta,i}$ are standardized. Therefore, in this case, testing whether $\rho_{\theta,i,t} = 0$ is equivalent to test whether $\beta_{\theta,i,t} = 0$ and require the same sample size. It should be noted that standardization is a common pre-processing technique for the SA [18] to reduce problems which arise from round-off errors and does not affect CPA, being the Pearson's correlation coefficient invariant to linear transformations of the inputs. Finally, Corollary 2 implies that, if single-bit models are used under the conditions stated, then the informative feedback of the SA is equivalent to the informative feedback provided by the Kocher's original DPA attacks and similar considerations regarding hypothesis testing hold, as in the previous case.

4   Empirical Validation

In this section, we evaluate the relationship between CPA and the SA from an *empirical* point of view, by considering the information feedback of CPA and the SA, when applied to simulated high-dimensional leakage data as well as to simulated power traces of an ASIC implementation of PRESENT [21].

Validation Using Simulated Leakage Data. Simulated high dimensional leakage data were generated by drawing inputs X uniformly at random and using the PRESENT S-box input $v_{Sim,t_0}(X,k) = X \oplus k$ and S-box output $v_{Sim,t_1}(X,k) = v_{Sim,t_2}(X,k) = S(X \oplus k)$ as sensitive intermediate values. Table 1 summarizes the results of conducted experiments by the way of three exemplary simulated leakage functions L^{SboxIN}_{Sim,t_0}, $L^{SboxOUT}_{Sim,t_1}$ and $L^{SboxOUT}_{Sim,t_2}$. For the sake of analysis, the very same intermediate values were targeted, using the $g_{Sim,j}$ model functions as defined by Eq. (5). When applying the SA, two different subspaces were considered, namely the so-called linear subspace $\mathcal{F}_5$ (c.f. $\widetilde{\beta}^{Lin}_{Sim,j,t}$) and the so-called full subspace $\mathcal{F}_{16}$ (c.f. $\widetilde{\beta}^{Full}_{Sim,j,t}$). Finally, bold faced fonts were used to mark values significantly different from zero with a confidence level of $\gamma = 0.999$ [13,18] and the coefficient of determination $\widetilde{R}^2$ [6,18] was used to quantify the model fit. From Table 1, it can be observed that only the SA is able to precisely identify each contribution to the leakages, given that the selected subspace properly accounts all the existing dependent contributions contained in the leakage function, c.f. $\widetilde{\beta}^{Lin}_{Sim,j,t_1}$.

Table 1. Simulated Leakage Data

$g_{Sim,j}$	v_1	v_2	v_3	v_4	v_1v_2	v_1v_3	v_1v_4	v_2v_3	v_2v_4	v_3v_4	$v_1v_2v_3$	$v_1v_2v_4$	$v_1v_3v_4$	$v_2v_3v_4$	$v_1v_2v_3v_4$	$\widetilde{R}^2$
$L^{SboxIN}_{Sim,t_0} = 5v_1 + 2.5v_1v_2 + 2.5v_1v_3 + 2.5v_1v_4 + \mathcal{N}(0,0.001)$																
$\widetilde{\rho}_{Sim,j,t_0}$	0.944	0.126	0.124	0.137	0.696	0.696	0.697	0.134	0.149	0.155	0.553	0.554	0.557	0.139	0.445	0.459
$\widetilde{\beta}^{Full}_{Sim,j,t_0}$	**5.000**	0.000	0.000	0.000	**2.500**	**2.500**	**2.500**	−0.000	−0.000	−0.000	0.000	−0.000	0.000	0.000	−0.000	1.000
$\widetilde{\beta}^{Lin}_{Sim,j,t_0}$	**8.751**	**1.234**	**1.252**	**1.267**												0.946
$L^{SboxOUT}_{Sim,t_1} = v_1 + v_2 + v_3 + v_4 + \mathcal{N}(0,0.001)$																
$\widetilde{\rho}_{Sim,j,t_1}$	0.497	0.503	0.497	0.495	0.577	0.570	0.573	0.571	0.571	0.569	0.559	0.562	0.557	0.557	0.506	0.848
$\widetilde{\beta}^{Full}_{Sim,j,t_1}$	**1.000**	**1.000**	**1.000**	**1.000**	0.000	−0.000	0.000	−0.000	0.000	−0.000	0.000	−0.000	0.000	0.000	−0.000	1.000
$\widetilde{\beta}^{Lin}_{Sim,j,t_1}$	**1.000**	**1.000**	**1.000**	**1.000**												1.000
$L^{SboxOUT}_{Sim,t_2} = 5v_1 - 5v_2 + 10v_1v_2 + \mathcal{N}(0,0.001)$																
$\widetilde{\rho}_{Sim,j,t_2}$	0.895	0.000	−0.000	−0.010	0.775	0.510	0.515	−0.002	−0.010	−0.009	0.502	0.507	0.328	−0.013	0.337	0.228
$\widetilde{\beta}^{Full}_{Sim,j,t_2}$	**5.000**	**−5.000**	0.000	−0.000	**10.000**	−0.000	0.000	−0.000	0.000	−0.000	0.000	−0.000	0.000	0.000	−0.000	1.000
$\widetilde{\beta}^{Lin}_{Sim,j,t_2}$	**10.039**	0.040	−0.029	−0.020												0.801

In contrast, if the employed subspace does not properly account the leakage contributions, c.f. $\widetilde{\beta}^{\mathsf{Lin}}_{\mathsf{Sim},j,t_0}$ or $\widetilde{\beta}^{\mathsf{Lin}}_{\mathsf{Sim},j,t_2}$, the information feedback delivered by the SA is biased and it is unable to identify the origins of the leakage correctly, although a notably high measure of model fit. In this sense, a biased leakage characteristic provides designers with wrong indications about the origins of the leakage and the flaws there of. On the other hand, it can be noted that CPA can only loosely explain the leakages in the three cases, since it can only consider contributions individually as if they were independent, although they are necessarily dependent when high-dimensional models are considered. Yet, it might be possible to grasp individual contributions using CPA by studying how the obtained individual contributions relate to each other. However, while this strategy would certainly be successful for relatively simple leakages, *e.g.* like those typically happening during the synchronous update of registers [12], it would not definitely be an option to explain arbitrary complicated leakage functions in general.

Validation Using Simulated Power Traces. In order to map previous experiments to a concrete application scenario, the leakage of an ASIC implementation of PRESENT [21] was investigated. Please note that only the analysis of an *unprotected* implementation is reported, since the goal here is to evaluate how CPA and the SA can *support* designers in the identification of design flaws by detecting each contribution to the leakages, and *not* to pin-point the flaws of a *specific* protected implementation. The design was synthesized using *Synopsys DesignCompiler* version *G-2012.06-SP3* in a TSMC 150nm process. The circuit was simulated at 25 MHz using *Synopsys VCS* version *F-2011.12-SP1* and power estimations were performed using *Synopsys PrimeTime* version *F-2011.06-SP3* with a resolution of 100 ps, resulting in 400 points per clock cycle. The data path processes 4 bits per clock cycle and performs one round in 17 clock cycles. The first 16 clock cycles perform $\mathsf{S}_i(X_i \oplus k_i)$ of input nibble $i \in [0, 15]$, while the 17th perform the permutation layer. The investigation focused on the processing of the first nibble in the first round and only the power consumption *after* the register updates was considered in the analysis. Hence, only the asynchronous switching activity of the combinational path was considered to validate the presence of bit interactions, due to glitches and different propagation delay characteristics.

Table 2 summarizes the results of conducted experiments by the way of three exemplary cases, obtained by targeting the intermediate values of the S-box output over a clock cycle. It can be observed that, the information feedback provided by CPA and the SA at time t_0 is fairly equivalent, since they both point to the same leakage contributions, although CPA only loosely. A similar situation can be observed a couple of hundreds picoseconds later, at time t_1, where the issue persists only for the second contribution, but it occurs that the $\widetilde{R}^2$ is halved. In this case, the selected subspace generated from the S-box output is not able to completely capture all the contributions in the leakages. This fact can be explained by observing that the considered implementation, though serialized, actually moves all the nibbles every clock cycles through a shift register

Table 2. Simulated Power Traces

$g_{Ser,j}$	v_1	v_2	v_3	v_4	v_1v_2	v_1v_3	v_1v_4	v_2v_3	v_2v_4	v_3v_4	$v_1v_2v_3$	$v_1v_2v_4$	$v_1v_3v_4$	$v_2v_3v_4$	$v_1v_2v_3v_4$	$\tilde{R}^2$
$\tilde{\rho}_{Ser,j,t_0}$	0.732	0.632	0.104	−0.102	0.779	0.528	0.338	0.469	0.272	0.067	0.607	0.424	0.355	0.315	0.424	0.458
$\tilde{\beta}^{Full}_{Ser,j,t_0}$	0.358	0.316	−0.001	0.001	0.002	0.003	0.003	0.000	−0.001	0.002	−0.002	0.002	−0.006	−0.003	0.000	0.990
$\tilde{\beta}^{Lin}_{Ser,j,t_0}$	0.360	0.315	−0.001	0.000												0.989
$\tilde{\rho}_{Ser,j,t_1}$	−0.053	0.731	0.049	−0.056	0.380	0.022	−0.088	0.469	0.383	0.022	0.299	0.202	0.014	0.298	0.202	0.110
$\tilde{\beta}^{Full}_{Ser,j,t_1}$	−0.004	0.116	−0.000	−0.003	−0.001	0.003	0.008	0.002	−0.000	0.002	−0.001	0.004	−0.009	−0.006	0.000	0.535
$\tilde{\beta}^{Lin}_{Ser,j,t_1}$	−0.002	0.115	0.000	−0.002												0.535
$\tilde{\rho}_{Ser,j,t_2}$	0.413	0.426	0.345	0.139	0.642	0.281	0.307	0.472	0.399	0.324	0.605	0.428	0.280	0.494	0.428	0.430
$\tilde{\beta}^{Full}_{Ser,j,t_2}$	0.414	0.266	0.601	0.092	−0.099	−0.862	−0.003	−0.676	0.007	−0.337	1.119	−0.857	0.446	0.660	0.000	0.935
$\tilde{\beta}^{Lin}_{Ser,j,t_2}$	0.205	0.210	0.127	0.084												0.483

producing surrounding activity which is not modelled by the targeted S-box. Finally, at time t_3, which happens closely before the end of the combinational logic activity, the $\mathcal{F}_{16}$ subspace clearly shows several high-dimensional contributions, which would be quite difficult to appreciate from either CPA or the SA in the $\mathcal{F}_5$ subspace. The propagation of the leakage characteristic over a clock cycle towards higher-degree polynomials results fairly clear and understandable if considering that the analysed implementation is unprotected and the sampling resolution used for power estimations is fine enough to be able to measure the effects of different path delays and the glitches there of, occurring during the switching activity of the logic gates in the combinational path.

5   Conclusion

In this work, we investigated the relationship between CPA and the SA as candidate tools to identify the leakage contributions and *support* hardware designers in the correction of design flaws. First, we investigated the mathematical relationship of CPA and the SA and showed how in some specific, yet practically relevant cases, they convey the same information feedback to designers. Secondly, we analysed the results of CPA and the SA when applied to simulated data and power traces, and showed the importance of high-dimensional leakage models when it comes to pinpoint the leakage of bit interactions during the switching activity of the combinational logic path. In particular, we have shown that the SA is able to precisely quantify high-dimensional leakages given that an adequate approximation subspace is selected, whereas CPA can only loosely point to the leakage contributions of high-dimensional leakages, being inherently unable to consider dependent variables jointly. On the other hand, we have shown that the SA has some notable limitations over CPA in practice, since establishing whether a selected subspace is adequate to properly explain the leakage contributions, using the coefficient of determination as a measure of model fit, is not an easy task. In this respect, we have shown that it is not always straightforward to interpret the measure of model fit in practice, since a notably high fit generated a false positive, cf. Table 1, while a relatively low fit provided a false negative, cf. Table 2.

Additionally, contrary to CPA which has quite good convergence properties, the estimation effort of the SA grows with the size of the selected subspace, which is exponential in the size of the considered target bits. Hence, the analysis of large datapath designs with the SA might be much more laborious, than the provided exemplary analysis of a 4-bit datapath design. In this case, the use of stepwise regression as proposed in [24] can be of help to systematically evaluate different subspaces, but still liable to similar interpretation issues in the context of side-channel security verifications. To conclude, the constructive usage of CPA and the SA offers a crucial *support* to designers for the identification and correction of design flaws, but ultimately the engineering experience and expertise are still decisive to determine the success of the correction phase.

Acknowledgements. This work has been funded in part by the German Federal Ministry of Education and Research 163Y1200D (HIVE) and 01DP12037A (SMERCS). The authors would like to thank Oscar Guillen and Stefan Rass for their useful comments.

References

1. Barenghi, A., Bertoni, G., De Santis, F., Melzani, F.: On the Efficiency of Design Time Evaluation of the Resistance to Power Attacks. In: DSD, pp. 777–785. IEEE (2011)
2. Batina, L., Gierlichs, B., Prouff, E., Rivain, M., Standaert, F.X., Veyrat-Charvillon, N.: Mutual Information Analysis: A Comprehensive Study. J. Cryptology 24(2), 269–291 (2011)
3. Bhasin, S., Guilley, S., Heuser, A., Danger, J.L.: From Cryptography to Hardware: Analyzing and Protecting Embedded Xilinx BRAM for Cryptographic Applications. Journal of Cryptographic Engineering, 1–13 (2013)
4. Brier, E., Clavier, C., Olivier, F.: Correlation Power Analysis with a Leakage Model. In: Joye, M., Quisquater, J.-J. (eds.) CHES 2004. LNCS, vol. 3156, pp. 16–29. Springer, Heidelberg (2004)
5. Doget, J., Dabosville, G., Prouff, E.: A New Second Order Side Channel Attack Based on Linear Regression. Cryptology ePrint Archive, Report 2011/505 (2011)
6. Doget, J., Prouff, E., Rivain, M., Standaert, F.X.: Univariate Side Channel Attacks and Leakage Modeling. J. Cryptographic Engineering 1(2), 123–144 (2011)
7. Goodwill, G., Jun, B., Jaffe, J., Rohatgi, P.: A testing methodology for side-channel resistance validation. In: NIST Non-invasive Attack Testing Workshop (2011)
8. Heuser, A., Schindler, W., Stöttinger, M.: Revealing Side-channel Issues of Complex Circuits by Enhanced Leakage Models. In: Rosenstiel, W., Thiele, L. (eds.) DATE, pp. 1179–1184. IEEE (2012)
9. Kasper, M., Schindler, W., Stöttinger, M.: A Stochastic Method for Security Evaluation of Cryptographic FPGA Implementations. In: Bian, J., Zhou, Q., Athanas, P., Ha, Y., Zhao, K. (eds.) FPT, pp. 146–153. IEEE (2010)
10. Kocher, P.C., Jaffe, J., Jun, B.: Differential power analysis. In: Wiener, M. (ed.) CRYPTO 1999. LNCS, vol. 1666, pp. 388–397. Springer, Heidelberg (1999)
11. Lemke-Rust, K., Paar, C.: Analyzing Side Channel Leakage of Masked Implementations with Stochastic Methods. In: Biskup, J., López, J. (eds.) ESORICS 2007. LNCS, vol. 4734, pp. 454–468. Springer, Heidelberg (2007)

12. Mangard, S.: Hardware countermeasures against DPA – A statistical analysis of their effectiveness. In: Okamoto, T. (ed.) CT-RSA 2004. LNCS, vol. 2964, pp. 222–235. Springer, Heidelberg (2004)

13. Mangard, S., Oswald, E., Popp, T.: Power Analysis Attacks - Revealing the Secrets of Smart Cards. Springer (2007)

14. Mangard, S., Oswald, E., Standaert, F.X.: One for All - All for One: Unifying Standard Differential Power Analysis Attacks. IET 5(2), 100–110 (2011)

15. Mangard, S., Pramstaller, N., Oswald, E.: Successfully Attacking Masked AES Hardware Implementations. In: Rao, J.R., Sunar, B. (eds.) CHES 2005. LNCS, vol. 3659, pp. 157–171. Springer, Heidelberg (2005)

16. Mangard, S., Schramm, K.: Pinpointing the Side-Channel Leakage of Masked AES Hardware Implementations. In: Goubin, L., Matsui, M. (eds.) CHES 2006. LNCS, vol. 4249, pp. 76–90. Springer, Heidelberg (2006)

17. Mather, L., Oswald, E., Bandenburg, J., Wójcik, M.: A Comparison of Statistical Techniques for Detecting Side-Channel Information Leakage in Cryptographic Devices. Cryptology ePrint Archive, Report 2013/298 (2013)

18. Montgomery, D.C., Peck, E.A., Vining, G.G.: Introduction to Linear Regression Analysis. Wiley & Sons (2012)

19. Regazzoni, F.: A Design Flow and Evaluation Framework for DPA-resistant Embedded Systems. Ph.D. thesis, University of Lugano, Lugano, Switzerland (2010)

20. Renauld, M., Standaert, F.-X., Veyrat-Charvillon, N., Kamel, D., Flandre, D.: A Formal Study of Power Variability Issues and Side-Channel Attacks for Nanoscale Devices. In: Paterson, K.G. (ed.) EUROCRYPT 2011. LNCS, vol. 6632, pp. 109–128. Springer, Heidelberg (2011)

21. Rolfes, C., Poschmann, A., Leander, G., Paar, C.: Ultra-Lightweight Implementations for Smart Devices – Security for 1000 Gate Equivalents. In: Grimaud, G., Standaert, F.-X. (eds.) CARDIS 2008. LNCS, vol. 5189, pp. 89–103. Springer, Heidelberg (2008)

22. Schindler, W.: Advanced Stochastic Methods in Side Channel Analysis on Block Ciphers in the Presence of Masking. J. Math. Cryptology 2(3), 291–310 (2008)

23. Whitnall, C., Oswald, E.: Profiling DPA: Efficacy and Efficiency Trade-offs. Cryptology ePrint Archive, Report 2013/353 (2013)

24. Whitnall, C., Oswald, E., Standaert, F.X.: The Myth of Generic DPA ... And the Magic of Learning. IACR Cryptology ePrint Archive 2012, 256 (2012)

Multi-precision Squaring for Public-Key Cryptography on Embedded Microprocessors[*]

Hwajeong Seo[1], Zhe Liu[2], Jongseok Choi[1], and Howon Kim[1,**]

[1] Pusan National University,
School of Computer Science and Engineering,
San-30, Jangjeon-Dong, Geumjeong-Gu, Busan 609–735, Republic of Korea
{hwajeong,jschoi85,howonkim}@pusan.ac.kr
[2] University of Luxembourg,
Laboratory of Algorithmics, Cryptology and Security (LACS),
6, rue R. Coudenhove-Kalergi, L–1359 Luxembourg-Kirchberg, Luxembourg
zhe.liu@uni.lu

Abstract. In the paper, we revisit the "Lazy Doubling" (LD) method for multi-precision squaring, which reduces the number of addition operations by deferring the doubling process so that it can be performed on accumulated results. The original LD method has to employ carry-catcher registers to store carry values, which reduces the number of general purpose registers available for optimization of the implementation. Furthermore, the LD method adopts the idea of hybrid multiplication to separate the partial products into several product blocks, which prevents the doubling process to be conducted on fully accumulated intermediate results. To overcome these deficiencies of the LD method and improve the performance of multi-precision squaring, we propose a novel and flexible method named "Sliding Block Doubling" (SBD). The SBD method delays the doubling process till the very end of the partial-product computation and then doubles the result by simply shifting it one bit to the left. In order to further reduce the overhead of doubling, we also optimize the execution process for updating carry values and adopt the product-scanning method for efficient computation of the partial products. Our experimental results on an AVR ATmega128 processor show that the SBD method outperforms state-of-the-art implementations by a factor of between 3.5% and 4.4% for operands ranging from 128 bits to 192 bits.

1 Introduction

Multiple-precision arithmetic is a performance-critical component of public-key cryptographic algorithms such as RSA [12], elliptic curve cryptosystems [7,11]

[*] This work was supported by the Industrial Strategic Technology Development Program (No.10043907, Development of high performance IoT device and Open Platform with Intelligent Software) funded by the Ministry of Science, ICT & Future Planning (MSIF, Korea).
[**] Corresponding author.

G. Paul and S. Vaudenay (Eds.): INDOCRYPT 2013, LNCS 8250, pp. 227–243, 2013.
© Springer International Publishing Switzerland 2013

and pairing-based schemes [15]. This is in particular the case for multiplication and squaring due to the high computational cost of these operations. When implementing multi-precision integer arithmetic in software, the operands are usually represented by arrays of single-precision words, i.e. w-bit digits such that w matches the word-size of the target processor. Given two m-bit integers A and B, the computation of the product $A \cdot B$ requires to execute n^2 word-level (i.e. $w \times w$-bit) multiply instructions on the underlying processor, whereby n denotes the number of single-precision words, i.e. $n = \lceil m/w \rceil$. Consequently, multi-precision multiplication has a complexity of $\mathcal{O}(n^2)$ when implemented in software. The square A^2 of an n-word integer A can be computed much faster (up to almost 50%) than the product of two distinct integers. More precisely, when $A = B$, a large number of $w \times w$-bit partial products of the form $A[i] \cdot B[j]$ appear twice during the execution of a multi-precision multiplication since $A[i] \cdot B[j] = A[j] \cdot B[i]$. In particular, when squaring a large integer A, all partial products of the form $A[i] \cdot A[j]$ appear once for $i = j$ and twice for $i \neq j$ [3]. Optimized squaring algorithms compute all these "duplicates" only once and then shift them left by 1 bit to double them. In this way, the computational cost for squaring an n-word integer amounts to $(n^2 + n)/2$ single-precision multiplications, which is just slightly more than half of that needed to compute $A \cdot B$.

1.1 Previous Work

There exist a large number of multiplication and squaring methods that aim to improve the execution time by reducing the number of memory accesses and/or word-level arithmetic instructions. In the case of multi-precision multiplication, one of the seminal techniques is the school-book method [10], also called operand-scanning method. The school-book method can be easily implemented on embedded microprocessors using a high-level language like C. It loads the operands and generates the partial products in a row-wise fashion. An alternative way to implement multiplication is the so-called product-scanning method. This method computes the partial products column by column and does not need to reload intermediate results [2]. The hybrid method combines the advantageous features of operand-scanning and product-scanning [4]. By adjusting the row and column width, the number of operand accesses and result updates are reduced. This method is particularly efficient on a microprocessor equipped with a large number of general purpose registers. At CHES 2011, the operand-caching method, which reduces the number of load operations by caching the operands, was presented [6]. Later, based on the operand-caching method, Seo and Kim [14] proposed the consecutive-operand-caching method, which is characterized by a continuous operand caching process.

All these multiplication methods can be straightforwardly applied to squaring. However, as mentioned before, it is not efficient to do so since computing all partial products and loading the words of both operands is not necessary for squaring. For this reason, specialized squaring methods have been studied in the literature. One of the first squaring methods, based on the operand-scanning technique, was developed for hardware implementation [5].

Unfortunately, the squaring technique from [5] is not really suited for software implementation on resource-constrained devices. In 2007, the so-called carry-catcher squaring method was presented, which aims to reduce the propagation of generated carry values up to the most significant word by introducing storage for saving carry values [13]. In 2012, the Lazy Doubling (LD) method, the fastest squaring technique so far, was proposed in [8]. The basic idea is that the partial products which need to be considered twice are doubled "in one pass" after they have been collected to the accumulator registers at the end of each column computation.

1.2   Our Contributions

This paper presents an efficient implementation of multi-precision squaring that achieves record-setting execution times on 8-bit AVR-based processors. Our optimized squaring technique can be used to accelerate the multi-precision arithmetic of public-key schemes, e.g. the modular squaring operation of RSA, squaring in prime fields operation for ECC. The research contribution of this paper is two-fold:

- *Novel sliding block doubling method for efficient implementation of multi-precision squaring on embedded processors.* We present a novel and flexible implementation methodology for multi-precision squaring named *Sliding Block Doubling (SDB)*, which yields high performance on a range of embedded platforms (e.g. 8-bit, 16-bit, 32-bit processors). The proposed method is inspired by the well-known LD method of Lee et al. [8] and also influenced by the state-of-art techniques for implementing multi-precision multiplication on micro-controllers, i.e. the operand-caching method [6] and consecutive operand-caching method [14]. Specifically, we make full use of the *lazy doubling* feature and delay the doubling process until the very end of the product computation and then conduct it by a simple 1-bit left shift. We also aim to reduce the overhead that may be introduced when using traditional squaring or the LD method. A third optimization is to calculate the partial products of each block by using the efficient product-scanning method. We also provide a simple formula to estimate the computational cost of our proposed SBD method depending on the operand-length.
- *New Speed record results achieved on 8-bit AVR embedded platforms.* In order to confirm the theoretical performance gain, we realized our squaring method on an 8-bit AVR embedded platform. We took the squaring of a 160-bit operand on an 8-bit ATmega128 as concrete examples for our experiments. Our results show that the SBD method takes only 1,456 clock cycles to square a 160-bit operand. This result represents the current speed record for multi-precision squaring on 8-bit platforms. When compared with the best previous results, our implementation achieves a performance enhancement by a factor of 3.5% to 4.4% for operands ranging from 128 to 192 bits.

The remainder of this paper is organized as follows. In Section 2, we recap the different approaches for implementing multi-precision multiplication and squaring. In Section 3, we present the new sliding block doubling method and analyse its computational complexity. In Section 4, we evaluate the performance of the proposed method in terms of clock cycles and compare with related work. Finally, Section 5 concludes the paper.

2 Multi-precision Multiplication and Squaring

In this section, we explore multiplication and squaring methods from the basic method (e.g. school-book method) to sophisticated method (e.g. operand caching multiplication and lazy doubling method). Then, we discuss the main differences of concrete implementation between multiplication and squaring to project considerations for efficient implementation on embedded processors.

2.1 Multi-precision Multiplication Techniques

In this section, we introduce various multi-precision multiplication techniques, including operand scanning method, product scanning method, hybrid scanning method, operand caching method as well as consecutive operand caching method. Each method has unique feature for reducing the number of load and store instructions and arithmetic operations.

Before describing the multi-precision multiplication method into details, we first define the following notations. Let A and B be two operands with a length of m-bit that are represented by multiple-word arrays. Each operand is written as follows: $A = (A[n-1], A[n-2], \ldots, A[1], A[0])$ and $B = (B[n-1], B[n-2], \ldots, B[1], B[0])$, whereby $n = \lceil m/w \rceil$, and w is the word size. The product of multiplication $A \cdot B$ is twice the length of A and can be represented by $C = (C[2n-1], C[2n-2], \ldots, C[1], C[0])$.

For clarity, we describe the method using a multiplication structure and rhombus form. As shown in Figure 1, each point represents a word-level multiplication, i.e. $A[i] \times B[j]$. The rightmost corner of the rhombus represents the lowest index $(i, j = 0)$, meanwhile the leftmost represents corner with highest index $(i, j = n - 1)$. The lowermost side represents result index $C[k]$, which ranges from the rightmost corner $(k = 0)$ to the leftmost corner $(k = 2n - 1)$.

Operand Scanning Method. Figure 1. (a) shows the operand scanning which consists of two parts, i.e., inner and outer loops. In the inner loop, operand $A[i]$ holds a value and computes the partial product by multipling all the multiplicands $B[j]$ $(j = 0 \ldots n - 1)$. While in the outer loop, the index of operand $A[i]$ increases by a word-size and then the inner loop is executed.

Product Scanning Method. Figure 1. (b) shows the product scanning method which computes all partial products in the same column by multiplication and addition [2]. Since each partial product in the column is computed and then accumulated, registers are not needed for intermediate results. The results are stored once, and the stored results are not reloaded since all computations have already been completed.

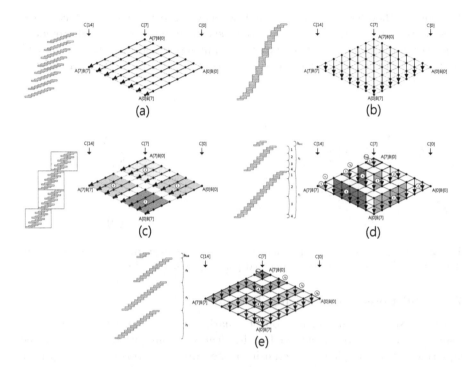

Fig. 1. Multi-precision multiplication techniques. (a) Operand scanning method [10]. (b) Product scanning method [2]. (c) Hybrid scanning method [4]. (d) Operand caching method [6]. (e) Consecutive operand caching method [14].

Hybrid Scanning Method. Figure 1. (c) shows the hybrid scanning method which combines both of the advantages of operand scanning and product scanning. Multiplication is performed on a block scale using product scanning. The number of rows within the block is defined as d, and inner block partial products follow the operand scanning rule. Therefore, this method reduces the number of load instructions by sharing the operands within the block [4].

Operand Caching Method. Figure 1. (d) shows the operand caching method which follows the product scanning method, but it divides the calculation into several row sections [6]. By reordering the sequence of inner and outer row sections, previously loaded operands in working registers are reused for the next partial products. A few store instructions are added, but the number of required load instructions is reduced. The number of row section is given by $r = \lfloor n/e \rfloor$, and e denotes the number of words used to cache digit in the operand.

Consecutive Operand Caching Method. Figure 1. (e) shows the consecutive operand caching which is based on characteristic of operand-caching method.

Previous method has to reload operands whenever a row is changed which generates unnecessary overheads. To avoid these shortcomings, this method provides a contact point among rows that share the common operands for partial products. As a result of this, one side of operands is continuously maintained in registers and used [14].

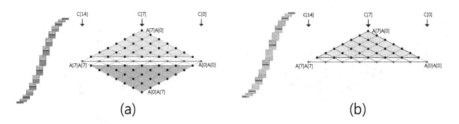

(a)   (b)

Fig. 2. Multi-precision squaring structure. (a) Before removing duplicated partial product results. (b) After removing duplicated partial product results.

2.2 Multi-precision Squaring Techniques

A typical software implementation of squaring method can be realized either using one of the above mentioned multiplication techniques or the specialized squaring method. Implementation using a specialized squaring method may have two advantages than simply using multiplication method for squaring as shown in described in Figure 2. Firstly, only one operand (A) is used for squaring computation, thus, the number of operand load is reduced to half times of multiplication, and many registers used for operand holding previously become idle status and can be used for caching intermediate results or other values. Second, there are duplicated partial products exist. In Figure 2. (a), the squaring structure consists of three parts including red dotted middle part, light and dark gray triangle parts. The red part is multiplying a same operand, which is computed once. The other parts including light and dark gray parts generate same partial product results. For this reason, these parts are multiplied once and added twice to intermediate results. This computation generates same results, we expected. After removing duplicated partial product results, we can describe the squaring structure as a triangular form in Figure 2. (b).

Yang-Hseih-Lair Method. Figure 4. case (a) describes Yang et al's method [5]. This squaring method is intended for hardware machine not for software implementation. The following is computation process in detail. First, duplicated partial products are computed using operand scanning. And then the intermediate results are doubled. Lastly, remaining partial products are computed. This method is not favorable for software implementation because the number of general purpose register is not enough to store all operands, carry catcher value[1] and

---

[1] This method is not introduced when this paper is published. To implement operand scanning method in software form, carry catcher method should be considered.

intermediate result during partial product computations using operand scanning. Furthermore, re-loading and re-storing the intermediate results for doubling conduct many memory accesses. Thus, straight-forward implementation of squaring method for hardware is not recommended for software implementation.

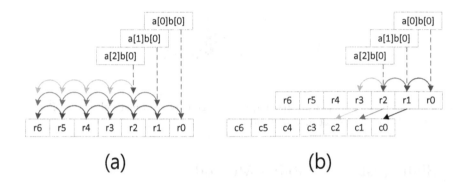

Fig. 3. Carry computation techniques. (a) Carry-propagation. (b) Carry-catcher.

Carry Catcher Method. Prime field multiplication or squaring consists of a number of partial products. When we compute partial products in ascending order, intermediate results generate carry values, accumulating the partial product results. Traditionally, carry values spread to end of intermediate results, which is described in Figure 3. (a). This case continuously updates result registers($r_6 \sim r_0$) so addition arithmetic is used in many times. To reduce the overheads, carry-catcher method, storing carry values to additional registers($c_6 \sim c_0$), was presented in [13] and is described in Figure 3. (b). The carry catching registers are updated at the end of computation at once. In Figure 4. (b), carry catcher based squaring was introduced by [13]. This method follows hybrid-scanning and doubles partial product results before they are added to results. This method is inefficient because all products should be doubled.

Lazy Doubling Method. In Figure 4. (d), efficient doubling method named lazy-doubling is described [8]. This method also follows hybrid scanning structure. The inner loop is computed in a operand scanning way, and then carry catcher method is used for removing consecutive carry updates. The strong feature of this method is doubling process which is delayed to end of inner structure and then computed. This method reduces number of arithmetic operations by conducting doubling computations on accumulated intermediate results. This technique significantly reduces a number of doubling process to one doubling process.

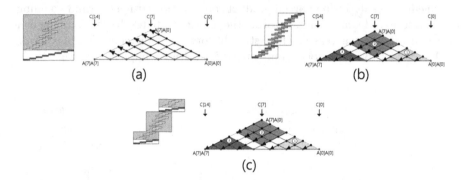

Fig. 4. Multi-precision squaring techniques. (a) Yang et al.'s method [5]. (b) Scott et al.'s method [13]. (c) Lee et al.'s method [8].

3   Sliding Block Doubling Method

Most of the previous squaring methods either employ the normally used operand-scanning method or directly follow the idea of hybrid-scanning when implementing the multi-precision squaring on resource constraint processors. However, these implementations may have two disadvantages, namely (1) lacking of optimal usage of working registers, and (2) inefficiently dealing with the carry bit produced when adding two partial products. In order to overcome the above shortcomings, we proposed a novel technique for efficient implementation of multi-precision squaring on embedded platforms, named "sliding block doubling" (SBD). On one hand, SBD method computes doubling using "1-bit left shifting" operation at the end of duplicated partial product computation, which accumulates all partial product results with only consuming few arithmetic operations. On the other hand, contrary to previously known solutions, SBD method adopts product-scanning method to compute duplicated product parts (see the black dots in Figure 5). After then the intermediate results are doubled, and added into the final results. The detailed process of proposed SBD method is described as follows.

Product-Scanning for Upper Part of Triangular Form. We adopt product-scanning method to execute partial products from the least significant part up to most significant part. As shown in Figure 5, the first black dot represents an execution of operation $A[2] \times A[1]$, after then the remaining black dots in the Figure 5 are computed. As mentioned before, we stored the intermediate results into memory rather than working registers similar as the works did in [6,14] for multiplication.

Sliding Block Doubling of Duplicated Products. After finishing the first step, we can then double the intermediate results accumulated from previous process by simply left-shifting 1-bit. This efficient operation is also the main difference between our SBD method and previous works in [13,8], namely, comparing to their works, we significantly saved the cost of doubling computation. Specially, both of Scott et al.'s [13] and Lee et al.'s [8] methods compute the doubling process in the middle of squaring process, while proposed SBD cunningly delayed this operation to the very end of duplicated partial products, in this way, we can double the accumulated intermediate results altogether. Compared to [5], our method separates the whole doubling process into several sub-doubling blocks due to limited number of working registers.

Remaining Partial Products for Middle Line of Triangular Form. The first two steps are used to calculate the blocks for the case of $A_i \times A_j$ where $i \neq j$, in which case each block is required to be computed twice. For the case of $i = j$, represented by the read dots in Figure 5, the multiplication is only computed once. And then the computed intermediate results are added to final results.

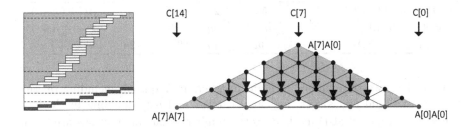

Fig. 5. Sliding-block-doubling squaring method

3.1   Computation Complexity

This section mainly discusses the computation complexity of SBD method, we took 8-bit AVR platform as an example to show the total number of operations. However, it is worth to note that similar works can also be extended to 16-bit MSP, 32-bit ARM platforms. On an AVR platform, each `mul`, `load` and `store` instruction consumes 2 clock cycles, while `add` and `shift` only needs 1 clock cycle.

In upper part of triangular form, n times `load` instructions are required for loading operands to registers as we load the operand byte by byte. After all operands are loaded to registers, each computation of partial product using product-scanning method to execute an operation of $(t, u, v) = (t, u, v) + A_i \cdot A_j$, whereby (t, u, v) represents three accumulator registers and A_i, A_j are the two registers allocated for operands. This operation requires one `mul` and three `add` (or `adc`) instructions, consuming five clock cycles altogether. An upper part of squaring operation needs to execute $\frac{n^2-2n}{2}$ iterations, therefore, the whole clock cycles are $\frac{5(n^2-2n)}{2}$. The results are needed to first store the intermediate result into memory. This process consumes $2n$ times of `store` and $4n$ clock cycles.

In sliding block doubling part, intermediate results are reloaded to registers which consumes $2n$ times of `load`, and thus costs $4n$ clock cycles. Then the full intermediate results are left-shifted by 1-bit. This shift operation is conducted by size of intermediate results, and roughly needs $2n$ clock cycles for `shift` operation.

In remaining partial products for middle line. Each block executes an operation of $A_i \cdot A_i$, costing 5 clock cycles and the operations are iterated by n times, therefore, $5n$ clock cycles are needed. During middle line computations, we catch carry values into registers and compute products using product-scanning. The values are updated after all computations and this is conducted by size of intermediate results, this process needs $2n$ clock cycles. After all computations, final results are stored to memory by $2n$ and it needs $4n$ clock cycles.

Table 1. Comparison of computation complexity with previous works

Algorithms	mul	load	store	add	shift	total
Scott et al. [13] (CC)	$\frac{n^2}{2}$	$5n$	$2n$	$\frac{6n^2}{2}$	-	$\frac{9}{2}n^2 + 6n + 5$
Lee et al. [8] (LD)	$\frac{n^2}{2}$	$\frac{15}{4}n - 26$	$2n$	$\frac{3n^2}{2}$	-	$3n^2 + \frac{54}{4}n + 55$
Our method (SBD)	$\frac{n^2}{2}$	$3n$	$4n$	$\frac{3n^2+4n}{2}$	$2n$	$\left(\frac{5n^2+36n}{2}\right) \times \alpha$

Table 1 shows the number of main instructions required, including of `mul`, `load`, `store`, `add` and `shift`, for carry catcher and lazy doubling methods as well as the proposed SBD method. Total number of `mul` instructions are $\frac{n^2}{2}$ including upper and middle part of triangular form. The memory-access operations are categorized into `load` and `store`. For `load` instruction, loading operands and intermediate results are iterated by $3n$ times. For `store` instruction, intermediate and final results are stored by $4n$ times. The addition instructions are used for accumulation and carry catcher update by $\frac{3n^2+4n}{2}$ times. Finally `shift` operations are executed by size of intermediate results to double duplicated results.

Besides of the above analyzed cost, proposed SBD method also have to pay additional overheads, e.g. integration of the blocks, setting or resetting working registers. For the sake of simplicity, we called the additional overheads "self-adjusting factor", represented by the symbol α. The concrete value of α depends on the block sizes adopted for implementation. To order to give an accurate estimation of the value α, we compared the real implementation cost C_I with the estimated results C_E obtained from Table 1, and then, computed the ratio as $\alpha = C_I/C_E$, we lists the value in Table 2.

Practical Implementation. We separate the whole process into three parts but for practical implementation we should combine the second and third part.

Table 2. The value of self-adjusting factor α

Operand length	C_I	C_E	$C_I - C_E$	α
128-bit	$1,003$	928	75	1.08
160-bit	$1,456$	$1,360$	96	1.07
192-bit	$2,014$	$1,872$	142	1.07

When we double the intermediate results, all results should be loaded into registers. After computation, results are stored into memory. To compute middle line of triangular form, intermediate results should be re-loaded. This costs lots of `load` and `store` operations. To overcome this drawback, we combine both processes and then compute part of combined process. The whole combined process is not computed at once due to limited number of registers so we separate combined process depending on available registers. Separated parts are computed in this order. First, intermediate results are loaded into registers. Second, the results are 1-bit left shifted. Third, middle line of triangular form is computed and then updated to intermediate results. This process is continued to the last separated block which is most significant byte. The detailed block structure example on 128-, 160-, 192-bit is available in Appendix. B. Furthermore during middle line computations, we can re-use operand registers for carry-catcher registers. For example, $A[0] \times A[0]$ product result is accumulated to intermediate results. During the process carry bit is generated. To catch the carry bit, we re-used a register storing operand $A[0]$.

4 Experimental Results

In this section, we evaluate the performance of proposed SBD method in term of execution time on 8-bit embedded platforms and then compare our results with related works.

4.1 Evaluation on 8-bit Platform ATmega128

We implemented the method on 8-bit AVR processor ATmega128 which is widely used in MICAz mote, and then simulated our implementation over AVR Studio 6.0. Normally, an ATmega128 processor runs at a frequency of 7.3728 MHz. It has a 128 KB EEPROM chip and 4 KB RAM chip [1]. The ATmega128 processor also supports a RISC architecture with 32 registers, among which 6 registers (R26 - R31) serve as the special pointers for indirect addressing. The remaining 26 registers are available for arithmetic operations. One arithmetic instruction incurs one clock cycle, and memory addressing (e.g. `load`, `store`) or 8-bit multiplication (e.g. `mul`) incurs two processing cycles [1]. We used four registers for the operand and result pointers, two registers for storing the result of multiplication, three registers for accumulating the intermediate result, one register for holding the zero value and the remaining registers for caching operands.

Table 3. Instruction counts for a 160-bit multiplication and squaring on the ATmega128 (excluding PUSH/POP), Unrolled the Loop (U-L)

Method	load	store	mul	add	shift	others	total
Multiplication							
Operand Scanning	820	440	400	1,600	-	466	5,427
Product Scanning [2]	800	40	400	1,200	-	161	3,957
Gura et al. [4]	200	40	400	1,250	-	311	2,904
Uhsadel et al. [16]	238	40	400	986	-	539	2,881
Liu et al. [9]	200	40	400	1194	-	391	2,865
Zhang et al. [17]	200	40	400	1092	-	473	2,845
Scott et al. [13] (U-L)	200	40	400	1263	-	108	2,651
Hutter et al. [6] (U-L)	80	60	400	1,240	-	70	2,395
Seo et al. [14] (U-L)	70	60	400	1,240	-	56	2,356
Squaring							
Yang et al. [5]	468	280	210	909	40	244	3,009
Scott et al. [13] (CC)	100	40	210	1,265	-	100	2,065
Lee et al. [8](LD)	51	40	210	804	-	103	1,509
Our method (SBD)	58	81	210	671	42	45	**1,456**

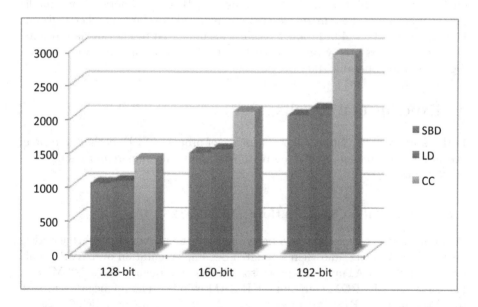

Fig. 6. Performance comparison in different operand size

Table 3 lists the performance comparison of the total clock cycles in case of 160-bit squaring. There are two main categories of methods, namely, the multi-precision multiplication and squaring methods. The multiplication methods are inefficient for squaring, since it does not take the advantage of main feature of squaring which can avoid duplicated partial products, exploiting doubling

Table 4. Performance enhancement of ATmega128 for squaring operation, our: proposed, LD: lazy-doubling, CC: carry-catcher

Bit	Clock Cycle			Performance Enhancement(%)	
	Our	LD	CC	$(1 - \frac{Our}{LD}) \times 100$	$(1 - \frac{Our}{CC}) \times 100$
128	**1,003**	1,039	1,365	3.465	26.520
160	**1,456**	1,509	2,065	3.512	29.492
192	**2,014**	2,107	2,909	4.414	30.767

operation. For this reason, when using the multiplication methods to conduct partial products, the efficiency is quite low.

In case of squaring, we compared with the three widely used methods. First, we compared with Yang et al.'s method. As mentioned before, this method is not suitable for software implementation. It conducts the multiplication with operand scanning method which requires lots of registers for maintaining intermediate results and carry catcher values. The registers in need are about $3n$. If number of register is lower than $3n$, performance is sharply plunged due to frequent memory access to restore the values.[2] Second, we compared with the carry catcher method. It enhances performance by computing partial products within specific inner multiplication blocks. Carry propagation is effectively reduced but doubling method is conducted to all duplicated partial products which computes lots of addition operations. Third, we compared with the best known previous result, namely LD method. LD method eliminates many number of doubling process by accumulating the intermediate results and then computing doubling at the end of inner multiplication blocks. However, this method does not fully accumulate intermediate results before doubling process. Compared to the three methods, SBD method is fully computing partial products using product-scanning and then shifting the intermediate results, which compute doubling with single 1-bit left shift operation, adding remaining partial products to intermediate results. Even though we conduct more number of memory accesses for load and store intermediate results, we efficiently compute doubling process and partial products, which draw higher performance enhancement by reducing arithmetic operations.

Table 4 and Figure 6 give the comparison details of these methods. The proposed SBD method only requires 1,456 clock cycles to accomplish an squaring operation of 160-bit, which is setting a new speed record for multi-precision squaring operation on 8-bit AVR micro-controllers. As a result of this, compared to previous best known result, lazy doubling, SBD method shows performance improvement by about 3.5 ~ 4.4%. It is also worth to notice that the performance enhancement of SBD appears in each operand length (128-bit to 192-bit), and the enhancement ratio shows an increased tendency with the increasing of operand length.

---

[2] Software implementation of Yang et al. is not reported in [5]. For pair comparison, we implemented this method following the their main idea and using carry-catcher method as well.

5 Conclusion

This paper presented a new technique to implement multi-precision squaring on resource-constrained embedded processors, named "sliding block method" (SBD). As the name suggests, the SBD method delays the doubling process to the very end of the partial-product computations so that it can be performed "in one pass" by a 1-bit left shift. In order to achieve high performance, we also optimized the usage of general purpose registers and reduced the overhead during the computation of each block by combining the advantages of the operand caching technique and lazy doubling method. We then theoretically analyzed the computational complexity of the proposed SBD method and provided a method to estimate the performance for arbitrary-length operands. To validate the theoretical results, we implemented the SBD method on an 8-bit AVR microcontroller for operands of different length. Our results show that the SBD method requires only 1456 clock cycles to perform a 160-bit squaring, which sets a new speed record for multi-precision squaring on an 8-bit platform. The proposed method outperforms the best previous results in the literature by a factor of between 3.5% and 4.4%, depending on the concrete bit-length. Moreover, the SBD method can be easily adapted to other embedded platforms with minor modifications, e.g. 16-bit MSP and 32-bit ARM processors. As a future work, we will port our method to various other platforms and show the impact of SBD squaring in real public-key algorithms, including RSA, ECC and pairing-based schemes.

References

1. Atmel Corporation. ATmega128(L) Datasheet (Rev. 2467O–AVR–10/06) (October 2006), http://www.atmel.com/dyn/resources/prod_documents/doc2467.pdf
2. Comba, P.G.: Exponentiation cryptosystems on the IBM PC. IBM Systems Journal 29(4), 526–538 (1990)
3. Großschädl, J., Avanzi, R.M., Savaş, E., Tillich, S.: Energy-efficient software implementation of long integer modular arithmetic. In: Rao, J.R., Sunar, B. (eds.) CHES 2005. LNCS, vol. 3659, pp. 75–90. Springer, Heidelberg (2005)
4. Gura, N., Patel, A., Wander, A., Eberle, H., Shantz, S.C.: Comparing elliptic curve cryptography and RSA on 8-bit cPUs. In: Joye, M., Quisquater, J.-J. (eds.) CHES 2004. LNCS, vol. 3156, pp. 119–132. Springer, Heidelberg (2004)
5. Hsieh, P.Y., Laih, C.S.: An exception handling model and its application to the multiple-precision integer library. Ph.D. Thesis, Master of Science, Japan (December 2003)
6. Hutter, M., Wenger, E.: Fast multi-precision multiplication for public-key cryptography on embedded microprocessors. In: Preneel, B., Takagi, T. (eds.) CHES 2011. LNCS, vol. 6917, pp. 459–474. Springer, Heidelberg (2011)
7. Koblitz, N.I.: Elliptic curve cryptosystems. Mathematics of Computation 48(177), 203–209 (1987)
8. Lee, Y., Kim, I.-H., Park, Y.: Improved multi-precision squaring for low-end RISC microcontrollers. Journal of Systems and Software 86(1), 60–71 (2013)

9. Liu, Z., Großschädl, J., Kizhvatov, I.: Efficient and side-channel resistant RSA implementation for 8-bit AVR microcontrollers. In: Proceedings of the 1st International Workshop on the Security of the Internet of Things (SECIOT 2010). IEEE Computer Society Press (2010), `https://www.nics.uma.es/seciot10/files/pdf/liu_seciot10_paper.pdf`

10. Menezes, A.J., Van Oorschot, P.C., Vanstone, S.A.: Handbook of Applied Cryptography. CRC Press Series on Discrete Mathematics and Its Applications. CRC Press (1996)

11. Miller, V.S.: Use of elliptic curves in cryptography. In: Williams, H.C. (ed.) CRYPTO 1985. LNCS, vol. 218, pp. 417–426. Springer, Heidelberg (1986)

12. Rivest, R.L., Shamir, A., Adleman, L.M.: A method for obtaining digital signatures and public key cryptosystems. Communications of the ACM 21(2), 120–126 (1978)

13. Scott, M., Szczechowiak, P.: Optimizing multiprecision multiplication for public key cryptography. Cryptology ePrint Archive, Report 2007/299 (2007) Available for download, `http://eprint.iacr.org`

14. Seo, H., Kim, H.: Multi-precision multiplication for public-key cryptography on embedded microprocessors. In: Lee, D.H., Yung, M. (eds.) WISA 2012. LNCS, vol. 7690, pp. 55–67. Springer, Heidelberg (2012)

15. Shamir, A.: Identity-based cryptosystems and signature schemes. In: Blakely, G.R., Chaum, D. (eds.) CRYPTO 1984. LNCS, vol. 196, pp. 47–53. Springer, Heidelberg (1985)

16. Uhsadel, L., Poschmann, A., Paar, C.: Enabling full-size public-key algorithms on 8-bit sensor nodes. In: Stajano, F., Meadows, C., Capkun, S., Moore, T. (eds.) ESAS 2007. LNCS, vol. 4572, pp. 73–86. Springer, Heidelberg (2007)

17. Zhang, Y., Großschädl, J.: Efficient prime-field arithmetic for elliptic curve cryptography on wireless sensor nodes. In: Proceedings of the 1st International Conference on Computer Science and Network Technology, ICCSNT 2011, pp. 459–466. IEEE (2011)

Appendix A. Algorithm for Sliding-Block-Doubling Squaring Method

Input: word size n, parameter e, where $n \geq e$, Integers $a \in [0, n), c \in [0, 2n)$.
Output: $c = a^2$.
$R_A[n-1, ..., 0] \leftarrow M_A[n-1, ..., 0]$.
$ACC \leftarrow 0$.
for $i = 1$ **to** $n - 1$
    for $j = 1$ **to** $\lceil \frac{i}{2} \rceil$
        $ACC \leftarrow ACC + R_A[i] \times R_A[j]$.
    end for
    $M_C[i] \leftarrow ACC_0$.
    $(ACC_1, ACC_0) \leftarrow (ACC_2, ACC_1)$.
    $ACC_2 \leftarrow 0$.
end for
for $i = n$ **to** $2n - 1$
    for $j = 2n - 1$ **to** $\lceil \frac{i}{2} \rceil$
        $ACC \leftarrow ACC + R_A[i] \times R_A[j]$.
    end for
    $M_C[i] \leftarrow ACC_0$.
    $(ACC_1, ACC_0) \leftarrow (ACC_2, ACC_1)$.
    $ACC_2 \leftarrow 0$.
end for
$ACC \leftarrow 0$.
for $i = 0$ **to** $n - 1$
    if $i \% d == 0$
        $R_C[i + d, ..., i] \leftarrow M_C[i + d, ..., i]$.
        $R_C[i + d, ..., i] \leftarrow R_C[i + d, ..., i] \ll 1$.
    end if
    $ACC \leftarrow ACC + R_A[i] \times R_A[i]$.
    $M_C[i] \leftarrow ACC_0$.
    $M_C[i + 1] \leftarrow ACC_1$.
end for

Appendix B. Example: Sliding-Block-Doubling Structure for 128-, 160-, 192-bit Case

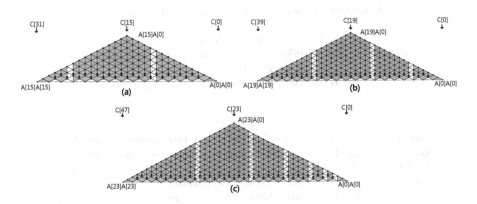

Fig. 7. Practical implementation of proposed method in case of, (a) 128-bit, (b) 160-bit, (c) 192-bit

8/16/32 Shades of Elliptic Curve Cryptography on Embedded Processors

Erich Wenger, Thomas Unterluggauer, and Mario Werner

Graz University of Technology
Institute for Applied Information Processing and Communications
Erich.Wenger@iaik.tugraz.at,
{T.Unterluggauer,M.Werner}@student.tugraz.at

Abstract. The decision regarding the best suitable microprocessor for a given task is one of the most challenging assignments a hardware designer has to face. In this paper, we make a comparison of cycle-accurate VHDL clones of the 8-bit Atmel ATmega, the 16-bit Texas Instruments MSP430, and the 32-bit ARM Cortex-M0+. We investigate their runtime, chip area, power, and energy characteristics regarding Elliptic Curve Cryptography (ECC), one of the practically most resource-critical public-key cryptography systems. If ECC is not implemented with greatest care, its implementation can lead to excruciating runtimes or enable practical side-channel attacks. Considering those important requirements, we present a constant runtime, side-channel protected, and resource saving scalar multiplication algorithm. To tap the full potential of all three microprocessors, we perform assembly optimizations and add carefully crafted instruction-set extensions. To the best of our knowledge, this is the first thorough software and hardware comparison of these three embedded microprocessors.

Keywords: ATmega, MSP430, Cortex-M0+, Elliptic Curve Cryptography, Instruction-Set Extension, Software and Hardware Evaluation.

1 Introduction

Motivation. It is a well-known fact that embedded microprocessors play a significant role within a huge number of consumer, industrial, commercial and military applications. Microprocessors are being produced and deployed in huge numbers and are the beating heart of, e.g., smart cards, wireless sensor networks, or in future even RFID tags. Those applications require solutions that are highly optimized in order to be cheap, energy-efficient, and/or power-efficient, while being versatile and delivering the necessary performance.

To meet all these requirements, the high demands of security and cryptography have too often been disregarded. Especially public-key cryptography needs to be implemented with great care in order to achieve small, performant, and energy-saving solutions. Since RSA and ElGamal based crypto systems simply require too much memory, Elliptic Curve Cryptography (ECC) seems to be the

G. Paul and S. Vaudenay (Eds.): INDOCRYPT 2013, LNCS 8250, pp. 244–261, 2013.

best choice. However, ECC is a highly demanding challenge within most applications, and therefore the decision regarding the most suitable microprocessor usually is the most discussed topic within a hardware manufacturer. To evaluate the performance of ECC in software and in hardware, we built VHDL clones of three of the most popular microprocessors.

Related Work. The research community recognized the challenge of efficiently implementing ECC. In this context, we want to cite [19,20,22,33,42,45], just to name a few. Those papers presented and used a lot of different approaches to improve the performance of ECC on embedded microprocessors. Unfortunately, in many papers, the authors sacrifice practical crucial properties, e.g., the memory footprint or practical side-channel security threats for the sake of fastest runtimes. Other characteristics like power and energy consumptions are also often neglected. Szczechowiak et al [42] is a welcome exception as they presented measured power values for the ATmega and the MSP430 microprocessor. However, how comparable are those values as both processors were manufactured in different ASIC technologies by different vendors? A fair comparison of the investigated microprocessors must utilize a common design flow, common technologies, and practically secured software implementations.

Our Contribution. In this paper, we perform a systematic and comprehensive approach to evaluate ECC on cycle-accurate VHDL clones[1] of three of the most popular microprocessors: the 8-bit Atmel AVR ATmega, the 16-bit Texas Instruments MSP430, and the 32-bit ARM Cortex-M0+. Our contribution is composed of the following points:

- We derive a point multiplication methodology from previous work which is light-weight and secure against (most) side-channel attacks. The resulting algorithm can be applied to any future embedded designs.
- All our software implementations for the three processors are secure against side-channel attacks and highly optimized using state-of-the-art multi-precision integer multiplication techniques. Runtime, chip area, power, and energy results are given for four different standardized elliptic curves (secp160-192-224-256r1).
- We built three cycle-accurate clones of three of the most popular microprocessors and evaluate them in an 130 nm ASIC manufacturing process. The hardware models are based on publicly available design documents and software simulators. It is quite unlikely that Atmel, Texas Instruments, or ARM would have given us their cores for such a comparison. Their chips are produced in different technologies, so any comparison of actual chips is impracticable for our purposes. Regarding code quality, we want to emphasize that Atmel, Texas Instruments, and ARM use similar libraries and tools as we do. Therefore our designs are probably very close to the real deal.
- We are the first to integrate instruction-set extensions (ISE) in actual clones of those microprocessors. The only common denominator of those three processors is the 16-bit instruction-set. In every other key aspect, they differ (e.g.

---

[1] Closed source for now, done by the authors.

8, 16, 32 bit datapaths, Harvard/Von Neumann architecture, ...). Therefore the multiply-accumulate ISEs have to be carefully crafted for each CPU core.
- We are the first to optimize ECC on the Cortex-M0+.
- Our results represent state-of-the-art of side-channel protected, fast, light-weight, and standardized asymmetric cryptography for embedded processors.

The paper is structured as follows: Section 2 presents and analyzes the side-channel protected elliptic-curve point multiplication algorithm. Within Section 3 the three processors are reviewed and compared on an architectural level. Sections 4 and 5 summarize the assembly and instruction-set optimizations. A rigorous analysis of all implementation results is performed in Section 6. Section 7 concludes the paper.

2 Elliptic Curve Cryptography

When implementing elliptic curve cryptography, a designer has a multitude of options. In the following we present an algorithm for the point multiplication which was chosen based on four characteristics:

- It is easy to **tamper** with embedded microprocessors. Timing attacks, power-analysis attacks and fault-analysis attacks are a real and omnipresent danger. For that matter we will not claim to be secure against all kinds of attacks, but by choosing a methodology that is aware of many kind of attacks, we emphasize the practical significance of the results presented later.
- ECC is a **feature**. Unlike, e.g., the work in [42] (Comb method with window size $w = 4$), we think that only a small fraction of the available program and data memory resource should be used for ECC so that the actual application is not hindered in its operation. Therefore we choose a point-multiplication formula which does not allocate the whole memory for pre-computed or temporary points. Reduced memory requirements further allows hardware designers to save money by equipping the chip with smaller memories.
- Standards were made to be used and simplify the **interoperability** of products. Thus, by choosing a NIST [35] or SECG [7] standard, any company can be sure that their product is compatible with products from other vendors.
- Achieving a **high speed** is an ubiquitous goal of nearly every designer. By getting the most out of an available hardware, one reduces latency times (important in real-time protocols) and saves energy (important for battery-powered devices and from an economic point of view). As we do not sacrifice our security requirements for speed, we concentrate on improving the finite-field operations by doing assembly and instruction-set optimizations.

In Algorithm 1, we present the point multiplication formula used for all our practical evaluations. A detailed analysis of Algorithm 1 is given in Appendix A. Our goal was to design an algorithm which can be used for Diffie-Hellman key exchanges (DHKE) and elliptic-curve based signatures (ECDSA [35]), which are the major features embedded applications actually require. The algorithm

---

Algorithm 1. Elliptic curve point-multiplication algorithm used for evaluation

---

Input: Domain parameters, secret scalar k with MSB $= 1$, point $P = (x, y)$.
Output: $R = k \times P$
1: if $y^2 \neq x^3 + ax + b$ then Perform Error Handling
2: $(X, Y, Z) \leftarrow (x \cdot \lambda, y \cdot \lambda, \lambda)$ ▷ Randomize Projective Coordinates
3: if $Y^2 Z \neq X^3 + aX Z^2 + bZ^3$ then Perform Error Handling
4: $Q[0] \leftarrow (X, Z), Q[1] \leftarrow 2 \cdot (X, Y, Z)$ ▷ Initial Point Doubling
5: for $i = |k| - 2$ downto 0 do   ▷ Montgomery Ladder
6:      $Q[k_i] \leftarrow Q[k_i] + Q[k_i \oplus 1]$
7:      $Q[k_i \oplus 1] \leftarrow 2 \cdot Q[k_i \oplus 1]$
8: end for
9: $(X, Y, Z) \leftarrow$ y-recovery$(Q[0], Q[1])$
10: if $Y^2 Z \neq X^3 + aX Z^2 + bZ^3$ then Perform Error Handling
11: $R = (x, y) \leftarrow (XZ^{-1}, YZ^{-1})$
12: if $y^2 \neq x^3 + ax + b$ then Perform Error Handling

---

is using a Montgomery ladder [34] with Randomized Projective Coordinates
(RPC) [10] and multiple point validation (PV) checks. After an initial PV check
the coordinates are randomized. In step 3, the point is again checked within the
projective coordinates. A fault attack on the randomized projective coordinates
is much more complex. Then, an initial point doubling within the RPC is performed. The double of the original point is needed for the following Montgomery
ladder. Here we use the common-z interleaved point addition and doubling formulas by Hutter, Joye, and Sierra [25]. As this is the most costly part of the
algorithm, no PV checks are performed within it. For the following recovery
of the y-coordinates, both $Q[0]$ and $Q[1]$ are used. Another two PV checks are
performed before and after the inversion of the Z-coordinate. One may argue
that several of the PV checks are redundant, but because they hardly have any
impact on the speed, we perform them anyways.

Runtimes of all finite-field operations are constant and data-independent.
Therefore, a finite-field inversion was implemented based on Fermat's little theorem (inversion by exponentiation). Particularly, the algorithm is based on the
exponentiation trick by Itoh and Tsujii [27]. Although this trick is usually applied
to elliptic curves over binary fields, we utilize it to optimize the inversion for the
standardized Mersenne-like primes, nearly halving the number of multiplications
needed for an exponentiation with a fixed exponent.

Summarizing, it is important to utilize the available resources. Therefore a
detailed knowledge of the used microprocessors is necessary to achieve competi-
tive results. Section 3 discusses the characteristics of the investigated embedded
microprocessors.

3 Microprocessor Architectures

This paper focuses on three of the most popular embedded microprocessors:
the 8-bit Atmel ATmega AVR, the 16-bit Texas Instruments MSP430 and the

32-bit ARM Cortex-M0+ microprocessors. All of them were designed for embedded applications, in which price and power consumption matter more than the maximum clock speed or the amount of available data or program cache. In fact, those RISC processors do not have any cache. In this section, we introduce the three processor architectures and discuss their capabilities relevant for ECC.

Atmel ATmega AVR Series. In 1996, two students from the Norwegian Institute of Technology developed the first AVR processor. Today, designers can choose from a vast range of descendants. Especially the ATmega series [2] has been and is used in a magnitude of commercial products.

The ATmega is a 8-bit RISC processor with separated program, data, and I/O memory buses (Harvard architecture). It comes with 32 general-purpose registers (GPR) and 91 (133 including simulated) instructions. To perform integer arithmetic, operands need to be loaded (2 cycles) to the GPRs, processed within the GPRs, and stored back (2 cycles) to the data memory. A for multi-precision integer arithmetic [9] interesting 8-bit multiply-accumulate operation (LD, LD, MUL, ADD, ADC, ADC) takes 9 cycles.

Texas Instruments MSP430 Series 1. One of the most successful, direct competitor of the ATmega is the MSP430 processor series [43] by Texas Instruments. With its six low-power modes it is most interesting for low power, and low-energy applications. This is why it is used for many wireless sensor nodes such as the EPIC Mote, TelosB, T-Mote Sky, and XM1000 platforms.

The original series-1 MSP430 is a 16-bit RISC processor with a single combined data and program bus. Merely 12 of its 16 16-bit registers are actually usable as general-purpose registers. The MSP430 series comes with a fully orthogonal instruction set of only 27 instructions with 7 addressing modes. Unfortunately, there is no dedicated multiplication instruction, but a memory mapped $16 \times 16 \rightarrow 32$-bit multiplier, with multiply-accumulate feature, is available. Despite the high costs introduced by transfering the operands from data memory to the multiplier, a 16-bit multiply-accumulate operation (MOV, MOV, NOP, ADD) can be performed in 13 cycles.

ARM Cortex-M0+ Series. In the recent years, ARM made a name for itself with supplying smart phones and tablets with powerful energy-saving processors, namely the Cortex-A series. For embedded applications however, Cortex-M series processors are more suitable. The Cortex-M0+ embedded microprocessor [1] is the smallest, most energy-efficient ARM ever built and supports a subset of the Thumb-2 instruction-set. This 32-bit RISC processor is designed as direct competitor for the ATmega and MSP430 processors. Launched in 2012, major companies (e.g., Freescale [15], Fujitsu [16], or NXP [36]) just started to introduce the Cortex-M0+ to their lineups.

Similar to the MSP430, the Cortex-M0+ comes with a Von Neumann architecture. Its 32-bit address and data buses enable the addressing of up to 4 GByte of data, preparing it perfectly for future memory requirements. Exactly 13 of its 16 32-bit registers can be used as general-purpose registers, but most of its 56 instructions can only access the lower 8 registers R0–R7. Registers R8–R15 are

Table 1. Summary of the embedded microprocessors

Characteristic	ATmega	MSP430 (1 Series)	Cortex-M0+
Data-Width	8 bits	16 bits	32 bits
Instruction-Word Size	16 bits	16 bits	16 bits
Architecture	Harvard	Von Neumann	Von Neumann
General-Purpose Registers	32	12/16	8/13/16
Number of Instructions	81	27	56
Max. Data Memory	16 kByte	10 KByte	4 GByte
Max. Program Memory	256 kByte	60 KByte	4 GByte
Multiply Accumulate[a]	9 cycles	13 cycles	29 cycles
Used Clone	JAAVR [47]	IDLE430 [50]	Xetroc-M0+ [44]
Core area[b]	6,140 GE	4,913 GE	15,262 GE
Registers	2,002 GE	1,732 GE	4,176 GE
Multiplier	372 GE	1,751 GE[c]	2,766 GE

[a] Load two operands, multiply and accumulate them.
[b] Including memory arbiter and necessary special function registers.
[c] Memory mapped and therefore not part of the core area.

accessible through a MOV instruction only. Optionally, the Cortex-M0+ comes with a bit-serial or a single-cycle $32 \times 32 \to 32$-bit multiplication instruction. Note that for ECC, also the upper half of the product is necessary for multi-precision integer arithmetic. In the following, we use this multiplier as $16 \times 16 \to 32$-bit multiplier. Section 4 illustrates the implementation of an efficient 29-cycle 32-bit multiply-accumulate operation.

Summary of the Embedded Microprocessors. The common denominators of the three embedded microprocessors are that they are RISC processors, support single-cycle register-to-register operations, and have 16-bit instruction sets (with some 32-bit exceptions). The major differences are summarized in Table 1. The three microprocessors utilize different architectures, have different amounts of available registers, clearly distinct instruction sets and support different amounts of data and program memory. Those differences become apparent when the actual hardware footprint is evaluated. Most remarkably, the 16-bit MSP430 (4,913 GE) requires less chip area than the 8-bit ATmega (6,140 GE). This is the price the ATmega has to pay for its three memory buses and the vast instruction set. To efficiently perform integer multiplications, the MSP430 additionally needs a memory mapped multiplier which is 1,751 GE in size. Compared to the ATmega and the MSP430, the 32-bit Cortex-M0+ is much larger. It requires 15,262 GE in a configuration with a single-cycle 32-bit multiplier. The optional 32-cycle bit-serial multiplier saves 1,363 GE which brings the Cortex-M0+ to a minimum size of 13,899 GE in the used 130 nm UMC process.

Related Work. ARM specifies that their Cortex-M0+ is only 12 kGE large in a 90 nm process. When synthesizing our clone in a 90 nm UMC process it requires 12,436 GE. So in terms of area, our Cortex-M0+ is (as aimed for) very close to the original. As neither Atmel nor Texas Instruments released characteristics of their processors, we can only compare our clones to the versions uploaded to opencores.org. Compared to the openMSP430 [37], our MSP430 is $5,958 - 4,913 = 1,045$ GE smaller. Compared to other (insufficiently tested) ATmega or AVR clones, our ATmega clone is similarly small.

4   Assembly Optimizations for ECC

As we already fixed the point arithmetic, we focus our effort on the finite-field operations. Most crucial is the finite-field multiplication as it contributes to 90 % of the runtime of a point multiplication. Hence, optimizing the runtime of the finite-field multiplication automatically improves the runtime of the point-multiplication algorithm. Additionally, it leads to a speedup of the finite-field squaring, exponentiation and inversion operation. To optimize the finite-field multiplication, one can either perform assembly optimizations or extend the instruction-set (see Section 5).

While the currently fastest multi-precision multiplication approaches for the ATmega and the MSP430 are based on related work, it was necessary to come up with a new technique for the Cortex-M0+ as it has not yet been investigated.

ATmega. In 2004, Gura *et al.* [22] presented an efficient multi-precision multiplication method and applied it to the ATmega. Hutter and Wenger [26] presented the "Operand Caching" method in 2011. It further reduced the number of memory load operations at the cost of some memory store operations. As it fully utilizes the available general purpose registers as caches and currently is one of the fastest ways to perform multi-precision multiplications on an ATmega, we used their technique.

MSP430. The MSP430 only has 12 useable GPRs, of which three registers have to be used as pointers and further three registers are necessary for the accumulation of intermediate results. With the remaining six registers, we applied the product-scanning technique by Comba [9]. This technique fully utilizes the multiply-accumulate functionality of the memory-mapped multiplier. It was first described by Gouvêa and López [19] and is fully tailored to the MSP430.

Cortex-M0+. ECC performance of the Cortex-M0+ has never been examined before. Most notable are the works of Aydos *et al.* [3], who optimized ECC for an ARM7TDMI processor, and Bernstein and Schwabe [4], who optimized the NaCl cryptographic library for a Cortex-A8. However, none of their work had to deal with the limitations of a Cortex-M0+: Its multiplier only computes 32-bit products, most instructions are restricted to registers R0–R7, and, for most instructions, the destination register must equal one of the source registers, i.e. in each multiplication one of the operands is overwritten by the product.

We evaluated several multiplication techniques and finally settled for a product-scanning multi-precision multiplication method. Its centerpiece is shown in Algorithm 2: the two operand references are moved from registers R8 and R9 to R1 and R2. Consequently, we can load their values from the memory. Then, five registers are available to perform four $16 \times 16 \rightarrow 32$-bit multiplications (steps

---

Algorithm 2. Multiply-Accumulate Operation on Cortex-M0+

Input: R8 and R9 are pointers.	14: MOV R7, #0
Output: R3, R4, R5 contain the sum.	15: ADD R3, R3, R0 ▷ Low–Low
1: MOV R1, R8	16: ADC R4, R4, R2 ▷ High–High
2: LDR R1, [R1, #offset1]	17: ADC R5, R5, R7
3: MOV R2, R9	
4: LDR R2, [R2, #offset2]	18: LSL R0, R6, #16 ▷ Low–High
	19: LSR R2, R6, #16
5: UXTH R6, R1	20: ADD R3, R3, R0
6: UXTH R7, R2	21: ADC R4, R4, R2
7: LSR R1, R1, #16	22: ADC R5, R5, R7
8: LSR R2, R2, #16	
	23: LSL R0, R1, #16 ▷ High–Low
9: MOV R0, R6	24: LSR R2, R1, #16
10: MUL R0, R0, R7 ▷ Low–Low	25: ADD R3, R3, R0
11: MUL R6, R6, R2 ▷ Low–High	26: ADC R4, R4, R2
12: MUL R2, R2, R1 ▷ High–High	27: ADC R5, R5, R7
13: MUL R1, R1, R7 ▷ High–Low	

9–13), whereby the 16-bit masking steps are performed only once (steps 5–7). Steps 14–27 accumulate the four 32-bit products into the registers R3–R5.

The stack is used to temporarily store the product of the multi-precision integer multiplication. Hence, we benefit from addressing relative to the stack pointer and avoid moving the address to one of the registers R0–R7. In a second step, a reduction is performed by taking advantage of the Mersenne-like primes.

Assembler Optimized Results. We did all assembly optimizations for four standardized elliptic curves (secp160-192-224-256r1). In order to keep the general view, Table 2 depicts the memory footprints, the runtimes for finite-field operations and the point multiplication over the secp160r1 elliptic curve.

In terms of **ROM** size the processors behave converse their word sizes. The implementation for the ATmega takes up 7,762 bytes in ROM, which is twice as much as for the Cortex-M0+. This is mainly a result of the unrolled integer multiplication. The MSP430 behaves well as it requires only 13% more ROM than the Cortex-M0+. With respect to **RAM**, the ATmega (402 byte) and the Cortex-M0+ (404 byte) perform similarly, consuming about 40% more RAM than the MSP430 (290 byte). The increased RAM footprint of the ATmega is due to the elliptic curve constants that need to be loaded to the RAM at startup. The root of the increased memory usage of the Cortex-M0+ lies within its calling hierarchy. Each PUSH operation stores four bytes of data within the RAM. These facts combined make the MSP430 an economic platform in terms of memory footprint and chip area.

Impressively, the **finite-field addition** on the Cortex-M0+ is 2.6 times faster than an addition on the MSP430. The main reason for that is the load-multiple LDM instruction of the Cortex-M0+, which allows loading multiple words into

Table 2. Benchmark data of assembly optimized implementations for `secp160r1`

Processor	ROM [Bytes]	RAM [Bytes]	Addition [Cycles]	Mult. [Cycles]	Inversion [Cycles]	Point Mult. [Cycles]	Core Area [kGE]
Atmega	8,358	402	291	3,024	519,217	9,230,048	6,140
MSP430	4,788	290	163	1,905	327,366	5,779,957	7,003
CortexM0+	4,256	404	62	942	162,500	2,809,619	15,262
Relative Performance							
Atmega	1.96	1.46	4.69	3.21	3.20	3.29	1.00
MSP430	1.13	1.00	2.63	2.02	2.01	2.06	1.14
CortexM0+	1.00	1.39	1.00	1.00	1.00	1.00	2.49

several registers requiring only $\#words + 1$ cycles. The load `LDR` instruction takes 2 cycles per word and therefore $2 \times \#words$ cycles would be needed.

As the runtime of **integer multiplication** scales quadratically, one expects the 32-bit Cortex-M0+ to be four times faster than the 16-bit MSP430 and the 16-bit MSP430 to be four times faster than the 8-bit ATmega. But they are not. The Cortex-M0+ is only twice as fast as the MSP430. The reason for that is the tremendous overhead needed to perform a $32 \times 32 \rightarrow 64$-bit multiplication using the $32 \times 32 \rightarrow 32$-bit integer multiplier (see the highly optimized Algorithm 2). But also the MSP430 is only 1.6 times faster than the ATmega. This is because the MSP430 has a memory mapped multiplier and the ATmega has an integrated multiplier.

By combining finite-field additions, multiplications, and inversions, the runtimes for `secp160r1` **point multiplications** were obtained. They are 9.2 million cycles for the ATmega, 5.8 million cycles for the MSP430, and 2.8 million cycles for the Cortex-M0+. As the finite-field multiplication contributes to the majority of this runtime, the ratios for the point multiplications are nearly identical to the ratios of the finite-field multiplication. Equipping the Cortex-M0+ with a bit-serial multiplier quadruples its runtime: With 11.9 million cycles the bit-serial multiplier simply defeats the purpose of having a 32-bit processor. Hence, we do not recommend implementing prime-field based ECC on a Cortex-M0+ without single-cycle multiplier. Consequently, instruction-set extensions were equipped to improve runtimes and to monitor how the performance ratios change.

5   Instruction-Set Modifications

We carefully crafted the VHDL clones of the ATmega, the MSP430, and the Cortex-M0+ to be cycle-compatible with its originals. During that process, we also observed some minor shortcomings regarding their respective potentials. This section is all about maximizing the performance by improving the runtime of existing instructions and adding multiply-and-accumulate [21] instructions. This `MULACC` instruction is optimal for multi-precision multiplication. It is used to multiply two n-bit registers and add the 2n-bit product to three accumulation registers. As the three processors differ significantly, MULACC had to be integrated differently for each processor.

ATmega. Our modifications of the ATmega are based on Wenger [46]. In this paper, we showed among other things how to improve load, store, and multiply instructions and execute them within a single cycle instead of two. Additionally, we added a single-cycle multiply-and-accumulate instruction, which was combined with the Operand-Caching multiplication method. In a special operating mode, activated by writing a memory-mapped configuration register, the existing MUL instruction is reinterpreted as MULACC instruction. Therefore, the software toolchain does not need to be modified. In fact, the trick of having a special mode for the instruction-set extension has also been applied for the MSP430 and Cortex-M0+.

MSP430. The advantage of the MSP430 is, that operands do not have to be explicitly loaded to core registers before their usage. The drawback is that the multiplier is only accessible via the memory. To get rid of this bottleneck, we removed the memory-mapped multiplier (saved 1,751 GE) and added a dedicated MULACC instruction within its core. Unfortunately, the 7 existing addressing modes were insufficient for our purposes. By perfectly utilizing the pre-existing auto-increment and a new auto-decrement addressing mode it is possible to load two operands, multiply-and-accumulate the data, and update the addressing registers. To omit manual pointer updates completely, we combined the new MULACC instruction with Wenger and Werner's [49] zig-zag product-scanning multiplication method. Other modifications with less impact on the ECC runtime improved move, jump, push, and call instructions by one to two cycles. This modifications do not only minimize the overhead of the C-calling convention, but also potentially improve the runtimes of any other algorithm run on the modified MSP430.

Cortex-M0+. As it is only possible to compute a $16 \times 16 \to 32$-bit product with the internal multiplier of the Cortex-M0+ and 29 cycles are necessary to perform a 32-bit (c.f. Algorithm 2) multiply-and-accumulate operation, it is specially important to equip the Cortex-M0+ with a MULACC extension. This extension reduced the for the product-scanning important sequence of LDR, LDR, MULACC instructions to mere 5 cycles. To save area, the pre-existing $32 \times 32 \to 32$-bit multiplier is reused and only extended to compute a 64-bit product. Therefore, the MULACC extension did only cost 3.4 kGE.

Results Using Instruction-Set Modifications. In general, the core idea of all modifications was to improve the performance without adding unnecessary hardware. So the modifications of the ATmega (+14.8 %) and the Cortex-M0+ (+22.5 %) only marginally increased the size of the CPU cores. The effective size of the MSP430 only increased by 2.8 %. The slow, memory-mapped multiplier was approximately as large as the new dedicated datapath to multiply-and-accumulate within a single cycle. While the size of the CPU cores increased, the size of the program memory decreased by 19-30 %. The rather large unrolled integer multi-precision multiplication functions shrunk significantly and therefore

Table 3. Benchmarks of processors with instruction-set modifications for `secp160r1`

Processor	ROM [Bytes]	RAM [Bytes]	Addition [Cycles]	Mult. [Cycles]	Inversion [Cycles]	Point Mult. [Cycles]	Core Area [kGE]
Atmega	5,828	402	176	984	170,053	3,268,486	7,039
MSP430	3,898	286	150	718	123,939	2,445,508	7,197
CortexM0+	3,088	408	62	369	64,859	1,231,946	18,700
Relative Performance of Modified Processors							
Atmega	1.89	1.41	2.84	2.67	2.62	2.65	1.00
MSP430	1.26	1.00	2.42	1.95	1.91	1.99	1.02
CortexM0+	1.00	1.43	1.00	1.00	1.00	1.00	2.66
Modified versus Assembly-optimized Implementations (Table 2)							
Atmega	−30.3%	±0.0%	−39.5%	−67.5%	−67.2%	−64.6%	14.6%
MSP430	−18.6%	−1.4%	−8.0%	−62.3%	−62.1%	−57.7%	2.8%
CortexM0+	−27.4%	1.0%	±0.0%	−60.8%	−60.1%	−56.2%	22.5%

the total chip areas actually decreased. However, the modifications only have very little impact on data memory utilization.

As intended, the modifications achieve a massive speedup of multiplications in the prime field (cf. Table 3). Throughout, the corresponding runtimes dropped by 60%, with the highest speedup achieved on the ATmega (-67%). As inversions are based on exponentiation to counteract side-channel attacks, the same impressing speedup is found there. Accordingly, point multiplication runtimes slumped by 65% on the ATmega and plunged by 57% on the others. Concerning addition, there are no performance gains for the Cortex-M0+ and the MSP430. Contrary to that, addition is performed 40% faster on the ATmega due to the improved timings of the load and store operations. Relating runtimes of the three modified processors, the Cortex-M0+ again achieves the best performance, being between 2-3 times faster than its competitors. However, its advantage diminishes slightly compared to the unmodified ATmega.

6   Discussion of Hardware Implementations

All our implementations for the three microprocessors, with and without instruction-set modifications, and over four elliptic curves were tested for correctness using externally generated test vectors, synthesized in a Faraday UMC 130 nm low-leakage ASIC library, placed-and-routed, and power-simulated (using Cadence RTL Compiler, Cadence Encounter). The huge number of results are accumulated within Table 4 and discussed in the following.

Memories. We used area-efficient single-port RAM macros as data memories and single-port Via-1 ROM macros as program memories. As their necessary sizes depend on the ECC implementation, they were chosen appropriately for each implementation. Experiments showed that synthesizing the program memories as standard logic cells resulted in smaller program memories after synthesis, but there were two problems: Firstly, it was virtually impossible to place and

Table 4. Summary of all experiments

Processor	Version	Program Memory [Bytes]	Data[a] Memory [Bytes]	ROM [GE]	RAM [GE]	Core [GE]	Total [GE]	Power @10 MHz [µW]	Energy [µJ]	Runtime @10 MHz [ms]
				secp160r1						
ATmega	ASM	8,358	402	11,807	3,754	6,140	21,701	545	503	923
MSP430	ASM	4,788	290	7,796	3,250	7,003	18,048	583	337	578
CortexM0+	ASM	4,256	404	8,270	4,308	15,262	27,840	718	202	281
ATmega	ISE	5,828	402	8,202	3,754	7,039	18,995	666	218	327
MSP430	ISE	3,898	286	6,363	3,225	7,197	16,786	794	194	245
CortexM0+	ISE	3,088	408	6,416	4,334	18,700	29,450	1,306	161	123
				secp192r1, NIST P-192						
ATmega	ASM	10,238	462	11,807	4,107	6,140	22,054	556	839	1,509
MSP430	ASM	5,408	330	8,202	3,475	7,003	18,679	581	533	918
CortexM0+	ASM	4,860	448	8,270	4,560	15,262	28,092	716	329	459
ATmega	ISE	6,564	462	10,040	4,107	7,039	21,186	670	336	502
MSP430	ISE	4,142	330	7,796	3,475	7,197	18,468	801	283	353
CortexM0+	ISE	3,164	444	6,416	4,535	18,700	29,652	1,318	241	183
				secp224r1, NIST P-224						
ATmega	ASM	12,570	526	15,484	4,485	6,140	26,109	571	1,326	2,321
MSP430	ASM	6,294	374	10,040	3,750	7,003	20,792	584	819	1,403
CortexM0+	ASM	5,672	496	8,270	4,838	15,262	28,369	716	496	693
ATmega	ISE	7,600	526	10,040	4,485	7,039	21,564	664	500	754
MSP430	ISE	4,588	370	7,796	3,725	7,197	18,718	805	419	521
CortexM0+	ISE	3,352	492	6,416	4,812	18,700	29,929	1,330	334	251
				secp256r1, NIST P-256						
ATmega	ASM	16,112	590	17,029	4,838	6,140	28,006	548	1,914	3,493
MSP430	ASM	8,378	418	11,878	4,000	7,003	22,881	580	1,286	2,217
CortexM0+	ASM	7,168	540	10,123	5,089	15,262	30,475	719	771	1,073
ATmega	ISE	9,596	590	11,807	4,838	7,039	23,684	655	779	1,190
MSP430	ISE	6,168	416	10,040	3,975	7,197	21,212	791	717	907
CortexM0+	ISE	4,124	536	8,270	5,064	18,700	32,034	1,339	546	408

[a] Including Stack.

route the program memories without significantly decreasing the cell density, which actually increased the effective size of the program memory. Secondly, the ROM macros have a significantly lower power consumption compared to the synthesized program memories.

Runtime. The runtime is measured at 10 MHz and visualized in Figure 1. The time for a single, side-channel secured point multiplication varies between 123–923 ms. As expected, the 32-bit processor is faster than the 16-bit processor, which in turn is faster than the 8-bit processor. Quite remarkably though is that the modified ATmega is nearly as fast as the native Cortex-M0+.

Area. The area visualized in Figure 1 accumulates the respective areas of the CPU, the ROM, the RAM, and core building blocks, such as an arbiter. Quite remarkably, the native and the modified MSP430 represent the smallest implementation, requiring around 16.8–18.0 kGE. Compared to that, the modified Cortex-M0+ (29 kGE) is 75 % larger.

Area-runtime-product. In the prestigious category of area-runtime-product, the modified implementations clearly outperform its native counterparts (see the

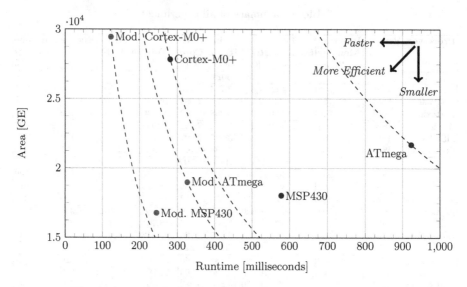

Fig. 1. Area-runtime-characteristics for `secp160r1` at 10 MHz

dashed lines within Figure 1). The modified Cortex-M0+ system performs best, and the native ATmega system performs worst. However, the modified ATmega system provides a better performance for the used chip area than the native Cortex-M0+. Consequently, if some commercial company evaluates whether to switch to a more powerful Cortex-M0+, we can clearly recommend to replace the native MSP430 or ATmega with its modified counterpart, presented within this paper. As nice side-effect, the software code-base does not have to be updated for a different processor.

Power. According to Figure 2, all designs require between 545–1,305 μW. The 8-bit ATmega requires the least amount of power, slightly less (6.5 %) than the MSP430. However, when their modified counterparts are compared, the modified ATmega needs 16 % less power than the modified MSP430. The Cortex-M0+ and the modified Cortex-M0+ need the most power.

Power-runtime-product: Energy. However, the same two processors shine within the energy-efficiency race. As represented by the dashed lines in Figure 2, the Cortex-M0+ based designs only need 161–202 μJ, while the other designs need 194–503 μJ. That is up to 60 % less. The MSP430 is 11–33 % more energy efficient than the ATmega.

Relating the Different Elliptic Curves. As initially stated and depicted in Table 4, we did not do our evaluation only with `secp160r1`, but also with `secp192r1`, `secp224r1`, and `secp256r1`. Most importantly, the results observed at the 80-bit security level are reproducible for the larger elliptic curves. On average, changing from one elliptic curve to the next larger one, costs 6 % of

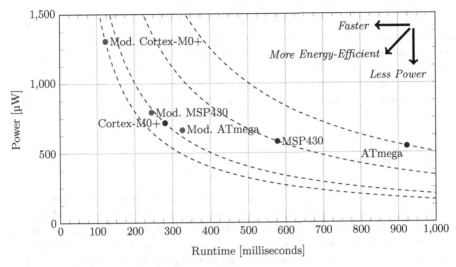

Fig. 2. Power-runtime-characteristics for `secp160r1` at 10 MHz

additional chip area, 53 % of additional runtime and 54 % of additional energy. The power consumption is not effected by the chosen elliptic curve.

Related Work. In terms of software implementations (c.f. Table 5), our implementations distinct themselves from related work with their low memory footprints and the side-channel countermeasures. In fact none of the implementations done by [20,22,33,42,45] have side-channel countermeasures built in. Therefore it is expected that, e.g., [20,22,42], achieve faster runtimes than we do. However, e.g., [20,42] need up to 7–10 times more program and data memory than we do.

Table 5. Comparison with related software implementations (80 bit security level)

Curve	ROM [Bytes]	RAM [Bytes]	Runtime [kCycles]
ATmega			
Custom [42]	46,100	1,800	9,376
secp160r1 [33]	20,768	1,774	15,060
secp160r1 [22]	3,682	282	6,480
Our secp160r1	8,358	402	9,230
MSP430			
Custom [42]	31,300	2,900	5,898
secp160r1 [20]	23,300	2,800	2,528
secp160r1 [33]	16,218	1,866	11,821
secp160r1 [45]	12,500	1,300	28,080
Our secp160r1	4,788	290	5,780

Table 6. Comparison with related hardware implementations

Implementation	Area [GE]	Runtime [kCycles]
96-bit security level		
Satoh et al. [39]	29,655	4,165
Hutter et al. [24]	19,115	859
Wenger et al. [48]	11,686	1,377
80-bit security level		
Öztürk et al. [38]	30,333	545
Fürbass et al. [17]	23,656	500
Kern et al. [29]	18,247	512
Our Mod. ATmega	18,995	3,268
Our Mod. MSP430	16,786	2,446
Our Mod. Cortex-M0+	29,450	1,232

For the sake of completeness, we also compare our modified processors with related hardware implementations (c.f. Table 6). Unfortunately, those dedicated hardware designs are faster than our flexible microprocessor based designs. However, in terms of chip area, our smallest modified MSP430 implementation is smaller than the work of [17,24,29,38,39]. Only the custom microprocessor design by Wenger *et al.* [48] is smaller. However, their microprocessor does not come with the vast (open-source) compiler toolchains, the ATmega, the MSP430, or the Cortex-M0+ provide.

7   Conclusion

In this work, three of the most popular micro-processors were evaluated regarding their runtime, chip area, power, and energy consumption on standard-compatible side-channel protected elliptic curve cryptography. By comparing them using a single design flow, the same application, and with a common technology, we achieve a fair comparison between the different architectures. Our work might help any system architect on their decision regarding best suitable processor, best suitable security level, and whether or not to implement hardware extensions. Our results show that the Cortex-M0+ is the fastest and most energy-efficient processor (e.g., ideal for Wireless Sensor Nodes), the MSP430 enables the smallest and least power consuming hardware design (e.g., ideal for RFID tags), and the ATmega gains the most performance when instruction-set modifications are applied (e.g., ideal for long-lived products that must be equipped with ECC). Any designer now has to define their own metric and weigh the characteristics with each other. To the best of our knowledge, such an comprehensive evaluation has not been done before.

Acknowledgments. This work has been supported in part by the Austrian Government through the research program FIT-IT under the project number 835917 (project NewP@ss) and by the European Commission through the ICT Programme under contract ICT-SEC-2009-5-258754 TAMPRES.

References

1. ARM. Cortex-M0+ Processor (2013),
   http://www.arm.com/products/processors/cortex-m/cortex-m0plus.php
2. Atmel Corporation. megaAVR Microcontroller (2013),
   http://www.atmel.com/products/microcontrollers/avr/megaavr.aspx
3. Aydos, M., Yanik, T., Koç, Ç.K.: A High-Speed ECC-based Wireless Authentication Protocol on an ARM Microprocessor. In: ACSAC, IEEE (2000)
4. Bernstein, D., Schwabe, P.: Neon crypto. In: CHES (2012)
5. Biehl, I., Meyer, B., Müller, V.: Differential Fault Attacks on Elliptic Curve Cryptosystems. In: Bellare, M. (ed.) CRYPTO 2000. LNCS, vol. 1880, pp. 131–146. Springer, Heidelberg (2000)

6. Brumley, B.B., Tuveri, N.: Remote timing attacks are still practical. In: Atluri, V., Diaz, C. (eds.) ESORICS 2011. LNCS, vol. 6879, pp. 355–371. Springer, Heidelberg (2011)

7. Certicom Research. Standards for Efficient Cryptography, SEC 2: Recommended Elliptic Curve Domain Parameters, Version 1.0 (2000)

8. Ciet, M., Joye, M.: Elliptic Curve Cryptosystems in the Presence of Permanent and Transient Faults. In: Designs, Codes and Cryptography (2005)

9. Comba, P.: Exponentiation cryptosystems on the IBM PC. In: IBM Systems Journal (1990)

10. Coron, J.-S.: Resistance against Differential Power Analysis for Elliptic Curve Cryptosystems. In: Koç, Ç.K., Paar, C. (eds.) CHES 1999. LNCS, vol. 1717, pp. 292–302. Springer, Heidelberg (1999)

11. Ebeid, N., Lambert, R.: Securing the Elliptic Curve Montgomery Ladder Against Fault Attacks. In: FDTC, pp. 46–50. IEEE Computer Society (2009)

12. Fan, J., Guo, X., Mulder, E.D., Schaumont, P., Preneel, B., Verbauwhede, I.: State-of-the-Art of Secure ECC Implementations: A Survey on known Side-Channel Attacks and Countermeasures. In: HOST. IEEE (2010)

13. Fan, J., Verbauwhede, I.: An Updated Survey on Secure ECC Implementations: Attacks, Countermeasures and Cost. In: Naccache, D. (ed.) Quisquater Festschrift. LNCS, vol. 6805, pp. 265–282. Springer, Heidelberg (2012)

14. Fouque, P.-A., Lercier, R., Réal, D., Valette, F.: Fault Attack on Elliptic Curve Montgomery Ladder Implementation. In: FDTC. IEEE Computer Society (2008)

15. Freescale Semiconductor. Kinetis L Series MCUs (2013),
    http://www.freescale.com/webapp/sps/site/taxonomy.jsp?code=KINETIS_L_SERIES

16. Fujitsu Semiconductors. Fujitsu Semiconductor Widely Expands Lineup of 32-bit General Purpose Microcontrollers with the Release of Products Adopting 2 New ARM Cores (November 2012); Press Release

17. Fürbass, F., Wolkerstorfer, J.: ECC Processor with Low Die Size for RFID Applications. In: IEEE International Symposium on Circuits and Systems (2007)

18. Goubin, L.: A Refined Power-Analysis Attack on Elliptic Curve Cryptosystems. In: Desmedt, Y.G. (ed.) PKC 2003. LNCS, vol. 2567, pp. 199–210. Springer, Heidelberg (2002)

19. Gouvêa, C.P.L., López, J.: Software Implementation of Pairing-Based Cryptography on Sensor Networks Using the MSP430 Microcontroller. In: Roy, B., Sendrier, N. (eds.) INDOCRYPT 2009. LNCS, vol. 5922, pp. 248–262. Springer, Heidelberg (2009)

20. Gouvêa, C.P.L., Oliveira, L., López, J.: Efficient Software Implementation of Public-Key Cryptography on Sensor Networks Using the MSP430X Microcontroller. Journal of Cryptographic Engineering (2012)

21. Großschädl, J., Savaş, E.: Instruction Set Extensions for Fast Arithmetic in Finite Fields GF(p) and GF(2^m). In: Joye, M., Quisquater, J.-J. (eds.) CHES 2004. LNCS, vol. 3156, pp. 133–147. Springer, Heidelberg (2004)

22. Gura, N., Patel, A., Wander, A., Eberle, H., Shantz, S.C.: Comparing Elliptic Curve Cryptography and RSA on 8-Bit CPUs. In: Joye, M., Quisquater, J.-J. (eds.) CHES 2004. LNCS, vol. 3156, pp. 119–132. Springer, Heidelberg (2004)

23. Heyszl, J., Mangard, S., Heinz, B., Stumpf, F., Sigl, G.: Localized Electromagnetic Analysis of Cryptographic Implementations. In: Dunkelman, O. (ed.) CT-RSA 2012. LNCS, vol. 7178, pp. 231–244. Springer, Heidelberg (2012)

24. Hutter, M., Feldhofer, M., Plos, T.: An ECDSA Processor for RFID Authentication. In: Ors Yalcin, S.B. (ed.) RFIDSec 2010. LNCS, vol. 6370, pp. 189–202. Springer, Heidelberg (2010)
25. Hutter, M., Joye, M., Sierra, Y.: Memory-Constrained Implementations of Elliptic Curve Cryptography in Co-Z Coordinate Representation. In: Nitaj, A., Pointcheval, D. (eds.) AFRICACRYPT 2011. LNCS, vol. 6737, pp. 170–187. Springer, Heidelberg (2011)
26. Hutter, M., Wenger, E.: Fast Multi-Precision Multiplication for Public-Key Cryptography on Embedded Microprocessors. In: Preneel, B., Takagi, T. (eds.) CHES 2011. LNCS, vol. 6917, pp. 459–474. Springer, Heidelberg (2011)
27. Itoh, T., Tsujii, S.: Effective recursive algorithm for computing multiplicative inverses in $GF(2^m)$. In: Electronic Letters (1988)
28. Joye, M., Yen, S.-M.: The Montgomery Powering Ladder. In: Kaliski Jr., B.S., Koç, Ç.K., Paar, C. (eds.) CHES 2002. LNCS, vol. 2523, pp. 291–302. Springer, Heidelberg (2003)
29. Kern, T., Feldhofer, M.: Low-Resource ECDSA Implementation for Passive RFID Tags. In: ICECS, pp. 1236–1239. IEEE (2010)
30. Kocher, P.C.: Timing Attacks on Implementations of Diffie-Hellman, RSA, DSS, and Other Systems. In: Koblitz, N. (ed.) CRYPTO 1996. LNCS, vol. 1109, pp. 104–113. Springer, Heidelberg (1996)
31. Kocher, P.C., Jaffe, J., Jun, B.: Differential Power Analysis. In: Wiener, M. (ed.) CRYPTO 1999. LNCS, vol. 1666, pp. 388–397. Springer, Heidelberg (1999)
32. Lenstra, A.K., Lenstra, H., Lovász, L.: Factoring Polynomials with Rational Coefficients. In: Mathematische Annalen (1982)
33. Liu, A., Ning, P.: TinyECC: A Configurable Library for Elliptic Curve Cryptography in Wireless Sensor Networks. In: International Conference on Information Processing in Sensor Networks (2008)
34. Montgomery, P.L.: Speeding the Pollard and Elliptic Curve Methods of Factorization. In: Mathematics of Computation (1987)
35. National Institute of Standards and Technology (NIST). FIPS-186-3: Digital Signature Standard, DSS (2009)
36. NXP Semiconductors. NXP Licenses ARM Cortex-M0+ Processor (March 2012); Press Release
37. Olivier Girard. openMSP430 (2013), http://opencores.org/project,openmsp430
38. Öztürk, E., Sunar, B., Savaş, E.: Low-Power Elliptic Curve Cryptography Using Scaled Modular Arithmetic. In: Joye, M., Quisquater, J.-J. (eds.) CHES 2004. LNCS, vol. 3156, pp. 92–106. Springer, Heidelberg (2004)
39. Satoh, A., Takano, K.: A Scalable Dual-Field Elliptic Curve Cryptographic Processor. In: IEEE Transactions on Computers (2003)
40. Schmidt, J.-M., Herbst, C.: A Practical Fault Attack on Square and Multiply. In: FDTC. IEEE Computer Society (2008)
41. Schmidt, J.-M., Medwed, M.: A Fault Attack on ECDSA. In: FDTC. IEEE (2009)
42. Szczechowiak, P., Oliveira, L.B., Scott, M., Collier, M., Dahab, R.: NanoECC: Testing the Limits of Elliptic Curve Cryptography in Sensor Networks. In: Verdone, R. (ed.) EWSN 2008. LNCS, vol. 4913, pp. 305–320. Springer, Heidelberg (2008)
43. Texas Instruments. MSP430 Ultra-Low Power 16-Bit Microcontrollers (2013), http://www.ti.com/msp430
44. Unterluggauer, T.: Xetroc-M0+. An implementation of ARMs Cortex-M0+. Master project, Graz University of Technology (2013)
45. Wang, H., Sheng, B., Li, Q.: Elliptic Curve Cryptography-based Access Control in Sensor Networks. International Journal of Security and Networks (2006)

46. Wenger, E.: A Lightweight ATmega-based Application-Specific Instruction-Set Processor for Elliptic Curve Cryptography. In: Avoine, G., Kara, O. (eds.) LightSec 2013. LNCS, vol. 8162, pp. 1–15. Springer, Heidelberg (2013)
47. Wenger, E., Baier, T., Feichtner, J.: JAAVR: Introducing the Next Generation of Security-Enabled RFID Tags. In: DSD, pp. 640–647. IEEE (2012)
48. Wenger, E., Feldhofer, M., Felber, N.: Low-Resource Hardware Design of an Elliptic Curve Processor for Contactless Devices. In: Chung, Y., Yung, M. (eds.) WISA 2010. LNCS, vol. 6513, pp. 92–106. Springer, Heidelberg (2011)
49. Wenger, E., Werner, M.: Evaluating 16-Bit Processors for Elliptic Curve Cryptography. In: Prouff, E. (ed.) CARDIS 2011. LNCS, vol. 7079, pp. 166–181. Springer, Heidelberg (2011)
50. Werner, M.: IDLE430 - an ImproveD msp LikE processor. Master project, Graz University of Technology (2013)
51. Yen, S.-M., Joye, M.: Checking Before Output Not Be Enough Against Fault-Based Cryptanalysis. IEEE Transactions on Computers. IEEE (May 2000)

A Analysis of Point Multiplication Formula

The following analysis discusses how Algorithm 1 holds up against the most common side-channel attacks. It is based on the overview papers of Fan et al. [12,13]. Attacks that are considered not to affect the security of the given algorithm:

Timing analysis [30] is not possible, because the used Montgomery Ladder [25] has a key-independent runtime, and all finite-field operations have a constant runtime as well. To avoid leading-zero-bits timing attacks [6] based on the LLL algorithm [32], we set the most-significant bit of the secret ephemeral scalar to one.

Simple power analysis [31] is hindered by using a Montgomery Ladder and Randomized Projective Coordinates.

Differential power analysis [31], Refined power analysis [18] are not possible as random ephemeral scalars are used for DHKE and ECDSA.

M & C safe-error analysis [28,51] are not possible because a Montgomery ladder in conjunction with random ephemeral scalars is used.

Invalid point analysis [5], Twist-curve based analysis [14] is not possible because in lines 1, 3, 10, and 12 point-validity checks are performed.

Subgroup analysis [5] is not possible because an y-recovery with subsequent point verification is performed. Ebeid and Lambert [11] provide a thorough analysis of the y-recovery as countermeasure.

Attacks that may affect the security of the given algorithm:

Program-flow fault analysis [40,41]. A fault attack applied on the program flow can hardly be detected by the program flow itself. To circumvent such paths of attacks, hardware countermeasures are recommended.

Invalid-curve analysis [8] has to be additionally handled by checking the validity of the stored curve parameters. This is not done within Algorithm 1, but the point-validity checks certainly handicap any invalid-curve attack.

Electromagnetic-emanation analysis [23] is possible if the attacker can detect which memory locations are accessed at certain points in time. A countermeasure would be to randomize the memory access patterns.

Accelerating Sorting of Fully Homomorphic Encrypted Data

Ayantika Chatterjee, Manish Kaushal, and Indranil Sengupta

Indian Institute of Technology, Kharagpur, India
{cayantika,manishkaushal163}@gmail.com, isg@iitkgp.ac.in

Abstract. Sorting is an age old problem in Computer Science. Recently with the advent of cloud computing this problem is revisited on encrypted data. This paper tries to evaluate the possibility of applying the recently discovered Fully Homomorphic Encryption schemes to sort encrypted text. The paper first develops fully homomorphic circuits for performing comparison based swaps and then employs them to realize conventional sorting algorithms. Since the sorting time grows exponentially with the input size, it is required to propose suitable measures to reduce it; the delay occuring due to the costly Recrypt operation which removes the noise in the Homomorphic computations. The paper then investigates the opportunity of reducing Recrypt by experimenting on the average errors introduced due to wrong comparisons, which arise due to the removal of the de-noising step. Results show that suitably choosing the number of Recrypt operations results in an almost sorted array. This motivates to develop a two-stage sorting called LazySort: the first phase performing a Bubble sort with reduced Recrypt operations to result in an almost sorted array, to be followed by a second stage which employs an Insertion sort with all Recrypt operations. Detailed experiments show that helps to obtain a significant speed up in the sorting time.

1 Introduction

Storage and management in cloud services are of growing importance due to its low cost approach of using large shared resources. However, with public access to the information in clouds security is a very important issue. Confidentiality of data can be preserved by encrypting critical data before storing it in the cloud. However using any encryption algorithm inhibits performing computations on the information stored in the cloud, as they are in the ciphertext domain. Bringing the data back and processing also leads to an overhead and outweighs the advantage of cloud computing. Homomorphic encryption which allows operations directly on the encrypted data is a major solution to reduce this overhead. The notion of delegating the ability to process secured data without giving away access to it was first introduced in [7] and vividly explained in Gentry's work [3]. In this paper, Gentry introduced the concept of performing arbitrary manipulations like addition, multiplication etc on encrypted data without the knowledge of secret key. The basic idea of this Fully Homomorphic Encryption (FHE) is

G. Paul and S. Vaudenay (Eds.): INDOCRYPT 2013, LNCS 8250, pp. 262–273, 2013.

as follows: Consider the messages $m_1, \ldots, m_t$, which are encrypted to the ciphertexts $c_1, \ldots, c_t$ with the FHE scheme under some key. For any efficiently computable function f, the FHE scheme allows anyone to efficiently compute a ciphertext that decrypts to $f(m_1, \ldots, m_t)$ under the secret key.

However there are several practical limitations of applying the FHE scheme to solve real life problems. One of the age old computer science problems is to sort information. This paper looks into the aspect of applying the FHE scheme to perform sorting of encrypted data. We investigate sorting algorithms based on comparisons. To achieve this we need further procedures and architectures based on the fundamental encrypted additions and multiplications on single bits defined in [3] and implemented using integers in [4] and [2]. Further works on fully homomorphic encryption has been reported on [6] and [9]. Some advances has been reported on [1] and [8].

Our work first develops a comparison based swap which utilizes a Fully Homomorphic Multiplexer circuit developed using the FHE primitives (like adder, multiplier). Results show that due to the costly Recrypt operations, which removes the noise of the FHE operations and produces correct results, the overall time of sorting grows exponentially with the number of elements, making it impractical. To alleviate this issue, the paper subsequently proposes a lazy two staged technique of sorting, LazySort. The proposed method is based on the observation that popular sorting techniques like Bubble sort are quite tolerant against erroneous comparisons, where around 30% error in the comparisons provide more than 50% correctly sorted data. Thus the LazySort algorithm performs first a Bubble sort with reduced Recrypt operations, followed by an Insertion sort stage with all the Recrypt operations present. Owing to the efficiency of Insertion sort for almost sorted data, the two staged approach leads to a remarkable improvement in the sorting process. Detailed experimental results are provided to demonstrate the above phenomena.

The overall paper is organised as follows: section 2 describes the basic concept of homomorphic encryption. Next, section 3 describes design of the comparison unit which is the basic building for sorting. Further, section 4 explains the design and timing requirement of sorting in homomorphic domain. Finally, section 5 mentions some future direction of this work.

2   Preliminaries: Fully Homomorphic Encryption

A homomorphism is a structure-preserving transformation between two sets, where an operation on two members in the first set is preserved in the second set on the corresponding members. Let P and C be sets with members $p_1, p_2 \in P$, t is a transformation between the two sets with its reverse function t' and an operation $\oplus$. The system is a homomorphism, if $\forall (p_1, p_2) \in P$, $(p_1 \oplus p_2) = t'(t(p_1) \ominus t(p_2))$. If there are two functions $\oplus$ and $\otimes$, such that $\forall (p_1, p_2) \in P$, $(p_1 \oplus p_2) = t'(t(p_1) \ominus t(p_2))$ and $\forall (p_1, p_2) \in P$, $(p_1 \otimes p_2) = t'(t(p_1) * t(p_2))$. This is called an algebraic homomorphism. Operations $\oplus$ and $\otimes$ on plaintext may be similar or may be different with the opearations $\ominus$ and $*$ performed on ciphertext.

The obvious practical implication is the possibility to transform the two members p_1 and p_2 into the range of C, thus applying some sort of encryption, and having the operations $\oplus$ and $\otimes$ (or equivalent operations) performed by a third party. The result can then be decrypted back into the range of P. An algebraically homomorphic crypto-system can be described as a 6-tuple $H_1 = (P, C, t, t', \oplus, \otimes)$ where P and C denote the plain-text space and the ciphertext space, respectively, whereas t and t' denote the encryption and decryption functions. $\oplus$ and $\otimes$ tag the two algebraic operations. Gentry's approach [3] of bootstrapping is to develop a fully homomorphic from a somewhat homomorphic system and provide addition and multiplication plus a normalization procedure that is supposed to allow unlimited chaining of operations in ciphertext space. This technique of reducing noise in the cipher-text space requires for an additional formal descriptive item, extending H_1 to $H_2 = (P, C, t, t', \oplus, \otimes, r)$, introducing a reduction-function r, which takes a noisy cipher-text and transforms it into an equivalent with reduced noise.

An encryption scheme ε consists of three algorithms: $KeyGen_\varepsilon$, $Encrypt_\varepsilon$ and $Decrypt_\varepsilon$. Each of these algorithms must be efficient, i.e. they must all run in polynomial time (λ), where λ is the security parameter which specifies the bit-length of the keys. $KeyGen_\varepsilon$ generates a key, which is used in both $Encrypt_\varepsilon$ and $Decrypt_\varepsilon$. In the next subsections, we shall discuss about two main homomorphic schemes: Somewhat homomorphic scheme and fully homomorphic scheme.

2.1   Somewhat Homomorphic Scheme

Consider the following encryption scheme. Here λ is the security parameter. We set $N = \lambda$, $P = \lambda^2$ and $Q = \lambda^5$.

- $KeyGen_\varepsilon(\lambda)$: Generate a random P-bit odd integer p, which acts as the key.
- $Encrypt_\varepsilon(p, m)$: Output a ciphertext $c \leftarrow m' + p * q$, where m' is a random N-bit number such that $m' = m \bmod 2$ and q is any random Q-bit number.
- $Decrypt_\varepsilon(p, c)$: Output $(c \bmod p) \bmod 2$.
- $Evaluate_\varepsilon(f, c_1, \ldots c_t)$: The boolean function f is first converted to an equivalent function f' with only AND and XOR gates. Then the AND and XOR operators are replaced with multiplication and addition operators respectively to generate the function f''. Compute and return $f''(c_1, \ldots, c_t)$.

2.2   Recrypt: Error Minimization in Ciphertext

One can observe that the ciphertexts from ε are near-multiples of p. ($c \bmod p$) is referred to as the noise associated with the cipher-text. It is the difference from the nearest multiple of p. Since the noise has the same parity as the message encrypted. Operations like $Add\_\varepsilon(c_1, c_2)$, $Sub\_\varepsilon(c_1, c_2)$ and $Mult\_\varepsilon(c_1, c_2)$ are computed as $(c_1 + c_2)$, $(c_1 - c_2)$ and $(c_1 * c_2)$ respectively.

In order to make it more convincing, an example is presented. For the computation of $Mult\_\varepsilon(c_1, c_2)$, where $c_1 \leftarrow Encrypt_\varepsilon(p, m_1) = m'_1 + p * q_1$, and

$c_2 \leftarrow Encrypt_\varepsilon(p, m_2) = m_2' + p * q_2$. The cipher-text output by $Evaluate\_\varepsilon$ is $c = c_1 * c_2$. So,

$$c = m_1' * m_2' + p * q' \tag{1}$$

where q' is some integer. As long as the noise $m_1' * m_2'$ is small, and not comparable to p, we have:

$$c \bmod p = m_1' * m_2' \tag{2}$$

Therefore, $(c \bmod p) \bmod 2 = m_1 * m_2$. This scheme works as long as the noise does not blow up too much and start affecting the result. It is easy to prove that this scheme is incomplete, because if the result of an operation between the two operands a and b exceeds the prime modulus p, the decryption fails. So starting with two clean plain-text items, the intermediate result grows towards the modulus with every operation and in this sense is polluted. To compensate for this, a fully homomorphic encryption scheme must define normalization (as mentioned reencryption procedure in [3]) of the intermediate result. In the case of the system shown here, a normalization would be any function that can minimize the remainder mod p of the result while preserving the parity mod p. Gentry addresses this problem by generating a public key that contains a decryption hint. This hint allows to homomorphically decrypt the intermediate result in the encrypted domain, which means that the plain-text of the argument remains unknown. With the plain-text at hand in cipherspace, it is possible to reencrypt the plain-text which generates a new cipher of the plain-text with reduced noise. Now reencryption can be defined as follows:

- $Recrypt_\varepsilon(pk_2, D_\varepsilon, sk_1, c_1)$: Compute $\overline{c_1} \leftarrow Encrypt_\varepsilon(pk_2, <c_1>)$ over the bits of c_1. Then output $c \leftarrow Evaluate_\varepsilon(pk_2, D_\varepsilon, \overline{sk_1}; \overline{c_1})$.

Here c_1 is the ciphertext encrypted under pk_1, $\overline{sk_1}$ are the bits of the secret key sk_1 encrypted under pk_2, and D_ε is the decryption circuit. If we observe carefully, we will find that $Recrypt_\varepsilon$ takes in a ciphertext encrypted in pk_1 and outputs another new ciphertext encrypted under pk_2. This recryption procedure basically refreshes the noise element, so that it once again becomes small enough. But for that, the scheme must be able to handle the decryption function $Decrypt_\varepsilon$. But the scheme that we just discussed does not have this property, and so the scheme is not appropriate.

2.3   Fully Homomorphic Scheme

In order to make the above scheme fully homomorphic, Gentry introduced the concept of bootstrapping. He defined a scheme to be bootstrappable if the set F_ε of permitted function includes the $Decrypt_\varepsilon$ function. The scheme ε is transformed to ε^* so that the new scheme becomes bootstrappable. This scheme requires two integer parameters $0 < \alpha < \beta$.

- $KeyGen_{\varepsilon*}(\lambda)$: Run $KeyGen_{\varepsilon*}(\lambda)$ to obtain p. A set $\overrightarrow{y} = \{y_1, y_2, \ldots y_\beta\}$ is generated such that $y_i \in [0, 2)$. Out of these elements, there must exist a sparse subset $S \subset \overrightarrow{y}$ of α elements, such that $\sum_{y_j \in S}(y_j) = \frac{1}{p} \bmod 2$. Set sk to be a binary encoding s of the sparse subset S, where $s = (0, 1)^\beta$. Set $pk \leftarrow (p, \overrightarrow{y})$.
- $Encrypt_{\varepsilon*}(pk, m)$: Run $Encrypt_\varepsilon(pk, m)$ to obtain the ciphertext c. Generate $\overrightarrow{z} : z_i \leftarrow c.y_i \bmod 2$. Return $c^* = (c, \overrightarrow{z})$. In the rest of the paper, we shall mention $Encrypt_{\varepsilon*}(pk, m)$ as $Encrypt$.
- $Decrypt_{\varepsilon*}(sk, c^*)$: Output LSB$(c)$ XOR LSB$(\lfloor \sum_t S_t z_t \rceil)$, where LSB() returns the least significant bit of the input, and $\lfloor . \rceil$ returns the nearest integer to the input. Decryption works since (up to small precision errors) $\sum_t S_t z_t = \sum_t c S_t y_t = \frac{c}{p} \bmod 2$.

The computations also get modified as $Add_{\varepsilon*}(c^*, c_1^*, c_2^*)$: Obtain c by running $Add_\varepsilon(c, c_1, c_2)$. Compute $\overrightarrow{z}$ from c and $\overrightarrow{y}$ in a manner similar to the one explained in $Encrypt_{\varepsilon*}$. $Mult_{\varepsilon*}$ and $Sub_{\varepsilon*}$ will be computed similarly.

3   Fully Homomorphic Swap

Comparison based sorting algorithms are based on conditional swap operations. When the data is encrypted this operation translates to a Fully Homomorphic Swap (FHS) operation. We use the following Fully Homomorphic primitive primitive circuits to realize the FHS circuit:

- fhe_add: Add ciphertexts (XOR).
- fhe_mul: Multiply ciphertexts (AND)
- fhe_fulladd: Add with carry in and carry out
- fhe_halfadd: Add with carry out

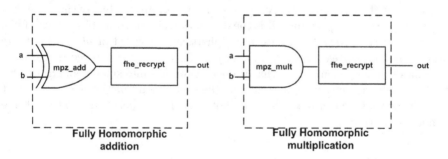

Fig. 1. Fully Homomorphic addition and multiplication

The FHS circuit depends on two main operations : subtraction operation and decision making based on the subtraction result. Fully Homomorphic subtraction, which is built using the fhe_add operation by performing homomorphic addition of one ciphertext with 2's complement of another ciphertext. The Subtraction can be implemented by adding one number with the 2's complement of another. For two plaintext numbers a and b, subtraction can be computed as:

$$a - b = a + \text{2's complement of b} \tag{3}$$

Now a homomorphic subtraction of a' and b' which are the encryptions of a and b respectively is computed using the homomorphic addition as follows:

$$a' - b' = a' + Encrypt(\text{ 2's complement of b}) \tag{4}$$

$$\tag{5}$$

The 2's complement of b in the encrypted domain is obtained as follows:

$$Encrypt((2's\ complement\ of\ b), pk) = b' \oplus$$
$$Encrypt(11\ldots 1, pk) \oplus Encrypt(1, pk)$$

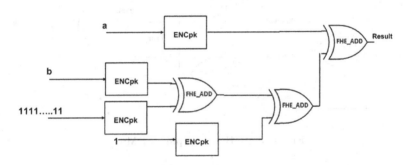

Fig. 2. Fully Homomorphic Subtraction

Figure 3 shows addition module in fully homomorphic domain and it is used to design the subtraction circuit as shown in figure 2. The MSB of the subtraction output is further fed to the decision making module as a selection line. The following equations represent how the swap operation takes place between two elements $A[i]$ and $A[i+1]$ depending on MSB (represented here as bt):

$$temp = bt * A[i] + (1 - bt) * A[i+1]$$
$$A[i+1] = (1 - bt) * A[i] + bt * A[i+1]$$
$$A[i] = temp$$

Figure 3 shows the overall swap operation in fully homomorphic domain. As the figure depicts, other than the fully homomorphic subtraction, FHS operation also depends on decision making of multiplexer(MUX) in homomorphic domain.

Figure 4 represents the fully homomorphic MUX (fhe_mux) designed with fhe_add and fhe_mul modules. In the figure, a' and b' are the encryptions of the

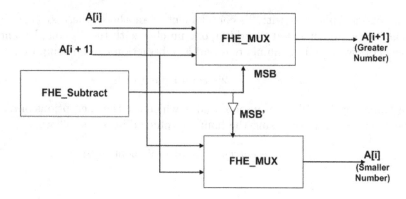

Fig. 3. Fully Homomorphic Swap

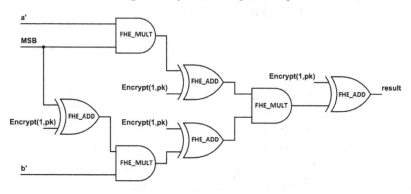

Fig. 4. Fully Homomorphic 2:1 Mux

two inputs a and b and MSB represents the MSB of the subtraction output. In every stage, to invert any input we add $Encrypt(1, pk)$ using fhe_add circuit. Finally, the output result of the MUX is computed as follows:

$$\overline{(a'.MSB).(b'.\overline{MSB})} = a'.MSB + b'\overline{MSB} \qquad [applying\ De\ Morgan's\ law]$$

$\overline{var}$ represents the inversion of var, where var is any variable. The overall module is designed with the inhand functions available to Scarab library [5]. With the help of this function we have developed the sorting operation in homomorphic domain. In the subsequent section, we explain the implementation of sorting algorithm in detail.

Next we shall discuss about the other submodule required for swap operation.

4   Homomorphic Form of Sorting

In this section, we consider two common sorting algorithms namely Bubble and Insertion sorts on encrypted data. We use the above developed FHS circuit for

Algorithm 1. Fully Homomorphic Bubble sort

```
void bubble_sort(mpz_t **enc_arr, int lenarr, fhe_pk_t pk){

int i, j, k, m;
mpz_t * temp1 = (mpz_t*)calloc(sizeof(mpz_t), sizeof(int) * 8);
char *ptext = (char*)calloc(sizeof(char), sizeof(int) * 8);
for (i = 0; i < lenarr − 1; i + +) do
    for (j = 0; j < lenarr − i − 1; j + +) do
        copy_mpz_arr(temp1, enc_arr[j]);
        copy_mpz_arr(temp2, enc_arr[j + 1]);
        fhe_Swap(enc_arr[j + 1], enc_arr[j], temp1, temp2, pk);

free(temp1);
free(temp2);
temp1 = NULL;
temp2 = NULL;
}
```

achieving the sorting functionalities. In Algorithm 1 we present an overview of fully homomorphic bubble sort.

In the algorithm mpz_t is the datatype mentioned in the library [5]. The function $copy\_mpz\_arr$ is to copy $enc\_arr[j]$ to the temp array. Finally, fhe_Swap is the function for above mentioned FHS operation and responsible for the main swap operation in the comparison based sorting. Further, we implement the Insertion sort of the encrypted data using the above FHS operation. The sorting was performed on input sizes of length $5 - 40$ for repeated runs of around 20 times. As can be observed that the average time for performing the encryptions increase exponentially with time.

Further, we investigate the ways to improve the performance of this sorting algorithm in fully homomorphic domain. We shall analyse how the number of recrypt operation can be reduced maintaining the overall functionality as this recrypt operation is the main reason of large timing requirement in homomorphic domain. Here are few techniques used in order to reduce number of recrypts.

- Recrypt operation is mainly required to refresh the ciphertext when error in the ciphertext increases beyond a certain threshold. Since, fhe_add function is the homomorphic implementtion of addition operation, error level is expected to be at most double, where it can be square for homomorphic multiplication. Hence, all the recrypts after addition operation are removed.
- To properly estimate the requirement of recrypt operation, measurement of noise is important. Hence, a noise measurement module is added and recrypt operation is performed once the noise level is crossing the threshold.

Table 1 shows required time for performing different sorting with increasing number of data. With the presence of all recrypt operations, initially around 807s was required for sorting only 5 data in homomorphic domain. From the reduced timing requirement in this table, it is clear that sorting using the fully

Table 1. Comparison of different sortings

Sorting	No. of elements	Average Timing requirement (sec)
Bubble Sort	5	235
	10	1527
	40	21565
Insertion Sort	5	290
	10	1702
	40	21757

homomorphic scheme is costly due to the presence of Recrypt operations. As we have taken size of integers as 32 bits, many functions/circuits on encrypted numbers have a constant overhead. Following table shows all the values of overhead in seconds.

Table 2. Estimate of different suboperations for sorting

	Operation	Overhead(sec)
1.	fhe add(XOR)	0.4
2.	fhe mul(AND)	0.5
3.	fhe swap(greater/smaller)	14.2
4.	fhe swap(greater+smaller)	26.5
5.	fhe recrypt	0.4

Using these values we have theoretically estimated the required time for sorting which mainly depends on time for each comparison, which in turn again depends on fhe_add, fhe_mul and Recrypt. For e.g. for $n = 40$, around n^2 comparisons are required. The total timing requirement in average case is around $((40^2) * 26.5/2)$s or 21,200s which is very close to practical time as observed in table 1. Figure 5 shows the comparison between theoretical and practical requirements.

Till now we have measured the possible minimization of recrypt properly maintaining the sorting operation. Next we shall introduce the concept of Lazy sorting and discuss about its possible advantages of it in sorting of encrypted data in terms of performance.

Lazy Sorting. In previous section recrypt operations are minimized but it is ensured that the sorting is errorless. However, as shown in the previous section the overall timing for sorting is quite slow.

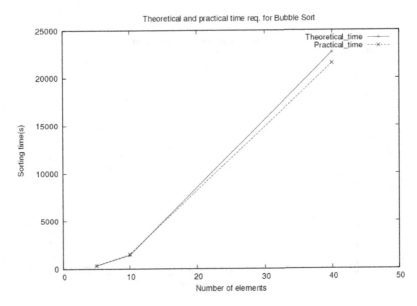

Fig. 5. Timing requirement for fully homomorphic Bubble sort

In this section we introduce the concept of lazy-sorting which is based on lazy fhe_swap. In this operation, we further reduce the number of recrypts. Reduction of recrypt operation leads to erroneous swap. In order to analyze the effect, we purposefully perform some erroneous swaps and analyze how much erroneous swaps can be tolerated to result in an almost sorted array. This almost sorted array is further converted to final sorted array but with an advantage of less number of recrypts. Figure 6 shows an average of several experiments with more than 1000 data to measure the allowable error. It shows that on an average with around 30% error, around 60% data are placed in proper position.

Thus, minimization of recrypt after a certain threshold may introduce some error in the comparison decision(swap) of fully homomorphic encrypted data. Hence, this will in turn introduce some error in the sorting decision. The term **error** indicates an element is placed in wrong position in the final sorted array. Now, if we perform any erroneous comparison sort with minimized recrypt, it will take comparatively less time due to the use of comparison circuit with reduced number of recrypts and results an almost sorted array. Finally, we apply insertion sort, which works in linear time for an almost sorted array.

4.1 Futher Reduction of Recrypt to Introduce Error

Now, according to the analysis in figure 6, it is evident that it is not possible to remove all the recrypts since it will introduce 100% error and result in positioning large number of elements in the wrong place in the sorted array. For this reason, careful choice of removable recrypts are necessary. We have identified the recrypts

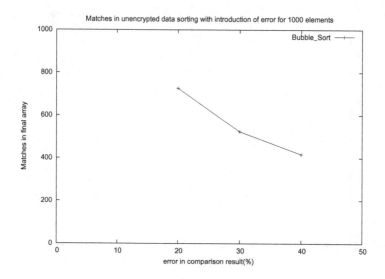

Fig. 6. Allowable Error analysis on unencrypted data

present in fhe_subtract, which is one of the main submodule of fhe_swap. In this function, we have removed the recrypt operations required to correct the values of carry bit(*cout*) of the addition result using fhe_fulladd. This in turn reduces the time requirement in every iteration of addition and finally reduces the time for swap operation. However, use of this modified swap operation results correct output with 70% accuracy. This results in an almost sorted array. Subsequently, we apply insertion sort, which has linear time complexity for almost sorted array.

Table 3. Timing analysis for Lazy sort

Sorting	No. of elements	Fully homomorphic sorting Time (sec)	Lazy sort time (sec)
Bubble (almost sorted) with insertion sort	10	1527	976
	40	21565	1399

Table 3 shows the advantage of this scheme, where general Bubble sort in homomorphic domain requires around 21500s, performing bubble sort with this erroneous technique reduces the time to 1350s.

5   Conclusion

In this paper, we have explained a technique for sorting on encrypted data using homomorphic encryption. To the best of our knowledge, there is no reported sorting technique on encrypted data. However, the fully homomorphic addition and multiplication operations are slow due to the presence of cipher refreshing recrypt technique. This in turn detoriates the overall performance. With this motivation, we have experimented the effect of eliminating recrypts, the error arising thereof and the effect of that on sorting. Finally, based on these observations, we propose a two stage lazy-technique for sorting which improves the time for sorting significantly. As a future work, we can further investigate various different ways of improving performance by applying parallelization and other techniques in software domain and perform a formal timing analysis for modified sorting schemes. Further, it can be investigated what is the relation between such sorting schemes and security of such homomorphic cryptosystems. Implementing the overall algorithm in a dedicated hardware can be looked in this context.

Acknowledgements. We would like to thank **Neucleodyne Systems, USA** for funding this project and anonymous reviewers for their constructive comments, which helped us to improve the manuscript.

References

1. Akinwande, M.: Advances in homomorphic cryptosystems 15(3), 506–522 (2009)
2. Coron, J.-S., Mandal, A., Naccache, D., Tibouchi, M.: Fully homomorphic encryption over the integers with shorter public keys. In: Rogaway, P. (ed.) CRYPTO 2011. LNCS, vol. 6841, pp. 487–504. Springer, Heidelberg (2011)
3. Gentry, C.: Computing arbitrary functions of encrypted data. Commun. ACM 53(3), 97–105 (2010)
4. Gentry, C., Halevi, S., Vaikuntanathan, V.: Fully homomorphic encryption over the integers (2010)
5. https://hcrypt.com//scarab~library
6. Naehrig, M., Lauter, K., Vaikuntanathan, V.: Can homomorphic encryption be practical? In: Proceedings of the 3rd ACM Workshop on Cloud Computing Security Workshop, CCSW 2011, pp. 113–124. ACM, New York (2011)
7. Rivest, R.L., Adleman, L., Dertouzos, M.L.: On data banks and privacy homomorphisms. In: Foundations of Secure Computation, pp. 169–179. Academia Press (1978)
8. Stehle, D., Steinfeld, R.: Faster fully homomorphic encryption. Cryptology ePrint Archive, Report 2010/299 (2010), http://eprint.iacr.org/
9. Vijaya Kumari, G., Govinda Ramaiah, Y.: Towards practical homomorphic encryption with efficient public key generation. ACEEE International Journal on Network Security 3(4), 8 (2012)

Construction of Recursive MDS Diffusion Layers from Gabidulin Codes*

Thierry P. Berger

XLIM (UMR CNRS 7252), Université de Limoges,
123 av. A. Thomas, 87060 Limoges Cedex, France
thierry.berger@unilim.fr

Abstract. Many recent block ciphers use Maximum Distance Separable (MDS) matrices in their diffusion layer. The main objective of this operation is to spread as much as possible the differences between the outputs of nonlinear Sboxes. So they generally act at nibble or at byte level. The MDS matrices are associated to MDS codes of ratio 1/2. The most famous example is the MixColumns operation of the AES block cipher.

In this example, the MDS matrix was carefully chosen to obtain compact and efficient implementations in software and hardware. However, this MDS matrix is dedicated to 8-bit words, and is not always adapted to lightweight applications. Recently, several studies have been devoted to the construction of recursive diffusion layers. Such a method allows to apply an MDS matrix using an iterative process which looks like a Feistel network with linear functions instead of nonlinear.

In this paper, we present a generic construction of MDS recursive diffusion layers as proposed in [1], [7], [10], [12], [15] but bridging this construction with the theory of Gabidulin codes. This construction uses Gabidulin codes which have the property to be not only MDS but also MRD (Maximum Rank Distance). This fact gives an additional property to diffusion layers which seems interesting for cryptographic applications.

Keywords: MDS matrices, diffusion, Gabidulin codes, rank distance, MixColumns.

1 Introduction

The MixColumns of the AES [5] is an important step in the diffusion of differences between the outputs of Sboxes. The MixColumns matrix is in fact a redundancy matrix of an MDS code of length 8, dimension 4 and minimum distance 5 over $GF(2^8)$. This matrix was carefully chosen to optimize software implementations. It remains suitable for hardware implementations. However, in some situations, the cost of the implementation may be too high in relation to available resources [10].

---

* This work was partially supported by the French National Agency of Research: ANR-11-INS-011.

G. Paul and S. Vaudenay (Eds.): INDOCRYPT 2013, LNCS 8250, pp. 274–285, 2013.

Moreover, MixColumns is efficient on 4 blocks of byte. In the lightweight block cipher KLEIN [9], the authors use this MixColumns operation on 8 nibble blocks. In this context, MixColumns is far from being optimal when considering the resistance against linear and differential attacks. In this case, its branch number is equal to 5 as shown in [3], while the optimum value is 9.

Following the work of Sajadieh et al. [12] and of Guo et al. [10], some recent papers [1], [7], [9], [15] are devoted to the construction of recursive diffusion matrices. This method consists in searching a companion matrix of size r with entries that are linear applications of $GF(2)^m$ into itself, where m is the size of the Sboxes, such that r iterations of this matrix is an MDS matrix. The main advantage of this approach is the fact that this MDS matrix can be implemented in hardware using a Feistel network with r rounds. In this case, the internal non-linear functions usually used in a Feistel network are replaced by linear applications which correspond to the last row of the companion matrix.

In this paper, we present a generic construction of MDS recursive diffusion layers. This construction comes from the theory of Maximum Rank Distance (MRD) codes and Gabidulin codes. So our MDS diffusion matrices have the additional MRD property.

This paper is organized as follows: in Section 2, we recall some results on the link between MDS codes and optimal diffusion layers and the construction of recursive diffusion layers. In Section 3 we first introduce some basic results on Gabidulin, we construct MDS matrices from Gabidulin codes and show that they are suitable for a recursive implementation. We discuss the interest of MRD property for cryptographic applications and we compare our results with existing works.

2 Recursive MDS Diffusion Layers

In this section we will recall some recent results on linear diffusion layers and their links with MDS codes.

2.1 MDS Matrices in Cryptography

The results concerning error coding codes and MDS codes are standard and can be found in [11]. To my knowledge, the link between MDS codes and optimal diffusion layers was introduced first in [13], [14] and was extensively studied in [4], [5].

Let K denotes the finite field $GF(2^m)$ and E denotes the $GF(2)$ vector space $GF(2)^m$ (there is no more multiplication by a scalar in E). The integer m corresponds in practice to the size of blocks, *i.e.* the binary size of the Sboxes of the non-linear part of a cryptographic scheme. A linear code of length n over K is a K-subspace of K^n. An additive code of length n over E is a $GF(2)$-subspace of E^n. Let k be the dimension of a linear code C over K or $\log_{2^m}(^\#C)$ for an additive code C over E.

The minimum distance of a code is the minimum number of non-zero coordinates of non-zero codewords. The MDS bound is the upper bound given by the relation $k + d \leq n + 1$. In other words, if we try to increase the size of a code, we decrease the distance between codewords. A code which meets this bound is called Maximum Distance Separable (MDS) code.

From a code of ratio $1/2$, *i.e.* $n = 2k$, we obtain some matrices of great interest for linear diffusion layers.

Definition 1. *A square matrix A of size r with coefficients in K is* MDS *(Maximum Distance Separable) if the code C over K generated by the matrix $M = (I_r | A)$ is MDS, where I_r is the $r \times r$ identity matrix.*

The following proposition gives a characterization of MDS matrices over a finite field K:

Proposition 1 ([11]). *A square matrix A of size r with coefficients in K is* MDS *if and only if every square submatrices of A are non singular.*

If a matrix A over a finite field K is MDS, then the matrices A^{-1} and A^t are MDS.

In the case of additive codes, the definition of MDS matrices is a little more complicated. Roughly speaking, the generator matrix M of Definition 1 becomes a matrix with entries in $\mathcal{L}(GF(2)^m, GF(2)^m)$, the set of $GF(2)$-endomorphisms of $GF(2)^m$. Sometimes, these endomorphisms are replaced by their $m \times$ binary matrices representations, in that case the diffusion layers is described by a $mr \times mr$ binary matrix which is MDS by blocks of size r.

One can remark that Proposition 1 does not hold in the general case, but remains true if the entries of the matrix are commutative endomorphisms, which is the case for example in [1], [7], [12], [15].

A major application of MDS matrices in cryptography is the design of linear diffusion layers in block ciphers or cryptographic hash functions. The best known example of the use of MDS matrices to design a linear layer is the AES Mix-Columns operation. It takes as input $r = 4$ blocks of byte ($m = 8$) and outputs 4 blocks of byte. The main requirement of such an operation is to diffuse any change into the maximum number of blocks.

If $\mathcal{A}$ is a $r \times r$ diffusion matrix with entries in K, the output is simply the image of the input $x \in K^r$ by $\mathcal{A}$: $y = (\mathcal{A}x^t)^t = x\mathcal{A}^t$, where $\mathcal{A}^t$ denotes the transpose of $\mathcal{A}$.

The resistance against linear or differential cryptanalysis of a diffusion layer is measured by the linear and differential branch numbers. As explained in [5], the linear branch number is the minimum distance of the linear code generated by the matrix $(I_r | A)$ and the differential branch number is the minimum distance of the linear code generated by the matrix $(I_r | A^t)$.

In consequence, a diffusion layer A has optimal linear and differential branch numbers if and only if it is an MDS matrix (either considered over a finite field or over E in the situation of additive codes).

So, there is a direct correspondence between optimal diffusion layers and MDS codes of ration $1/2$.

2.2 Recursive MDS Diffusion Layers

The construction and implementation of efficient MDS diffusion layers is a major problem in symmetric cryptography. Reference [8] is a good one for the design of MDS matrices for software applications.

Following the example of MixColumns, in that case the size of the binary MDS diffusion layer is 32×32. Even if MixColumns was well chosen to optimize the implementations, especially in software, in the context of limited resources or hardware implementation the size of this matrix becomes a problem.

To avoid this difficulty, the designers of Photon [10] proposed first the use of a companion matrix D such that $A = D^r$ is MDS. The implementation of D is then compact, and the full diffusion is obtained after r iterations of D.

This approach was generalized by many authors. A nice presentation under a Feistel-like scheme was introduced in [12] and was reused in many papers (see e.g. [7], [15]).

The papers [1], [7], [12], [15] are devoted to the construction of such recursive diffusion layers. The results are obtained by combining theoretical results and exhaustive search. All these papers (except [1]) concern MDS matrices that are associated to additive codes.

We will present this approach in our context which is those of linear codes over K. Moreover, we use the transpose of the traditional companion matrix which corresponds to source-heavy Generalized Feistel Networks (GFN) instead of target-heavy GFN [16].

Let D be a companion matrix of size r over K:

$$D = \begin{pmatrix} 0 & \cdots\cdots & 0 & a_1 \\ 1 & 0 & \ddots & \vdots & a_2 \\ 0 & 1 & \ddots & \vdots & a_3 \\ \vdots & \ddots & \ddots & 0 & \vdots \\ 0 & \cdots & 0 & 1 & a_r \end{pmatrix}.$$

Let $x = (x_1, ..., x_r) \in K^r$ and $y = xD^t$ the image of x by the linear application defined by D. The y_i's can be computed from the x_i's using the following network:

This network can be interpreted as a round of a generalized Feistel network with linear components instead of nonlinear. Note that this function is bijective if and only if a_1 is invertible, since $\det(D) = a_1$. The matrix D^{-1} corresponds also to a generalized Feistel network.

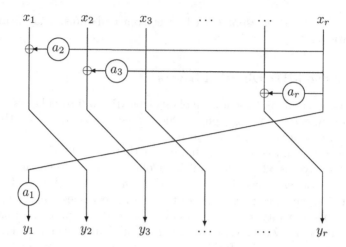

The application of r rounds of this Feistel scheme corresponds to the computation of the matrix $A = D^r$ applied to the input x. In [1], [12], [7], [15], the coefficients a_i are not necessary elements of a finite field, but could be $GF(2)$-linear mappings from $GF(2)^m$ into itself. In this paper, we only consider the case where the linear operations correspond to multiplications in the field K, for example, the symbol a_i in our network means the $GF(2)$-linear application $u \mapsto a_i u$ in K.

3   MDS Matrices from Gabidulin Codes

In this section we introduce some basic properties on the rank metric and the construction of Gabidulin codes, that are optimal for this metric. A complete description of the theory of rank metric and Gabidulin codes can be found in [6].

3.1   Rank Metric and Gabidulin Codes

Let $K = GF(p^m)$ be a finite field which is an extension of degree m of the base field $F = GF(p)$. For our applications, we will restrict ourself to the case $p = 2$.
The field K can be viewed as a vector space of dimension m over F.

Definition 2. *Let $x = (x_1, \ldots, x_n)$ be an element of $E = K^n$, the* rank weight *$rk(x)$ of x is the dimension of the F-vector space generated by $\{x_1, \ldots, x_n\}$.*

For example, let $K = GF(2^3) = GF(2)(\alpha)$ with $\alpha^3 = \alpha + 1$, and $n = 5$. Set $x = (\alpha^6, \alpha, 0, \alpha^5, \alpha) = (\alpha^2 + 1, \alpha, 0, \alpha^2 + \alpha + 1, \alpha)$. The rank of x is $rk(x) = 2$.
A simple way to compute the rank of a codeword x is to use a basis $\mathcal{B} = (b_1, \ldots, b_m)$ of K over F. The rank of x is then the rank of the $m \times n$ matrix M_x with entries in F replacing each coordinate x_i by the column vector of its decomposition over the basis $\mathcal{B}$. Following the previous example, if we use the natural

polynomial basis $\mathcal{B} = (1, \alpha, \alpha^2)$, we obtain the matrix $M_x = \begin{pmatrix} 1 & 0 & 0 & 1 & 0 \\ 0 & 1 & 0 & 1 & 1 \\ 1 & 0 & 0 & 1 & 0 \end{pmatrix}$, which

is of rank 2.

The relation $d_r(a, b) = rk(a - b)$ defines a distance over E. We have the following properties: $d_r(x, y) \leq m$ and $d_r(x, y) \leq d_h(x, y)$, where $d_h(x, y)$ is the Hamming distance between x and y. The rank distance d_r of a linear code C is then the minimum rank weight of its non-zero codewords. There exists a Singleton-like bound for the rank distance:

Proposition 2 ([6]). *If C is a linear code of length n, dimension k and rank distance d_r, then*
- *if $n \leq m$, then* $k + d_r \leq n + 1$
- *if $n > m$, then* $km + d_r n \leq (m + 1)n$.

A maximum rank distance (MRD) code is a code reaching this bound. Note that, if $n \leq m$, then any MRD code is also an MDS code. Following the definition of MDS matrices, we say that a square matrix A has the MRD property if the code generated by $(I_r | A)$ is MRD. As for the Hamming distance, it is easy to verify that, if A has the MRD property, then both A^t and A^{-1} have the MRD property.

In his original article, Gabidulin gives a construction of a family of codes that are MRD, the so-called Gabidulin codes.

Definition 3. *Let $\mathcal{B} = (b_1, b_2, \ldots, b_n)$ be an ordered set of $n \leq m$ elements of K, which are linearly independent over F. The Gabidulin code $\mathcal{G}_{\mathcal{B},k}$ of support $\mathcal{B}$ and dimension k is the code generated by the generator matrix*

$$G_{\mathcal{B},k} = \begin{pmatrix} b_1^{[0]} & b_2^{[0]} & \cdots & b_n^{[0]} \\ b_1^{[1]} & b_2^{[1]} & \cdots & b_n^{[1]} \\ \vdots & \vdots & \ddots & \vdots \\ b_1^{[k-1]} & b_2^{[k-1]} & \cdots & b_n^{[k-1]} \end{pmatrix} \quad \text{with the convention } b_j^{[i]} = b_j^{p^i}.$$

These codes can be viewed as evaluation of linearized polynomials of linear degree strictly less than k over a set of linearly independent points. Using a similar reasoning than for Reed Solomon codes, it is easy to show that these codes are MRD (and so are MDS).

3.2   Construction of MDS Matrices with the MRD Property

As soon as $n \leq m$, a MRD code is MDS. So, from any Gabidulin code of ratio $1/2$, it is direct to construct a MDS matrix as explained in Section 2.1.

In practice, we fix $p = 2$ and $m = 2r$ even. We choose a basis $\mathcal{B} = (b_1, ..., b_m)$ of K over $F = GF(2)$. The Gabidulin code $\mathcal{G}_{\mathcal{B},r}$ is a MRD code of parameters $[m = 2r, r, r + 1]$ over K.

If A is the square matrix of size r over K such that $(I_k | A)$ is the systematic generator matrix of $\mathcal{G}_{\mathcal{B},r}$, then A is an MDS matrix over K.

This matrix is optimal for diffusion on r blocks of size $m = 2r$ and have the additional MRD property.

Example. For example, we set $m = 8$ and $r = 4$. Let α be a root of the primitive polynomial $X^8 + X^4 + X^3 + X^2 + 1$. The set $\mathcal{B} = (1, \alpha, \alpha^2, ..., \alpha^7)$ is a basis of K over F.

The MDS matrix A constructed from the Gabidulin code $\mathcal{G}_{\mathcal{B},4}$ is:

$$A_4 = \begin{pmatrix} \alpha^{15} & \alpha^{253} & \alpha^{205} & \alpha^{153} \\ \alpha^{168} & \alpha^{49} & \alpha^{246} & \alpha^{252} \\ \alpha^{235} & \alpha^{170} & \alpha^{92} & \alpha^{3} \\ \alpha^{238} & \alpha^{190} & \alpha^{138} & \alpha^{18} \end{pmatrix}.$$

This matrix A have the same parameters as MixColumns. Note that $r = 4$ is the maximum size of an MDS matrix with MRD property over $GF(2^8)$.

Note that it is possible to choose $n < m$ linearly independent points of K. In this case, we obtain a $r \times r$ diffusion matrix over K, with $n = 2r$. For instance, if we fix $m = 16$, it is possible to construct an MDS diffusion matrix of size r, $2 \leq r \leq 8$.

The condition $n \leq m$ is very strong and limits the number of MDS matrices with the MRD property. Suppose that $n > m$ and $n = 2k$. In this situation an MRD code is not necessary MDS (in fact, it is generally not MDS). In a previous work [2], we constructed MDS codes of length $n > m$ by extending the evaluation points of linearized polynomial using binary optimal codes. Unfortunately, these codes are no more MRD. Moreover, their parameters are constrained, so it is not possible to attempt a ration $1/2$. These extended Gabidulin codes seem not suitable to construct MDS diffusion layers and have no specific additional properties compared to Reed Solomon codes.

3.3   Analysis of the MRD Property

In this section, we will discuss the meaning of the MRD property for an MDS diffusion matrix. For clarity, we focus on our previous example. The following considerations can be generalized to any block size.

Let C be the Gabidulin code over $K = GF(2^8)$ generated by the matrix $(I_4 | A_4)$. The parameters of this code are $[8, 4, 5]$ where $d = 5$ is both the minimum Hamming distance and the minimum rank distance of C.

Let $x = (x_1, ..., x_4) \in K^4$ be the input of the diffusion process and $y = (y_1, ..., y_4) = xA^t$ be the associated output. The corresponding codeword is $c = (x|y)$. In a differential cryptanalysis, x is the differential in input and y is the differential in output.

In practice each x_i or y_i is a byte, *i.e.* $x_i = (x_{i,1}, ..., x_{i,8}) \in F^8 \simeq K$ (idem for y_i). In the following, we use the letter z to refer generically to both the input x and the output y. The MDS property means that, from all the 8 bytes z_i, if c is non-zero, then at least 5 of them are non-zero. The MRD property means that, not only 5 of them are non-zero, but at least 5 of them are F-linearly independent when considered as elements of F^8.

A similar property does not exist for the MixColumns matrix because it is not an MRD matrix. More precisely, the word $c = (1, 1, 1, 1, 1, 1, 1, 1) \in (F^8)^8$ is a codeword of the MDS code associated to MixColumns. This means that the input differential which consists in swapping the low weight bit of each byte leads to the same property in output. This differential corresponds to a codeword of rank 1. So the rank distance of the MDS code corresponding to the MixColumns matrix is only 1, which is the weakest value.

Another interesting differential for the Mixcolumns is the particular input $x = (1, 0, 0, 0)$ which leads to the output $y = (2, 3, 1, 1)$ (with the convention $3 = (1, 1, 0, 0, 0, 0, 0, 0)$, and so on). The codeword over K corresponding to this differential has an Hamming weight of 5, but remains of rank 2. In particular it is localized on the two bits of low weight of each byte. In addition, when interpreting this codeword as a binary word of length 32, its Hamming distance is only 6.

If our diffusion matrix A_4 is used instead of the MixColumns, at least 5 of the 8 bits of each byte is modified by any differential. The minimum distance of the underlying binary code is 10.

To the best of our knowledge, we do not know any attack against the AES which uses this particular property. However, MixColumns is often used in the design of lightweight block ciphers. For example, KLEIN [9] applies nonlinear Sboxes at nibble level and then uses MixColumns as a diffusion layer by regrouping two nibbles in one byte. This is a clear weakness of this cipher exploited in the attack presented in [3], which would be discarded by the use of the diffusion matrix A_4.

In conclusion, the MRD property is a local one at bit level. For a well-designed cryptosystem with an ideal Sbox, this property does not probably augment the level of security against known attacks so far. However, for some specified cryptosystems, it increases the diffusion of Sboxes and may help to discard some attacks using the potential weakness of Sboxes. This MRD proprty is an additional ones, and preserves the MDS optimality of the diffusion layers and the resistance against linear and differential attacks.

3.4   An Infinite Class of Recursive MDS Diffusion Layers with the MRD Property

In this section, we will show that if we choose a polynomial basis to construct our Gabidulin code, it is possible to construct a companion matrix which is a recursive diffusion layer corresponding to our MDS matrix A.

Let $\alpha \in K = GF(2^m)$ be a root of an irreducible polynomial $P(X)$ of degree m. This implies in particular $K = GF(2)(\alpha)$. The set $\mathcal{B} = (1, \alpha, \alpha^2, ..., \alpha^{m-1})$ is a basis of K over F. Such a basis is called a polynomial basis.

For i from 0 to $m - 1$, we set $a_i = \alpha^i$. In particular, the a_i's verify $a_i a_j = a_{i+j}$ for all i and j such that $0 \leq i + j < m$.

Using the notation $a^{[i]} = a^{2^i}$, we obtain the following generator matrix of the Gabidulin code $\mathcal{G}_{\mathcal{B},r}$, with $m = 2r$.

$$G_{\mathcal{B},r} = \begin{pmatrix} a_0 & a_1 & a_2 & \cdots & a_{m-1} \\ a_0^{[1]} & a_1^{[1]} & a_2^{[1]} & \cdots & a_{m-1}^{[1]} \\ a_0^{[2]} & a_1^{[2]} & a_2^{[2]} & \cdots & a_{m-1}^{[2]} \\ \vdots & \vdots & \vdots & \vdots & \vdots \\ a_0^{[r-1]} & a_1^{[r-1]} & a_2^{[r-1]} & \cdots & a_{m-1}^{[r-1]} \end{pmatrix}$$

We define the square matrices U and S of size r as follows:
U is the matrix $G_{\mathcal{B},r}$ restricted to its r first columns.
S is the diagonal matrix with coefficients $(a_1, a_1^{[1]}, a_1^{[2]}, ..., a_1^{[r-1]})$.

Lemma 1. *For $0 \le i \le r$, we have*

$$S^i U = \begin{pmatrix} a_i & a_{i+1} & a_{i+2} & \cdots & a_{i+r-1} \\ a_i^{[1]} & a_{i+1}^{[1]} & a_{i+2}^{[1]} & \cdots & a_{i+r-1}^{[1]} \\ \vdots & \vdots & \vdots & \vdots & \vdots \\ a_i^{[r-1]} & a_{i+1}^{[r-1]} & a_{i+2}^{[r-1]} & \cdots & a_{i+r-1}^{[r-1]} \end{pmatrix}.$$

In particular, $G_{\mathcal{B},r} = (U|S^r U)$ and $M = (I_r|U^{-1}S^r U)$ is the systematic generator matrix of the Gabidulin code $\mathcal{G}_{\mathcal{B},r}$.

Proof. This is a direct consequence of the relations $a_i a_j = a_{i+j}$ and $(ab)^{[s]} = a^{[s]}b^{[s]}$ for all $i + j \le m$, for any integer s and for all elements a and b of K.

Now, we are interested by the MDS diffusion matrix $A = U^{-1}S^r U$. We set $A = (a_{i,j})$ for $0 \le i, j < r$. We define the companion matrix Δ as follows:

$$\Delta = \begin{pmatrix} 0 \cdots\cdots 0 & a_{0,0} \\ 1 \quad 0 \quad \ddots \vdots & a_{1,0} \\ 0 \quad 1 \quad \ddots \vdots & a_{2,0} \\ \vdots \ddots \ddots 0 & \vdots \\ 0 \cdots 0 \quad 1 \, a_{r-1,0} \end{pmatrix}$$

The main result of this section is the fact that Δ is a companion diffusion layer in r rounds associated to the matrix A.

Theorem 1. *The following property is satisfied: $\Delta^r = U^{-1}S^r U = A$.*

Proof. The equality $\Delta^r = U^{-1}S^r U = A$ is equivalent to $U\Delta^r U^{-1} = S^r$. So, it is sufficient to prove that $U\Delta U^{-1} = S$ since $(U\Delta U^{-1})^r = U\Delta^r U^{-1}$. Finally, our result is equivalent to show that $U\Delta = SU$.

From Lemma 1, we have

$$SU = \begin{pmatrix} a_1 & a_2 & a_3 & \cdots & a_r \\ a_1^{[1]} & a_2^{[1]} & a_3^{[1]} & \cdots & a_r^{[1]} \\ \vdots & \vdots & \vdots & \vdots & \vdots \\ a_1^{[r-1]} & a_2^{[r-1]} & a_3^{[r-1]} & \cdots & a_r^{[r-1]} \end{pmatrix}.$$

For i from 0 to $m - 1$, we denote by C_i the column $(a_i, a_i^{[1]}, ..., a_i^{[r-1]})^t$. With this notation, we have $SU = (C_1|C_2|...|C_r)$.

Note that $U = (C_0|C_1|...|C_{r-1})$. Since Δ is a companion matrix, the $r - 1$ first columns of $U\Delta$ are just a shift of one position of the $r - 1$ last columns of U. So we have $U\Delta = (C_1|C_2|...|C_{r-1}|D_r)$ with $D_r = U\Delta_r$ where Δ_r is the last column of Δ, i.e. the first column of A.

To complete our proof, we have to show that $D_r = C_r$. Recall that $A = U^{-1}S^rU$. This implies $UA = S^rU$. The first column of the matrix U is C_0, that is the all one column. In consequence, the first column of UA is $(a_r, a_r^{[1]}, ..., a_r^{[r-1]})^t$ which is C_r.

If we continue the example of Section 3.2, we obtain

$$\Delta = \begin{pmatrix} 0 & 0 & 0 & \alpha^{15} \\ 1 & 0 & 0 & \alpha^{168} \\ 0 & 1 & 0 & \alpha^{235} \\ 0 & 0 & 1 & \alpha^{238} \end{pmatrix} \text{ with } \Delta^4 = A.$$

If we change the basis $\mathcal{B}$ in the construction of Gabidulin, we obtain distinct MDS matrices with the MRD property. In particular, for $m = 8$ and $r = 4$ it is possible to construct some MDS matrices of order 51, 85 or 255.

3.5   Comparison with Previous Constructions

The MRD condition is a very strong constraint on the research of MDS matrices. So, it will not be as efficient as results of [7], [10], [12], [15]. However, from an implementation aspect, it is close to the results of [1].

Moreover, our approach is quite different from previous works in the meaning that our original starting point is not the search of companion matrices leading to MDS matrices, but is a MDS matrix for which we are able to exhibit a corresponding companion matrix.

If someone needs to construct a MDS matrix over blocks of size m, due to the MDS conjecture on the length of MDS codes [11], the maximum number of blocs is $r = 2^m$. For instance, if $m = 8$ then number of blocks is upper bounded by 256, however, the typical values for applications a $r = 4$ or $r = 8$. So there is a large choice of MDS matrices, and it is possible to exhibit some matrices with goods properties from the implementation aspects. The MRD constraint limits the size of blocs to $r = m/2$, so, for $m = 8$ the maximum number of blocks is $r = 4$ and the choice of MRD matrices is restricted.

In [7], [10], [12], [15], authors have imposed additional constraints on companion matrices to obtain efficient implementations. For example, some of coefficients a_i defined in Section 2.2 are fixed to 1 (the identity map), and the others are of low density. In our situation, if we fix any a_i equals to 1, it is easy to show that the resulting MDS matrix cannot be MRD.

4   Conclusion

In this paper, we introduced a new infinite class of MDS diffusion matrices which can be computed using recursive diffusion layers. These matrices have the additional MRD property, which seems interesting for cryptographic applications. However, it remains an open problem to determine the impact of this additional property in concrete cryptanalyzes of existing cryptosystems.

Even if practical implementations are possible, the MRD property implies that this construction cannot be as efficient as previous one. So this work remains at the present moment a bit theoretical, however, it is a potential tool to increase the security against some specific attacks.

Acknowledgments. The author want to thanks Marine Minier for her helpful comments and remarks.

References

1. Augot, D., Finiasz, M.: Exhaustive search for small dimension recursive MDS diffusion layers for block ciphers and hash functions. In: Proceedings of the 2013 IEEE International Symposium on Information Theory. IEEE (2013)
2. Berger, T.P., Ourivski, A.: Construction of new MDS codes from Gabidulin codes. In: Proceedings of ACCT 2009, Kranevo, Bulgaria, pp. 40–47 (June 2004)
3. Aumasson, J.-P., Naya-Plasencia, M., Saarinen, M.-J.O.: Practical attack on 8 rounds of the lightweight block cipher KLEIN. In: Bernstein, D.J., Chatterjee, S. (eds.) INDOCRYPT 2011. LNCS, vol. 7107, pp. 134–145. Springer, Heidelberg (2011)
4. Daemen, J., Knudsen, L.R., Rijmen, V.: The block cipher SQUARE. In: Biham, E. (ed.) FSE 1997. LNCS, vol. 1267, pp. 149–165. Springer, Heidelberg (1997)
5. Daemen, J., Rijmen, V.: The Design of Rijndael: AES - The Advanced Encryption Standard. Information Security and Cryptography. Springer (2002)
6. Gabidulin, E.M.: Theory of codes with maximum rank distance. Problems of Information Transmission (English translation of Problemy Peredachi Informatsii) 21(1) (1985)
7. Gupta, K.C., Ray, I.G.: On constructions of MDS matrices from companion matrices for lightweight cryptography. In: Cuzzocrea, A., Kittl, C., Simos, D.E., Weippl, E., Xu, L. (eds.) CD-ARES Workshops 2013. LNCS, vol. 8128, pp. 29–43. Springer, Heidelberg (2013)
8. Junod, P., Vaudenay, S.: Perfect diffusion primitives for block ciphers. In: Handschuh, H., Hasan, M.A. (eds.) SAC 2004. LNCS, vol. 3357, pp. 84–99. Springer, Heidelberg (2004)
9. Gong, Z., Nikova, S., Law, Y.W.: KLEIN: A new family of lightweight block ciphers. In: Juels, A., Paar, C. (eds.) RFIDSec 2011. LNCS, vol. 7055, pp. 1–18. Springer, Heidelberg (2012)
10. Guo, J., Peyrin, T., Poschmann, A.: The PHOTON family of lightweight hash functions. In: Rogaway, P. (ed.) CRYPTO 2011. LNCS, vol. 6841, pp. 222–239. Springer, Heidelberg (2011)
11. MacWilliams, F.J., Sloane, N.J.A.: The Theory of Error-Correcting Codes. North Holland Publishing Co. (1988)

12. Sajadieh, M., Dakhilalian, M., Mala, H., Sepehrdad, P.: Recursive diffusion layers for block ciphers and hash functions. In: Canteaut, A. (ed.) FSE 2012. LNCS, vol. 7549, pp. 385–401. Springer, Heidelberg (2012)
13. Schnorr, C.-P., Vaudenay, S.: Black box cryptanalysis of hash networks based on multipermutations. In: De Santis, A. (ed.) EUROCRYPT 1994. LNCS, vol. 950, pp. 47–57. Springer, Heidelberg (1995)
14. Vaudenay, S.: On the need for multipermutations: Cryptanalysis of md4 and safer. In: Preneel, B. (ed.) FSE 1994. LNCS, vol. 1008, pp. 286–297. Springer, Heidelberg (1995)
15. Wu, S., Wang, M., Wu, W.: Recursive diffusion layers for (lightweight) block ciphers and hash function. In: Knudsen, L.R., Wu, H. (eds.) SAC 2012. LNCS, vol. 7707, pp. 355–371. Springer, Heidelberg (2013)
16. Yanagihara, S., Iwata, T.: Improving the permutation layer of type 1, type 3, source-heavy, and target-heavy generalized Feistel structures. IEICE Transactions 96-A(1), 2–14 (2013)

Polynomial Structures in Code-Based Cryptography

Vlad Dragoi[1,2], Pierre-Louis Cayrel[1,*],
Brice Colombier[1], and Tania Richmond[1,*]

[1] Laboratoire Hubert Curien, UMR CNRS 5516,
University of Lyon, Saint-Etienne, France
{pierre.louis.cayrel,tania.richmond}@univ-st-etienne.fr
[2] Normandie Univ, France, UR, LITIS, F-76821 Mont-Saint-Aignan, France

Abstract. In this article we discus a probability problem applied in the code based cryptography. It is related to the shape of the polynomials with exactly t different roots. We will show that the structure is very dense and the probability that this type of polynomials has at least one coefficient equal to zero is extremelly low. We treated this issue in our research of natural countermeasures to a timing attack against the polynomial evaluation.

Keywords: *McEliece, Galois field, Monte-Carlo method, the simple roots problem.*

Introduction

One of the main threats in modern cryptography is the arrival of the quantum computers, it was shown that cryptosystems based on factorisation of large numbers would be compromised [18]. Therefore, new concepts like hash-based cryptography, code-based cryptography, lattice-based cryptography, and multivariate cryptography were proposed as possible solutions. The new aspects of the post-quantum cryptography are well illustrated in [2].

Even though code-based cryptosystems exist since 1978, being introduced by Robert J. McEliece in [15], they weren't used in real life because of the key length problem. Nowadays, these problems are partially solved as new variants of the classical McEliece using shorter keys, without compromising the security, were proposed in [6,4,5,16] and more recently in [3]. The latest proposal for embedded devices proposed in [12] is based on QC-MDPC codes.

Here we will focus our attention on the last step in the decoding algorithm. If Patterson algorithm [17] or Berlekamp-Massey algorithm [14] is used, the last step is the same : finding the roots of the error locator polynomial. This polynomial has a particular form and it will be detailed in Section 1.

McBits [3] is the latest implementation and uses some new algorithms in order to provide a fast constant-time decoding. Other existing implementations like:

* Supported in part by NATO's Public Diplomacy Division in the framework of "Science for Peace", SPS Project 984520.

G. Paul and S. Vaudenay (Eds.): INDOCRYPT 2013, LNCS 8250, pp. 286–296, 2013.
© Springer International Publishing Switzerland 2013

HyMes [6], CCA2-secure variant of McEliece [7], QD for embedded devices [10], Low-reiter [11], CFS [13], MicroEliece [9] use the mentioned decoding algorithms and manipulate the type of polynomials treated in this paper.

Our Contribution

We will provide an answer the following problem :

What is the probability that all the coefficients of a monic polynomial $P(X)$ of degree t with t distinct roots over $\mathbb{F}_{2^m}$ are different from zero ?

Thefinal probability will be bounded by theoretical and experimental results. We will show how this result can be used in the context of side-channel attacks against the McEliece cryptosystem.

As shown, this problem has a direct application in code-based cryptography but it could be also usefull in many other scientific fields e.g. those where error correcting codes are used.

Organization of the Paper

In Section 1, we give the required notations and some definitions and properties for the Goppa codes. The Section 2 details the simple roots problem and give the theoretical approach. We provide in Section 3 the experimental results. Section 4 shows how to apply this result and we wonclude in Section 5.

1   Preliminaries

1.1   Notations

We will use the following notations :

- The partial permutations $A_n^k = n(n-1)\ldots(n-k+1)$.
- The Galois field $\mathcal{L} : \mathbb{F}_{2^m} = \{0, 1, \alpha, \alpha^2, \ldots, \alpha^{n-2}\}$
- Let $P(x)$ be a monic polynomial of degree t over $\mathcal{L}$ with t distinct roots a_i :

$$P(x) = x^t + S_{t-1}^t x^{t-1} + S_{t-2}^t x^{t-2} + \ldots + S_2^t x^2 + S_1^t x + S_0^t$$

where the coefficients $S_i \in \mathbb{F}_q^m$ correspond to :

$$S_{t-1}^t = \sum_{i=1}^{t} a_i, \qquad S_{t-2}^t = \sum_{\substack{i=1,j=1 \\ i \neq j}}^{t} a_i a_j, \qquad \ldots$$

$$\ldots \qquad S_1^t = \sum_{j=1}^{t} \prod_{\substack{i=1 \\ i \neq j}}^{t} a_i, \qquad S_0^t = \prod_{i=1}^{t} a_i.$$

- The subset of all roots for a given polynomial $\mathcal{R}_{f(x)} = \{ a_i \mid f(a_i) = 0 \}$.

1.2 Goppa Codes

Definition :

The Goppa code $\Gamma(\mathcal{L}, g)$ consists of all vectors $c = (c_0, c_1, ..c_{n-1})$ over $\mathbb{F}_q$ such that $\mathcal{S}_c(x) \equiv 0 \mod g(x)$. Here $g(x)$ is a polynomial over $\mathbb{F}_{2^m}$ and $\mathcal{L} = \{\alpha_0, \alpha_1, .., \alpha_{n-1}\}$ a subset so that $g(\alpha_i) \neq 0$ for all $i = 0 \ldots n - 1$. $\mathcal{S}_c(x) = \sum_{i=0}^{n-1} \frac{c_i}{x - \alpha_i}$ is called the syndrome of c and $\mathcal{L}$ the support of the Goppa code.

The syndrome polynomial $\mathcal{S}_c(x)$ satisfies the following property :

$$\mathcal{S}_c(x) = \frac{\omega(x)}{\sigma(x)} \mod g(x)$$

$\sigma(x)$ is called the error locator polynomial : $\sigma(x) = \prod_{i=1}^{t} (x + a_i)$.

$\omega(x) = \sigma'(x)$ for binary Goppa codes.

2 Simple Roots Problem

Problem : Let $P(x)$ be a monic polynomial of degree t with t distinct roots over $\mathbb{F}_{2^m}$.
What is the probability that all its coefficients are different from zero ?

Proposition 1 : This probability is independent of the primitive generator polynomial $G(x)$ of degree m where $\mathbb{F}_{2^m} = \mathbb{F}_2[x]/G(x)$.

Proof. This is due to:

$$\mathbb{F}_2[x]/G_1(x) \cong \mathbb{F}_2[x]/G_2(x) \cong \mathbb{F}_2[x]/G_3(x) \cong \ldots \mathbb{F}_2[x]/G_{\mathcal{N}}(x)$$

where $G_i(x)$ are primitive polynomials $\forall i \in \{1, 2, .., \mathcal{N}\}$ of degree $= m$. □

2.1 General Properties

Let $n = 2^m$.

1. $\boxed{\mathcal{P}(S_0^t = 0) = \frac{t}{n}}$

   Proof. If $S_0^t = 0$ then $0 \in \mathcal{R}_{P(x)}$. There are t different positions for any possible root. We can choose any of those t positions for zero. □

2. $\boxed{\mathcal{P}(S_1^t = 0 \cap S_0^t = 0) = 0}$

   Proof. If $S_0^t = 0$ then $0 \in \mathcal{R}_{P(x)}$. So $S_1^t = \prod_{i=1}^{t-1} a_i = 0$. It means that zero is a root of order 2 of $P(x)$ and that's impossible. □

3. $\boxed{\mathcal{P}(S_i^t \in \mathbb{F}_{2^m} \cap S_1^t \neq 0 \cap S_0^t = 0) = \mathcal{P}(S_i^{t-2} \in \mathbb{F}_{2^m} \cap a_i \neq 0) \times \mathcal{P}(S_0^t = 0)}$

Proof. If $S_0^t = 0$ then $0 \in \mathcal{R}_{P(x)}$ This implies that the two following events are equivalent :

$$\{S_1^t \neq 0 \cap S_0^t = 0\} \Leftrightarrow \{S_0^{t-1} \neq 0 \cap a_t = 0\}.$$

The only information we obtain with this event is that $a_t = 0$ then :

$$\mathcal{P}(S_1^t \neq 0 \cap S_0^t = 0) = \mathcal{P}(S_0^t = 0).$$

$\square$

4. $\boxed{\text{If } S_i^t = 0 \text{ then } S_{i-1}^{t-1} = a_t S_i^{t-1} \quad \forall \, 0 < i < t}$

Proof. The proof can easily be done by induction.
Suppose that $S_{t-1}^t = 0$. It means that we can express a_t as :

$$a_t = \sum_{i=1}^{t-1} a_i \Rightarrow a_t = S_{t-2}^{t-1}.$$

If $S_{t-2}^t = 0 \Rightarrow a_t \sum_{i=1}^{t-1} a_i = \sum_{i \neq j, 1}^{t-1} a_i a_j \Rightarrow a_t S_{t-2}^{t-1} = S_{t-3}^{t-1}.$

If $S_{t-3}^t = 0 \Rightarrow a_t \sum_{i \neq j, 1}^{t-1} a_i a_j = \sum_{i \neq j \neq k, 1}^{t-1} a_i a_j a_k \Rightarrow a_t S_{t-3}^{t-1} = S_{t-4}^{t-1}$

By induction, we obtain $S_1^t = 0 \Rightarrow a_t S_1^{t-1} = S_0^{t-1}.$ $\square$

In the following paragraph we will give two bounds for the probability. The lower bound is very close to our experimental results (see Section 3).

2.2   The Bounds

We propose a lemma concerning the last coefficient (the sum) and we observe that the probability can be bounded. We consider for $\forall i \geq 3$ the probability $\mathcal{P}(S_{i-1}^i = 0)$. We give a general formula with the following consideration :

Lemma 1 :

$$\text{Even } i : \mathcal{P}(S_{i-1}^i = 0) = \sum_{k=1}^{\lfloor \frac{i-1}{2} \rfloor} (-1)^{k-1} \frac{1}{n+2k-i} + (-1)^{\lfloor \frac{i-1}{2} \rfloor - 1} \left(\frac{1}{n-3} - \frac{1}{n-2} \right)$$

$$\text{Odd } i : \mathcal{P}(S_{i-1}^i = 0) = \sum_{k=1}^{\lfloor \frac{i-1}{2} \rfloor} (-1)^{k-1} \frac{1}{n+2k-i} + (-1)^{\lfloor \frac{i-1}{2} \rfloor - 1} \left(\frac{1}{n} - \frac{1}{n-1} \right)$$

We will give some simple examples and observe that the general behavior of the sum suits the formula given above. We will use induction in order to prove it.

Main idea :
• Let $i = 3$. The probability associated to this event is $\mathcal{P} = \frac{A_{n-1}^2}{A_n^3} = \frac{1}{n}$. Consider (a_1, a_2, a_3) so that $\forall i \in \{1, 2, 3\} \, a_i \in \mathcal{R}_{P(x)}$.
The number of all posible combinations is : $A_n^3 = n(n-1)(n-2)$.
The number of good cases is :

$$\#\{((a_1, a_2, a_3) \mid a_1 + a_2 + a_3 = 0\} = \#\{((a_1, a_2, a_3) \mid a_1 + a_2 = a_3\} = \mathcal{A}^2_{(n-1)} = (n-1)(n-2).$$

- Let $i = 4$. The probability is $\mathcal{P} = \frac{A_n^3}{A_n^4} = \frac{1}{n-3}$.

Consider (a_1, a_2, a_3, a_4) so that $\forall i \in \{1, 2, 3, 4\}$ $a_i \in \mathcal{R}_{P(x)}$.

The number of all posible combinations is : $\mathcal{A}_n^4 = n(n-1)(n-2)(n-3)$.

The number of good cases is :

$$\#\{((a_1, a_2, a_3, a_4) \mid a_1 + a_2 + a_3 + a_4 = 0\} = \#\{((a_1, a_2, a_3, a_4) \mid a_1 + a_2 + a_3 = a_4\} = \mathcal{A}_n^3 = n(n-1)(n-2).$$

Is it possible that for a given (a_1, a_2, a_3, a_4) solution, the choice of a_4 might cause repetitions? We know that a_4 is fixed as $a_4 = a_1 + a_2 + a_3$ and all the elements are different (because $P(X)$ has 4 distincts roots).

Example: If $a_4 = a_1$ then $a_2 = a_3$. But a_2 and a_3 must be different. So it is impossible that $a_4 = a_1$. Therefore we have the exact probability $\mathcal{P} = \frac{1}{n-3}$

- Let $i = 5$

If $a_2 \neq a_3 \neq a_4 \neq a_2$ then the event related to $a_1 + \cdots + a_5 = 0$ has the following form:

$$\bullet \ \{s = \sum_{i=1}^5 a_i = 0\} = \{s = 0 \cap a_1 = a_5\} \cup \{s = 0 \cap a_1 \neq a_5\}$$

The event $\{s = 0 \cap a_5 = a_1\}$ was treated in the case $i = 3$. So $\mathcal{P}(\{s = 0 \cap a_5 = a_1\}) = \frac{1}{n}$.

The event $\{s = \sum_{i=1}^5 a_i = 0\}$ has the following probability:

$$\mathcal{P}(\{s = \sum_{i=1}^5 a_i = 0\}) = \frac{n(n-1)(n-2)(n-3)}{n(n-1)(n-2)(n-3)(n-3)} = \frac{1}{n-3}$$

Finally we obtain the probabillity $\mathcal{P} = \frac{1}{n-3} - \frac{1}{n}$.

For $i \in 6, 7, 8$ we will only give the final result. The idea and the calculus are the same as for the explained cases.

- Let $i = 6$ the probabillity is : $\mathcal{P} = \frac{1}{n-4} - \frac{1}{n-3}$.
- Let $i = 7$ the probabillity is : $\mathcal{P} = \frac{1}{n-5} - (\frac{1}{n-3} - \frac{1}{n})$.
- Let $i = 8$ the probabillity is : $\mathcal{P} = \frac{1}{n-6} - (\frac{1}{n-4} - \frac{1}{n-3})$.

Proof. By induction :

- For the *even* case : The hypothesis is satisfied for

$$i = 4 \text{ as we have } \mathcal{P}(S_3^4 = 0) = \frac{1}{n-3}.$$

Suppose that $i = 2p$ and

$$\mathcal{P}(S_{2p-1}^{2p} = 0) = \sum_{k=1}^{\lfloor \frac{2p-1}{2} \rfloor} (-1)^{k-1} \frac{1}{n + 2k - 2p} + (-1)^{\lfloor \frac{2p-1}{2} \rfloor - 1}(\frac{1}{n-3} - \frac{1}{n-2}).$$

We will search the $\mathcal{P}(S_{2p+1}^{2p+2} = 0)$

As before we distinguish the case where $a_{2p} = a_1$ and the case where $a_{2p} \neq a_1$ (the general case in ❶).

So we have $\mathcal{P}(S^{2p+2}_{2p+1} = 0) + \mathcal{P}(S^{2p}_{2p-1} = 0) = \frac{1}{n-2p}$

We finally obtain :

$$\mathcal{P} = \frac{1}{n-2p} - \left[\sum_{k=1}^{\lfloor \frac{2p-1}{2} \rfloor} (-1)^{k-1} \frac{1}{n+2k-2p} + (-1)^{\lfloor \frac{2p-1}{2} \rfloor - 1}\left(\frac{1}{n-3} - \frac{1}{n-2}\right) \right] =$$

$$\sum_{k=1}^{\lfloor \frac{2p+1}{2} \rfloor} (-1)^{k-1} \frac{1}{n+2k-(2p+2)} + (-1)^{\lfloor \frac{2p+1}{2} \rfloor - 1}\left(\frac{1}{n-3} - \frac{1}{n-2}\right)$$

- For the *odd* case on can easilly use the same proof.

Asymptotically, $\mathcal{P} \approx \frac{1}{n-i+2}$.   □

Lemma 2 :

$$\mathcal{P}(S^t_i = 0) \approx \mathcal{P}(S^t_{t-1} = 0) \ \forall i \in \{1, 2, .., t-2\}$$

Proof. Using properties 3 and 4 from 2.1 we get :

$$S^t_i = 0 \Rightarrow S^{t-1}_{i-1} = a_t S^{t-1}_i \quad \forall \ 0 < i < t$$

So we have all the possible choices on the first $t-1$ elements, as for the last one it has to be defined as in the formula above. We get the same number of possible choices for $(a_1, a_2, ..., a_t)$ as in the case $S^t_{t-1} = 0$.   □

Proposition 2 : For a given polynomial with t different roots the probability that all coefficients are different from zero can be bouded by the two following quantities :

The two bounds:

$$1 + f(n,t) - \left[\frac{t}{n} + (t-1)\mathsf{ub} \right] \leq \mathcal{P} \leq 1 + f(n,t) - \left[\frac{t}{n} + (t-1)\mathsf{lb} \right]$$

Proof From **Lemma 1** we have :

$$\mathcal{P}(S^t_{t-1} = 0) = \frac{1}{n-t+2} - \frac{1}{n-t+4} + \frac{1}{n-t+6} - \frac{1}{n-t+8} + \frac{1}{n-t+10} + \cdots$$

So :

$$\mathsf{lb} \leq \mathcal{P}(S^t_{t-1} = 0) \leq \mathsf{ub}$$

where

$$\mathsf{lb} = \frac{1}{n-t+2} - \frac{1}{n-t+4}$$

and

$$\mathsf{ub} = \frac{1}{n-t+2} - \frac{1}{n-t+4} + \frac{1}{n-t+6}$$

Using property 1 from 2.1 we have $\mathcal{P}(S_0^t = 0) = \frac{t}{n}$.
From **Lemma 2** we can approach

$$\mathcal{P}(S_i^t = 0) \approx \mathcal{P}(S_{t-1}^t = 0) \ \forall i \in \{1, 2, .., t-2\}$$

We will be able to approach the sum :

$$\sum_{i=0}^{t-1} \mathcal{P}(S_i^t = 0) \approx \mathcal{P}(S_0^t = 0) + (t-1)\mathcal{P}(S_{t-1}^t = 0)$$

Givind the bounds for the sum it becomes a simple task :

$$\frac{t}{n} + (t-1) \times \mathsf{lb} \le \sum_{i=0}^{t-1} \mathcal{P}(S_i^t = 0) \le \frac{t}{n} + (t-1) \times \mathsf{ub}$$

Finally :

$$\mathcal{P}(\bigcap_{i=0}^{t-1}\{S_i^t \neq 0\}) = 1 - \mathcal{P}(\exists i \ S_i^t = 0)$$

Notation : $f(n, t)$ represents the sum of the probabilities associated to all the possible intersections between $S_i^t \ \forall i$ so that at least two coefficients equal zero.
Example for $t = 3$:

$$\{S_0^3 = 0\} = \bigcup\{S_0^3 = 0, S_1^3 \in \{0, \neq\}, S_2^3 \in \{0, \neq\}\}$$

We have the same relation for S_1^3 and S_2^3. So all the possible combinations where at least two members equal zero will constitute the function.

$$\begin{aligned} f(n, 3) = 2 \times \mathcal{P}(S_0^3 = S_1^3 = \quad S_2^3 = 0) \\ + \mathcal{P}(S_0^3 = S_1^3 = 0, S_2^3 \neq 0) \\ + \mathcal{P}(S_0^3 = S_2^3 = 0, S_1^3 \neq 0) \\ + \mathcal{P}(S_1^3 = S_2^3 = 0, S_0^3 \neq 0) \end{aligned}$$

We use the following relation in order to finalize our proof :

$$\sum_{i=0}^{t-1} \mathcal{P}(S_i^t = 0) = \mathcal{P}(\exists i \ S_i^t = 0) + f(n, t)$$

$$\mathcal{P}(\bigcap_{i=0}^{t-1}\{S_i^t \neq 0\}) = 1 + f(n, t) - \sum_{i=0}^{t-1} \mathcal{P}(S_i^t = 0)$$

So :

$$1 + f(n, t) - \left[\frac{t}{n} + (t-1)\mathsf{ub}\right] \le \mathcal{P}(\bigcap_{i=0}^{t-1}\{S_i^t \neq 0\}) \le 1 + f(n, t) - \left[\frac{t}{n} + (t-1)\mathsf{lb}\right]$$

That sets the two bounds but doesn't allow having a graphic representation since the quantity $f(n,t)$ is unknown.   □

One of the ideas was to consider the following result :

$$1 - \left[\frac{t}{n} + (t-1) \times \mathsf{ub}\right] \leq 1 + f(n,t) - \left[\frac{t}{n} + (t-1) \times \mathsf{ub}\right] \leq \mathcal{P}(\bigcap_{i=0}^{t-1}\{S_i^t \neq 0\})$$

We represented in Section 3 the lower bound $1 - \left[\frac{t}{n} + (t-1) \times \mathsf{ub}\right]$ and the experimental values using the Monte Carlo method. As expected the quantity represented by $f(n,t)$ could be neglected in the formula. Therefore we used two following bounds in Section 3 :

$$\mathsf{LB} = 1 - \left[\frac{t}{n} + (t-1) \times \mathsf{ub}\right] \text{ and } \mathsf{UB} = 1 - \left[\frac{t}{n} + (t-1) \times \mathsf{lb}\right]$$

3   Experiments

Simulations were made using PariGP, a free software used especially for its abillity to generate finite fields in the Galois field theory.

For the experimental approach we used the Monte-Carlo method. It uses the Central Limit Theorem and applied in our case to estimate the number of coefficients equal to zero for a given polynomial. We will detail in the next

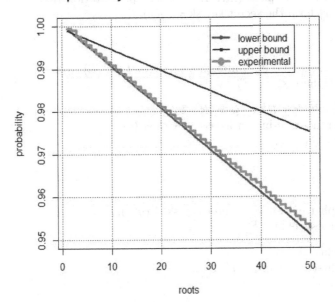

The probability that all coefficients are different from 0

Fig. 1. Experimental and theoretical bounds for $n = 2048$

paragraph the procedure used in order to obtain the results. After that we will give the graphical representation of the simulated variables and the theoretical bounds. We will see that the possible distribution is very close to one of the bounds.

First of all we simulated for a given number t of roots the corresponding polynomial. Then we counted the number of coefficients that equal zero. We repeated the simulation 3.000.000 times for each t. In our case the Monte Carlo method was applied to the variable : *number of coefficients that equal zero.*

Results *:* The figure illustrates the importance of the lower bound. Since we are interested in having less coefficients equal to zero the lower bound gives the folowing values :

> classical parameters $n = 2048$ and $t \leq 50$ we obtain $\mathcal{P} \geq 0.95$;
> 128-bit security $[2960; 2288]$ Goppa code ($t = 56$) we obtain $\mathcal{P} \geq 0.9622$;
> 256-bit security $[6624; 5129]$ Goppa code ($t = 115$) we obtain
> $$\mathcal{P} \geq 0.9651.$$

4 Applications

4.1 The McEliece Cryptosystem [15]

KeyGen *:* The first step is to generate the support $\mathcal{L}$ and the Goppa polynomial $g(x)$. Once this step is achieved, we can build the parity check matrix and bring it into systematic form $\mathsf{pk} = (m, t, R^T, \mathcal{L})$. The permutation $\varPi$ and the Goppa polynomial $g(x)$ form the secret key $\mathsf{sk} = (g(x), \varPi)$.

Encrypt *:*

- *Input* : message $\mathsf{m} \in \mathbb{F}_2^k$, public key $\mathsf{pk} = (m, t, R^T, \mathcal{L})$
- *Output* : ciphertext $\mathsf{z} \in \mathbb{F}_2^n$

1. Expand public key R^T to $\mathcal{G} = [R^T | \mathcal{I}_k]$;
2. Choose a random n-bit error-vector with $\mathsf{wt}(e) = t$;
3. Encode $\mathsf{z} = \mathsf{m}\mathcal{G} \oplus e$;
4. Return z.

Decrypt *:*

- *Input* : ciphertext $\mathsf{z} \in \mathbb{F}_2^n$, secret key $\mathsf{sk} = (g(x), \varPi)$
- *Output* : message $\mathsf{m} \in \mathbb{F}_2^k$

1. Find e' using $\mathcal{D}ecode(\mathsf{z}, \mathsf{sk})$
2. $\mathsf{m} \leftarrow$ the first k bits of $\mathsf{z} \oplus e'$
3. Return m.

$\mathcal{D}ecode(.,.)$ is a decoding algorithm used for the Goppa codes.

4.2   Side-Channel Attacks

The most important side-channel attacks treated in the scientific literature are timing attacks. They operate on the software implementation of the McEliece PKC and can be classified by their goal:

1. Recover the secret message (in [22,1])
2. Recover the secret key, fully or partially (in [21,20,19])

The type of attacks aiming to recover the secret message exploit timing differences between $\deg(\sigma_1) = t$ and $\deg(\sigma_2) = t - 1$. The countermeasures proposed manipulate $\sigma(x)$ so that if $\deg(\sigma) < t$ the designer should either

1. deterministicaly add coefficients so that $\deg(\sigma) = t$ and all coefficients are non zero
2. use coeffcients from the non-support so that $\deg(\sigma) = t$ and all coefficients are non zero

Countermeasure Our idea is that the second part of the statement *make sure that all coefficients are non zero* is already verified by 2. So we should only manipulate the degree of σ. Then the probability of having at least one coefficient equal to zero in σ is extremely low.

4.3   CFS Signature Scheme

In the CFS signature scheme, a small number t is used due to the density of the Goppa codes. It was proven in [8] that the decoding algorithm must be repeated in average $t!$ times. Decoding Goppa Codes for CFS with the recommended values gives the following result :

$$\text{for } n = 2^{16} \text{ and } t \leq 10 \text{ we obtain } \mathcal{P} > 0.999.$$

5   Conclusion

In this article, we have treated the simple roots polynomial problem. We have shown that the structure is such that timing attacks are difficult to be applied, since most of the σ-coefficient are different from 0. The security comes directly from the structure of the Galois field and the form of the error-locator polynomial.

Acknowledgements. We would like to thank Alain Couvreur and Michael Bulois for their help and comprehension. We would also like to thank Florent Bernard for his support.

References

1. Avanzi, R., Hoerder, S., Page, D., Tunstall, M.: Side-channel attacks on the McEliece and Niederreiter public-key cryptosystems. In: Cryptology ePrint Archive, Report 2010/479 (2010)

2. Bernstein, D.J., Buchmann, J., Dahmen, E.: Post-Quantum Cryptography. Springer (2009)
3. Bernstein, D.J., Chou, T., Schwabe, P.: McBits: fast constant-time code-based cryptography, 0616 (2013)
4. Bernstein, D.J., Lange, T., Peters, C.: Wild MCEliece. In: Biryukov, A., Gong, G., Stinson, D.R. (eds.) SAC 2010. LNCS, vol. 6544, pp. 143–158. Springer, Heidelberg (2011)
5. Bernstein, D.J., Lange, T., Peters, C.: Wild MCEliece incognito. In: Yang, B.-Y. (ed.) PQCrypto 2011. LNCS, vol. 7071, pp. 244–254. Springer, Heidelberg (2011)
6. Biswas, B., Sendrier, N.: McEliece cryptosystem implementation: Theory and practice. In: Buchmann, J., Ding, J. (eds.) PQCrypto 2008. LNCS, vol. 5299, pp. 47–62. Springer, Heidelberg (2008)
7. Cayrel, P.-L., Hoffmann, G., Persichetti, E.: Efficient implementation of a CCA2-secure variant of MCEliece using generalized Srivastava codes. In: Fischlin, M., Buchmann, J., Manulis, M. (eds.) PKC 2012. LNCS, vol. 7293, pp. 138–155. Springer, Heidelberg (2012)
8. Courtois, N.T., Finiasz, M., Sendrier, N.: How to achieve a MCEliece-based digital signature scheme. In: Boyd, C. (ed.) ASIACRYPT 2001. LNCS, vol. 2248, pp. 157–174. Springer, Heidelberg (2001)
9. Eisenbarth, T., Güneysu, T., Heyse, S., Paar, C.: MicroEliece: McEliece for embedded devices. In: Clavier, C., Gaj, K. (eds.) CHES 2009. LNCS, vol. 5747, pp. 49–64. Springer, Heidelberg (2009)
10. Heyse, S.: Implementation of McEliece based on Quasi-dyadic Goppa Codes for Embedded Devices. In: Yang, B.-Y. (ed.) PQCrypto 2011. LNCS, vol. 7071, pp. 143–162. Springer, Heidelberg (2011)
11. Heyse, S.: Low-reiter: Niederreiter encryption scheme for embedded microcontrollers. In: Sendrier, N. (ed.) PQCrypto 2010. LNCS, vol. 6061, pp. 165–181. Springer, Heidelberg (2010)
12. Heyse, S., von Maurich, I., Guneysu, T.: Smaller Keys for Code-based Cryptography: QC-MDPC McEliece Implementations on Embedded Devices (2013)
13. Landais, G., Sendrier, N.: CFS Software Implementation. Indocrypt 2012 and Cryptology ePrint Archive, Report 2012/132 (2012)
14. Massey, J.L.: Shift-register synthesis and bch decoding. Transactions on Information Theory IT-15(1), 122–127 (1969)
15. McEliece, R.J.: A public-key cryptosystem based on algebraic coding theory. In: Jet Propulsion Laboratory DSN Progress Report 42-44, pp. 114–116 (1978)
16. Misoczki, R., Tillich, J.-P., Sendrier, N., Barreto, P.S.L.M.: Mdpc-McEliece: New McEliece variants from moderate density parity-check codes. In: Cryptology ePrint Archive, Report 2012/409 (2012)
17. Patterson, N.J.: The algebraic decoding of goppa codes. IEEE Transactions on Information Theory IT-21, 203–207 (1975)
18. Shor, P.W.: Polynomial-time algorithms for prime factorization and discrete logarithms on a quantum computer (1994)
19. Shoufan, A., Strenzke, F., Molter, H.G., Stöttinger, M.: A Timing Attack against Patterson Algorithm in the McEliece PKC. In: Lee, D., Hong, S. (eds.) ICISC 2009. LNCS, vol. 5984, pp. 161–175. Springer, Heidelberg (2010)
20. Strenzke, F.: A Timing Attack against the Secret Permutation in the McEliece PKC. In: Sendrier, N. (ed.) PQCrypto 2010. LNCS, vol. 6061, pp. 95–107. Springer, Heidelberg (2010)
21. Strenzke, F.: Timing attacks against the syndrome inversion in code-based cryptosystems. In: Cryptology ePrint Archive, Report 2011/683 (2011)
22. Strenzke, F., Tews, E., Molter, H.G., Overbeck, R., Shoufan, A.: Side channels in the mcEliece PKC. In: Buchmann, J., Ding, J. (eds.) PQCrypto 2008. LNCS, vol. 5299, pp. 216–229. Springer, Heidelberg (2008)

Security Analysis of the RC4+ Stream Cipher

Subhadeep Banik[1], Santanu Sarkar[2], and Raghu Kacker[2]

[1] Applied Statistics Unit, Indian Statistical Institute,
203 B T Road, Kolkata 700 108, India
s.banik_r@isical.ac.in
[2] National Institute of Standards and Technology, 100 Bureau Drive, Stop 8930
Gaithersburg, MD 20899-8930, USA
santanu.sarkar@nist.gov

Abstract. The RC4+ stream cipher was proposed by Maitra and Paul at Indocrypt 2008. The authors had claimed that RC4+ ironed out most of the weaknesses of the alleged RC4 stream cipher and was only marginally slower than RC4 in software. In this paper we show that it is possible to mount a distinguishing attack on RC4+ based on the bias of the first output byte. The distinguisher requires around 2^{26} samples produced by different keys of RC4+. In the second part of the paper we study the possibility of mounting the differential fault attack on RC4 proposed by Biham et. al. in FSE 2005, on RC4+. We will show that that the RC4+ is vulnerable to differential fault attack and it is possible to recover the entire internal state of the cipher at the beginning of the PRGA by injecting around $2^{17.2}$ faults.

Keywords: Cryptanalysis, Differential Fault Attack, Distinguishing Attack, RC4, RC4+, Stream Cipher.

1 Introduction

There has been extensive research in recent years to come up with RC4-like stream ciphers that while marginally slower in software, would wipe out the known shortcomings of RC4. Many such ciphers like RC4A [10], NGG [9], GGHN [4], VMPC [14] have been proposed to fulfil this objective. However, all the aforementioned ciphers have had distinguishing attacks reported against them [7,11–13]. RC4+ is another stream cipher that belongs to this family. The cipher was proposed by Maitra and Paul at Indocrypt 2008 [5]. The authors had claimed that RC4+ while marginally slower than RC4 in software, would resist all the known distinguishing and state recovery attacks against RC4. To the best of our knowledge, no cryptanalytic advance has been made against this cipher.

Description of the Cipher. The physical structure of RC4+ is the same as that of RC4. It consists of a permutation S of $N = 256$ elements from the integer ring $\mathbb{Z}_{256}$. It also uses two index pointers i, j of size 1 byte each. As in RC4, during the Key Scheduling Algorithm(KSA), S is initialized to the identity permutation

G. Paul and S. Vaudenay (Eds.): INDOCRYPT 2013, LNCS 8250, pp. 297–307, 2013.

and mixed using a Secret Key K of size l bytes (typically $l = 16$). Then, the array S is further scrambled using an l byte IV, after which another layer of zig-zag scrambling is performed. The exact details of the KSA are given in Table 1. Note that all addition operations are performed in $\mathbb{Z}_{256}$, and $\oplus$ denotes bitwise-XOR. The array V used in the KSA is defined as

$$V[i] = \begin{cases} IV[127 - i], & \text{if } 128 - l \leq i \leq 127, \\ IV[i - 128], & \text{if } 128 \leq i \leq 127 + l \\ 0, & \text{otherwise.} \end{cases}$$

Table 1. KSA routine for RC4+

Input: Secret Key K, Initial Vector IV
Output: Permutation S on $\mathbb{Z}_{256}$
for $i = 0$ to 255 do
  | $S[i] = i$;
end
$j \leftarrow 0$
Key Loading
for $i = 0$ to 255 do
  | $j \leftarrow j + S[i] + K[i \bmod l]$;
  | Swap $S[i], S[j]$;
end
IV Loading
for $i = 127$ to 0 do
  | $j \leftarrow$
  | $(j + S[i]) \oplus (K[i \bmod l] + V[i])$;
  | Swap $S[i], S[j]$;
end

for $i = 128$ to 255 do
  | $j \leftarrow$
  | $(j + S[i]) \oplus (K[i \bmod l] + V[i])$;
  | Swap $S[i], S[j]$;
end

Zig-Zag Scrambling
for $y = 0$ to 255 do
  | if $y \equiv 0 \bmod 2$ then
    | $i = \frac{y}{2}$;
  | end
  | else
    | $i = 128 - \frac{y+1}{2}$;
  | end
  | $j \leftarrow j + S[i] + K[i \bmod l]$;
  | Swap $S[i], S[j]$;
end

The PRGA routine of RC4+ deviates slightly from the simplistic structure of RC4. In order to protect against the well known second output byte bias of Mantin-Shamir [6] and the permutation recovery attack of Maximov and Khovratovich [8], the designers propose to make the output keystream byte functions of a few other locations of the permutation array S. The details of the PRGA routine are given in Table 2. Note that $\gg$ and $\ll$ denote right and left bitwise shifts respectively.

Table 2. PRGA routine for RC4+

Input: Permutation S on $\mathbb{Z}_{256}$
Output: Output Keystream bytes Z

$i = j = 0$;
while *Keystream is required* **do**
    $i \leftarrow i + 1$;
    $j \leftarrow j + S[i]$;
    Swap $S[i], S[j]$;

    $t \leftarrow S[i] + S[j]$;
    $t' \leftarrow (S[i \gg 3 \oplus j \ll 5] + S[i \ll 5 \oplus j \gg 3]) \oplus \texttt{0xAA}$;
    $t'' \leftarrow j + S[j]$;

    $Z_i = (S[t] + S[t']) \oplus S[t'']$;
end

Our Contribution and Organization of the Paper. In this paper we will show that the first output byte produced by RC4+ is negatively biased towards 1. In fact we will prove that the probability that the first output byte is equal to 1 is around $\frac{1}{N} - \frac{1}{2N^2}$, where $N = 256$ is the number of elements of the array S used in the design. Using this observation we will mount a distinguishing attack against RC4+ that requires around 2^{26} output keystreams produced by **(a)** Secret Keys chosen uniformly at random or **(b)** any fixed Secret Key used with IVs chosen unformly at random. In the second part of the paper we revisit the Differential Fault Attack on RC4 proposed by Biham et. al. in FSE 2005 [1]. We explore the possibility of mounting such a fault attack on RC4+. We will show that by injecting around $2^{17.2}$ faults, it is possible to recover the internal state of the cipher efficiently.

2 Distinguishing Attack on RC4+

In this section we will prove that the first output byte Z_1 (when the value of the index $i = 1$) is negatively biased towards 1. We will prove that $\Pr(Z_1 = 1) = \frac{1}{N} - \frac{1}{2N^2}$. The initial state of the RC4+ PRGA is denoted by S_0.

Lemma 1. *Let S_0 be a random permutation on $\{0, 1, 2, \ldots, 255\}$. If $S_0[1] = 1$ and $S_0[2]$ is even, then Z_1 can never take the value 1.*

Proof. We refer to the PRGA algorithm in Table 2. Initially $i = j = 0$. After the increment operations the new values of i, j are as follows: $i = 0 + 1 = 1$ and $j = 0 + S_0[i] = 0 + S_0[1] = 1$. Since $i = j$ even after the increment operations, the subsequent swap operation does not bring about any change in the array S_0. Thereafter the values of t, t', t'' are calculated as follows:

$$t = S_0[i] + S_0[j] = 2 \cdot S_0[1] = 2.$$

$$t' = (S_0[i \gg 3 \oplus j \ll 5] + S_0[i \ll 5 \oplus j \gg 3]) \oplus \texttt{0xAA}$$
$$= (S_0[1 \gg 3 \oplus 1 \ll 5] + S_0[1 \ll 5 \oplus 1 \gg 3]) \oplus \texttt{0xAA}$$
$$= (2 \cdot S_0[32]) \oplus \texttt{0xAA}$$

Finally $t'' = j + S_0[j] = 1 + S_0[1] = 1 + 1 = 2$. Therefore we have $Z_1 = (S_0[2] + S_0[t']) \oplus S_0[2]$. Suppose that $Z_1 = 1$, then we will have

$$(S_0[2] + S_0[t']) \oplus S_0[2] = 1 \quad \Rightarrow \quad S_0[2] + S_0[t'] = S_0[2] \oplus 1$$

Since $S_0[2]$ is even, we must have $S_0[2] \oplus 1 = S_0[2] + 1$. Hence the previous equation reduces to:

$$S_0[2] + S_0[t'] = S_0[2] + 1 \quad \Rightarrow \quad S_0[t'] = 1$$

S_0 is a permutation and hence injective. So $S_0[t'] = S_0[1] = 1$ can only imply that $t' = 1$. Thus we have

$$(2 \cdot S_0[32]) \oplus \texttt{0xAA} = 1$$

The LHS of the above equation is clearly an even number whereas the RHS is odd. This gives rise to a contradiction, and therefore $Z_1 = 1$ can clearly not hold.   □

Corollary 1. *The above Lemma would still hold if any even pad instead of 0xAA were used in the design.*

Theorem 1. *Let S_0 be a random permutation on $\{0, 1, 2, \ldots, 255\}$. The probability that $Z_1 = 1$ is given by the equation $\Pr(Z_1 = 1) = \frac{1}{N} - \frac{1}{2N^2}$ (where $N = 256$).*

Proof. Let E denote the event: "$S_0[1] = 1$ and $S_0[2]$ is even". Then it is clear that $\Pr[\mathsf{E}] = \frac{\frac{N}{2} \cdot (N-2)!}{N!} \approx \frac{1}{2N}$. From Lemma 1, we have $\Pr[Z_1 = 1 | \mathsf{E}] = 0$. By standard randomness assumptions, we have $\Pr[Z_1 = 1 | \mathsf{E}^c] = \frac{1}{N}$ (this has been verified by extensive computer experiments with 2^{20} random keys). Therefore we have

$$\Pr[Z_1 = 1] = \Pr[Z_1 = 1 | \mathsf{E}] \cdot \Pr[\mathsf{E}] + \Pr[Z_1 = 1 | \mathsf{E}^c] \cdot \Pr[\mathsf{E}^c]$$
$$= 0 \cdot \frac{1}{2N} + \frac{1}{N} \cdot \left(1 - \frac{1}{2N}\right) = \frac{1}{N} - \frac{1}{2N^2}.$$

□

We now state the following theorem from [6], which outlines the number of output samples required to distinguish two distributions X and Y.

Theorem 2. *(Mantin-Shamir [6]) Let X, Y be distributions, and suppose that the event e happens in X with probability p and in Y with probability $p(1 + q)$. Then for small p and q, $O\left(\frac{1}{pq^2}\right)$ samples suffice to distinguish X from Y with a constant probability of success.*

Distinguishing RC4+ from Random Sources. Let X be the probability distribution of Z_1 in an ideal random stream, and let Y be the probability distribution of Z_1 in streams produced by RC4+ for randomly chosen keys. Let the event e denote $Z_1 = 1$, which occurs with probability of $\frac{1}{N}$ in X and $\frac{1}{N} - \frac{1}{2N^2} = \frac{1}{N} \cdot \left(1 - \frac{1}{2N}\right)$ in Y. By using the Theorem 2 with $p = \frac{1}{N}$ and $q = -\frac{1}{2N}$, we can conclude that we need about $\frac{1}{pq^2} = 4 \cdot N^3 = 2^{26}$ output samples to reliably distinguish the two distributions.

Experimental Results. By performing extensive computer simulations with **(a)** one billion random keys, and **(b)** a fixed key with one billion random IVs, the probability $\Pr[Z_1 = 1]$ was found to be around $2^{-8} - 2^{-17.03}$. This is consistent with the theoretical value of $\frac{1}{N} - \frac{1}{2N^2}$ proven in Theorem 1.

3 Differential Fault Analysis of RC4+

In [1], a Differential Fault Attack and an Impossible Fault Attack of the RC4 stream cipher was proposed. The Impossible Fault Attack uses random faults on the i or j indices of the RC4 PRGA to drive the cipher into a special state called Finney state [3]. The Finney states are called impossible states because they can not occur under normal mode of operation of RC4 and hence the unusual name of the attack. By injecting around 2^{16} faults on either the i or j register, the cipher is expected to enter a Finney State. From observing the faulty output bytes of RC4 it is possible to assess if the cipher has indeed entered a Finney State. Since any Finney state cycles back after $255 \cdot 256 = 65280$ iterations of the cipher, the attacker selects one of the interleaved cycles in the output stream as the internal state. Once the internal state is obtained at some point in time, it is possible to backtrack and find the initial state at the beginning of the PRGA. Note that, since the PRGA update operations of RC4 and RC4+ are exactly similar, an impossible fault attack on RC4+ may also be carried out using the same techniques outlined in [1].

Applying the Differential Fault Attack (DFA) of [1] to RC4+, however, is not so straightforward. Before proceeding, we note that the PRGA of RC4 is exactly the same as that of RC4+, the only difference being that RC4 outputs $S[t]$ instead of $(S[t] + S[t']) \oplus S[t'']$. We will state in brief the DFA algorithm in [1].

A. Perform a key setup (KSA) with the unknown key and run the RC4 PRGA for around 1000 iterations, and record the output stream Z_i, $(1 \leq i \leq 1000)$ for later analysis.

B. Process the following 256 times with l being set from 0 to 255, giving 256 faulty output streams
  1. Restart the cipher and perform a key setup with the same unknown key.
  2. Make a fault in $S[l]$.
  3. Run the RC4 PRGA 30 steps, and record the faulty output stream $Z_i^1[l]$ for later analysis.

C. Repeat Step **B** with fault injection in k^{th} $(2 \leq k \leq 1000)$ PRGA iteration instead of just after key setup. Record the faulty keystream sequence $Z_i^k[l]$ in each case (thus $Z_i^k[l]$ is the faulty i^{th} keystream byte when the location $S[l]$ has been faulted at PRGA round k).

For any i, the output byte Z_i is a function of just 3 locations of the S array: i, j, $S[i] + S[j]$. So evidently, the output byte of all the $Z_i^i[l]$'s (note $Z_i^i[l]$ is the first output byte obtained after faulting $S[l]$ at round i), except for three of them, are the same as in the faultless output byte Z_i. The identification of these three streams leak the values of i, j, $S[i] + S[j]$, but not which is which. Of course, the value of i is always known, thus the only task is to identify which is j and which is $S[i] + S[j]$. After the values of j, $S[i] + S[j]$ are obtained for sufficiently many PRGA rounds i, a cascade guessing technique is employed in [1] to eliminate incorrect guesses of j from j, $S[i] + S[j]$ and thereafter reconstruct the initial permutation S. For more details, we refer the reader to [1].

However in RC4+, the output byte is a function of 7 locations of the S array: i, j, $S[i] + S[j]$, $j + S[j]$, $i \gg 3 \oplus j \ll 5$, $i \ll 5 \oplus j \gg 3, (S[i \gg 3 \oplus j \ll 5] + S[i \ll 5 \oplus j \gg 3]) \oplus$ 0xAA. Therefore repeating the above procedure in the case of RC4+ would leak a maximum of 7 indices in each round, of which only the value of i is known with certainty. The values of the other 6 indices can not be assigned with certainty. Thus, on the face of it, performing DFA on RC4+ seems to be more difficult than RC4. However as we will see in Section 3.1, this is not so.

3.1   Inferring the Values of j in Each Round

As we have seen, performing steps **A, B, C** for RC4+, leaks the values of 6 indices. Although the attacker knows that these are the values of the indices j, $S[i] + S[j]$, $j + S[j]$, $i \gg 3 \oplus j \ll 5$, $i \ll 5 \oplus j \gg 3, (S[i \gg 3 \oplus j \ll 5] + S[i \ll 5 \oplus j \gg 3]) \oplus$ 0xAA, he is unable to ascertain which of these 6 values correspond to which index. We will later see in Section 3.2, that if the attacker can correctly establish the value of only the index j, it will be enough to reconstruct the permutation S at the beginning of the PRGA. Before we outline our strategy to find the value of j, we will look at a result that will help us build the attack.

Lemma 2. *For any value of i, consider two values j_1, j_2. If $i \gg 3 \oplus j_1 \ll 5 = i \gg 3 \oplus j_2 \ll 5$, and $i \ll 5 \oplus j_1 \gg 3 = i \ll 5 \oplus j_2 \gg 3$, then $j_1 = j_2$.*

Proof. Rearranging the terms in both equations we get $(j_1 \oplus j_2) \ll 5 = 0 = (j_1 \oplus j_2) \gg 3$. Then, $j_1 \oplus j_2 = 0$ is the only solution to the equation and so $j_1 = j_2$.

Ascertaining j. For any round i, the attacker has with him 6 values corresponding to the indices j, $S[i] + S[j]$, $j + S[j]$, $i \gg 3 \oplus j \ll 5$, $i \ll 5 \oplus j \gg 3, (S[i \gg 3 \oplus j \ll 5] + S[i \ll 5 \oplus j \gg 3]) \oplus$ 0xAA. Let us call these six values $k_1, k_2, \ldots, k_6$. He of course does not know the correspondence between the

$k_1, \ldots, k_6$ and the indices. Without loss of generality let k_1 be the correct value of j. Then evaluating the functions $i \gg 3 \oplus k_1 \ll 5$ and $i \ll 5 \oplus k_1 \gg 3$ will lead to two of the values in $k_2, k_3, \ldots, k_6$ i.e. those corresponding to $i \gg 3 \oplus j \ll 5$ and $i \ll 5 \oplus j \gg 3$. The probability that any other k_a, $2 \leq a \leq 6$ will on evaluating $i \gg 3 \oplus k_a \ll 5$ and $i \ll 5 \oplus k_a \gg 3$ will lead to two elements of $\{k_1, k_2, \ldots, k_6\}$ is very low. Therefore given any i the strategy will be as follows

- For $a = 1$ to 6

  1. Compute $M_a = i \gg 3 \oplus k_a \ll 5$ and $N_a = i \ll 5 \oplus k_a \gg 3$.
  2. If $M_a, N_a \in \{k_1, k_2, k_3, k_4, k_5, k_6\}$ then $j = k_a$.

The strategy of the attacker will be to determine the values of j for around 602 consecutive values of i. As will be seen in Section 3.2, this will suffice to reconstruct the permutation S at the beginning of the PRGA.

Error Analysis. Lemma 2 guarantees that any value k_a different j, when used to calculate M_a, N_a will result in values $\neq i \gg 3 \oplus j \ll 5$ and $i \ll 5 \oplus j \gg 3$. Therefore, a confusion will only occur when some value $k_a \neq j$ on evaluating $i \gg 3 \oplus k_a \ll 5$ and $i \ll 5 \oplus k_a \gg 3$ also leads to two elements of $\{k_1, k_2, \ldots, k_6\}$ (which are not equal to $i \gg 3 \oplus j \ll 5$ and $i \ll 5 \oplus j \gg 3$). In such an event the attacker must guess one from the multiple values of j extracted by the algorithm. Experiments with 2^{20} random keys show that in the first 602 rounds there are around 5 to 6 confusions on average, and each confusion usually gives no more than 2 values of j to choose from. The attacker can simply guess the values of j during these rounds and use it in the algorithm for state recovery that will be discussed in the next subsection.

Fault Requirement. As we will see in the next subsection, around 602 values of j are required to reconstruct S. Since each round requires 256 faults, the total fault requirement is around $602 \times 256 \approx 2^{17.23}$.

3.2   Reconstructing the Permutation S

We will now present the Algorithm 1 that will be used to reconstruct the state S. The technique used here is similar to the algorithm presented in [2]. The algorithm works under the principle that if j_1, j_2 are the values of j in two successive PRGA rounds then the the value of $S[i_1]$ is given as $j_2 - j_1$.

We assume that the algorithm starts from PRGA round t armed with M values of j in consecutive PRGA rounds. First, a two dimensional array acc is used, whose r-th row contains the triplet (i_r, j_r, z_r). After each subsequent round $t + r$, the algorithm reverts to the initial round t and in the process uses new entries to check if the array $guess$ (which is the temporary array used to guess the state S) can be populated further. Thereafter the algorithm again performs a *forward pass* up to the round $t + r + 1$ to further populate the array $guess$ as much as possible. The strategy is formally presented in Algorithm 1.

Input: $(i_t, j_t), \{(i_{t+r}, j_{t+r}, z_{t+r} : r = 1, \ldots, M-1)\}$.
Output: Permutation array S_{t+m} for some $m \in [0, M-1]$.

0.1 $numKnown \leftarrow 0$;
0.2 $m \leftarrow 0$;
0.3   **for** u *from* 0 *to* $N-1$ **do**
0.4 | $guess[u] \leftarrow EMPTY$;
      end
0.5 $acc[0][0] \leftarrow i_t$;
0.6 $acc[0][1] \leftarrow j_t$;
0.7   **for** u *from* 1 *to* $M-1$ **do**
0.8 | $acc[u][0] \leftarrow i_{t+u}$;
0.9 | $acc[u][1] \leftarrow j_{t+u}$;
0.10 | $acc[u][2] \leftarrow z_{t+u}$;
      end
0.11 **repeat**
0.12 | $i_{t+m+1} \leftarrow acc[t+m+1][0]$, $j_{t+m+1} \leftarrow acc[t+m+1][1]$,
      | $z_{t+m+1} \leftarrow acc[t+m+1][2]$;
0.13 | **if** $guess[i_{t+m+1}] = EMPTY$ **then**
0.14 | | $guess[i_{t+m+1}] \leftarrow j_{t+m+1} - j_{t+m}$;
      | **end**
0.15 | $backtrack(t+m, t)$;
0.16 | $processForward(t, t+m+1)$;
0.17 | $m \leftarrow m+1$;
0.18 | $numKnown \leftarrow$ Number of non-empty entries in the array $guess$;
      until $numKnown = N-1$ *OR* $m = M-1$;
0.19 **if** $numKnown = N-1$ **then**
0.20 | Fill the remaining single EMPTY location of the array $guess$;
0.21 | **for** u *from* 0 *to* $N-1$ **do**
0.22 | | $S_{t+m}[u] \leftarrow guess[u]$;
      | **end**
      end

Algorithm 1. The algorithm for state recovery with backward and forward passes.

Algorithm 1 uses two subroutines. The subroutine $backtrack(r, t)$ presented in Algorithm 2 performs a backward pass, tracing all state information back from the current round r to a previous round $t < r$. On the other hand, the subroutine $processForward(r, t)$, presented in Algorithm 3 evolves the state information in the forward direction from a past round r to the current round $t > r$. Note that Algorithm 1 returns the array S_{t+m} (the value of S at PRGA round $t+m$) where m is the minimal value for which S_{t+m} can be fully constructed. Thereafter the value of S at any previous round can be easily calculated as the state update of RC4+, like RC4, is one-one and invertible.

Subroutine $backtrack(r, t)$

1.1 **repeat**
1.2 $\quad i_r \leftarrow acc[r][0];$
1.3 $\quad j_r \leftarrow acc[r][1];$
1.4 $\quad swap(guess[i_r], guess[j_r]);$
1.5 $\quad r \leftarrow r - 1;$
$\quad$ **until** $r = t$;

Algorithm 2. Subroutine $backtrack$

Experimental Results. We present some experimental evidences. Experimental result showing the average number of bytes recovered (over 100 random simulations) against the number of rounds used is shown in Table 3. It shows that around 602 consecutive values of j are required to reconstruct the entire of S.

Table 3. No. of rounds vs. average no. of bytes recovered for Algorithm 1

Rounds M	100	200	300	400	500	602
#Bytes Recovered	84	144	194	233	249	255

4   Conclusion

The paper presents some weaknesses of the RC4+ stream cipher proposed by Maitra and Paul in Indocrypt 2008. Firstly, a distinguishing attack requiring around 2^{26} output samples is presented, based on the bias of the first output byte. In the second part of the paper, a Differential Fault Attack requiring around $2^{17.2}$ faults is reported against the cipher. The results show that designing reinforcements to strengthen RC4 is not an easy task. It would be worthwhile to discover a design paradigm that not only rids RC4 of its weaknesses but also preserves its innate simplicity.

Subroutine $processForward(r,t)$

2.1 **repeat**

2.2 $\quad i_r = acc[r][0];$

2.3 $\quad j_r = acc[r][1];$

2.4 $\quad z_r = acc[r][2];$

2.5 $\quad t_r = S_r[i_r] + S_r[j_r];$

2.6 $\quad t'_r = (S_r[i_r \gg 3 \oplus j_r \ll 5] + S_r[i_r \ll 5 \oplus j_r \gg 3]) \oplus 0xAA;$

2.7 $\quad t''_r = j_r + S_r[j_r];$

2.8 $\quad swap(guess[i_r], guess[j_r]);$

2.9 $\quad$ **if** $\Big(guess[i_r] \neq EMPTY \wedge guess[j_r] \neq EMPTY \wedge guess[t_r] \neq$
$\qquad EMPTY \wedge guess[i_r \gg 3 \oplus j_r \ll 5] \neq EMPTY \wedge guess[i_r \ll$
$\qquad 5 \oplus j_r \gg 3] \neq \quad EMPTY \wedge guess[t'_r] \neq EMPTY \Big)$ **then**

2.10 $\qquad$ **if** $guess[t''_r] = EMPTY$ **then**

2.11 $\qquad\quad$ $guess[t''_r] \leftarrow z_r \oplus (guess[t_r] + guess[t'_r]);$
$\qquad$ **end**
$\quad$ **end**

2.12 $\quad$ **if** $\Big(guess[i_r] \neq EMPTY \wedge guess[j_r] \neq EMPTY \wedge guess[t_r] \neq$
$\qquad EMPTY \wedge guess[i_r \gg 3 \oplus j_r \ll 5] \neq EMPTY \wedge guess[i_r \ll$
$\qquad 5 \oplus j_r \gg 3] \neq \quad EMPTY \wedge guess[t''_r] \neq EMPTY \Big)$ **then**

2.13 $\qquad$ **if** $guess[t'_r] = EMPTY$ **then**

2.14 $\qquad\quad$ $guess[t'_r] \leftarrow (z_r \oplus guess[t''_r]) - guess[t_r];$
$\qquad$ **end**
$\quad$ **end**

2.15 $\quad$ **if** $\Big(guess[i_r] \neq EMPTY \wedge guess[j_r] \neq EMPTY \wedge guess[i_r \gg 3 \oplus j_r \ll$
$\qquad 5] \neq EMPTY \wedge guess[i_r \ll 5 \oplus j_r \gg 3] \neq EMPTY \wedge guess[t'_r] \neq$
$\qquad EMPTY \wedge guess[t''_r] \neq EMPTY \Big)$ **then**

2.16 $\qquad$ **if** $guess[t_r] = EMPTY$ **then**

2.17 $\qquad\quad$ $guess[t_r] \leftarrow (z_r \oplus guess[t''_r]) - guess[t'_r];$
$\qquad$ **end**
$\quad$ **end**

2.18 $\quad r \leftarrow r + 1;$

until $r = t$;

Algorithm 3. Subroutine $processForward$

References

1. Biham, E., Granboulan, L., Nguyen, P.Q.: Impossible Fault Analysis of RC4 and Differential Fault Analysis of RC4. In: Gilbert, H., Handschuh, H. (eds.) FSE 2005. LNCS, vol. 3557, pp. 359–367. Springer, Heidelberg (2005)
2. Das, A., Maitra, S., Paul, G., Sarkar, S.: Some Combinatorial Results towards State Recovery Attack on RC4. In: Jajodia, S., Mazumdar, C. (eds.) ICISS 2011. LNCS, vol. 7093, pp. 204–214. Springer, Heidelberg (2011)
3. Finney, H.: An RC4 cycle that can't happen. Posting to sci.crypt (September 1994)
4. Gong, G., Gupta, K.C., Hell, M., Nawaz, Y.: Towards a General RC4-Like Keystream Generator. In: Feng, D., Lin, D., Yung, M. (eds.) CISC 2005. LNCS, vol. 3822, pp. 162–174. Springer, Heidelberg (2005)
5. Maitra, S., Paul, G.: Analysis of RC4 and Proposal of Additional Layers for Better Security Margin. In: Chowdhury, D.R., Rijmen, V., Das, A. (eds.) INDOCRYPT 2008. LNCS, vol. 5365, pp. 27–39. Springer, Heidelberg (2008)
6. Mantin, I., Shamir, A.: A Practical Attack on Broadcast RC4. In: Matsui, M. (ed.) FSE 2001. LNCS, vol. 2355, pp. 152–164. Springer, Heidelberg (2002)
7. Maximov, A.: Two Linear Distinguishing Attacks on VMPC and RC4A and Weakness of RC4 Family of Stream Ciphers. In: Gilbert, H., Handschuh, H. (eds.) FSE 2005. LNCS, vol. 3557, pp. 342–358. Springer, Heidelberg (2005)
8. Maximov, A., Khovratovich, D.: New State Recovery Attack on RC4. In: Wagner, D. (ed.) CRYPTO 2008. LNCS, vol. 5157, pp. 297–316. Springer, Heidelberg (2008)
9. Nawaz, Y., Gupta, K.C., Gong, G.: A 32-bit RC4-like Keystream Generator. IACR Cryptology ePrint Archive 2005, 175 (2005)
10. Paul, S., Preneel, B.: A New Weakness in the RC4 Keystream Generator and an Approach to Improve the Security of the Cipher. In: Roy, B., Meier, W. (eds.) FSE 2004. LNCS, vol. 3017, pp. 245–259. Springer, Heidelberg (2004)
11. Paul, S., Preneel, B.: On the (In)security of Stream Ciphers Based on Arrays and Modular Addition. In: Lai, X., Chen, K. (eds.) ASIACRYPT 2006. LNCS, vol. 4284, pp. 69–83. Springer, Heidelberg (2006)
12. Tsunoo, Y., Saito, T., Kubo, H., Shigeri, M., Suzaki, T., Kawabata, T.: The Most Efficient Distinguishing Attack on VMPC and RC4A. In: SKEW (2005), http://www.ecrypt.eu.org/stream/papers.html
13. Tsunoo, Y., Saito, T., Kubo, H., Suzaki, T.: A Distinguishing Attack on a Fast Software-Implemented RC4-Like Stream Cipher. IEEE Transactions on Information Theory 53(9), 3250–3255 (2007)
14. Zoltak, B.: VMPC One-Way Function and Stream Cipher. In: Roy, B., Meier, W. (eds.) FSE 2004. LNCS, vol. 3017, pp. 210–225. Springer, Heidelberg (2004)

On the Security of *Piccolo* Lightweight Block Cipher against Related-Key Impossible Differentials[*]

Marine Minier

Université de Lyon, INRIA
INSA-Lyon, CITI, F-69621, Villeurbanne, France
marine.minier@insa-lyon.fr

Abstract. *Piccolo* is a new lightweight block cipher proposed at CHES 2011 [13]. It ciphers plaintext blocks of length 64 bits under keys of lengths 80 or 128 bits. It is based on a modified Feistel structure with a variable number of rounds.

In this paper, we present two related key impossible differential attacks against 14 rounds of *Piccolo*-80 and 21 rounds of *Piccolo*-128 without the whitening layers. The attack against *Piccolo*-80 has a time and data complexity of $2^{68.19}$ whereas the time/data complexity of the attack against *Piccolo*-128 is $2^{117.77}$.

Keywords: Lightweight block ciphers, *Piccolo*, related-key impossible differential attack.

Introduction

Due to the emergence of new highly constrained systems such as RFID tags, many lightweight block ciphers dedicated to those environments have been recently proposed. Among them, let us mention: PRESENT [4], DESXL [12], KATAN & KTANTAN [7], SEA [14], LED [8], LBlock [17], TWINE [15], PRINCE [6] and finally *Piccolo* [13].

Even if some cryptanalytic results (see [5,11] for example) have already been published concerning the security of those block ciphers, it still remains necessary to study more deeply their security and their efficiency.

In this paper, we focus on the security evaluation of the new lightweight block cipher *Piccolo* [13]. We present two related key impossible differential attacks against 14 rounds of *Piccolo*-80 and 21 rounds of *Piccolo*-128 without the whitening layers. Of course, an attack in the related key security model is much weaker than an attack in the secret key setting but this result provides a better understanding of the *Piccolo* security evaluation, especially its key schedule. Table 1 compares the already published attacks against *Piccolo*.

---

[*] This work was partially supported by the French National Agency of Research: ANR-11-INS-011.

G. Paul and S. Vaudenay (Eds.): INDOCRYPT 2013, LNCS 8250, pp. 308–318, 2013.
© Springer International Publishing Switzerland 2013

Table 1. Comparison table of cryptanalytic results against *Piccolo*

Attack	Nb rounds	In	time complexity
MIM	21/*Piccolo*-128	[9]	2^{121}
MIM	14/*Piccolo*-80	[9]	2^{73}
Biclique	28/*Piccolo*-128	[16]	$2^{126.79}$
Biclique	full/*Piccolo*-80	[16]	$2^{78.95}$

This paper is organized as follows: Section 1 gives a short description of *Piccolo*; In Section 2 we describe the related key impossible differential attacks on 21 rounds of *Piccolo*-128 and 14 rounds of *Piccolo*-80 while Section 3 concludes the paper.

1   Description of *Piccolo*

Piccolo is a new lightweight block cipher proposed by K. Shibutani, T. Isobe, H. Hiwatari, A. Mitsuda, T. Akishita and T. Shirai at CHES 2011 [13]. It ciphers blocks of length 64 bits under keys of length 80 or 128 bits. The number of rounds is variable and depends on the key lengths. It is equal to 25 for a 80-bit key and to 31 for a 128-bit key. Those rounds are surrounded at the top and at the bottom by key additions with two 16-bit whitening keys. The encryption function is illustrated on Fig. 1. The round function is a modified Generalized Feistel with 4 branches. It is composed of an *F*-function that acts at 16-bit level composed of the application of a 4-bit S-box applied four times in parallel, followed by a MixColumns-like transformation acting at nibble level, finally followed by the reapplication of the S-box layer. A subkey addition is applied after the *F*-function as shown on Fig. 1. The RP transformation acts at byte level and permutes the bytes of the current block $X^i = (x_0, x_1, x_2, x_3, x_4, x_5, x_6, x_7)$ into $(x_2, x_7, x_4, x_1, x_6, x_3, x_0, x_5)$.

The key schedule of *Piccolo* is linear. The key is seen as 5 or 8 16-bit words $k_{i(16)}$ for i from 0 to 4 or 0 to 7. For a 80-bit key, the key schedule extracts the subkeys as described in Algorithm 1 where con_i^{80} are round constants. For a 128-bit key, the key schedule works as shown in Algorithm 2 where con_i^{128} are round constants.

Finally, Table 2 sums up the key words extracted at each round for the two possible key lengths.

2   Related Key Impossible Differential Attacks

In this section, we first introduce our attack model then we present our related key impossible attacks against 14 rounds of *Piccolo*-80 and 21 rounds of *Piccolo*-128. We first describe the related keys, then the impossible differentials and we conclude with the full attacks.

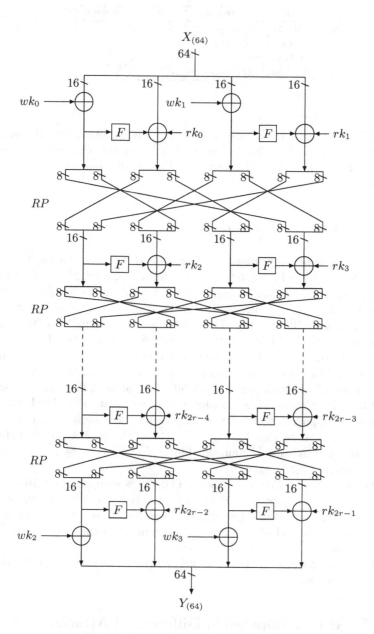

Fig. 1. Encryption function of *Piccolo*

Algorithm 1. The *Piccolo* Key Schedule for a 80-bit key

Data: The master key $k_{0(16)}, k_{1(16)}, k_{2(16)}, k_{3(16)}, k_{4(16)}$.
Result: The whitening keys $wk_0, \cdots, wk_3$, the round keys $rk_0, \cdots, rk_{49}$.
$wk_0 \leftarrow k_0^L \| k_1^R, \ wk_1 \leftarrow k_1^L \| k_0^R, \ wk_2 \leftarrow k_4^L \| k_3^R, \ wk_3 \leftarrow k_3^L \| k_4^R$
for i *from 0 to* $r - 1$ **do**

$$(rk_{2i}, rk_{2i+1}) \leftarrow (con_{2i}^{80}, con_{2i+1}^{80}) \oplus \begin{cases} (k_2, k_3) & (\text{if } i \mod 5 = 0 \text{ or } 2) \\ (k_0, k_1) & (\text{if } i \mod 5 = 1 \text{ or } 4) \\ (k_4, k_4) & (\text{if } i \mod 5 = 3) \end{cases}$$

Algorithm 2. The *Piccolo* Key Schedule for a 128-bit key

Data: The master key $k_{0(16)}, \cdots, k_{7(16)}$.
Result: The whitening keys $wk_0, \cdots, wk_3$, the round keys $rk_0, \cdots, rk_{61}$.
$wk_0 \leftarrow k_0^L \| k_1^R, \ wk_1 \leftarrow k_1^L \| k_0^R, \ wk_2 \leftarrow k_4^L \| k_7^R, \ wk_3 \leftarrow k_7^L \| k_4^R$
for i *from 0 to* $r - 1$ **do**
  if $i + 2 \mod 8 = 0$ **then**
    $(k_0, k_1, k_2, k_3, k_4, k_5, k_6, k_7) \leftarrow (k_2, k_1, k_6, k_7, k_0, k_3, k_4, k_5)$
  $rk_i \leftarrow k_{(i+2) \mod 8} \oplus con_i^{128}$

Table 2. Key expansion function for *Piccolo*-128 and *Piccolo*-80

Piccolo-128

Round	1	2	3	4	5	6	7	8	9	10	11	12	13	14	15	16
Key Word	2, 3	4, 5	6, 7	2, 1	6, 7	0, 3	4, 5	6, 1	4, 5	2, 7	0, 3	4 ,1	0, 3	6, 5	2, 7	0, 1
Round	17	18	19	20	21	22	23	24	25	26	27	28	29	30	31	
Key Word	2, 7	4, 3	6, 5	2, 1	6, 5	0, 7	4, 3	6, 1	4, 3	2, 5	0, 7	4, 1	0, 7	6, 3	2, 5	

Piccolo-80

Round	1	2	3	4	5	6	7	8	9	10	11	12	13	14	15	16
Key Word	2, 3	0, 1	2, 3	4, 4	0, 1	2, 3	0, 1	2, 3	4, 4	0, 1	2, 3	0, 1	2, 3	4, 4	0, 1	2, 3
Round	17	18	19	20	21	22	23	24	25							
Key Word	0, 1	2, 3	4, 4	0, 1	2, 3	0, 1	2, 3	4, 4	0, 1							

2.1   The Attack Model

Impossible differential attacks have been introduced by E. Biham et al. in [2] in 1998. Impossible differential cryptanalysis, in contrast with ordinary differential cryptanalysis, exploits differences with probability 0 at some intermediate state of a cipher. The related key attacks introduced by E. Biham in [1] in 1993 allow an attacker to know some relations between different keys without knowing the keys themselves and to cipher under those keys some plaintexts. From those pairs of plaintexts/ciphertexts, the aim of the attacker is to recover the key.

The idea of combining both techniques has been first introduced by G. Jakimoski and Y. Desmedt in [10] in 2003 against AES-192. In this model, an attacker introduces a difference in the keys and produces an impossible differential in the middle of the cipher considering only differences between the keys. Some variants of this attack where differences are also introduced in the plaintext/ciphertext could also be considered. The most interesting differences in the plaintexts/ciphertexts are in general the ones that could partially cancel the ones in the key as proposed against AES-192 in [3].

2.2   The Considered Related Keys

Piccolo-128. For *Piccolo*-128, we consider the following related keys. Given two master keys K and K' such that $K \oplus K' = (0, 0, X, 0, 0, 0, 0, 0)$ where X denotes a byte difference in the lower bits of k_2, then the differences in the subkeys are summed up in Table 3.

Piccolo-80. For *Piccolo*-80, we consider the following related keys. Given two master keys K and K' such that $K \oplus K' = (X, 0, 0, 0, 0)$ where X denotes a byte difference in the lower bits of k_0, then the differences in the subkeys are summed up in Table 3.

2.3   The Considered Impossible Differentials

The Impossible Differential for *Piccolo*-128. We propose the following impossible differential for *Piccolo*-128 taking into account the injection of differences coming from the subkeys.

If we consider an input difference at round 5 of the form $(0, 0, 0, 0, 0, 0, 0, 0)$ seen at byte level, this input difference gives after 8 rounds the following output difference $(0, 0, *, *, *, *, *, *)$ where $*$ denotes an unknown (possibly null) difference. In the same way and in the backward direction, if the output of round 16 is of the form $(0, *, 0, 0, 0, 0, 0, 0)$ then deciphering 4 rounds gives an input of the form $(\neq 0, \neq 0, *, *, 0, 0, *, *)$ when $\neq 0$ means a difference that could not be null.

Thus we can construct the following related key impossible differential on 12 rounds, between the rounds 5 and 16, for *Piccolo*-128: $(0, 0, 0, 0, 0, 0, 0, 0)$ could not lead to $(0, *, 0, 0, 0, 0, 0, 0)$.

Table 3. Subkey differences for *Piccolo*-128 on the left and *Piccolo*-80 on the right

Round Number	Piccolo-128 Subkey	Differences	Piccolo-80 Subkey	Differences
1	(rk_0, rk_1)	(X,0)	(rk_0, rk_1)	(0,0)
2	(rk_2, rk_3)	(0,0)	(rk_2, rk_3)	(X,0)
3	(rk_4, rk_5)	(0,0)	(rk_4, rk_5)	(0,0)
4	(rk_6, rk_7)	(X,0)	(rk_6, rk_7)	(0,0)
5	(rk_8, rk_9)	(0,0)	(rk_8, rk_9)	(X,0)
6	(rk_{10}, rk_{11})	(0,0)	(rk_{10}, rk_{11})	(0,0)
7	(rk_{12}, rk_{13})	(0,0)	(rk_{12}, rk_{13})	(X,0)
8	(rk_{14}, rk_{15})	(0,0)	(rk_{14}, rk_{15})	(0,0)
9	(rk_{16}, rk_{17})	(0,0)	(rk_{16}, rk_{17})	(0,0)
10	(rk_{18}, rk_{19})	(X,0)	(rk_{18}, rk_{19})	(X,0)
11	(rk_{20}, rk_{21})	(0,0)	(rk_{20}, rk_{21})	(0,0)
12	(rk_{22}, rk_{23})	(0,0)	(rk_{22}, rk_{23})	(X,0)
13	(rk_{24}, rk_{25})	(0,0)	(rk_{24}, rk_{25})	(0,0)
14	(rk_{26}, rk_{27})	(0,0)	(rk_{26}, rk_{27})	(0,0)
15	(rk_{28}, rk_{29})	(X,0)		
16	(rk_{30}, rk_{31})	(0,0)		
17	(rk_{32}, rk_{33})	(X,0)		
18	(rk_{34}, rk_{35})	(0,0)		
19	(rk_{36}, rk_{37})	(0,0)		
20	(rk_{38}, rk_{39})	(X,0)		
21	(rk_{40}, rk_{41})	(0,0)		

The Impossible Differential for *Piccolo*-80. We found the following impossible differential for *Piccolo*-80 taking into account the injection of differences coming from the subkeys.

If we consider an input at round 3 of the form $(0,0,0,0,0,0,0,0)$, this input difference gives after 5 rounds the following output difference $(0,0,*,*,*,*,*,*)$ where $*$ denotes an unknown (possibly null) byte difference. In the same way and in the backward direction, if the output of round 12 is of the form $(*,0,0,0,0,0,0,0)$ then deciphering 5 rounds gives an input of the form $(\neq 0, \neq 0, *, *, *, *, *, *)$ when $\neq 0$ means a byte difference that could not be null.

Thus we can construct the following related key impossible differential on 10 rounds, between the rounds 3 and 12, for *Piccolo*-80: $(0,0,0,0,0,0,0,0)$ could not lead to $(*,0,0,0,0,0,0,0)$.

2.4   Adding Rounds at the Beginning and at the End

Piccolo-128. We can add 4 rounds at the beginning and 5 rounds at the end to the related key impossible differential described in the previous subsection. The two extensions are shown respectively in Fig. 2 and 3 with the number of byte conditions required for the attack to succeed (i.e. to find a differential of the form $(0,0,0,0,0,0,0,0)$ at the output of round 4 taking into account the differences

314   M. Minier

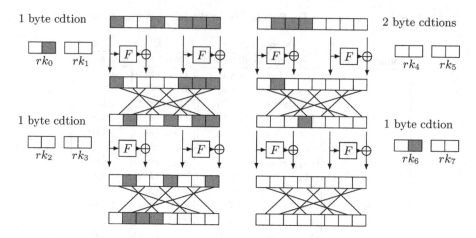

Fig. 2. The 4 rounds added at the beginning. The gray nibbles designate nibbles with differences.

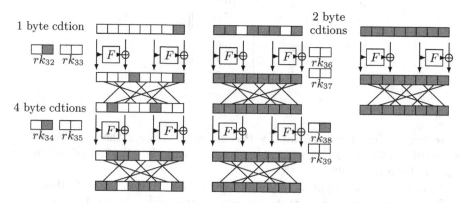

Fig. 3. The 5 rounds added at the end. The gray nibbles designate nibbles with differences.

coming from the subkeys and a differential of the form $(0, *, 0, 0, 0, 0, 0, 0)$ at the output of round 16).

***Piccolo*-80.** We can add 2 rounds at the beginning and 2 rounds at the end to the related key impossible differential described in the previous subsection. The two extensions are shown respectively in Fig. 4 with the number of byte conditions required for the attack to succeed (i.e. to find a differential of the form $(0, 0, 0, 0, 0, 0, 0, 0)$ at the output of round 2 taking into account the differences coming from the subkeys and a differential of the form $(*, 0, 0, 0, 0, 0, 0, 0)$ at the output of round 12).

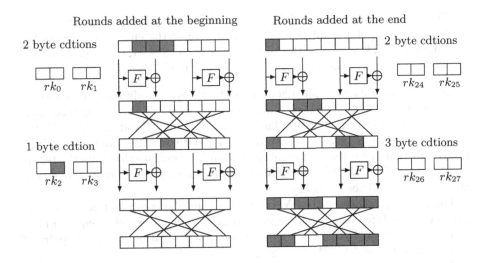

Fig. 4. The 2 rounds added at the beginning on the left and the 2 rounds added at the end. The gray nibbles designate nibbles with differences.

2.5   Attack Procedure

Piccolo-128. The procedure of our attack is as follows:

- For the differential path in the key schedule, we find N good pairs of input messages that satisfy the extended differential path on 21 rounds (N pairs with differences of the form $(*, 0, 0, *, 0, *, *, *)$ at the input and with differences everywhere at the output). This can be done with a complexity equal to C_N that will be explained at the end. As the partial keybits will be determined only in a second step, we need to build the N set and repeat the following procedure for each of the two keys involved in the differential path in the key schedule.
- For each of the N good pairs (and for the two possible keys involved in the differential path in the key schedule), we check if the conditions of getting from the input pair to the beginning of the impossible differential on the 4 initial rounds, and from the output to the end of the impossible differential on the 5 rounds, can be verified by some values of the keybits that intervene in these conditions. In total, we have 112 keybits involved in the subkey search.
- The keybits that make both transitions possible for at least one of the N good pairs will be filtered out of the possible key guesses as otherwise they would imply that the impossible differential had occurred.
- From Fig. 2, we can see that there are 5 byte conditions for erasing the active bytes and obtaining the differential configuration at the input of the impossible differential. The 16-bit words of the key involved in the process are $k_1, k_2, k_3, k_4, k_5, k_6, k_7$. Thus, in total, we need to determine 112 keybits.

– From Fig. 3, we can see that there exist 7 byte conditions for obtaining from the output the differential configuration of the end of the impossible differential. They involve the 16-bit words of the key $k_1, k_2, k_3, k_4, k_5, k_6, k_7$. These are exactly the same keybits as for the initial rounds.

As the probability that for a good pair the 12 byte conditions are verified is 2^{-96}, for each key guess the probability that none of the N good pairs verifies all the conditions is $P = (1-2^{-96})^N$. Thus, we take $N = 2^{102}$. And, $P = 2^{-92,33}$. We have 2^{112} possibilities for the involved keybits. With $N = 2^{102}$ and $P = 2^{-92,33}$, this means that the estimated number of wrong key guesses that pass the test is equal to $2^{112-92,33} = 2^{19,67}$. These keys will be directly tested in a second step at low cost to find the good key.

The cost C_N for generating N valid pairs could be computed according the number of bit differences at the input and at the output, which is equal, in our case, to $64 + 40 = 104$. Thus the total cost for generating $N = 2^{102}$ pairs of differences is $C_N = N2^{64+1-104} = 2^{63}$.

The complexity of the attack, where we recover 112 keybits (and then the remaining ones with much lower complexity) is then

$$2 * (2^{63} + 2^{102}2^{112-96}) \approx 2^{119}$$

partial ciphering operations corresponding to approximatively $\frac{9}{21} \cdot 2^{120} \approx 2^{117.77}$ encryptions. In this equation, the first term represents the complexity of obtaining the 2^{102} pairs with the wanted input-output differences for the 2 related keys, and the second term comes from the fact that, for each of the 2^{102} pairs of messages, and for the 2 possible keys, we filter out all the partial keys that verify the conditions.

The data complexity is about the same as the time complexity. This attack works without the whitening keys that could not be added due to the presence of the whole 16-bit word k_0 in the whitening keys. If we try to add the whitening keys at the beginning and at the end of our attack, the complexity of the attack becomes more expensive than the exhaustive key search.

Piccolo-80. The attack procedure for *Piccolo*-80 is exactly the same, so we do not describe it in details. We only mention that a total of 64 keybits coming from the 16-bit word subkeys $rk_0 = k_2, rk_1 = k_3, rk_2 = k_0, rk_{24} = k_2, rk_{25} = k_3, rk_{26} = k_4, rk_{27} = k_4$ must be guessed under 8 byte conditions, 3 at the beginning and 5 at the end. As the probability P is equal to $P = (1 - 2^{-64})^N$, we take $N = 2^{69}$ which leads to $P = 2^{-46.16}$. The total cost for generating $N = 2^{69}$ pairs of differences is $C_N = N2^{64+1-24-48} = 2^{62}$. The complexity of the attack, where we recover 64 keybits (and then the remaining ones with much lower complexity) is then $2 * (2^{62} + 2^{69}2^{64-64}) \approx 2^{70}$ partial ciphering operations corresponding to approximatively $\frac{4}{14} \cdot 2^{70} \approx 2^{68.19}$ encryptions. The data complexity is about the same as the time complexity. This attack works without the whitening keys that could not be added due to the presence of the whole 16-bit word k_0 in the whitening keys. If we try to add the whitening keys at the beginning and at the end of our attack, the complexity of the attack becomes more expensive than the exhaustive key search.

3 Conclusion

We have presented in this article two related key impossible differential attacks against the two reduced versions of *Piccolo*. Even if those attacks are in the related key settings, they improve the previous complexities of the best attack known against *Piccolo* except the biclique attacks. But the biclique attacks are much more improvements of the key exhaustive search than classical attacks in the common sense of the term.

As part of our future work, we consider improving our analysis on *Piccolo* by considering more number of rounds and whitening keys.

References

1. Biham, E.: New types of cryptanalytic attacks using related keys. In: Helleseth, T. (ed.) EUROCRYPT 1993. LNCS, vol. 765, pp. 398–409. Springer, Heidelberg (1994)
2. Biham, E., Biryukov, A., Shamir, A.: Cryptanalysis of skipjack reduced to 31 rounds using impossible differentials. In: Stern, J. (ed.) EUROCRYPT 1999. LNCS, vol. 1592, pp. 12–23. Springer, Heidelberg (1999)
3. Biham, E., Dunkelman, O., Keller, N.: Related-key impossible differential attacks on 8-round AES-192. In: Pointcheval, D. (ed.) CT-RSA 2006. LNCS, vol. 3860, pp. 21–33. Springer, Heidelberg (2006)
4. Bogdanov, A.A., Knudsen, L.R., Leander, G., Paar, C., Poschmann, A., Robshaw, M., Seurin, Y., Vikkelsoe, C.: PRESENT: An Ultra-Lightweight Block Cipher. In: Paillier, P., Verbauwhede, I. (eds.) CHES 2007. LNCS, vol. 4727, pp. 450–466. Springer, Heidelberg (2007)
5. Bogdanov, A., Rechberger, C.: A 3-subset meet-in-the-middle attack: Cryptanalysis of the lightweight block cipher KTANTAN. In: Biryukov, A., Gong, G., Stinson, D.R. (eds.) SAC 2010. LNCS, vol. 6544, pp. 229–240. Springer, Heidelberg (2011)
6. Borghoff, J., Canteaut, A., Güneysu, T., Kavun, E.B., Knezevic, M., Knudsen, L.R., Leander, G., Nikov, V., Paar, C., Rechberger, C., Rombouts, P., Thomsen, S.S., Yalçın, T.: PRINCE – A low-latency block cipher for pervasive computing applications. In: Wang, X., Sako, K. (eds.) ASIACRYPT 2012. LNCS, vol. 7658, pp. 208–225. Springer, Heidelberg (2012)
7. De Cannière, C., Dunkelman, O., Knežević, M.: KATAN and KTANTAN — A Family of Small and Efficient Hardware-Oriented Block Ciphers. In: Clavier, C., Gaj, K. (eds.) CHES 2009. LNCS, vol. 5747, pp. 272–288. Springer, Heidelberg (2009)
8. Guo, J., Peyrin, T., Poschmann, A., Robshaw, M.: The LED block cipher. In: Preneel, B., Takagi, T. (eds.) CHES 2011. LNCS, vol. 6917, pp. 326–341. Springer, Heidelberg (2011)
9. Isobe, T., Shibutani, K.: Security analysis of the lightweight block ciphers XTEA, LED and piccolo. In: Susilo, W., Mu, Y., Seberry, J. (eds.) ACISP 2012. LNCS, vol. 7372, pp. 71–86. Springer, Heidelberg (2012)

10. Jakimoski, G., Desmedt, Y.: Related-key differential cryptanalysis of 192-bit key aes variants. In: Matsui, M., Zuccherato, R.J. (eds.) SAC 2003. LNCS, vol. 3006, pp. 208–221. Springer, Heidelberg (2004)

11. Leander, G., Abdelraheem, M.A., AlKhzaimi, H., Zenner, E.: A cryptanalysis of printcipher: The invariant subspace attack. In: Rogaway, P. (ed.) CRYPTO 2011. LNCS, vol. 6841, pp. 206–221. Springer, Heidelberg (2011)

12. Leander, G., Paar, C., Poschmann, A., Schramm, K.: New lightweight DES variants. In: Biryukov, A. (ed.) FSE 2007. LNCS, vol. 4593, pp. 196–210. Springer, Heidelberg (2007)

13. Shibutani, K., Isobe, T., Hiwatari, H., Mitsuda, A., Akishita, T., Shirai, T.: *piccolo*: An ultra-lightweight blockcipher. In: Preneel, B., Takagi, T. (eds.) CHES 2011. LNCS, vol. 6917, pp. 342–357. Springer, Heidelberg (2011)

14. Standaert, F.-X., Piret, G., Gershenfeld, N., Quisquater, J.-J.: SEA: A scalable encryption algorithm for small embedded applications. In: Domingo-Ferrer, J., Posegga, J., Schreckling, D. (eds.) CARDIS 2006. LNCS, vol. 3928, pp. 222–236. Springer, Heidelberg (2006)

15. Suzaki, T., Minematsu, K., Morioka, S., Kobayashi, E.: TWINE: A Lightweight Block Cipher for Multiple Platforms. In: Knudsen, L.R., Wu, H. (eds.) SAC 2012. LNCS, vol. 7707, pp. 339–354. Springer, Heidelberg (2013)

16. Wang, Y., Wu, W., Yu, X.: Biclique cryptanalysis of reduced-round piccolo block cipher. In: Ryan, M.D., Smyth, B., Wang, G. (eds.) ISPEC 2012. LNCS, vol. 7232, pp. 337–352. Springer, Heidelberg (2012)

17. Wu, W., Zhang, L.: LBlock: A lightweight block cipher. In: Lopez, J., Tsudik, G. (eds.) ACNS 2011. LNCS, vol. 6715, pp. 327–344. Springer, Heidelberg (2011)

Author Index